Data Structures and Algorithms in Java

Learn with confidence with this hands-on undergraduate textbook for CS2 courses. Active learning and real-world projects underpin each chapter, briefly reviewing programming fundamentals then progressing to core data structures and algorithms topics, including recursion, lists, stacks, trees, graphs, sorting, and complexity analysis. Creative projects and applications put theoretical concepts into practice, helping students master the fundamentals. Dedicated project chapters supply further programming practice using real-world, interdisciplinary problems which students can showcase in their own online portfolios. Example Interview Questions sections prepare students for job applications. The pedagogy supports self-directed and skills-based learning with over 250 "Try It Yourself" boxes, many with solutions provided, and over 500 progressively challenging end-of-chapter questions. Written in a clear and engaging style, this textbook is a complete resource for teaching the fundamental skills that today's students need. Instructor resources are available online, including a test bank, solutions manual, and sample code.

Dan S. Myers is Associate Professor of Computer Science at Rollins College in Winter Park, Florida, where he has taught Data Structures and Algorithms for 10 years.

"An intuitive and engaging introduction to foundational content; a terrific source for anyone looking to dive deeper into computer science!"

Remzi Arpaci-Dusseau, University of Wisconsin–Madison

"This book teaches data structures with an active learning approach. Students will first learn the constructs, then get hands-on experience by applying what they learned in real projects. In addition, the try-it-yourself sections are really helpful as simple brain teasers to ensure that students got the point. Students will be more engaged by learning this way."

Mohammed Farghally, Virginia Tech

"*Data Structures and Algorithms in Java* by Dan Myers is a carefully crafted book for second-level CS students, right after learning the rudiments of at least one programming language (be it Python, C/C++, or Java) and doing basic programming. To fill the gap from simple programming to serious CS, art, and natural science applications programming, a fundamental course is needed. Often named 'Data Structures and Algorithms,' this course helps students to learn beyond basic data structures such as numbers and arrays, and to move to the world of lists, stacks, hash tables, trees, queues, heaps, and graphs. There are also the fundamental algorithms, such as searching, sorting, hashing, and binary tree traversal algorithms, which are the building blocks of more complicated algorithms needed to develop applications programs. Here is an excellent book that skillfully brings students to serious programming, by providing meaningful explanations, beautiful figures, and short but to-the-point code fragments. The exercises at the end of every chapter are very helpful. Fascinating projects every few chapters make even an experienced programmer want to try, such as particle effects, generative art, fractals, logic puzzles, and specialized search engines. I strongly urge the CS instructor to consider this book before making commitment to their often-used textbook."

Çetin Kaya Koç, University of California, Santa Barbara

"With beautifully accessible prose, Professor Myers opens the door wide to a field known for its formidable jargon and subtle technical detail. This text offers scaffolded, incremental learning as well as innovative and engaging projects, all well designed and supported by a wealth of diverse exercises. His rich, interdisciplinary contexts also demonstrate the centrality of algorithms in many human endeavors."

Trevor Kearns, Greenfield Community College

"I wholeheartedly endorse *Data Structures and Algorithms in Java*. Its unique project-based approach effectively merges theory with practical application, making it an invaluable resource for undergraduate students. The book's emphasis on hands-on learning through Java programming projects elevates the understanding and deepens the knowledge of the applicability of data structures."

Tajmilur Rahman Md, Gannon University

"*Data Structures and Algorithms in Java* is a must-read for aspiring programmers. The book bridges theory and practice seamlessly using real-world projects illustrating key concepts. The book covers a wide array of data structures from the simple stack to the more complex graph. The author's beginner-friendly approach makes it an excellent companion for self-learners and computer science students alike."

Lilian Blot, University of York

"The examples of projects offer a fun yet insightful way to boost students' creativity and enhance their problem-solving skills following the 'Try It Yourself' approach, ensuring the understanding of each concept."

Jeong Yang, Texas A&M University–San Antonio

"Dr. Myers carefully balances teaching students the Java they need after an introductory programming course with building more complex projects that students can use in their job portfolios. It covers the fundamental data structures and algorithms students need to know while immediately applying those ideas to longer-form projects in areas of student interest."

Brian Patterson, Oglethorpe University

"A stand-out feature of this book is its project-based approach, which bridges theoretical content with real-world applications. This method not only enhances students' understanding of data structures and algorithms, but also prepares them for technical roles through a variety of creative projects."

Bailin Deng, Cardiff University

"This book goes beyond the typical scope of a data structures and algorithms textbook. The carefully described projects are excellent examples of how to structure large programs."

Christian Trefftz, Grand Valley State University

"I have developed many techniques, tools, and examples to facilitate learning in my data structures classes. Dan Myers' textbook incorporates many similar strategies – it is conversational, establishes a foundation for new concepts and techniques then builds upon the foundation. It also incorporates numerous examples and problems, including historical references, making the material more interesting. This is a refreshing take on a potentially dry subject."

Dave Rosenberg, Wentworth Institute of Technology

"The project-based approach in the book highlights the real-world applications of topics presented, and facilitates greater understanding and clarity. The interview questions included underscore the importance of the concepts beyond the classroom. Several sections introduce new topics in simple terms along with relevant fun facts which draw the reader in and make the learning process an engaging one. Highly recommended!"

Omofolakunmi Olagbemi, Hope College

"Professor Myers' project-based approach not only motivates students but also offers a practical framework for applying complex concepts effectively. The projects in this text provide context for decision-making and enhance understanding through practical applications. Each project builds a solid foundation fostering thoughtful engagement with challenging material."

Michael Penta, Northern Essex Community College

Data Structures and Algorithms in Java A Project-Based Approach

Dan S. Myers

Rollins College, Florida

Shaftesbury Road, Cambridge CB2 8EA, United Kingdom

One Liberty Plaza, 20th Floor, New York, NY 10006, USA

477 Williamstown Road, Port Melbourne, VIC 3207, Australia

314–321, 3rd Floor, Plot 3, Splendor Forum, Jasola District Centre, New Delhi – 110025, India

103 Penang Road, #05–06/07, Visioncrest Commercial, Singapore 238467

Cambridge University Press is part of Cambridge University Press & Assessment, a department of the University of Cambridge.

We share the University's mission to contribute to society through the pursuit of education, learning and research at the highest international levels of excellence.

www.cambridge.org
Information on this title: www.cambridge.org/highereducation/isbn/9781009260336

DOI: 10.1017/9781009260350

When citing this work, please include a reference to the DOI 10.1017/9781009260350

First published 2025

A catalogue record for this publication is available from the British Library

A Cataloging-in-Publication data record for this book is available from the Library of Congress

ISBN 978-1-009-26033-6 Hardback

Additional resources for this publication at www.cambridge.org/myers

For Chelsea, who helped make it possible

Contents

Preface

Teaching our students how to understand and use algorithms is the heart of the computer science curriculum. The relevance of algorithms to the modern world may seem obvious, but the unfortunate reality is that many of our students will finish their data structures and algorithms coursework with no idea how the material applies to actual software development. This book fills a gap in the data structures and algorithms literature by offering students and instructors an engaging and carefully curated text that presents all of the fundamental material of the data structures and algorithms course while also emphasizing meaningful applications in CS, the arts, and the natural sciences. Every content-based chapter is paired with at least one significant project or application illustrating how to use the chapter's theory in a creative context.

Motivation and Content

This book is aimed at the standard undergraduate "CS2" course that presents the core content of data structures and algorithms (sorting, lists, trees, complexity analysis, etc.) to students who have already completed introductory programming. It emerged as a response to real challenges I've encountered while teaching CS2 over the past 10 years, which I think will resonate with instructors at a broad range of institutions:

- **Review of CS1 material**. Many universities expect students to take CS2 as their second programming-focused course, typically after one semester covering the fundamentals of programming. Therefore, the CS2 course needs to begin with a review of fundamental concepts and a deeper presentation of object-oriented programming before introducing new material. This problem has become more acute in recent years as programs have shifted their introductory class to Python while keeping the data structures course in Java.
- **Developing students' project portfolios**. Job-market demand for CS graduates remains high, but competition for the best internships and full-time jobs is intense. Students are under pressure to develop a portfolio of significant projects that they can showcase in job and internship applications. Because students now seek internships earlier, there is often a need to include significant portfolio-ready projects earlier in the curriculum. The CS2 course is an ideal place to incorporate creative projects for early CS majors.
- **Relevance**. Many data structures resources, including the popular online practice sites, emphasize abstract puzzle-style problem solving. While solving algorithmic puzzles

can certainly build students' skills, they don't do much to generate enthusiasm for the subject or show how data structures and algorithms connect to interesting applications. Professional developers often associate the subject solely with preparing for technical interviews.

The CS2 course, therefore, needs to do several things: build fundamental programming skills, teach theoretical content, prepare students for electives, and get students ready for job and internship applications, while also nurturing their growing engagement with the discipline. Over the coming years, we will likely see the current emphasis on student success and persistence in the CS1 course continue up to the rest of the computer science curriculum. In addition to a greater emphasis on active learning, we'll see a desire for relevance, interdisciplinary applications, and social awareness throughout the CS major. The content of this book was designed with those goals in mind. It features:

- coverage of fundamental data structures and algorithms topics, including recursion, lists, stacks, trees, graphs, sorting, and complexity analysis;
- project-based chapters that apply content in significant software projects, of the kind that could be major assignments or featured in a student's resume and portfolio;
- emphasis on interdisciplinary application areas;
- early review of object-oriented programming for recent CS1 students;
- active learning using reflective questions and solutions integrated throughout the text, informed by extensive undergraduate teaching experience; and
- an additional section in each theoretical chapter illustrating techniques that frequently show up in technical interview questions – working through these examples will help students engage with other technical interview resources.

In return, the book makes a careful trade-off to de-emphasize niche data structures, as well as limit coverage of advanced topics in algorithm design and analysis that are more likely to be featured in an upper-level course.

A Project-Based Approach

Every topic includes at least one significant Java programming project illustrating how the theoretical content can apply to interdisciplinary problems. Some of these examples are time-tested standards that will be familiar from previous books, but most are new. The goal of these projects is not only to give students programming practice, but to illustrate how data structures and algorithms are used to solve interesting problems. Examples include:

- a turtle graphics system using the Java Graphics API and object-oriented techniques (Chapter 3);
- particle-based graphic effects and artificial life simulations (Chapter 7);
- writing graphical applications to produce recursive generative art and fractal images, including the famous Mandelbrot set (Chapter 9);
- a small HTML viewer and web browser (Chapter 11);
- password cracking and hashing (Chapter 14);

- a text-based search engine for a Shakespeare play (Chapter 16); and
- a recommendation system using random walks on a bipartite graph (Chapter 21).

The theoretical chapters feature smaller application sections that can be covered as part of a topical lecture. The larger projects are in stand-alone chapters and have been designed to be extensible, so that instructors can present the basic design of each project, work through the example code, and then assign modifications to the basic project as homework. The project chapters are written in a follow-along style that develops each application incrementally. Laboratory or small discussion sections are an ideal environment for presenting and coding the initial project solutions.

The projects and examples do not require any specific platform, development environment, or specialized software libraries. Any desktop or cloud-based editor that can compile and run Java is suitable for the course. All of the projects use straightforward object-oriented Java programming and the Java standard library; there are no projects that rely on custom libraries or elaborate prewritten code that exists outside of the text. After working through the examples and projects in this book, students will be comfortable writing moderate-sized Java programs and will be prepared for upper-level courses on object-oriented software design and algorithm analysis.

Student Background

This book is aimed at early-career computer science students with at least one semester of programming experience and some familiarity with object-oriented programming. It assumes that students have seen (but not yet mastered) the core concepts of structured programming – variables, data types, functions, control structures, I/O, etc. – typically covered in the standard "CS1" course, and that students are comfortable working with moderate-sized programs that combine those features into one application.

Students entering without previous Java experience should spend the first weeks of the class working through the material of Chapters 1 and 2, which introduce the basic elements of Java and object-oriented programming. Chapter 4 presents one-dimensional and two-dimensional arrays. After completing those chapters, students should be comfortable writing CS1-level programs in Java. Students who have already completed a Java course can move a little faster, but reviewing the core material on object-oriented programming and arrays is still recommended. This book focuses on using Java to implement data structures and algorithms topics, so it isn't intended to be a comprehensive guide to all of Java, or to object-oriented software design. For the most part, Java topics are introduced when they're required for a project.

Course Design

Instructors have a number of options when designing a class with this book. Covering every chapter is too much for a one-semester course, so you may prefer to focus on your favorite examples and projects. Additional resources for instructors, including full implementations of all projects and major examples, solutions to the end-of-chapter questions, a test bank, and teaching guide are available online. The text is organized as follows:

- Chapters 1–4 present Java fundamentals. If students have had a previous course in Java, this can be covered efficiently. Chapter 3, the turtle graphics project, introduces the graphics framework that will be used throughout the first half of the book, so you should include it if you plan to use any of the projects from Chapters 4–9.
- Chapters 5–7 introduce algorithm analysis, Big-O notation, and lists. This is core content for any data structures course. Chapters 6 and 7 also demonstrate interfaces and graphical applications with user input.
- Chapter 8 presents recursion. If students have already seen standard recursive examples in an earlier course, you could cover this material quickly, in preparation for sorting algorithms in Chapter 10. Chapter 9 is a major project covering recursive art and the Mandelbrot fractal viewer.
- Chapters 10–17 cover the fundamental algorithms and data structures: sorting (10), stacks (11), backtracking search (12), queues (13), hashing (14), hash tables (15), and binary search trees (17). These will likely form the core of any CS2 course and you could realistically expect to spend 10 weeks on this material.
- Chapters 18–22 are additional material that may not fit into a one-semester course: self-balancing trees (18), heaps (19), and graphs (20–22).

The following table shows an example 14-week schedule for a course that starts with a review of Java and touches on all of the core content. This sequence covers roughly one chapter per week, with the vision that students will complete one guided project from the text (independently or in a weekly lab meeting), then complete assigned project extensions or a set of end-of-chapter questions for further practice.

Week	Topic	Chapter	Project
1	Java basics	1	Monte Carlo simulation
2	Java basics cont.	1	Substitution ciphers
3	Objects	2	Card games
4	Graphical applications	3	DIY turtle graphics
5	Arrays	4	Conway's Life
6	Algorithm analysis	5	Ch. 5 practice questions
7	Lists	6	*Snake* game or particle graphics (Ch. 7)
8	Recursion	8	Fractal art (Ch. 9)
9	Sorting	10	Ch. 10 practice questions
10	Stacks	11	Tiny web browser
11	Backtracking search	12	Logic puzzles
12	Hashing	14	Password cracker
13	Hash tables	15	Text search engine (Ch. 16)
14	Trees	17	Ch. 17 practice questions

This book has enough material for a two-course sequence. Many programs have made the choice to use a "bridge" course that sits between CS1 and CS2, with the goal of helping students transition between early programming and the full data structures course. With this model, the bridge course could cover Chapters 1–9, with their projects, at a moderate pace. The CS2 course would review analysis and recursion and then cover the remaining topics from Chapters 10–22.

Self-Teaching

This book can also serve as a useful companion for working software developers who want to improve their data structures and algorithms knowledge. Many developers without a formal computer science background find it difficult to bridge the gap between early programming and upper-level theoretical texts on algorithm analysis intended for graduate students. This book was created to provide a smooth introduction to important theoretical topics and also serve as an antidote to the popular view that algorithms are only important for "whiteboard" technical interviews.

If you are using this book to teach yourself, simply start wherever you feel appropriate and work through the material at your own pace. If you have no or limited Java experience, you should definitely start with Chapters 1 and 2. Follow the directions for the example projects and, if time permits, add a few of the extensions. It isn't necessary, or even desirable, to complete every project or end-of-chapter question, so don't force yourself and allow yourself to move on if you become stuck. The sequence of topics and projects given above would also be appropriate for a self-taught developer. Completing that schedule will equip you with the core knowledge required for technical interviews and give a solid base for further study in more advanced books.

Responding to AI

ChatGPT was publicly released while I was halfway through writing this book. Although it remains to be seen how far large-language models will develop, it's fair to say that they're already powerful enough to have a disruptive effect on introductory CS courses. Our traditional model of assessment – leave class, write some small programs, and run them against test cases – fails in the face of automated tools that can solve those problems better than most undergraduates. As teachers, we have to strike a balance between remaining open to AI tools – which are going to be a key part of professional software development going forward – while still equipping our students with fundamental skills.

Although it wasn't originally planned with AI in mind, I believe the approach of this book is one part of that balance. The presentation here emphasizes *context*, rooting the discussion of data structures and algorithms in meaningful larger-scale projects and emphasizing connections across disciplines. Asking students to develop in a hands-on way, by building and extending the specific solutions given in the text, lessens their ability to rely only on an AI tool. Ultimately, though, nothing is safe. It seems likely that every piece of public code will eventually be absorbed into one language model or another, and clever students will always use every tool at their disposal. Now, at this moment, I see this book as one contribution to a conversation about how to continue evolving the curriculum and pedagogy of our discipline.

Sell your cleverness and buy bewilderment instead.
Cleverness is mere opinion. Bewilderment
brings intuition.
Rumi

Algorithms+Data Structures = Programs

OVERVIEW

There's a perception that computer science is constantly changing, and in some respects that's true: There are always new languages, frameworks, and application domains rising up and old ones sinking down. All of this change that we see around us, though, is like the *top part of an iceberg*. The most visible elements of our field are built upon and supported by a deeper layer of knowledge that's mostly invisible to the casual observer. This book is about what's under the water, *the fundamental things that make programming possible*, even if we don't see them right away.

LEARNING OBJECTIVES

This chapter introduces the topics ahead. By the end of it, you'll understand:

- How algorithms and data structures work together to create programs.
- Key points from the history of algorithms that are still relevant to us today and the definition of an algorithm.
- Why data structures and algorithms matter to real-world programmers.
- Suggestions for improving your own learning and tips for teaching yourself.

Goals

Consider just a few examples of challenging real-world programming problems:

- predicting moves for a game-playing program;
- implementing a compiler for a new programming language;
- creating digital special effects for an animated movie;
- generating procedural content in an open-world game;
- routing data through the network of devices that make up the Internet; and
- building a large language AI model like ChatGPT.

These problems are all different, but in order to solve them you need an understanding of both **algorithms** and **data structures**. You've probably encountered both of these terms before, even if you haven't studied them in depth yet. An algorithm, in plain words, is a precisely specified procedure for solving a problem. Computer programs are algorithms, but the term could be applied to any series of steps that accomplishes a goal, from assembling modular furniture to baking a key lime pie. Data structures are standard ways of organizing a program's information so that it can be easily accessed and manipulated. You've probably already encountered some standard data structures, like arrays in Java or C, or lists and dictionaries in Python.

With that in mind, this book focuses on three major topics:

- A set of *fundamental data structures* that are essential for every computer scientist and programmer. Each of the data structures we'll cover – including lists, stacks, queues, hash tables, trees, and graphs – represents a particular way of arranging and manipulating data, and they each have their own strengths and important applications. These are the most important data structures that occur over and over again throughout computer science.
- A collection of *standard algorithmic techniques* that are building blocks of more complex programs, including recursion, sorting, backtracking, and hashing.
- A *framework for comparing algorithms*. If two methods solve the same problem, can we say that one is "better" in a rigorous way? This question is addressed by the techniques of **algorithm analysis**, which we'll use to evaluate the quality of our solutions.

Finally, it's not enough to simply understand data structures theoretically: you have to use them! Each chapter of this book will show you how to implement data structures and use them in Java applications. Some chapters feature larger stand-alone projects that you can feature on a resume or project portfolio.

A Brief History of Algorithms

The concept of an algorithm has existed since ancient times, although the term itself did not come into its modern use until the nineteenth century. Clay tablets from Mesopotamia (approximately 2000–1800 BCE) discuss procedures for performing arithmetic by hand and solving equations that are relevant to agriculture and building (Knuth, 1972). Greek mathematicians described methods for finding roots and divisors, estimating π, and solving some classes of equations.

What, though, is an algorithm, really? Scientists have wrangled over a formal definition, but it's generally agreed that a procedure must meet some criteria in order to be called an algorithm (Shaffer, 1997; Cormen et al., 2022):

- It must have *well-defined inputs and outputs.*
- Each step must be *concrete and feasible.* That is, there should be no ambiguity about what is to be performed at each step and each step must be something that a computer (or other agent executing the algorithm) can actually do. Further, the order of the steps must be unambiguous.

- It must be *correct*. For its given inputs, the algorithm must produce correct outputs.
- It should have only a *finite* number of instructions. Programs can contain loops or other control structures, but it has to be possible to write the algorithm down in a form that allows it to be executed.
- It must *terminate*. The running time may be infeasibly large, but the method must eventually end and produce an output.

Try It Yourself

The physicist Richard Feynman is credited with the following algorithm for solving any problem:

1. Write down the problem.
2. Think very hard.
3. Write down the solution.

Explain why Feynman's method, clever though it may be, is not really an algorithm.

The term **algorithm** itself is derived from the ninth-century Islamic Persian scholar Muḥammad ibn Mūsā al-Khwārizmī. The name al-Khwārizmī means "from Khwarazm," which is located in present-day Uzbekistan. He was a true polymath, active in all the scientific fields of his day, but his legacy is connected to writing on mathematics. His most important work is *al-Kitāb al-Mukhtaṣar fī Ḥisāb al-Jabr wal-Muqābalah*, translated as *The Compendious Book of Calculation by Completion and Balancing*, which provided general methods for solving quadratic equations. The book named the field of algebra, from *al-Jabr*, meaning "completion," which refers to the process of moving terms between the two sides of an equation (Gandz, 1926). al-Khwārizmī also wrote texts describing arithmetic using the now-standard system of Indian-Arabic numerals, which were compiled and translated into Latin as *Algoritmi de numero Indorum* – "Algoritmi on the Indian numbers." In Europe, the term *algorismus* came to refer to the techniques for doing calculation on decimal numbers; by the nineteenth century it had acquired its modern form and meaning.

Although mathematicians and engineers continued to develop new computational techniques, algorithms didn't emerge as a distinct field of study until the post-World War II period and the development of electronic computers. The early pioneers of computer science began to investigate not just algorithms for specific problems, but the design and evaluation of algorithms as its own field of study. The study of data structures as a distinct subject developed as computer science and software engineering matured in the 1960s.

Programming in the earliest days was done in low-level machine languages that gave programmers a great deal of control but lacked support for abstractions such as variables. As a result, it was often hard to reason about the correctness of programs, and debugging was painful and time-consuming. By the late 1960s, a group of computer scientists led by Edsger Dijkstra began to advocate for **structured programming** in "high-level" languages like Fortran, ALGOL, and C. These languages were more abstract than machine language and allowed programmers to think more about the *meaning* of a program and how that meaning should be best expressed in code. Along with these ideas came an increased focus on the relationship between a program's code and the data that it operates on. The Swiss computer scientist Niklaus Wirth described it like this (Wirth, 1976):

> *Programs*, after all, are concrete formulations of abstract *algorithms* based on particular representations and structures of *data*.

Data structures are important because they provide the basis on which the program's algorithm executes. This insight led to considerable research into the best ways to organize information in programs, which by the 1980s had become a core part of the computer science curriculum.

Why Do Data Structures and Algorithms Matter to Real-World Programmers?

"That sounds interesting," you may say, "but do I need to learn this material to be a highly paid software professional?" I'll tell you the truth, reader: *You don't have to learn any of this stuff to be a working software developer*. Even if you can get paid without reading this book, though, there are still good reasons to spend time engaging with this material, whether you're doing that in a formal course or for self-study.

- Algorithms and data structures are *foundational to all of programming*. Foundational knowledge, in any field, is important because it's transferable. If you understand, for example, how to use a data structure like a hash table,[1] that knowledge can then be applied to any language, framework, or problem. Mastering the material in this book will make it easier for you to see the connections and patterns that reoccur over and over again throughout computer science.
- Second, as your career advances, you'll eventually encounter hard problems. The closer you get to the cutting edge of the field – in areas like AI, scientific computing, or programming language design – the less your success depends upon knowing a specific language or tool and the more it depends on having *strong core computer science skills*.
- If you play sports, you've probably spent time in the gym lifting weights or stretching as preparation for training on the field. Athletes train muscles and movements that aren't part of their sport because they want to be strong and injury-free. In the same way, knowing algorithms and data structures will help you *avoid common design mistakes*. In particular, algorithm analysis will help you avoid wasting time from choosing bad, inefficient solutions that can't scale.
- Finally, like a jazz musician building chops by practicing technical exercises and solos by other musicians, working through the projects in this book will *make you better at programming* and prepare you for larger projects.

1 Covered in Chapters 14–16.

Learning from This Book

If you're using this book for a course, your instructor will provide you with a schedule of suggested readings and assignments. If you're a working programmer using it to teach yourself, then you have more freedom to explore the material at your own pace. In either case, here are some tips for getting the most out of this (or any) text.

Orient yourself. Read the introduction and section headings for a chapter and read the learning goals in the introduction, which will give you an overview of the intended outcomes. When you finish a chapter, return and review its outcomes.

Focus on the problem. Data structures and algorithms exist to solve interesting problems. When you're learning a new technique, always ask yourself, "What applications benefit from this?"

Use active learning. Every chapter contains *Try It Yourself* sections integrated into the text that allow you to think about the parts you've just read. When you encounter these, stop and think about them. Don't immediately move on to the solution without trying the question for a few minutes. Read the example programs carefully and reflect on how they work.

Implement the projects. The larger example projects are a key element of this book. If you're a relatively new Java programmer, they'll show you how to use the language's features and develop your coding style and organization skills. Resist the temptation to simply copy the project code and then run it – build the projects step by step and focus on the reasoning behind each implementation.

Do the exercises but don't get stuck. Each chapter ends with several exercises and extensions you can try. These are helpful, but it isn't necessary to do every one. Pick the ones that seem interesting. I recommend doing most of the "Understand" questions, several of the "Apply" questions, and at least a few of the more difficult "Extend" questions. If you get stuck on a question, give it a fair try then move on to something else. You'll likely find that returning to it later, after you have some more practice, will help you get unstuck. If you're using this book as part of a class, don't be afraid to ask your professor or teaching assistants for help, even on questions that aren't assigned to you.[2]

Revisit and compare. As you work through each topic, think about how it relates to the other topics you've already seen. For example, the early chapters of the book cover arrays and lists, which are similar to each other, but used for different applications. As you complete each new topic, read back through the introduction and ending sections of earlier chapters and think about how what you've just learned is similar to and different from the earlier material. Doing this will help you build a richer mental map of the important concepts and their relationships.

Try It Yourself

Think about your previous programming experience. What worked well for you when you were learning new concepts? What didn't work well?

2 We like it when you do this.

SUMMARY

This chapter has introduced our major theme: data structures and algorithms working together to make programs possible. As you're reading, consider the following points:

- There is often no "best" solution to a particular programming problem, but rather multiple solutions with their own trade-offs. Understanding data structures and algorithm analysis will help you evaluate these trade-offs in an intelligent way.
- Even if you use higher-level libraries and frameworks, understanding the fundamentals of computer science will improve your programming and help you learn.
- The concepts from this book are relevant to every area of computer science, including programming language design, systems, AI, and networking.

We'll start the next chapter with an introduction to Java.

EXERCISES

Understand

1. List three examples of algorithms that aren't programming or cooking related.
2. Give an example of a procedure that isn't an algorithm by our criteria.
3. Other than execution time, what are some qualities we might consider in determining whether an algorithm is good or not?
4. Sorting data is an important problem and many sorting algorithms have been developed. What is a real-world problem that requires sorting data?
5. Consider your previous programming experience. What data structures and algorithms have you already studied?
6. Do some research on the difference between active and passive learning. What makes learning active?

Apply

7. I wrote an algorithm that uses a `random` function to make a choice. Explain why the program is still an algorithm, even if the output is not the same every time it runs.
8. I wrote another program that runs and terminates but doesn't display any output or save any results. Is that an algorithm?
9. Think about a classic 2D video game like *Pac-Man*. What data do you need to keep track of for the different elements on the screen? What about a modern 3D game?
10. Many languages support a basic data type for character strings. List some common operations that you would expect to perform on character strings.
11. Explain why any program executing on a computer is automatically composed of concrete, feasible steps. Tip: Think about what happens when a program runs. What is the CPU actually doing?

12. Do some research on genealogies. What kind of data structure could you consider using to model a person's family history?
13. Do some research on social networks. What kind of data structure might you use to model the connections between users on a social media platform?

Extend

14. **Bloom's taxonomy** is a model for structuring learning goals based on their complexity. It arranges engagement with a topic into a hierarchy, where the lowest level is memorizing basic facts and the highest is creating new original knowledge. Do some research on Bloom's taxonomy, then give an example of a question or project about algorithms that fits into each of its categories.
15. Do some research on difficult problems. Identify and describe one problem for which there is no known efficient algorithm.
16. Look up the word "metacognition." How does metacognition apply to learning?
17. Think about your own learning process in programming or another area. What lessons have you learned about how **you** learn best?

NOTES AND FURTHER READING

The title of this chapter is a reference to Niklaus Wirth's book, *Algorithms + Data Structures = Programs* (Wirth, 1976). Wirth designed Pascal, one of the most important programming languages of the 1970s and 1980s, and contributed to the development of object-oriented programming with the Modula family of languages. The book was influential and widely used in education. It contains a great overview of building a tiny compiler for a small Pascal-like language. After you finish this book, there are a number of other excellent resources you can read. Cormen et al.'s *Introduction to Algorithms* is a classic upper-level book that covers algorithm design, analysis, and advanced data structures (Cormen et al., 2022). Skiena's *Algorithm Design Manual* features a catalog of important problems and approaches for tackling each one, along with a number of entertaining stories about his experience designing algorithms for real-world problems (Skiena, 1998).

Java is a blue collar language. It's not PhD thesis material but a language for a job.
James Gosling

1 Java Fundamentals

INTRODUCTION

Java is one of the world's most popular programming languages. Widely used in enterprise software development, Java's strengths lie in its combination of performance and portability, as well as its large, robust library of built-in features, which allow developers to create complex applications entirely within the language. Java was developed in the early 1990s by a team from Sun Microsystems led by James Gosling. Initially called Oak (after a tree outside Gosling's office), the new language was intended to be a development environment for interactive TV, but pivoted to the emerging World Wide Web after its public release in 1995. Since then, Java has expanded into almost every area of software development. It is the default programming language for Android mobile devices, the Hadoop large-scale data processing system, and *Minecraft*. Java is one of the most well-known **object-oriented** programming languages.

This chapter surveys the core elements of Java programming, assuming some familiarity with programming in any language. If you already have Java experience, it will be a refresher on important points. If your experience is with Python, JavaScript, or other languages, this chapter will help you understand how Java does things differently.

LEARNING OBJECTIVES

By the end of this chapter you'll be able to

- Write programs using the core elements of Java: variables, types, conditionals, loops, and methods.
- Use built-in classes from the standard library to represent text, read input, and do calculations.
- Combine these features to implement simulation programs and historical cryptographic algorithms.

The next chapter extends these fundamentals and focuses on object-oriented programming. After completing both chapters, you'll be well-prepared to move forward with the rest of the book.

1.1 Hello, Java!

Let's write some code! This section will show you how to write your first Java program.

1.1.1 The First Program

The traditional first program prints "Hello, World!" to the screen. This may seem trivial, but simply coding and running this program verifies that it's possible to compile and run a valid program that produces output. Copy the code below to a file named `HelloWorld.java` in your Java environment, run it, and verify that it produces the expected output.

```
// The first program: print a hello message

// All Java code is contained in a class
public class HelloWorld {

  // Main is the entry point for the program
  public static void main(String[] args) {

    // Print a message to the standard output
    System.out.println("Hello, World!");
  }
}
```

Every Java program is enclosed in a `class` block. The class name is the name of the program, and the name of the class must match the name of the `.java` file that contains it. This class is named `HelloWorld`, so it must be in a file named `HelloWorld.java`. By convention, *class names always start with an uppercase letter*. Multi-word names are created by capitalizing each word. The top of the program also illustrates Java's basic comment: Two forward slashes tells the compiler to ignore everything on the same line. Java also supports multiline comments; we'll see an example shortly.

Every Java application must contain one method called `main`, which is the *entry point* for the program. When `HelloWorld` executes, it begins at the first line of `main`. Java is more verbose than Python, and programming the `main` method requires chanting an invocation to the Java verbosity gods. That invocation is:

```
public static void main(String[] args)
```

The signature for `main` must contain all of these keywords. For now, don't worry about the meaning of `public`, `static`, and `void` – we'll come to them soon.[1] The `main` method always takes one input argument, a `String[]` called `args`, used to pass command-line arguments into

1 `void` will be discussed in Section 1.6; `public` and `static` will be covered in Chapter 2.

the program.[2] Note that `args` is required even if the program doesn't use any command-line arguments.

Like its C/C++ ancestors, Java uses curly braces to mark blocks of code. We prefer to place the left curly brace on the same line as the block declaration, but other style guides place it on the next line (Google, 2022a). Whitespace is not syntactically significant in Java – unlike Python, Java does not require spacing to indicate the structure of your program – but you should always *indent each new block* to show the logical structure of the program.

The basic printing method is `System.out.println`, which outputs a string to the terminal and then moves to the next line. The input is a text string, denoted using *double quotes*; Java does not allow single-quoted strings.

```
System.out.println("Hello, World!");
```

Every Java statement is terminated by a semicolon. `System` is a special built-in Java object that provides access to the computer's operating system and lower-level utility methods. Every Java program automatically has access to `System` and its methods. Notice that `System` starts with a capital `S`, which is required.

Try It Yourself

- Write a new program called `Haiku.java` that contains a class called `Haiku`. Use three print statements to output this haiku by the poet Kobayashi Issa, famous for his poems about insects and small creatures:

  little snail,
  inch by inch –
  climb Mount Fuji!

- Java's printing supports the standard set of special characters: `\n` for a newline, `\t` for a tab, `\"` for a literal double quote within a string, and `\\` for a literal backslash. Use multiple print statements and `\"` to print this version of *The Raven* as a limerick (Doctorow, 2007). Put your program in a file named `Raven.java` in a class named `Raven`.

  There once was a girl named Lenore,
  And a bird, and a bust, and a door,
  And a guy with depression,
  And a whole lot of questions,
  And the bird always says, "Nevermore."

2 Programs that run in a Linux shell may get inputs this way.

1.1.2 How Java Programs Execute

A computer can't execute Java – or any other high-level source code – directly. Different languages handle the problem of moving from source code to executable program in different ways.

- Systems programming languages such as C, C++, and Rust are *compiled* all the way down to a sequence of basic machine language instructions that then execute directly on the computer's processor. Compiled programs generally have high performance, but the executable is tied directly to the processor's architecture, so porting across multiple platforms is difficult.
- Scripting languages like JavaScript, Ruby, Perl, and BASIC are traditionally *interpreted*. A special program, the interpreter, scans the source code and executes it directly without doing any additional translation or generating low-level machine code (Nystrom, 2021). Interpreted languages can run on any platform that supports the interpreter, but these languages are often slower than their fully compiled counterparts.[3]

Java combines elements of both compilation and interpretation. The Java compiler, called `javac`, first translates your source code file into a lower-level format called **Java Byte Code** (JBC). The JBC form of the program is similar to the basic machine language instructions used by a computer's processor, but JBC is actually a *virtual* machine language that isn't tied to any specific real-world processor. Instead, the byte code program is executed by the **Java Virtual Machine** (JVM), a software program that emulates the registers, memory, and other low-level details of a virtual computer. This system allows Java programs to be *platform independent*. Software developers can write applications using Java, which can then be run by any end-user with a JVM program installed on their system – the actual architecture of the end-user's computer is irrelevant. The ability to write platform-independent web applets was a major feature that drove adoption of Java in its early years.

Java's designers did not invent the virtual machine concept; it was originally developed in the 1970s for the Pascal language. The reference implementation of Python, CPython, uses a similar approach, where Python source code is first converted into an internal byte code format, which is then interpreted (Python, 2022). There are now a number of languages – notably Clojure, Kotlin, and Scala – that are not Java but compile to JBC and execute on the JVM.

1.2 Variables and Data Types

As in other languages, a Java variable is a *name associated with a value*. Java requires that every variable have an explicitly declared **type**, indicating what kind of data is valid for the variable. If your previous experience was with Python or JavaScript, the way Java handles variables may seem complex at first.

3 The distinction between compiled and interpreted languages can be thin. Modern high-performance interpreters, like the Chrome browser's V8 JavaScript engine, use techniques like *just-in-time compilation* to convert source code to machine language as the program executes (V8 Dev, 2010).

1.2.1 Declaring Variables

The following statement declares an integer variable and assigns 5 to it:

```
int fingersPerHand = 5;
```

Conceptually, think of a variable as a little "box" of memory that holds a piece of data. The name of the variable is bound to the box as its identifier. The type specifies what kinds of values are allowed in the box. In this case, the memory box associated with `fingersPerHand` can only hold `int` values.

```
                int
fingersPerHand [ 5 ]
```

Declaring a type for every variable in the program's code is called *static typing*. The alternative approach is *dynamic typing*, where variables do not have explicit, fixed types and the type of a variable depends on its current value. Java's compiler checks the types of all data and variables and will flag any operations that violate the type system. For example, the string `"5"` is not the same as the integer number `5`, so the following statement results in a compiler error:

```
// Type error: cannot assign a String value to an int variable
int fingersPerHand = "5";
```

1.2.2 Variable Names

By convention, Java variable names start with a lowercase letter and can contain lowercase and uppercase letters, numbers, and the underscore character. Like classes, multi-word variable names are created by capitalizing subsequent words:

```
int brainWeightInGrams = 1400;
int numberOfBones = 206;
int litersOfBlood = 5;
```

This style of variable naming is often called **camelCase**, because it makes multi-word variable names "bumpy." The alternative of separating multiple words with underscores (e.g., `number_of_bones`) is sometimes called **snake_case**, which is – appropriately – preferred for Python. Remember that variable names should never start with an uppercase letter; that style is reserved for class names.

1.2.3 Primitive and Object Types

Java has eight basic **primitive types**, summarized in Table 1.1. Each primitive type represents a single value in a specific underlying data format.

- `int`: The basic 32-bit integer type, representing signed integers in the range of approximately ±2.14 billion. Use `int` for most data and calculations involving whole numbers.
- `short`: A smaller integer type. A `short` is half the size of an `int` (16 bits) and has a range of −32,768 to 32,767. The most common use case for `short` values is saving memory in large arrays.

Table 1.1 **Java's eight basic primitive types**

Type	Format	Range	Example values
`int`	32-bit signed integer	-2^{31} to $2^{31} - 1$	`10, 0, -101`
`short`	16-bit signed integer	-2^{16} to $2^{16} - 1$	`10, 0, 32767`
`long`	64-bit signed integer	-2^{64} to $2^{64} - 1$	`12345L, -6789L`
`byte`	8-bit signed integer	−128 to 127	`0, -101`
`double`	64-bit floating point	±1.7E308	`-1.0, 3.14, 2e100`
`float`	32-bit floating point	±3.4E38	`-1.0f, 3.14F`
`char`	16-bit Unicode	A single text character	`'z', '0', 'n'`
`boolean`	Logical value	N/A	`true, false`

- `long`: A signed 64-bit integer value. Its range is approximately ±9.2 quintillion.
- `byte`: A signed 8-bit integer, with a range of −128 to 127. It can be used as a very small integer type or to represent low-level data from files and networks.
- `double`: The basic type for real numbers. The name stands "double-precision floating point," the data format used to store decimal numbers on computers, which spans a range of approximately ±1.7E308. Any number with a decimal point is automatically a `double` in Java. For example, `1` is an `int` and `1.0` is a `double`, even though the two are mathematically the same. The minimum nonzero `double` value is 4.9E-324.
- `float`: The single-precision 32-bit floating point number. Like `short`, its main use is saving memory in large arrays. To encode a `float` literal, append `f` or `F` to the number. For example, `3.1415f`. The minimum nonzero float value is 1.45E-45.
- `char`: A single text character, encoded using 16-bit Unicode representation. This encoding allows `char` to represent what Unicode calls the "Basic Multilingual Plane" containing characters for almost all modern languages, including the Latin and Cyrillic alphabets, Hebrew, Arabic, Indian and East Asian scripts, as well as common symbols (Everson et al., 2021). Enclose `char` literals in *single quotes*. For example, `'a'`, `'A'`, and `'\n'`.
- `boolean`: A single logical value that can only take on one of the two special values `true` or `false`. The `boolean` type is used for relational comparisons, conditional execution, and flags that control loops.

Any Java variable that isn't one of the eight basic primitive types is an **object**. Object types always start with a capital letter. For example, `String` is Java's built-in type for representing a sequence of text characters.[4] You can declare `String` variables in a manner similar to primitive type variables, using double quotes to enclose each character sequence:

```
String bookTitle = "The Enormous Room";
String bookAuthor = "e.e. cummings";
```

Just like the integer example, think of each `String` object as representing a little box of memory that holds the data of the object – in this case, the sequence of `char` values that make up the

4 This is a common point of confusion, particularly if you're coming from a Python background: `char` is a primitive type but `String` isn't!

string. The variables `bookTitle` and `bookAuthor` serve as **object references** that refer to their underlying `String` objects in memory. It's helpful to think of `bookTitle` as a variable that stores a little pointer to the object. Maintaining this mental model will help you reason about the relationships between names and the objects they refer to, which is important for comparing objects.

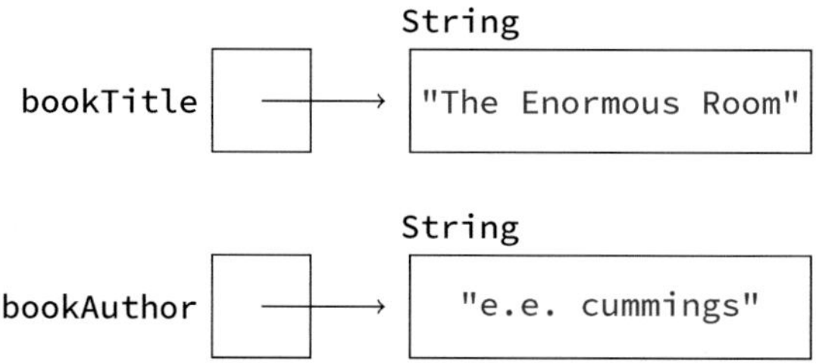

1.2.4 Arithmetic

Java supports the standard arithmetic operators: `+`, `-`, `*`, and `/`. There is no built-in exponentiation operator. These operators work the way you would expect, with one important exception for division: *dividing two integer values always produces an integer result.* The answer is truncated down to the next lowest integer:

```
// This calculation yields 3
double approxPi = 22 / 7;


// This calculation yields zero
double fraction = 3 / 4;
```

To perform exact division, make at least one value a `float` or `double`:

```
// All of these statements yield fractional results
double approxPi1 = 22.0 / 7;
double approxPi2 = 22 / 7.0;
double approxPi3 = 22.0 / 7.0;
```

Try It Yourself

Write a short program (you can choose the class and file name) to simply print the sum of 0.1 and 0.2 as a `double`.

```
double result = 0.1 + 0.2;
System.out.println(result);
```

Do you get what you expect?

Solution

The program prints `0.30000000000000004`, rather than the correct value of 0.3. Floating point numbers can only represent some numbers approximately, so fractional calculations may result in very small errors. Managing numerical errors can be a significant problem in scientific computing, linear algebra, and simulation programming. Can you find some more calculations that exhibit small numerical errors?

Try It Yourself

The beard-second is an incredibly scientific unit of length defined as the distance an average beard grows in 1 second, which is approximately 5 nanometers (Sullivan, 2009). Using this definition, it would take an average beard 55.55 hours to grow one millimeter. The longest beard in the world is 17 feet (5.18 meters) long and is housed in the Smithsonian Institution in Washington, DC. In life, it belonged to Hans Langseth, who immigrated to the United States from Norway in 1864; he died in North Dakota in 1927 (Geiling, 2014). He would wrap his beard around a corncob and carry it in his pocket. Under the (completely unrealistic) assumption that Hans Langseth grew his entire beard at the average rate of 1 mm every 55.55 hours, how many years would it take him to grow 5.18 meters of beard? Write a Java class named `BeardLength` in a file named `BeardLength.java` to perform the calculation and output your answer.

Solution

Unit conversion problems like this one are a great way to practice using basic variables, types, and calculations. In this case, Hans Langseth's beard is 5.18 meters long and grew at a rate of 1 mm every 55.55 hours. The solution converts meters to millimeters, then converts the number of hours to years. The result is about 32.8 years. Observe that the program uses descriptive variable names – not single letters – and breaks up calculations into multiple operations.

```
// The growing time of Hans Langseth's beard

public class BeardLength {
  public static void main(String[] args) {
    double lengthInMeters = 5.18;
    double lengthInMillimeters = lengthInMeters * 1000;

    double hours = lengthInMillimeters * 55.55;
    double days = hours / 24;
    double years = days / 365;
```

```
        // Use + to concatenate output into one string
        System.out.println(years + " years");
    }
}
```

1.2.5 Casting

Sometimes you need to convert a single value between different data types. A **cast** is an explicit operation that instructs the compiler to temporarily treat a value of one type as a different type. Casting is frequently used to "promote" a value from its base type so it can combine with a value of another type. For example, suppose you are performing an experiment and need to calculate a fraction of successful trials. If the data are integers, straightforward division won't work, but you can cast one value to a double to enable exact division. To cast, put the temporary type in parentheses next to its value. Casting has lower priority than arithmetic, so you may need to use parentheses to apply the cast to one value, rather than to the calculation as a whole.

```
int successes = 789;
int trials = 1500;

// This expression results in 0 because of integer division
double incorrectFraction = successes / trials;

// Cast one variable to a double to get the correct answer
double correctFraction = ((double) successes) / trials;
```

1.3 Working with Objects

One of Java's strengths is its large and well-implemented *standard library*, the set of built-in classes that are automatically available to any program that needs them. The standard library includes reference implementations for many of the data structures and algorithms that we'll discuss throughout this book, as well as utilities for useful tasks like reading user input, working with files, and performing advanced calculations. This section gives an overview of a few important built-in classes, including more detail on how to use object variables.

1.3.1 Reading User Input with `Scanner`

`Scanner` is a built-in class that can be used to read both typed user input and input from files. It can automatically format the values it reads as `int`, `double`, and other types. The following example shows how to create a new `Scanner` and use it to read input.

```
1 // Reading user input with Scanner
2
3 import java.util.Scanner;
4
5 public class ScannerDemo {
6   public static void main(String[] args) {
7     // Create a new Scanner --  System.in is the standard input
8     Scanner input = new Scanner(System.in);
9
10    // Read a String using the nextLine method
11    System.out.println("What is your name?");
12    String name = input.nextLine();
13
14    // Print a message using the name
15    System.out.printf("Hello, " + name + ".");
16  }
17 }
```

Creating and initializing a `Scanner` is more complex that declaring a basic primitive type variable. You must first import `Scanner` from the `java.util` package:

```
import java.util.Scanner;
```

Notice that `import` statements go at the very beginning of the program, before the declaration of the `public class` block. Line 8 declares a new `Scanner` variable.

```
Scanner input = new Scanner(System.in);
```

The left-hand side looks like other variable declarations, creating a variable named `input` that has type `Scanner`. The name `input` is not significant; we could have used any valid variable name. The right-hand side has two parts:

- The `new` keyword, which indicates that Java should create a new object.
- A call to the special **constructor method**, which initializes the new object. Every Java class has at least one constructor, which always has the same name as the class. The constructor for `Scanner` takes one argument, which is the input source that the new `Scanner` will read from. Here, `System.in` is a built-in reference to the standard system input.

The remainder of the method prints a prompt for the user, then reads the response as a `String` using the `nextLine` method (line 12):

```
String name = input.nextLine();
```

The nextLine method is invoked using the name of the object and a dot. This is the standard way to invoke methods of a Java object. It may be helpful to think of the dot as representing a message or command given to the object:

> "Scanner named input, use your nextLine method to read a line of text from your source and return it as a String."

The Scanner class supports a number of methods that can read and return values of different types: nextInt to read an integer value, nextDouble to read a double, and so forth. You'll have the chance to practice using these methods in future examples.

Try It Yourself

Oliver R. Smoot is an MIT graduate and former head of the American National Standards Institute (ANSI) and the International Organization for Standards (ISO). In 1958, as part of his initiation into the ΛXA fraternity, Smoot and his brothers measured the entire length of Harvard Bridge over the Charles River in Cambridge, MA, using Smoot's body as the ruler. He was at the time 170 cm tall (5 feet, 7 inches), and the bridge was declared to be 364.4 Smoots, "plus or minus one ear" (about 2,034 feet or 620 meters). Since that time, the measurement of Harvard Bridge has always been denominated in Smoots, with the markings repainted each year by the incoming ΛXA pledge class at MIT. The Cambridge police use the Smoot markings to identify the location of accidents on the bridge. Write a Java program that reads an input number of centimeters (as a double) and converts it to Smoots. Tip: Create a new Scanner to read from System.in, then use its nextDouble method to read a single number from the user.

Solution

Before looking at the code, contemplate for a moment the fact that Oliver R. Smoot established himself as a leader in the field of international standardization when *he himself is a unit of measurement*. The following program creates a Scanner to read from System.in, reads the user's input using the nextDouble method, and then performs the conversion into Smoots.

```
// Convert centimeters to Smoots

import java.util.Scanner;

public class Smoots {
  public static void main(String[] args) {
    // Create a Scanner
    Scanner input = new Scanner(System.in);

```

```
        // Prompt the user to enter a number of cm
        System.out.println("Enter a length in centimeters.");

        // Use nextDouble to read the response as a double value
        double cm = input.nextDouble();

        // Convert to Smoots
        double smoots = cm / 170.0;

        // Output
        System.out.println("That is " + smoots + " Smoots.");
    }
}
```

There's one additional point to consider: What do you do with `Scanner` when you've finished using it? It's possible to close a `Scanner` object using its `close` method:

```
// Close the Scanner
input.close();
```

This action frees up the resources allocated to the `Scanner` and it also closes the underlying input stream. This latter point can be a problem if you're reading from `System.in` – closing the `Scanner` also closes `System.in`, which means that you can't reopen another `Scanner` to read from it later in the program. Java will automatically reclaim open unused resources at the end of the program.

1.3.2 Constants and Formatted Printing

The Smoot program can be improved in a few ways. First, consider the conversion factor of 170.0 cm per Smoot. It's generally better to declare constants as dedicated variables with descriptive names. In Java, the `final` keyword declares a constant. A `final` variable can only be assigned a value one time; any attempt to reassign it later results in an error. By convention, `final` constants have their names written in ALL_CAPS with underscores separating consecutive words.[5]

```
final double CM_PER_SMOOT = 170.0;
```

The output calculation then becomes:

```
double smoots = cm / CM_PER_SMOOT;
```

5 LOUD_SNAKE_CASE.

Further, suppose we'd like to restrict the output to only two decimal places. Java supports an alternate *formatted printing* function, `System.out.printf`. Here's an example:

```
System.out.printf("%.2f Smoots, plus or minus one ear.", smoots);
```

`System.out.printf` takes a string input, followed by zero or more variables that should be substituted into the string. The substitutions are controlled by special **format specifiers** that begin with `%`. Here, `%.2f` indicates that the corresponding variable should be formatted as a floating point type with two digits after the decimal place.

Try It Yourself

Update the program to use constants and `printf`, then experiment with changing the number of decimal places in the output.

1.3.3 Run-Time Exceptions

What happens if you run the program above and try to enter a non-`double` value? For example, suppose you type the length in words:

```
Enter a length in centimeters.
one hundred
```

The result is an `InputMismatchException` with output similar to the following:

```
Exception in thread "main" java.util.InputMismatchException
    at java.base/java.util.Scanner.throwFor(Scanner.java:939)
    at java.base/java.util.Scanner.next(Scanner.java:1594)
    at java.base/java.util.Scanner.nextDouble(Scanner.java:2564)
    at Smoots.main(Smoots.java:15)
```

Exceptions are Java's way of handling **run-time errors** – problems that occur while the program is executing, as opposed to errors that are identified at compile time. In this case, the `nextDouble` method expected to read a sequence of numeric characters that could be converted into a `double`, but received an incompatible text string instead. The output shows the sequence of method calls that led to the error. When a program generates an exception, look carefully at the output trace and identify the line of your code that's responsible. In some cases, it's possible to "catch" an exception to deal with it in a controlled way, as opposed to simply crashing the program. We'll defer the discussion of exception handling for now and cover it in future projects.

1.3.4 Calculations with `Math`

`Math` is Java's built-in class providing important mathematical methods and constants, including trigonometric functions, exponents, logarithms, and random number generation. `Math` works a bit differently from `Scanner`. You don't instantiate it using `new` and, in fact, like the built-in

`System` class, it would be impossible to do so.[6] Instead, call methods of `Math` by name. For example,

```
// Math.pow calculates powers
// Math.PI is the built-in double value of pi
double r = 5.0;
double area = Math.PI * Math.pow(r, 2);

// Trigonometric functions
double s = Math.sin(Math.PI / 2);
double c = Math.cos(3 * Math.PI / 2);
```

Other useful methods include `log` (the natural logarithm), `log10` (the base-10 logarithm), and rounding functions `floor`, `ceil`, and `round`.

The `random` method generates a random uniformly distributed `double` value in the range [0.0, 1.0) – that is, 0.0 is included in the range, but 1.0 is not. It's a useful tool for generating randomized choices in programs. For example, to simulate a coin flip, you could use

```
double flip = Math.round(Math.random());
```

The output is either 0.0 or 1.0. The following statement generates a random `int` die roll from 1 to 6:

```
int roll = (int) (Math.random() * 6) + 1;
```

Multiplying the random value by 6 yields a uniformly distributed value in the range [0.0, 6.0). Casting to an `int` truncates that value, giving an integer from 0 to 5. Adding 1 shifts to the range 1 to 6.

Try It Yourself

Recall the famous Fibonacci sequence, where each term is calculated by adding the two previous terms:

$$0, 1, 1, 2, 3, 5, 8, 13, 21, 34, \ldots.$$

Surprisingly, there's a single formula that will calculate the terms of the Fibonacci sequence. The result is know as **Binet's formula**, and it says that the nth Fibonacci number f_n is given by

$$f_n = \frac{1}{\sqrt{5}}\left(\left(\frac{1+\sqrt{5}}{2}\right)^n - \left(\frac{1-\sqrt{5}}{2}\right)^n\right).$$

The special number $\frac{1+\sqrt{5}}{2}$ is the famous *golden ratio*, the most aesthetically pleasing of all proportions. It's sometimes denoted by the Greek letter ϕ (phi) after the ancient architect

6 Technically, `Math` and `System` are created one time when the program begins and can't be modified or reinitialized.

and sculptor Phidias, credited with using it in the design of the Parthenon. Write a Java class called `Binet` that uses a `Scanner` with `nextInt` to read a value of n from the standard input, then calculates f_n. Use `Math.sqrt` to calculate $\sqrt{5}$ and `Math.pow` to calculate the powers.

Solution

Don't try to fit a complex expression into one statement! Instead, use intermediate variables to break it into parts, then combine the parts together to get the final result. Here is a code fragment showing the core part of the program, which you can put into the full `main` method.

```
// Read input
Scanner input = new Scanner(System.in);
System.out.println("Enter a value of n: ");
int n = input.nextInt();

// Calculate F_n
double phi = (1 + Math.sqrt(5)) / 2;
double phi2 = (1 - Math.sqrt(5)) / 2;
double pow1 = Math.pow(phi, n);
double pow2 = Math.pow(phi2, n);
double fib = (1 / Math.sqrt(5)) * (pow1 - pow2);

System.out.println(fib);
```

1.4 Conditional Execution

We've now considered the basics of Java variables and statements. This section describes conditional execution using Java's `if` and `else` statements, and using those features to write more complex programs.

1.4.1 Relational and Logical Operators

Like other languages, Java uses the six standard **relational operators** to support comparisons. The output of a relational comparison is always a `boolean` value – either `true` or `false`.

- < and > test for strict inequality.
- <= and >= test for less-than-or-equal and greater-than-or-equal relationships.

- `==` tests for equality. Note that "equality" in Java depends on the nature of the items you're comparing. For primitive types, this operator is `true` if the two items under comparison have the same value, which is what you would expect. For object types like `String`, testing for equality is more complicated and the `==` operator is usually not what you want. Section 1.4.4 discusses this behavior in more detail.
- `!=` tests for inequality. Like `==`, this is appropriate for primitive types, but generally not used for object types.

More complex tests can be constructed using the three logical operators: `&&` (logical-*and*), `||` (logical-*or*), and `!` (inversion, or logical-*not*).

- The `&&` operator combines two boolean tests and returns `true` if both tests are `true` and `false` otherwise.
- The `||` operator returns `true` if one or both tests are `true` and `false` if both are `false`.
- The final operator, `!`, inverts the result of a single test. One application is turning an expression using `&&` into one using `||`, or vice versa. For example, consider testing if a variable `x` is outside the range 0 to 10, which could be done with logical-or:

  ```
  // true if x is outside the range 0 to 10
  x < 0 || x > 10
  ```

  This is equivalent to testing if `x` is not within the range:

  ```
  // true if x is outside the range 0 to 10
  !(0 <= x && x <= 10)
  ```

  Consider using inversion when one form of the test is easier to read and understand than another.

1.4.2 The `if-else` Statement

Like other programming languages, Java uses `if-else` statements to support conditional execution. Java's `if` statement has the following form

```
if (boolean expression) {
  // Code block that is executed if
  // the statement is true
}
```

The statement has four required parts:

- the keyword `if`;
- an expression that evaluates to `true` or `false`. The expression must be enclosed in a pair of parentheses;
- a pair of curly braces;
- a block of one or more statements inside the braces. The code block is executed only if the expression evaluates to `true`. If it evaluates to `false`, the entire block is skipped.

Use `if-else` to create a conditional statement with two mutually exclusive branches.

```
if (boolean expression) {
  // Block that is executed if the expression is true
} else {
  // Block that is executed if the expression is false
}
```

Try It Yourself

Testing if a number is odd or even (or more generally if it's divisible by some integer *k*) is a common problem. Java supports the **modulus operator**, `%`, which returns the remainder after division.

- If a number `n` is even, then `n % 2` is 0.
- If it's odd, `n % 2` is 1.

Write a code fragment that can read a number from the terminal using `nextInt` and print whether it's even or odd.

Solution

There are two mutually exclusive paths, so the `if-else` structure is the appropriate choice.

```
// Initialize Scanner
Scanner input = new Scanner(System.in);

// Read a value from the terminal
int n = input.nextInt();

// Test if n is even or odd
if (n % 2 == 0) {
  System.out.println("Even.");
} else {
  System.out.println("Odd.");
}
```

An `if-else` block can be extended to arbitrarily many conditions by adding `else if` clauses. For example, suppose that we want a program to output a randomized message. One way to do this is to generate a random number in [0, 1) using `Math.random`, then use its value to choose among the options. The following code fragment selects from among four different messages.

```
double r = Math.random();

if (r < 0.25) {
  System.out.println("Have a nice day.");
} else if (r < 0.50) {
  System.out.println("Hasta la vista.");
} else if (r < 0.75) {
  System.out.println("Fare thee well.");
} else {
  System.out.println("Log off already.");
}
```

The first case executes when `r` is between 0.0 and 0.25, the second when `r` is between 0.25 and 0.50, and so forth.

1.4.3 Cho-han

Let's work on a larger example that combines all of the features we've seen so far. Cho-han ("even-odd") is a traditional Japanese dice game with simple rules:

- The player bets if the sum of two six-sided dice will be odd or even.
- If the player's guess is correct, he wins. If not, he loses.

Let's write a program for cho-han. The program should prompt the user to choose even or odd by picking from a menu, then simulate the roll of two dice and announce if the player's choice was correct. Here's example output that we'll use as a model:

```
Welcome to Cho-Han.
1. Even
2. Odd
Select a bet.
1
The dice are 1 and 5.
The sum is 6.
You win.
```

Try It Yourself

Work on your own implementation of the cho-han program using the techniques we've discussed so far. Here is some starter code to show the basic structure of the program. Tip: Look back through the previous sections for relevant examples that show how to create a `Scanner`, read input, and simulate die rolls.

```
// Cho-han

import java.util.Scanner;

public class ChoHan {
  public static void main(String[] args) {
    // Create a new Scanner to read standard input

    // Print welcome message and options

    // Read the player's input

    // Roll the two dice

    // Print the die rolls using formatted output
    // %d is the format specifier for an integer value

    // Print the outcome message

  }
}
```

Solution

Here's an implementation based on the starter code.

```
// Cho-han

import java.util.Scanner;

public class ChoHan {
  public static void main(String[] args) {
    // Create a new Scanner to read standard input
    Scanner input = new Scanner(System.in);

    // Print welcome message and options
    System.out.println("Welcome to Cho-Han.");
    System.out.println("1. Even");
```

```
13     System.out.println("2. Odd");
14     System.out.println("Select a bet.");
15
16     // Read the player's input
17     int bet = input.nextInt();
18
19     // Roll the two dice
20     int die1 = (int) (Math.random() * 6) + 1;
21     int die2 = (int) (Math.random() * 6) + 1;
22     int sum = die1 + die2;
23
24     // Print the die rolls using formatted output
25     // %d is the format specifier for an integer value
26     System.out.printf("The dice are %d and %d.", die1, die2);
27     System.out.printf("The sum is %d.\n", sum);
28
29     // Print the outcome message
30     if (bet == 1 && sum % 2 == 0) {  // Winning even bet
31       System.out.println("You win.");
32     } else if (bet == 2 && sum % 2 == 1) {  // Winning odd bet
33       System.out.println("You win.");
34     } else {  // Every other combination loses
35       System.out.println("You lose.");
36     }
37   }
38 }
```

The first two parts are straightforward and similar to the previous examples: Create a `Scanner` that reads from `System.in` and use its `nextInt` method to read the user's choice as an `int` (lines 8–17). Generating die rolls can be done using `Math.random` (lines 20 and 21). The final part of the program uses a three-part conditional block to determine the output. There are two winning conditions, one for the even bet and one for the odd bet; any other combination of outcomes results in a loss.

Try It Yourself

Rewrite the conditional block program to combine both winning conditions into a single expression.

Solution

A player can only win or lose, so the three-part block can be rewritten as an `if-else` statement with both winning conditions in one test:

```
if ((bet == 1 && sum % 2 == 0) || (bet == 2 && sum % 2 == 1)) {
  System.out.println("You win.");
} else {
  System.out.println("You lose.");
}
```

Here are a few additional things to consider when writing conditional blocks:

- The structure of the conditions is always determined by the application. In particular, beginning programmers sometimes try to include an `else` clause in every conditional, even when there's no logical need for a default branch.
- Notice that Java uses `else if` as two separate words. This is different from Python, which uses a dedicated `elif` keyword.
- You're technically allowed to omit the curly braces around a conditional block that contains only one statement. For example, you could use the following code to test if `n` is even:

  ```
  if (n % 2 == 0)
    System.out.println("Even");
  else
    System.out.println("Odd");
  ```

  This can lead to errors, though, particularly in multi-part or nested conditionals. It's always safer to include the braces, even when the body of your conditional branch contains only one statement (Google, 2022a).

1.4.4 Comparing Strings and Other Objects

Many languages support direct comparisons between strings. In Python, for example, the `==` operator can test if two strings have identical sequences of characters, and the `<` and `>` operators can be used to compare strings lexicographically. Java does allow you to compare strings and other objects using `==`, but the results will probably not be what you expect. The following fragment prints `Not equal` even though the two strings have the same characters.

```
// Construct two new Strings with the same characters
String s1 = new String("Tyrannosaurus Rex");
String s2 = new String("Tyrannosaurus Rex");

// Test if the two strings are equal
```

```
if (s1 == s2) {
  System.out.println("Equal");
} else {
  System.out.println("Not equal");
}
```

Recall that a variable is, conceptually, a labeled box of memory that holds a value. Comparing two objects with == tests if *their variables refer to the same object in memory*. This is called **reference equality**. Recall that the new keyword allocates space for an object.[7] After executing the first two lines, Java will have allocated two String objects in memory, with the object reference s1 pointing to the first and s2 to the second.

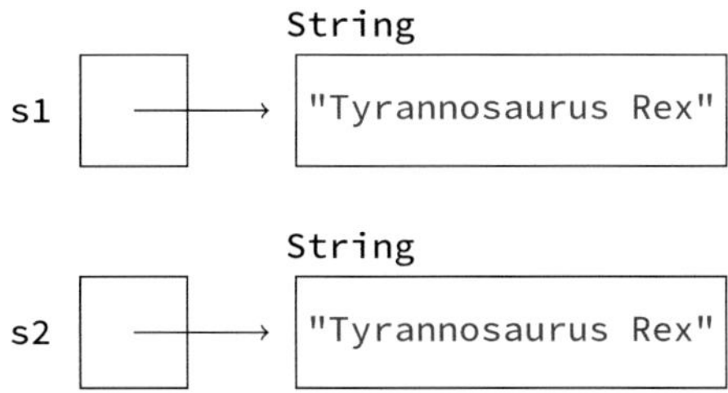

In this case, s1 and s2 have the same data, but refer to different underlying objects, so the == comparison evaluates to false. How about the following example?

```
String s1 = new String("Tyrannosaurus Rex");
String s2 = s1;
```

These statements create two names, s1 and s2, that refer to the same object in memory. Therefore, s1 == s2 evaluates to true.

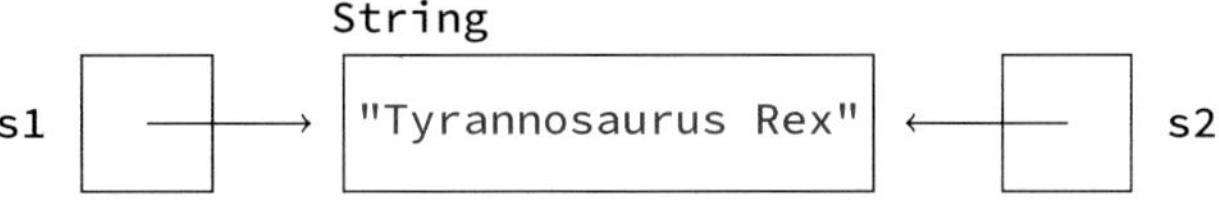

In most cases, though, you don't care about the underlying object references and just want to know if two objects have equal data – that is, if they have **value equality**. The String class has an equals method that tests if two objects have the same sequence of characters.

```
// Two strings with the same characters
String s1 = new String("Tyrannosaurus Rex");
String s2 = new String("Tyrannosaurus Rex");

// Test for value equality
if (s1.equals(s2)) {
```

7 Sharp-eyed readers will recall that it's possible to create String objects using double-quotes and avoid using the new keyword. An end-of-chapter question asks you to think about how reference equality plays out in that case.

```
    System.out.println("Equal");
} else {
    System.out.println("Not equal");
}
```

This fragment will output `Equal`. The `equals` method is case-sensitive; use `equalsIgnoreCase` if you want to test for value equality without considering case. Every Java class has its own version of `equals`, which defines a test for equality in a way that makes sense for the class's data. Unless you know that you need to test for equality of the underlying object references, always use `equals` rather than the == relational operator to compare objects.

1.5 Loops

Java uses the standard `while` and `for` loops to repeat blocks of statements. The `while` loops is functionally similar to its counterparts in other languages. The `for` loop has the same syntax and behavior as the `for` loop in C/C++ and JavaScript, but is different from Python's `for` loop.

1.5.1 The `while` Loop

Java's `while` loop functions the same as its counterparts in Python, JavaScript, and C/C++. The loop evaluates a `boolean` expression and executes the associated code block as long as the expression is `true`. For example, suppose you want the user to enter input from a restricted set of possible values, like entering `yes` or `no` in response to a prompt. The following example combines `Scanner` and a `while` loop to force valid input.

```
// Input validation with a while loop

import java.util.Scanner;

public class InputExample {
  public static void main(String[] args) {

    // Setup
    Scanner in = new Scanner(System.in);
    System.out.println("Coffee (y/n)?");
    boolean checkingInput = true;

    // Read the initial response
    String response = in.next();

    // Loop until the user inputs a valid choice
```

```
    while (checkingInput) {
      // If response is "y" or "n", end the loop
      if (response.equalsIgnoreCase("y") ||
          response.equalsIgnoreCase("n")) {
        checkingInput = false;
      }

      // Otherwise, prompt and read again
      else {
        System.out.println("Enter y or n.");
        response = in.next();
      }
    }

    //*** Do something with the response ***//
  }
}
```

This example illustrates a common technique: a `while` loop controlled by a `boolean` variable. The loop control variable is initially `true` and is reevaluated on every iteration of the loop. When the user's input satisfies the loop's stopping condition (in this case, that the user has typed `y` or `n`), the variable is set to `false` to end the loop.

1.5.2 The `for` Loop

Java's `for` loop combines declaration, condition checking, and a variable update into a single statement. The most common use is iterating through a range of numbers. Here's an example of a basic `for` loop that prints the numbers 0 through 9.

```
for (int i = 0; i < 10; i = i + 1) {
  System.out.println(i);
}
```

The `for` loop has the following elements:

- The keyword `for`.
- Three statements enclosed in a pair of parentheses and separated by semicolons.
- The first statement is the declaration of the **loop index variable**. In this example, the variable is named `i` and is initialized to 0. Single-letter variables like `i` are traditional for loops, but the variable can have any name. Note that this is a full variable declaration, so the type is required.[8]

8 An answer to a common question: It's possible to declare the loop index variable to be a `double` or another type, but this is not common; non-`int` loop variables should be viewed with suspicion.

- The second statement is a `boolean` test. The body of the loop executes as long as this statement evaluates to `true`. In the example, the loop will continue to execute as long as `i` is strictly less than 10.
- The final statement is an update to the loop index variable, which is automatically applied at the end of every iteration of the loop body. The most common update is to add 1 to the variable, but any valid expression is possible.
- The body of the loop is enclosed in a pair of curly braces, as in the `if` and `while` statements.

Here's a common loop pattern: using an "accumulator" variable to add up a range of values:

```
int sum = 0;
for (int j = 1; j < 101; j++) {
  sum += j;
}
```

This fragment uses some common Java statements:

- `j++` is a shortened statement that adds 1 to `j`.[9]
- `+=` adds a value to a variable and stores the result back in the variable. Here, each loop iteration adds the current value of `i` to the running total represented by `sum`.

Also notice that `j` is declared to start at 1 and the loop runs as long as `j` is strictly less than 101. Therefore, the loop steps through the numbers from 1 to 100.

Try It Yourself

Find the sum of all the even numbers from 1 to 100.

Solution

Combine a `for` loop that iterates from 1 to 100 with an `if` statement that tests for divisibility:

```
int sum = 0;
for (int i = 1; i < 101; i++) {
  if (i % 2 == 0) {
    sum += i;
  }
}
System.out.println(sum);
```

9 Java allows for `j++` and the similar `++j` operator, which both increment `j` but in slightly different ways; see the end-of-chapter questions.

1.5.3 Monte Carlo Simulation

Sic bo is a traditional Chinese dice game, now offered in many Western casinos that cater to Asian gamers. Play is similar to other dice games like craps: The player rolls three six-sided dice and bets on the outcome. There are a variety of possible bets, but the two main ones are called "big" and "small." The big bet wins if the sum of the three dice is strictly greater than 10, but not a triple, and the small bet wins if the sum is less than or equal to 10, but also not a triple.

What is the probability of winning the big bet in sic bo? We could approach this problem theoretically, by reasoning about the combinatorics of the dice rolls and the winning and losing outcomes. Another option is to estimate the winning probability using *simulation*:

- Perform a large number of random trials, each simulating the roll of three dice.
- Keep a count of the number of trials that would win the big bet.
- The fraction of simulated trials that result in a win should be a good estimate for the true theoretical win probability.

This kind of program – using a simulation to estimate the answer to a difficult calculation – is called a **Monte Carlo simulation**, named after the famous Monte Carlo casino complex in the European principality of Monaco. The Monte Carlo concept relies on the idea that, for many problems, sampling random trials can approximate the complete distribution of possible outcomes.

The origin of Monte Carlo simulation is credited to Stanislaw Ulam (1909–1984), a Polish scientist who came to America, worked on the Manhattan Project, and continued to be involved in nuclear research after World War II. While recuperating from an injury, he became interested in solitaire[10] and decided to calculate the probability that an arbitrary game was winnable. The combinatorics of solitaire proved too challenging to work out exactly, so Ulam hit upon the idea of using one of the very new computers to simply simulate a large number of solitaire games, keeping track of the percentage that could be won.[11] Once Ulam explained his idea to his fellow scientists, it became clear that random sampling could be used to find answers to other complex calculations that were more directly related to nuclear research (Eckhardt, 1987).

The following program uses a Monte Carlo approach to estimate the probability of winning the big bet in sic bo. Look at it carefully; it combines all of the features we've discussed so far.

```
// Estimate the winning probability of sic bo's big bet

public class SicBo {
  public static void main(String[] args) {

    // Constant number of trials
    final int NUM_TRIALS = 10000;

```

10 A single-player card game, also known as patience. There are many variants that all involve the player dealing out the cards in some configuration and then attempting to arrange them in sorted order.

11 Surprisingly, the true fraction of winnable games for Klondike, the most popular solitaire variant, is still unknown. It has been experimentally shown to be less than 40%, even for the most skilled players (Yan et al., 2004).

```
9      // Count the number of trials that result in a win
10     int numWins = 0;
11
12     // Iterate over the number of trials
13     for (int trial = 0; trial < NUM_TRIALS; trial++) {
14
15       // Simulate three dice
16       int die1 = (int) (Math.random() * 6) + 1;
17       int die2 = (int) (Math.random() * 6) + 1;
18       int die3 = (int) (Math.random() * 6) + 1;
19
20       // The bet loses on a triple
21       if (die1 == die2 && die2 == die3) {
22         continue;
23       }
24
25       // Otherwise, the bet wins on a sum greater than 10
26       else if (die1 + die2 + die3 > 10) {
27         numWins++;
28       }
29     }
30
31     // Calculate the total fraction of wins
32     //
33     // Cast one value to a double to get a fractional result
34     double winPercentage = ((double) numWins) / NUM_TRIALS;
35
36     // Output
37     System.out.printf("Winning prob. =  %.4f.", winPercentage);
38   }
39 }
```

The program combines many of the features we've introduced so far:

- Define a constant at the beginning of the program representing the number of simulated trials (line 7). This variable controls the number of iterations for the core `for` loop (line 13).
- Simulate the die rolls with `Math.random`.
- Test the winning condition and keep count of the number of trials resulting in a win (line 27). Triple rolls lose, which is implemented here using `continue` to move immediately to the next loop iteration.
- Finally, print the fraction of total trials that result in a win (line 37).

Running the program will show that the bet has a winning probability of about 48.6%.

Try It Yourself

Sic bo also has odd and even bets. The odd bet wins if the sum of the three dice is odd but not a triple, and similarly for the even bet. Modify the program to estimate the probability of winning the odd bet in sic bo.

1.6 Static Methods

We've now seen several examples of methods from built-in Java classes. Like other languages, Java allows you to write your own methods.[12] This section discusses **static methods**. A Java static method is declared using the keyword `static` and functions similarly to a Python or JavaScript function, in that it can be called by name, take input arguments, and return a result. Chapter 2 will discuss non-static methods and explain the difference between the two.

1.6.1 Writing Methods

Here's an example static method that takes the radius of a circle as a `double` and returns its area:

```
public static double circleArea(double radius) {
  return Math.pow(radius, 2) * Math.PI;
}
```

The standard static Java method has the following elements:

- The keywords `public` and `static`.
- A **return type**, which is the data type that the method returns. This can be any primitive or object type, or the special keyword `void`, which indicates a method does not return any result.[13]
- The name of the method, which follows the same rules as variable naming.
- A pair of parentheses enclosing the list of input parameters. Every input parameter declaration specifies both a type and a parameter name. The parentheses are required even if the method does not take any inputs.
- A pair of curly braces enclosing the body of the method.

If the method is not `void`, it must contain a `return` statement that outputs a value of the declared return type. Here's another static method that generates the roll of a six-sided die. The return type is `int` and the method takes no inputs.

12 If you have previously programmed in Python, JavaScript, or other languages, you may be more familiar with the term *functions* to describe named blocks of code that take inputs and return outputs. *Method* is the preferred name in object-oriented languages.

13 This is one piece of the mysterious `public static void main` incantation taken care of: `main` is a method that doesn't return a value, so its return type is `void`.

```
public static int dieRoll() {
  return (int) (Math.random() * 6) + 1;
}
```

It's possible, of course, for a method to include more complex operations and intermediate local variables:

```
public static int sumOfTwoDice() {
  int die1 = dieRoll();
  int die2 = dieRoll();
  return die1 + die2;
}
```

Here is an example that demonstrates a conditional with multiple return paths. Every path through the method must return a value of the declared return type.

```
public static boolean isEven(int n) {
  if (n % 2 == 0) {
    return true;
  } else {
    return false;
  }
}
```

However, for a simple test like `isEven`, it's usually better to return the result of the comparison directly:

```
public static boolean isEven(int n) {
  return n % 2 == 0;
}
```

Try It Yourself

Write a static method called `rollDice` that takes a parameter `n` as input and returns the sum of that many six-sided dice. Bonus: Modify your method to take a second input, `faces`, controlling the number of faces on each die.

Solution

Here's the full version, using a `for` loop to accumulate the sum.

```
public static int rollDice(int n, int faces) {
  int sum = 0;
```

```
    for (int i = 0; i < n; i++) {
      sum += (int) (Math.random() * faces) + 1;
    }
    return sum;
  }
```

1.6.2 Automatic Documentation with JavaDoc

As we've seen, the basic Java comment is two forward slashes, `//`, which causes the compiler to ignore all following text on the same line. Java also allows for **multiline comments** delimited by `/*` and `*/`.

```
/* This is a multiline comment.

Everything after the slash-star is ignored until the closing
star-slash.
*/
```

Multiline comments are typically used for headers or other large blocks of high-level descriptive documentation. It's common to use additional characters to give the comment structure and improve readability. For example, a header for the `HelloWorld.java` program might be written as follows:

```
/**
 * HelloWorld
 *
 * The first program. Prints the string "Hello, World!".
 */
```

JavaDoc is a utility that automates the creation of web-based documentation for Java programs.[14] When you run JavaDoc on your source code, it scans the program looking for special multiline comments describing details of the program, which it then converts into formatted HTML pages. JavaDoc's main use is providing details on the input parameters and return values of methods. The basic JavaDoc header is a multiline comment with the form shown above: an opening `/**` followed by `*` characters on each line. Typically, there is one header for the class as a whole and individual headers for each method. Method headers specify the input parameters using an `@param` tag with the following form:

```
@param  name  description
```

14 JavaDoc is provided as part of the Java Development Kit (JDK). If you're using a Java IDE such as Eclipse, JavaDoc is provided as a built-in feature. If you're using a command-line interface, you can run it using the `javadoc` command.

Information on the return value can be specified using `@return`. Here's an example:

```
/**
 * Utility class to roll multiple dice
 */

public class Dice {

  /**
   * Roll a group of dice and return their sum
   *
   * @param  n  number of dice
   * @param  faces  number of faces on each die
   * @return  the sum of n random rolls in [1, faces]
   */
  public static int rollDice(int n, int faces) {
    int sum = 0;
    for (int i = 0; i < n; i++) {
      sum += (int) (Math.random() * faces) + 1;
    }
    return sum;
  }
}
```

From this point forward, we'll use JavaDoc style comments to annotate classes in all of our examples.

1.7 Project: Substitution Ciphers

Sir Arthur Conan Doyle wrote "The Adventure of the Dancing Men" in 1905. In it, Sherlock Holmes receives a request for help from a man whose wife has been receiving strange messages. The notes terrify her, but appear to contain only drawings of dancing stick figures. Holmes realizes that the stick men are actually a code: each dancing figure corresponds to a letter of the alphabet. Holmes breaks the code and learns the sinister truth – which you'll have to learn for yourself by reading the story. The Dancing Men are an example of a **substitution cipher**, one of the oldest techniques for encoding secret messages. Each letter in the input *plaintext* message is mapped to a letter or other symbol to yield the output *ciphertext* message. Knowing the substitutions allows the encryption to be reversed. This project will allow you to explore four classical substitution-based encryption techniques. Although these methods aren't secure enough for modern information systems, they still provide interesting insight into the history of codes and codebreaking. Along the way, we'll get further practice using Java's loops, conditions, methods, and string processing features.

1.7.1 The Caesar Cipher

The simplest substitution cipher is also one of the oldest. The **Caesar cipher** rotates each letter a fixed number of positions in the alphabet. The name comes from Julius Caesar, who used a three-position rotation to encrypt his personal communications (Lyons, 2012). For example, the phrase `TRAVELEAST`, using Caesar's three-position rotation, would become `WUDYHOHDVW` – it's traditional to write the plain and ciphertext messages in capital letters with no spaces or punctuation. Decryption is done by reversing the rotation.

In general, you can rotate by any number of positions; if the rotation would move a letter beyond the end of the alphabet, just wrap back around to the beginning. The *ROT13* encoding, a 13-place rotation, was often used to obscure jokes or spoilers on USENET and the early Internet.

Let's write a program to implement the Caesar-style cipher. Here is the starting code that we'll fill in one step at a time. There are three methods:

- `main`, the entry point.
- `encrypt`, which takes the plaintext `String` and shift value as inputs and returns the encrypted ciphertext `String`.
- `decrypt`, which undoes the encryption and returns the original plaintext. Note that the `rotation` parameter for `decrypt` should be the value used for the original encryption.

```
/**
 * Implement the substitution ciphers
 */
public class Cipher {

  static final String ALPHABET = "ABCDEFGHIJKLMNOPQRSTUVWXYZ";

  /**
   * encrypt -- perform Caesar-style rotation
   *
   * @param  plaintext  the input String of uppercase letters
   * @param  shift  number of positions to rotate
   * @return  the encrypted ciphertext String
   */
  public static String encrypt(String plaintext, int shift) {

  }

  /**
```

```
   * decrypt -- reverse rotation
   *
   * @param  ciphertext  the input String
   * @param  shift  rotation used for the encryption
   */
  public static String decrypt(String ciphertext, int shift) {

  }

  /**
   * main -- entry point for the program
   */
  public static void main(String[] args) {

    String message = "TRAVELEAST";
    int rotation = 3;

    System.out.println(message);

    // Encrypt the message
    String cipher = encrypt(message, rotation);
    System.out.println(cipher);

    // Decrypt
    String decrypted = decrypt(cipher, rotation);
    System.out.println(decrypted);
  }
}
```

The challenge of this program is performing the character rotations efficiently. Our approach will take advantage of Java's built-in `String` methods to make the operations easy. The top of the class defines a `String` containing the uppercase alphabet:[15]

```
static final String ALPHABET = "ABCDEFGHIJKLMNOPQRSTUVWXYZ";
```

Given a particular uppercase character `ch` that we want to encrypt, we can look up its index in the alphabet using the `indexOf` method, which returns the first place a given character occurs in a `String`.

15 `ALPHABET` doesn't change, so it can be declared `final`. Making it `static` allows our methods to access it. Chapter 2 discusses the use of `static` in more detail.

```
int index = ALPHABET.indexOf(ch);
```

Shift the index, wrapping around the alphabet if necessary, then look up the ciphered character in the alphabet string.

```
int rotIndex = (index + shift) % ALPHABET.length();
char cipherChar = ALPHABET.charAt(rotIndex);
```

The method below uses this approach in a loop to process each character of the input plaintext string.

```
/**
 * encrypt -- perform Caesar-style rotation
 *
 * @param  plaintext  the input String of uppercase letters
 * @param  shift  number of positions to rotate
 * @return  the encrypted ciphertext String
 */
public static String encrypt(String plaintext, int shift) {
  // Start with an empty output String
  String ciphertext = "";

  // Loop through the plaintext letters
  for (int i = 0; i < plaintext.length(); i++) {

    // Plaintext character at position i
    char ch = plaintext.charAt(i);

    // Look up its alphabetical index
    int index = ALPHABET.indexOf(ch);

    // Rotate and convert back to a char
    int rotIndex = (index + shift) % ALPHABET.length();
    char cipherChar = ALPHABET.charAt(rotIndex);

    // Append to the output String
    ciphertext += cipherChar;
  }

  return ciphertext;
}
```

This version uses only uppercase letters, but we could extend the alphabet to use a different character set if we wanted to.

Try It Yourself

Use `encrypt` as a model to implement `decrypt`.

Solution

The steps are the same as `encrypt`, with a negative shift value. You need to implement wrapping around from the front of the alphabet to the back. If the rotated index is negative, subtract from the end of the alphabet:

```
int rotIndex;
if (index < shift) {
  rotIndex = ALPHABET.length() + (index - shift);
} else {
  rotIndex = index - shift;
}
char plaintextChar = ALPHABET.charAt(rotIndex);
```

1.7.2 The Vigenère Cipher

Basic substitution ciphers are insecure because they only manipulate the symbols of the plaintext without concealing its true information content. The basic attack strategy – used by Holmes in "The Adventure of the Dancing Men" – is **frequency analysis**. English letters are not uniformly distributed: E is the most common, accounting for about 12% of occurrences in real text, followed by T (9%), and then A (8%). *Q* and *Z* occur less than 0.1% of the time in normal usage. Therefore, given a large amount of ciphertext, the most frequently occurring symbol is likely to represent E, the second most frequent T, and so forth. Even if the probabilities aren't perfect, frequency analysis can yield a starting point for manual decryption.

The **Vigenère cipher** is an improved substitution method. It was first described by the Italian cryptographer Giovan Bellaso in the mid-sixteenth century, but later incorrectly attributed to his French contemporary, Blaise de Vigenère, who had designed a different substitution cipher around the same time (Martin, 2012). The Vigenère cipher is a *polyalphabetic substitution cipher*, where different letters in the plaintext message may be encrypted using different substitutions. This approach is stronger than the Caesar cipher, which used one rotation for all characters. Using multiple alphabets defeats simple frequency analysis, and the general approach was considered quite strong in the early modern era. Vigenère-style ciphers (which should really be called Bellaso-style ciphers, but the name has stuck) were difficult to break until a general method was introduced in the 1860s.

The Vigenère cipher is a series of Caesar-style rotational ciphers with the encryption controlled by a *keyphrase*. Suppose that we'd like to encrypt the message `TRAVELEAST` using the keyphrase `CAT`. First, match up each letter of the input with a letter of the keyphrase, repeating the keyphrase as many times as necessary:

```
plaintext: TRAVELEAST
keyphrase: CATCATCATC
```

Now, encrypt each letter of the plaintext using its corresponding key letter to determine the shift: a key of `A` corresponds to a shift of 1, `B` to a shift of 2, and so forth. Here, the first letter of the message, `F`, is paired up with key letter `C`, so it's shifted forward three positions to become `I`. The next letter, `L` is paired with `A` and is therefore shifted forward one position. Shifts wrap around the alphabet if necessary.

Try It Yourself

Finish the encoding of the Vigenère cipher in the example.

```
plaintext: TRAVELEAST
keyphrase: CATCATCATC
           ------------
output:    WS
```

The final answer should be `WSUYFFHBMW`.

Since the Vigenère cipher is a series of Caesar-style rotations, we can reuse the `encrypt` method that we've already developed to create a `vigenere` encryption method. We only need to use the keyphrase to choose the appropriate shift for each character of the plaintext. Consider the following implementation.

```
/**
 * Vigenere cipher encryption
 *
 * @param  plaintext  the input String
 * @param  key  the key String
 * @return  the encrypted ciphertext String
 */
public static String vigenere(String plaintext, String key) {
  // Start with an empty output
  String output = "";

  // Iterate over the letters in the plaintext
  for (int i = 0; i < plaintext.length(); i++) {

```

```
15       // Get the next letter of the input
16       char ch = plaintext.charAt(i);
17
18       // Determine the matching letter of the key
19       //
20       // Use the mod operation to wrap around the key
21       int keyIndex = i % key.length();
22       char keyCh = key.charAt(keyIndex);
23
24       // Use the key letter's alphabet position for the shift
25       int shift = ALPHABET.indexOf(keyCh) + 1;
26
27       // Encrypt the letter and append it to the output
28       //
29       // encrypt needs a String input
30       // Character.toString converts a char to a String
31       output += encrypt(Character.toString(ch), shift);
32     }
33
34     return output;
35 }
```

Performing the Vigenère cipher by hand required repeating the key string as many times as required to match the length of the plaintext. Rather than attempting to do that, lines 25 and 26 use modular arithmetic to select the appropriate key character. Line 35 calls the `encrypt` method to perform a rotation on a single character. Note that `encrypt` expects a `String` input, so we can't pass the plaintext `char` to it directly. The built-in `Character.toString` method converts a `char` into its `String` counterpart.

Try It Yourself

Implement a decryption method for the Vigenère cipher. Again, use the `vigenere` method as a guide and take advantage of the fact that you have a Caesar-style `decrypt` function. Put both functions in the `Cipher` class, then add test cases to `main`.

1.7.3 The Polybius Square

Polybius was an ancient Greek scholar of the second century BCE. His writings touched on a variety of topics, including politics and government, but he's best known for describing a surprisingly durable method used in encryption algorithms even into the twentieth century. The **Polybius square** is an arrangement of the alphabet into a 5 × 5 grid, such as the one in

Table 1.2 The English-language Polybius square

	0	1	2	3	4
0	A	B	C	D	E
1	F	G	H	I/J	K
2	L	M	N	O	P
3	Q	R	S	T	U
4	V	W	X	Y	Z

Table 1.2. It's traditional to combine *I* and *J* into a single entry to fit the standard Latin alphabet into the grid.[16] The Polybius encoding maps each letter to the row and column numbers of its grid position. For example, M would be mapped to `21`, because M occurs at row two and column one – notice that the example uses zero-based indexing.

Try It Yourself

Use the square in Table 1.2 to encode the message `TRAVELEAST`.

There are other ways of generating the square; one approach is to use a five-letter key word to fill in the first row, then fill in the remaining letters of the alphabet after it. No matter how you make the square, the Polybius cipher is still a substitution, mapping letters to two-digit numbers, so it offers no protection against frequency analysis. It does, however, provide a simple way to convert a single character into a sequence of multiple characters, which can then be rearranged or further manipulated.

We could implement the Polybius encoding by constructing the square, then searching it to find the place where each letter occurs. For the alphabetical square, though, it's possible to directly calculate the row and column position for a letter:

- Map the letter to its corresponding place in the alphabet, indexed from 0. For example, H would be mapped to position 7.
- There are five letters per row, so the row position (indexed from 0) can be calculated using integer division by 5. H is in row 7 / 5 = 1.
- The letter position modulo 5 gives the zero-indexed column number. H is at column 7 % 5 = 2.

There's one catch: I and J have been combined into one entry, so any letter greater than I must be shifted down by one. Therefore, I and J are both at position 8, K is at position 9, and so forth, up to Z at position 25. The implementation below uses this approach.

```
/**
 * Polybius encoding
 *
 * @param  plaintext  the input String
```

16 Polybius's actual writings are in Greek, which has 24 letters, so his square had one empty position.

```
   * @return  the plaintext encoded using the standard English square
   */
  public static String polybius(String plaintext) {
    String output = "";

    for (int i = 0; i < plaintext.length(); i++) {
      // Determine the alphabet position of letter i
      char ch = plaintext.charAt(i);
      int index = ALPHABET.indexOf(ch);

      // Letters J or higher are shifted down by one position
      if (index >= 9) {
        index--;
      }

      // Calculate row and column positions
      int row = index / 5;
      int col = index % 5;

      // Append to output
      // Integer.toString converts an int to a String
      output += Integer.toString(row);
      output += Integer.toString(col);
    }

    return output;
}
```

Try It Yourself

Consider the problem of reversing the Polybius encoding. Given an input `message` that contains the two-digit encodings, convert each pair of digits back to its corresponding letter. The code fragment below loops through the string two characters at a time and uses each row–column pair to calculate a corresponding letter position. The built-in `getNumericValue` method converts a digit `char` to its `int` equivalent. As with the encryption, letters greater than I are shifted by one to account for I and J taking the same position in the square.

```
for (int i = 0; i < message.length(); i += 2) {
  int row = Character.getNumericValue(message.charAt(i));
  int col = Character.getNumericValue(message.charAt(i + 1));

  int position = row * 5 + col;
  if (position >= 9) {
    position++;
  }

  output += ALPHABET.charAt(position);
}
```

Use the loop to implement the complete decryption method.

1.7.4 The Russian Nihilist Cipher

The Russian Nihilists were an intellectual and radical movement that began in the 1850s, primarily among middle-class students at Russian universities. The name refers not to a "belief in nothing," but to their all-encompassing critique of Russian society and rejection of traditional values. By the 1880s, the Nihilist name had become associated with radical groups that carried out attacks against the Russian state, including the assassination of Tsar Alexander II in 1881. The Nihilist cipher is a real-world encryption technique used by these groups; variations continued to be used by Soviet intelligence networks into the Cold War.

The Nihilist cipher is a combination of the Polybius square and Vigenère cipher. The input plaintext and keyphrase are converted to two-digit codes using the Polybius square, then added together as in the Vigenère cipher. For example, to encode `TRAVELEAST` using the keyphrase `CAT`, first align each letter of the plaintext with a letter of the codeword, repeating as necessary. This is the same as the first step in the Vigenère cipher.

```
plaintext: T R A V E L E A S T
keyphrase: C A T C A T C A T C
```

Next, convert each letter to its two-digit Polybius encoding. Here, we'll use the standard square, but it's also possible to use a custom square or let the square be generated from the keyphrase.

```
plaintext: 33 31 00 40 04 20 04 00 32 33
keyphrase: 02 00 33 02 00 33 02 00 33 02
```

Add the corresponding entries using standard arithmetic to obtain the output. The basic Nihilist cipher keeps its output as a series of separated numbers.

```
plaintext: 33 31 00 40 04 20 04 00 32 33
keyphrase: 02 00 33 02 00 33 02 00 33 02
----------------------------------------
output:    35 31 33 42 04 53 06 00 65 35
```

Decryption reverses the process. Given the sequence of ciphered numbers, subtracting the two-digit codes for the keyphrase recovers the two-digit codes for the plaintext characters, which can then be decoded by reversing the Polybius step.

Try It Yourself

Encode the message `CALLYOURMOTHER` using the keyphrase `DOG`.

Implementing the Nihilist cipher requires combining techniques from the previous cipher examples. The overall format is similar to the `vigenere` method. For each letter of the plaintext, the basic steps are:

- Extract each plaintext character and its associated key letter using the same strategy as `vigenere`.
- Generate the Polybius encoding of each letter.
- Add the encodings to get a two-digit output. This step requires representing the outputs of the Polybius encoding step as `int` values.
- Append the result to the output string.

Try It Yourself

Using `vigenere` as a model, write the `nihilist` encryption method. Tips:

- You can use the `polybius` method to encode the plaintext and key letters. Note that `polybius` takes a `String` as input and returns a `String`.
- Use the built-in `Integer.parseInt` method to convert numeric strings to their `int` equivalents.

Solution

Here's an implementation of `nihilist`.

```
/**
 * The Russian Nihilist cipher
 */
public static String nihilist(String plaintext, String key) {
  String output = "";

  for (int i = 0; i < plaintext.length(); i++) {
```

```
    // Get the next letter of the input
    char textCh = plaintext.charAt(i);

    // Determine the matching letter of the key
    int keyIndex = i % key.length();
    char keyCh = key.charAt(keyIndex);

    // Polybius encoding
    String textEnc = polybius(Character.toString(textCh));
    String keyEnc = polybius(Character.toString(keyCh));

    // Add
    //
    // Integer.parseInt converts a numeric String to int
    int textInt = Integer.parseInt(textEnc);
    int keyInt = Integer.parseInt(keyEnc);
    int cipher = textInt + keyInt;

    // Encrypt the letter and append it to the output
    // Single-digit numbers get a leading zero
    if (cipher < 10) {
      output += "0";
    }
    output += cipher + " ";
  }

  return output;
}
```

SUMMARY

This chapter has reviewed the most important Java topics that we'll need to go forward with the projects in the rest of this book. After working through it, you should be comfortable writing moderately large Java programs consisting of a `main` with static methods and using standard variables, loops, and conditional statements. We've also reviewed how to read user input, perform calculations, and generate random numbers. All of these features will be used in future chapters. As you're reviewing this material, keep the following ideas in mind:

- Java's syntax may be new for you, but the problem-solving process remains the same. If you get stuck, think about solutions in other languages you may know.
- Use good programming style, comments, and descriptive variable names. If you haven't been emphasizing those things in your code, you need to start right now. The next chapters will scale up the size of our programs, and they'll quickly become unmanageable if your code is not clean.
- If you're coming from a background in a dynamic language like Python or JavaScript, Java will feel more restrictive and verbose. Remember that the rules of the language are (mostly) there to prevent you from hurting yourself.
- Java's large standard library is one of its strengths. Although we'll be looking at how many built-in Java classes are implemented, you should always think about leveraging preexisting classes to make your programs simpler.

The next chapter will take on core features of Java that we didn't discuss in this introductory chapter: object-oriented programming.

EXERCISES

Understand

1. List Java's eight primitive types.
2. Convert the following `for` loop to an equivalent `while` loop.

```
for (int j = 25000; j > 999; j = j - 9) {
  if (j % 2 == 0) {
    System.out.println(j);
  }
}
```

3. Write a program that finds the sum of all numbers between 1 and 2,000 that are divisible by 11 or 13, but not both.
4. Write a program that uses a `while` loop to prompt the user to enter a `String`. Keep prompting until the user types one of the following words:

```
nitwit
blubber
oddment
tweak
```

Tips: Create a `Scanner` and use its `nextLine` method to read input. Use `equalsIgnoreCase` to test for `String` equality.

5. Crickets are a naturally renewable (albeit noisy) resource and contain proportionally more protein than chicken or beef. The average cricket weighs half a gram and consists of about 60% protein (Collavo et al., 2005). Suppose an iron-slinging bodybuilder wants to consume 200 grams of protein per day. How many crickets would be required to generate that amount? Write a Java class called `Entomophagy` with a `main` method to calculate and output the answer.

6. Here's a strange method. What is `weird(weird(11))`?

```
public static int weird(int n) {
  if (n % 7 != 0) {
    return n / 3;
  } else {
    int count = 0;
    for (int i = 1; i < n; i = i * 2) {
      count++;
    }
    return count;
  }
}
```

7. Write a static method called `min` that takes two `int` values as input and returns the minimum of the two. Don't use the built-in `Math.min` method.

8. Write a static method called `tripleMin` that takes three `int` values and returns the minimum. Again, don't use the built-in `Math.min`.

9. The seventh-century Indian mathematician Bhaskara developed the following approximation for the sine of an angle in degrees (Stroethoff, 2014):

$$\sin\theta \approx \frac{4\theta(180-\theta)}{40,500-\theta(180-\theta)}.$$

Write a method named `bhaskara` that takes a `double` as input and returns the approximate sine as its output.

10. Now write a program that uses a loop to iterate through the angles from 0 degrees to 360 degrees in units of 30 degrees. For each angle, print the values obtained by Bhaskara's approximation, `Math.sin`, and the difference between the two. Among these values, what's the maximum error attained by Bhaskara's approximation?

11. Recall that an individual cricket contains about 0.30 grams of protein. Write a program that reads a number of grams of protein as input from the terminal and outputs the equivalent number of crickets.

12. Write a program that can read in a number of kilometers as input and print the corresponding number of miles. There are 1.60934 kilometers in 1 mile. The Comrades Marathon in South Africa is the world's oldest and largest ultramarathon race, established in 1921. It is run between the cities of Durban and Pietermaritzburg in South Africa, a distance of about 87 km. What is the length of the Comrades Marathon in miles?

13. Write a program to read in a weight in kilograms and convert it to pounds. There are about 2.20462 lb in 1 kg. Display the result to one decimal place. The current world record for weight lifted overhead in the clean and jerk is 267 kg, held by the colossal Georgian superheavy weightlifter Lasha Talakhadze. Use your program to calculate the weight of Talakhadze's record lift in pounds.

14. Write a method called `stairs` that takes an `int n` as input and prints a descending staircase of `n` levels. For example, if `n` is five, the method should print

```
#
##
###
####
#####
```

15. It's common to use the *post-increment* addition operator `i++` to represent `i = i + 1`, but Java also supports a *pre-increment* operator, `++i`. What's the difference between the two? Do some research and identify at least one case where you might want the pre-increment version instead of the post-increment.

16. Write a static method called `onlyConsonants` that takes a `String str` as input and returns `true` if it contains no vowels and no `y`. Use a loop to iterate over the characters in the string and test each one.

Apply

17. The main unit of currency in Great Britain is the pound sterling, represented by the £ symbol. Similar to the US dollar, each pound is divided into 100 pence. However, this straightforward system only went into effect in 1971. Prior to that date, the British used a different system descended from the ancient Romans. The £sd system, as it was known, had three basic units:

    - The pound, which was the main unit, just as it is today.
    - The shilling, with 20 shillings to a pound.
    - The penny, with 12 pennies to the shilling, or 240 to a pound.

    Old-style £sd coins are no longer legal tender, but can still be exchanged for their face value. Write a program that can take in a number of shillings and pennies and return the number of modern pounds. Each shilling is worth 0.05 pounds and each old penny is worth 0.0041667 pounds. You can assume that the user will only enter positive integer values. Report your answers to two decimal places. Here's an example:

```
Enter a number of shillings: 25
Enter a number of pennies: 40
That's 1.42 pounds
```

18. Find the sum of the first 50 terms of the Fibonacci sequence.

19. Write a method named `pyramid` that takes an `int n` as input and prints a pyramid of stars with `n` levels. For example, if `n` is five, print

```
    *
   ***
  *****
 *******
*********
```

20. Of course, my pyramid must be hollow to hold all the precious objects that will accompany me to the afterlife. Modify your previous program to print a hollow pyramid.

```
    *
   * *
  *   *
 *     *
*********
```

21. Write one more program to print a ziggurat/pyramid that alternates stars and spaces.

```
    *
   * *
  * * *
 * * * *
* * * * *
```

22. Write a function called `isPrime` that takes an integer `n` as input and returns `true` if the number is prime and `false` otherwise. The easiest way to test if a number is prime is to use a loop over the numbers from 2 to `Math.sqrt(n)`. If any number divides `n` then it can't be prime. If you make it to the end of the loop and haven't returned `false`, then you can return `true`.

23. Write a method called `isLeapYear` that takes a year (as an integer number) as input and returns `true` if that year is a leap year and `false` otherwise. A year is a leap year if it's divisible by 4, except for years divisible by 100, which are not leap years. Years divisible by 400 are an exception and are still leap years. For example, 2020 was a leap year; 1900 was not a leap year, because it's divisible by 100; 2000 was a leap year, because it's divisible by 400.

24. Passe-dix (French for "pass ten") is an ancient dice game. The rules are simple: roll three dice and add their sum. The player wins if the sum is strictly greater than 10, loses if the sum is strictly less than 10, and draws if the sum equals 10. Write a simulation program to estimate the probability of winning at passe-dix.

25. Craps is the most popular dice game in American casinos. The most common of its numerous bets is called the "pass" bet, and it works as follows:

- A player (the "shooter") rolls two six-sided dice.
- If their sum is 7 or 11, the bet immediately wins. If the sum is 2, 3, or 12, the bet immediately loses.
- If the sum is any other number, that number becomes the *point* and the bet enters a second phase.
- During the second phase, the shooter continues rolling the dice with the goal of rolling the point value again before rolling a 7. If the point comes up first, the bet wins; if a 7 comes up first, the bet loses. The shooter will re-roll as many times as required until either the point or 7 comes up.

Write a simulation program to estimate the probability of winning the pass bet in craps. Tip: Write a `simulate` method that simulates one round of the game and returns `true` if the player wins. You can repeatedly call `simulate` in a loop and keep count of how many trials result in a win. The answer should be about 49%.

26. Samuel Pepys (pronounced "Peeps") was a seventeenth-century British naval administrator, best known for the detailed diary he kept describing his life in the 1660s. In 1693 he corresponded with Isaac Newton regarding a wager: Which of the following three propositions has the greatest chance of success?

1. Six fair dice are tossed independently and at least one six appears.
2. Twelve fair dice are tossed independently and at least two sixes appear.
3. Eighteen fair dice are tossed independently and at least three sixes appear.

Write a simulation program to answer Pepys' question. Tips: Write a `toss` method that tosses `n` dice and returns the number of sixes that result. For each proposition, call `toss` in a loop with the appropriate value of `n` and keep count of the number of trials that succeed. Notice that the statements are "at least," not "exactly."

27. Write a method called `constructAlphabet` that takes a keyword as input and uses it to construct a custom encryption alphabet by starting with the letters of the keyword, then following with the remaining letters of the alphabet. For example, if the keyword is `"GHOST"`, the alphabet would be `"GHOSTABCDEFIJKLMNPQRUVWZYZ"`. You can assume the keyword contains only unique letters with no duplicates.

28. Heron's formula, named after the ancient Greek engineer and inventor Heron of Alexandria, is a method of calculating the area of a triangle given the lengths of its three sides. If the three side lengths are a, b, and c, the formula is:

$$A = \sqrt{s(s-a)(s-b)(s-c)},$$

where s is the "semi-perimeter":

$$s = \frac{a+b+c}{2}.$$

Write a function called `heron` that takes three `double` inputs `a`, `b`, and `c` and returns the area calculated by the formula.

Extend

29. Let's revisit the string comparison example from Section 1.4.4. What happens if you declare the strings using double quotes instead of the `new` keyword?

```
String s1 = "Tyrannosaurus Rex";
String s2 = "Tyrannosaurus Rex";

if (s1 == s2) {
  System.out.println("Equal");
} else {
  System.out.println("Not equal");
}
```

Are these two strings equal or not equal by the == operator? Do some research and figure out an explanation for what you observe.

30. Here is a trickier question that has shown up on technical interviews for coding jobs. Write a function called `reverseInt` that takes a three-digit nonnegative integer `n` as input and returns the number with the digits reversed. For example, `reverse_num(123)` will return 321 and `reverse_num(742)` will return 247. One way to approach this question is to convert the number to a `String`, reverse it, then convert the result back to an `int`. Java strings don't have a built-in reverse method, so you may want to do a little research to find an efficient solution.

31. Repeat the previous problem, but don't use a `String`. Perform the reversal using only arithmetic. Here's a tip: You can isolate the hundreds digit using `n / 100`. If you have that, you can reduce the number to two digits, then continue identifying the other two digits. `n % 10` will identify the ones digit.

32. Write a decryption method for the Nihilist cipher. You'll need to extract the sequence of two- or three-digit numbers from the input `String`. Use the fact that the numbers are separated by whitespace and use the `String` class's `split` method.

33. In practice, hand ciphers that used the Polybius square encoding technique preferred to map the rows and columns to phonetically distinct letters rather than numbers, in order to facilitate transmission of messages over radio. Write a variation of the Polybius encryption method that uses the 5×5 square with the letters `ADFGX` in place of the numbers zero to four.

34. Now write the corresponding decryption method that can take a sequence of characters encoded using the ADFGX square and recover the original message.

NOTES AND FURTHER READING

This chapter is only a condensed overview of important elements of Java programming. The next chapters will discuss objects and classes in more detail, but there are still several features that we haven't touched on. For a thorough overview of programming in Java, Anderson and Franceschi (2014) is a good reference.

If you have done some web development, you may be wondering about the relationship between Java and JavaScript. Despite its name, JavaScript is not directly related to Java: Its true intellectual heritage is from older functional languages, notably the Scheme dialect of

LISP. JavaScript was originally created to be a scripting language for the Netscape browser (Peyrott, 2017). The new language was named JavaScript after Netscape entered a partnership with Sun Microsystems, the creators of Java. Sun and Netscape intended that JavaScript would be for control of small page elements and Java would become the language for serious web app development. That plan didn't work out, however, because of the technical difficulty of implementing a JVM on early web browsers. Java web applets did have a presence on the early Internet, but its role there has faded as JavaScript has matured into a full-featured development language.

Object-oriented programming is an exceptionally bad idea which could only have originated in California.
Attributed to Edsger Dijkstra

2 Object-Oriented Programming

INTRODUCTION

Java is an **object-oriented programming language**. Java programs are implemented as collections of **classes** and **objects** that interact with each other to deliver the functionality that the programmer wants. So far, we've used "class" as being roughly synonymous with "program," and all of our programs have consisted of one `public class` with a `main` method that may call additional methods. We've also talked about how to use the `new` keyword to initialize objects like `Scanner` that can perform useful work. It's now time to talk about the concepts of objects and classes in more depth and then learn how to write customized classes.

LEARNING OBJECTIVES

This chapter focuses on the motivation for object-oriented programming and how to write your own classes in Java. After completing it, you will be able to:

- Explain the concept of encapsulation as it's used by classes and objects.
- Write custom Java classes that represent a set of related variables, including the use of constructors, access modifiers, and class methods.
- Use the built-in `ArrayList` class to represent a collection of objects.

This chapter concludes with a classic example: using object-oriented techniques to implement card games. The next chapter builds on these concepts to introduce Java's built-in graphics framework.

2.1 The Concept of Object-Oriented Programming

Programming language developers have always sought to create languages that are expressive and capable of representing higher-level abstract concepts, freeing programmers from managing the low-level details of their software. The object-oriented programming (OOP) paradigm developed gradually as programmers thought about how to best represent the relationships between data and behaviors for real-world things in their software.

2.1.1 Classes and Objects

An object is a group of related variables and a set of methods that operate on those variables. An object "wraps up," into a single unit, a group of variables that are conceptually related to each other and provides a set of methods that other parts of the program can use to interact with those variables. A **class** is a template or blueprint for creating objects of a specific type. Like a construction blueprint or a design document, a class file describes the parts of an object: the data variables that it contains and the behaviors that it implements.

An individual object is an **instance** of its class. In the same way that builders can use blueprints to construct many houses according to the same basic design, we can **instantiate** multiple copies of the same class, each with their own specific data. For example, suppose we create two new `String` variables:

```
// s1 is an instance of the String class
String s1 = new String("I'm an instance of the String class.")

// s2 is a different instance with different data
String s2 = new String("So am I!");
```

It's correct to say that "`s1` is a `String` object" and also that "`s1` is an instance of the `String` class." Both statements mean the same thing.

Here's another metaphor: a class is like a position on a sports team. If you say that a certain player is a goalkeeper, you're describing a particular set of attributes, roles, and skills that player provides to the team. A player of a different class – say, a forward – fulfills a different role and has different skills. An individual goalkeeper object (an instance of the Goalkeeper class) would represent a single unique player. All goalkeepers have the same role on their teams, but are distinguished by their individual attributes – such as name, team, height, and career statistics – in the same way that individual objects belong to the same class but have unique data.

Try It Yourself

Pick a team sport, then think about how to divide the players on a team into classes based on their roles. Are there common attributes shared by all players across all the different classes? Are there some class-specific attributes? What kinds of behaviors or skills should each class provide to the team?

2.1.2 Encapsulation

It's often helpful to think of an object as *providing a service* that other parts of the program can call upon (Anderson and Franceschi, 2014). For example, a `Scanner` object provides the service of reading data from an input source. Calling `nextInt` is an easy way to read an `int`:

```
// Scanner makes it easy to read data from the terminal
Scanner input = new Scanner(System.in);
int date = input.nextInt();
```

Consider this: You, as an application programmer, don't have to understand how `nextInt` is implemented in order to use it. Instead, the `Scanner` object *hides its complex behavior behind a simple method call.* All of the data and operations required to perform the read are handled internally by the object. This is amazing! We, as higher-level programmers, only have to call the method to make something useful happen.

Try It Yourself

We've seen several other examples where Java allows us to access complex behaviors by calling methods. Give some examples of built-in objects providing useful behaviors.

If you want to be fancy – which you do – you can say that an object **encapsulates** data and then allows controlled access to that data through its methods.[1] A `String` object, for example, encapsulates a sequence of text characters. This data is *private*: The only way to interact with a `String`'s data is by using the methods defined by the `String` class. Encapsulating private data behind a set of methods ensures that the data can only be accessed and modified in safe, logically appropriate ways.[2]

2.1.3 Advantages and Disadvantages

Object-oriented programming has several advantages. The concept of encapsulating data behind a well-defined interface supports several goals of good software design. Major commercial software applications may have tens of millions of lines of code divided into several components. Object-oriented programming provides one way[3] to separate the different logical parts of the application into different bodies of code, so that the different parts of the application can be developed independently.

Object-oriented programming can also be useful for modeling real-world problems. If you can describe the "things" that make up a problem – people, items, processes, places, etc. – you can often map each "thing" to a class by defining its important properties and behaviors. Java supports features that allow you to mirror the real-world relationships between things as relationships between your classes.

Advanced OOP allows one class to serve as a template for another. The "child" class automatically *inherits* useful properties and methods of its "parent" class, like a customized building plan that is based on another, more general blueprint. Inheritance is quite powerful, because it allows for hierarchies of objects that all share common features, and can model relationships among classes.

Finally, OOP supports *code reuse*, where useful classes can be repurposed across multiple projects. Once you write a self-contained class, it can ideally be easily incorporated into future projects that need the same functionality. Java, in effect, takes advantage of this feature with its standard library, providing a huge number of prewritten classes that you can draw upon to simplify your applications.

1 If you really understand this concept you will get an A in this class. Guaranteed.

2 Seriously, read this section again and meditate on it. **These ideas are truly important.**

3 But not the only way, or the best way for every problem.

The major disadvantage of OOP is complexity. Encapsulation, by its very nature, is all about separating information into distinct components. As programs become more complex, it's hard to reason about the actual state of any particular object – what data does it have and what is it actually doing? It's difficult to reason about the correctness of object-oriented programs.[4] Advanced OOP emphasizes **design patterns**: useful architectural models for designing large programs (Freeman et al., 2004). Code reuse was often cited as one of the major benefits of OOP in early writing, but it's now known that effective code reuse requires designing classes with future reuse in mind, which may not always be practical.

2.2 Developing a Class Step by Step

This section will lead you through the process of developing a class incrementally. Starting with a basic shell that contains a few related variables, we'll gradually introduce a series of features, first to make the class easier to use, then to enforce encapsulation of its contents.

2.2.1 The Simplest Class: A Collection of Related Variables

The simplest class represents a group of variables that are conceptually related to each other: that is, the variables are attributes of a single "thing." Here is a Java class that represents a book with a title, author, and price.

```
/**
 * A basic Book class with a title, author, and price
 */

public class Book {
  // Declare instance variables of the class
  String author;
  String title;
  double price;
}
```

This is the simplest class definition: a group of variables declared inside the `class` block. Notice that the class contains no methods yet, not even a `main`. The three variables represent properties of an example `Book` object. In OOP, a class's internal variables are called its **fields** or **instance variables**.

Using `Book` requires writing a `main` method that can instantiate `Book` objects. The code below shows a class that contains a `main` method that creates and uses `Book` objects. This kind of class

4 In fact, formally verifying the correctness of programs was a major emphasis of Edsger Dijkstra's research and writing (Dijkstra, 1976). The source of our opening quote is unknown, but Dijkstra did see the difficulty of proving correctness in object-oriented programs as a critical flaw.

is sometimes called a **driver class** because it contains the entry point that "drives" execution of the program (Deitel and Deitel, 2005).

```
/**
 * BookDriver --- class with a main that tests Book
 */

public class BookDriver {
  public static void main(String[] args) {
    // Create a new Book object
    Book prideAndPrejudice = new Book();

    // Assign values to its instance variables using dot notation
    prideAndPrejudice.author = "Jane Austen";
    prideAndPrejudice.title = "Pride and Prejudice";
    prideAndPrejudice.price = 9.99;
  }
}
```

The program instantiates a fresh `Book` object named `prideAndPrejudice`. Recall that creating an object requires using the `new` keyword and the special constructor method, which always has the same name as the class. Here, we're using the default `Book()` constructor. Once it's constructed, `prideAndPrejudice` has three internal variables – `title`, `author`, and `price` – but they haven't yet been assigned any particular values. The second group of statements assigns a value to each field. Java uses dot notation to access the properties of an object.

Try It Yourself

Modify the `BookDriver` class to create a second `Book` variable using `new` and the constructor, then assign values to its properties.

Solution

These statements will create a second example `Book`:

```
// Create a second Book
Book dracula = new Book();
dracula.author = "Bram Stoker";
dracula.title = "Dracula";
dracula.price = 5.99;
```

It's important to note that each instance of the `Book` class that we create is allocated *its own independent variables* for `author`, `title`, and `price`. Conceptually, think of each `Book` object being an independent block of memory containing its own copy of each of the three fields. Also remember that `dracula` and `prideAndPrejudice` are references to the underlying `Book` objects in memory:

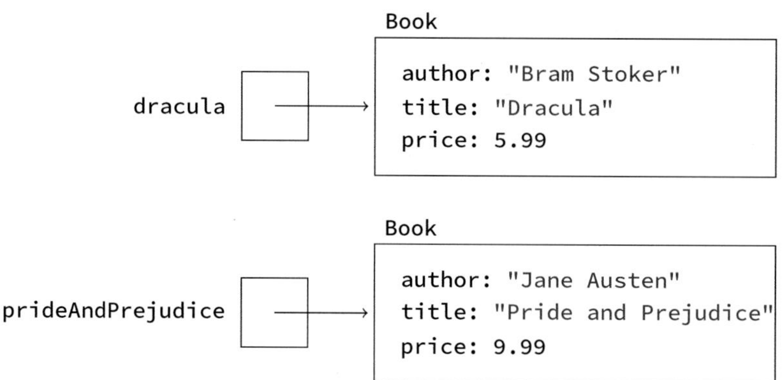

This property is the origin of the name *instance variables*: They are the set of internal variables that "belong" to an object – which is, recall, an instance of its class – and give it a unique identity.

2.2.2 Custom Constructors

Instantiating an object requires calling the constructor method to initialize the object. As we've seen, the name of the constructor is always the same as the name of the class. Java's default constructor simply allocates memory to hold the new object and its instance variables, but doesn't do any further initialization. It's usually convenient to assign values to an object's fields when it's created, which we can do by adding a custom constructor method to `Book` to replace the default constructor. The new constructor will take three parameters, representing the title, author, and price of the new `Book` object, and then assign those values to the new object's instance variables.

Here's an updated `Book` with a constructor method. Observe that the constructor method has *no return type*, not even `void`.

```
/**
 * Adding a constructor to the Book class
 */

public class Book {
  // Instance variables are declared before any class methods
  String author;
  String title;
  double price;
```

```

    /**
     * Constructor
     *
     * @param   newAuthor   author of this new Book
     * @param   newTitle   title of this new Book
     * @param   newPrice   price of this new Book
     */
    public Book(String newAuthor, String newTitle, double newPrice) {
      this.author = newAuthor;
      this.title = newTitle;
      this.price = newPrice;
    }
}
```

The body of the constructor assigns each input parameter to its corresponding instance variable. The keyword `this` is the *object self-reference*, a way to refer to the class's internal variables from within its own code. Here, `this.author` refers to the `author` field of the new object that is currently being constructed. It's often useful, though not strictly required, to use `this` when referring to internal fields from within a class's own methods.[5] Now, let's revise `BookDriver` to use the new constructor:

```
// Use the constructor to create new Book objects
Book prideAndPrejudice = new Book("Jane Austen",
                                  "Pride and Prejudice",
                                  9.99);

Book dracula = new Book("Bram Stoker", "Dracula", 5.99);
```

These calls replace the earlier version that used the default `new Book()` constructor call. Once you add a custom constructor to a class, Java no longer allows the use of the default constructor.

Try It Yourself

Use the new constructor method to create at least two more `Book` objects.

5 Different style guides have different opinions about when and where `this` should be used. We'll generally use it to make clear that a variable is an object's instance variable rather than a local variable.

2.2.3 The `toString` Method

Try It Yourself

Add print statements to `BookDriver`:

```
System.out.println(prideAndPrejudice);
System.out.println(dracula);
```

Compile both classes and then run `BookDriver`. What output do you observe?

Solution

Instead of printing the `Book`'s properties, you'll see something like:

```
Book@1c655221
```

The output value `1c655221` is called the **hash code** of the object. The exact value depends on your system and will probably change each time you run the program. A hash code is like an object summary, and Java requires that equal objects have equal hash codes. The default hash code is based on the internal memory address where the object is stored – so two variables with the same hash code must be the same object in memory – but it's also possible for a class to have its own custom hash code method that makes sense for that class's data. We'll talk much more about hashing in Chapters 14 and 15.

Java allows you to define a special method called `toString`, which returns a `String` representation of an object. When you print an object using `System.out.println` or another printing method, Java automatically runs its `toString` method behind the scenes and then prints the result. The `toString` method takes no inputs and must have a return type of `String`. Here's one for the `Book` class:

```
/**
 * Return a String representation of this Book
 *
 * @return  String describing title, author, and price
 */
public String toString() {
  // Construct a summary String for this book
  String summary = String.format("%s by %s, %.2f",  this.title,
                                       this.author, this.price);

  // Return that string
  return summary;
}
```

`String.format` is similar to `System.out.printf`: It creates a `String` by substituting the given variables into the formatting string.

Try It Yourself

Add the `toString` method to the `Book` class, then modify `BookDriver` to print each `Book` object. Run the program to verify that you can print your objects.

2.2.4 Access Modifiers

We've now created a class that represents a collection of related variables, but we haven't actually enforced encapsulation of `Book`'s fields. This section introduces an important concept, **access modifiers**, which can be used to control when and how an object's internal variables can be used by other parts of the program. Suppose you add a line to update the `price` of the `dracula` book to `BookDriver`:

```
dracula.price = -3.99;
```

Is this allowed? Yes, it is – from Java's perspective it's just an assignment to a `double` variable.[6] It doesn't make logical sense, though, because a real-world price shouldn't be negative.

Java supports four access modifiers that control how class fields can be used. The two most important are `public` and `private`:

- `public` fields have no access restrictions. They can be accessed and changed by code within their own class or from any other class.
- `private` fields can only be accessed by code within their own class. They can't be used or modified by code in other classes.

There are two other access modifiers that are used less frequently:

- `protected` fields can be accessed by code within the same class, other classes in the same package, or by subclasses, but not by the general world outside those categories.
- Any field that isn't declared `public`, `private`, or `protected` has a default level of protection that allows access from within the same class or from other classes in the same package.

Update `Book` to make its fields `private`:

```
/**
 * Book class with private fields
 */

public class Book {
```

6 Using a `double` is a reasonable choice for this example, but if you're writing a program that uses monetary values you should probably use a dedicated class that supports fixed-point arithmetic.

```

  private String author;
  private String title;
  private double price;

  //*** Constructor and toString methods appear below here ***//
}
```

The Book class's internal variables are now private, so they can only be accessed by code within the class itself. If you attempt to access a Book variable from a different class, like main in BookDriver, you'll get an error.

```
Book dracula = new Book("Bram Stoker", "Dracula", 5.99);

dracula.price = -3.99;  // Compiler error -- price is private
```

2.2.5 Accessor and Mutator Methods

Making author, title, and price private enforces the goal of encapsulation, but it also makes those fields inaccessible to any other part of the program. As written, we can create a new Book object and assign values to its fields using the constructor, but can't make any changes to them after that moment. Fields that cannot be changed after creation are said to be *immutable*. We probably don't want to change the author or title of a Book after it's been created, so immutability makes sense for those fields. Suppose, however, that we want the option to change a Book's price after it's created, but in a controlled and safe way. We can provide this functionality by creating new methods, called **accessor** and **mutator** methods.

An accessor method – also called a **get** method – returns the value of a private field. All accessor methods have the same form:

- The name is get followed by the name of the variable.
- The return type is always the type of the variable.
- The method takes no input parameters.
- The body returns the variable and does nothing else.

Here's an example that would return the current value of a Book's price field:

```
/**
 * Get the current value of price
 *
 * @return  the price of this Book
 */
public double getPrice() {
  return this.price;
}
```

You can then call `getPrice` on an object to retrieve its `price` field.

```
// Create a new Book object
Book leaves = new Book("Walt Whitman", "Leaves of Grass", 19.99);

// This statement would give a compiler error -- price is private
double leavesPrice = leaves.price;

// Instead, call the accessor method to get its value
double leavesPrice = leaves.getPrice();
```

Try It Yourself

Add `getAuthor` and `getTitle` methods to the `Book` class, then add test code to `BookDriver` that calls each one and prints the results.

A **mutator** method – often called a **set** method – changes the value of a private variable, and may include additional logic to verify that the change makes sense. Mutator methods always have the following form:

- The name is `set` followed by the name of the variable.
- The return type is `void` – mutators don't return a result, they modify their associated instance variable.
- The method takes one input parameter, which will be the new value.

Here is an example `setPrice` method. It has an additional check that returns without making a change if the input is negative.

```
/**
 * Change the price of this Book
 *
 * @param  newPrice  the updated price value
 */
public void setPrice(double newPrice) {
  // Ignore negative prices
  if (newPrice < 0.0) {
    return;
  }

  // Set the new price
  this.price = newPrice;
}
```

Try It Yourself

Add a new field to `Book` called `genre` of type `String`. Make the new field `private`, add a parameter to the constructor to initialize it, and give it `get` and `set` methods.

2.2.6 Throwing Exceptions

That version of `setPrice` just ignores negative inputs. That might make sense in some cases, but it provides no feedback that a problem has occurred. Java allows a method to "throw" an exception indicating that a run-time error has taken place. Here's an updated `setPrice` that throws an exception if it receives negative input. The header uses the `throws` keyword to declare the exception and the body uses `throw` to generate it in response to bad input.[7]

```
/**
 * Change the price of this Book
 *
 * @param  newPrice  the updated price value
 */
public void setPrice(double newPrice) throws IllegalArgumentException{
  // Throw an exception on negative inputs
  if (newPrice < 0.0) {
    throw new IllegalArgumentException("setPrice: negative input");
  }

  // Set the new price
  this.price = newPrice;
}
```

Now, if `BookDriver` calls `setPrice` with a negative input, the result will be an exception that crashes the program.

It's possible to "catch" a thrown exception and handle it using a `try-catch` block, instead of simply printing an error and terminating the program. For example, suppose we prompt the user to enter a new price for a book `b` and then pass it to `setPrice`. One way to handle the possibility of negative input is the following:

```
// Enter a new price for a book b and attempt to set it

System.out.println("Enter the new price for " + b.getTitle());
double newPrice = input.nextDouble();
```

7 Detail: `IllegalArgumentException` is a type of `RuntimeException`. The JVM allows any method to throw `RuntimeException` objects without any special declarations, so the `throws` clause could be omitted and the method would still work.

```
// Try the setPrice method with newPrice as its input
//
// If it throws an exception, run the catch block
try {
  b.setPrice(newPrice);
} catch (IllegalArgumentException e) {
  System.out.println("Negative prices are not allowed.");
}
```

Logically, this is similar to an `if` statement.[8] Java executes the code in the `try` block. If that code throws an exception, the `catch` block handles it. In some cases Java requires the use of `try-catch` to ensure the program is prepared to handle exceptions that might occur during execution. We'll see examples when we work with files and some built-in classes.

2.2.7 More on the `static` Keyword

You may have noticed that none of the methods in the `Book` class used the `static` keyword, which we used for methods in Chapter 1. Understanding the use of `static` is one of the trickier parts of OOP in Java.

The standard explanation of `static` in Java is that static methods and variables *belong to the class as a whole* and not to any particular instance of the class. Recall that instantiating an object allocates memory and allows the new object to have its own copies of the class member variables, like giving each new `Book` object its own personal `title`, `author`, and `price` fields.

What does it mean, then, for a static method to belong to the class as a whole? Methods that are declared `static` *cannot make use of class instance variables*. That is, a static method can't access any data that might change from object to object. For example, we couldn't write a static method that accesses the `author` field, because each `Book` may have a different value of `author`, which would make the behavior of that method instance-dependent, rather than consistent for all objects of the `Book` class.

Static methods are useful when you want to write procedural methods whose outputs depend only on their inputs and not on any instance-specific data. `Math.sin`, for example, takes an angle as input and returns its sine: the output depends only on the input and not on any private state being maintained by an object.

Try It Yourself

The `Scanner` class contains methods like `nextLine` that read values from the input stream. Explain why these methods cannot be static.

8 And, as you'll observe, we could have used an `if` statement to test if the price was valid.

Solution

Reading from the input requires interacting with some lower-level stream, which might be `System.in`, a file, or another source. The `Scanner` object maintains a connection to the input source and tracks its state — for example, whether there is still unread data in the input. `Scanner` methods can't belong to the class as a whole, because they depend on data that's inherently object-specific.

It's less common, but possible, to declare a static field. Like methods, static fields belong to the class as a whole. For fields, this means that *there is one copy of the field variable shared among all objects of the class.* For example, suppose that we have a class with a single static field.

```
/**
 * An example class with one static field
 */
public class StaticExample {
  static String word;
}
```

Every instance of class `StaticExample` will share the same underlying `word` value. Changes made to any one object are shared with the others.

```
StaticExample a = new StaticExample();
StaticExample b = new StaticExample();

a.word = "aardvark";
System.out.println(b.word); // prints "aardvark"

// Changing the word in b makes the same change in a
b.word = "bandicoot";
System.out.println(a.word);  // prints "bandicoot"
```

You can even access a static field using only the class name, without going through an object.

```
StaticExample.word = "caiman";
System.out.println(a.word);  // now prints "caiman"
```

Try It Yourself

Based on what we've said about the key concepts of OOP, explain why static fields should generally be avoided.

Solution

Static fields *break encapsulation*. Allowing changes to propagate unrestricted between different parts of the program is a recipe for hard-to-diagnose bugs. A constant, on the other hand, can be declared `static final`: It's one fixed value shared among all instances of a class, and it can't change.

2.2.8 Null Objects

One more point about objects and keywords. Take a look at the following code fragment. Does it seem okay?

```
Book b;
System.out.println(b.getAuthor());  // What does this print?
```

The first line *declares* a `Book` variable, but does not *instantiate* it. Therefore, `b` is only a name, not a real `Book` object with allocated memory and fields of its own. Running a program with that code gives an error:

```
Exception in thread "main" java.lang.NullPointerException: Cannot
invoke "Book.getAuthor()" because "<local1>" is null
```

A **null** object is one that has not been initialized. Attempting to access the fields or methods of a null object results in a `NullPointerException` because the thing that you're trying to access has never been allocated and doesn't exist.

Most compilers will detect uninitialized objects like `b` and generate an error. If you really want to compile a program with an uninitialized object variable, you can assign it the special keyword `null`, indicating that the reference is deliberately being left unassigned for now.

```
Book b = null;  // b refers to nothing
```

Attempting to use any of the methods or data of `b` would still result in a `NullPointerException`. This technique is sometimes necessary when you want to create a name that will later be assigned to an object.

2.3 The ArrayList Class

Java supports several ways to store groups of data items. One-dimensional arrays, discussed in detail in Chapter 4, are low-level, fixed-size sequences of values. Java also provides a number of built-in classes that can represent collections, including lists and sets. The `ArrayList` class is one of Java's built-in data structures, similar to Python's lists and JavaScript's arrays. An `ArrayList` represents a *resizable ordered sequence* of items. An `ArrayList` can grow and shrink over the life of the program by adding, inserting, or removing data items. This section introduces `ArrayList` as a way to manage a collection of objects, which we can then use to implement the projects in this chapter and the next. Chapter 6 discusses `ArrayList` in detail.

2.3.1 Creating an `ArrayList`

To use `ArrayList`, import it from the `java.util` package at the top of the class.

```
import java.util.ArrayList;
```

Declaring a new `ArrayList` is similar to initializing other objects. The following statement creates an empty list of `String` values named `composers`:

```
ArrayList<String> composers = new ArrayList<String>();
```

`ArrayList` uses *angle brackets* to specify the element type. This is required: Java demands that you specify the type of data in the list so that the compiler can verify the type safety of anything that you might add or remove from it. A class that takes a type as a parameter is called a **generic**. Note that an `ArrayList`, unlike a Python list, can only have one type.

2.3.2 Useful Methods

Here's a quick overview of the most important `ArrayList` methods. If you have worked with Python's lists, most of these behaviors will be similar. Use `add` to append a new item to the end of the list.

```
composers.add("Wolfgang Amadeus Mozart");
composers.add("Scott Joplin");
composers.add("Clara Schumann");
composers.add("Iannis Xenakis");
```

The `size` method returns the number of items in the list:

```
int numComposers = composers.size();  // 4
```

`ArrayList` has a `toString` method, which produces formatted output when you print the list:

```
["Wolfgang Amadeus Mozart", "Scott Joplin", "Clara Schumann",
 "Iannis Xenakis"]
```

Indexing starts at 0, similar to Python, JavaScript, and C/C++. Use the `get` method to retrieve the element at a given position:

```
String clara = composers.get(2);  // "Clara Schumann" is at position 2
```

`ArrayList` allows dynamic insertion and removal. The `remove` method takes an index and removes the item at the position; the `add` method can insert at a specified position:

```
// Remove the first element
String mozart = composers.remove(0);

// Insert a new value into the first position
composers.add(0, "Francisco Tarrega");
```

After performing the above operations, the list will be

```
["Francisco Tarrega", "Scott Joplin", "Clara Schumann",
"Iannis Xenakis"]
```

Removing an element shrinks the list; there are never any holes. Likewise, inserting automatically grows the list to accommodate the new item. If you insert into the front or middle, items will be moved out of the way to make room for the new entry.

Try It Yourself

Modify `BookDriver` to initialize an `ArrayList<Book>` named `inventory`. Add three `Book` objects to it, then print the resulting list.

Solution

Here is an example. Remember to add `import java.util.ArrayList` to the top of the program.

```
// Instantiate an ArrayList<Book>
ArrayList<Book> inventory = new ArrayList<Book>();

// Create three new Book objects
Book austen = new Book("Jane Austen", "Emma", 19.95);
Book verne = new Book("Jules Verne",
                      "Around the World in 80 Days", 6.99);
Book wells = new Book("H.G. Wells", "The War of the Worlds",
                      11.99);

// Add to the ArrayList
inventory.add(austen);
inventory.add(verne);
inventory.add(wells);

// Print -- automatically invokes toString
System.out.println(inventory);
```

2.3.3 Working with Primitive Types

Every primitive type is paired with a class that provides an object wrapper around the primitive value: `Integer` for `int`, `Double` for `double`, and so forth. A Java `ArrayList` can only hold objects, not primitive types. Use the wrapper class as the generic parameter:

```
// This will fail -- you can't use a primitive type in a generic
ArrayList<int> primes = new ArrayList<int>();

// Use the capital-I Integer wrapper type
ArrayList<Integer> primes = new ArrayList<Integer>();
```

Java is able to automatically convert between a primitive type and its corresponding wrapper object. This feature is called **autoboxing** and simplifies adding and removing elements from the list:

```
// int values are automatically converted to Integer
primes.add(2);
primes.add(3);
primes.add(5);
primes.add(7);

// Conversions also work the other way -- "auto-unboxing"
int firstPrime = primes.get(0);
```

2.4 Project: Deck of Cards

Let's look at a classic example: using object-oriented techniques to create a deck of playing cards. Each card has two attributes: a suit (spades, diamonds, hearts, or clubs) and a rank (ace, two, three, etc.). In addition to demonstrating class-design principles, this project also shows how to use an `ArrayList` to manage a collection of items, including features like using random permutations to shuffle the deck.

2.4.1 Enumerated Types

Consider the problem of representing a single `Card` object. We know it needs two fields, the `rank` and `suit`, but what types should those attributes have? We could encode each one as a `String`, so that the suit values would be `"Spades"`, `"Hearts"`, and so forth, and likewise for the ranks. This is awkward, however, because comparing or testing `suit` values would require a `String` comparison. Another choice is to encode each suit as a constant number:

```
final int CLUBS = 0;
final int DIAMONDS = 1;
final int HEARTS = 2;
final int SPADES = 3;
```

With this approach, we could compare values using ==. Also, the encoding enforces an ordering on the suits, so that `CLUBS` is the lowest valued suit and `SPADES` is the highest, which is standard in games like bridge.

An **enumerated type** is a special data type that can only take on a value from a finite, fixed set of values. Playing card suits and ranks are enumerated types: There are only 4 possible suits and 13 possible ranks. The days of the week, months of the year, or the compass directions are other examples of common enumerated types. The `enum` keyword defines an enumerated type as a set of constants:

```
public enum Suit {
  CLUBS, DIAMONDS, HEARTS, SPADES;
}
```

Once `Suit` is defined, it can be used like any other data type.

```
// Declare a Suit variable and assign it SPADES
// Use dot notation to access enum elements
Suit s = Suit.SPADES;
```

The statement below checks if two `Card` objects named `card1` and `card2` have equal suits, which can be done using the == operator.

```
if (card1.suit == card2.suit) {
  // Do something for the case where the Cards are equal
}
```

Less than/greater than comparisons are trickier. They're discussed in more detail in Section 2.4.4.

Try It Yourself

Write an enumerated type for the set of playing card ranks, starting with `ACE`, then `TWO`, `THREE`, and so forth.

Solution

The format is the same as for `Suit`. Here, `ACE` is the first entry and therefore the lowest rank; moving it to the end would make `ACE` the high card.

```
public enum Rank {
  ACE, TWO, THREE, FOUR, FIVE, SIX, SEVEN, EIGHT, NINE, TEN,
  JACK, QUEEN, KING;
}
```

2.4.2 The `Card` Class

The `Card` class uses the same set of features we previously developed for `Book`.

- The two enumerated types for `Suit` and `Rank` are defined at the top of the file.
- `Card` has private `suit` and `rank` fields.
- The constructor takes `Suit` and `Rank` values of the new `Card` as inputs.
- The `toString` returns a printable description of the object.

```
/**
 * Card
 *
 * Represents a single playing card with suit and rank
 */

enum Suit {
  CLUBS, DIAMONDS, HEARTS, SPADES;
}

enum Rank {
  ACE, TWO, THREE, FOUR, FIVE, SIX, SEVEN, EIGHT, NINE, TEN, JACK,
  QUEEN, KING;
}

public class Card {

  private Suit suit;
  private Rank rank;

  /**
   * Constructor
   *
   * @param  newSuit  Suit for this new Card
```

```
     * @param  newRank  Rank for this new Card
     */
    public Card(Suit newSuit, Rank newRank) {
      this.suit = newSuit;
      this.rank = newRank;
    }

    /**
     * Return a String representation of this Card
     *
     * @return  a String describing the suit and rank
     */
    public String toString() {
      return this.rank + " of " + this.suit;
    }
}
```

Try It Yourself

Add `get` methods for `suit` and `rank`; the fields are read-only, so we don't need `set` methods. Write a `CardTest` class with a `main` that creates and prints a few `Card` objects. For example,

```
Card aceOfSpades = new Card(Suit.SPADES, Rank.ACE);
Card queenOfHearts = new Card(Suit.HEARTS, Rank.QUEEN);
```

Solution

Here's the `getRank` method. It follows the same format as all other `get` methods. The return type is `Rank`.

```
/**
 * @return  the rank of this card
 */
public Rank getRank() {
  return this.rank;
}
```

2.4.3 The Deck Class

The `Deck` class is a wrapper around an `ArrayList<Card>`, with methods to shuffle the deck and deal out individual cards. Here is starter code for the class, which we'll fill in one method at a time:

```
/**
 * Deck -- a deck of 52 playing cards
 */
import java.util.ArrayList;
import java.util.Collections;

public class Deck {

  /**
   * Represent the deck as a list of Card objects
   */
  private ArrayList<Card> deck;

  /**
   * Constructor -- create an ArrayList of 52 Cards
   */
  public Deck() {

  }

  /**
   * Deal a Card from this Deck
   * @return  the first Card in this Deck
   */
  public Card deal() {

  }

  /**
   * Randomly permute the Cards in this Deck
   */
  public void shuffle() {

```

```
    }

    /**
     * Return a String representation of this Deck
     * @return  a String listing all Cards in the Deck
     */
    public String toString() {

    }
}
```

Constructor

The constructor initializes the `ArrayList<Card>`, then fills it with `Card` objects representing all 52 suit–rank combinations. Take a look at the following implementation:

```
/**
 * Constructor -- create an ArrayList of 52 Cards
 */
public Deck() {
  this.deck = new ArrayList<Card>();  // Initialize empty ArrayList

  // Loop through all 52 cards using the enhanced for loop
  for (Suit s : Suit.values()) {
    for (Rank r : Rank.values()) {
      Card c = new Card(s, r);
      deck.add(c);
    }
  }
}
```

This constructor demonstrates a helpful feature, the **enhanced `for` loop**. Similar to Python's `for`, the enhanced loop is an easy way to iterate through a sequence of items. Here, `Suit.values` is a built-in helper method that returns all of the elements in the `enum`. The enhanced loop uses the variable `s` to step through each of those values one at a time. The inner loop works similarly, with `r` iterating through all values of `Rank`. Each combination is used to create a new `Card`, which is then appended to the `ArrayList` using `add`.

Dealing Cards

To deal a card, simply remove and return one item from the list:

```
/**
 * Deal a Card from this Deck
 * @return  the first Card in this Deck
 */
public Card deal() {
  return this.deck.remove(0);
}
```

Notice that dealing a card removes it from the deck, so it can't be dealt again until the deck is refreshed. This is an important detail if you're writing a game like blackjack using a single deck of cards and want to accurately model the probabilities involved.

Try It Yourself

This implementation of `deal` removes and returns the first card. How would you modify the method to return the last card? Does the choice of index really make a difference?

Solution

The list is indexed from 0, so the last card is at position `deck.size() - 1`:

```
return this.deck.remove(this.deck.size() - 1);
```

Removing the first vs. last card doesn't matter from a dealing standpoint, but it turns out dealing from the end is actually more efficient. We'll see why when we implement `ArrayList` in Chapter 6.

Shuffling

Shuffling the deck is implemented by randomly permuting the contents of the `ArrayList`. This is trickier than it might seem; simply exchanging randomly selected elements won't guarantee a statistically uniform permutation (Atwood, 2007). One option is to write our own implementation of `shuffle` using a correct permutation algorithm. However, that sounds like a lot of work, so let's be lazy and use a built-in feature of Java to do the permutation for us.

Try It Yourself

Take a look at the documentation for Java's `Collections` class and find a method that you can use to permute an `ArrayList`.

Solution

The `Collections` class has a `shuffle` method. With it, shuffling the deck is trivial:

```
/**
 * Randomly permute the Cards in this Deck
 */
public void shuffle() {
  Collections.shuffle(this.deck);
}
```

Notice that `shuffle` is a static method.

toString

Writing a `toString` method could also be difficult if we had to write all of our own code to format the `ArrayList` and each `Card` object it contains. As we've seen, though, `ArrayList` has its own `toString` method. Here's a neat feature: When you call an `ArrayList`'s `toString` method, it will automatically invoke the `toString` for each item in the list. The result is a fully formatted printable list containing the string representation of each `Card` object.

```
/**
 * Return a String representation of this Deck
 * @return  a String listing all Cards in the Deck
 */
public String toString() {
  return this.deck.toString();
}
```

Try It Yourself

Write a class called `DeckTest` that initializes a new `Deck`, calls its `shuffle` method, and then prints it to verify that the cards are shuffled.

Solution

Because we've implemented the methods efficiently, these steps require only a few lines. Here's how they might be done within `main`:

```
// Create a new Deck
Deck d = new Deck();
```

```
// Shuffle -- rearranges the deck internally, no return
d.shuffle();

// Print using toString
System.out.println(d);
```

That's it! The output will be randomized, but will look something like

```
[SIX of DIAMONDS, TWO of HEARTS, TWO of CLUBS, QUEEN of HEARTS, FOUR
        of DIAMONDS, EIGHT of SPADES, SIX of CLUBS, FIVE of CLUBS,
        ACE of HEARTS, NINE of DIAMONDS,

//*** And so forth ***//
```

2.4.4 Hi-Lo

Let's write a simple game that uses the `Card` and `Deck` classes. After creating and shuffling the deck, the player is shown a card, then guesses whether the next card will be higher in rank or lower in rank. The novel part of the program is the comparison between the `Rank` values of the two `Card` objects.

Enumerated types support equality testing using `==`, but don't support the basic `</>` operators. Instead, there is a special method called `compareTo` that returns the *difference between two objects*. Many Java classes implement their own `compareTo`, which always uses ordering rules that make sense for the class. For an `enum`, the comparison uses the ordering of the enumerated values. To compare two ranks, first extract them from their `Card` objects, then use the `compareTo` method of one with the other as input.

```
Rank firstRank = firstCard.getRank();
Rank secondRank = secondCard.getRank();
int diff = secondRank.compareTo(firstRank);
```

The result `diff` is equal to `secondRank - firstRank`. If the difference is zero, the two ranks are equal; if it's positive, then `secondRank` is greater, and if it's negative, then `firstRank` is greater.

Try It Yourself

The code below shows a skeleton of the program with comments for each step. Fill in each part to complete the working Hi-Lo game. Put the program in the same location as your `Card` and `Deck` classes so it has access to them.

```
/**
 * Hi-Lo -- Guess if the next card will be higher or lower
```

```
 */

import java.util.Scanner;

public class HiLo {

  public static void main(String[] args) {
    // Initialize and shuffle the deck

    // Create a Scanner for user input

    // Deal and print the first card

    // Prompt the user for a guess
    System.out.println("The next card will be:");
    System.out.println("1. Higher");
    System.out.println("2. Lower");
    System.out.println("Enter your choice:");

    // Read the user's choice with nextInt

    // Deal and print the next card

    // Extract the ranks and compare them
    Rank firstRank = firstCard.getRank();
    Rank secondRank = secondCard.getRank();
    int diff = secondRank.compareTo(firstRank);

    // Print the result
    //
    // There are four options: two ways to win,
    // a tie between the ranks, or a loss

  }
}
```

Solution

Review the previous chapter for examples using `Scanner`. Deal each `Card` by calling the `deal` method of the `Deck`.

```
Card firstCard = deck.deal();
System.out.println("The first card is: " + firstCard);
```

Determine the result by testing the values of `choice` and `diff`.

```
if (choice == 1 && diff > 0 || choice == 2 && diff < 0) {
  System.out.println("Winner, winner, chicken dinner!");
} else if (diff == 0) {
  System.out.println("It's a tie!");
} else {
  System.out.println("You have chosen...poorly.");
}
```

SUMMARY

This chapter has explored both the concepts of OOP and their implementation in Java. If you're coming from another language background, these ideas may be new to you, but they're very much what makes Java *Java*, and not just a verbose version of C. As you're studying, keep these ideas in mind:

- The concept of encapsulation and the value of protecting data behind a well-defined interface is fundamental, both to the rest of this book and programming in general.
- The standard library of built-in classes is an important part of Java programming. Understanding how standard data structures are implemented is critically important; it's rarely necessary to reimplement them from scratch.
- Designing large software applications is hard. Very hard. In the long run, you've got to work just as hard at building up your design skills – the ability to "see" the scope of a problem and how it can be modeled in software – as you do at low-level algorithmic manipulations.

EXERCISES

Understand

1. Define the term encapsulation as it applies to OOP. Why is encapsulation useful for programmers?

2. Come up with a concrete case where encapsulation might be harmful rather than helpful.
3. Explain the meaning of the phrase "instance of" as it's used in the sentence, "`s1` is an instance of the `String` class."
4. Are class fields the same thing as instance variables? Why or why not?
5. Add an `equals` method to the `Book` class that takes a second `Book` as input and returns `true` if the two objects have equal values. Tip: Review the section in Chapter 1 on testing `String` equality.
6. We've now defined most pieces of the `main` incantation. Explain why `main` must be static and why a non-static `main` wouldn't make sense.
7. Consider the following sequence of `ArrayList` commands. What are the final contents of the list?

```
ArrayList<String> dinosaurs = new ArrayList<String>();
dinosaurs.add("T-Rex");
dinosaurs.add("Triceratops");
dinosaurs.add("Stegosaurus");
dinosaurs.add("Plesiosaurus");
dinosaurs.add("Deinonychus");

// Oops! Plesiosaurus is a marine reptile, not a dinosaur!
dinosaurs.remove(3);

String trex = dinosaurs.remove(0);
dinosaurs.add(3, trex);
dinosaurs.add(0, "Brachiosaurus");
dinosaurs.add(2, "Pachycephalosaurus");
```

8. Add an `empty` method to the `Deck` class that returns `true` if there are no more cards remaining to deal and `false` otherwise. Tip: Test the length of the internal `ArrayList`.
9. Take a look at the following method call. Reconstruct the signature of the method.

```
String message = example.f("Alligator", 1.4804, 9);
```

10. How about this method call? How is its signature different from the previous one?

```
String message = Example.f("Alligator", 1.4804, 9);
```

11. Define an `enum` type representing the oceans of the world.
12. Take a look at the following constructor, which uses the same names for both parameters and assignment variables. Explain why there is no confusion about which versions of `x` and `y` are being assigned.

```
public Example(int x, double y) {
  this.x = x;
  this.y = y;
}
```

13. Write a method called `dictFirst` that takes two `String` parameters as input and returns the one that would come first in a dictionary. Tip: Look at the `compareToIgnoreCase` method in the `String` class.
14. Imagine that you've finally graduated and gone on to your dream coding job (if that is in fact your dream). One day, your boss proposes designing a class that includes a static member variable. Thinking back to what you've learned here, how do you respond?
15. Find another example of a static member variable in a built-in Java class other than `Math`. Why does it make sense for that variable to be declared `static`?
16. Suppose that we made the `author` and `title` attributes of the `Book` class `final`. What would that choice imply about how we expect those fields to be used?

Apply

17. Write a class that encapsulates the concept of a player on a football team[9] with `name` and `position` attributes. Make the attributes `private` and write a constructor, `toString`, and `get` methods.
18. Write a class called `Guitar` that represents a guitar. Give it the following private variables: `String make`, `String model`, `int year`, `int numStrings`. Write a constructor that sets those properties, a `toString`, and `get` methods for each one.
19. Write a class representing a university course. It should have a `String prefix` (e.g., `"CS"`), `String number`, `String instructor`, and `int enrollment`. Write an appropriate constructor, `toString`, and `get` methods. Write `set` methods for the fields that you believe should have them.
20. Write a `Rectangle` class with `x` and `y` values for the upper-left corner, `width`, and `height`. Add a constructor and methods to return the area and perimeter of the `Rectangle`.
21. Write a class named `Circle` with fields representing a 2D center point (using two `double` values) and a `double radius`. Add a constructor and methods to calculate and return the area and circumference of the `Circle`
22. Add a method to `Circle` called `overlaps` that takes another `Circle` as input and returns `true` if the two objects overlap in 2D space. Tip: Calculate the distance between the centers.
23. If you have experience with Python, you probably miss being able to print by typing `print`, rather than `System.out.println`. Write an `IOHelper` class with a static method called `print` that takes a `String` and passes it to `System.out.println`.
24. Add a `printNPlaces` method to `IOHelper` that wraps around `System.out.printf`. The inputs should be a `double` to print and an `int` number of places.

9 American or metric.

25. Add a readInt method to the IOHelper class. Your method should take an input String message, print the message, then create a Scanner that reads one int value from System.in. Note: You don't want to close the Scanner at the end of the method because that would close the connection to System.in.

26. Write a class named Library that functions as a container for an ArrayList<Book>. Give it the following methods:
   - A constructor that initializes an empty ArrayList<Book>.
   - An add method that takes a Book and appends it to the list.
   - A searchByAuthor method that takes a String as input and returns an ArrayList <Book> containing any Book objects in the library whose author field matches (you can use an exact match).
   - A searchByTitle method that takes a String as input and returns an ArrayList< Book> containing any Book objects in the library whose title field matches (again, you can use an exact match).
   - A toString that prints the contents of the Library.

27. Add a searchByKeyword method to the Library that takes a String input and returns all Books that *contain* the input in either the title or author fields.

Extend

28. In blackjack, number cards count for their values, all face cards count for 10, and aces have a default value of 11. Add a method to the Card class called blackjackValue that returns the value the card would have in a game of blackjack.

29. Baccarat is another card-based table game offered at casinos. It's traditionally played in special roped-off areas with high bets and has a reputation as the province of high-rollers. When scoring baccarat hands, number cards count for their values, aces count for 1, and face cards count for 0. Add another method called baccaratValue to Card that returns the value of the card in baccarat.

30. Write a class called Hand that represents an ArrayList<Card> with the following methods:
   - A constructor that initializes an empty ArrayList<Card>.
   - An add method that takes a Card and appends it to the list.
   - A toString that prints the contents of the Hand.

31. Add a second version of the deal method to Deck that takes an int n as input and returns a Hand containing n cards. Consider how to handle the situation where n is larger than the number of remaining cards or negative.

32. In blackjack, a game begins with the player receiving two cards. The best possible outcome – a "blackjack" – is for the value of the two cards to sum to 21. This is achieved if one card is an ace and the other has a value of 10. What is the probability of the player drawing a blackjack on the first two cards of a game? Write a simulation program to find the answer. Tips:
   - As in the other simulation programs, perform a large number of simulated trials and record the number that result in a blackjack.

- Start each trial with a full, freshly shuffled `Deck`.
- You can deal two individual cards or use the enhanced deal method to get a `Hand` of two cards. The choice doesn't matter.

33. Like blackjack, baccarat also starts with dealing two cards to the player. In baccarat, the score of a hand is the *sum of its cards modulo 10*. For example, a hand of 9 and 7 has a score of 6, because (9 + 7) modulo 10 is 6. The best outcome for the player is a "natural," which is obtained with a score of 8 or 9 on the first two cards. What is the probability of drawing a natural at the beginning of a hand of baccarat? Write a simulation program to find the answer using the same format as the previous problem.

34. Add a method to the `Hand` class called `blackjackValue` that returns the value of the `Hand` according to the rules of blackjack. Each card's value is its `blackjackValue`, except for the ace, which has a default value of 11, unless that would make the hand go over 21, in which case the ace counts for only 1. Note that a hand with multiple aces can have one count for 11 and the other for 1. For example, a hand of two aces has a value of 12.

35. Now use the `Card`, `Deck`, and `Hand` classes to implement a game of blackjack between one player and a dealer. The basic flow of the game is as follows:

- Shuffle the deck and deal two cards to the player and two cards to the dealer. Print both of the player's cards but print only the dealer's first card.
- If the player achieves a blackjack, the game ends immediately with a win.
- If the player has any other score, they may choose to "stand" or to "hit". If the player hits, they receive one additional card. If they stand, their turn ends and they keep their current hand.
- If the player hits and the additional card pushes their score over 21, they "bust" and the game ends immediately.
- The player may continue to repeatedly hit until they either bust or choose to stand.
- Once the player stands, the dealer reveals their second card. The dealer then repeatedly draws cards from the deck as long as their hand has a value less than 17. If the dealer busts, they immediately lose.
- Once the dealer stands, the values of the two hands are compared. The player wins if their hand has a higher score than the dealer's.

Here is a starting program. Think about any additional features that you might need to add to complete the project.

```
/**
 * BLACKJACK
 */

import java.util.Scanner;

public class Blackjack {

  public static void main(String[] args) {
```

```

    // Initialize a Scanner for input

    // Create and shuffle a Deck

    // Deal two-card Hand to the player

    // Deal two-card Hand to the dealer

    // Print the player's two cards
    // Tip: think about adding a method to the Hand class

    // Print the dealer's first card
    // Again, think about adding a method to Hand

    // Calculate the score of the player's hand

    // If score == 21, the player wins immediately

    // Use a loop to prompt the player to hit or stand
    boolean looping = true;

    while (looping) {
      // Calculate and print the player's current score

      // Print choices
      System.out.println("1. Hit");
      System.out.println("2. Stand");
      System.out.println("Hit or Stand?");

      // Read the player's move

      // If the player chooses to hit,
      //     Deal a new card
      //     Add it to the player's hand
      //     Calculate the score of the hand
      //     Check if the score is greater than 21.

```

```
      // Else if the player chooses stand,
      //     Set looping = false to end the loop

      // Else, the player has chosen an option that isn't 1 or 2,
      //     Print an error message and repeat
    }

    // Reveal the dealer's second card

    // Use a second loop to make the dealer hit on < 17
    // If the dealer's score goes over 21, they bust

    // Compare the scores of the two hands
    // The hand with the higher score is the winner

  }
}
```

NOTES AND FURTHER READING

The first OOP language was Simula, which was created for simulation programming and modeling and debuted in 1967 (Dahl, 2004). Several previous languages supported the idea of grouping related variables into a single unit – often called a structure or record – but Simula went further by combining methods and data within the same class and also introducing new features like subclassing. Another significant early OOP language was Smalltalk, developed as a research language in the early 1970s by Alan Kay and a team at the Xerox Palo Alto Research Center (PARC). Objects in Smalltalk interact with each other by passing messages that represent requests for services or data (Goldberg and Robson, 1983). Object-oriented programming finally took off and became a dominant programming paradigm in the 1990s, driven by the development of Java, C++, and other competitive object-based languages, as well as the rising popularity of graphical user interfaces. Graphical applications are a great fit for the object-based approach, because it's natural to model each "thing" in the application – windows, components, menus, etc. – as an object with internal properties describing position, style, and other qualities, as well as methods that specify how to update and interact with it. Java has a robust library of built-in graphics classes, which we'll start exploring in the next chapter.

3 Project: Mindstorms

Should the computer program the kid, or the kid program the computer?
Seymour Papert

INTRODUCTION

Seymour Papert published *Mindstorms* in 1980. Subtitled *Children, Computers, and Powerful Ideas*, the book advocated for making computational thinking a core part of the curriculum for young children (Papert, 1980). *Mindstorms* was influential in computer education circles, and the approaches it described were the first exposure to programming and computer science for many children. LEGO later adopted the name for a line of programmable building sets.

Mindstorms built on earlier educational programming environments, notably the Logo language, which introduced **turtle graphics** as a tool for teaching programming. The user writes programs to move a drawing tool – the "turtle" – around the screen. As the turtle moves and turns, it leaves behind a trail, which then creates an image on the screen.

LEARNING OBJECTIVES

In this chapter, you'll implement your own version of Logo using Java's built-in graphics libraries. After completing the project, you'll be able to:

- Create visible applications with Java's built-in graphics classes.
- Use the `Canvas` and `Graphics` classes to draw shapes and colors.
- Use OOP concepts and `ArrayList` to implement the turtle.
- Extend the turtle and draw new shapes by writing custom methods.

In addition to reviewing important OOP concepts from the last chapter, this project introduces key graphics concepts that we'll use in several future projects.

3.1 Introduction to Java Graphics

Java includes a variety of classes for creating graphical applications. This section will show you how to use Java's graphics framework to create geometric drawings using basic colored shapes.

3.1.1 Drawing Shapes

Learning to use graphics in Java can be challenging because there are a large number of relevant classes and often multiple ways of accomplishing the same goal. Java actually has three different frameworks for building graphical apps, each focusing on a different use case. We're going to focus on a standard set of features that we can use in future projects. Our first goal is to create a visible window and draw onto it using the `Graphics` class.

```
/**
 * FirstDrawing
 *
 * Demonstrates how to draw using JFrame and Graphics
*/

import java.awt.Canvas;
import java.awt.Graphics;
import javax.swing.JFrame;

public class FirstDrawing extends Canvas {

  // Size of the display window
  final int WIDTH = 640;
  final int HEIGHT = 480;

  /**
   * Constructor
   */
  public FirstDrawing() {
    setSize(WIDTH, HEIGHT);
  }

  /**
   * paint -- contains all drawing operations
   *
   * @param  g  Graphics object that refers to the
   *            drawable surface
   */
  public void paint(Graphics g) {
    g.fillRect(100, 125, 320, 240);
  }

```

```
34   /**
35    * main -- sets up frame and makes it visible
36    */
37   public static void main(String[] args) {
38     // Construct the driver object
39     FirstDrawing app = new FirstDrawing();
40
41     // Create a JFrame and attach the driver to it
42     // These steps are required to make the window visible
43     JFrame frame = new JFrame();
44     frame.add(app);
45     frame.pack();
46     frame.setVisible(true);
47     frame.setDefaultCloseOperation(JFrame.EXIT_ON_CLOSE);
48   }
49 }
```

Let's break it down. The first lines import three required classes:

- `Canvas` represents a drawable surface.
- `Graphics` implements drawing operations.
- `JFrame` is a utility class that creates a visible application window.

`Graphics` is in the `java.awt` package. AWT stands for **Abstract Windowing Toolkit**, and contains classes for building graphical applications from basic low-level components. `JFrame` is part of Java's Swing library, which was created to facilitate building platform-independent graphical user interfaces that don't need the low-level control of the AWT framework. Java now has a third framework, JavaFX, which is an updated version of Swing. Our projects will focus primarily on drawing with the AWT classes, with a few features of Swing/JavaFX.[1]

The class declaration introduces a new keyword: `extends`. Recall from the last chapter that it's possible to use one class as a template for another, which is called **inheritance**. Here, the `extends` keyword indicates that `FirstDrawing` is a kind of `Canvas`; that is, it inherits the useful properties of being a displayable, drawable surface from the built-in `Canvas` class. This setup allows us to gain the benefits of `Canvas`'s properties and methods without implementing them ourselves, but with the ability to write our own drawing methods to make `FirstDrawing` produce the graphics we want.

3.1.2 Graphics Methods

Start by looking at `main`, the entry point for the program. Notice that `main` is defined within the class, instead of being in a separate file, like some of our previous examples.

- The first statement (line 39) constructs a `FirstDrawing` object named `app`.

1 Chapter 11 uses Swing to build a tiny web browser.

- The `add` method (line 44) attaches `app` to a `JFrame`.
- The `pack` method (line 45) automatically adjusts the size of the `JFrame` to match the size of the drawable surface.
- The remaining calls (lines 46 and 47) make the window visible and specify that the program should end when the visible window closes.

The constructor sets the size of the new drawing surface. `WIDTH` and `HEIGHT` are constants that define the dimensions of the surface in units of pixels.

The creative work happens in the `paint` method, which is where the actual graphics operations take place. Notice that there is no call to `paint` within `main`. *Do not call `paint` directly.* Instead, `paint` is called *automatically* by the Java graphics framework when the application window becomes visible. The framework automatically obtains a `Graphics` object, which is the interface to the drawing surface, then passes it as the input of `paint`. We'll later see ways to call `paint` on demand when we need to make a change to the graphics.

Drawing is done in units of pixels. Pixel (0, 0) is located at the *upper-left* of the window. Increasing the x-coordinate moves to the right, as you would expect, but increasing the y-coordinate moves *down*. The statement

```
g.fillRect(100, 125, 320, 240);
```

draws a filled rectangle at a position 100 pixels to the right and 125 pixels down. The width of the rectangle is 320 pixels and the height is 240.

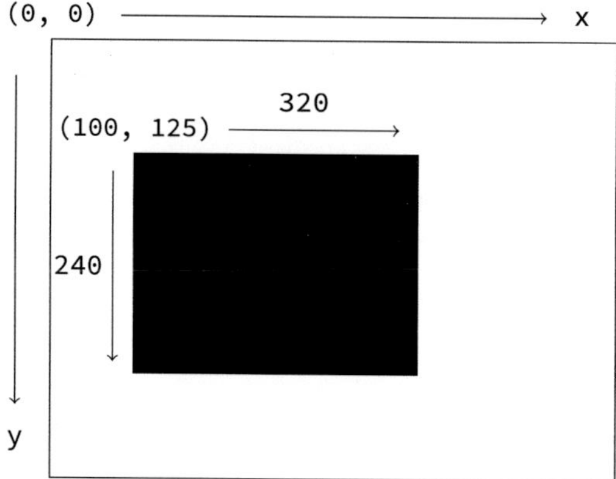

Try It Yourself

Experiment with changing the `WIDTH` and `HEIGHT` parameters to make the drawing window larger or smaller. Change the inputs to `fillRect` to change the position and size of the rectangle. `Graphics` can also draw other shapes and even text. Use `drawRect` to create an outlined (unfilled) rectangle. Use `drawString` to make a message appear on the screen. For example,

```
g.drawString("Hello, friend.", 100, 125);
```

Again, experiment with changing the text and its position.

3.1.3 Colors

By default, the `draw` and `fill` methods paint in black. It isn't possible to specify the color as a parameter to an individual drawing operation. Instead, the `Graphics` object has one active color, which is controlled by the `setColor` method. After calling `setColor`, everything you draw will be in the new color until you call `setColor` again to switch to a different one. The `Color` class contains constants representing common colors. First, import it at the top of your program:

```
import java.awt.Color;
```

Now call `g.setColor` to change the color before drawing. For example, to draw a blue rectangle:

```
g.setColor(Color.BLUE);
g.fillRect(100, 125, 320, 240);
```

Try It Yourself

Modify the method to draw a blue rectangle with a red boundary. Tip: After drawing the rectangle, change the color to `Color.RED` and then use `drawRect`.

You can also construct new `Color` objects representing custom colors. The standard red–green–blue (RGB) color space encodes every color as a triple of values representing the mixture of red, green, and blue, each in the range of 0–255. To create a new RGB color, pass the three values to the `Color` constructor:

```
Color c = new Color(red, green, blue);
```

For example, you could define a purple color as the triple (128, 0, 128): a mixture of moderate, equal amounts of red and blue with no green:

```
// Draw a purple rectangle
g.setColor(new Color(128, 0, 128));
g.fillRect(100, 125, 320, 240);
```

`Color` also accepts RGB mixtures expressed as `float` values between 0.0 and 1.0, which is convenient for creating random colors:

```
// Math.random returns a double -- cast it to a float for Color
float red = (float) Math.random();
float green = (float) Math.random();
float blue = (float) Math.random();

Color randCol = new Color(red, green, blue);
g.setColor(randCol);
```

Try It Yourself

Use a color wheel app (there are several available online) to look up the integer RGB values for a few colors that you like. Experiment with changing the drawing color. You can use multiple `setColor` and `fillRect` commands in `paint` to draw multiple rectangles of different colors.

3.2 Project: Do-It-Yourself Turtle Graphics

Let's build on the basic graphic ideas to implement our own turtle drawing program. This section will lead you through implementing a simple turtle that can draw lines by moving and turning, then show you how to write custom methods for complex shapes. Throughout this section, focus on how the methods of the turtle interact with the internal variables that describe its position and direction.

3.2.1 Basic Commands

Turtle programs are written as instructions to the turtle, which allows the student to reason about the program's behavior by thinking about (or physically acting out) the movements that the turtle makes.The simplest turtle programs are built around straight-line movements and turns.

- The `move` command moves the turtle forward a certain distance in its current direction, drawing a line between its starting and ending positions. For example, if the turtle starts facing right, the `move` command would make it draw to the right.

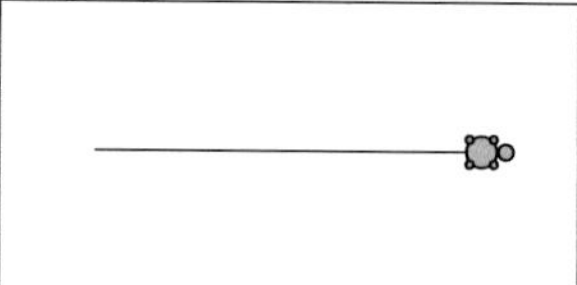

- The `turnLeft` command rotates the turtle left by a given angle, relative to its current angle. For example, the command `turnLeft 90` would make the turtle turn 90 degrees to the left.

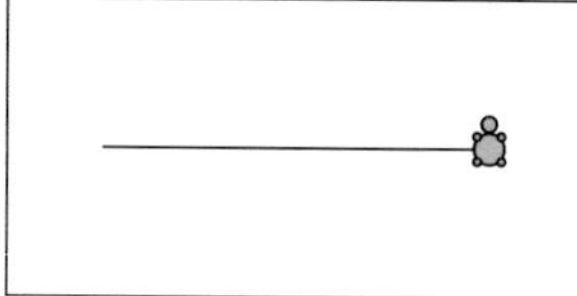

Combining the basic commands allows for more complex drawings. For example, to draw a square you could issue the following commands:

```
move 100
turnLeft 90
move 100
turnLeft 90
```

```
move 100
turnLeft 90
move 100
turnLeft 90
```

The program draws four lines of 100 units each, with a 90 degree turn after each movement. A typical turtle programming exercise asks the student to write custom methods to draw progressively more complex patterns.

Try It Yourself

By hand, work out a sequence of `move` and `turnLeft` commands that would allow the turtle to draw an equilateral triangle.

Solution

The internal angles of the triangle are all 60 degrees, so you can draw it by moving forward, then turning 120 degrees to the left, then repeating those steps two more times.

3.2.2 Setup

Our basic turtle will have three attributes required to move it around the screen:

- `x` and `y`, representing its position within the drawing window. Moving the turtle changes `x` and `y`.
- An `angle`, keeping track of the turtle's direction. Rotating the turtle changes the angle. We'll represent this angle in units of *degrees*, which will be important in a moment when we need to use it for calculations.

We'll start with the following methods.

- `move(double dist)`: move the turtle a length of `dist` in its current facing direction. This action generates a line segment beginning at the turtle's current position. It also changes the turtle's position to the endpoint of the segment.
- `turnLeft(double degrees)`: rotate the turtle left by an angle of `degrees`.
- `paint(Graphics g)`: the standard painting method that draws the lines created by the turtle to the window.

We need a way, though, to connect the movements of the turtle to the `paint` method. `paint` always clears the drawing window when it runs, so we'll need a way to maintain the history of the turtle's movements so we can reconstruct its path. Java has a built-in class called `Line2D` that represents a segment with a starting and ending position. Use the following strategy:

- Give the turtle an `ArrayList<Line2D>`, representing its history of movements.
- Every time the turtle moves, create another `Line2D` and add it to the list.
- When `paint` runs, iterate through the list and draw every line segment. This will reconstruct the turtle's entire path.

The project starter code is below. It uses the same overall format as the previous project, built around a `JFrame`. Notice that there are a few new imports at the top. We'll fill in each method one at a time.

```
/**
 * Turtle graphics using Java classes
 *
 * Key idea: the Turtle maintains an  ArrayList<Line2D>
 * describing the lines that it has drawn over the course of
 * the program
 *
 * On a paint, draw each line in the ArrayList to produce the
 * complete figure
 */

import java.awt.Canvas;
import java.awt.Graphics;
import javax.swing.JFrame;
import java.awt.Color;
import java.util.ArrayList;
import java.awt.geom.Line2D;

public class Turtle extends Canvas {

  /**
   * Instance variables
   */
final int WIDTH = 500;
final int HEIGHT = 400;

  /**
   * Constructor
   */
  public Turtle() {

  }

  /**
   * turnLeft -- adjust the Turtle's angle
```

```
 *
 * @param  degrees  counter-clockwise change in angle
 */
public void turnLeft(double degrees) {

}

/**
 * Helper method -- calculate cosine of an angle in degrees
 *
 * @param  theta  angle in degrees
 * @return cos(theta)
 */
public double cosDeg(double theta) {

}

/**
 * Helper method -- calculate sine of an angle in degrees
 *
 * @param  theta  angle in degrees
 * @return sin(theta)
 */
public double sinDeg(double theta) {

}

/**
 * move -- move the Turtle in its current facing direction
 *
 * @param  dist  the linear distance for the move
 *
 */
public void move(double dist) {

}

/**
```

```
  * paint -- contains all drawing operations
  *
  * @param  g  Graphics object that refers to the drawable surface
  */
 public void paint(Graphics g) {

 }

 /**
  * main -- creates and tests the Turtle
  */
 public static void main(String[] args) {

   // Create a new Turtle object
   Turtle t = new Turtle();

   // Setup the JFrame
   JFrame frame = new JFrame();
   frame.add(t);
   frame.pack();
   frame.setVisible(true);
   frame.setDefaultCloseOperation(JFrame.EXIT_ON_CLOSE);

   // Issue commands to the Turtle to draw

   // Draw a rectangle
   t.move(100);
   t.turnLeft(90);
   t.move(50);
   t.turnLeft(90);
   t.move(100);
   t.turnLeft(90);
   t.move(50);

   // Use repaint to trigger a call to paint
   t.repaint();
 }
}
```

The starter code has an example `main` method. It creates a new `Turtle` object (line 88) and displays the window, as in the previous examples. Lines 100–106 draw a rectangle using a sequence of `move` and `turnLeft` calls. The final line calls `repaint`, which triggers an internal call to the `paint` method. This is the way to trigger a paint operation on-demand – remember that you can't call `paint` directly.

3.2.3 Instance Variables and Constructor

Start by adding fields to the top of the class (in the instance variables section) that maintain the `Turtle`'s state.

```
// Position and direction variables
private double x;
private double y;
private double angle;

// List of segments generated by moving
private ArrayList<Line2D> lines;
```

Notice that `x` and `y` have been declared `double`. It turns out to be easier to work with `double` values even though the actual position has to eventually be turned into an integer number of pixels for the drawing operations. Java's `Line2D` classes expect either `double` or `float` coordinates.

The constructor needs to set the size of the window, then initialize the other fields. Let's assume that the turtle will start in the middle of the window at an angle of zero degrees. We'll also initialize an empty `ArrayList`.

```
/**
 * Constructor
 */
public Turtle() {
  setSize(WIDTH, HEIGHT);

  // Turtle starts in the center
  this.x = WIDTH / 2.0;
  this.y = HEIGHT / 2.0;
  this.angle = 0.0;

  // Initialize the list of Line objects
  this.lines = new ArrayList<Line2D>();
}
```

3.2.4 Moving and Angles

The `turnLeft` method is simple. It takes a change in angle as its input and adds it to the turtle's `angle` parameter.

```
/**
 * turnLeft -- adjust the Turtle's angle
 *
 * @param  degrees  counter-clockwise change in angle
 */
public void turnLeft(double degrees) {
  this.angle += degrees;
}
```

Moving the turtle requires reasoning about the relationship between position, angle, and distance. Suppose the turtle is currently centered over position (x, y) and facing at an angle θ. We'd like to move in that direction for a distance of d.

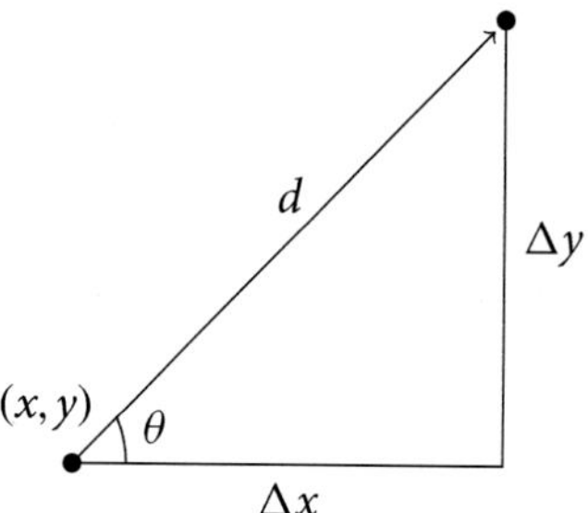

From trigonometry, the horizontal and vertical displacements are given by

$$\Delta x = d \cos \theta$$
$$\Delta y = d \sin \theta .$$

The `move` method performs those calculations, then uses them to create a `Line2D` connecting the starting position to the ending position.[2]

```
/**
 * move -- move the Turtle in its current facing direction
 *
 * @param  dist  the linear distance for the move
 */
public void move(double dist) {
```

2 You can verify that this approach continues to work correctly when θ is greater than 90 or negative.

```
7
8     // Calculate new position -- note: angle is in units of degrees
9     double newX = this.x + cosDeg(this.angle) * dist;
10
11    // Remember: y axis is reversed for pixel
12    // coordinates -- subtract to move up
13    double newY = this.y - sinDeg(this.angle) * dist;
14
15    // Construct a Line2D representing the movement
16    Line2D newLine = new Line2D.Double(this.x, this.y, newX, newY);
17
18    // Append to the ArrayList of movements
19    this.lines.add(newLine);
20
21    // Update position
22    this.x = newX;
23    this.y = newY;
24 }
```

Line 16 creates a new `Line2D` object representing the segment. Java provides two forms of `Line2D`, with either `double` or `float` coordinates. There is no generic `Line2D` constructor, so the right side of line 16 calls `Line2D.Double`.

The most complicated lines are the calculations of `newX` and `newY` (lines 9 and 13). Recall that the turtle's `angle` parameter is in units of degrees. However, `Math.sin` and `Math.cos` expect inputs in units of *radians*. Therefore, we'll create two helper methods, `cosDeg` and `sinDeg`, to calculate those values on degree inputs.

```
/**
 * Helper method -- calculate cosine of an angle in degrees
 *
 * @param  theta  angle in degrees
 * @return cos(theta)
 */
public double cosDeg(double theta) {
  return Math.cos(Math.toRadians(theta));
}
```

The method converts the current angle to radians and returns its cosine; `sinDeg` is similar.

3.2.5 Drawing

Finally, the `paint` method, which loops over the list of lines and draws each one using `drawLine`.

```
/**
 * paint -- contains all drawing operations
 *
 * @param  g  Graphics object that refers to the drawable surface
 */
public void paint(Graphics g) {

  // Paint the background white
  g.setColor(Color.WHITE);
  g.fillRect(0, 0, WIDTH, HEIGHT);
  g.setColor(Color.BLACK);

  // Loop over the set of lines
  for (Line2D line : this.lines) {
    // Extract coordinates -- convert to int for units of pixels
    int startX = (int) line.getX1();
    int startY = (int) line.getY1();
    int endX = (int) line.getX2();
    int endY = (int) line.getY2();

    // Draw
    g.drawLine(startX, startY, endX, endY);
  }
}
```

This method uses the enhanced `for` loop to iterate through every element of `lines`. For each line, it extracts the coordinates (as `int` values), then draws each segment using `g.drawLine`.

Try It Yourself

Use the starter code and descriptions of each method to complete the `Turtle` class. When you're done, run it and verify that it draws the rectangle described in `main`. Try changing the `move` and `turnLeft` commands to create your own shapes.

3.2.6 Adding New Commands

The basic turtle only knows how to move and turn left. You can implement new behaviors by defining more methods in the `Turtle` class. For example, to make the turtle turn right, define a `turnRight` method that adjusts the angle in the opposite way from `turnLeft`.

```
/**
 * turnRight -- adjust the Turtle's angle
 *
 * @param  degrees  clockwise change in angle
 */
public void turnRight(double degrees) {
  this.angle -= degrees;
}
```

Another useful set of methods make the turtle face a particular direction:

```
/**
 * faceNorth -- set angle to 90 degrees
 */
public void faceNorth() {
  this.angle = 90;
}
```

Try It Yourself

Add more methods: `faceEast`, `faceWest`, `faceSouth`, and `turnAround`. Add code to `main` to test each method.

Try It Yourself

Add a method called `moveTo` that takes two `double` inputs named `newX` and `newY` and then sets the turtle's position to those coordinates without drawing a segment.

3.2.7 Complex Shapes

Let's finish this project by working through a few examples from the original *Mindstorms* book. In addition to showing how to write more complex methods, they show off a variety of interesting patterns that can be built from a simple "move and turn" approach.

Rosettes

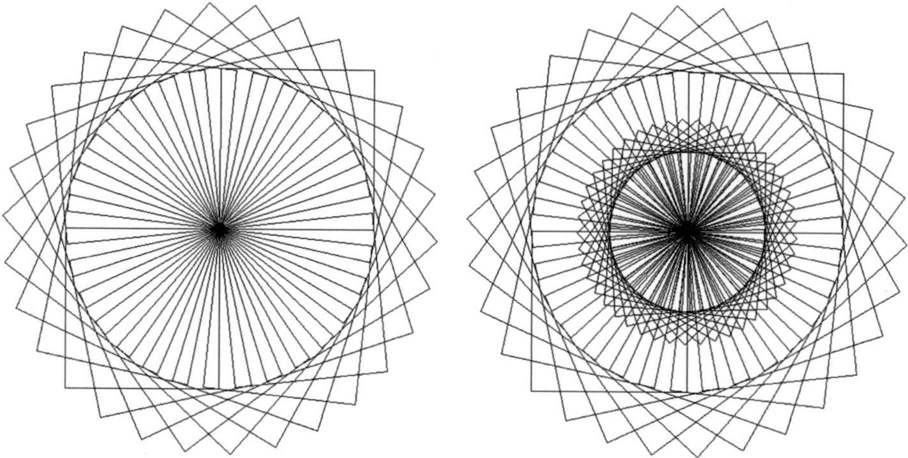

These attractive rosette figures are built from rotated overlapping squares. To begin, write a method called `square` that takes a `double side` as input and then draws a square with that side length by making four moves and four 90 degree turns. The turtle starts and ends with the same position and orientation.

```
/**
 * Draw a square based on the turtle's current orientation
 *
 * @param  side  side length of the square
 */
public void square(double side) {
  for (int i = 0; i < 4; i++) {
    move(side);
    turnLeft(90);
  }
}
```

The `rosette` method repeatedly calls `square` followed by a turn. The method takes two parameters: the number of squares in the rosette and the side length. Notice how the turn angle is calculated from the number of squares in order to make a full rotation.

```
/**
 * Draw a rosette made from overlapping squares
 *
 * @param  n  the number of squares
 * @param  side  the side length of each square
 */
public void rosette(int n, double side) {
```

```
  double turnAngle = 360.0 / n;

  for (int i = 0; i < n; i++) {
    square(side);
    turnLeft(turnAngle);
  }
}
```

To create the second image, draw two overlapping rosettes with different values of `n` and `side`.

Spirals

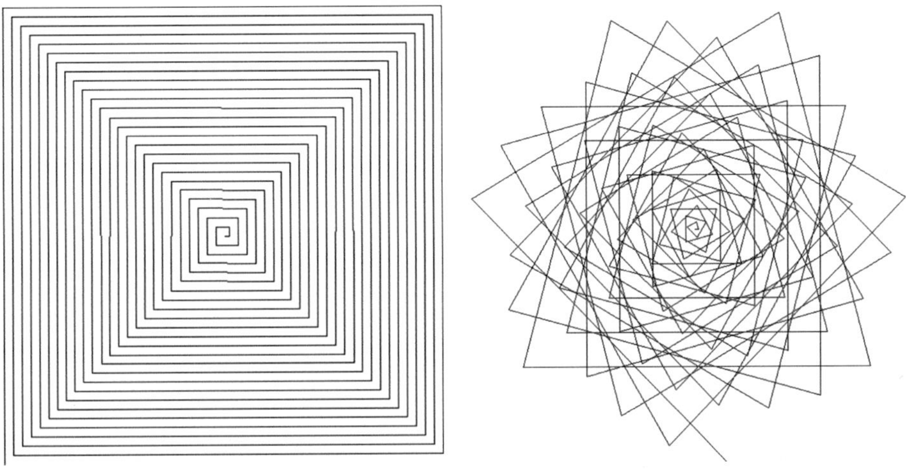

Create an outward spiral by repeatedly moving and then turning, but increasing the size of the move on each step.

```
/**
 * Draw a spiral
 */
public void spiral() {
  double dist = 5;
  for (int i = 0; i < 100; i++) {
    move(dist);
    turnLeft(90);
    dist += 5;
  }
}
```

The left example makes 90 degree turns for a right-angled spiral. More interesting results happen if you make the turn angle something other than 90. The right example makes a 105 degree turn between each move.

Flowers

These flowers are similar in structure to the rosettes: Each one is built from spear-shaped petals with a turn between each. The petal, though, uses a curved shape. Consider: How would you use the turtle to draw a circle? A true circle is a continuous curve, which we can't really create out of linear move operations, but we can approximate a curve by making very small movements and turning between each one.

```
// Make a circle out of 360 tiny steps and turns
for (int i = 0; i < 360; i++) {
  move(1);
  turnLeft(1);
}
```

Try It Yourself

Write a method called `quarterCircle` that draws a quarter-circle by performing 90 step-and-turn operations. Give your method a `double step` input to control the size of the move.

When you have `quarterCircle` you can combine two quarter-circles to draw a petal:

```
/**
 * Draw a flower petal out of two quarter-circles
 *
 * @param  scale  the size of the petal
 */
public void petal(double scale) {
  quarterCircle(scale);
  turnLeft(90);
```

```
    quarterCircle(scale);
    turnLeft(90);
  }
```

Finally, the `flower` method calls `petal` repeatedly in a loop, turning after each call. This version takes two inputs: `n` for the number of petals and `scale`, which is passed to `petal` and then `quarterCircle` to determine the size of each leaf.

```
/**
 * Draw a flower out of petals
 *
 * @param  n   number of petals
 * @param  scale  size of this flower
 */
public void flower(int n, double scale) {
  double turnAngle = 360.0 / n;

  for (int i = 0; i < n; i++) {
    petal(scale);
    turnLeft(turnAngle);
  }
}
```

Notice how the result is similar to `rosette`. Like the rosettes, you can create attractive designs by combining multiple flowers. The second example above is made from three flowers with different values of `n` and `scale`.

Try It Yourself

Write a method called `triangle` that draws an equilateral triangle using three moves and three turns, similar to `square`. Then write a method called `triangleRing` that uses the "draw and turn" approach to create a ring of overlapping triangles. Give each method appropriate parameters similar to `square` and `rosette`.

SUMMARY

As you're working on this project, keep these ideas in mind:

- The turtle illustrates the concepts of OOP: it maintains a set of related variables and "wraps up" changes to those variables behind a set of well-defined methods. Other parts of the program can call the turtle's methods to make it move and draw, but can't directly modify its internal data.

- We used `ArrayList` as a dynamic data structure that continually grows as the turtle moves and adds more `Line2D` objects. Consider that it would be basically impossible to implement the turtle if we didn't have some kind of dynamic resizable list class. This is one of our first examples of the way that data structure choice contributes to program design.

We'll use the built-in Java graphics classes in several future projects, so you may want to return to this chapter periodically to review these examples.

EXTENSIONS

Additional Shapes

You can experiment with creating more methods to draw additional shapes. These are a good way to practice using OOP concepts: Each method is built from a composition of simpler methods, but you don't have to directly manipulate the internal state of the turtle.

- Add a `tile` method that takes an input `n` and uses `square` to produce an `n`-by-`n` grid of squares.
- Add a method that can draw a regular five-pointed star. Give it a `size` parameter that controls the length of each segment.
- Add a `drawHexagon` method that draws a regular hexagon, with a `size` input that determines the length of each edge. Write another method called `hexagonRing` that uses the "draw and turn" approach to create a ring of hexagons.[3]
- Write a method called `polygon` that takes an input `n` and makes the turtle draw an `n`-sided regular polygon. You'll need to determine the moves and turn angles as a function of `n`.

Moving without Drawing

In the old Logo language it was possible to give the turtle a `penUp` command that allowed it to move without drawing. The corresponding `penDown` command would turn drawing back on. Add a `boolean` variable called `drawing` to `Turtle` that keeps track of whether drawing is on or not, then implement `penUp` and `penDown` methods to set its status. Modify `move` to check the value of `drawing`.

Visible Turtle

Modify `paint` to draw the turtle at the end of its path. The simplest turtle is just a green circle centered over the current position. A better turtle will have a little head that shows the angle it's currently facing. Think about how to calculate the position of the head relative to the current center of the body. Tip: It's similar to how we calculated the displacements to make the turtle move.

3 These look really cool.

NOTES AND FURTHER READING

Seymour Papert's work on Logo was influenced by the constructionist theories of the French education researcher Jean Piaget. A major theme of *Mindstorms*, and turtle graphics in general, is creating an environment where children can develop their own understanding of computational concepts through play and exploration. The idea that computer-based tools can enable ways of learning that are difficult to implement in traditional classrooms has continued as a major emphasis of education technology research.

4 Arrays

Should array indices start at 0 or 1? My compromise of 0.5 was rejected without, I thought, proper consideration.
Stan Kelly-Bootle

INTRODUCTION

Arrays are Java's fundamental low-level data structure, used to manage fixed-size collections of items. Chapter 2 introduced `ArrayList`, which implemented a resizable sequential collection of data items, similar to Python's lists. Arrays are lower-level, but they're often the best choice for representing fixed-size collections of items, such as matrices. Arrays are also the basic building block of many higher-level data structures. Therefore, understanding how to create and manipulate basic arrays is an essential skill.

LEARNING OBJECTIVES

At the end of this chapter, you'll have experience:

- Creating and manipulating one-, two-, and higher-dimensional arrays in Java.
- Using arrays for one- and two-dimensional data in an object-oriented program.

The final projects of this chapter will allow you to use arrays in a larger graphical simulation program to implement **cellular automata** – abstract models of living systems that can produce surprisingly complex behavior from simple inputs. These projects build upon the object-oriented concepts we introduced in Chapters 2 and 3. After completing this project, you'll be well-versed in the fundamentals of Java and ready to shift to implementing and analyzing more complex data structures.

4.1 One-Dimensional Arrays

An array represents a *fixed-size sequence of elements of the same type*. The number of elements in the array is set when the array is created and can't change after that point. The basic one-dimensional array represents a linear sequence of values, with a first element, second element, and so forth. Java also allows the creation of *multi-dimensional arrays*, which can be used to represent two-dimensional matrices, three-dimensional data cubes, and other structures.

4.1.1 Creating and Accessing Arrays

The following statement creates a one-dimensional array that holds five `int` values:

```
int[] primes = new int[5];
```

The basic array declaration has the following components:

- The type data stored within the array, which is `int` in this case, followed by square brackets to indicate an array.
- The name of the array, which is a regular variable name.
- The `new` keyword.
- A second statement of the array type, which also specifies the number of elements in the array.

As the use of the `new` keyword suggests, Java arrays are *objects*. The right-hand side initialization is similar to a normal object initialization, but there is no special constructor method for arrays. Conceptually, you should think of a Java array as a fixed-size sequence of data items. Following its initialization, the name of the array functions as an *object reference* that points to the underlying array object.[1] Java arrays created using the default `new` declaration are always initialized to zero. Therefore, following its creation, `primes` has the following configuration:

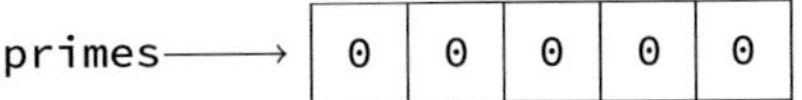

Try It Yourself

Write statements to declare an array of 20 `double` values, an array of 12 `String` values, and an array of 2 `boolean` values.

Use square brackets to access individual elements of the array. Like `String` and `ArrayList`, array elements are *indexed starting at zero*. For example, to assign elements to the `primes` array:

```
primes[0] = 2;
primes[1] = 3;
primes[2] = 5;
primes[3] = 7;
primes[4] = 11;
```

If you find zero-based indexing unnatural, it may be helpful to think of the array index as an **offset** relative to the beginning of the array.

- `primes[0]` is the element located zero `int`-sized elements beyond the beginning of the array. That is, it's the element at the first position of the array.
- `primes[1]` is the element one `int`-sized unit from the beginning of the array, which is the second position.

1 From this point forward, we'll represent this relationship using the name and an arrow pointing to the object.

- `primes[2]` is the element offset two `int`-sized units from the beginning of the array, which is the third position, and so forth.

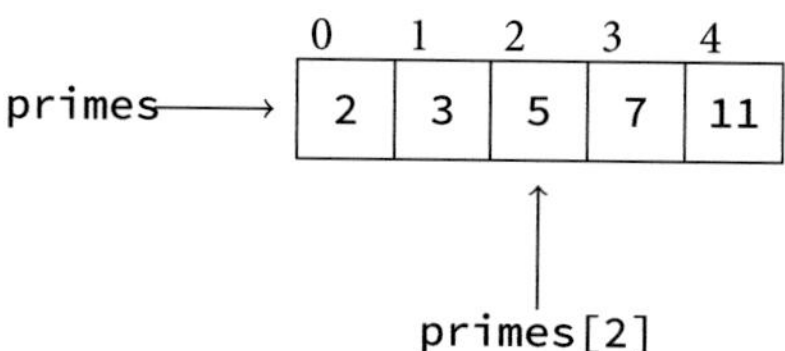

If you know the array's contents, you can specify them at creation using curly braces.

```
// An alternate declaration of primes
int[] primes = {2, 3, 5, 7, 11};
```

The compiler will automatically allocate an array large enough to hold the given number of elements, so specifying the size isn't required.

Try It Yourself

Use curly brace-style declaration to create two `char[]` called `vowels` and `consonants` containing the lower-case vowel and consonant letters.

Solution

Here is the statement that declares vowels. Declaring `consonants` is similar.

```
char[] vowels = {'a', 'e', 'i', 'o', 'u'};
```

4.1.2 Looping over Arrays

The following `for` loop prints all of the elements in an array `a`:

```
for (int i = 0; i < a.length; i++) {
  System.out.println(a[i]);
}
```

The `length` property returns the number of elements in the array. Note that it's a property of the array, not a method, so parentheses aren't required.[2]

2 It's easy to get confused about this: Arrays have a `length` property, strings have a `length` *method*, and `ArrayList` has a `size` method.

Try It Yourself

Write a code fragment to calculate the mean of the elements in a `double[]` named `d`.

Solution

This is a straightforward use of the `for` loop:

```
double sum = 0;
for (int i = 0; i < d.length; i++) {
  sum += d[i];
}
double mean = sum / d.length;
```

You could also use the enhanced `for` loop to iterate over the values directly:

```
double sum = 0;
for (double value : d) {
  sum += value;
}
double mean = sum / d.length;
```

Try It Yourself

Write a static method called `isSorted` that takes an `int[] a` as input and returns `true` if the elements are sorted in increasing order and `false` otherwise.

Solution

Iterate through the array and compare `a[i]` to `a[i + 1]`. If any pair of elements is out of order, return `false`. If the loop completes without returning, then every pair of elements is in sorted order and the method returns `true`. Notice the stopping condition for the loop: using `a.length - 1` prevents the error of checking beyond the end of the array on the last iteration.

```
/**
 * Check if an array is in sorted order
 *
 * @param  a  input array
 * @return  true if a is in sorted order, false otherwise
 */
```

```
public static boolean isSorted(int[] a) {
  for (int i = 0; i < a.length - 1; i++) {
    // Check if a[i] and a[i + 1] are in the correct order
    // If not, return false immediately
    if (a[i] > a[i + 1]) {
      return false;
    }
  }

  // If the loop completes, all pairs are sorted
  return true;
}
```

In practice, you often want to print the elements of an array in a formatted style. Java has a built-in `Arrays` class that contains a number of useful static methods, including a `toString` that takes an array as input and turns it into a formatted `String`. Import `Arrays` using

```
import java.util.Arrays;
```

and print the elements of the `primes` array:

```
System.out.println(Arrays.toString(primes));
```

The output is similar to printing an `ArrayList`:

```
[2, 3, 5, 7, 11]
```

4.1.3 Modifying an Array in a Method

Consider the following pair of methods. The `addOne` method takes an array as input, then modifies the elements of the array within the method. What do you think the third line of `main` will print when the program runs? Will the effect of `addOne` be applied to `nums` or will it remain unchanged?

```
/**
 * Add one to each element of a
 */
public static void addOne(int[] a) {
  for (int i = 0; i < a.length; i++) {
    a[i]++;
  }
```

```
}

public static void main(String[] args) {
  int[] nums = {1, 2, 3, 4, 5};

  // Call addOne --- notice that it doesn't return anything
  // What will be the effect of this method on nums?
  addOne(nums);

  System.out.println(Arrays.toString(nums));
}
```

If run this example, you'll find that the output is `[2, 3, 4, 5, 6]`. The changes made to `a` in the `addOne` method are also applied to the `nums` array in `main`! This may seem surprising: Method parameters are usually thought of as local variables and – at least for primitive types – changes to a local variable should affect only that variable. Recall that the variable `nums` functions as a reference to the array:

```
nums ───→ | 1 | 2 | 3 | 4 | 5 |
```

Passing `nums` as an input to `addOne` creates another reference that refers to the same underlying object in memory:

```
nums ───→ | 1 | 2 | 3 | 4 | 5 |
   a ───→
```

Therefore, both `nums` and `a` refer to the same array in memory, and changes made through `a` have a *permanent effect* that persists outside the scope of the `addOne` method. This behavior can lead to unexpected bugs. If you aren't careful, it's easy to write a method that accidentally modifies an input array or other data structure when that isn't what you want to do. Always define the expected behavior of a method carefully and decide whether a method is allowed to make changes to its input. As a general rule, a method that operates on a mutable data structure can either:

- make changes to its input that persist outside of the method's local scope; or
- leave the input unmodified, but create and return a new data structure.

But you shouldn't do both at the same time.

Try It Yourself

Write a method called `reverse` that takes an `int[] a` as input and reverses it *in place*; that is, modify the input array without allocating and returning any new arrays.

Solution

This is a good warm-up for more complex array problems. Reversing the array in place requires moving the first element to the last position, and vice versa. Likewise, the second element and the next-to-last element should exchange positions, and so forth. Therefore, a strategy is as follows:

- Use two variables called `left` and `right`. At the beginning of the method `left = 0` and `right = a.length - 1`.
- Exchange the items pointed to by `left` and `right`, then advance to the next inner pair of elements.
- The method ends when the two references reach the middle and `left >= right`.

```
/**
 * Reverse an array in place
 *
 * @param  a  input array
 * @return  nothing, a is reversed in place
 */
public static void reverse(int[] a) {
  int left = 0;
  int right = a.length - 1;

  // Loop until left and right meet or pass in the middle
  while (left < right) {
    // Exchange items
    int temp = a[left];
    a[left] = a[right];
    a[right] = temp;

    // Advance to next inner pair
    left++;
    right--;
  }
}
```

4.2 Multidimensional Arrays

Java arrays can have more than one dimension. A two-dimensional array, for example, can be used to represent a matrix of values, an image, or an array of one-dimensional arrays. Arrays with three dimensions can represent three-dimensional volumes in space, or "cubes" of data, such as a sequence of images taken over time.

4.2.1 Creating Multidimensional Arrays

The basic two-dimensional array declaration looks like the standard array declaration with a second pair of square brackets and a second size:

```
double[][] m = new double[4][5]
```

Think of a two-dimensional array as a rectangular matrix of values. By convention, the first dimension represents the rows and the second represents the columns. Array `m` is therefore a four-by-five matrix with its elements initially set to zero:

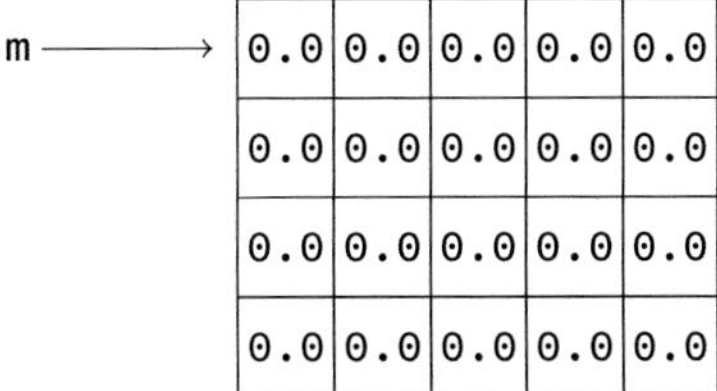

Individual elements are accessed using two pairs of square brackets and specifying the row and column index. As with one-dimensional arrays, indexing starts from zero, so the first row is `m[0]`, the second row is `m[1]`, and so forth.

```
// Upper-left element
m[0][0] = 0.1;

// Third element of first row
m[0][2] = 0.3;

// Last element of second row
m[1][4] = 0.5;

// Lower-right element
m[3][4] = 0.7;
```

You can also declare a two-dimensional array using nested curly braces.

```
// Declare a 3x3 grid with values 1 through 9
int[][] grid = {{1, 2, 3},
                {4, 5, 6},
                {7, 8, 9}};
```

The outer pair of braces represents the array as a whole and each inner pair of braces represents one row. The compiler automatically determines the appropriate dimensions.

The same syntax for declaring two-dimensional arrays can be extended to higher dimensions by adding additional pairs of square brackets. For example, to declare a three-dimensional array:

```
int[][][] cube = new int[10][10][10];
```

Three-dimensional arrays can represent "layers" of two-dimensional data. For example, a standard color image consists of three layers, representing the red, green, and blue color components of each pixel.

4.2.2 The "Array of Arrays" Model and Ragged Arrays

It's common to think of two-dimensional arrays as representing a matrix or grid of values. Many array operations are easier to understand, however, if we consider the complete two-dimensional array as an "array of arrays." In this model there is one "outer" array, each element of which is a reference to a second-tier "inner" array. For example, consider the following declaration:

```
int[] a = new int[3][4];
```

The array can be thought of as a three by four matrix, as in the previous examples, or as an outer array of three elements, each containing a reference to an inner array of four elements.

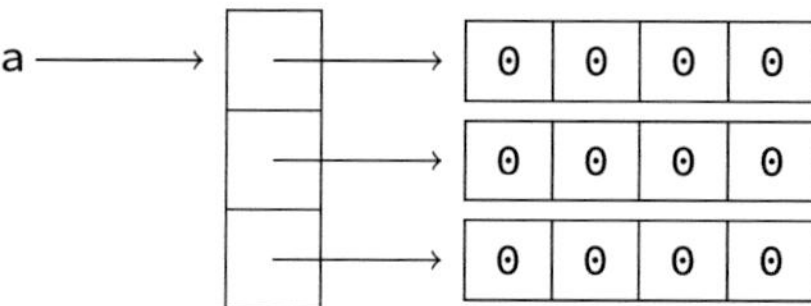

Now consider an array access, like `a[1][2]`. The first dimension, which we previously interpreted as the rows of the matrix, can also be interpreted as an entry in the outer array. The second dimension refers to a specific element within the second-level array. It's possible to exploit this feature to create uneven arrays, which Java calls **ragged arrays**. For example, suppose we want to create an array of daily sales figures, divided by month. The first row of the array, representing sales for January, should have 31 entries. The second row, for February, should have 28, and so forth.[3]

To create the ragged array, first declare the size of the outer array, but leave the second dimension unspecified.

```
double[][] dailySales = new double[12][];
```

This statement allocates a two-dimensional array of `double` values, but specifies only the size of the outer array. Declare the inner arrays individually:

```
dailySales[0] = new double[31];  // January
```

3 A two-dimensional array is not the only data structure that could solve this problem, and may not be the best for some applications. We'll later talk about creating structures that could map each month's name to a list of its daily sales values.

```
dailySales[1] = new double[28];  // February
dailySales[2] = new double[31];  // March

// And so forth for the other nine months
```

Ragged arrays can be useful when you need fast access to a matrix-like data set that isn't rectangular. Processing the entire array can be complex, though, because you have to account for the variable number of columns in each row. In this example, processing daily sales per month would be easy – for example, find the total sales for March – but summing the sales that occur on, say, the last day of each month is more challenging.

Try It Yourself

Consider the `dailySales` array. Write statements to access the sales for the following dates:

- March 13
- October 31
- December 25
- June 24.

4.2.3 Looping over Two-Dimensional Arrays

Iterating over all the elements of a two-dimensional array is a common pattern. For example, the following code fragment prints all of the elements of a two-dimensional array as a rectangular matrix.

```
// Print elements of two-dimensional array a
for (int row = 0; i < a.length; i++) {
  for (int col = 0; col < a[row].length; col++) {
    // Print element at position (row, col)
    System.out.print(a[row][col] + "\t");
  }
  System.out.println();  // Move to the next line
}
```

The outer loop iterates over the rows of `a` and `a.length` gets the number of rows. The inner loop iterates over the columns within each row; `a[row].length` is the size of the inner array associated with `a[row]`. Notice that the iterations of the inner loop are adjusted automatically for each row; this detail is important if you're working with ragged arrays with unequal numbers of columns.

Try It Yourself

Write a code fragment that calculates and prints the sum of each row within a two-dimensional `double` array named `a`.

Solution

Combine a pair of `for` loops with an accumulator variable. Each iteration of the outer loop performs one sum.

```
for (int row = 0; row < a.length; row++) {
  double sum = 0.0;

  for (int col = 0; col < a[row].length; col++) {
    sum += a[row][col];
  }

  System.out.println(sum);
}
```

Try It Yourself

Write a code fragment that calculates the sum of each *column* within a two-dimensional rectangular `double` array named `a`.

Solution

Sometimes it's useful to iterate over a two-dimensional array in column order. Reverse the order of the two loops. Because the array is rectangular, it's sufficient to use `a[0].length` to get the number of columns.

```
for (int col = 0; col < a[0].length; col++) {
  double sum = 0.0;

  for (int row = 0; row < a.length; row++) {
    sum += a[row][col];
  }

  System.out.println(sum);
}
```

Iterating over a ragged array in column order is more challenging, because you need to know the maximum number of columns in advance and then account for rows that have fewer columns. The end-of-chapter questions will allow you to practice looping over ragged arrays.

4.2.4 Ancient Algorithms: Magic Squares

A **magic square** is a square matrix where all rows, columns, and diagonals sum to the same value. The Sagrada Família basilica in Barcelona has the following magic square inscribed on one of its exterior façades, dedicated to scenes of the Passion narrative. The rows, columns, and diagonals all sum to 33, held to be the traditional age of Jesus at the time of the Crucifixion.

1	14	14	4
11	7	6	9
8	10	10	5
13	2	3	15

There are a number of methods, some of ancient origin, for generating magic squares. The most well-known is called the **Siamese method** (Kraitchik, 1942). It was brought to Europe in the seventeenth century by the French diplomat Simon de la Loubère, who learned of it during his trip as an ambassador to the Kingdom of Siam. The Siamese method generates an n by n magic square where n is odd. By default, the square is filled with the numbers from 1 to n^2. The method proceeds as follows.

1. Beginning with an empty square, place a 1 in the top-center.

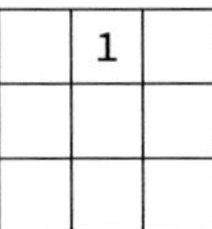

2. Move *up and to the right* to find the next square to fill. If moving up and to the right moves you off of the grid, wrap around to the other side. Here, moving up and to the right from the top-center square wraps around to the bottom, which places the second number in the bottom-right square.

	1	
		2

3. Continue moving up and to the right, wrapping around as necessary. Here, another move up and to the right places the three in the middle-left square.

	1	
3		
		2

4. If moving up and to the right would cause you to land on a square that is already occupied, move down by one square instead of moving up and right.

	1	
3		
4		2

5. Continue this process of moving up and right and moving down to avoid occupied squares, placing the numbers in sequential order until the entire square has all n^2 entries filled.

8	1	6
3	5	7
4	9	2

Try It Yourself

Use the method to construct (by hand) a magic square with $n = 5$.

Implementation

Let's write a program to implement the Siamese magic square method. The code below shows the basic structure of the program. It reads a value of n from the user, then initializes an n by n matrix. The variables `row` and `col` keep track of the current placement in the square, starting with the center of the top row. The main loop, which we'll fill in shortly, iterates over the values from 1 to n^2.

```
/**
 * Magic squares
 */

import java.util.Scanner;

public class MagicSquare {
  public static void main(String[] args) {

    // Read a value of n from the user
    Scanner in = new Scanner(System.in);
    System.out.println("Enter a value for n: ");
    int n = in.nextInt();

    // n must be odd
    if (n % 2 == 0) {
      System.out.println("n must be odd.");
```

```
      return;
    }

    // Create the matrix
    int[][] square = new int[n][n];

    // Keep track of the current row and column
    int row = 0;
    int col = n / 2;  // Integer division

    // Main loop
    for (int i = 1; i <= n * n; i++) {
      // Complete this loop to construct the square
    }

    // Print the final square
  }
}
```

The `for` loop needs to do two things: assign the current value of `i` to the current position, then determine the position for the next value. The next position may be found by moving up and right, wrapping around if necessary, or by moving down if the up-and-right position is occupied. Here is a version of the loop body that tries moving up and right and then backtracks if that spot is occupied.

```
// Assign the current value of i to the current position
square[row][col] = i;

// Save the current value of row and col
int oldRow = row;
int oldCol = col;

// Move up and right, wrapping around
row = row == 0 ? n - 1 : row - 1;  // Ternary operator
col = (col + 1) % n;

// If that square is occupied, backtrack and move down
if (square[row][col] != 0) {
  row = oldRow + 1;
  col = oldCol;
}
```

The update to `row` shows off another feature that's sometimes useful: the **ternary operator**, a one-line replacement for an `if-else` assignment.

```
row = row == 0 ? n - 1 : row - 1;
```

It evaluates a `boolean` expression, then chooses one of two options based on the result. The first expression after the `?` is the `true` result; the expression after the colon is the `false` result. Here, the first part tests if `row == 0`. If so, wrap around to the bottom row by assigning `n - 1`; if not, move up by assigning `row - 1`.

4.3 Project: Cellular Automata

A **cellular automaton** (CA) is a computational model built from a grid of cells, typically a one-dimensional array or a two-dimensional rectangular matrix. At each discrete time step, a cell may be either "alive" or "dead," represented by the color of the cell. The cells evolve over time, with the evolution of the model determined by a set of rules that determine whether cells "live" or "die" in each new generation based on the states of their neighbors.

Cellular automata were originally developed out of research into biology and self-replicating systems, but have attracted interest from computer scientists and mathematicians because they illustrate how complex behavior can emerge from relatively simple sets of rules. Biologists and physicists have used CAs to model natural phenomena, and philosophers have used them to make arguments about emergent complexity in systems. This project will lead you through the creation of two CA models:

- a one-dimensional elementary CA; and
- an implementation of **Life**, the most famous and widely studied two-dimensional cellular automata model. Originally created by the mathematician John Conway in 1970 (Gardner, 1970), Life is famous for its ability to create complex emergent structures out of simple initial configurations.

In addition to revisiting the graphics and OOP techniques we introduced in Chapter 3, this project will allow you to practice using arrays to store the state of a complex model. We'll also extend our basic painting program to create an *animation* of a cellular automata model as it evolves over time.

4.3.1 One-Dimensional Elementary Cellular Automata

The simplest CA model is built on top of a one-dimensional array. At each generation, some of the cells are alive and colored black and the others are dead and colored white. In the classic model, which we'll consider here, the state of a cell in the next generation depends on its state in the current generation and the state of its two neighbors. Let's work through the evolution of an example one-dimensional CA (Berto and Tagliabue, 2006). Suppose that we start with an array containing only one active central cell.

Consider the following update rule set:

- A cell is active in the next generation if it is currently inactive and exactly one, but not both, of its two neighbors is active in the current generation.
- Otherwise a cell is dead.
- All transitions from one generation to the next happen *simultaneously*. That is, we determine whether each cell in the next generation is alive or dead based on the current state, then apply all of those updates at the same time as a discrete event.

In the first update, the two immediate neighbors of the single active cell come to life. By the update rules, the active cell itself must die. Showing the first and second generations as two consecutive rows, the evolution of the model is as shown.

In the third generation, two more cells on the edge come to life and the two living cells die. Continuing the pattern for a few more generations begins to show a structure.

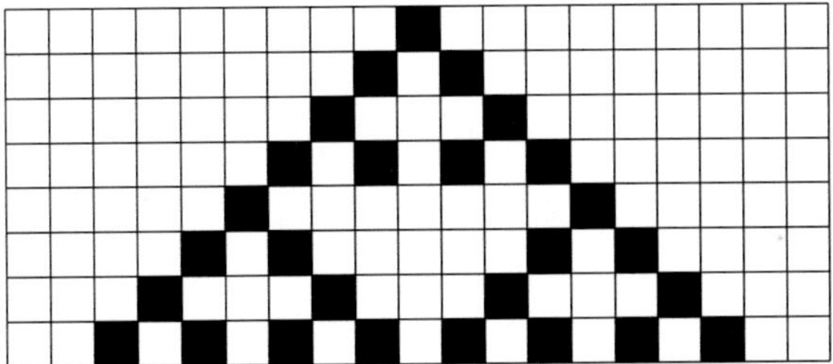

Try It Yourself

Continue applying the pattern for eight more generations. What structure do you observe?

Continuing for further iterations reveals a surprising pattern that could never have been predicted from just the description of the rules.

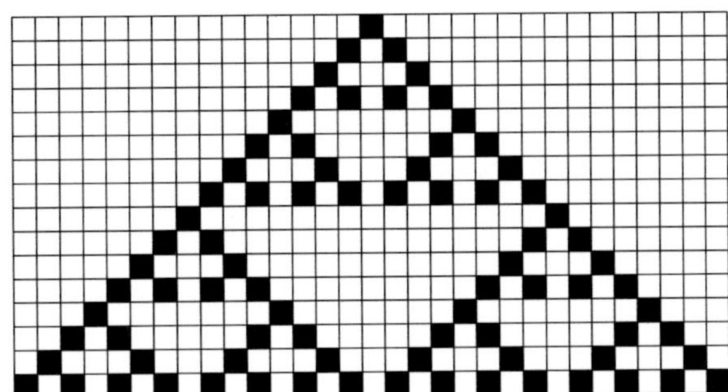

This is, in fact, a **fractal** pattern – a repeating, self-similar structure – generated from a simple initial state and rules.[4] We'll have much more to say about fractals and see several examples in Chapter 9.

4.3.2 Visualizing Elementary Cellular Automata

Let's write a program that can visualize a one-dimensional elementary CA. The starting code below contains the constructor, `main`, and `paint` methods.

```
/**
 * Visualizing a one-dimensional elementary cellular automaton
 */

import java.awt.Canvas;
import java.awt.Graphics;
import java.util.Arrays;
import javax.swing.JFrame;

public class CellularAutomata extends Canvas {

  final int WIDTH = 512;
  final int ITERATIONS = WIDTH / 2;

  /**
   * Constructor
   */
  public CellularAutomata() {
    setSize(WIDTH, ITERATIONS);
  }

  /**
   * main -- sets up frame and makes it visible
   */
  public static void main(String[] args) {
    // Construct the driver object
    CellularAutomata ca = new CellularAutomata();

    // Create a JFrame and attach the driver to it
```

4 This fractal is a cellular version of one called Sierpinski's Triangle. Chapter 9 will introduce Sierpinski's Carpet, another similar fractal.

```
    // These steps are required to make the window visible
    JFrame frame = new JFrame();
    frame.add(ca);
    frame.pack();
    frame.setVisible(true);
    frame.setDefaultCloseOperation(JFrame.EXIT_ON_CLOSE);
  }

  /**
   * paint -- contains all drawing operations
   *
   * @param  g  Graphics object that refers to the
   *            drawable surface
   */
  public void paint(Graphics g) {

  }
}
```

The program has four basic elements:

- The `CellularAutomata` class extends the built-in `Canvas` class to create a surface.
- The `main` method creates a new `CellularAutomata` object and attaches it to a `JFrame`, which makes the surface visible.
- The constructor simply sets the size of the surface. Here, the size is determined by `WIDTH`, which will be the number of elements in the one-dimensional array. The second constant value, `ITERATIONS`, will be the number of generations to compute. Setting `ITERATIONS` to `WIDTH / 2` makes the resulting image yield a nice triangle that's twice as wide as it is tall.
- The `paint` method performs the actual drawing work. Recall that `paint` is called automatically by the Java graphics framework, which generates a `Graphics` object that's then used to interact with the drawable surface.

Our goal is to complete the `paint` method, which needs to initialize a starting array of `WIDTH` total elements, then compute `ITERATIONS` total generations of the CA, drawing each one to the surface. We'll use a `boolean` array to track the binary state of each cell. The method uses an outer loop that iterates over the required number of generations. Within that loop, repeatedly draw the current array to the surface, then compute the values of the cells in the next generation. Examine the following program carefully:

```
/**
 * paint -- contains all drawing operations
 *
```

```
 * @param  g  Graphics object that refers to the
 *            drawable surface
 */
public void paint(Graphics g) {
  // Initialize the array of cells
  boolean[] cells = new boolean[WIDTH];

  // Make the middle cell alive
  cells[cells.length / 2] = true;

  // Loop for the chosen number of iterations
  for (int i = 0; i < ITERATIONS; i++) {

    // Draw the current set of cells
    for (int c = 0; c < cells.length; c++) {
      if (cells[c]) {
        // Draw a 1x1 square at position (c, i)
        // On iteration i, the cells are i pixels from the top
        g.fillRect(c, i, 1, 1);
      }
    }

    // Update the cells
    boolean[] next = new boolean[cells.length];

    for (int c = 1; c < WIDTH - 1; c++) {
      if (cells[c - 1] && cells[c] && cells[c + 1]){
        next[c] = false;
      } else if (cells[c - 1] && cells[c] && !cells[ c + 1]) {
        next[c] = false;
      } else if (cells[c - 1] && !cells[c] && cells[ c + 1]) {
        next[c] = false;
      } else if (cells[c - 1] && !cells[c] && !cells[ c + 1]) {
        next[c] = true;
      } else if (!cells[c - 1] && cells[c] && cells[ c + 1]) {
        next[c] = false;
      } else if (!cells[c - 1] && cells[c] && !cells[c + 1]) {
        next[c] = false;
```

```
      } else if (!cells[c - 1] && !cells[c] && cells[c + 1]) {
        next[c] = true;
      } else if (!cells[c - 1] && !cells[c] && !cells[c + 1]) {
        next[c] = false;
      }
    }

    // Make the next generation the active generation
    cells = next;

  }
}
```

The method seems long, but look at it carefully. The first few lines set up the array. The main `for` loop has two sections. The first part paints the current row of cells to the surface using `fillRect`. The second part applies the rules of the model to determine whether each cell is alive or dead in the next generation. It uses a secondary array called `next` to store the state of each cell during the next generation. Each iteration of the loop checks the value of a cell and its two neighbors, then assigns the appropriate result to `next` based on the current rule set. The output of the program is shown in Figure 4.1.

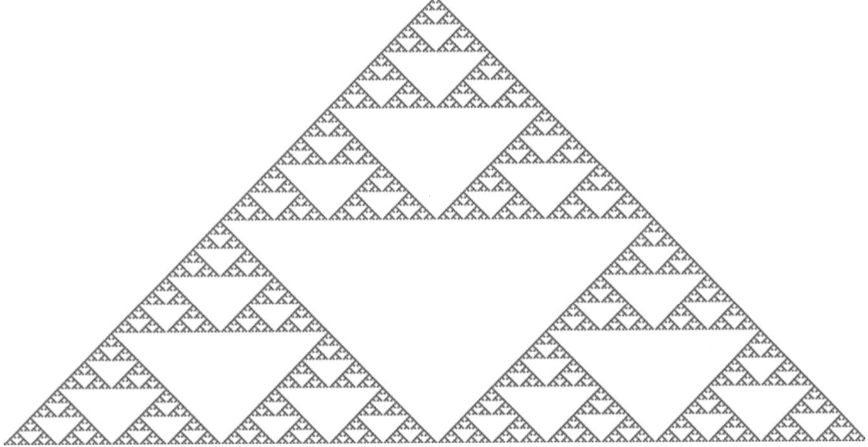

Figure 4.1 Visualizing a one-dimensional cellular automaton.

The mathematician Stephen Wolfram developed a standard way of describing the rules for elementary one-dimensional CA (Wolfram, 1983). If we consider a cell and its two neighbors, there are eight possible on/off configurations those three cells could have:

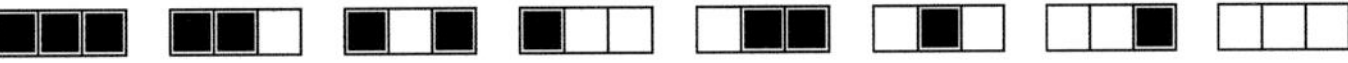

The leftmost configuration corresponds to the case where all three cells are on, and the rightmost to where all three are off, with the other six states representing the other possible on/off patterns. In our example program, a cell came to life only if it was currently dead and had exactly one living neighbor; all other cells died in the next generation. That rule set can be expressed graphically by marking which of the eight cell patterns correspond to a living cell in the next generation and which correspond to a dead cell:

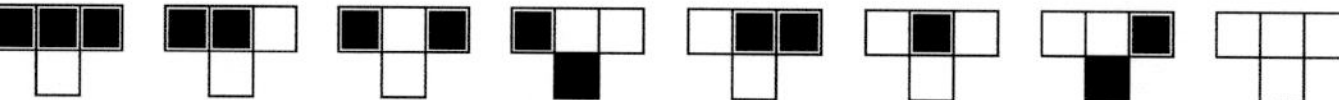

Wolfram's system treats the eight output states as a binary number. The bit pattern `00010010` corresponds to 18 in unsigned binary, so this CA is referred to as Rule 18.

Try It Yourself

Modify the visualization program to implement the following rule, which creates structured but nonrepeating triangular patterns. Figure 4.2 shows the output. This pattern is called Rule 30 in Wolfram's notation.

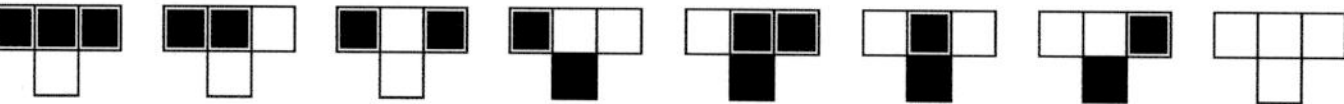

This pattern is similar to the shell of the textile cone snail, shown in Figure 4.3. Cells in the snail's shell decide whether to produce pigment or not based on the activity of their neighbor cells, creating a real-life version of an abstract CA model.

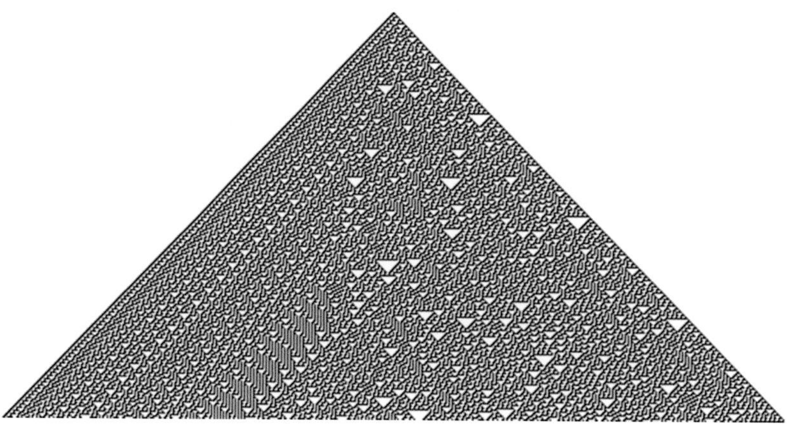

Figure 4.2 Visualizing a CA rule with structured but irregular output.

4.3.3 Conway's Life

Life is the most well-known cellular automaton. It was invented by the mathematician John Conway in 1970 and is famous for the complex and infinitely repeating patterns it can produce. Conway was a professor of mathematics at Cambridge. He had a long academic research career but is best known for his contributions to recreational mathematics, including Life and the "Doomsday Rule" for calculating the day of the week for a given date (Conway, 1973). He died of COVID-19 on April 11, 2020.

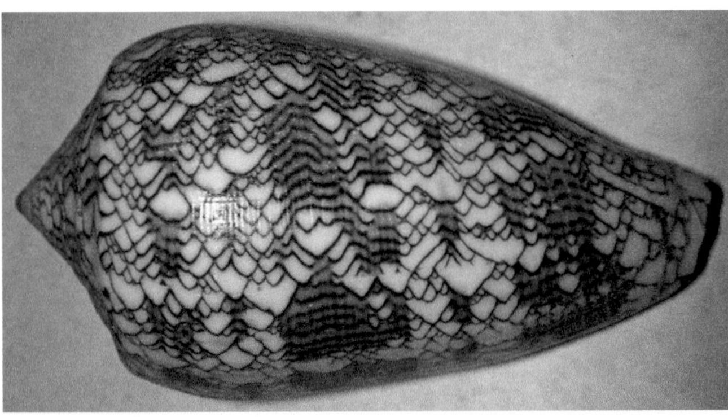

Figure 4.3 **CA patterns on the shell of the textile cone snail (St. John, 2016).**

The universe of Life is an infinite two-dimensional grid of cells. At each iteration, a cell is either alive or dead. Each cell has eight neighbors: the cells to its left, right, top, bottom, and to its four corners. At each step in time, cells change state from alive to dead or vice versa based on the following rules:

- A living cell that has fewer than two living neighbors dies from isolation.
- A living cell with more than three living neighbors dies from overcrowding.
- A living cell that has exactly two or three living neighbors remains alive into the next generation.
- A dead cell with exactly three live neighbors comes to life in the next generation.

Another way of stating the rules is that all living cells die unless they have exactly two or three neighbors. Dead cells remain dead unless they have exactly three neighbors. Like in the one-dimensional cellular automaton, all births and deaths happen *simultaneously*.

Example

The best way to get familiar with Life is to use an online tool to explore patterns and run simulations. Spend some time playing around with one before working through this example. Consider the following three-by-three grid. We'd like to apply the rules of Life to update this grid to the next state.

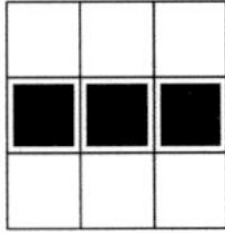

The first phase is to count the living neighbors of each cell. Neighbor counting is done by considering all eight positions surrounding a cell. Any neighbors that would fall outside of the grid are automatically treated as dead.

- The cell at position (0, 0) (the upper-left position) has two living neighbors, one directly below and one to its lower right. All of its other neighbors, including the ones that would lie outside the grid, are dead.
- The cell at position (0, 1) (upper-middle position) has three living neighbors, all in the row below.
- The cell at position (0, 2) (upper-right position) has two living neighbors, one directly below and one to its lower-left.

Try It Yourself

Determine the number of living neighbors for each of the remaining cells in the example.

Solution

The bottom row is a mirror of the top row. The center cell has two neighbors (its left and right sides) and the left and right middle cells have only one neighbor, the central cell. Representing the number of living neighbors as a matrix:

2	3	2
1	2	1
2	3	2

The next phase applies the rules of Life to determine which cells live and die in the next generation. Remember that births and deaths happen simultaneously, so if we determine that a cell should come to life or die in the next generation, that decision has no effect on the neighbor counts for the current generation. By the rules:

- The upper-left cell remains dead, because it has only two living neighbors.
- The upper-middle cell comes to life in the next generation, because it is currently dead and has exactly three neighbors.
- The upper-right cell remains dead, because it has two neighbors.
- The center-left cell dies, because it is currently alive and has fewer than two living neighbors.
- The center-middle cell survives, because it is currently alive and has two living neighbors.

And so forth. Take a moment to verify the reasoning for each cell in the grid. When you're done, you should be certain that the state of the grid in the next generation is:

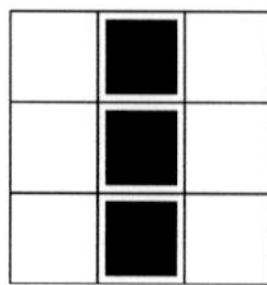

Try It Yourself

Repeat the neighbor-counting and update steps to show that applying the rules of Life to the vertical pattern results in switching back to the original horizontal pattern. This simple three-cell pattern, alternating between horizontal and vertical, is called a **blinker**.

Try It Yourself

The most famous Life pattern is the **glider**. It continually repeats itself on a four-step cycle, moving down and right. Use the starting pattern below and apply the rules of Life to observe the glider's movement.

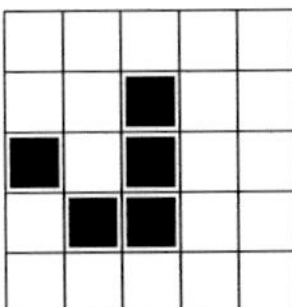

Tip: Determine and write down the number of living neighbors for each cell in the grid, then use those numbers to determine if the cell is alive or dead in the next generation. You should see the glider cycle through the four patterns below, moving one square down and one square right on each cycle.

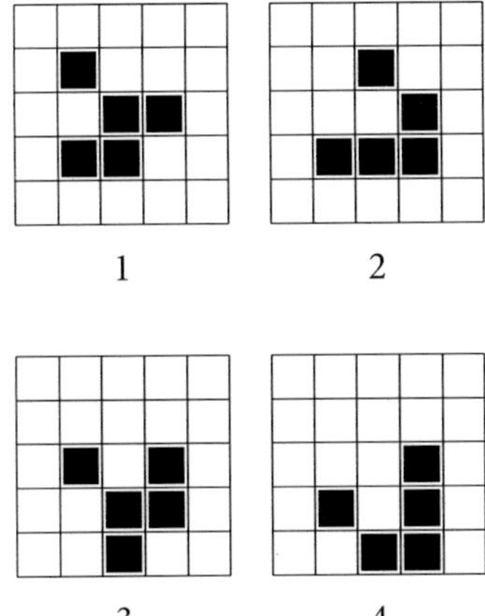

It's possible to construct a **glider gun**, which produces an infinite stream of gliders. The first glider gun was discovered by Bill Gosper in 1970 (Gardner, 2001). The discovery resulted in a $50 prize from John Conway for identifying the first finite Life pattern that could produce a theoretically infinite number of living cells.

4.3.4 Animating Life

Implementing Life is more complex than our previous graphical projects. Life is interesting because of the *evolution* of the patterns it produces, so we need the ability to create not just a static image but an *animation*, which is really just a series of images displayed one after the other. Our program will use a `run` method that performs the following actions in a loop:

- Update the current grid to the next generation.
- Invoke the `paint` method to draw the current grid to the screen.
- Pause for a few milliseconds.

Most of the work will end up being done in the `update` and `paint` methods. The basic structure of the program is shown below, with stubs for the methods that we'll complete. Notice the `boolean[][] cells`: This is the class variable that maintains the state of the grid on each iteration. The `paint` method will use `cells` to determine which cells are alive and dead every time it draws the current image.

```
/**
 * Conway's Game of Life
 */

import java.awt.Canvas;
import java.awt.Graphics;
import javax.swing.JFrame;
import java.awt.Color;

public class Life extends Canvas {

  final int WIDTH = 25;
  final int HEIGHT = 25;
  final int SIZE = 8;  // Size of each cell in pixels

  boolean[][] cells;

  /**
   * Constructor - set size and starting pattern
   */
  public Life() {

  }

  /**
   * Compute the next generation of the grid of cells
   *
   * @return  nothing - changes are made to this.cells
   */
  public void update() {

  }

```

```
34   /**
35    * Run the main animation loop
36    */
37   public void run() {
38
39   }
40
41   /**
42    * Main
43    */
44   public static void main(String[] args) {
45     Life life = new Life();
46
47     JFrame frame = new JFrame();
48     frame.add(life);
49     frame.pack();
50     frame.setVisible(true);
51     frame.setDefaultCloseOperation(JFrame.EXIT_ON_CLOSE);
52
53     // Call the run method -- this is the actual main loop
54     life.run();
55   }
56
57   /**
58    * Draw the current grid of cells
59    *
60    * @param  g  Graphics object that refers to
61    *            the drawable surface
62    */
63   public void paint(Graphics g) {
64
65   }
66 }
```

Setting Up the Animation

The `main` method should be familiar by this point. Notice that the last line of `main` (line 54) calls `run`, the method with the core animation loop. The constructor is straightforward. It sets the size of the window, initializes `cells`, and then enters an initial pattern of living cells for the animation. The constant values `WIDTH` and `HEIGHT` control the numbers of rows and columns in the grid. The extra parameter `SIZE` controls the visible size of a cell in units of pixels.

```
/**
 * Constructor - set size and starting pattern
 */
public Life() {
  setSize(WIDTH * SIZE, HEIGHT * SIZE);

  this.cells = new boolean[WIDTH][HEIGHT];

  // Store starting pattern -- glider
  cells[1][2] = true;
  cells[2][3] = true;
  cells[3][1] = true;
  cells[3][2] = true;
  cells[3][3] = true;
}
```

The Animation Loop

The `run` method is a simple loop that repeatedly pauses, updates, and then calls `repaint` to draw the next image. Java provides a built-in `Thread.sleep` method that can pause the program for a given number of milliseconds. The method can fail or be interrupted by the operating system, so it has to be wrapped in a `try-catch` block.

```
/**
 * Run the main animation loop
 */
public void run() {

  while (true) {
    try {
      Thread.sleep(200);  // Sleep for 200 ms
    } catch(Exception e) {
      e.printStackTrace();
    }

    // Update the current grid
    update();
```

```

    // Trigger a call to paint
    repaint();
  }
}
```

Updating the Grid

The actual logic for Life is contained in the `update` method, which needs to count the number of neighbors for each cell, then apply the rules of Life to determine whether each cell lives or dies in the next generation. We'll take a direct approach of looping over the grid of cells and checking the state of each of the eight neighbors. The code below shows a pair of `for` loops that iterate over the rows and columns of the grid and a few example `if` statements that check the status of the neighbors. To simplify neighbor-checking, let's assume that the outer ring of cells around the edge of the grid is permanently dead. Assuming that the pattern is restricted to the inner cells allows us to avoid the special cases of checking whether a cell is on the grid and then determining which of its neighbors lie outside the grid.

```
/**
 * Compute the next generation of the grid of cells
 *
 * @return  nothing - changes are made to this.cells
 */
public void update() {
  // Grid that holds the states of the next generation
  boolean[][] next = new boolean[WIDTH][HEIGHT];

  // Loop over all cells in the grid
  //
  // Ignore the outer ring of cells -- treat them as
  // permanently dead
  for (int r = 1; r < HEIGHT - 1; r++) {
    for (int c = 1; c < WIDTH - 1; c++) {
      int neighbors = 0;

      // Upper-left
      if (this.cells[r - 1][c - 1]) {
        neighbors++;
      }

      // Upper-middle
```

```
      if (this.cells[r - 1][c]) {
        neighbors++;
      }

      // Upper-right
      if (this.cells[r - 1][c + 1]) {
        neighbors++;
      }

      // Add more cases to process the other neighbors


      // Apply the rules of Life to determine if the cell
      // lives or dies in the next generation

    }
  }

  // Make the next generation of cells the current active generation
  this.cells = next;
}
```

Try It Yourself

Complete the method by adding five more cases to evaluate the status of the five remaining neighbors. Then add statements at the end of the method to determine the correct value of `next[r][c]` based on the values of `cells[r][c]` and `neighbors`.

Solution

The five neighbor-checking cases are similar to the ones shown in the example code; just modify the row and column indices. The rules of Life state that a cell is alive in the next generation if it is current alive with two or three neighbors, or currently dead with exactly three neighbors. The following statements determine if a cell should be alive or dead based on the value of `neighbors`:

```
// Apply the rules of Life to determine if the cell lives or
// dies in the next generation

```

```
// Living cells that remain alive
if (this.cells[r][c] && (neighbors == 2 || neighbors == 3)) {
  next[r][c] = true;
}

// Dead cells that come to life
else if (!this.cells[r][c] && neighbors == 3) {
  next[r][c] = true;
}

// All other cases result in death
else {
  next[r][c] = false;
}
```

Painting the Grid

The final method is `paint`, which draws the current grid. Living cells are drawn as filled squares and dead cells are drawn as outlined squares.

```
/**
 * Draw the current grid of cells
 *
 * @param  g  Graphics object that refers to
 *            the drawable surface
 */
public void paint(Graphics g) {

  // Clear the window
  g.setColor(Color.WHITE);
  g.fillRect(0, 0, WIDTH * SIZE, HEIGHT * SIZE);

  g.setColor(Color.BLACK);

  // Draw the cells
  // Remember that fillRect uses (x, y) positions
  for (int r = 0; r < HEIGHT; r++) {
    for (int c = 0; c < WIDTH; c++) {
      if (this.cells[r][c]) {
```

```
                g.fillRect(c * SIZE, r * SIZE, SIZE, SIZE);
            } else {
                g.drawRect(c * SIZE, r * SIZE, SIZE, SIZE);
            }
        }
    }
}
```

The two `for` loops iterate over the row and column combinations in the grid of cells. Look carefully at the call to `g.fillRect`.

```
g.fillRect(c * SIZE, r * SIZE, SIZE, SIZE);
```

The first argument to the method is the *x-coordinate* of the rectangle, which depends upon the *column* index of the cell in the two-dimensional grid. Multiplying by `SIZE` converts the column index into a horizontal x-position in pixels. Likewise, `r * SIZE` converts the row index into a vertical y-position in pixels. The last two arguments control the width and height of the rectangle, which is `SIZE` pixels in both dimensions.

Try It Yourself

Finish coding the complete Life program and run it. You should see the classic glider pattern march from the upper-left to lower-right. You can then modify the constructor to try a few more patterns.

The **acorn**, one of the best known "Methuselah" patterns. The initial seven cells create a chain reaction that persists for more than 5,000 generations before finally stabilizing.

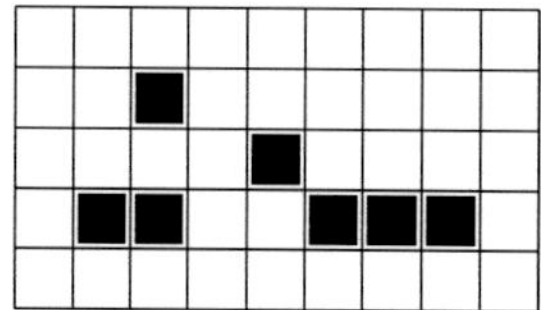

The **R-pentomino**, another Methusaleh that survives for over 1,100 generations. It was one of the first interesting patterns discovered by John Conway and is the most active small pattern. It sometimes emerges naturally from the evolution of other patterns.

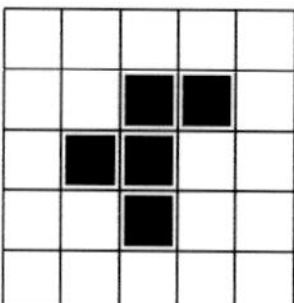

The **lightweight spaceship (LWSS)**, the smallest moving pattern other than the glider. It moves horizontally to the left, so place it on the right side of the starting grid. Like the glider, the LWSS often emerges naturally from the evolution of other patterns.

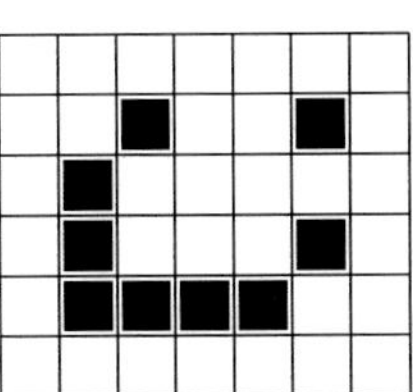

4.4 Example Interview Questions Using Arrays

4.4.1 Removing Elements

Write a method called `remove` that takes an `int[] a` and `int index` as inputs and returns a new array with the item at position `index` removed.

Arrays are of a fixed size, so there's no way to dynamically modify them in ways that would change their length.[5] This question, therefore, asks you to allocate a new, smaller array that will hold `a.length - 1` values. The method needs to copy all of the values up to, but not including, the `index` value to the new array, then copy the remaining values, which we do in two stages.

```
/**
 * Remove an element from an array
 *
 * @param  a  the input array
 * @param  index  the position of the element to remove
 *
 * @return  a new array with a.length - 1 elements
 */
public static int[] remove(int[] a, int index) {
  // Allocate a new array
  int[] newA = new int[a.length - 1];

  // Copy elements up to the index
  for (int i = 0; i < index; i++) {
    newA[i] = a[i];
  }

  // Copy the remaining elements after the index
  for (int i = index + 1; i < a.length; i++) {
```

5 `ArrayList`, as you'll recall, doesn't have this limitation.

```
    newA[i - 1] = a[i];
  }

  return newA;
}
```

Try It Yourself

There are a number of variations on this concept, which all involve making modifications that change the size of an input array. Try writing a method called `append` that takes an array and a new element and returns a new array with the new value appended to the end.

4.4.2 Rotate an Array

Write a method called `rotate` that takes an array `a` and an `int k` and returns `a` rotated by `k` positions. Each rotation step moves the current front element to the back of the array. For example, if `a = {1, 2, 3, 4, 5, 6}` and `k = 2`, the output should be `{3, 4, 5, 6, 1, 2}`.

This problem would be trivial with a list, which makes it easy to dynamically move elements from the front to the back, or vice versa. The fixed-size nature of arrays, however, requires thinking carefully about how to perform the move. There are two ways to perform this action: a general iterative approach, or a "clever" approach that uses reversals. The iterative method does rotation by repeatedly saving the value of the first element, moving all of the other elements forward in the array, then placing the first value into the last position.

```
// Iterative array rotation

// Perform k total rotations
for (int step = 0; step < k; step++) {
  // Get the value of the first element
  int first = a[0];

  // Slide the other elements forward one position
  for (int i = 1; i < a.length; i++) {
    a[i - 1] = a[i];
  }

  // Put the original first element into the last position
  a[a.length - 1] = first;
}
```

The "clever" approach is to use partial rotations: Reverse the order of the first k elements in the array, then reverse the remaining `a.length - k` elements, then reverse the entire array. It's not obvious that this should work, but it does. For example, using the example above and performing the first two reversal steps yields

2	1	6	5	4	3

Reversing the entire array then yields the rotated version:

4.4.3 Maximum Subarray Sum

Given an `int[] a`, which may contain both positive and negative values, find the subarray of sequential elements having the maximum sum. For example, if `a = {2, 3, -1, -4, 5, -2, 6, -3}`, the maximum subarray is `[5, -2, 6]`, with a sum of 9.

This is a more challenging problem, and one that would be hard to reason about in a high-pressure situation, but thinking through it provides a good example of a higher-level array-based algorithm. The solution is called Kadane's algorithm, named after its creator, Joseph Kadane, and described by Bentley (2016). First, consider the fact that the maximum sum subarray must have one element that is its *final* element. Suppose that some element `a[k]` is the final element of the maximum sum subarray. There are two ways that this could happen:

- Item `k` extends a subarray that also includes `a[k - 1]`. That is, the subarray that ended at `a[k - 1]` was not maximal, adding `a[k]` increased the subarray sum, but adding `a[k + 1]` does not yield a further improvement.
- Item `k` is the maximum subarray by itself. Adding elements on either side does not yield a larger subarray sum.

Kadane's algorithm works from left to right, identifying the maximum sum subarray that *ends at each position*. For an array position `j`, the best sum ending there is the maximum of either

- the best subarray ending at position `j - 1` plus `a[j]`; or
- `a[j]` by itself.

The implementation below uses an extra array called `bestSum` to keep track of the best possible subarray sum ending at each array position. At the conclusion of the method, the final result is the maximum of `bestSum`.

```
/**
 * Maximum subarray sum
 *
 * @param  a  input array
 * @return  the maximum sum obtained by any subarray of a
 */
```

```
public static int maxSubarraySum(int[] a) {

  // The best sum of a subarray ending at each array position
  int[] bestSum = new int[a.length];
  bestSum[0] = a[0];

  // The overall best sum
  int overallBestSum = a[0];

  for (int i = 1; i < a.length; i++) {
    // The best subarray for position i is either the extension
    // of the previous position, or a[i] by itself
    bestSum[i] = Math.max(bestSum[i - 1] + a[i], a[i]);

    // Update the overall best if necessary
    overallBestSum = Math.max(bestSum[i], overallBestSum);
  }

  return overallBestSum;
}
```

Try It Yourself

Execute `maxSubarraySum` on the example array given in the problem description.

Sharp-eyed readers will notice that the use of the `bestSum` array is actually unnecessary: The algorithm only needs to refer to the best sum for the previous array position, so there's no need to maintain a record of the results for every position. Therefore, it's possible to simplify the bookkeeping to one variable called `currentSum` that keeps track of the maximum subarray sum for the current position:

```
currentSum = Math.max(currentSum + a[i], a[i]);
overallBestSum = Math.max(currentSum, overallBestSum);
```

SUMMARY

This chapter has covered one- and two-dimensional arrays, Java's basic data structure for representing fixed-size collections of items. As we go forward, we'll be using arrays in projects, examples, and data structure implementations, including `ArrayList` in Chapter 6 and sorting in Chapter 10. As you're working through the exercises, keep the following ideas in mind:

- Arrays are often the best choice when you can easily determine the number of items you need. They're not suitable for collections that need to change over the lifetime of a program. For those cases, a list is a better choice.
- Java's arrays are still objects, even though they have a special syntax. Remember that the name of an array is really a reference to the underlying object in memory.
- Many array-based programs ultimately involve looping over the array's contents and counting, comparing, or modifying values. Review the sections on loops carefully and make sure that you're comfortable writing with Java's standard `for` loop constructions.

EXERCISES

Understand

1. List some important differences between a one-dimensional array and `ArrayList`.
2. Is the following statement a valid array declaration? Why or why not?

```
int[] a = new int[];
```

3. What is the default value of the elements in a new `int[]`? How about an array of `boolean`? How about an array of `String`?
4. Write a method called `range` that takes an array of integers as input and returns the difference between the maximum and minimum elements. Don't use any built-in Java methods and make sure that your solution works for arrays with negative values.
5. Write a method called `evenArray` that takes an `int[]` as input and returns `true` if every element in the array is even and `false` otherwise.
6. Write a method called `constantArray` that takes an `int n` and `int value` as inputs and returns an `int[]` containing `n` elements all set to `value`.
7. Write a method called `rangeArray` that takes an `int min` and `int max` as inputs and returns an array containing the consecutive integers starting at `min` and going up to and including `max`. Tip: Think about the number of elements that the array will contain.
8. Write a method called `flips` that takes a number `n` and returns a `boolean[]` with `n` randomly generated `true`/`false` values, representing `n` coin flips.
9. Write a method called `randomArray` that takes three `int` values named `n`, `min`, and `max`. Return an array with `n` randomly generated elements in the range from `min` to `max`, inclusive.
10. Write a method called `stringToArray` that takes a `String` as input and returns a `char[]` containing its characters. The `String` class has a built-in `toCharArray` method, but can you write your own code to perform the conversion without using it?
11. Write a method that performs the reverse operation from the previous problem: Take a `char[]` as input and return its associated `String`. Tip: Look at `StringBuilder` for a useful class that makes it easy to concatenate characters to a string.

12. Write a method called `asArrayList` that takes an `int[]` as input and returns an `ArrayList<Integer>` containing its values. As with the previous problems, write your solution without using any built-in Java class methods.
13. Write a method called `copyRange` that takes an `int[]` as input, along with two index values, `int left` and `right`. Return a new array that contains the values of `a` starting at position `left` and going up to position `right`, including both ends. Return `null` if either `left` or `right` lies outside of `a` or if `left > right`.
14. The `Arrays` class has a method called `equals` that can compare two arrays and determine if they contain equal elements at all positions. Write your own version of this method for arrays of integers.
15. Modify your `equals` method to work for two `String[]`. Tip: Remember how to test if two `String` objects are equal to each other.
16. Is it true that the `Arrays.equals(a, b)` will always be `true` if `a == b` is `true`? Why or why not?
17. Write a code fragment to find and print the minimum elements in each *row* of a two-dimensional matrix of integers.
18. Write a code fragment to find and print the minimum element in each *column* of a two-dimensional matrix of integers.
19. Write a code fragment to check if a two-dimensional array `a` is ragged. That is, output `true` if there is at least one row with a different number of columns from the others and `false` if all rows have the same number of columns.
20. Write a code fragment to find and print the minimum in each *column* of a ragged array, assuming that the maximum number of columns in any subarray is given by a constant named `MAX_COLS`.

Apply

21. Modify the `CellularAutomata` class to visualize the following rule set:

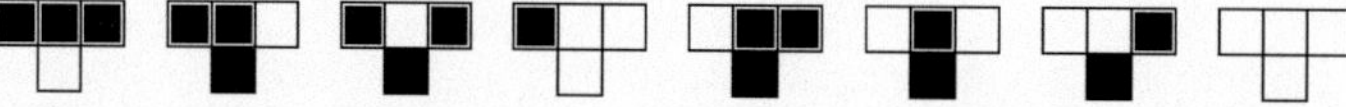

22. Write a method called `addToFront` that takes an `int[]` and an `int newValue` and returns a new array with `newValue` at index 0. The other elements in the array are moved to accommodate the new item; nothing is overwritten.
23. Next, write a method called `insert` that takes three parameters: an array, a new value, and an index position. Return a new array with the given item inserted at the specified index. Elements shift to make room for the new item.
24. Suppose that you have a ragged array (as a `double[][]`) recording sales for each day of each month. Write a code fragment to calculate and print the total sales in the first seven days of each month.
25. Repeat the previous problem, but calculate the total sales in the *last* seven days of each month.

26. Write your own version of `Arrays.toString` that can take an `int[]` as input and print it in formatted style – for example,

```
[2, 3, 5, 7, 11, 13]
```

27. Repeat the previous problem, but allow the input to be `Object[]`, a generic array of any object type. Remember that every class either has its own `toString` method or has access to the default `toString`.

28. The **dot product** of two vectors is defined to be the sum of the products of the corresponding elements. That is, if a and b are vectors of equal length,

$$a \cdot b = \sum_{i=1}^{n} a_i b_i.$$

Write a method called `dot` that takes two `double[]` as input and returns their dot product. You can assume the two inputs have the same length.

29. Write a method that takes two `int[][]` named `a` and `b` as inputs and returns a new `int[]` containing the element-wise sums of `a` and `b`. That is,

```
c[i][j] = a[i][j] + b[i][j]
```

for each position `(i, j)` in the matrices. Return `null` if the two matrices are different sizes.

30. Write a method that takes an `int n`, `int min`, and `int max` as inputs and returns an `n`-by-`n` matrix containing random values in the range `min` to `max`, inclusive.

31. The **trace** of a square matrix is defined to be the sum of its main diagonal elements; that is, the sum of the elements on the diagonal from upper-left to lower-right. Write a method to calculate and return the trace of a square matrix of `double` values.

32. Write a method called `isMagic` that takes an `int[][] m` as input and returns `true` if `m` is a magic square and `false` otherwise. Start by checking if `m` is a square.

33. Write a method called `rowCheck` that takes a `boolean[][]` as input and returns `true` if any *row* in the matrix contains all `true` values. Return `false` otherwise.

34. Repeat the previous problem, but check the *columns* for any column containing all `true` values.

35. A matrix A is **lower triangular** if $A_{ij} = 0$ for all $j > i$. That is, all of the nonzero elements form a triangle that lies on or below the diagonal.

1	0	0	0
1	1	0	0
1	1	1	0
1	1	1	1

Write a method called `isLowerTriangular` that takes an `int[][]` as input and returns `true` if the matrix is lower triangular and `false` otherwise. Note that the definition only requires that the upper triangle be zero, not that all elements of the lower triangle be nonzero.

36. Write a method called `print3d` that prints an `int[][][]`. Treat the three-dimensional array as a stack of two-dimensional arrays. For each value in the first dimension, print the values in the second and third dimensions as a rectangular matrix.

```
// Iterate through the outermost dimension
for (int i = 0; i < a.length; i++) {

  // Print the values in the second and third dimensions
  // of a[i] as a rectangular matrix

}
```

37. Here's a popular interview question with a "clever" solution. You're given an array that contains 99 of the numbers 1 to 100. Identify the one number that's missing. The "clever" answer is to calculate the sum of the array and compare it to the sum of the numbers 1 to 100. Write a method that implements this strategy. Tip: The sum of the first n natural numbers is

$$\sum_{i=1}^{n} = \frac{n(n+1)}{2}.$$

This is an important summation that shows up in many different contexts so it's worth memorizing.

38. What if the array is allowed to contain duplicate values, or has more than one missing value? Now you have no choice but to keep track of which elements are in the array. Write a method that iterates through the input array and uses a `boolean[]` to keep track of which numbers are present. If you wanted a more space-efficient implementation you could achieve the same result using Java's `BitSet`, which represents an array of `boolean` values using individual bits.

Extend

39. One hundred passengers are waiting to board a train with 100 seats. Every passenger has been assigned a seat, with the assigned seat numbers given on the passengers' tickets. The passengers will board one at a time and each passenger must take their seat before the next one can board. However, the first passenger has lost their ticket and can't remember their assigned seat number, so they just choose a seat 1–100 at random and sit there. Each subsequent passenger will board in the following way:

- If their assigned seat is open, the passenger sits there.
- If their seat has already been taken, they choose a random open seat instead.

Write a simulation program to determine the probability that passenger 100 gets to sit in her originally assigned seat. Perform 100 trials and keep track of the fraction that result in passenger 100 being able to sit in the correct seat. Use an array to keep track of which seats are occupied. Note that you can always renumber the seats, so it's fine to assume that passenger 2 should be assigned seat 2, passenger 3 should be assigned seat 3, and so forth.

40. **Treblecross** is a one-dimensional tic-tac-toe variant. Both players take turns marking Xs on a line of n squares. The object is to be the first player to complete a grouping of three Xs:

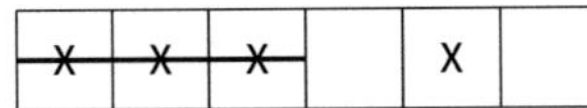

Finish the implementation of Treblecross given below. Your program should:

- prompt for the size of the playing array;
- quit if the input value is negative;
- print the board and read input on each turn;
- successfully alternate between the two players; and
- detect the three winning conditions and declare the appropriate player the winner.

```
// Starting main for Treblecross
public static void main(String[] args) {

  // Create a Scanner and get an input value of n
  // If n is negative, quit the program immediately

  boolean[] board = new boolean[n];
  int player = 1;

  // Main game loop
  boolean playing = true;
  while (playing) {

    // Print the current board

    // Ask the player to choose an open position

    // Read the player's move

    // If that square is occupied, continue

    // Set the position to true

    // Check if there is now a line of three

    // If a group of three exists, declare the
```

```
        // current player the winner and set
        // playing = false

        // Otherwise, switch to the other player
        player = (player % 2) + 1;
    }
}
```

41. **Nim** is a classic mathematical strategy game. There are many variations, but a common version is played with multiple piles of stones. On each turn, a player may remove as many stones as he or she wishes from any single pile. The player who takes the final stone is the *winner*. Write a program to allow two players to play Nim against each other. Your program should have the following features:
    - Use an `int[]` to represent three piles. Each pile starts with 20 stones.
    - On each turn, prompt the current player to select one of the piles, then a number of stones to remove from that pile. Use a loop to force the player to select a valid, nonempty pile, and take a valid number of stones; remember that you can't take more stone than the pile contains.
    - Update the number of stones in the pile, then check if there are any stones remaining. If not, the current player has just won the game.
42. Modify the Nim game so that the player who takes the last stone is the *loser*. This is called a *misère* game.
43. Now modify the Nim game so that the players can choose the number of piles at the beginning of the game. After reading in the number of piles and initializing the underlying array, prompt the players to enter a number of starting stones for each pile.
44. **Notakto** is a tic-tac-toe variant where there are only Xs. Both players take turns marking Xs on a 3×3 grid and the first one to make a move that completes a row, column, or diagonal line of Xs *loses*. Implement a Java program to allow two players to play Notakto.
    - Use a `boolean[][]` to represent the state of the board. Mark a position `true` when a player selects it.
    - On each turn, prompt the user for a position in the grid and read the response with a `Scanner`. You can use a loop to force the user to input a valid, unoccupied location. You can decide how you want to accept input; one reasonable choice is to accept a number 1 to 9 and map each of those input values to one of the nine squares in the grid.
    - Write a method that prints the board. If an entry in the `boolean[][]` is `true`, print an `X` for that location, otherwise leave the location blank.
    - After each move, check if there is now a complete row, column, or diagonal. Two of the earlier questions in this chapter are a relevant warm-up for this question.

NOTES AND FURTHER READING

Cellular automata are fun to explore – accessible but containing enormous depth if you're interested. Life has been a fixture of recreational mathematics since its invention in the 1970s, and there are extensive online repositories of patterns, classification systems, and high-performance simulation software (LifeWiki, 2022). There is an active community of researchers, many of them nonprofessional mathematicians and computer scientists, who continue to develop new patterns and variations of Life and other CA models. Life was initially popularized through Martin Gardner's recreational mathematics column in *Scientific American*, which published both the first public overview of the model and several early discoveries of interesting patterns. The archives of his column, "Mathematical Games" (republished in the *Colossal Book of Mathematics* (Gardner, 2001)) are a great source of puzzles, theories, and applications.

5 Searching and an Introduction to Algorithm Analysis

The answer, of course, is "it depends." In engineering, it turns out "it depends" is almost always the answer . . . However, it is almost always better to know why it depends, which is what we discuss here.
Andrea and Remzi Arpaci-Dusseau,
Operating Systems: Three Easy Pieces

INTRODUCTION

Very often, software developers need to evaluate the trade-offs between different approaches to solving a problem. Do you want the fastest solution, even if it's difficult to implement and maintain? Will your code still be useful if you have to process 100 times as much data? What if an algorithm is fast for some inputs but terrible for others? **Algorithm analysis** is the framework that computer scientists use to understand the trade-offs between algorithms. Algorithm analysis is primarily *theoretical*: It focuses on the fundamental properties of algorithms, and not on systems, languages, or any particular details of their implementations.

This chapter introduces the key concepts of algorithm analysis, starting from the practical example of searching an array for a value of interest. We'll start by making experimental comparisons between two searching methods: a simple linear search and the more complex binary search. The second part of the chapter introduces one of the most important mathematical tools in computer science, **Big-O notation**, the primary tool for algorithm analysis.

LEARNING OBJECTIVES

At the end of this chapter, you will be able to:

- Describe the linear and binary search algorithms.
- Use Java's built-in timing tools to compare programs experimentally.
- Define Big-O notation and uses it to describe the order of growth of a mathematical function or program.
- Prove that an algorithm is correct using a loop invariant.

5.1 Linear Search and Algorithm Performance

Let's begin by considering the fundamental problem of searching an array to find an item of interest. Given a one-dimensional array `a` (which can be of any type) and a value of interest `val`, search the array and return the first index where `val` occurs, or -1 if it's not present. A straightforward algorithm for solving this problem is **linear search**: Iterate through each element of the array and check for `val`. The following implementation searches an array of `int` values.

```
/**
 * Linear search
 *
 * @param  a  one-dimensional array
 * @param  val  search value of interest
 *
 * @return  first index of val in a or -1
 */
public static int linearSearch(int[] a, int val) {
  for (int i = 0; i < a.length; i++) {
    if (a[i] == val) {
      return i;
    }
  }

  return -1;  // Default if search value is not found
}
```

Take a moment to examine the code for `linearSearch`: How good is this method? It is certainly compact and easy to understand, which are nice properties. The number of lines of code in an algorithm's implementation, however, is not a reliable predictor of its performance on real computers. When computer scientists analyze an algorithm, we are primarily interested in how its performance *scales* as its input size increases. For example, suppose you implemented and ran `linearSearch` on an array of 1 million elements – it would take only a fraction of a second on a modern computer. How is your code likely to perform if the size of your input array increases to 2 million, 10 million, or 1 billion elements? Increasing the size of the input array requires consuming more resources to execute the algorithm. The two most important resources for algorithm analysis are *time* and *space*.

- The **time complexity** of an algorithm is an estimate of the amount of work the algorithm requires, expressed as a function of its input size. This could be presented as the expected execution time of the algorithm on a real computer, but real execution times are system-dependent and hard to predict, so analysts usually express the time complexity of algorithms in terms of the number of steps or statements that the program must execute.
- Some algorithms must allocate additional memory for intermediate results as they execute. The **space complexity** of an algorithm measures how this additional space requirement scales as the input size increases. Linear search does not require any additional space, but we'll see later examples of algorithms that do.

In general, a "good" algorithm is one that scales efficiently as its input size increases. There can be other considerations, but choosing an algorithm with good scaling behavior means that your code will continue to be useful over time, even as it's required to process more data or solve bigger problems.

5.2 Binary Search

Is there a search algorithm that's better than linear search? In general, the answer is no – given no additional information about the elements or ordering of the array, the only possible solution is to check every element – but a faster algorithm exists when the array is sorted. Like linear search, the **binary search** algorithm takes a sorted array `a` and a value of interest `val` as input and returns either an index where `val` occurs in `a`, or -1 if `val` is not present. It searches the array by checking the middle element to identify the half containing the search value:

- Start by checking the middle element. In the best case, this will be the search value and the algorithm terminates immediately.
- Determine whether the search value is in the left or right half of the array.
- Check the middle element of the chosen half to narrow the search range to one-quarter of the array. Repeat this step, checking the middle of the remaining data and dividing in half, until you've either located the matching item or discovered that it isn't present.

The standard strategy uses two pointers, `left` and `right`, to keep track of the active search region. Each step checks the middle element, then adjusts `left` and `right` to narrow the search window. The main search loop ends when `left` and `right` cross, indicating that the search has failed.

```
/**
 * Binary search
 *
 * @param  a  sorted array
 * @param  val  search value
 *
 * @return  an index where val occurs in a, or -1
 */
public static int binarySearch(int[] a, int val) {
  int left = 0;
  int right = a.length - 1;

  while (left <= right) {
    int mid = (left + right) / 2;  // Calculate midpoint

    // Case 1: success
    if (a[mid] == val) {
```

```
      return mid;
    }

    // Case 2: search value is in left half
    else if (val < a[mid]) {
      right = mid - 1;
    }

    // Case 3: search value is in right half
    else {
      left = mid + 1;
    }
  }

  // Default: loop ends without finding search value
  return -1;
}
```

Try It Yourself

Execute binary search on the following array with a search value of 11:

2	3	5	7	11	13	17

Solution

The first iteration sets `left` and `right` to the first and last elements in the array. The initial midpoint is `a[3]`, the 7.

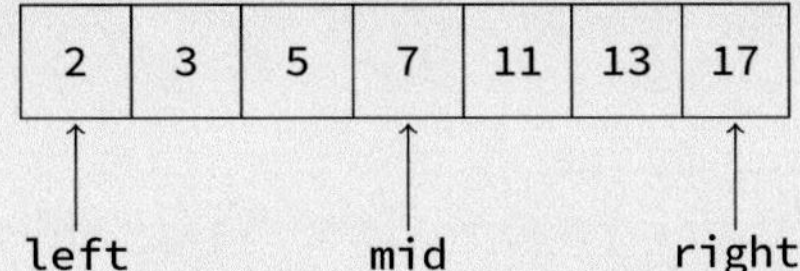

11 must be in the right half of the array; set `left = mid + 1`. The next midpoint is `a[6]`, the 13.

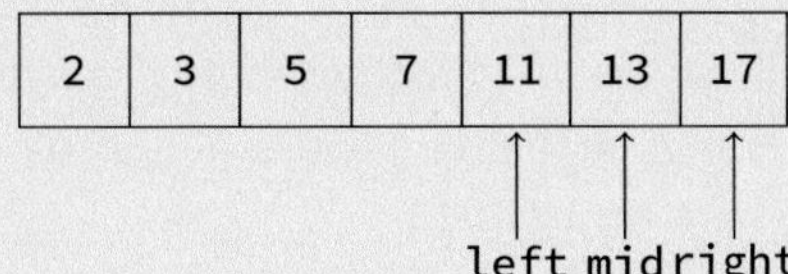

The search value must be left of 13. On the third iteration, we discover that `left` and `right` are equal and that `a[4]` is the search value. The method ends and returns 4 as the result.

Binary search is conceptually straightforward but famously tricky to implement. Programming author Jon Bentley, in his book *Programming Pearls*, cites an experience with a group of professional programmers, 90% of whom could not produce a fully functioning binary search after several hours of coding (Bentley, 2016). Common errors include:

- Testing `left < right`, instead of `left <= right`. Including equality in the condition is required to deal with the stopping condition where `left` and `right` converge on the search value.
- Setting `right = mid` instead of `mid - 1`, and likewise for `left = mid + 1`.
- Initializing `right` to `a.length` instead of `a.length - 1`, which will cause an `ArrayIndexOutOfBounds` error.

Try It Yourself

Look carefully at the line that calculates the midpoint. Could this lead to a problem? Tip: Think about what happens to the `int` sum if both `left` and `right` are very large.

Solution

If the array is larger than one billion elements, then it's possible for `left + right` to *overflow* the maximum positive `int` value, which is $2^{31} - 1$, or about 2.147 billion. This bug would not have been observed in earlier eras, but arrays with a billion or more elements are possible in modern big data applications. The overflow bug was present in the standard Java binary search, `Arrays.binarySearch`, for more than nine years before it was discovered and fixed in 2006. Joshua Bloch, the original author of `Arrays.binarySearch`, recommends the following overflow-proof formulation for the midpoint calculation (Bloch, 2006):

```
int mid = low + ((high - low) / 2);
```

Try It Yourself

The default binary search assumes the array is sorted in increasing order. How would you modify the method if the array is sorted in decreasing order?

Solution

Use the same strategy, but switch the left and right sides. If the search value is *less* than the middle element, it will be in the right half of the search region; if it's *greater than* the middle element, it will be in the left half.

5.3 Project: Experimental Performance Analysis

How do the time complexities of the two search algorithms scale as their input sizes increase? It seems clear that binary search should be more efficient, but its code is nontrivial. One way to engage with this question is to perform an experiment: Code up each method, measure the time required for input arrays of increasing size, and identify any trend in the results.

5.3.1 Best, Worst, and Average Case Performance

Before starting, it's important to describe exactly what we'll be measuring and how the experiment will be carried out. First, what kind of inputs should we analyze? Depending on the elements in the array and the choice of search value, `linearSearch` and `binarySearch` could take more or fewer steps to execute. Algorithm analysis considers three different classes of inputs, each of which corresponds to a different measure of performance.

- The **best case** occurs when the algorithm terminates after completing the minimum amount of work. For both algorithms, the best case occurs when the search value is the first item examined (the first array element for `linearSearch` or the midpoint element for `binarySearch`). In both cases, the answer will be returned immediately after checking only one element.
- The **worst case**, on the other hand, occurs when the algorithm requires the maximum amount of work to terminate. For both methods, the worst case occurs when the search fails. For `linearSearch`, failure requires iterating through every element of the array. For binary search, failure requires performing enough iterations to identify that the search value isn't in the array.
- The **average case** is the expected time needed to execute the algorithm on "typical" inputs. Average case analysis is harder, because it requires defining the distribution of possible inputs and search values.

Most algorithm analyses, including the majority of the results in this book, focus on worst-case performance. That is, when we consider how an algorithm's performance scales, we are interested in the *most challenging inputs that require the maximum amount of work*. Worst-case analysis establishes bounds on performance – things could get *this bad*, but not any worse. In practice, best-case analysis is often trivial, because the best case for many algorithms is to immediately find a solution and stop. Average-case analysis requires defining the distribution of "typical" inputs, which may not be easy. It's also often true that the difference between worst- and average-case performance is only a constant factor, which usually doesn't affect performance scaling that much.

5.3.2 Measuring Execution Time

Java includes two built-in functions that can measure the execution time of programs. The first is `System.currentTimeMillis`, which returns your operating system's estimate of the current **system time**, which is defined to be the number of milliseconds since midnight,

January 1, 1970.[1] This way of measuring computer time originated with the UNIX operating system and has become an international standard for computer timekeeping. `System.currentTimeMillis` suffers from two limitations for performance analysis:

- The granularity of the measurement depends on the OS; many platforms only report system time in 10–100 ms increments, which makes it hard to time brief events.
- Elapsed time measured by `System.currentTimeMillis` includes the time for your program to execute, but also the time for any overhead added by the OS and other programs sharing the same system.

The second function, `System.nanoTime`, uses a high-resolution timer to measure elapsed nanoseconds within an individual JVM instance. The value it reports can be used to measure the elapsed time for a specific Java program exclusive of any OS or system-related overhead. Therefore, `nanoTime` is the preferred function for performance experiments.

The following program measures the worst-case execution time for linear search against arrays of increasing size. It uses `nanoTime` to measure the elapsed time for 100 search iterations, then calculates the average time array size.

```
/**
 * Time search algorithms for increasing array lengths
 */
public class SearchTiming {
  public static void main(String[] args) {
    for (int i = 1; i <= 256; i = i * 2) {
      // Construct an array of i million elements
      int[] a = new int[i * 1000000];
      for (int j = 0; j < i * 1000000; j++) {
        a[j] = j;
      }

      // Time 100 worst-case trials of linear search
      //
      // Measure the total elapsed time for all trials
      final int NUM_TRIALS = 100;

      long startTime = System.nanoTime();
      for (int trials = 0; trials < NUM_TRIALS; trials++) {
        linearSearch(a, -1);  // Worst-case search
      }
      long elapsedTime = (System.nanoTime() - startTime);
```

1 This date is referred to as "The Epoch." The measurement is made with respect to Universal Coordinated Time.

```
      // Calculate the average time per trial in milliseconds
      double timeInMillis = elapsedTime / 1000000.0 / NUM_TRIALS;
      System.out.println(i + " million\t\t" + timeInMillis);
    }
  }
}
```

Try It Yourself

Add the `linearSearch` method into the class, then run it to collect some timing measurements. How do you think the performance of binary search will compare to linear search for large arrays? Will it be significantly faster, a little bit faster, or take about the same time? Modify the code to time binary search. What results do you observe?

Executing the two algorithms on a 2021 M1 MacBook Pro with 16 GB of memory[2] yields the following measurements:

Array elements	Linear search time (ms)	Binary search time (ms)
1 million	0.3000	0.0011
2 million	0.4482	0.0010
4 million	0.7769	0.0030
8 million	1.5716	0.0000
16 million	3.1979	0.0000
32 million	5.9213	0.0000
64 million	11.8582	0.0001
128 million	23.6208	0.0000
256 million	47.4238	0.0001

The behavior of linear search is straightforward: Doubling the array size roughly doubles the worst-case execution time. There is a little inconsistency for the smallest array values, but the pattern is clear once the array size reaches 4 million. This makes sense: The worst case for linear search requires checking every array element, so doubling the number of elements doubles the required time. What about binary search? All of the arrays take, essentially, no time at all to search – even for an array of 128 million elements, the average search time was less than 0.0001 ms. The variability that we do observe is most likely due to memory access overhead within the system.

These results, rough though they are, reveal an important difference between the two algorithms. Binary search is not just a little more efficient than linear search: It belongs to a *completely*

2 If it is the future and you are reading an old copy of this book in your university library, I hope you find these system specs amusingly ancient, the way my generation used to chuckle when we read about implementing something on, like, a PDP-8.

different class of complexity. The scaling behavior of binary search must operate according to fundamentally different rules than the easy-to-understand scaling behavior of linear search. What are those rules that govern the performance scaling of binary search? To answer that question, we need to develop *analytical* methods for describing algorithm performance.

5.4 The Growth of Functions

Although experimentation can be useful, there are still good reasons to develop purely mathematical tools of algorithm analysis.

- Experimental results always depend on the execution conditions: how the algorithm is coded, the language, the operating system, and the specs of the machine. It can be hard to interpret results in a way that yields generalized insight into an algorithm's performance.
- Our first-cut experimental results are still not very precise. We'd like to have more detailed insight into how binary search scales.

Let's begin by considering a simple mathematical function and reasoning about how it changes as its input increases. Consider the behavior of the following function. How does the value of $f(n)$ change as n increases?

$$f(n) = 2n^2 + 3n + 1.$$

As n increases, $f(n)$ becomes dominated by $2n^2$, the fastest-growing term. If n is very large, it's reasonable to say that $f(n)$ is approximately equal to $2n^2$ and the other terms behave like a small error. Consider another polynomial function of a higher power:

$$h(n) = 0.001n^3 + 1,000n^2.$$

$h(n)$ is initially dominated by $1,000n^2$, which is the largest term when n is small. However, once n becomes sufficiently large ($n > 1,000,000$), the $0.001n^3$ term becomes dominant. Because n^3 grows more quickly than n^2, the first term will eventually dominate $h(n)$ as n becomes bigger and bigger, just as the $2n^2$ term dominated $f(n)$.

This type of reasoning is called **asymptotic analysis**, because it focuses on describing a function's approximate behavior when its input becomes very large. The asymptotic behavior of a function is determined by its fastest-growing term, which is called the **order of growth**. In our examples, $f(n)$ has order of growth n^2, because its fastest-growing term is a multiple of n^2; $h(n)$ has order of growth n^3. Notice also that $f(n)$ is going to be a little bit greater than $2n^2$ for large values of n, but less than $3n^2$. Therefore, it's correct to reason that $f(n)$ "grows like" n^2. More specifically, $f(n)$ is bounded above and below by constant multiples of n^2 once n becomes large. Likewise, $h(n)$ is eventually bounded above and below by multiples of n^3.

Reasoning about the order of growth for simple functions is easy:

- Ignore all constants.
- Identify the fastest-growing term. In polynomial functions this will be the highest-powered term, but you may need to think carefully about functions that are not basic polynomials.
- That term is the dominant order of growth for sufficiently large inputs.

Try It Yourself

Identify the dominant order of growth for each of the following functions:

1. $n^4 + 100n^3 + 1,000n^2 + 10,000$
2. $n^{0.1234} + n^{0.5678}$
3. $n \log n + n + \log n$
4. $n + \sin n$.

Solution

(1) and (2) are straightforward: the highest-powered terms are n^4 and $n^{0.5678}$, respectively. (3) is trickier. The log function grows slowly as a function of n, but does increase without bound as its input increases. Therefore, $n \log n$ grows more quickly than n by itself and is the dominant order of growth. (4) is dominated by n, because $\sin n$ is bounded by $[-1, 1]$ for all n.

5.5 Big-O Notation

Big-O notation is the most important tool for making statements about the growth of algorithms. The examples in the previous section established the concept of an order of growth that bounds the value of a mathematical function as its input increases. Big-O notation formalizes this concept, relating a function $f(n)$ to another function $g(n)$ according to the following definition:

> A function $f(n)$ is in the set $O(g(n))$ if there exist constants c and m such that $f(n) < cg(n)$ for all $n > m$.

The definition states that a constant multiple of $g(n)$ is an upper bound for $f(n)$ once n becomes sufficiently large. For example, consider the initial example function

$$f(n) = 2n^2 + 3n + 1.$$

It's easy to see that once n is large enough – say, greater than 5 – $f(n)$ is always less than $3n^2$. Therefore, $f(n) < 3n^2$ for all $n > 5$, which satisfies the formal definition of Big-O notation and allows us to state that $f(n)$ belongs to the set $O(n^2)$. There are other values of c and m that could satisfy the definition. Big-O notation does not require finding the "best" or smallest values of c and m, only that two values exist that establish $g(n)$ as an upper bound for $f(n)$. Big-O notation therefore formalizes our earlier intuitive concept of the dominant order of growth. If $f(n)$ is in the set $O(n^2)$, then it "grows like" n^2 and its value is bounded by some multiple of n^2 as n becomes large. Figure 5.1 illustrates the definition of Big-O notation graphically.

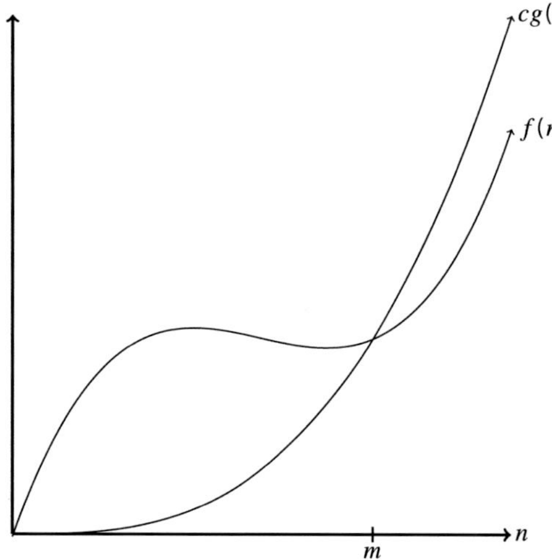

Figure 5.1 **Visualizing the definition of Big-O notation. The cubic function $f(n)$ is upper-bounded by a multiple of $g(n) = n^3$ once n becomes sufficiently large. Notice that it's acceptable for $f(n)$ to be greater than $cg(n)$ for small values of n, but the asymptotic relationship takes over once $n > m$.**

A quick note on terminology. $O(n^2)$ is properly a set: It's the set of functions that share the property of being upper-bounded by a multiple of n^2. It's correct to write

$$f(n) \in O(n^2)$$

to state that $f(n)$ is a member of that set and therefore has that property. In practice, though, it's common to say "$f(n)$ is $O(n^2)$" or to write

$$f(n) = O(n^2).$$

Try It Yourself

Find values of c and m that satisfy the formal definition of Big-O notation to show that

$$f(n) = n^3 + 10n^2 + n + 1$$

is in the set $O(n^3)$.

Solution

This problem could be solved by fixing a value of c, such as 2, and then solving for the value of m that makes $f(n) < cn^3$ for all $n > m$. Here is another, more mechanical approach. Create another function that has the same coefficients as $f(n)$, but with lower powers of n replaced by n^3:

$$f(n) < n^3 + 10n^3 + n^3 + n^3$$
$$f(n) < 13n^3.$$

This relationship holds for all $n > 1$, so the formal definition of Big-O notation is satisfied when $c = 13$ and $m = 1$. Remember: We don't have to find the "best" values, only two that work, so this is sufficient to satisfy the definition.

Try It Yourself

Is the function $z(n) = 10n^2 + 5n + 3$ in the set $O(n^3)$? Explain your reasoning.

Solution

$z(n)$ is clearly $O(n^2)$, so it is bounded above by a multiple of n^2 for large values of n. Because n^3 grows even faster than n^2, $z(n)$ must also be bounded by a multiple of n^3 and is therefore also $O(n^3)$. The same reasoning would apply to any power of n greater than 2.

Big-O notation describes upper bounds, but doesn't set any restrictions on how tight or loose those bounds might be. It's technically correct[3] to say that $z(n)$ is $O(n^3)$, but that statement is not useful, because the bound is too loose to capture the function's true behavior. In general, algorithm analysis seeks the *tightest possible complexity bound*, which is $O(n^2)$ for $z(n)$.

5.6 Applying Big-O Analysis to Programs

So far, our analysis has only focused on basic mathematical functions. What we really care about, though, are algorithms. The next goal is to use the concept of asymptotic order of growth and Big-O notation to bound the work required by an algorithm as a function of its input size. The simplest way to do this is by **counting statements**. Given an implementation of an algorithm in pseudocode or a programming language, write down an expression for the total number of statements required to execute the algorithm as a function of its input size. The order of growth of that function then describes how the work required by the algorithm scales as its input increases.

For example, consider the following simple code fragment to add up the numbers from 1 to n in a loop.

```
int sum = 0;

for (int i = 0; i < n; i++) {
   sum += i;
}

return sum
```

There are four statements to consider:

1. The first line declaring `sum`. This statement executes only one time.

3 The best kind of correct.

2. The `for` statement, which executes $n + 1$ times: n times while the loop is running and one final time when `i = n` to terminate the loop.
3. The body of the loop, which executes n times.
4. The final `return` statement, which executes only one time.

By this reasoning, the total number of program statements required to execute the code fragment is $2n + 3$, which is $O(n)$. In other words, the time required to execute the fragment is dominated by the parameter n, which controls the number of loop iterations. Doubling the value of n roughly doubles the expected running time.

Try It Yourself

This analysis assumes that each statement in the program takes an equivalent amount of time. Explain why that simplification is not really correct, but also why it doesn't affect the result.

Solution

Different high-level program statements map to different sequences of low-level machine language instructions, which will take different amounts of time to execute. Evaluating the `for` statement, for example, requires testing the loop index variable and updating its value on each iteration. Big-O notation ignores constant factors, so it's fine to ignore differences in the execution times of individual program statements when performing this type of analysis. Evaluating the `for` loop takes more time than a basic assignment statement, but the difference is at most a constant factor that doesn't depend on n.

Try It Yourself

Analyze, using Big-O notation, the worst-case complexity of linear search. Let the input size n be the length of the input array `a`.

Solution

The core of linear search is the `for` loop that iterates over each element of `a`:

```
for (int i = 0; i < a.length; i++) {
  if (a[i] == val) {
    return i;
  }
}
```

Like the previous example, linear search contains a loop from 1 to `a.length`, but there is a conditional `return` statement in the body of the loop. How to reason, then, about the number of loop executions? Recall that worst-case analysis assumes an input that requires the maximum amount of work to process. In the worst case, the body of the loop must execute `a.length` times, once for each element of the array. Therefore, the worst-case complexity of linear search is $O($`a.length`$)$.

Try It Yourself

Here's an example that uses two loops to fill an $n \times n$ matrix with all pairs of products of the numbers 0 to $n - 1$.

```
int[][] a = new int[n][n];


for (int i = 0; i < n; i++) {
  for (int j = 0; j < n; j++) {
    a[i][j] = i * j;
  }
}
```

What is the complexity of this fragment as a function of n?

Solution

This fragment has a pair of nested loops, each iterating through the numbers 1 to n. The outer loop executes n times, and the inner loop executes n times for each iteration of the outer loop. Therefore, the innermost statement executes n^2 total times and the complexity of the fragment as a whole is $O(n^2)$.

5.7 Detailed Analysis of Binary Search

Analyzing programs that contain simple loops is straightforward: Figure out how many times each statement executes as a function of the input size and use the results to bound the execution time for the entire program. An algorithm like binary search, though, poses a challenge: It isn't easy to determine how many times the main loop executes. We would like to show two things: first, that binary search is *correct*, and second, that it has *logarithmic time complexity*, $O(\log n)$, where n is the array length.

5.7.1 Correctness Using a Loop Invariant

First, recall the core of the binary search algorithm:

```
/**
 * The core of binary search
 */
```

```
int left = 0;
int right = a.length - 1;

while (left <= right) {
  int mid = (left + right) / 2;  // Calculate midpoint

  if (a[mid] == val) {  // Success
    return mid;
  } else if (val < a[mid]) {  // Search left half
    right = mid - 1;
  } else {  // Search right half
    left = mid + 1;
  }
}

// Default: loop ends without finding search value
return -1;
```

Showing that binary search is correct requires establishing that it can only terminate by either finding the value of interest or confirming that the value doesn't exist in the input array. This section introduces a standard method for proving the correctness of a loop-based algorithm called an **invariant**. A loop invariant is a condition that is guaranteed to be true on each iteration of the loop. The basic argument has three parts:

1. State an invariant that can be used to reason about the correctness of the algorithm. Coming up with this is often the hardest part and may require trial and error as you work out the details of the proof.
2. Argue that the invariant must be true on every iteration of the loop.
3. Show that maintaining the invariant ensures that the algorithm can only terminate under correct conditions.

Here's a statement that we can use to reason about the correctness of binary search:

> If `val` exists in `a`, it must be within the range of indices defined by the two references `left` and `right`. More specifically, if `val` occurs at an index `i`, then `i` $\geq$ `left` and `i` $\leq$ `right`.

We now need to argue two things:

1. The invariant is guaranteed to be true the first time the loop executes.
2. If the invariant is true at the beginning of one loop iteration, it's guaranteed to be true at the beginning of the next iteration. The body of the loop can never execute in a way that breaks the invariant.

The first part is easy. The initial values of `left` and `right` are set to the first and last elements of the array at the beginning of the method. Therefore, the first requirement is satisfied – the starting values of `left` and `right` span the entire array, so any index *i* must be between them.

The second part is more challenging, but still mechanical: Look at the body of the loop, reason about each execution case, and show that each path through the body must maintain the invariant. Binary search has three cases:

- The first case checks the midpoint and discovers that `a[mid] == val`. This case terminates the method and returns `mid` as the result.
- The second case occurs when `val < a[mid]`. The array is sorted, so if `val` occurs within the array, it must occur in the range defined by `left` and `mid - 1` and not at all in the range `mid` to `right`. Therefore, setting `right = mid - 1` shrinks the search range by half and still maintains the invariant.
- The third case is the mirror of the second. If `val > a[mid]`, then it is acceptable to set `left = mid + 1`, which again shrinks the search range by half without violating the invariant property.

Therefore, we can reasonably conclude that the invariant property is true when the `while` loop begins executing and continues to be true on every subsequent iteration.

The final step is to argue that this property guarantees correct termination. The loop is constructed so that the range of indices defined by `left` and `right` strictly decreases on every iteration. The invariant property guarantees that `val` must be in this range, if it exists, so there are only two possible outcomes. Binary search will either eventually find a location where `val` occurs and then end the method, or the range will shrink until it becomes empty – that is, `left` > `right` – in which case we have established that `val` can't be present and the loop ends.[4]

If you haven't spent much time reasoning about the formal correctness of programs, this kind of argument may seem a bit wonky. This is not the kind of thing you need to do every time you write a program with a loop, but invariants are a useful tool for proving the correctness of algorithms. If you go from having no awareness of loop invariants to understanding the reasoning of a few invariant proofs, you'll have made a solid step toward writing more rigorous code.

5.7.2 Complexity

Analyzing the worst-case time complexity of binary search requires figuring out how many times the `while` loop executes as a function of the input array size. One solution to this problem is to use the technique of recurrence relations, discussed in Chapter 8. In this case, though, let's use a simpler strategy: Reason about small, concrete examples and then look for a general pattern. If the array is only a single element, the search takes one operation in the worst case: Check the element and discover that it is or is not the search value. If the array has three elements, then the search requires two comparisons in the worst case: one to check the middle element and a second to check either the first or last element. You can verify that searching an array of seven elements requires at most three comparisons.

---

4 It may be helpful to think of this as a "squashing" argument: The range defined by `left` and `right` continually shrinks, but the array is finite, so the method must eventually squash down to a single array element that either is or is not the value of interest.

Try It Yourself

How many binary search steps are required for a 15-element array in the worst case? How about 31 elements?

Solution

Four steps are required for a 15-element array. In fact, any array of size 8–15 can be searched in at most four steps. Continuing examples will show that any array of size 16–31 can be searched in five steps, and arrays of 32–63 can be searched in six steps. In general, an array of size up to $2^k - 1$ can be searched in at most k steps.

There is clearly a connection between powers of 2 and the amount of work required by binary search, because the method discards half of the remaining search space on each iteration.

- The input array is of length n and the first step reduces the search space by half, so there are at most $n/2$ remaining elements.[5]
- The second step reduces the search space to at most $n/4$ elements.
- The third step reduces the search space to at most $n/8$ elements.

This dividing process is characteristic of algorithms that exhibit **logarithmic complexity**. Each step reduces the amount of remaining work by a constant factor.

Let r represent the number of remaining elements in the search space. After k iterations of binary search,

$$r \leq \frac{n}{2^k}$$

by the reasoning given above. The final iteration of the method occurs when there is only one remaining element to consider – that is, when $r = 1$. Therefore, the maximum number of iterations is the value of k that satisfies

$$\frac{n}{2^k} = 1.$$

The value of k is the number of times n can be halved before reaching one element, which is

$$k = \log n.$$

Here, $\log n$ is the base-2 logarithm, which is the most commonly used one in algorithm analysis. We'll always assume that standard logarithm is taken base-2 unless we specify otherwise. Note that $\log n$ might be fractional – for example, if $n = 15$, then $k \approx 3.9$ – but the algorithm can't perform a fractional number of steps. It's standard to use the ceiling function to indicate that we need the whole number of steps that's at least as large as $\log n$:

$$k = \lceil \log n \rceil.$$

5 The exact number of remaining elements depends on whether the array length is odd or even, and, in the even case, whether the value is in the left or right half. Try some examples and verify that $n/2$ is the maximum number of remaining elements.

Therefore, the work required by binary search scales logarithmically with n and the worst-case complexity is $O(\log n)$.

5.8 Common Complexities

- $\boldsymbol{O(n)}$. Linear complexity. This generally occurs when the core loop of an algorithm must process each data item one time. Doubling n doubles the execution time.
- $\boldsymbol{O(n^2)}$. Quadratic complexity. Examples include comparing all pairs of elements in an array or processing an $n \times n$ matrix. Doubling n quadruples the execution time.
- $\boldsymbol{O(\log n)}$. Logarithmic complexity. Each operation reduces the problem size by a constant factor. The log function is usually base-2, but all logarithms differ by only a constant, so any algorithm with logarithmic scaling can be called $O(\log n)$, regardless of base.
- $\boldsymbol{O(1)}$. Constant complexity. This notation is used for an operation that does not depend on the size of the input. For example, accessing a single array element is $O(1)$ because the time required for an array access does not change with the size of the array. Note that $O(1)$ operations are not necessarily fast. Because Big-O notation ignores constant factors, a piece of code – such as a loop that runs for a high but fixed number of iterations – can still be $O(1)$ even if it takes a long time to execute.
- $\boldsymbol{O(n^k)}$. Polynomial complexity. This category includes all algorithms that scale according to a polynomial function of n. This is an important class in higher-level complexity theory.
- $\boldsymbol{O(n \log n)}$. An unusual function, but one that occurs in many algorithms that use a divide-and-conquer strategy, where the complete problem is broken into smaller subproblems that are solved separately. Two important algorithms in this class are Quicksort and merge sort, discussed in Chapter 10.
- $\boldsymbol{O(2^n)}$. Exponential complexity. Algorithms of this complexity often occur in combinatoric problems, such as generating all binary strings of length n or generating all possible subsets of n items. The amount of work required grows extremely quickly as n increases: 2^{100} exceeds the number of elementary particles in the entire universe. Algorithms with exponential complexity are intractable for anything other than small values of n. This fact is unfortunate, because this category includes many problems of real-world importance in logistics, optimization, and operations research.
- $\boldsymbol{O(n!)}$. Factorial complexity. This complexity occurs in algorithms that must consider all permutations of n items, such as evaluating all possible routes among n locations on a map. $n!$ grows even faster than 2^n, so practical work on these problems focuses on developing accurate approximations that are still tractable.

5.9 Other Notations: Ω and Θ

Big-O notation is the most frequently used method of describing algorithm performance, but there are two other important notations, denoted by the Greek letters Ω (capital Omega) and Θ (capital Theta).

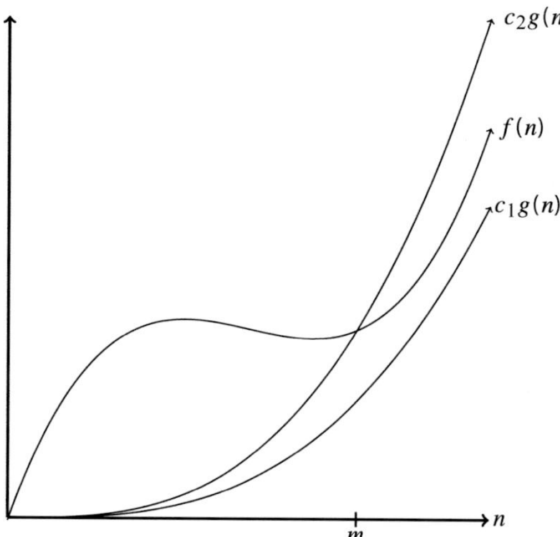

Figure 5.2 Visualizing the definition of Θ notation. Once n becomes sufficiently large, $f(n)$ is bounded both above and below by multiples of $g(n) = n^3$. The upper bound, $f(n) < c_2g(n)$, is equivalent to saying that $f(n)$ is $O(g(n))$. The lower bound, $f(n) > c_1g(n)$, is equivalent to saying that $f(n)$ is $\Omega(g(n))$.

5.9.1 Ω Notation for Lower Bounds

Omega notation (Ω) is the lower-bound equivalent of Big-O notation. Its definition states that $f(n)$ is bounded *below* by some multiple of $g(n)$ once n becomes sufficiently large.

> A function $f(n)$ is in the set $\Omega(g(n))$ if there exist constants c and m such that $f(n) > cg(n)$ for all $n > m$.

Lower bounds are theoretically interesting because they establish limits on algorithm performance. For example, a standard result in the theory of sorting says that comparison-based sorting algorithms (a category that includes all of the important algorithms discussed in Chapter 10) are $\Omega(n \log n)$. Many algorithms require sorting their data as an initial step, so this bound tells us something useful about the practical limits to improvement for a wide class of algorithms.

Try It Yourself

Find values of c and m to show that $f(n) = 2n^2 + n + 1$ is $\Omega(n^2)$.

Solution

There are many possible solutions, but it's easy to see that ignoring the linear and constant terms gives $f(n) > 2n^2$ when $n \geq 1$. Therefore, $f(n)$ satisfies the definition of $\Omega(n^2)$ with $c = 2$ and $m = 1$.

5.9.2 Θ Notation for Exact Bounds

An algorithm is $\Theta(g(n))$ if it's both $O(g(n))$ and $\Omega(g(n))$. Theta notation gives an *exact* bound: The algorithm's performance is bounded both above and below by multiples of $g(n)$. This is the "best" type of analytical result, because it establishes that $g(n)$ is neither too tight nor too loose – $f(n)$ grows exactly like a multiple of $g(n)$. Formally,

A function $f(n)$ is in the set $\Theta(g(n))$ if there exist constants c_1, c_2, and m such that $c_1 g(n) < f(n) < c_2 g(n)$ for all $n > m$.

Figure 5.2 depicts these relationships graphically. The cubic function $f(n)$ is bounded both above and below by a multiple of $g(n) = n^3$ once n becomes larger than m. As with Big-O notation, the bounds may not hold for smaller values of n, but the asymptotic behavior takes over once n is sufficiently large.

5.10 Limitations of Asymptotic Analysis

Asymptotic analysis is a useful theoretical framework for reasoning about algorithm performance and making comparisons between algorithms, but it does have limitations. Keep the following facts in mind when you reason about an algorithm's performance using Big-O notation.

- *Worst case vs. average case.* Asymptotic analysis focusing on worst-case behavior, like our examples so far, may be too pessimistic if there is a significant gap between worst-case and average-case performance. There are some algorithms that perform very well on "typical" problems and only attain their worst-case theoretical behavior for pathological inputs that are unlikely to occur in practice.
- *System considerations.* Standard Big-O analysis does not take into account the actual design or capabilities of the system executing the algorithm. This is an *advantage*, in that it allows to evaluate performance trade-offs in a neutral way, but risks ignoring things that might matter when the algorithm executes on a real computer. In particular, the role of the memory hierarchy and caching can have a significant impact on performance that Big-O notation never considers.
- *Small vs. large constants.* Asymptotic analysis ignores constant factors that affect an algorithm's performance. Two algorithms that are both $O(g(n))$ are "equal" from an asymptotic perspective, but there's a practical difference between an algorithm with a constant factor of 2 and one with a constant of 10,000, particularly for small values of n.
- *Overall design.* Finally, algorithm complexity is only one element of good design. A less efficient algorithm may be a better choice if it's easier to code, understand, and maintain.

SUMMARY

We've now taken two important steps on our path to understanding data structures and algorithms. First, we've introduced binary search, our first major nontrivial algorithm. Second, we've introduced the concept of computational complexity, with Big-O notation as the main tool for describing the performance of algorithms. Almost every chapter from this point forward will feature Big-O analysis. As you're reviewing this material, here are a few points to keep in mind:

- Binary search is a fundamental concept that reoccurs in many variations and guises throughout computer science. Serious students will memorize its implementation.
- The formal definition of Big-O notation is tricky, but not something that we need for simple algorithm analysis. In many cases, you can understand the basic complexity of an algorithm by looking at the number of iterations of its deepest loop.
- More sophisticated algorithms can require more complex analysis techniques, which we'll develop in future chapters.
- We'll make only limited use of Ω and Θ notation, but you'll see them frequently in books on advanced algorithm analysis.

EXERCISES

Understand

1. State the formal definition of Big-O notation.
2. Explain, intuitively, why $f(n) = 0.00000001n^2 + 100,000,000$ is $O(n^2)$.
3. Describe the differences between best-, worst-, and average-case time complexities.
4. Draw a picture that illustrates the definition of Ω notation.
5. Write a version of linear search that takes a `String[]` and `String` as inputs.
6. What is the complexity of the following code fragment, expressed in Big-O notation?

```
int count = 0;
for (int k = 1; k < n; k = k * 2) {
    count++;
}
```

7. Suppose that you have (finally) finished this course and have gone on to your dream job at a prominent tech company. One day, your boss (who has forgotten everything he learned in his own data structures course) asks you to code an algorithm that requires you to generate all possible subsets of n items. How do you respond?
8. True or false: Every function in the set $O(n)$ is also in the set $O(n^2)$.
9. Give an example of a function that is $\Omega(n)$ but not $\Theta(n)$.
10. In general, which of the following approaches to searching an unsorted array for a single value is more efficient? You only need to perform the search one time.
    - Use linear search.
    - Sort the array first using insertion sort, then apply binary search. Insertion sort has time complexity $O(n^2)$.
11. What is the complexity of adding two n-digit positive integers? What about multiplying them, using the standard by-hand multiplication technique?
12. What is the *space* complexity of multiplying two n-digit integers by hand?
13. Summarize the loop invariant method for proving correctness.

14. Find values of c and m to show that

$$f(n) = 15n^3 + 10n^2 + 3^n + 1$$

is formally $O(n^3)$.

15. Suppose that you completed the previous problem and your friend says that you should find a smaller constant c. How do you respond?

Apply

16. Consider the following code fragment, which compares all pairs of elements in array a to each other but does not repeat comparisons that have already been made. Show that the fragment is $O(n^2)$. Tip: Think about the number of inner iterations performed on each outer iteration. You may need to look up a common summation.

```
for (int i = 1; i <= n - 1; i++) {
    for (int j = i + 1; j <= n; j++) {
        // do something with a[i] and a[j]
    }
}
```

17. Prove that the function

$$f(n) = n^5 + 3n^4 + 5n^3 + 10n^2 + 25n + 15$$

is $O(n^5)$, $\Omega(n^5)$, and $\Theta(n^5)$ using the formal definitions of the three notations.

18. If $f_1(n)$ is $O(g_1(n))$ and $f_2(n)$ is $O(g_2(n))$, show that $f_1(n)f_2(n)$ is $O(g_1(n)g_2(n))$. Tip: Use the formal definition with constants c_1 and c_2.

19. Suppose two functions $f_1(n)$ and $f_2(n)$ are both $O(g(n))$. Prove that the sum $f_1(n) + f_2(n)$ is also $O(g(n))$.

20. Suppose you have two polynomial functions $f(n)$ and $g(n)$. Show that, if $f(n)$ is $O(g(n))$, then $g(n) = \Omega(f(n))$.

21. Suppose that a certain algorithm has complexity $O(\log_a n)$, where $\log_a$ denotes the base-a logarithm. Show that this algorithm is also $O(\log_b n)$. Tip: Use the formal definition of Big-O notation and review the properties of logarithms.

22. Show that $f(n) = n!$ is $O(n^n)$.

23. Show that $f(n) = \log(n!)$ is $O(n \log n)$.

24. Suppose you have a computer running a certain program that implements an algorithm that has complexity $O(n^2)$. In some length of time T, the computer can process a problem of size s using your code. Suppose you purchase a new computer that is 100 times as fast as your current computer. What size problem would you expect to be able to solve in the same time T with the new machine without changing the code? What if the algorithm had been $O(n)$? What about $O(n \log n)$?

25. Use the loop invariant method to argue that this loop must terminate:

```
int n = 100;
```

```
while (n > 0) {
  n--;
}
```

Extend

26. Give an argument that linear search is $\Theta(n)$.

27. Given a positive integer a, what is the complexity of calculating a^2 by hand? Note: The earlier question asked about the complexity of multiplication when you knew the number of *digits* in a. Can you relate the value of a to its number of digits?

28. Suppose that I measured the execution time of an algorithm with order of growth $O(n^2)$. Fill in the right-hand column of the table below with reasonable measurements that could have occurred if execution time of my program scales quadratically with input size.

Input size (n)	Execution time (ms)
1,000	10
2,000	
4,000	
5,000	
10,000	

29. (Shaffer, 1997.) Our version of binary search finds a location where the search value occurs in array a (if one exists), but isn't guaranteed to find the *first* location. Modify the binary search algorithm to return the first location (that is, the smallest index) where the search value appears. Tip: If the same value appears multiple times, all of its occurrences must be grouped together. Binary search is guaranteed to find one element within the group, but it may not find the first one. Therefore, an easy way to solve this problem is to use the basic binary search to find any element in the group, then perform a linear search to the left to identify the first element, but that won't be $\Theta(\log n)$. Design a version that is guaranteed to have logarithmic performance.

30. Consider a *ternary* search algorithm. Given a sorted input array of length n, examine the elements at positions $n/3$ and $2n/3$ to determine which third of the array contains the search value, then repeat the process. Implement this method.

31. Make an argument that ternary search is still $O(\log n)$.

32. Use a loop invariant to prove that your method is correct.

33. Suppose that you want to perform an *average* case analysis of linear search. Consider the following problem. You are given an n-element array that contains the numbers 1 to n, each of which may be chosen as the search value with equal probability. Show that the expected number of operations required by linear search under these assumptions is $O(n)$. Tip: If each element can be the search value with equal probability, there is a $1/n$ chance that the first element is chosen, in which case the search requires only one iteration and then terminates. There is a $1/n$ chance that the second element may be chosen, in which case the search requires two iterations, and so forth.

34. Java contains a built-in sorting routine called `Arrays.sort`. Write a program that uses `System.nanoTime` to time the execution of `Arrays.sort` for random arrays of increasing lengths. Using a spreadsheet, or other software package, plot your observed sorting times (in milliseconds) as a function of array length. Your results should show that `Arrays.sort` scales like $n \log n$.

NOTES AND FURTHER READING

The German number theorist Paul Bachmann is credited with introducing O notation to represent the growth of a function – he used it to stand for *Ordnung*, the German word for "order" (Bachmann, 1894). Asymptotic notations were adapted into the analysis of algorithms in the 1960s and 1970s and were popularized by Donald Knuth's mega-influential text *The Art of Computer Programming*, which did more than any other work to establish and standardize the core concepts of the field (Knuth, 2014a). Knuth also popularized the use of Ω and Θ notations for lower bounds and exact order of growth (Knuth, 1976).

Anecdotes about the difficulty of binary search are taken from Jon Bentley's *Programming Pearls*, a fun book based on columns that Bentley authored for the *Communications of the Association for Computing Machinery* (Bentley, 2016). It covers data structures, algorithm design, and practical performance calculations. It's well worth picking up or seeking out at your local library.

6 Lists

Bad programmers worry about the code. Good programmers worry about the data structures and their relationships.
Linus Torvalds

INTRODUCTION

Up to this point we've focused on introducing the Java language and – starting with the previous chapter – the technique of algorithm analysis. We're now ready to put that machinery to work by describing our first important new data structure: **lists**. A list is like an array, in that it represents an ordered sequence of data values, but lists are more flexible: They support operations for dynamically inserting and removing data as the program executes. We've already used Java's built-in `ArrayList` class to manage a collection of values; now we're ready to talk about how it's implemented internally.

LEARNING OBJECTIVES

After studying this chapter, you will be able to:

- Discuss the concept of an abstract data type and the difference between the higher-level behaviors of a data structure and its lower-level implementation.
- Implement the two important types of lists – array lists and linked lists – as Java classes and write new methods to extend the behaviors of each list.
- Use Big-O notation to analyze the complexity of list methods and reason about the trade-offs between linked and array lists.

We'll put all these concepts together to build the classic *Snake* game, which will demonstrate how to manage a set of objects with a list and read keyboard input in a graphical program.

6.1 Abstract Data Types

Some of the challenge of studying data structures comes from the fact that there are often multiple ways to solve the same problem. Java, for example, includes multiple implementations of standard data structures that provide the same operations, but in different ways and with different intended applications. Before discussing lists in detail, we need to develop a framework for the relationship between a data structure's behaviors and its implementation.

6.1.1 Separating Behaviors from Implementation

It's helpful to think of a data structure as a combination of three things:

1. a relationship among a group of data items, such as a linear sequence, a set, or a hierarchical tree;
2. a collection of operations that can be performed on those data items; and
3. an implementation of that relationship and those operations in a particular program.

This three-layer classification scheme separates a *description* of the data structure – what it is and can do – from its internal *implementation*.

For example, think about arrays. The basic relationship between the items in a one-dimensional array is that of a *fixed-size ordered sequence of values*: There is a first element in the array, a second element, and so forth up to the maximum size, and each element is individually accessible. A one-dimensional array allows you to get the value at an index position, set the value at a position, or get the fixed length of the array, but no other operations. Notably, you can't grow or shrink the array by removing an item, appending to the end, or inserting at an interior position. In Java, both the get and set operations are implemented using square bracket notation:

```
int x = a[0];  // Get first element of array a
a[1] = 537; // Set second element of a
```

Python's lists use similar syntax, but are dynamically resizable and heterogeneous: A Python list implements *fundamentally different behaviors* than a Java array. JavaScript has a data structure that it calls "arrays" that also use square bracket syntax, but aren't actually arrays at all!

6.1.2 The List Abstract Data Type

A list data structure is a resizable ordered sequence of values. Like an array, a list has a first item, a second item, and so forth, and it can grow and shrink as items are added or removed. There are two basic strategies for implementing a list data structure:

- An array-based list, which adds resizability on top of a basic one-dimensional array. We saw Java's built-in `ArrayList` class in Chapter 3, but we haven't discussed how it's implemented internally.
- A **linked list**, which implements the list as a chain of independent nodes. Java has a `LinkedList` class that provides an alternative to `ArrayList`.

Both implementations support the same methods – `add`, `get`, `remove`, and so forth – but have *different internal implementations*. Therefore, some operations are better supported by a linked list and others are more efficient on an array list.

If you want to be fancy,[1] you can use the term **abstract data type** (ADT) to refer to a description of a data structure's properties and operations, independent of its implementation. Therefore, we could say that array-based and linked lists are two different implementations of the "list abstract data type." We'll use this terminology in future chapters when we discuss the general concept of a data structure, independent of the details of its implementation. An ADT presents a summary of a data structure from the perspective of a *user* – it describes what the structure is and what it can do, without presenting specific internal details.

Try It Yourself

Think about the behaviors that should be part of the list ADT. What kinds of operations would we like to perform on lists, without worrying yet about how they'll be implemented in a Java program?

Solution

The earlier comparison with arrays has described a few important list operations:

- Getting and setting the item at a particular index.
- Getting the number of items in the list.
- Inserting or removing items at a particular index. We might distinguish between insert and remove operations to the interior of the list and operations that add or remove from the ends.

We could add others, such as testing if the list contains a certain value, getting a sublist, or combining lists.

Try It Yourself

Java defines a `List` interface, which lays out a set of methods that all lists agree to implement, including `get`, `add`, `insert`, and `remove`. The three standard Java classes that implement `List` are `ArrayList`, `LinkedList`, and `Vector`. Look at the documentation for `List` and review the methods that it describes.

6.2 Array Lists

We've already seen how to use the built-in `ArrayList` to represent a dynamic sequence of items. This section discusses the internal implementation and analysis of `ArrayList`.

1 Which you do.

6.2.1 Array List Structure

`ArrayList`, as its name implies, implements the methods of the list ADT on top of a one-dimensional backing array. When you add or remove items from the list, the `ArrayList` automatically modifies the backing array in an appropriate way, which might include *resizing* the backing array to hold more elements.

Consider the problem of appending an item to the end of the list. When you create a new `ArrayList`, it contains an initial, empty backing array. Java distinguishes between the **capacity** of the list, which is the length of the internal array, and the **size**, which is the number of elements in the list. The `ArrayList` maintains a reference to the next unoccupied position in the backing array, which is initially the first position. The new list below has a capacity of 10 and a size of 0.

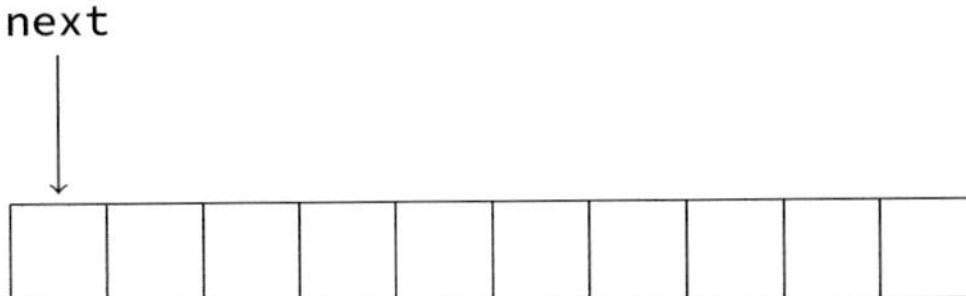

Appending a new item is easy: Fill the position pointed to by `next`, then advance it to the next open location. For example, after appending 2, 3, and 5, we'd have the following backing array:

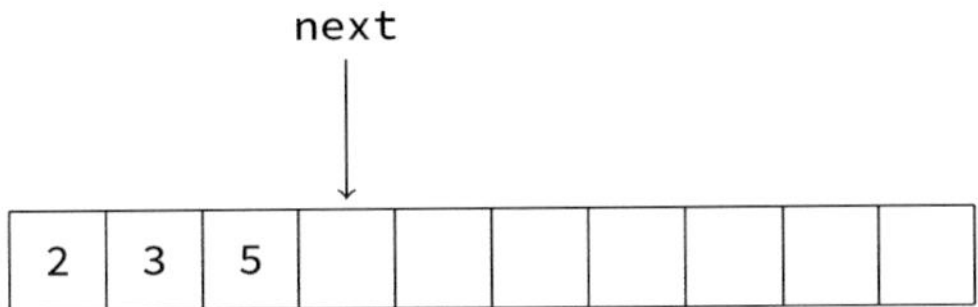

Appending when there are open spaces requires one array access, which is $O(1)$, then updating `next` and the list's `size`, which are also $O(1)$ operations. Therefore, the simple append operation is $O(1)$.

What if the backing array fills? In this case, we allocate a new, larger backing array, copy all of the elements from the old array to the new one, and then append the new item to the next open spot in the larger array. It's common to double the size of the backing array each time you perform this step. In the example below, we've filled the original 10-element array and would like to append 31 as the eleventh value, which requires copying all 10 values from the original array to a new 20-element array.

Try It Yourself

What is the complexity of the `add` operation under these conditions?

Solution

Let the size of the list be n. The operation is dominated by the time required to copy n values from the old array to the new array, which is $O(n)$.

6.2.2 Implementing an `ArrayList` Class

Let's implement our own version of `ArrayList`. The example below shows the basic outline of the class with an empty constructor and `add` methods, which we'll complete in a moment.

```
/**
 * A custom version of ArrayList
 */

// The generic type T is the type of data held by the list

public class ArrayList<T> {

  // The 1-D backing array
  private T[] array;

  // Number of elements added to the list
  private int size;

  /**
   * Constructor -- allocate a default backing array
   */
  public ArrayList() {

  }

  /**
   * Append a new item to the list
   *
   * @param  item  the new item of generic type T
   */
  public void add(T item) {

  }
}
```

Generic Types

The class declaration introduces a new feature: a **generic type** `T` enclosed in angle brackets. Recall that declaring an `ArrayList` requires specifying the type of values it contains with angle brackets:

```
ArrayList<String> names = new ArrayList<String>;
```

In our class, `T` functions as a placeholder and refers to whatever type of data are being held in the list. For example, when performing operations on an `ArrayList<String>`, `T` would be `String`; for an `ArrayList<Double>`, it would be `Double`. Using the generic parameter allows Java to enforce the requirement that all elements in the list have the same type, and that operations that add or remove items from the list are type safe, in a way that works for any underlying element type.

Constructor

The default constructor allocates the initial backing array, which is a `T[]`. This turns out to be a bit tricky: `T` is a *parameter*, not a specific type, so simply stating

```
this.array = new T[10];
```

will fail. Instead, allocate an `Object[]` and then *cast* it to `T[]`.

```
/**
 * Constructor -- allocate a default backing array
 */
@SuppressWarnings("unchecked")
public ArrayList() {
  // Default capacity of 10
  this.array = (T[]) new Object[10];

  // A new list contains no elements
  this.size = 0;
}
```

This action can generate a warning: Since `T` is a generic type, there's no way for the compiler to confirm that casting an `Object[]` to a `T[]` is safe. Adding `@SuppressWarnings` tells the compiler to allow the unchecked cast.[2]

The `add` Method

The `add` method implements the strategy described in the previous section: Put the new item in the next open space, allocating a larger backing array if the current one fills. Rather than declaring a `next` field, we'll use `size` to determine the next open position.

2 Imagine telling the compiler in your most businesslike manner: "The situation is under control."

```
/**
 * Append a new item to the list
 *
 * @param  item  the new item of generic type T
 */
@SuppressWarnings("unchecked")
public void add(T item) {
  // If the array is full, double its capacity
  if (this.size == this.array.length) {
    T[] newArray = (T[]) new Object[this.size * 2];

    // Copy items to the new array
    for (int i = 0; i < this.array.length; i++) {
      newArray[i] = this.array[i];
    }

    // Make the new array the backing array
    this.array = newArray;
  }

  // Append the new item to the next open spot
  this.array[this.size] = item;

  // Don't forget to increase the size!
  this.size++;
}
```

Try It Yourself

Add a `get` method that takes an `int index` as input and returns the item at that position. What could you do if the given index is out of bounds?

Solution

One option for an out of bounds index is to return `null`, but that might not be safe. Instead, let's `throw` an `IndexOutOfBoundsException` to indicate that the index was invalid. If the index is in bounds, then `get` is simply a wrapper around an array access.

```
/**
 * Get the item at the given index position
 *
 * @param  index  position in the list
 * @return  the item at the index
 */
public T get(int index) {
  // Check if the index is in bounds
  if (index < 0 || index >= this.size) {
    throw new IndexOutOfBoundsException("Index " + index);
  }

  return this.array[index];
}
```

Notice that the method signature doesn't declare that `get` throws the `IndexOutOfBoundsException`. Technically, `IndexOutOfBoundsException` is a type of `RuntimeException`, and Java allows a method to throw any `RuntimeException` without any special declarations. Likewise, other parts of the program can call `get` without wrapping it in a `try-catch` block.

6.2.3 Amortized Analysis of the Append Operation

The `add` method has a new behavior that we haven't seen before: It's usually $O(1)$, but sometimes $O(n)$, depending on the state of the backing array. Many data structures have this property, where operations are usually fast, but you have to pay an occasional higher cost to update or balance the structure. It turns out that the *expected time* for appending to an array list is $O(1)$. That is, the time required to increase the backing array adds no more than a constant factor to the total workload, averaged over a large number of appends.

Consider the following reasoning. Let's start with an empty array list of capacity 1, then determine the *total work* required to append k elements. Dividing by k will then give the average work per append. This is called an **amortized analysis**, a term that comes from accounting and refers to spreading the cost of something over its lifetime. In this case, we're going to average out the cost of the expensive $O(n)$ appends with the cheaper $O(1)$ operations. The work to perform k appends has two parts:

- inserting each of the k elements into an open array position, which is $O(k)$ total: every item must be inserted into the array; and
- the total time spent enlarging the backing array each time it fills during the k insertions, which is dominated by the number of times items must be copied from a filled array to a larger array.

If we start with a single-element array and double the size each time it fills, how many times does it need to be enlarged to insert k elements?

- Consider $k = 5$: The array must double three times to insert five elements, at sizes of 1, 2, and 4, for a total of seven data movements.
- If $k = 21$, the array will double five times, at sizes of 1, 2, 4, 8, and 16, for a total of 31 data movements.

In general, to insert k elements, the array must double $\lceil \log k \rceil$ times. This is equivalent to saying that the array will double at every power of 2 size less than k.

Try It Yourself

How many total data movements will be performed if we start with an array of size 1 and then insert enough elements to double at every power of 2 size less than k?

Solution

From the examples above, and a little experimentation, you can verify that the number of movements $M(k)$ is equal to

$$M(k) = 2^{\lceil \log k \rceil} - 1.$$

For example, if $k = 17$, the total number of data movements is $1 + 2 + 4 + 8 + 16 = 31$, which is equal to $2^5 - 1$.

The ceiling function is hard to work with; replace it with a simpler bound:

$$\lceil \log k \rceil < \log k + 1$$

$$M(k) < 2^{\log k + 1} - 1.$$

Simplifying the exponent gives an easy bound: $M(k) < 2k - 1$. This expression says that the work spent copying elements when performing k appends is only linear in k. Therefore, the complete amount of work required to insert k elements, including the time to put each element into the array, is bounded by

$$T(k) < 2k - 1 + k,$$

which is $O(k)$. Therefore, the average time required to insert a single element is $O(1)$.

Try It Yourself

This argument assumed that we started with an array of size 1. What if the starting capacity had been larger? Make an argument that it wouldn't change the result.

6.2.4 Removing and Inserting

Our array list should also provide methods to remove and insert at a given position. The basic `remove` operation takes an `int index` and removes and returns the item at that position. Items are shifted to fill the open space left by the removed item. Take a look at the following implementation.

```
/**
 * Remove and return an item from the list
 *
 * @param  index  position of the removed element
 * @return  the item at the given position
 */
public T remove(int index) {
  // Check if the index is in bounds
  if (index < 0 || index >= this.size) {
    throw new IndexOutOfBoundsException("Index " + index);
  }

  // Save the item so it can be returned later
  T removedItem = this.array[index];

  // Shift items to the left
  // This step overwrites the removed item
  for (int i = index + 1; i < this.size; i++) {
    this.array[i - 1] = this.array[i];
  }

  // Clear the item that was at the previous last position
  this.array[this.size - 1] = null;

  // Reduce the size
  this.size--;

  return removedItem;
}
```

The core of the method is a loop that shifts all items from positions `index + 1` to `size - 1` to the left to fill the space opened by removing the item. The last step clears the final position that was previously occupied by the last element.

Try It Yourself

What is the worst-case complexity of the `remove` method?

Solution

The worst case occurs when removing the first element, which requires every other element in the array to shift left. If the size of the list is n, removing is $O(n)$ in the worst case.

Inserting uses a similar strategy: Shift elements to the right to make room for the new value. The method below takes an `int index` and a `T value` as inputs and puts the new element at that position, shifting other values out of the way to make room. Observe that shifting the elements starts from the *back* of the list.

```
/**
 * Insert a new item at the given position
 *
 * @param  index  insertion position
 * @param  value  the new item
 */
public void insert(int index, T value) {
  // TODO: Check if the index is in range

  // TODO: Enlarge the backing array if it's full

  // Shift elements right, starting from the back
  for (int i = this.size - 1; i >= index; i--) {
    this.array[i + 1] = this.array[i];
  }

  // Add the new element and increase the size
  this.array[index] = value;
  this.size++;
}
```

Try It Yourself

Finish the `insert` method by adding statements to check if the `index` is valid and to enlarge the backing array if it's full.

Try It Yourself

Make an argument that insertion is also $O(n)$.

6.3 Linked Lists

The second kind of list, the **linked list**, represents its data as a *sequence of linked nodes*:

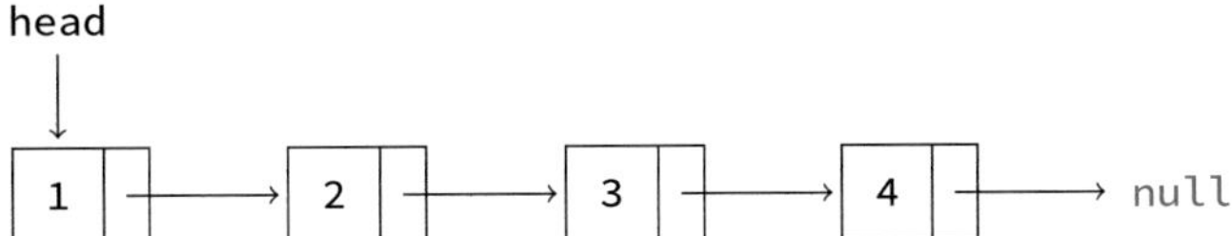

Think of a linked list as a *chain* of data. Each node stores a piece of data – which may be called the `value` or `key` – and has a `next` field that points to the following node. Given a reference to the head element, you can start at the head of the list and follow the chain to reach the other elements. The final node in the chain has its `next` field set to `null`, which marks the end of the list.

6.3.1 Linked List Implementation

Each item in the list is a `ListNode` object, which stores both the data value and the reference to the following node. The top-level `LinkedList` object maintains a reference to the first node in the list, which we'll call the `head`. The class below implements this basic structure. As in the `ArrayList`, it uses a generic type `T` to represent the type of the items in the list. This class has yet another new feature: `ListNode` is implemented as a private "inner" class inside of `LinkedList`. This arrangement ensures that `ListNode` objects can only be created and used by `LinkedList` methods; you can't create a `ListNode` as an independent object.

```
/**
 * Custom version of a linked list
 */
public class LinkedList<T> {

  // Maintain a reference to the head node
  private ListNode head;
  private int size;

  /**
   * Constructor -- the head is initially null
   */
  public LinkedList() {
```

```
    this.head = null;
    this.size = 0;
  }

  /**
   * ListNode is a private "inner" class
   */
  private class ListNode {
    private T value;
    private ListNode next;

    public ListNode(T newValue) {
      this.value = newValue;
      this.next = null;
    }
  }
}
```

A new, empty list simply has its `head` reference set to `null`.

6.3.2 Adding to the Front

The basic linked list insertion operation puts a new item at the head of the list. Suppose that we have the existing list shown below and want to add 2 to its front. Inserting at the head of a list takes $O(1)$ time and has three steps. First, initialize the new node, which will have a `next` field of `null`.

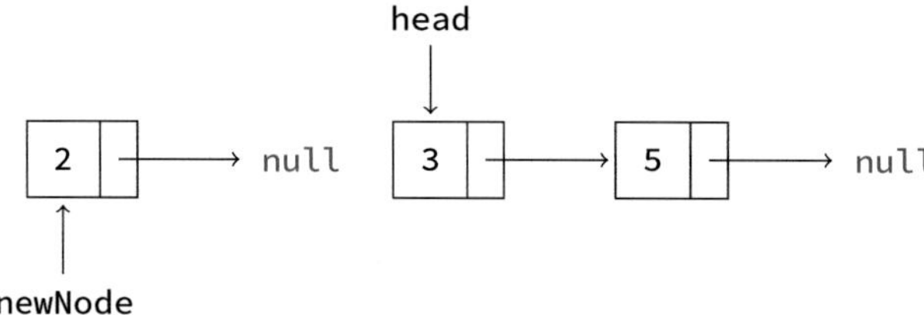

Second, connect the new node to the current head.

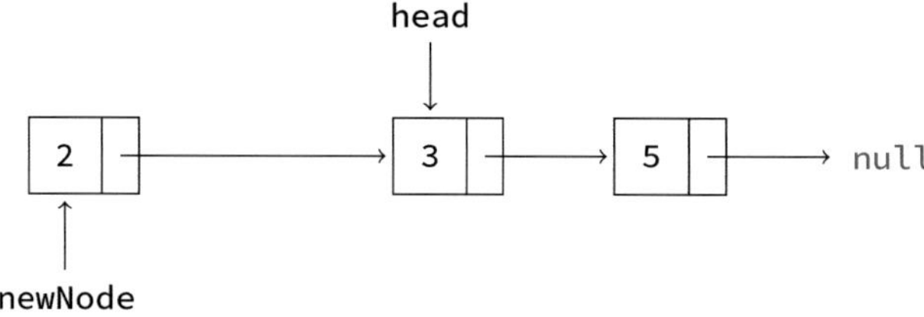

Finally, move the head reference to make the new node the head of the list.

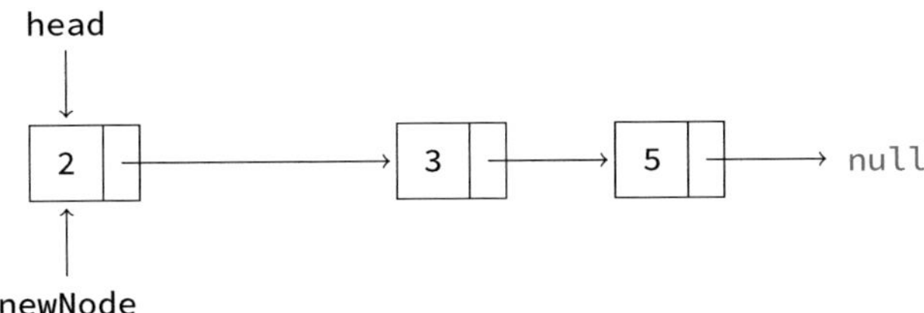

Here is a Java implementation of this process. The code is simple, but remember that the order of steps is important. If you reposition `head` before connecting the new node, you'll lose access to all of the nodes in the initial list.

```
/**
 * Insert a new item at the head of the list
 *
 * @param  value  the value of the new list node
 */
public void addToFront(T value) {
  // Make a new list node
  ListNode newNode = new ListNode(value);

  // Point the new node to the current head
  newNode.next = this.head;

  // Move the head reference
  this.head = newNode;

  // Don't forget the size!
  this.size++;
}
```

6.3.3 Getting an Item

Linked lists are indexed from 0, just like arrays and `ArrayList`. Getting an item is more complex, however, because accessing the node at a given position requires starting at the head and *iterating through the chain* one node at a time. Examine the following implementation:

```
/**
 * Get an item in a linked list
 *
 * @param  index  return the item at this position
 * @return  the item at the given index position (of type T)
```

```
 */
public T get(int index) {
  // Check if the index is in bounds
  if (index < 0 || index >= this.size) {
    throw new IndexOutOfBoundsException("Index " + index);
  }

  // Start at the head node
  ListNode current = this.head;

  // Iterate through the chain, following the links
  for (int i = 0; i < index; i++) {
    current = current.next;
  }

  // current now points to the node at position index
  return current.value;
}
```

This method illustrates a typical pattern for moving through a linked list:

- Initialize a reference to the head node, which is called `current` in the example.
- Use a loop to step through the list, following the `next` references, until you reach the desired position. The key move is setting `current = current.next` to advance one position in the chain.

In some cases we need to interact with a node and its neighbors, which might require stepping through the list with more than one reference.

Try It Yourself

What is the complexity of the `get` method?

Solution

In the worst case, the method has to iterate through the entire list. Therefore, if there are n nodes, `get` is $O(n)$. This is worse than `ArrayList`, which had $O(1)$ `get` operations via its backing array.

6.3.4 Inserting at an Arbitrary Location

Now consider the problem of inserting at an arbitrary position: Iterate through the list to find the right index, then tie a new node in at that spot. The general `insert` method takes a `value` and inserts it at a given `index`. Consider the list below. We'd like to insert the new value 2.5 at index 2. As before, the first step is to create a new node that is not initially connected to the list.

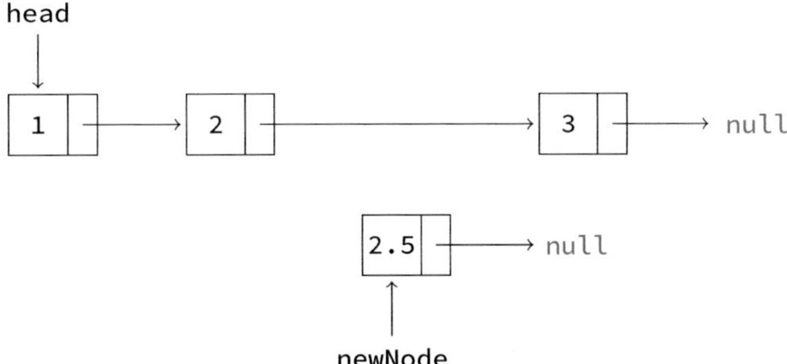

The second step is to iterate through the list to find a reference to the node *before* the position where we want to insert. In this case, that's position 1. Once the reference is in position, set `newNode.next = current.next` to connect the new node to the rest of the list.

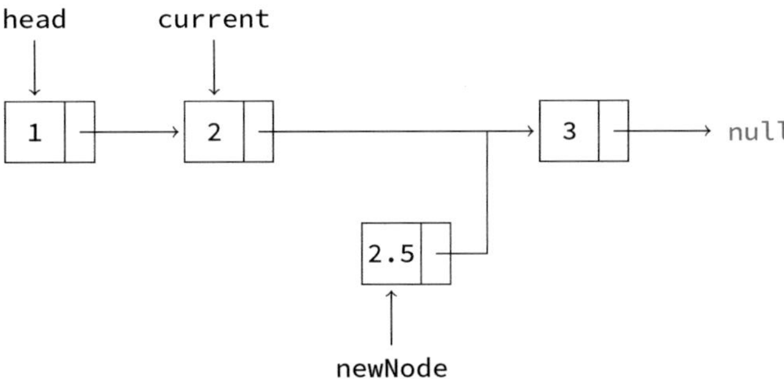

The final step is to set `current.next = newNode`.

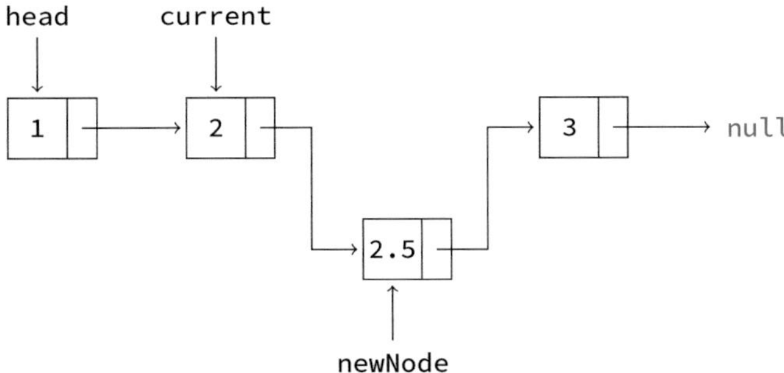

Try It Yourself

Implement the `insert` method that takes an `int index` and a `T value` and inserts a new node using the steps above. Can you use the general insert method to add to the front of the list?

Solution

The method is a combination of `addToFront` and `get`.

```
/**
 * Insert a value at a given position
 *
 * @param  index  the insertion position
 * @param  value  the new value to insert
 */
public void insert(int index, T value) {
  // TODO: Special case for index == 0

  // Check the index
  if (index < 0 || index >= this.size) {
    throw new IndexOutOfBoundsException("Index " + index);
  }

  // Make a new node
  ListNode newNode = new ListNode(value);

  // Iterate through the list to index - 1
  ListNode current = this.head;
  for (int i = 0; i < index - 1; i++) {
    current = current.next;
  }

  // Connect
  newNode.next = current.next;
  current.next = newNode;

  // Size
  this.size++;
}
```

This looks good, but it won't work for the head because it requires a reference to the node before the head, which (for this style of list) doesn't exist. Add a special case for `index == 0`:

```
if (index == 0) {
  addToFront(value);
  return;
}
```

6.3.5 Removing

Removing the node at a given position requires delinking it from the list. For the head node, this is straightforward: Extract the return value from the current head, then advance the head reference to the next node. If the head is the only node, this will set the head to `null`, which is correct.

```
if (index == 0) {
  T returnVal = this.head.value;
  this.head = this.head.next;
  return returnVal;
}
```

Suppose that we want to remove the node at position 2 in the list below. Begin by advancing two pointers, one for the node that will be removed and the other for the previous node.

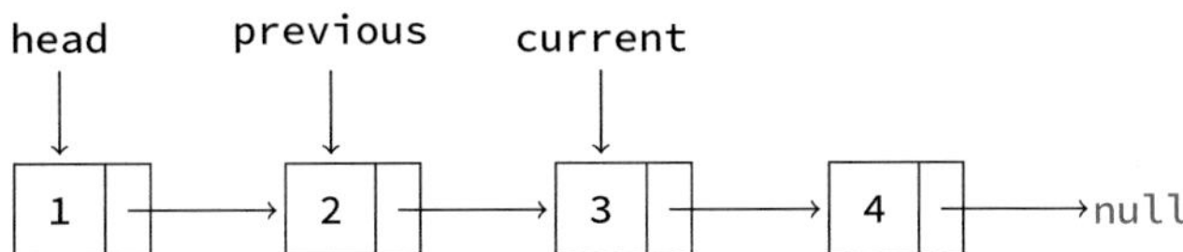

Setting `previous.next = current.next` will delink `current` from the chain.

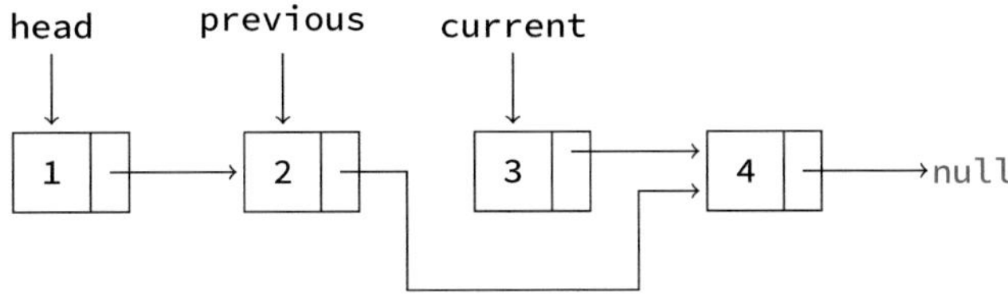

A final optional step is to set `current.next = null`.

Try It Yourself

Here's a partial version of the `remove` method. Complete the implementation.

```
/**
 * Remove value from an arbitrary position
```

```
 *
 * @param  index  the removal position
 */
public T remove(int index) {
  // Check for an out of bounds index

  // Check for index == 0

  // Create two references -- the head is a special case, so
  // we can start at i = 1
  ListNode current = this.head.next;
  ListNode previous = this.head;

  // Loop to the index position
  for (int i = 1; i < index; i++) {
    previous = current;
    current = current.next;
  }

  // Get the value from current

  // Update pointers

  // Reduce size

  // Return value
}
```

Try It Yourself

What happens to the removed node after it's delinked from the list?

Solution

Recall that Java uses a **garbage collector** to reclaim objects that are no longer being used by the program. The garbage collector runs periodically in the background of the JVM and looks for objects that no longer have any active references; that is, objects that exist in memory but aren't referred to by anything else, and are therefore unreachable. In the case of the `remove` method, delinking `current` from `previous` removes the single external reference to `current`, so it will be reclaimed when the garbage collector runs.

Try It Yourself

What are the worst-case complexities of the `insert` and `remove` methods?

Solution

The time for both methods is dominated by the time to iterate through the list to find the required index position. In the worst case, this might require iterating through the entire list, which is $O(n)$.

6.3.6 Doubly Linked and Circular Lists

The basic linked list has a single head reference and forward links to each node in the chain. This arrangement makes interacting with the head node $O(1)$, but most other list operations $O(n)$. Changing the link structure and adding more references can improve performance for some applications.

Doubly Linked Lists

First, consider a list with a **tail reference**, a counterpart to the head reference that always points to the *last* element in the list. If the list has only one element, it is both the head and the tail simultaneously. With the tail pointer, it's now possible to add to the end of the list in $O(1)$ time.

Try It Yourself

Write a code fragment to append a new item to the end of the list using a `tail` reference.

Solution

There are three required steps: make the new node, make it the `next` node of the current tail, then advance the tail reference.

```
ListNode newNode = new ListNode(value);
this.tail.next = newNode;
this.tail = newNode;
```

The tail reference by itself, though, doesn't allow $O(1)$ removal from the list, since removing a node requires a reference to the previous node. A solution to this problem – as well as other issues related to the ordering of nodes – is to make the list **doubly linked**. In a doubly linked list, each node maintains references to both its next and previous nodes.

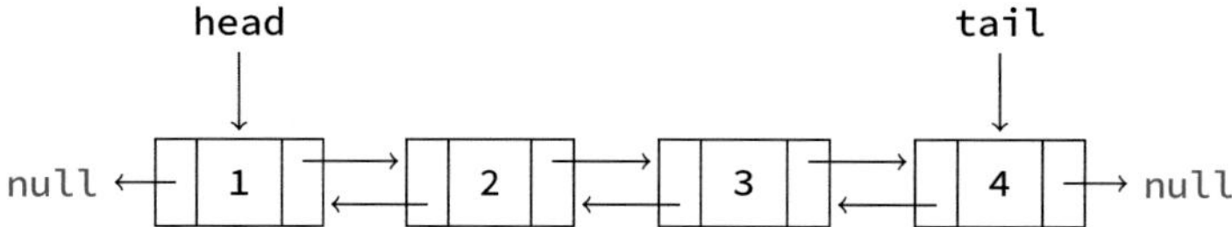

The class below updates `LinkedList` to the doubly linked version. The updated `ListNode` adds a `previous` reference.

```
/**
 * An example doubly linked list
 */

public class DoublyLinkedList<T> {

  ListNode head;
  ListNode tail;
  int size;

  /**
   * Constructor -- create an empty list
   */
  public DoublyLinkedList() {
    this.head = null;
    this.tail = null;
    this.size = 0;
  }

  /**
   * Internal node class with next and previous fields
   */
  private class ListNode {
    private T value;
    private ListNode next;
    private ListNode previous;

    public ListNode(T newValue) {
      this.value = newValue;
      this.next = null;
```

```
            this.previous = null;
        }
    }
}
```

Try It Yourself

Use the method below as a guide to implement `addToFront`.

```
/**
 * Add a new node to the front
 *
 * @param  value  the new value
 */
public void addToFront(T value) {
  // Create a new node with the new value

  // Empty list: head and tail are the same node

  // newNode points to the current head

  // Current head's previous is now the new node

  // Move the head reference

  // Increase size
}
```

Solution

The method is similar to the single-linked version: It creates a new node, connects it to the current head, then moves the head reference to the new node. The new node becomes the `previous` of the old head.

```
/**
 * Add a new node to the front
 *
 * @param  value  the new value
 */
public void addToFront(T value) {
```

```
  // Create a new node with the new value
  ListNode newNode = new ListNode(value);

  // Empty list: head and tail are the same node
  if (this.head == null) {
    this.head = newNode;
    this.tail = newNode;
    return;
  }

  // newNode points to the current head
  newNode.next = this.head;

  // Current head's previous is now the new node
  this.head.previous = newNode;

  // Move the head reference
  this.head = newNode;

  // Increase size
  this.size++;
}
```

Try It Yourself

Most operations in a doubly linked list are similar to their singly linked counterparts, but with the added ability to access the predecessor of any node. With that in mind, consider a `removeFromEnd` method on a doubly linked list with a tail pointer. What is the complexity of that method?

Try It Yourself

Removing from the tail is now $O(1)$. The general procedure (when the list has more than one element) is to get a reference to the node before the current tail, then delink the current tail:

```
// Removing from the end of a doubly linked list

// Reference to the next-to-last node
ListNode newTail = this.tail.previous;
```

```
// Delink the current tail
newTail.next = null;
tail.previous = null;

// Reposition the tail reference
tail = newTail;
```

The end-of-chapter exercises will give you a chance to practice writing more methods for doubly linked lists.

Circular Lists

A **circular list** is one where the `next` reference of the tail node points back to the head.

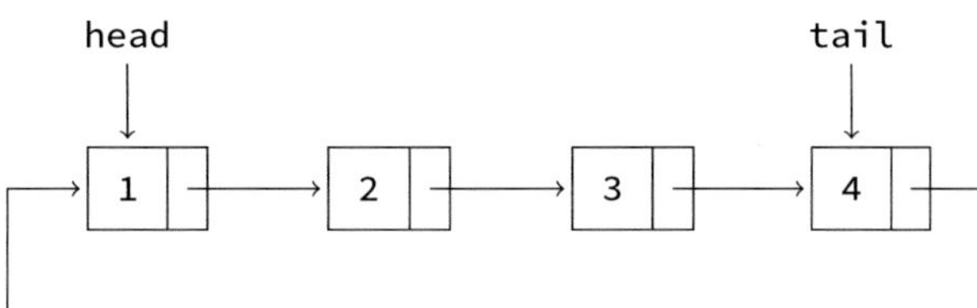

A circular list can also be doubly linked, where the `previous` reference of the head points back to the tail. This is the implementation used by Java's `LinkedList`:

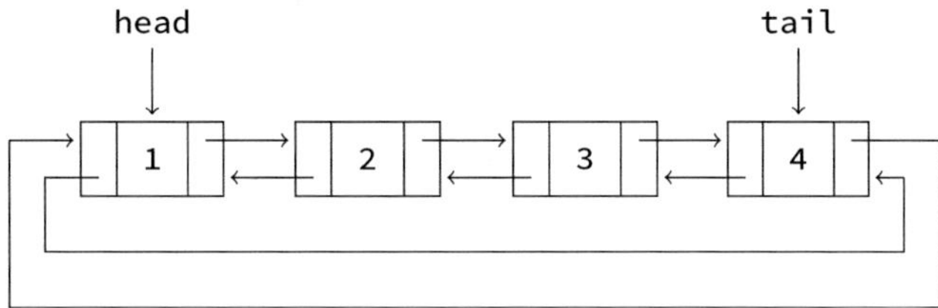

Making a list circular simplifies applications that need to repeatedly cycle through its elements: Every operation simply processes the current node and then advances to the next node, with no special case required to identify the tail and return to the head. Conceptually, such a list functions as a *ring*. A doubly linked circular list also has the small, but nice, advantage that all insert and remove operations use the same steps, without the need for special cases at the head and tail.

6.4 Project: *Snake*

Let's use our new list powers and build the classic *Snake* game. The player controls a "snake" of square blocks. The snake moves continuously in one of the four cardinal directions and changes direction when the player presses an arrow key. "Pellets," represented by square blocks, appear on the screen at random locations. When the snake "eats" a pellet by passing over it, the body grows by one block. The game ends if the snake collides with its own body. In addition to illustrating how to use a list to manage data that grow over the life of the program, this example will also show how to add keyboard input to a graphical application using `KeyListener`, and how to use the `Rectangle` class to represent interactions between game objects. Figure 6.1 shows an image of the finished game.

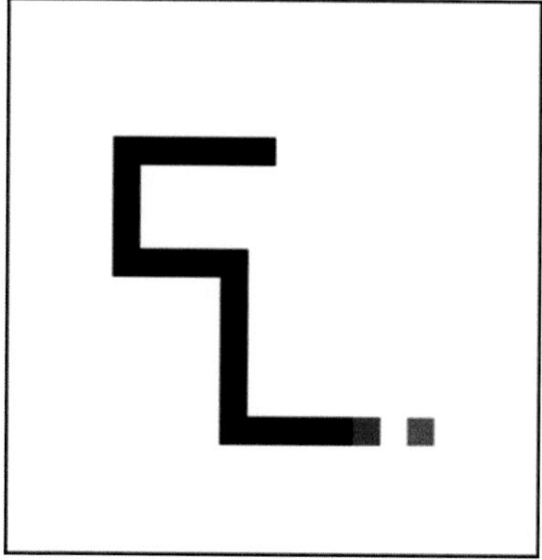

Figure 6.1 Picture of the final *Snake* game.

6.4.1 The `Snake` class

`Snake` illustrates some general strategies for simple 2D games. The basic setup is the following:

- Initialize the `JFrame` and `Canvas` that provide the game window. These steps are similar to our earlier graphical programs from Chapters 3 and 4.
- Implement `KeyListener` and use the `keyPressed` method to respond to keyboard input. The next section will explain how this works.
- Call a `run` method that implements the main game loop. This method will repeatedly update the positions of each game element, check for interactions, and call `repaint` to draw the screen.

Starter code for `Snake` is given below. We'll fill in the constructor, `keyPressed`, `run`, and `paint`.

```
/**
 * SNAKE
 */

import java.awt.Graphics;
import java.awt.Image;
import java.awt.Canvas;
import java.awt.Color;
import java.awt.Rectangle;
import java.awt.event.KeyListener;
import java.awt.event.KeyEvent;
import javax.swing.JFrame;
```

```
import java.util.LinkedList;

// Enumerated type representing the snake's direction
enum Direction {
 RIGHT, LEFT, UP, DOWN;
}

public class Snake extends Canvas implements KeyListener {

  // Game objects
  private LinkedList<Rectangle> snake;
  private Rectangle pellet;
  private Direction direction;

  // Constants
  private final int WIDTH = 400;
  private final int HEIGHT = 400;
  private final int SIZE = 10;  // Side length of squares

  /**
   * Constructor - set initial positions of snake and pellet
   */
  public Snake() {

  }

  /**
   * Listen for keyboard input
   */
  public void keyPressed(KeyEvent e) {

  }

  public void keyTyped(KeyEvent e) { /* Empty */ }
  public void keyReleased(KeyEvent e) { /* Empty */ }

  /**
   * Draw each object to the screen
```

```
     */
    public void paint(Graphics g) {

    }

    /**
     * The main game loop
     */
    public void run() {

    }

    /**
     * Main
     */
    public static void main(String[] args) {
      // Construct the driver object
      Snake game = new Snake();

      // Create a JFrame and attach the driver to it
      JFrame frame = new JFrame();
      frame.add(game);
      frame.pack();
      frame.setVisible(true);
      frame.setDefaultCloseOperation(JFrame.EXIT_ON_CLOSE);

      // Call the run method -- this is the main game loop
      game.run();
    }
}
```

6.4.2 Class Members and Constructor

We're using the built-in `java.awt.Rectangle` class to represent the on-screen game elements. `Rectangle`, as you'd expect, represents a rectangular region of space on the screen, identified by the `x` and `y` coordinates of its *upper-left corner*, its width, and its height. A `Rectangle` can also test for intersections with other `Rectangle` objects, which we'll use to check for interactions between the game's objects. Our game only has two on-screen elements:

- The `pellet` is a single `Rectangle`.
- The snake's body is a `LinkedList<Rectangle>`.

The constructor creates these objects and assigns their initial positions in the game window. Update the method to the version below.

```
/**
 * Constructor - set initial positions of snake and pellet
 */
public Snake() {
  // Set up game window and listen for keyboard
  setSize(WIDTH, HEIGHT);
  addKeyListener(this);

  // Starting locations
  this.snake = new LinkedList<Rectangle>();
  this.snake.add(new Rectangle(90, 90, SIZE, SIZE));
  this.snake.add(new Rectangle(90 - SIZE, 90, SIZE, SIZE));
  this.pellet = new Rectangle(300, 240, SIZE, SIZE);

  // Initial direction
  this.direction = Direction.RIGHT;
}
```

6.4.3 Keyboard Input with the `KeyListener` Interface

Let's give the user the ability to provide keyboard input using the `KeyListener` and `KeyEvent` classes. The top of the program declares an `enum Direction` that represents the four cardinal directions, and the game has a `direction` variable that controls the snake's current orientation. We're going to write a method that uses the keyboard's arrow keys to change the value of `direction`.

`KeyListener` is an **interface**. An interface is like a contract: When a class implements `KeyListener` it is required to provide certain methods that can handle keyboard input. In return, `KeyListener` will check for keyboard activity and automatically call those methods in response to user actions. Specifically, the class must implement three methods:

- `keyPressed`: called when the user presses down on a key. The event records the key and any modifying keys – e.g., shift or control – held at the same time.
- `keyReleased`: called when the user releases a key that was previously pressed down. Like `keyPressed`, it records the triggering key and any modifying keys.
- `keyTyped`: called when a single character has been generated from the keyboard and sent to the system. This is a higher-level event and considers only the output character, which might be generated from a combination of multiple keys.

For each method, the input `KeyEvent` object records information about the keyboard interaction. The `addKeyListener` method called in the constructor is required to make the application receive input. For `Snake`, we only need `keyPressed`. The other methods are still required, but are left empty.

```
/**
 * Listen for keyboard input
 */
public void keyPressed(KeyEvent e) {
  int code = e.getKeyCode();

  if (code == KeyEvent.VK_RIGHT) {
    this.direction = Direction.RIGHT;
  }
}
```

The method uses `getKeyCode` to retrieve the underlying numeric code corresponding to the pressed key. The predefined constant `KeyEvent.VK_RIGHT` refers to the right arrow key. Pressing the right arrow key changes the value of `direction` to `Direction.RIGHT`.

Try It Yourself

Update the `keyPressed` method in `Snake`, then add three more `if` statements to check for the other three directions.

6.4.4 The `paint` Method

Drawing to the screen is straightforward and similar to our previous programs. Use `fillRect` to put each `Rectangle` object on the screen. Notice the use of the enhanced `for` loop to iterate over the contents of the body list.

```
/**
 * Draw each object to the screen
 */
public void paint(Graphics g) {
  // Clear the screen
  g.setColor(Color.WHITE);
  g.fillRect(0, 0, this.getWidth(), this.getHeight());

  // Draw the snake's body segments
  g.setColor(Color.BLACK);
  for (Rectangle segment : this.snake) {
    g.fillRect(segment.x, segment.y, SIZE, SIZE);
  }
```

```

  // Draw the pellet
  g.setColor(Color.RED);
  g.fillRect(pellet.x, pellet.y, SIZE, SIZE);
}
```

6.4.5 The Main Game Loop

Finally, let's write the `run` method, which implements core logic for the game. The loop has four steps:

- Use `Thread.sleep` to pause for a moment.
- Move the snake in its current direction, extending the snake's body if it intersects with the pellet.
- Check if the snake collides with its own body and, if so, end the game.
- Call `repaint` to draw everything.

Consider the problem of moving the snake. We could iterate through the list and update the position of every body segment, but that would be challenging because the body of the snake might bend and twist as it grows. Instead, consider this approach: move the snake by *adding a new head segment* and *deleting the current tail segment*.

With this strategy, almost all of the body segments remain in the same place. The value of `direction` controls the placement of the new head block. This approach also makes it easy to extend the body. On each iteration, check if the snake collides with the pellet block. If it does, grow by adding a new head block *without deleting the current tail*.

Try It Yourself

We could have used an `ArrayList` for the body segments, but a `LinkedList` is a more natural choice. Why?

Solution

Adding to the front of the list is $O(1)$ on a linked list but $O(n)$ on an array list. The performance difference is minor in this case, since the list is always small, but a linked list is generally a better choice when you expect to repeatedly interact with the head and tail.

The implementation of `run` is given below. It uses `addFirst` and `removeLast` to interact with the linked list and `intersects` to test if two `Rectangle` objects collide with each other.

```
/**
 * The main game loop
 */
public void run() {

  boolean running = true;
  while (running) {

    // Sleep for a moment
    try {
      Thread.sleep(250);
    } catch(Exception e) {
      e.printStackTrace();
    }

    // Get the current head segment
    Rectangle head = this.snake.getFirst();
    int newX = head.x;
    int newY = head.y;

    // Use the current head and direction to find
    // the coordinates of the new head segment
    if (this.direction == Direction.RIGHT) {
      newX += SIZE;  // Move one square right
    } else if (this.direction == Direction.LEFT) {
      newX -= SIZE;  // Move one square left
    } else if (this.direction == Direction.UP) {
      newY -= SIZE;  // Move one square up
    } else if (this.direction == Direction.DOWN) {
      newY += SIZE;  // Move one square down
    }

    // Put the new head segment on the front of the list
    Rectangle newHead = new Rectangle(newX, newY, SIZE, SIZE);
    this.snake.addFirst(newHead);

    // If the snake does not eat the pellet, remove the tail
```

```
    if (!head.intersects(pellet)) {
      this.snake.removeLast();
    }

    // Check for self-collision
    for (Rectangle segment : this.snake) {
      if (segment != head && head.intersects(segment)) {
        running = false;
      }
    }

    // Draw
    repaint();
  }
}
```

Examine the code carefully until it's clear what each section is doing. The `if` statements in the middle calculate the position of the new head based on the current head and direction.

Try It Yourself

Complete the `Snake` class and run the game. Experiment with playing it, then make a few modifications:

- Move the `pellet` to a random location each time the snake eats it.
- Modify the `paint` method to draw the snake's head in a different color.
- Add another check to end the game if the snake goes offscreen.

The strategies for this game can be used to build other 2D arcade games.

- Think about the on-screen elements. Represent each one as an object and use lists to manage groups of objects of the same class.
- Use `KeyListener` and the `keyPressed` method to respond to input. Respond to each key press by changing variables that control the state of the game.
- Write a `run` method that implements the main game loop. The method should sleep for a moment (the sleep time determines the frame rate), move the game objects, check for interactions (including the stopping condition), and then call `repaint` to draw every object to the screen.

The next chapter will demonstrate more programs that combine graphics, input, objects, and lists.

6.5 Example Interview Questions Using Lists

6.5.1 Comparing Linked and Array Lists

Think about the complexities of the array and linked list methods we've discussed. In what cases is an array-based list better? How about a linked list? Use a doubly linked list with a tail pointer for your analysis.

Recall that the beginning of this chapter established that an abstract data type might have multiple implementations, with each having its own strengths and weaknesses. We've now seen that both array-based and link-based lists provide the same behaviors, but in different ways. As you might expect, neither list is clearly superior to the other. The table below summarizes the major differences between the two kinds of lists. In general, array lists are good for workloads that require getting internal values; linked lists are better for tasks that require repeatedly modifying the head and tail. Array lists also benefit if you know the maximum possible capacity in advance. The linked list column assumes the doubly linked implementation with a tail pointer.

Behavior	**Array list**	**Linked list**
`get`	$O(1)$	$O(1)$ for the head and tail $O(n)$ for internal nodes
`insert`, `remove`	$O(1)$ for the tail $O(n)$ for the head $O(n)$ for internal positions	$O(1)$ for the head and tail $O(n)$ for internal positions
Memory use	May allocate extra space beyond the size of the list	One node per item, but each node must store links to its neighbors
Contiguity	Items are stored in one contiguous array	Nodes are not contiguous in memory

6.5.2 Reversing a List

Write a method named `reverse` that uses a loop to reverse the order of the nodes in a singly linked list.

Reversing the order of a singly linked list is a classic question. Here, we'll consider the iterative solution, which uses three pointers. Consider the following portion of the list, assuming that `previous` has already been reversed.

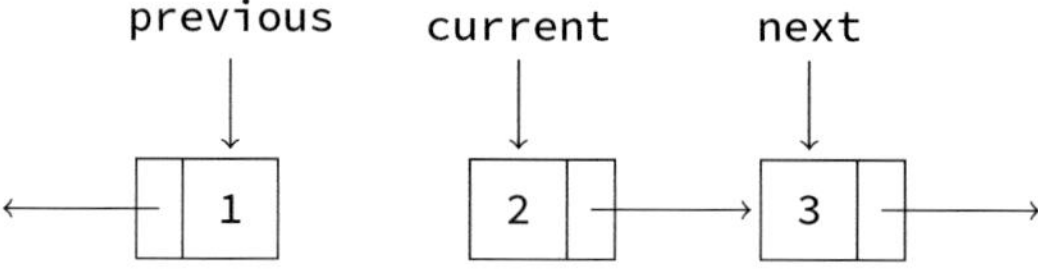

The goal is to reverse the links so that `current` points to `previous`. The `next` reference is used to maintain a connection to the rest of the list so that we can continue to advance after reversing `current`.

```
// Reverse the link for the current node
current.next = previous;

// Move forward
previous = current;
current = next;
next = current.next;
```

Note that the order of adjusting the pointers is important: Once `current.next` has been changed, `next` is the only thing maintaining a reference to the remainder of the list. To initialize the three pointers, start with

```
ListNode previous = null;
ListNode current = this.head;
ListNode next = current.next;
```

This setup will correctly reverse the head's reference to point to `null` and make it the new tail.

Try It Yourself

When does the reversing loop stop? What node becomes the new head when the list is reversed?

Solution

The loop stops when `current.next == null`. At that point, `current` is pointing to the tail node, which will then become the new head.

Try It Yourself

Implement the complete `reverse` method.

6.5.3 The Tortoise and Hare Algorithm

Describe an algorithm for testing if a noncircular linked list contains a cycle.

This question has become popular despite its tricky and not-obvious answer. If you know the size, it's easy to loop through the list and make sure you reach the end in the correct number of steps. If you don't know the size, the preferred solution is the "tortoise and hare" algorithm (Knuth, 2014b):

- Initialize two pointers called `fast` and `slow` to the head of the list.
- The `slow` reference advances through the list one step at a time, while `fast` moves two steps at a time.

- If there is a cycle, it will eventually happen that `fast` loops around and catches `slow` from behind. This may not happen on the first pass through the cycle.
- If `fast` reaches the end of the list, there can't be a cycle.

The core of the algorithm looks like this:

```
ListNode slow = this.head;
ListNode fast = this.head;

// Loop until fast reaches the end of the list
while (slow.next != null && fast.next.next != null) {
  slow = slow.next;
  fast = fast.next.next;

  if (slow == fast) {
    return true;  // Cycle!
  }
}

// Made it to the end without a cycle
return false;
```

SUMMARY

Lists illustrate many of the key data structures techniques that we'll revisit multiple times throughout future chapters. As you're working on the questions for this section, keep the following points in mind:

- The concept of an abstract data type separates the outward-facing behaviors of a data structure from the details of its internal implementation. This is closely related to the idea of encapsulation in OOP, where an object "wraps" internal variables and only allows access to them through a well-defined interface. The ADT defines what operations are possible on a data structure.
- Building a complex structure out of nodes and links is fundamental and we'll use it to implement hash tables, trees, and graphs in future chapters. Make sure you understand the example `LinkedList` class.
- You can analyze many data structure methods by simply considering whether the code interacts with only one data item or with (in the worst case) every data item. However, methods that have a fast and a slow option, like appending to `ArrayList`, might need more complex analysis.

The next chapter will lead you through a guided project to build several graphical applications that require managing groups of objects.

EXERCISES

Understand

1. Give some advantages that lists have over arrays and vice versa.
2. Write a Java statement that declares an `ArrayList<Double>` with a starting capacity of 100 elements.
3. Look up Java's `Vector` class. How does it relate to `LinkedList` and `ArrayList`?
4. I implemented the following code to print the contents of a `LinkedList`. However, the performance of this code fragment scaled quadratically with the list length, even though there's only a single `for` loop over the contents of the list. Why?

```
for (int i = 0; i < list.size(); i++) {
  System.out.print(list.get(i) + " ");
}
```

5. Review the table of comparisons between linked and array lists. How would the table change if we had a singly linked list with a tail pointer?
6. Repeat the previous question for a basic singly linked list with no tail pointer.
7. Suppose you need to iterate through a list in a single pass. That's $O(n)$ for both array and linked lists, but would you expect one to be faster than the other? Tip: Which is typically faster, iterating linearly through an array or through random memory locations? Why?
8. Suppose you need to read n entries from a file and you know the size of n in advance. Which type of list might be the best choice?
9. Write an `addToEnd` method for the basic singly linked list.
10. What is the complexity of `removeFromEnd` in a singly linked list with a tail reference? Why is it not $O(1)$?
11. Add a `toString` method to `ArrayList`. Tip: Look at the `Arrays.toString` method. Can you use that to avoid iterating through the array?
12. Add a method to `ArrayList` called `toLinkedList` that returns the contents of the `ArrayList` in linked form.
13. Repeat the previous question, but go the other way, from a `LinkedList` to an `ArrayList`.
14. Add a method called `ensureCapacity` to `ArrayList`. The method takes an `int minCapacity` as input and enlarges the internal array to ensure it can hold at least that many elements. The method does not add or remove any items.

Apply

15. Add a `toString` method to the `LinkedList` class. You'll have to iterate through the list to get the value of each node and construct a formatted `String`.

16. Modify your `toString` method to work on a singly linked circular list. How do you know when to stop iterating through the list?
17. Add a `toArray` method to `ArrayList` to return the contents of the list as an array. Note that you can't just return the backing array.
18. Repeat the previous question for `LinkedList`.
19. Write an `addAll` method that takes another `List` as input and adds all of its items to the current list.
20. Modify the `get` method of `LinkedList` to use a doubly linked list with a tail reference. Start at the end that is closest to the node you want to retrieve.
21. Suppose that you implement the improved `get` method that starts from the closest end. Does that change the method's overall Big-O complexity?
22. Write a method called `contains` that takes a `T value` as input and returns `true` if the list contains an item equal to `value` and `false` otherwise. Tip: Think about how to test for equality!
23. Write a `replace` method that takes a `T oldValue` and a `T newValue` as inputs and replaces every occurrence of `oldValue` in the list with `newValue`.
24. Implement the `subList` method, which takes a `beginIndex` and `endIndex` as inputs and returns a new list with all items starting at `beginIndex` and going up to, but not including, `endIndex`.
25. Implement the `containsAll` method, which takes a `List otherList` as input and returns `true` if the list contains every item in `otherList` and `false` otherwise.
26. What is the average case of the insert or remove operation on a linked list when all elements are equally likely to be chosen? Tip: Add up the total amount of work required to insert to any of the n positions and then divide by n.
27. Write an `insert` method for a doubly linked list.
28. Write a `remove` method for a doubly linked list.
29. Repeat the two previous questions on a singly linked circular list.

Extend

30. Reverse a doubly linked list. Tip: This one can be painful, but it's a rite of passage. Use three pointers, as in the singly linked example, and think carefully about how to adjust both pointers on each step.
31. Create a class called `SortedList` to represent a list of values that are in sorted order. Use `LinkedList` as a template and write an `insert` method that takes a `T value` as input and inserts at the appropriate position in the list.
32. Modify `SortedList` to use a `boolean ascending` to specify whether the list should be sorted in ascending or descending order. Allow the user to specify the value of `ascending` as input to the constructor and modify `insert` to work appropriately.
33. Add obstacles to *Snake*. The game ends if the snake's head collides with any obstacle. Tip: Use an `ArrayList<Rectangle>` to represent the obstacles. You can start by putting a few blocks in fixed locations, then experiment with randomizing their positions.

34. Make the pellet move around the screen. The easiest way to do this is to move it horizontally or vertically on each frame, wrapping around to the other side when it goes off screen.
35. Add a second type of pellet that makes the snake shrink by removing an extra tail segment. Give it a different color.
36. Add a score counter that increases as the player eats pellets. You can add it to the screen using the `drawString` method of `Graphics`.
37. Modify the *Snake* game to use *two snakes*, one controlled by the arrow keys and the other by the WASD keys. The game ends when one snake collides with itself or the opponent snake.
38. Use two score counters, one per snake, and display both on each iteration.
39. Write a game called `Escape`. Let the player be a `Rectangle` and create a goal `Rectangle` that the player is trying to reach. Update the player's `x` and `y` position in response to keyboard input. End the game when the player touches the goal square.
40. Now add obstacles to the previous game that the player has to navigate around. Touching an obstacle ends the game. Tip: Use an `ArrayList<Rectangle>` to represent the objects. You can start with static ones, then experiment with making them move on each frame.
41. Finally, add a timer. Keep track of the number of frames that the game has generated and convert them to a number of elapsed seconds that you display on the screen using `drawString`. Race to the finish!

NOTES AND FURTHER READING

Linked lists are one of the oldest data structures, having been introduced in the mid-1950s. Several languages developed at that time adopted lists as their main data representation, with the most famous of these being John McCarthy's LISP (*list processing*) of 1960. LISP enjoyed a long period of success as a major AI programming language and has remained relevant through an extended family of dialects that includes Scheme and Racket. If you want to experiment with LISP-style languages, a classic starting point is *The Little Schemer* (Friedman and Felleisen, 1995).

Isn't it a pleasure to study and practice what you've learned?
Confucius

7 Project: Particle Effects

INTRODUCTION

Computer animators have always sought to push boundaries and create impressive, realistic visual effects, but some processes are too demanding to model exactly. Effects like fire, smoke, and water have complex fluid dynamics and amorphous boundaries that are hard to recreate with standard physical calculations. Instead, animators might turn to another approach to create these effects: **particle systems**. Bill Reeves, a graphics researcher and animator, began experimenting with particle-based effects in the early 1980s while making movies at Lucasfilm. For a scene in *Star Trek II: The Wrath of Khan* (1982), he needed to create an image of explosive fire spreading across the entire surface of a planet. Reeves used thousands of independent particles, each one representing a tiny piece of fire (Reeves, 1983). The fire particles were created semi-randomly, with attributes for their 3D positions, velocities, and colors. Reeves' model governed how particles appeared, moved, and interacted to create a realistic effect that could be rendered on an early 1980s computer. Reeves would go on to work on other Lucasfilm productions, including *Return of the Jedi* (1983), before joining Pixar, where his credits include *Toy Story* (1995) and *Finding Nemo* (2003).

LEARNING OBJECTIVES

This project chapter features particle-based systems. You'll get more practice with Java's graphical applications, OOP, and lists by completing two projects:

- A *falling sand simulator*. Clicking on the screen with the mouse drops "sand" particles that fall to the bottom of the window and pile up. This program will show off more coloring and a graphics technique called **double buffering**, which is useful for creating smooth animations.
- A particle swarm simulator called *Boids*, which models a flock of birds using only three simple rules. This project will demonstrate managing a list of independent objects, each of which maintains its own position, velocity, and movement rules.

The end-of-chapter extensions will show you how to use the particle concept to create some neat old-school visual effects.

7.1 Falling Sand

Figure 7.1 shows some example landscapes with different color schemes created by the falling sand simulator. Start by taking a look at the `FallingSand` class below. Like our previous graphical applications, the class uses `JFrame` and `Canvas` to implement a drawing surface. The image is controlled by a 2D `boolean[][]`, where each entry represents one pixel that either does or does not have a sand particle.

Figure 7.1 **Sand landscapes created with the `FallingSand` program.**

```
/**
 * FALLING SAND
 */

import java.awt.Graphics;
import java.awt.Canvas;
import java.awt.Color;
import java.awt.event.MouseListener;
import java.awt.event.MouseMotionListener;
```

```
import java.awt.event.MouseEvent;
import javax.swing.JFrame;

public class FallingSand extends Canvas implements MouseListener,
      MouseMotionListener {

  private final int WIDTH = 640;
  private final int HEIGHT = 240;

  private final boolean[][] sand = new boolean[HEIGHT][WIDTH];

  private boolean active = false;
  private int x;
  private int y;

  /**
   * Constructor
   */
  public FallingSand() {
    setSize(WIDTH, HEIGHT);

    addMouseListener(this);
    addMouseMotionListener(this);
  }

  /**
   * Add methods to listen for mouse input
   */

  /**
   * Draw each object to the screen
   */
  public void paint(Graphics g) {

  }

  /**
   * The main game loop
```

```
   */
  public void run() {

  }

  /**
   * Main -- set up the window and run the main game loop
   */
  public static void main(String[] args) {
    // Construct the driver object
    FallingSand game = new FallingSand();

    // Create a JFrame and attach the driver to it
    JFrame frame = new JFrame();
    frame.add(game);
    frame.pack();
    frame.setVisible(true);
    frame.setDefaultCloseOperation(JFrame.EXIT_ON_CLOSE);

    // Run the main loop
    game.run();
  }
}
```

The `main` method and constructor should be familiar from our previous graphical projects. We'll fill in the `run` and `paint` methods shortly. In addition to the `boolean[][] sand`, there are three other variables: `active`, `x`, and `y`. These are used to create sand in response to mouse actions as follows:

- The `active` variable will be set to `true` when the mouse button is pressed and `false` when it's released. As long as it's `true`, the user is holding down the button.
- Variables `x` and `y` track the position of the mouse cursor; they're updated whenever the mouse is clicked or dragged.
- On every iteration, the main loop checks if the mouse button is `active`. If so, drop a particle of sand at the current (`x`, `y`) position.

7.1.1 Listening for Mouse Input

Reading mouse input uses two classes: `MouseListener`, which checks for button presses, and `MouseMotionListener`, which checks for mouse motion and dragging events. As with `KeyListener`, a class that implements the two interfaces makes a contract to implement a specified set of methods. In return, the `Listener` classes will monitor the mouse for events and automatically call the appropriate methods. Implementing both listeners requires *seven* methods, but we'll only use three: `mousePressed`, `mouseReleased`, and `mouseDragged`. Add the following code to the `FallingSand` class.

```
/**
 * Listen for mouse events
 */
public void mousePressed(MouseEvent e) {
  this.x = e.getX();
  this.y = e.getY();
  this.active = true;
}

public void mouseDragged(MouseEvent e) {
  this.x = e.getX();
  this.y = e.getY();
}

public void mouseReleased(MouseEvent e) {
  this.active = false;
}

public void mouseClicked(MouseEvent e) {}
public void mouseExited(MouseEvent e) {}
public void mouseEntered(MouseEvent e) {}
public void mouseMoved(MouseEvent e) {}
```

7.1.2 Falling Physics

Now for the fun part. Simulating the falling sand doesn't require any complex physical model, just two simple rules. First, if the space below a particle is open, it moves down.

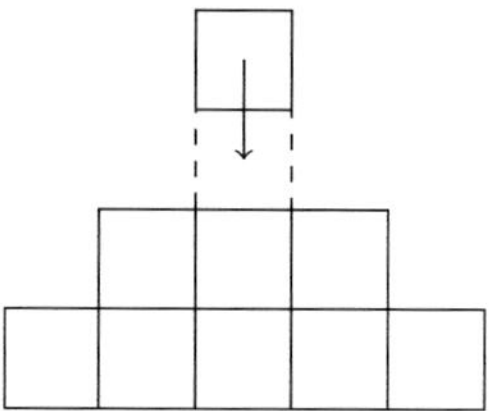

If the space below is occupied, but the down-left or down-right spaces are open, the particle should move to one of those:

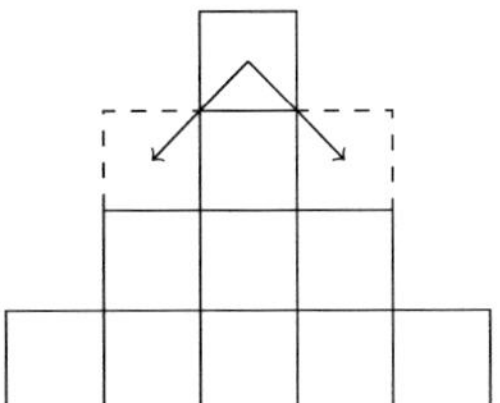

This turns out to be sufficient to generate nice heaping piles from a stream of falling sand. The choice of moving down-left or down-right first doesn't matter, since a stream will quickly fill any open position.

Let's put these behaviors into the simulation. The `run` method does two things. First, it checks if the mouse is `active` and, if so, drops sand at the current mouse position. Second, it loops over the `sand` array and implements the two falling rules. An implementation of the method is shown below; examine it carefully and look at the structure of the `for` loop.

```
/**
 * The main game loop
 */
public void run() {

  boolean running = true;
  while (running) {
    try {
      Thread.sleep(1);
    } catch(Exception e) {
      e.printStackTrace();
    }

    // Drop sand at the current mouse position
    //
    // Notice: the y position is used as the row of the
    // sand matrix and x is the column!
    if (this.active) {
      this.sand[this.y][this.x] = true;
    }

    // Falling physics
```

```
    for (int r = this.HEIGHT - 2; r >= 0; r--) {
      for (int c = 1; c < this.WIDTH - 1; c++) {

        if (!this.sand[r][c]) {
          continue;
        }

        // Try to move down
        if (!this.sand[r + 1][c]) {
          this.sand[r][c] = false;
          this.sand[r + 1][c] = true;
        }

        // Try to move down-left
        else if (!this.sand[r + 1][c - 1]) {
          this.sand[r][c] = false;
          this.sand[r + 1][c - 1] = true;
        }

        // Try to move down-right
        else if (!this.sand[r + 1][c + 1]) {
          this.sand[r][c] = false;
          this.sand[r + 1][c + 1] = true;
        }
      }
    }

    // Draw
    repaint();
  }
}
```

There are a couple subtleties in this implementation. First, observe that the `sand` matrix is indexed using `y` for the row dimension and `x` for the column dimension. This makes sense – row 0 of the matrix corresponds to a `y` value of 0 – but it's easy to overlook. Second, the sand-dropping loop starts from the bottom and works its way up through the matrix; if you have multiple grains of sand in the same column, the lower ones will fall first and make room for the upper ones to move down. To finish the program, add a `paint` method that draws each sand particle as a pixel.

```
/**
 * Draw each object to the screen
 */
public void paint(Graphics g) {
  // Fill the background
  g.setColor(Color.WHITE);
  g.fillRect(0, 0, this.WIDTH, this.HEIGHT);
  g.setColor(Color.BLACK);

  // Draw each sand particle
  for (int r = 0; r < this.HEIGHT; r++) {
    for (int c = 0; c < this.WIDTH; c++) {
      if (this.sand[r][c]) {
        g.fillRect(c, r, 1, 1);
      }
    }
  }
}
```

Try It Yourself

Finish implementing the falling sand program and run it. You should be able to drop black sand by clicking on the window. Try dragging the mouse to create lines of sand across the screen.

7.1.3 Better Performance with Double Buffering

Once you have the program working, you may notice a problem: The screen is prone to flickering as the `paint` method tries to draw every particle. A solution to this problem is a standard technique from graphics programming called **double buffering**:

- Create an "offscreen" image that has the same size as the visible window and obtain a `Graphics` object to draw onto it.
- Paint the entire frame onto the offscreen image rather than onto the visible window.
- Draw the offscreen image onto the visible window as a single operation.

Double buffering separates the action of *changing* the pixels of the visible surface from the action of *displaying* those changes. The first version of `paint` tries to do those things at the same time, which can lead to artifacts and flickering if the rate of change is too high. Use the `Image` class to create the offscreen image. First, add

```
import java.awt.Image;
```

to the beginning of the program. Next, at the beginning of `paint`, create a new `Image` and add a `Graphics` object for drawing on it:

```
// Create an offscreen Image
Image offscreen = createImage(this.WIDTH, this.HEIGHT);

// Get a Graphics to draw onto the image
Graphics og = offscreen.getGraphics();
```

Change the drawing methods in `paint` to use the offscreen `Graphics` object `og` instead of the regular `Graphics g`. Finally, at the very end of `paint`, draw the `offscreen` image onto the visible window with the `drawImage` method:

```
g.drawImage(offscreen, 0, 0, this);
```

The first argument is the image. The second and third arguments are the coordinates where the upper-left corner of the image should be placed, which in this case is the origin of the entire visible window. The fourth argument is a bit wonky: It's an `ImageObserver`, which is an interface that can respond to changes in the state of the image as it's being drawn.[1] The `Canvas` class, which we extended to create our drawing surface, implements `ImageObserver`, so `this` – that is, the object that is executing the `paint` method – can go in the fourth position.

Try It Yourself

Modify `paint` to implement double buffering. Run the program again and enjoy the relaxing vibes of falling sand.

7.1.4 Adding Colors

Now let's modify the painting method so that the sand's color depends on its position. Recall from Chapter 3 that the basic RGB color model represents each color as a mixture of red, green, and blue. It's possible to create custom colors by specifying a combination of these:

```
// Mix red and blue to make purple
Color purple = new Color(128, 0, 128);
```

The RGB components can be either `int` values in the range 0–255 or `float` values in the range 0.0–1.0.

Here's a version of the sand-drawing loop that sets the red amount based on the pixel's horizontal position and green amount based on its vertical position. The amount of blue is constant:

1 For example, if the window is resized while the image is being drawn, the image needs to be resized also.

```
// Draw each sand particle
for (int r = 0; r < this.HEIGHT; r++) {
  for (int c = 0; c < this.WIDTH; c++) {
    if (this.sand[r][c]) {
      float red = c / (float) this.WIDTH;
      float green = r / (float) this.HEIGHT;
      float blue = 0.5f;
      og.setColor(new Color(red, green, blue));
      og.fillRect(c, r, 1, 1);
    }
  }
}
```

To generate a grayscale palette, make all values the same. Here's a version that puts pure black at the bottom of the window and fades up to pure white at the top:

```
float gray = (this.HEIGHT - r) / (float) this.HEIGHT;
og.setColor(new Color(gray, gray, gray));
```

Try It Yourself

Experiment with different coloring calculations and make your own rules.

7.2 Boids

Boids is an artificial flocking simulation method invented by Craig Reynolds in 1987 (Reynolds, 1987). Each boid – short for "bird-oid" object – is a particle representing a single member of a flock, school, or swarm. The goal of the model is to create realistic emergent flocking behavior that could be used in computer animations. The boids technique was used to animate animal groups in films and games, including the 1992 film *Batman Returns* and the 1998 first-person shooter *Half-Life* (Reynolds, 2001). More broadly, boids is an example of an **artificial life** model, a category which also includes cellular automata and Conway's Life, which we implemented in Chapter 4. Artificial life models are interesting because they generate *emergent behavior*, where the dynamics of the group can't be predicted from the rules governing individuals.

For us, this project introduces another useful technique: using a list to manage a collection of graphical elements. We'll create a `Boid` class that represents a single particle with a position and velocity. Each `Boid` will have methods to update its position and draw itself to the screen. The entire flock will be an `ArrayList<Boid>`.

7.2.1 Flocking with Particles

Each boid is a spherical particle defined by four parameters: x and y coordinates and dx and dy velocity components. On each time step, the boid adjusts its current position in the direction determined by its velocity.

(x + dx, y + dy)

(x, y)

Boids adjust their velocities on each time step according to three rules. First, boids want to move toward the average position of their flock.

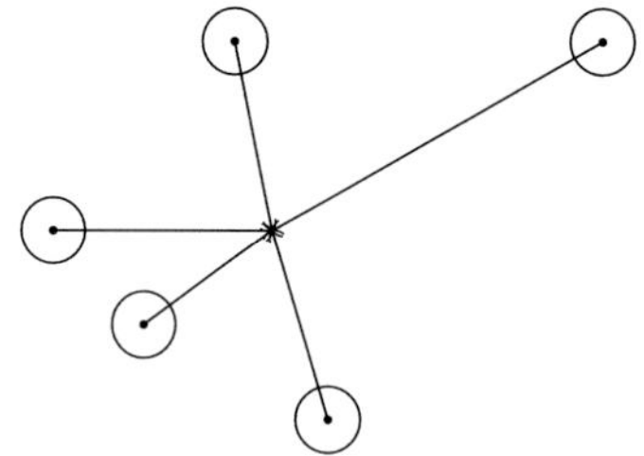

Second, boids want to match the velocities of other boids. Here, the highlighted boid will adjust its current direction and speed to more closely match its neighbors.

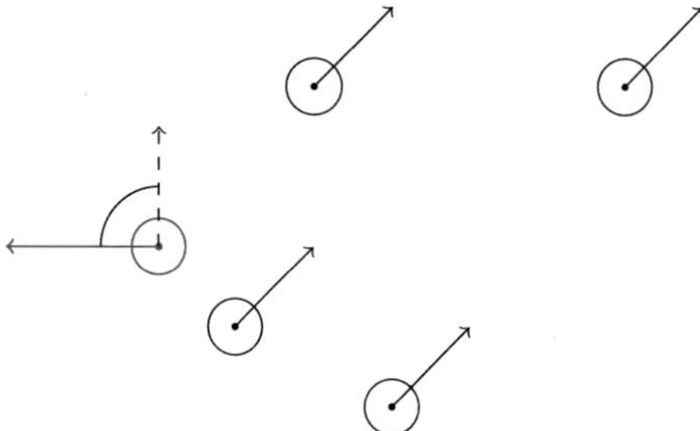

Finally, boids want to maintain separation from nearby boids in order to avoid collisions. Each boid has a radius that it uses to determine how close is "too close" for the purposes of maintaining separation. In the figure below, the boid in the bottom center checks the distances to its three neighbors and moves away from them to create more separation.

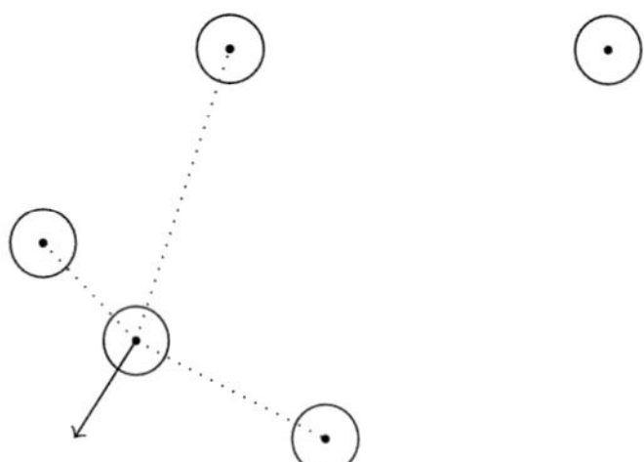

Together, these three rules create flocking dynamics: Boids tend toward a central point and heading, but boids are constantly adjusting themselves in unpredictable ways to maintain separation. The model uses weights to control the relative strength of the three rules; different weights lead to different flocking behaviors.

7.2.2 Starting Code

Here is the starting `FlockingBoids` class. It contains a standard `main` and a constructor, which initializes an `ArrayList<Boid>` that represents all of the particles in the flock. The `paint` method is also simple: It uses the double buffering strategy and simply calls a `draw` method for each `Boid` object. We'll fill in the internal `Boid` class and the body of `run` in the next sections.

```
/**
 * Flocking with Boids
 */

import java.awt.Graphics;
import java.awt.Canvas;
import java.awt.Color;
import java.awt.Image;
import javax.swing.JFrame;
import java.util.ArrayList;

public class FlockingBoids extends Canvas {

  private final int WIDTH = 640;
  private final int HEIGHT = 480;
  private ArrayList<Boid> boids;

  // Parameters for flocking behavior -- experiment with these
  private final double FLOCK_AVERAGE_STRENGTH = 0.001;
  private final double FLOCK_VELOCITY_STRENGTH = 0.001;
  private final double LOCAL_AVOID_STRENGTH = 0.005;

  /**
   * Constructor
   */
  public FlockingBoids() {
    setSize(WIDTH, HEIGHT);
    this.boids = new ArrayList<Boid>();
```

```

    // Initialize some boids
    for (int i = 0; i < 20; i++) {
      this.boids.add(new Boid());
    }
  }

  /**
   * Draw each object to the screen
   */
  public void paint(Graphics g) {
    Image offscreen = createImage(WIDTH, HEIGHT);
    Graphics og = offscreen.getGraphics();
    og.setColor(Color.WHITE);
    og.fillRect(0, 0, WIDTH, HEIGHT);
    og.setColor(Color.BLACK);

    for (Boid b : this.boids) {
      b.draw(og);
    }

    g.drawImage(offscreen, 0, 0, this);
  }


  /**
   * The main loop
   */
  public void run() {
    boolean running = true;
    while (running) {
      try {
        Thread.sleep(20);
      } catch(Exception e) {
        e.printStackTrace();
      }

      //*** Add in the flocking rules ***//
```

```

      // Update positions
      for (Boid b : this.boids) {
        b.update();
      }

      // Draw
      repaint();
    }
  }

  /**
   * Main -- set up the window and run the main game loop
   */
  public static void main(String[] args) {
    // Construct the driver object
    FlockingBoids flock = new FlockingBoids();

    // Create a JFrame and attach the driver to it
    JFrame frame = new JFrame();
    frame.add(flock);
    frame.pack();
    frame.setVisible(true);
    frame.setDefaultCloseOperation(JFrame.EXIT_ON_CLOSE);

    flock.run();
  }

  /**
   * Internal class representing a boid particle
   */
  private class Boid {
    // Fill in the class
  }
}
```

Note: This is a lot of code! By this point, though, you should be feeling comfortable with the structure of the class and the techniques it uses. Read through each method carefully before moving on.

7.2.3 The Boid Class

Boid is implemented as an internal private class. Each Boid will have four double variables – x, y, dx, and dy – and a constructor that initializes them to random values. The other two methods will be update, which simply changes the position based on the current velocity, and draw, which draws the Boid using a given Graphics object.

```
private class Boid {
  double x, y, dx, dy;
  private final int RADIUS = 10;

  Boid() {
    this.x = Math.random() * WIDTH;
    this.y = Math.random() * HEIGHT;
    this.dx = (Math.random() - 0.5) * 2;
    this.dy = (Math.random() - 0.5) * 2;
  }

  void update() {
    this.x += this.dx;
    this.y += this.dy;
  }

  void draw(Graphics g) {
    int ulX = (int) (this.x - RADIUS);
    int ulY = (int) (this.y - RADIUS);
    g.drawOval(ulX, ulY, RADIUS * 2, RADIUS * 2);
    g.drawLine((int) this.x, (int) this.y,
               (int) (this.x + this.dx),
               (int) (this.y + this.dy));
  }
}
```

The position and velocity variables are implemented as double so that they can vary continuously as the simulation runs. However, the drawing methods use integer pixel coordinates. Therefore, we have to cast x and y to int in the draw method. Further, Graphics doesn't provide a drawCircle method. Instead, you can drawOval, which takes the *upper-left corner* of the rectangle containing the oval as its input, plus the width and height of that rectangle.

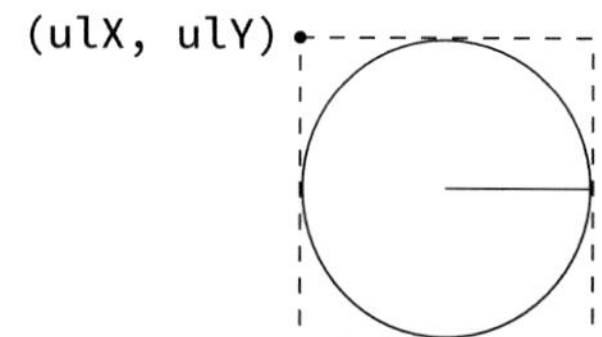

The `drawLine` method adds a line to the `Boid` showing its velocity.

Try It Yourself

At this point you should be able to run the program. It will create some boids at random locations and they'll drift off in random directions.

7.2.4 Implementing the Flocking Rules

To implement the flocking behavior, we're going to add three more blocks of code to the `run` method. First, we'll update each boid's velocity to move it closer to the center of the group. One way to do this is to calculate the average position of all boids, but a simpler approach that works well for this program is to simply move all boids toward the center of the window.[2]

```
double centerX = this.WIDTH / 2.0;
double centerY = this.HEIGHT / 2.0;
for (Boid b : this.boids) {
  b.dx += (centerX- b.x) * FLOCK_AVERAGE_STRENGTH;
  b.dy += (centerY - b.y) * FLOCK_AVERAGE_STRENGTH;
}
```

The parameter `FLOCK_AVERAGE_STRENGTH` (set at the beginning of `FlockingBoids`) controls how aggressively boids are pulled toward the center point.

Try It Yourself

Add the code fragment above to `run`, before the loop that updates the boids, and then run the program. You should see the boids all fly toward the center, overshoot it, then fly back toward it, over and over again. You can experiment with changing the weight parameter to see what effect it has.

The second rule forces boids to match the velocities of the flock. For this step, we're going to calculate the average velocity of all boids, then use it to modify the velocities of each individual.

```
// Calculate average flock velocity
double totaldX = 0.0;
double totaldY = 0.0;
for (Boid b : boids) {
  totaldX += b.dx;
  totaldY += b.dy;
}
```

2 Fixing the central point stops the boids from gradually wandering off. You can also experiment with moving the center point to create a moving flock – see the end-of-chapter extensions.

```
double avgdX = totaldX / this.boids.size();
double avgdY = totaldY / this.boids.size();

// Update boid velocities to point toward the average
for (Boid b : this.boids) {
  b.dx += (avgdX - b.dx)  * FLOCK_VELOCITY_STRENGTH;
  b.dy += (avgdY - b.dy) * FLOCK_VELOCITY_STRENGTH;
}
```

Try running the program again, and you should see that the flock starts to gradually converge. Increasing the velocity weight pulls the boids into a single point.

The final step pushes boids away from their neighbors. Rather than checking against the entire flock, let's define a radius and only move away from neighbors that are within that distance.

```
// Avoid nearby boids
final double AVOID_RADIUS = 40;

for (Boid b : this.boids) {
  double totalLocalX = 0.0;
  double totalLocalY = 0.0;
  int numLocal = 0;

  // Calculate average location of neighbor boids
  for (Boid otherBoid : this.boids) {
    if (otherBoid == b) {
      continue;
    }

    // Distance to the other boid
    double distX = b.x - otherBoid.x;
    double distY = b.y - otherBoid.y;
    double dist = Math.sqrt(distX * distX + distY * distY);

    if (dist > AVOID_RADIUS) {
      continue;
    }

    totalLocalX += otherBoid.x;
    totalLocalY += otherBoid.y;
```

```
            numLocal += 1;
        }

        // Move in the opposite direction of neighbors
        if (numLocal > 0) {
            double avgX = totalLocalX / numLocal;
            double avgY = totalLocalY / numLocal;
            b.dx -= (avgX - b.x) * LOCAL_AVOID_STRENGTH;
            b.dy -= (avgY - b.y) * LOCAL_AVOID_STRENGTH;
        }
    }
```

Look carefully at the calculations that update `b.dx` and `b.dy`: They're written to move the boid *away* from the average of its neighbors.

Try It Yourself

Add the last step into `run`, then view the simulation. Try experimenting with the weight parameters: what happens when you make one larger or smaller relative to the others?

SUMMARY

These projects have demonstrated how simple systems of interacting particles can create complex effects. As you're working on the extensions, think about these ideas:

- Develop incrementally! Start with a simple framework that produces a little bit of output, then add the next feature, then the next one. Don't try to write a huge amount of code without testing it!
- Object-oriented programming is good at modeling "things" that manage their own collections of attributes. Think about keeping the main animation loop and `paint` method high-level and pushing the actual operations down into object-specific `update` and `draw` methods.

We'll return to the graphics and algorithmic art in Chapter 9, which will show off recursive images and fractals.

EXTENSIONS

Dune

Here are a few suggestions for the falling sand model:

- Modify the sand-creating statement to invert the value of a pixel, so you can remove existing sand by clicking on it.
- Add wind to the model: If a particle has nothing to its right, move it in that direction, stopping at the edge. Play around with making drifts and dunes.
- Once you have wind, apply it only to pixels that have nothing above them, so the top layer of a dune can continuously erode away.
- Add keyboard support and let the user choose the color by pressing a number key. To do this, change the `sand` array to an `int[][]`. Use a variable to keep track of the most recently pressed number, then enter it in the array when you create a new sand particle. When you draw a particle, use its `int` value to choose its color.
- Now disable the falling physics and you have a paint program!

More Boids

Modify the boid program to make the center position move around the window. You can give it a velocity and make it follow a path or simply move it to a random location every few seconds. If you get the settings right, the flock will chase the center point around the screen. You may need to increase the strength of the center point to pull the boids toward it more aggressively.

Old-School Fire Effect

Here's another graphic effect that uses a simple pixel-based model. We're going to create a system that simulates a "fire" like the one in Figure 7.2. This effect was frequently used in graphics demos and on the early Internet since it could be generated by a program that was smaller than a comparable animated image (Vandevenne, 2007). The algorithm uses a `float[][]` to store intensity of the fire at each location. The `paint` method will map those intensities to a red–orange–yellow color palette – more on that in a moment. On each iteration of the `run` method, do the following:

Figure 7.2 The old-school pixel fire effect.

- Set the bottom two rows of the image to random `float` values. Use `Math.random()` and cast the result to a `float`.
- Iterate *downward* through the rows, from row 0 to row `HEIGHT` −2.
- For each pixel, add the values of its three neighbors on the next lower row and the pixel two rows directly below it. Think about how to handle the edge columns.

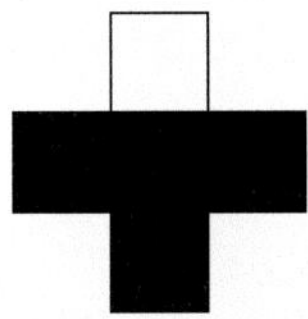

- Divide the sum by a value a little greater than 4.0 so that the averages gradually drop off to zero as you move from the bottom to the top rows.

The `paint` method is similar to `FallingSand`: Iterate through the matrix and draw each pixel. However, to get the right effect, we need to map each `float` value to the red–orange–yellow color palette. The example below calculates three parameters, called `hue`, `sat`, and `bright`, then maps them to an RGB color value.

```
// Paint each pixel -- this.fire is the float[][] of pixels
for (int r = 0; r < this.HEIGHT - 2; r++) {
  for (int c = 0; c < this.WIDTH; c++) {
    float hue = this.fire[r][c] / 4.0f;
    float sat = 1.0f;
    float bright = Math.min(1.0f,  this.fire[r][c] * 3.0f);

    int rgb = Color.HSBtoRGB(hue, sat, bright);
    og.setColor(new Color(rgb));

    og.fillRect(c, r, this.SIZE, this.SIZE);
  }
}
```

The key method is `HSBtoRGB`. *HSB* stands for **hue–saturation–brightness**, an alternative way of defining colors compared to the standard RGB model.

- The first parameter, the hue, selects the color from its position on a color wheel. A hue of 0.0 corresponds to red; increasing the argument moves around the color wheel to yellows, then greens, blues, and purples before returning to red. Here, we're using `this.fire[r][c]` to control the hue. Pixels with values close to 0.0 get red hues; pixels with values closer to 1.0 get mapped to a hue of 0.25, which is in the yellow region.
- The other two arguments – saturation and brightness – control the tone of the color. Saturation values close to 1.0 corresponds to richer, "purer" colors of the given hue; reducing saturation yields softer, less intense shades. Decreasing the brightness parameter makes the color darker and more muted; a brightness of 0.0 is simply black. Here, brightness scales with the pixel value, so that pixels closer to 1.0 come out as bright yellow, fading into progressively less bright oranges and then muted reds.

Starfield

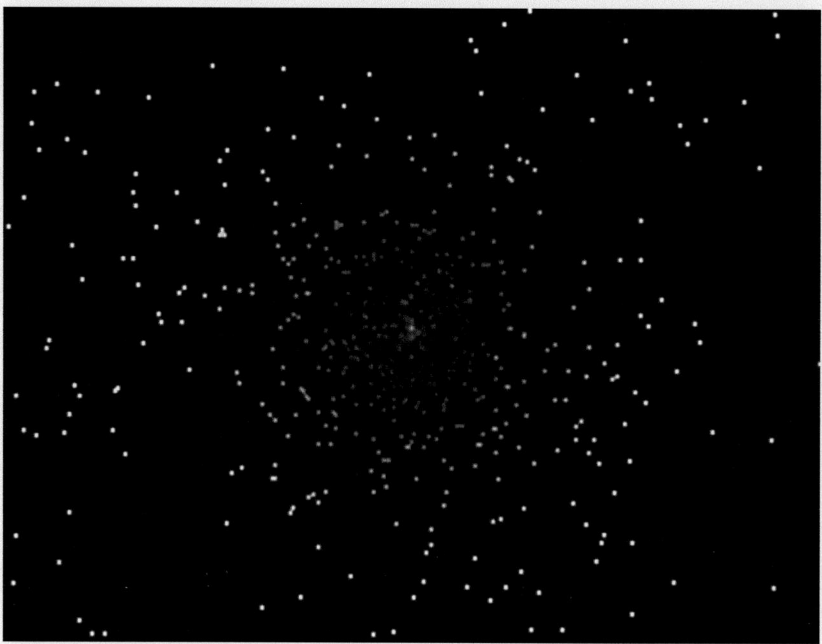

Figure 7.3 Stars emerge from the center point and zoom toward the boundary.

Another classic visual effect: You're zooming through space as the stars fly toward you. This program is similar to `FlockingBoids`: We're going to use an `ArrayList` to manage a collection of `Star` objects, each of which keeps track of its own position and velocity. The star positions are defined using **polar coordinates**. Each star has an offset angle θ and a distance r from the center of the image.

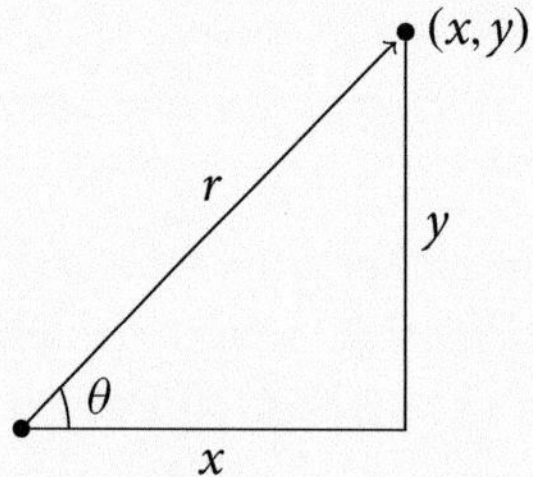

From trigonometry, the corresponding Cartesian coordinate values are:[3]

$$x = r\cos\theta$$
$$y = r\sin\theta.$$

You're in charge of writing the `main`, constructor, `run`, and `paint` methods:

- The constructor should set the size of the window (640 by 480 is a good choice), then create the `ArrayList<Star>` and fill it with new `Star` objects – 200 is a good starting number.

3 You may remember using these formulas for the `Turtle` class in Chapter 3.

- The `run` method loops repeatedly, calling `update` on each `Star` and then calling `repaint`.
- The `paint` method calls `draw` on each `Star`. You'll need double buffering.
- Color the screen `BLACK` at the start of `paint` then set the color to `WHITE`.

Most of the work is in the `Star` class, which has the following structure:

```
/**
 * A star in the Starfield
 */
private class Star {
  private double theta, r, dr;

  // Approximation of the max distance from center
  private double MAX_R = HEIGHT / 2 + WIDTH / 2;

  /**
   * Constructor -- random initialization
   */
  Star() {
    this.theta = Math.random() * 2 * Math.PI;
    this.r = Math.random() * MAX_R;
    this.dr = Math.random() * 0.1;
  }

  /**
   * Move the star
   */
  void update() {
    // Move outwards from the center and accelerate
    this.r += this.dr;
    this.dr *= 1.02;

    // When the star leaves the field, reinitialize it
    if (this.r > MAX_R) {
      this.theta = Math.random() * 2 * Math.PI;
      this.r = 0.0;
      this.dr = Math.random() * 0.1;
    }
  }

```

```
  /**
   * Draw this star to the given Graphics
   */
  void draw(Graphics g) {
    double centerX = WIDTH / 2;
    double centerY = HEIGHT / 2;

    // Convert (r, theta) coordinates into integer (x, y)
    int x = (int) (Math.cos(this.theta) * this.r + centerX);
    int y = (int) (Math.sin(this.theta) * this.r + centerY);

    // Scale the transparency of the star so it gets
    // "brighter" as it moves closer to the edge
    float alpha = (float) (this.r / MAX_R);
    alpha = Math.min(1.0f, alpha * 2.0f);

    Color c = new Color(1.0f, 1.0f, 1.0f, alpha);
    g.setColor(c);
    g.fillRect(x, y, 3, 3);
  }
}
```

The constructor initializes each `Star` to a random position in the field. The star's movement is controlled by a random `dr`; stars with higher values move away from the center more quickly. The `update` method moves the star, then checks the value of `r` and resets it to the center of the starfield when it goes beyond the maximum distance. The stars gradually accelerate as they move.

The `draw` method converts the polar coordinates to their integer counterparts and fills the appropriate pixel on the screen. It's nice if the stars become more prominent as they move "toward" the viewer, which the example method implements by scaling the transparency of each pixel – also called **alpha** – based on its distance from the center. Pixels close to the center are very faint and get brighter as they reach the edge.

For one last flourish, make the stars turn as they move. Put the following statement in `update`:

```
this.theta += 0.02;
```

Engage!

NOTES AND FURTHER READING

Boids, along with other artificial life models, went on to inspire work in other areas of computer science. In 1995, James Kennedy and Russell Eberhart proposed **particle swarm optimization** (PSO), a global optimization technique based on – you guessed it – particle swarms (Kennedy and Eberhart, 1995). The goal of PSO is to maximize or minimize a function of interest. PSO seeks to find *global* optimal values; that is, the best values that exist anywhere in the search space, which is typically difficult to do with standard techniques from calculus or numerical optimization. PSO imagines the optimization process as a flock of birds searching for food. The flock needs to balance *exploiting* known good areas of the parameter space vs. *exploring* for new areas that might be better than the current best results. Like the boids, each PSO particle has a position and velocity. Each particle keeps track of the best point it has seen so far, as well as the overall best point seen by any member of the swarm, and uses those two locations to influence its movement. It turns out that this system balances exploration with exploitation – if the global and individual bests are similar, particles tend to stay in their local areas, but will still move toward a new area if a significantly better global optimum is discovered.

8 Recursion

Life can only be understood by looking backward;
but it must be lived looking forward.
Søren Kierkegaard

INTRODUCTION

Recursion is a fundamental concept in computer science. A recursive algorithm is one that *defines a solution to a problem in terms of itself.* That is, recursive techniques solve large problems by building up solutions of smaller instances of the same problem. This turns out to be a powerful technique, because many advanced algorithmic problems and data structures are fundamentally *self-similar*.

LEARNING OBJECTIVES

This chapter will equip you with the fundamental skills to write and analyze recursive methods. After working through its examples and exercises, you will be able to:

- Implement a recursive method given a description of its recursive and base cases.
- Model the execution of a recursive method.
- Derive the complexity of a recursive method, which is more challenging than simply reasoning about the number of iterations in a loop.

The second part of the chapter illustrates several recursive applications, including combining the `Turtle` class from Chapter 3 with recursion, and recursive implementations of list and string algorithms.

8.1 Writing Recursive Methods

A recursive method is *one that calls itself.* Reasoning about recursive methods may seem challenging at first, because they break the "linear" model of computation that we've generally relied on up to this point. Recursive programs add an extra dimension – you now have to think more critically about the relationship between *how a method is written* and *what it actually does.* The advantage of recursion is that it makes many algorithms easier to understand and code compared to using only basic loops.

8.1.1 Mathematical Functions

Let's start with a mathematical example. Recall that the factorial function, $n!$, is defined as the product of the numbers from the positive integer n down to 1:

$$n! = n \cdot (n-1) \cdot (n-2) \cdot \ldots \cdot 2 \cdot 1.$$

Observe that the terms from $(n-1)$ to 1 are in fact $(n-1)!$, so it's possible to define the factorial function in terms of itself:

$$n! = n \cdot (n-1)!\,.$$

This is a recursive definition: The calculation for $n!$ is expressed in terms of the calculation of a smaller problem. In order to complete the definition, we need to specify a **base case**: the point at which the recursion stops. For the factorial function, $0! = 1$, so an input of zero is a natural base case. The complete function definition is

$$n! = \begin{cases} 1 & n = 0 \\ n \cdot (n-1)! & n > 0 \end{cases}.$$

Given the definition, it's easy to turn it into a method by simply converting the two cases into Java expressions. The base case becomes an `if` statement that returns its value immediately. The recursive case invokes the `factorial` function on `n - 1`.

```
/**
 * Recursive factorial calculation
 *
 * @param  n  positive input integer
 * @return  n!
 */
public static int factorial(int n) {
  // Base case
  if (n == 0) {
    return 1;
  }

  // Recursive case
  return n * factorial(n - 1);
}
```

This is the basic template for recursive methods:

- There is at least one base case, which returns a result immediately. Often, but not always, the base case occurs at a small value of the input, like 0 or 1.
- There is at least one recursive case, which calls the method again with a different input. Sometimes, as in the factorial example, the method uses the recursive result in another calculation to produce the final result. In other cases, the recursive result is returned immediately, with no further work required.

To write a recursive method, *always start by identifying the base and recursive cases*, then translate them into program statements.

Try It Yourself

Like the builders of old, I enjoy constructing stone ziggurats in my back yard. A ziggurat of n levels starts with an $n \times n$ square of stones, then a layer of $(n-1) \times (n-1)$ stones, and so forth, until I finally place a single stone on top. Let $s(n)$ represent the number of stones in an n-layer ziggurat:

$$s(n) = \begin{cases} 1 & n = 1 \\ n^2 + s(n-1) & n > 1 \end{cases}.$$

That is, a single-layer ziggurat is just one stone, and an n-layer one has a base of n^2 stones plus the stones for the $n-1$ higher layers. Convert the definition of $s(n)$ to a `static` Java method called `stones`. The method will take a single `int n` as input and return an `int`.

Solution

The base case is clearly the single-level ziggurat with $n = 1$. The recursive case calculates the total number of stones in the $n-1$ level ziggurat.

```
/**
 * Stones in an n-level ziggurat
 *
 * @param  n  positive integer number of levels
 * @return  number of stones
 */
public static int stones(int n) {
  // Base case
  if (n == 1) {
    return 1;
  }

  // Recursive case
  return n * n + stones(n - 1);
}
```

As you begin writing recursive methods, keep the following key points in mind:

- Every recursive method must have at least one base case and at least one recursive case.

- The base case is often for a small-sized input and allows you to return a result immediately with minimal calculation.
- The recursive case calls the method again with a different input. In general, in order for the process to eventually terminate, the input to the recursive method call should move in the direction of the base case.
- Every path through the method, both the base case and recursive case, involves a `return` statement. It's easy to forget that the recursive path does not simply call the method, but rather *returns the result* of the recursive call, possibly after performing additional work with the result.

8.1.2 Recursive Binary Search

Simple mathematical functions are easy to convert to code. Let's look at converting binary search, which we previously examined as an iterative algorithm in Chapter 5, into a recursive example. Recall that each step of binary search checks the middle of the current search region, then, based on the result, continues searching either its left or right half. Because binary search discards half of the remaining search space on every iteration, it takes in the worst case only $O(\log n)$ iterations to terminate. Although we didn't phrase it this way initially, the process of continuing to search half of the remaining space is recursive. The recursive implementation takes four inputs:

- the array `a`;
- the search value `v`; and
- values of `left` and `right`, which define the current search region.

The base case occurs when `left > right`; that is, there are no more elements to examine and the search value was never found.

```
/**
 * Recursive binary search
 *
 * @param  a  sorted integer array
 * @param  v  the search value
 * @param  left  left index of the search region
 * @param  right  right index of the search region
 * @return  index where v occurs or -1
 */
public static int binarySearch(int[] a, int v, int left, int right) {

  // Base case -- terminate the search with no result
  if (left > right) {
    return -1;
  }
```

```
16
17    // Calculate the middle element
18    int mid = (left + right) / 2;
19
20    // Success
21    if (a[mid] == v) {
22      return mid;
23    }
24
25    // Recursive case #1 -- left half
26    else if (a[mid] > v) {
27      return binarySearch(a, v, left, mid - 1);
28    }
29
30    // Recursive case #2 -- right half
31    else {
32      return binarySearch(a, v, mid + 1, right);
33    }
34 }
```

The first part of the method is similar to the iterative version: Calculate the midpoint element and check if it's the search value.[1] The recursive calls (lines 27 and 32) continue the search by calling `binarySearch` with different input values of `left` and `right`.

8.1.3 How Recursive Methods Execute

It's easy to say, as we did at the beginning of this chapter, that "a recursive method is one that calls itself." But how does that actually work? In particular, how does the system keep track of the different variables involved in the sequence of recursive calls and manage the sequence of returns correctly? Consider the `factorial` function. Suppose we have the following, which calls `factorial(3)` from within `main`.

```
/**
 * Executing a recursive method
 */
public class RecursiveExecution {

  /**
   * Calculate n! recursively
```

1 For simplicity, we're still using the average calculation for the midpoint, but review the details in Chapter 5 on midpoint calculation for the overflow-proof solution.

```
  */
  public static int factorial(int n) {
    // Base case
    if (n == 0) {
      return 1;
    }

    // Recursive case
    int f = n * factorial(n - 1);
    return f;
  }

  public static void main(String[] args) {
    int n = 3;
    int fact = factorial(n);
    System.out.println(fact);
  }
}
```

When a program executes, the system allocates a special region of memory called the **stack** to keep track of both local variables allocated within methods, as well as method calls and returns. Every method has a **stack frame** that stores the values of its local variables. When our example program begins executing, the system automatically creates a stack frame which will hold the local variables defined in `main`, which are `n` and `fact`. Assigning a value to `fact` requires calling `factorial(3)`.

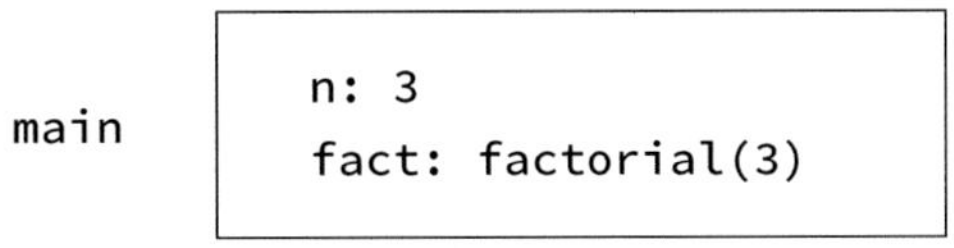

```
main            n: 3
                fact: factorial(3)
```

Every method call allocates *another stack frame* to hold parameters and local variables. Notice that `factorial` has its own input parameter named `n`, which gets the value that was passed as the function argument from `main`. The frame for the most recent method is always at the top of the stack and the oldest frame is at the bottom.

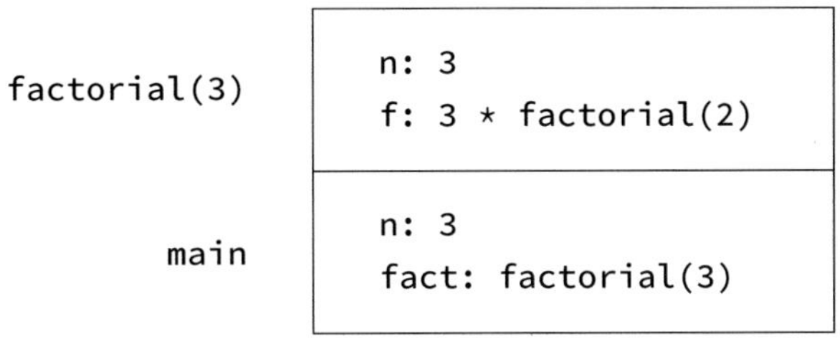

```
factorial(3)    n: 3
                f: 3 * factorial(2)

main            n: 3
                fact: factorial(3)
```

This process continues for each subsequent recursive call: `factorial(3)` calls `factorial(2)`, which calls `factorial(1)` and then `factorial(0)`. Each call allocates a new frame. By the time we reach the base case, the stack looks like the following, where the top frame represents the base case with `n = 0`.

`factorial(0)`	`n: 0`
`factorial(1)`	`n: 1` `fact: 1 * factorial(0)`
`factorial(2)`	`n: 2` `fact: 2 * factorial(1)`
`factorial(3)`	`n: 3` `fact: 3 * factorial(2)`
`main`	`n: 3` `fact: factorial(3)`

Now that we've reached the base case, it's time to unwind and return from the sequence of recursive method calls. Observe that function evaluations lower in the stack are in a kind of suspended state, waiting on methods higher up the stack to finish and return their results. Reaching the base case is what finally stops the "building up" process and triggers the sequence of returns back down the call stack.

- Returning from the base case (the `factorial(0)` frame) "pops" the top frame off the stack and returns the base result, which is 1.
- The next frame, `factorial(1)`, uses that result to calculate its own result, `1 * factorial(0)`, which is also 1.

Try It Yourself

Work through the remaining sequence of method returns. Verify the order in which frames are popped off the stack and the result returned by each one.

Solution

The next frame down is `factorial(2)`, which returns 2 as its result. Next is `factorial(3)`, which calculates a result of 6 and passes that result back to `main`, where it becomes the value of the local variable `fact`, which is then printed.

8.1.4 Stack Overflow Errors

Awareness of the stack allows you to understand and fix one of the most common recursive bugs: the **stack overflow**. Suppose that you write a method like the one below, which makes a recursive call, but omits the base case.

```
/**
 * A recursive method with no base case
 */
public static int factorial(int n) {
  int f = n * factorial(n - 1);
  return f;
}
```

Try It Yourself

What will happen to the stack when you call this method?

Solution

Each recursive call allocates a new stack frame, but there's no base case to stop the recursive process. The stack grows and grows until it eventually exceeds the system's built-in limit on the size of the stack. The stack region "overflows" and the program crashes.

Fortunately, stack overflow errors are usually easy to diagnose and fix. If you see one, it almost always means that you've formulated the base case incorrectly and your recursive calls are not terminating. Think carefully about the base case logic and double-check your code to make sure it's implemented correctly.

8.1.5 Recursion vs. Iteration

Here is a second way in which recursion can go wrong. Consider the Fibonacci sequence, where each number is the sum of the two previous numbers:

$$0, 1, 1, 2, 3, 5, 8, 13, 21, \ldots$$

It's natural to think of defining the Fibonacci series recursively. If $F(n)$ is the nth Fibonacci number, then

$$F(n) = \begin{cases} 0 & n = 0 \\ 1 & n = 1\,. \\ F(n-1) + F(n-2) & n > 1 \end{cases}$$

The recursive implementation is straightforward:

```
/**
 * Recursive Fibonacci
```

```
 *
 * @param  n  number of the sequence
 * @return  F_n
 */
public static int fib(int n) {
  if (n == 0) {
    return 0;
  } else if (n == 1) {
    return 1;
  } else {
    return fib(n - 1) + fib(n - 2);
  }
}
```

Try It Yourself

Code the `fib` method with a `main` that calls it for increasing input values. What do you observe about the performance of the method as `n` increases?

This method seems perfectly fine when `n` is small, but its performance rapidly degrades for values in the range 50–100. In fact, although it seems simple, this implementation is terrible: Its running time grows *exponentially* with the size of `n`. To understand the issue, consider just the top of the tree of recursive calls for `fib(50)`:

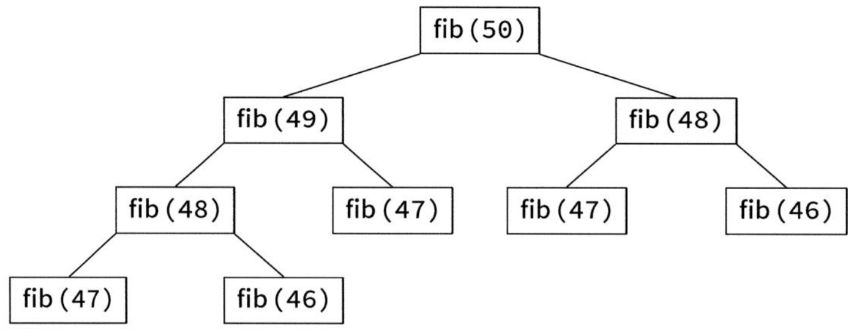

Notice the huge amount of repeated work: `fib(48)` has to be evaluated twice, `fib(47)` three times, and so forth. The bottom of the tree consists of a huge number of evaluations of `fib(0)` and `fib(1)`, each consuming a small amount of time and method call overhead. An iterative implementation would require only `n` iterations. This example illustrates how recursion is only useful if the *underlying computational structure* of the problem supports efficient recursive evaluations. In some cases, you can make the recursive implementation efficient by saving the result of each evaluation, so you never need to calculate the same term more than once. This approach is called *memoization*.

8.2 Analyzing Recursive Algorithms

The algorithms we've analyzed up to this point have been built around simple loops. For the most part, analysis amounted to reasoning about the number of times each statement could execute, then translating the overall amount of work the algorithm could perform into Big-O notation. Recursive algorithms, however, pose a problem for the statement-counting approach, because it's not easy to figure out how many times a recursive method can execute before it terminates. This section presents a useful technique for analyzing recursive algorithms. The key concept is the **recurrence relation**: an equation that expresses the amount of recursive work the problem requires as a function of the problem size n. Given a recurrence relation, we can apply standard mathematical techniques to derive an equation that satisfies the relationship, then convert that result to Big-O notation.

8.2.1 Recurrence Relations

Consider the binary search algorithm. For an input array of size n, binary search will perform a constant amount of work to check the middle element, then recursively search either the left or right half.[2] Let $T(n)$ represent the *total amount of work* that binary search must perform on an input array of size n, inclusive of all recursive searches. The base case is an array of one element, which requires one comparison. A larger array of size n requires one comparison, then searching an array of size at most $\frac{n}{2}$. Therefore, the work required for binary search is described by

$$T(n) = \begin{cases} 1 & n = 1 \\ T\left(\frac{n}{2}\right) + 1 & n > 1 \end{cases}.$$

This is a **recurrence relation**. It expresses the amount of work required for an input of size n in terms of the work required for a smaller problem. Here, $T(\frac{n}{2})$ is the *total* work required to binary search an array of size $\frac{n}{2}$.

The recurrence relation is the starting point for deriving the complexity of a recursive algorithm. The overall goal of the analysis is to find a closed-form function of n that satisfies the relation. We'll do this using the "guess-and-check" approach or, more formally, the *substitution method*:

- Reason about the behavior of the relation by considering the base case and other small values of n.
- Identify a candidate function that matches the observed behavior.
- Using mathematical induction, prove that the candidate function is a valid solution to the relation.
- Convert the function into Big-O form.

This process may seem long at first, but it's mostly mechanical. Consider the recursive case of the binary search recurrence relation:

$$T(n) = T\left(\frac{n}{2}\right) + 1.$$

---

2 We're assuming worst-case behavior throughout this section, ignoring the case where the algorithm finds the search value and terminates immediately.

The relation says that solving a problem of size n (the left side) requires solving a problem of size $\frac{n}{2}$ plus a constant amount of additional work (the right side). We're going to show, eventually, that this recurrence relation is satisfied by

$$T(n) = \log n + 1,$$

and that binary search is therefore $O(\log n)$.

The first step is to get a handle on the behavior of $T(n)$. Start by trying some evaluations for small inputs. We already know that $T(1) = 1$ is the base case, so we can use it to calculate $T(2)$:

$$T(2) = T(1) + 1 = 2.$$

$T(2)$ can then be used to calculate $T(4)$:

$$T(4) = T(2) + 1 = 3.$$

And so forth for increasing values of n. The goal here is not to reason about every possible value of n, but rather to try out some numbers and get a feel for how the recurrence behaves.

Try It Yourself

Fill out the table below, then think about $T(n)$. What is a function that satisfies the relationship that you see between n and $T(n)$?

n	$T(n)$
1	1
2	2
4	3
8	
16	
32	
64	

Solution

Unsurprisingly, $T(n)$ appears to scale logarithmically: Doubling n increases $T(n)$ by only 1. The observed results are satisfied by

$$T(n) = \log n + 1,$$

where the logarithm is taken base-2.

8.2.2 Proving Correctness Using Mathematical Induction

We're not quite done! In order to show that this choice of $T(n)$ is correct, we must prove that it satisfies the relationship for *all values* of n, not just the particular values that we've tested. The technique for doing this is **mathematical induction**. A proof by induction has two parts:

- Show that the guess of $T(n)$ satisfies the recurrence relation for the specific value of n defined by the base case.
- Assuming that $T(n)$ satisfies the recurrence for all values less than some value k, show that it must also hold for k itself.

Induction is like climbing a ladder. The first step establishes, through a specific value, that you can get on the ladder at the bottom rung. The second step establishes that if you have managed to climb up to $k-1$ rungs, then you can continue to ascend to rung k: starting at rung 1 allows you to climb to 2, reaching 2 allows you to climb to 3, and so forth, all the way up to infinity.

The first step is to show that our choice of $T(n)$ is correct for the base case, $T(1) = 1$:

$$T(1) = 1 = \log 1 + 1.$$

We've now established that our candidate function is correct for at least one value of n and agrees with the base case. The second step requires showing that the relation holds for general k:

$$T(k) = T\left(\frac{k}{2}\right) + 1.$$

The induction assumption allows us to assume that T is valid for all inputs less than k, which includes $\frac{k}{2}$. This step is done algebraically by substituting $T(k)$ and $T(\frac{k}{2})$ on the left and right sides, then showing that the two sides are equal:

$$\log k + 1 = \left(\log \frac{k}{2} + 1\right) + 1.$$

Note: Be careful with these substitutions. There are two $+1$ terms on the right – one is from the recurrence relation and the other is from the definition of T. Accidentally omitting one would give an incorrect result. Simplify using the properties of logarithms on the right:

$$\begin{aligned}\log k + 1 &= (\log k - \log 2 + 1) + 1\\ &= \log k + 1.\end{aligned}$$

We've now verified that our choice of $T(n)$ satisfies the relation for any $n \geq 1$. Therefore, the amount of work required by binary search is proportional to $\log n + 1$, which is $O(\log n)$. This process may feel elaborate at first, but remember that the only "hard" step was deciding on a good guess for $T(n)$. If your guess is correct, the proof by induction will usually go through very smoothly.

Try It Yourself

Using induction, show that the recurrence

$$T(n) = 2T\left(\frac{n}{2}\right) + n$$

is satisfied by $T(n) = n \log n$. Use $T(1) = 0$ for the base case.

Solution

This is an important recurrence. It shows up frequently in divide-and-conquer algorithms that split an input into two subproblems, recursively solve those subproblems, then do $O(n)$ work to glue the recursive results back together and calculate the final output. Start by showing that the choice of $T(n)$ is correct for the base case:

$$T(1) = 0 = 1 \log 1.$$

The second step is to show that the relationship holds for a general k, assuming that it's valid for smaller values:

$$k \log k = 2\left(\tfrac{k}{2} \log \tfrac{k}{2}\right) + k.$$

Simplifying the right-hand side:

$$\begin{aligned} k \log k &= k \log k - k \log 2 + k \\ &= k \log k. \end{aligned}$$

8.3 Example: Drawing Recursive Trees

The turtle is back! This extension will work through a classic recursive algorithm using the `Turtle` class from Chapter 3. The recursive tree-drawing algorithm grows realistic or otherworldly trees by successive branching. Each branch has the same structure as the larger tree.

8.3.1 Symmetric Trees

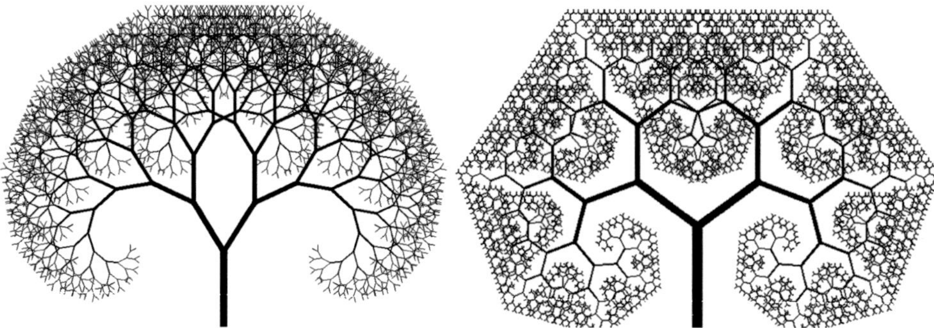

The basic tree-drawing procedure is simple:

- Start with the turtle at the bottom center of the canvas, facing north.
- Move forward to draw the trunk of the tree.
- Turn left, then recursively draw the left side.
- After finishing the left branch, turn right and recursively draw the right side.

- When both sides are complete, return to the base of the tree, facing in the same direction as at the start. This step is important in order for the turtle to be aligned properly to draw the next recursive subtree.

The following method illustrates the basic procedure. It takes three parameters: the length of the trunk, the angle for the left and right turns, and a scale factor that shrinks the trunk length for each successive branch.

```
/**
 * Draw a recursive tree using the turtle
 *
 * @param  count  the number of remaining recursive steps
 * @param  length  trunk length
 * @param  angle  turn angle for the left and right branches
 * @param  scale  reduces the trunk length on each step
 */
public void tree(int count, double length, double angle, double scale) {
  if (count == 0) {
    return;
  }

  // Draw the trunk
  move(length);

  // Left subtree
  turnLeft(angle);
  tree(count - 1, length * scale, angle, scale);

  // Turn back to center
  turnRight(angle);

  // Right subtree
  turnRight(angle);
  tree(count - 1, length * scale, angle, scale);

  // Return to the base of the tree
  turnLeft(angle);
  turnLeft(180);
  move(length);
  turnLeft(180);
}
```

Add this method to the `Turtle` class and experiment with drawing some trees. The right example tree above has an angle of 45 degrees and a scale of 0.80. Angles close to 90 create very artificial geometric shapes.

8.3.2 Adjusting Branch Thickness

The trees look a little spindly, since all of their branches are the same thickness. To create more aesthetic trees, modify the `Turtle` class's `paint` method to make the thickness of each line proportional to its length. Recall from Chapter 3 that the `Turtle` object maintains an `ArrayList<Line2D>` that it uses to paint the image. Each `Line2D` has four coordinates representing its start and end points. Modify the `paint` method to calculate the length of the line segment and then adjust the thickness of the line before drawing:

```
1  // Main drawing loop in Turtle's paint method
2  for (Line2D line : this.lines) {
3    int startX = (int) line.getX1();
4    int startY = (int) line.getY1();
5    int endX = (int) line.getX2();
6    int endY = (int) line.getY2();
7
8    // Set the width of the line as a function of its length
9    double length = Math.sqrt(Math.pow(endX - startX, 2) +
10                             Math.pow(endY - startY, 2));
11
12   // Make the line's thickness proportional to its length
13   Graphics2D g2 = (Graphics2D) g;
14   g2.setStroke(new BasicStroke((int) length / 10));
15
16   // Draw
17   g.drawLine(startX, startY, endX, endY);
18 }
```

Line 13 takes the `Graphics` object `g` and casts it to a `Graphics2D`, which has access to more methods. One of those methods is `setStroke`, which takes a `BasicStroke` object describing the width of the line. Line 14 creates a `BasicStroke` and sets its stroke size proportional to the length of the line. Add import statements for both classes:

```
import java.awt.Graphics2D;
import java.awt.BasicStroke;
```

You can vary the scaling by changing the divisor; 10 is a good starting value.

8.3.3 Asymmetric and Randomized Trees

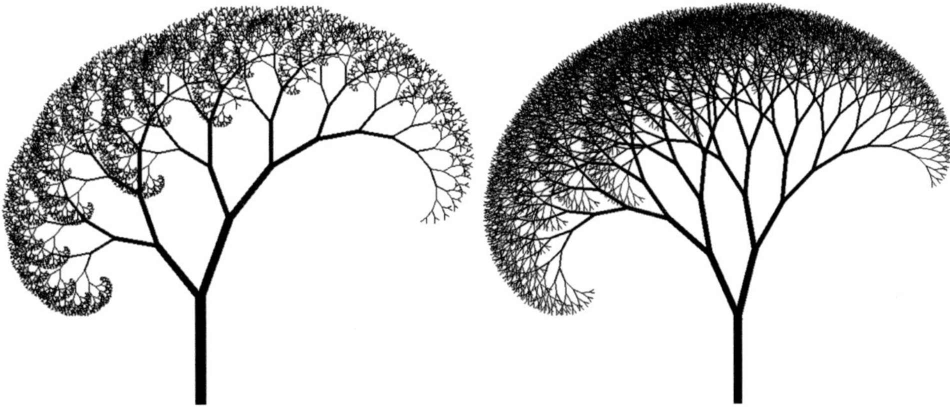

Real trees, of course, are not perfectly symmetric. Modify the `tree` method to take separate scale and angle parameters for the left and right branches: `leftAngle`, `leftScale`, `rightAngle`, and `rightScale`. Adjust the body of the method to turn at the appropriate angles and pass in the appropriate trunk lengths when making the recursive method calls. For example, when you draw the left subtree:

```
// Draw the left subtree
turnLeft(leftAngle);
tree(count - 1, length * leftScale, leftAngle, leftScale,
     rightAngle, rightScale);

// Turn back to center -- undo the previous turn by leftAngle
turnRight(leftAngle);
```

And likewise for the right subtree. With this version, you can create some nice sweeping trees by letting one side grow longer than the other with a shallower turn angle, as shown in the examples above. Try starting with:

```
// Make Turtle t draw a gently sweeping tree
t.tree(13, 60, 33, 0.77, 15, 0.82);
```

To go further, slightly randomize the turn angles and scale lengths. The full method below adds two more parameters, `angleWidth` and `scaleWidth`, and uses them to randomly adjust the angle and scale on each step:

```
/**
 * Draw a recursive tree using the turtle
 *
 * @param  count  the number of remaining recursive steps
 * @param  length  trunk length
```

```
 * @param  leftAngle  turn angle for the left branch
 * @param  leftScale  scale for the left branch
 * @param  rightAngle  turn angle for the right branch
 * @param  rightScale  scale for the rightBranch
 * @param  angleWidth  maximum random change in angle
 * @param  scaleWidth  maximum random change in scale
 */
public void tree(int count, double length, double leftAngle,
                 double leftScale, double rightAngle,
                 double rightScale, double angleWidth,
                 double scaleWidth) {

  // Base case
  if (count == 0) {
    return;
  }

  // Draw the trunk
  move(length);

  // Randomized angle and length scaling for the left side
  double randLeftAngle = (Math.random() - 0.5) * angleWidth
                         + leftAngle;
  double randLeftScale = (Math.random() - 0.5) * scaleWidth
                         + leftScale;

  // Left subtree
  turnLeft(randLeftAngle);
  tree(count - 1, length * randLeftScale, leftAngle, leftScale,
       rightAngle, rightScale, angleWidth, scaleWidth);

  // Turn back to center
  turnRight(randLeftAngle);

  // Randomized angle and length scaling for the right side
  double randRightAngle = (Math.random() - 0.5) * angleWidth
                          + rightAngle;
  double randRightScale = (Math.random() - 0.5) * scaleWidth
```

```
                              + rightScale;

    // Right subtree
    turnRight(randRightAngle);
    tree(count - 1, length * randRightScale, leftAngle, leftScale,
         rightAngle, rightScale, angleWidth, scaleWidth);

    // Return to the base of the tree
    turnLeft(randRightAngle);
    turnLeft(180);
    move(length);
    turnLeft(180);
}
```

With this version, you can create tree structures that range from the natural to the chaotic. Try the following call as a starting point then experiment with making the turns and scales asymmetric:

```
// Make Turtle t draw a chaotic tree
t.tree(13, 60, 33, 0.77, 33, 0.77, 66, 0.05);
```

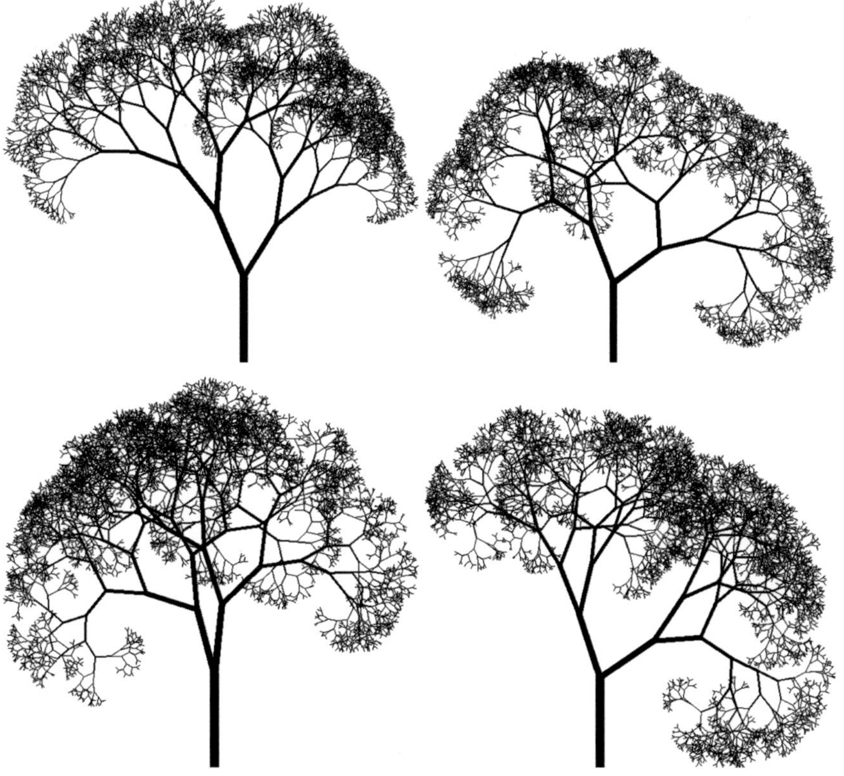

8.4 Example Interview Questions Using Recursion

8.4.1 Reverse a List

Write a recursive method that takes a list as input and returns its reversal.

This question illustrates a useful strategy for recursive methods that operate on sequences: Separate the input into its first element and the sublist (or substring) of the remaining elements, recursively perform the procedure on the sublist, then add back in the first element. For reversal, the procedure can look like this:

- Separate the first element from the remaining elements.
- Reverse the sublist.
- Add the first element onto the back end to get the complete reversed list.

Thus, the complete reversal of the list is defined in terms of the reversal of the sublist, plus a bit of work involving the first element. The base case is a list of one element, which is its own reversal. The program below shows an example solution that reverses a `List<Integer>`. Here, `List` is a general, top-level data type that can be used to refer to any Java list,[3] without worrying about whether it's an `ArrayList` or `LinkedList`. The `subList` method takes a starting and ending index and returns a `List` of all items beginning at the start and going up to, but not including, the end.

```
/**
 * Reverse a list recursively
 *
 * @param  a  the input list
 * @return  the reversed list
 */
public static List<Integer> reverse(List<Integer> a) {
  // Base case:
  if (a.size() <= 1) {
    return a;
  }

  // Get first element
  int first = a.get(0);

  // Extract sublist
  List<Integer> rest = a.subList(1, a.size());

```

3 That is, any class that implements the `List` interface, which describes all the common methods that Java lists should provide.

```
    // Recursive operation
    rest = reverse(rest);

    // Append first element to reversed sublist
    rest.add(first);
    return rest;
}
```

8.4.2 Decimal to Binary Conversion

Write a recursive method called `convert` that takes a nonnegative integer `n` as input and returns its unsigned binary representation as a `String`. For example, `convert(10)` should return `"1010"` and `convert(32)` should return `"100000"`.

This problem seems like it should be easier than it really is. It's intuitive that the solution must somehow involve calling `convert(n / 2)`, but determining the correct recursive relationship is tricky. Let's think through a few cases.

- `convert(1)` is `"1"`. We can treat this as a base case.
- `convert(2)` is `"10"`, which is equivalent to `convert(1) + "0"`.
- `convert(3)` is `"11"`, which is equal to `convert(1) + "1"`.
- `convert(4)` is `"100"`, which is equal to `convert(2) + "0"`.
- `convert(5)` is `"101"`, which is equal to `convert(2) + "1"`.

Working through the cases begins to reveal a pattern. For even values of `n`,

```
convert(n) = convert(n / 2) + "0"
```

For odd values,

```
convert(n) = convert(n / 2) + "1"
```

Conceptually, given the result of `convert(n / 2)`, you can determine `convert(n)` by left-shifting and then appending the correct value of the rightmost bit.

```
/**
 * Decimal to binary conversion
 *
 * @param  n  positive integer to convert
 * @return  binary string form of n
 */
public static String convert(int n) {
  // Base cases
```

```
    if (n == 0) {
      return "0" ;
    } else if (n == 1) {
      return "1";
    }

    // Recursive case
    String bits = convert(n / 2);

    if (n % 2 == 0) {
      return bits + "0";
    } else {
      return bits + "1";
    }
}
```

8.4.3 Moving on a Chessboard

Place a pawn on the upper-left square of a standard 8×8 chessboard. Suppose you'd like to move the pawn from the upper-left to the lower-right square by moving only *right or down*. How many different paths can you take between the upper-left and lower-right squares on the board if you can only move right or down?

This problem is representative of a category of recursive questions that might be described as *count the ways*. The general strategy is to consider the desired final state – in this case, being on the lower-right square of the chessboard – and then reason about where the pawn must have been *on the previous step*. The pawn could only have reached the final position by moving right or down, so there are two possibilities:

- It could have been one square above the final square, and then moved down.
- It could have been one square left, and then moved right.

Let `paths(r, c)` be the number of ways to reach the square at row `r` and column `c`. In general:

```
paths(r, c) = paths(r - 1, c) + paths(r, c - 1)
```

The base case occurs at the first row or first column. There is only one way to reach a square in the first row – moving continuously right – and likewise with moving down for the first column. Therefore, a code implementation of `paths` could look like the following. This code assumes zero-based indexing.

```
/**
 * Number of ways of reaching square (r, c)
```

```
   * if you can only move right or down
   *
   * @param  r  zero-based row index
   * @param  c  zero-based column index
   * @return  number of ways of reaching (r, c)
   */
  public static int paths(int r, int c) {
    // Base cases: first row or first column
    if (r == 0  || c == 0) {
      return 1;
    }

    // Recursive case
    return paths(r - 1, c) + paths(r, c - 1);
  }
```

Running `paths(7, 7)` will show that there are 3,432 ways to move from the upper-left to the lower-right while moving only right or down.

SUMMARY

Recursion is a fundamental concept in computer science. Developing the ability to think recursively is an essential skill for working with more advanced algorithms and data structures. As you're working through the examples and exercises in this chapter, keep the following points in mind:

- Every recursive method must have at least one base case and at least one recursive case. The base case is an input that allows you to return a result immediately. When in doubt, return to thinking about the base and recursive cases.
- Proving the complexity of a recursive algorithm is not something you'll need to do on a daily basis, but working through a few problems will deepen your understanding and prepare you for other kinds of advanced algorithm analysis.
- The "take off the first element" and "count the ways" strategies are useful templates for many recursive list and string algorithms.

We'll continue to work with recursive algorithms throughout the rest of this book. In particular, the next chapter focuses on recursive graphics programs and Chapter 10 introduces recursive sorting algorithms.

EXERCISES

Understand

1. Review the `stones` method from Section 8.1.1. What is the result of `stones(8)`?
2. What is the result of the following recursive method when the input is 24?

```
public static int rec(int a) {
  if (a > 25) {
    return a - 25;
  }

  return rec(a + 5);
}
```

3. The following method is recursive but includes a randomized choice. Make an argument that it will still successfully terminate for any input.

```
public static int randRec(int x) {
  if (x <= 0) {
    return x;
  }

  if (Math.random() < 0.50) {
    return randRec(x - 1);
  } else {
    return randRec(x / 2);
  }
}
```

4. Review the example `fib` method that calculates Fibonacci numbers. What happens if the input argument `n` is negative?
5. Draw out, step by step, a stack diagram for the evaluation of `fib(3)`.
6. Write a method called `power` that takes two positive integer inputs `a` and `b` and recursively calculates a^b. Tip: $a^b = a \cdot a^{b-1}$.
7. Review the example that reverses a list recursively. Modify it to reverse a `String`.
8. Return to the example of moving from the upper-left to the lower-right square on a chessboard. How many possible paths are there if you can only move right, down, or diagonally down-right?
9. What if you can move right, down, diagonally down-right, or in a down-down-right L-shape, like a knight?

10. Write a recursive method that takes a `String` as input and returns a count of the vowels it contains. Don't use any loops. Tip: Yes, there is no real reason to do this recursively, but thinking about the relationship between simple iterative algorithms and their recursive equivalents will help develop your intuition for recursive solutions.

11. Write a recursive method that takes two `String` values as input and returns `true` if they are equal and `false` otherwise. Don't use any loops.

Apply

12. Write a method that reverses a `List<String>` and also reverses its individual strings. That is, the method returns a reversed list of the reversed strings.

13. Given a positive integer x_n, the *hailstone sequence* defines the next number in the sequence, x_{n+1} to be

$$x_{n+1} = \begin{cases} x_n/2 & \text{if } x \text{ is even} \\ 3x_n + 1 & \text{if } x \text{ is odd} \end{cases}.$$

The Collatz conjecture, named after the mathematician Lothar Collatz, proposes that this sequence will always terminate at 1 for any starting value. There are no known counter-examples, but the result has never been formally proven. Write a recursive implementation that prints out the values in the hailstone sequence for a given input `n`, terminating at 1.

14. Modify your program to return the *length* of the sequence starting at `n`. Tip: The length of the sequence is 1 for `n` itself plus the length of the rest of the sequence.

15. The Ackermann function is defined as

$$A(m,n) = \begin{cases} n+1 & \text{if } m = 0 \\ A(m-1,1) & \text{if } m > 0 \text{ and } n = 0 \\ A(m-1, A(m, n-1)) & \text{if } m > 0 \text{ and } n > 0 \end{cases}.$$

Fun fact: It grows rapidly, even for small values of m and n. For example,

$$A(4,3) = 2^{2^{65536}} - 3.$$

Write a recursive method that evaluates the Ackermann function.

16. The Euclidean algorithm, named after the famous Greek mathematician Euclid, is a method for finding the greatest common divisor of two numbers. It's an important result in number theory and cryptography and is probably the oldest nontrivial algorithm that's still in modern use. Given $x \geq y \geq 0$:

$$gcd(x,y) = \begin{cases} x & \text{if } y = 0 \\ gcd(y, \text{remainder of } x/y) & \text{if } y > 0 \end{cases}.$$

Write a recursive method that evaluates the Euclidean algorithm according to the definition above.

17. Show that

$$T(n) = \begin{cases} 1 & n = 1 \\ 2T(\frac{n}{2}) + 1 & n > 1 \end{cases}$$

is satisfied by $T(n) = 2n - 1$.

18. Show that

$$T(n) = \begin{cases} 1 & n = 1 \\ T(n-1) + n & n > 1 \end{cases}$$

is satisfied by

$$T(n) = \frac{n(n+1)}{2}.$$

19. Show that

$$T(n) = \begin{cases} 0 & n = 1 \\ T(n) = 4T(\frac{n}{2}) + n^2 & n > 1 \end{cases}$$

is satisfied by $T(n) = n^2 \log n$.

20. Consider a variant of binary search that checks the elements at the positions one-third and two-thirds of the way through the search region, and uses them to narrow the search to one-third of the remaining array. Write down a recurrence relation for the work required by this algorithm.

21. Consider the problem of getting from 1 to a given positive integer n by repeatedly either adding 1 or doubling the current value. For example, you can get from 1 to 15 with the sequence 1, 2, 3, 6, 7, 14, 15, but that isn't the only way. Write a recursive method that calculates the *number of ways* to get from 1 to an input value of n under these rules. Tip: If the final number is n, think about what the previous number might have been.

22. Write a recursive method to find the number of binary strings of length k that contain exactly n 1s. For example, if $k = 3$ and $n = 2$, there are three possible strings: 110, 101, 011. Tip: There are two cases to consider. Either the last digit is a 1 – in which case the first $k - 1$ characters must have $n - 1$ 1s – or it's a 0.

23. Write a recursive version of `Integer.parseInt`, which takes a numeric `String` as input and returns its corresponding `int` value.

Extend

24. Consider the recurrence defined by

$$T(n) = \begin{cases} 1 & n = 1 \\ 2T(n-1) + 1 & n > 1 \end{cases}.$$

Find a $T(n)$ that satisfies this recurrence.

25. The definition of the Fibonacci sequence is

$$F(n) = \begin{cases} 0 & n = 0 \\ 1 & n = 1 \\ F(n-1) + F(n-2) & n > 1 \end{cases}.$$

The last rule can be rearranged into

$$F_{n-2} = F_n - F_{n-1},$$

or equivalently

$$F_n = F_{n+2} - F_{n+1}.$$

This new rule extends the Fibonacci sequence to negative numbers:

$$F_{-1} = F_1 - F_0 = 1$$
$$F_{-2} = F_0 - F_{-1} = -1$$
$$F_{-3} = F_{-1} - F_{-2} = 2.$$

Write an updated recursive `fib` method that can evaluate both positive and negative inputs. Tip: The base cases are still the same but there are now two possible recursive cases depending on whether the input `n` is positive or negative.

26. Write a recursive method called `removeDuplicates` that takes a `List<String> words` as input and returns a `List` containing only the unique items from `words`. That is, the method should remove any extra copies of any items in `words` that occur more than once, leaving only one copy in the final result.

27. Show that the two-test version of binary search (question 20) is still $O(\log n)$ in the worst case, where n is the length of the input array.

NOTES AND FURTHER READING

The literature on recursion is vast, encompassing mathematics, every aspect of computer science, art, and philosophy. A classic meditation on the relationships among these areas is Douglas Hofstadter's *Gödel, Escher, Bach: An Eternal Golden Braid* (Hofstadter, 1979). The book deals with questions of logic, music, self-reference, and the problem of self-awareness in human consciousness. It includes a famous recursive aphorism, *Hofstadter's Law*, which states, "It always takes longer than you expect, even when you take into account Hofstadter's Law."

Those who do not want to imitate anything,
produce nothing.
Salvador Dali

9 Project: Generative Art and Fractals

INTRODUCTION

Computers have always mixed with art and music. Even in the earliest days of computing, when machines were the size of entire rooms, artists and composers began to harness them to create original works that could only exist in the digital realm. "Generative art" or "algorithmic art" is a term for works created according to a process that evolves with no or limited guidance from a human creator. Rather than directly making choices, the artist instead focuses on the design and initialization of a system that produces the final work. The appeal of algorithmic art lies in its combination of detail, technical complexity, and variation. Generative art frequently incorporates ideas from biology, physics, and mathematics.

LEARNING OBJECTIVES

The previous chapter introduced the idea of recursion and worked through several examples showing how to write recursive methods for mathematical functions, lists, and strings. This chapter will allow you to practice recursion through a different lens: creating generative art and fractal images. After completing these projects, you will be able to:

- Write Java graphics programs that generate images recursively. This requires reasoning about the relationships between the recursive processes and their outputs.
- Discuss the concept of fractal images that exhibit self-similarity at different scales and implement programs for drawing several famous fractals.
- Create a viewing program for the Mandelbrot set, the iconic fractal image. The Mandelbrot set is not defined recursively, but it exhibits an intricate self-similar structure.

These projects build upon the Java graphics concepts that we've explored in earlier chapters. After completing these programs, you should be well-prepared to build original graphical applications.

9.1 Homage to *Homage to the Square*

Josef Albers was a German-American painter, art educator, and theorist, known for his contributions to abstract painting and his writings on color interaction. Born in 1888 in Westphalia, Germany, into a family of crafts people, he first learned trade skills, then trained as a painter and stained-glass maker. He enrolled in the Bauhaus[1] as a student in 1920, then joined the faculty as a stained-glass maker in 1922. Albers married his wife Anni, a weaver, in 1925. She would become one of the twentieth century's leading textile artists. The Albers fled Germany in 1933 after the Bauhaus closed under Nazi pressure and Josef accepted a new position at Black Mountain College in North Carolina, an experimental liberal arts school that emphasized hands-on learning and art making. Before closing in 1957, the college would go on to host a number of figures from the mid-century avant-garde, including the composer John Cage and architect Buckminster Fuller, who constructed the first geodesic domes at Black Mountain. Albers moved to Yale in 1949.

Albers began the *Homage to the Square* series in 1949, accumulating more than 1,000 entries before his death in 1976. The pieces use a formal composition of three or four nested squares and were created to investigate the properties of colors and their interactions. Figure 9.1 shows an example, *Persistent*, from 1976. Let's write a graphical program that will create our own nested square images inspired by *Homage*. Our version will use recursion to construct the square arrangement. Here is a template for the program, which we'll fill in one step at a time.

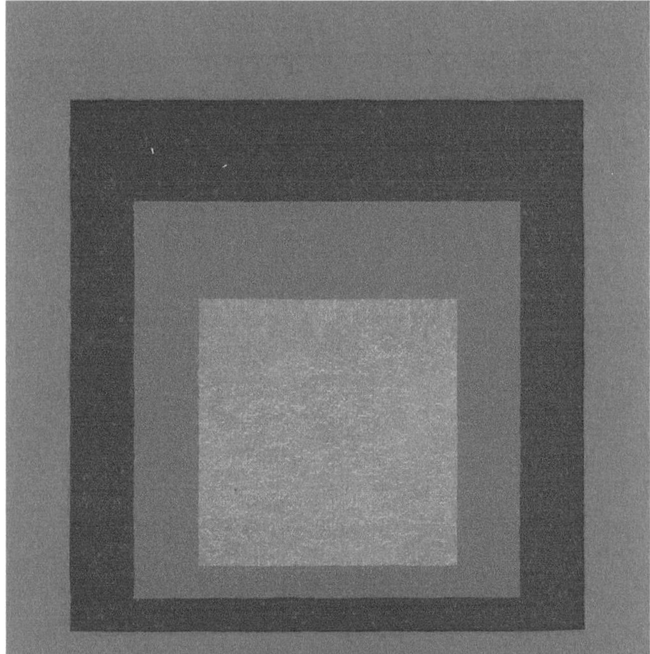

Figure 9.1 **Josef Albers, *Persistent* from *Homage to the Square* (1976). © The Josef and Anni Albers Foundation/DACS 2023.**

1 An important art and design school founded by the architect Walter Gropius. The Bauhaus ("building house") was famous for combining traditional art with industrialization, including new materials and mass production. The school had a major influence on mid-twentieth-century design (Droste, 2002).

```
/**
 * Homage to Homage to the Square
 *
 * Recursively draw nested squares in the style of Josef Albers
 */

import java.awt.Canvas;
import java.awt.Graphics;
import java.awt.Color;
import javax.swing.JFrame;

public class Homage extends Canvas {

  private final int WIDTH = 400;
  private final int HEIGHT = 400;

  /**
   * Constructor -- set the drawing surface's size
   */
  public Homage() {
    setSize(WIDTH, HEIGHT);
  }

  /**
   * Recursively draw nested squares
   *
   * @param  g  The Graphics object for the drawing surface
   * @param  count  Number of squares to draw
   * @param  x  Starting x position
   * @param  y  Starting y position
   * @param  size  Starting square side length
   */
  public void drawSquares(Graphics g, int count, int x, int y,
                          int size) {

  }

  /**
```

```
   * Paint the surface
   *
   * @param  g  Graphics object for the drawable surface
   */
  public void paint(Graphics g) {

  }

  /**
   * Main
   */
  public static void main(String[] args) {

    // Construct the driver object
    Homage h = new Homage();

    // Create a JFrame and attach the driver to it
    // These steps are required to make the window visible
    JFrame frame = new JFrame();
    frame.add(h);
    frame.pack();
    frame.setVisible(true);
    frame.setDefaultCloseOperation(JFrame.EXIT_ON_CLOSE);

    h.repaint();
  }
}
```

Recall, from our previous graphics programs, a few important details about Java graphics:

- The `Homage` class extends `Canvas`, which is one of the built-in Java classes representing a drawable surface. `Homage` inherits the useful properties and built-in methods of `Canvas`, but has its own custom drawing code. The `Homage` constructor sets the size of the drawing surface.
- The `main` method uses `JFrame` to create a visible window.
- The `paint` method contains the code that actually does the drawing work. Remember that you can't invoke `paint` directly; instead, call `repaint`, which triggers the call to `paint` and passes it a `Graphics` object for interacting with the drawing surface.

Rather than putting all of the `Graphics` commands in `paint`, we'll use a helper method named `drawSquares` to perform the drawing operations. The basic strategy of `drawSquares` is as follows:

- Draw a square at position (`x`, `y`) with side length `size`.
- Calculate values for the next nested square's `x`, `y`, and `size`, then recursively invoke `drawSquare` with those new arguments.

The `count` input keeps track of the number of remaining squares. The base case occurs when `count` is 0. The first argument to `drawSquares` is the `Graphics` object provided by `paint`, which allows `drawSquares` to interact with the surface.

```
/**
 * Recursively draw nested squares
 *
 * @param  g  The Graphics object for the drawing surface
 * @param  count  Number of squares to draw
 * @param  x  Starting x position
 * @param  y  Starting y position
 * @param  size  Starting square side length
 */
public void drawSquares(Graphics g, int count, int x, int y,
                        int size) {
  // Base case
  if (count == 0) {
    return;
  }

  // Recursive case

  // Random color
  float red = (float) Math.random();
  float green = (float) Math.random();
  float blue = (float) Math.random();
  g.setColor(new Color(red, green, blue));

  // Fill the square at (x, y) with given size
  g.fillRect(x, y, size, size);

  // Recursively fill a smaller region
  int nextSize = 3 * size / 4;
  int nextX = x + size / 8;
  int nextY = y + size / 6;
  drawSquares(g, count - 1, nextX, nextY, nextSize);
}
```

Lines 29–32 perform the recursive method call. In this case, each nested square is three-fourths the size of its parent. Adjusting `x` and `y` by different amounts makes the squares slightly off-center, similar to the positioning in Albers' original painting. All that remains is to add a statement to `paint` to call `drawSquares` for the first time. Figure 9.2 shows an example output with five nested squares.

```
public void paint(Graphics g) {
  drawSquares(g, 5, 0, 0, WIDTH);
}
```

Figure 9.2 Example output of the `Homage` program with five nested squares.

Try It Yourself

Experiment with changing the calculations of `nextX`, `nextY`, and `nextSize` to create different square arrangements.

9.2 In the Style of Piet Mondrian

Piet Mondrian (1872–1944) was a Dutch painter, famous for his geometrical abstract works. Although he began his career with realistic paintings and landscapes, he shifted toward abstract art while living in Paris after World War I, which then dominated his output for the rest of his life. Mondrian is best known for works like *Composition in red, yellow, blue and black* from 1921 (Figure 9.3), featuring irregular rectangular grids drawn in strong black lines with a simple palette. Mondrian did not employ any particular generative process to create his works, but a recursive method can create images in a similar style (Stephenson, 2018):

Figure 9.3 **Piet Mondrian, *Composition in red, yellow, blue and black* (1921).**

- Start with an empty rectangular canvas.

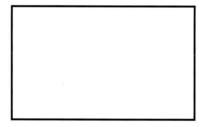

- Randomly select horizontal and vertical splits to divide the canvas into four parts.

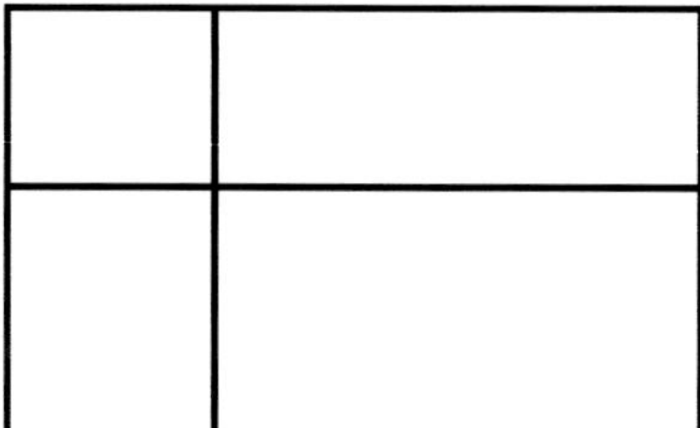

- Recursively split each subrectangle, continuing until either the rectangles reach a minimum size, or a set number of splits have been performed.

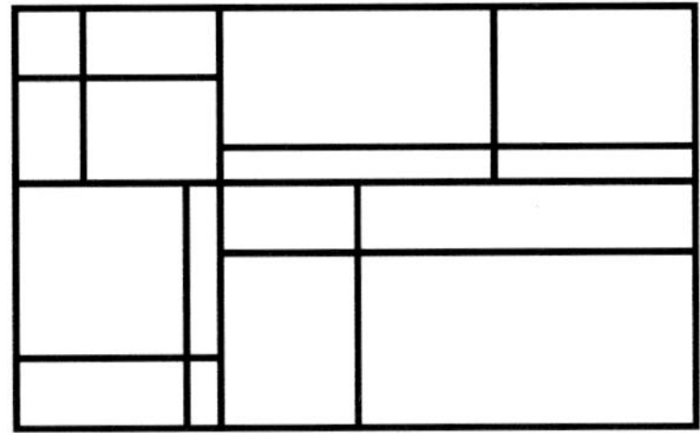

- At the base case, choose a color for each rectangle. This can be done randomly so that most rectangles remain white and a few are colored.

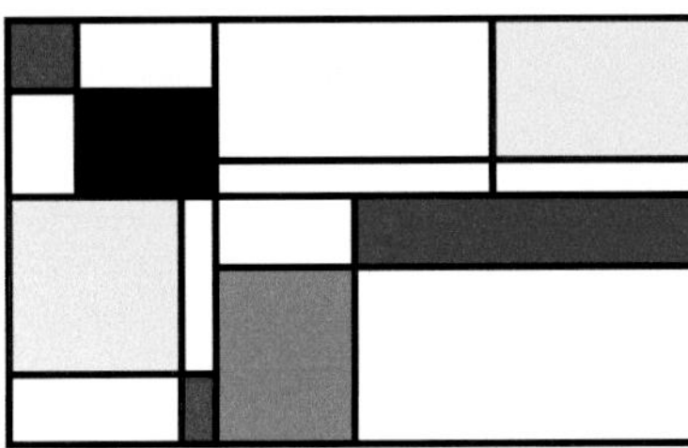

Start by creating a class named `Mondrian` that uses the same setup as `Homage`. Your `paint` should call `drawMondrian`, using the starter code given below.

```
/**
 * Recursively subdivide and color rectangles
 *
 * @param  g  The Graphics object for the drawing surface
 * @param  count  Remaining recursive splits
 * @param  x  Current rectangle's x position
 * @param  y  Current rectangle's y position
 * @param  width  Current rectangle's width
 # @param  height  Current rectangle's height
 */
public void drawMondrian(Graphics g, int count, int x, int y,
                         int width, int height) {
  // Base case -- draw this rectangle, then return
  if (count == 0) {
    // Decide if the rectangle should be colored
    if (Math.random() < FRAC_COLORED) {
      // Choose a random color
    } else {
      // Set color to white
    }

```

```
    // Draw using g.fillRect

    // Outline the rectangle in black using g.drawRect

    return;
  }

  // Generate randomized splits
  int xSplit = (int) (Math.random() * width);
  int ySplit = (int) (Math.random() * height);

  // Upper-left subrectangle
  drawMondrian(g, count - 1, x, y, xSplit, ySplit);

  // Upper-right subrectangle

  // Lower-left subrectangle

  // Lower-right subrectangle

}
```

Try It Yourself

Finish the `drawMondrian` method by adding the missing parts of the base and recursive cases. Tip: Think carefully about the inputs to each recursive call. You'll need to identify the upper-left corner, width, and height of each subrectangle.

The base case uses code similar to `Homage` to generate random colors:

```
// Base case -- draw this rectangle, then return
if (count == 0) {

  // Decide if the rectangle should be colored
  if (Math.random() < FRAC_COLORED) {
    // Choose a random color
    float red = (float) Math.random();
    float green = (float) Math.random();
    float blue = (float) Math.random();
```

```
      g.setColor(new Color(red, green, blue));
    } else {
      g.setColor(Color.WHITE);
    }

    // Draw using g.fillRect
    g.fillRect(x, y, width, height);

    // Outline the rectangle in black using g.drawRect
    g.setColor(Color.BLACK);
    g.drawRect(x, y, width, height);

    return;
  }
```

With this setup, only some rectangles are colored and the others have a white interior. The constant `FRAC_COLORED` controls how dense or sparse the coloring is. Declare it at the top of the class.

```
final double FRAC_COLORED = 0.3333;
```

The second part of the program makes four recursive calls to `drawMondrian` to process the four subrectangles. The drawing below shows the corners of the four subrectangles based on the values of `xSplit` and `ySplit`.

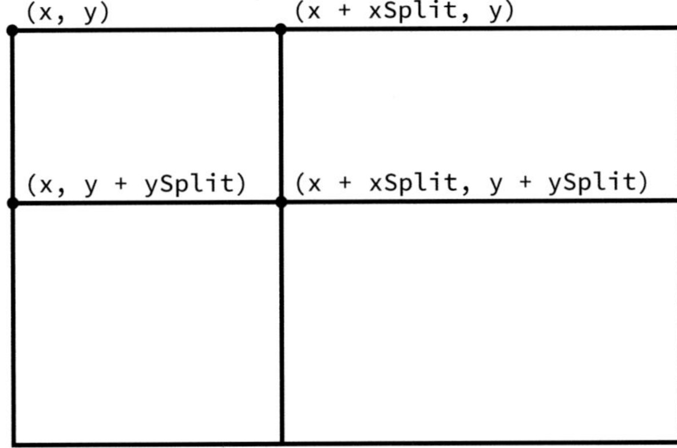

The four recursive calls are

```
// Upper-left subrectangle
drawMondrian(g, count - 1, x, y, xSplit, ySplit);

// Upper-right subrectangle
```

```
drawMondrian(g, count - 1, x + xSplit, y, width - xSplit, ySplit);

// Lower-left subrectangle
drawMondrian(g, count - 1, x, y + ySplit, xSplit, height - ySplit);

// Lower-right subrectangle
drawMondrian(g, count - 1, x + xSplit, y + ySplit, width - xSplit, height
    - ySplit);
```

Figure 9.4 shows an example of an image produced by the complete `drawMondrian` method.

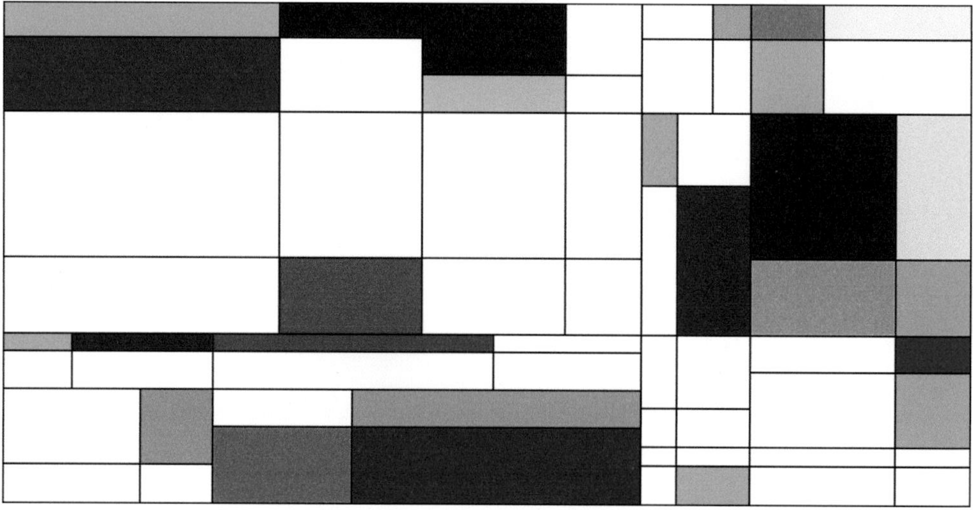

Figure 9.4 Example output of `drawMondrian` with three recursive subdivisions.

Try It Yourself

Add `drawMondrian` to the `Mondrian` class and finish the program. After you've run the program a few times, try the following modifications:

- The default splitting method can result in very thin rectangles. Modify it to eliminate random splits that are too close to 0.0 or 1.0. Can you come up with a method that restricts the split ratios to only a limited set of choices, such as `[0.25, 0.33, 0.66, 0.75]`?
- Modify the color selection to choose from a fixed palette.

9.3 Fractals

A **fractal** is a shape that exhibits self-similar details at arbitrarily small scales. That is, zooming in on a part of the shape reveals a structure that is like, or even identical to, the shape as a whole.

Fractals are often defined by a recursive process, such that, in theory, the fractal pattern could be repeated down to infinitely small scales. Fractals are mathematically interesting because they play with notions of space and topology. A fractal shape could, for example, occupy a finite area within the plane (that is, you could draw a box around it), but also have an infinite perimeter, due to the infinite twists and turns occurring at smaller and smaller scales. This is the kind of thing that drives mathematicians bonkers.[2]

Fractals are a relatively modern area of mathematics, and their popularity has been connected to advances in computer graphics, which make it possible to visualize fractal shapes that would be impossible to graph by hand. Mathematicians like Georg Cantor began investigating objects that exhibited self-similar behavior in the late nineteenth and early twentieth centuries, but the word "fractal" was only introduced in the 1970s by Benoit Mandelbrot. We'll investigate the Mandelbrot set fractal named for him in Section 9.4.

9.3.1 Sierpiński's Carpet

Let's start with a simple 2D fractal: Sierpiński's Carpet, named after the Polish mathematician Wacław Sierpiński and shown in Figure 9.5. The process for generating the Carpet is as follows.

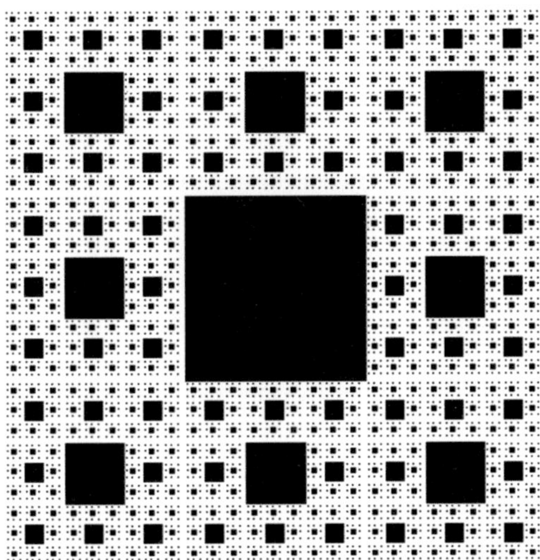

Figure 9.5 The Sierpiński's Carpet fractal.

- Begin with an empty square and subdivide it into nine equal pieces.

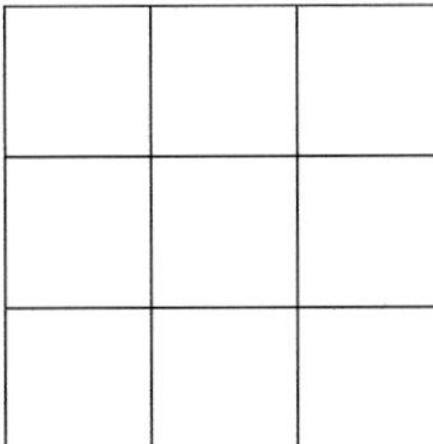

2 In a good way.

- Color the middle subsquare.

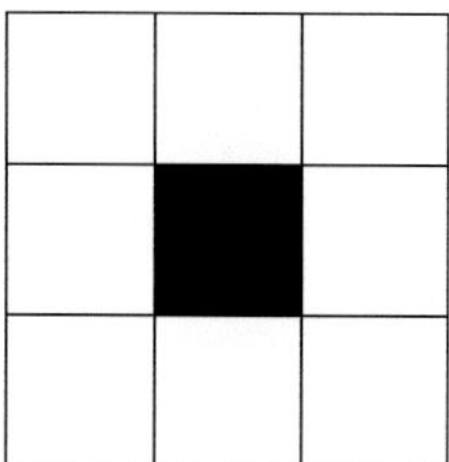

- Recursively divide the remaining eight subsquares and fill the middle of each one.

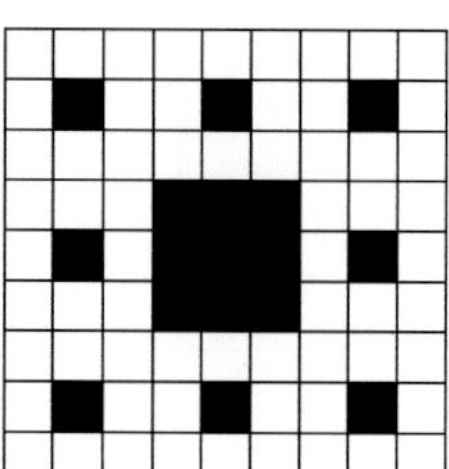

- Continue the process, recursively dividing each square and filling its center, until a stopping condition is reached.

You may recall the cellular automaton from Chapter 4 that generated a triangular version of this fractal.

Try It Yourself

Write a class called `Sierpinski` that sets up a `Canvas` using the same techniques as the previous projects. In the `paint` method, call a method named `carpet` that will draw the fractal. Using the code below as a starting point, complete the `carpet` procedure. Tip: You'll need to make recursive calls for each of eight subsquares. Think about how to calculate the corners and sizes of each subsquare based on the position, width, and height of the parent square.

```
/**
 * Recursively draw the carpet fractal
 *
 * @param  g  The Graphics object for the drawing surface
 * @param  count  Recursive iterations from the base case
 * @param  x  Current square's x position
 * @param  y  Current square's y position
 * @param  side  Current square's side length
 */
public void carpet(Graphics g, int count, int x, int y,
                   int side) {

  // Base case, return when count == 0
```

```

  // Calculate the x, y, width, and height
  // of the middle subsquare

  // Fill the middle subsquare using g.fillRect

  // Recursively call carpet on the other eight subsquares

}
```

Most of the work is in making the recursive calls. Rather than making eight separate calls with different arguments, this version uses the slightly pretentious approach of constructing a pair of arrays holding the three required x-coordinates and three required y-coordinates. It then iterates over the arrays to process all nine subsquare locations.

```
/**
 * Recursively draw the carpet fractal
 *
 * @param  g  The Graphics object for the drawing surface
 * @param  count  Recursive iterations from the base case
 * @param  x  Current square's x position
 * @param  y  Current square's y position
 * @param  side  Current square's side length
 */
public void carpet(Graphics g, int count, int x, int y, int side) {

  // Base case
  if (count == 0) {
    return;
  }

  // Generate subsquare coordinates
  int step = side / 3;

  int[] xCoords = {x, x + step, x + 2 * step};
  int[] yCoords = {y, y + step, y + 2 * step};

  // Fill the middle subsquare using g.fillRect
```

```
  g.fillRect(xCoords[1], yCoords[1], step, step);

  // Recursively call carpet on the other eight subsquares
  for (int i = 0; i < xCoords.length; i++) {
    for (int j = 0; j < yCoords.length; j++) {

      // Skip the middle square
      if (i == 1 && j == 1) {
        continue;
      }

      carpet(g, count - 1, xCoords[i], yCoords[j], step);
    }
  }
}
```

9.3.2 Vicsek's Cross

The Vicsek's Cross fractal is a variation of the strategy used to create Sierpiński's Carpet, named for Hungarian physicist Tamás Vicsek. Like the carpet, it works by subdividing the initial starting square, coloring some of its elements, then repeating recursively.

- Start with a black square, then subdivide it into nine parts.
- Color the four corner subsquares white to "remove" them from the shape.
- Recursively repeat the process on the remaining five squares.

Figure 9.6 shows the fractal that results from this process.

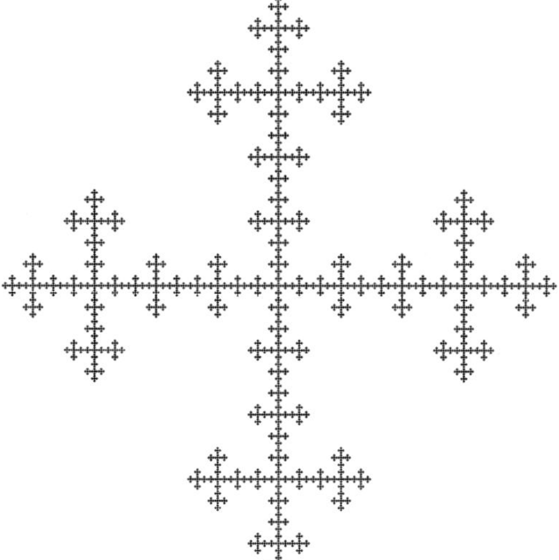

Figure 9.6 The Vicsek Cross fractal.

Try It Yourself

Implement a method named `vicsek` that draws the Vicsek Cross fractal. Your method should take five inputs: `Graphics g`, `int count`, `int` values for the `x` and `y` coordinates of the square, and an `int side` representing the side length of the square. Tip: Make the size of the starting square a power of three, which avoids the problem of artifacts caused by drawing subsquares with fractional sizes. Setting the dimensions to

```
final int WIDTH = 729;
final int HEIGHT = 729;
```

will allow for up to six recursive calls. Remember to paint the complete square black before calling `vicsek` for the first time.

By this point, the necessary steps should feel familiar. The method only needs to paint the four corner squares, then recursively call `vicsek` on the remaining five squares.

```
/**
 * Recursively draw Vicsek's Cross
 *
 * @param  g  The Graphics object for the drawing surface
 * @param  count  Recursive iterations from the base case
 * @param  x  Current square's x position
 * @param  y  Current square's y position
 * @param  side  Current square's side length
 */
public void vicsek(Graphics g, int count, int x, int y, int side) {

  // Base case
  if (count == 0) {
    return;
  }

  // Size of the subsquare -- make sure the top-level
  // canvas size is a power of three
  int step = side / 3;

  // Corner coordinates
  int[] xCorners = {x, x + step, x + 2 * step};
  int[] yCorners = {y, y + step, y + 2 * step};

```

```
  g.setColor(Color.WHITE);

  for (int i = 0; i < xCorners.length; i++) {
    for (int j = 0; j < yCorners.length; j++) {
      // Paint the corners white -- exclude middle row and col
      if (i != 1 && j != 1) {
        g.fillRect(xCorners[i], yCorners[j], step, step);
      }

      // Non-corner squares get a recursive call
      else {
        vicsek(g, count - 1, xCorners[i], yCorners[j], step);
      }
    }
  }
}
```

This version uses the same looping strategy as the Mondrian method. The `if` statement distinguishes between subsquares that are in the middle row or column, which are processed recursively, and the ones on the corners, which are painted white. The `paint` method should color the entire surface black and then call `vicsek`:

```
public void paint(Graphics g) {
  // Paint it black
  g.setColor(Color.BLACK);
  g.fillRect(0,  0, WIDTH, WIDTH);

  // Start the recursive process
  vicsek(g, 6, 0, 0, WIDTH);
}
```

Try It Yourself

Fractals that follow the general strategy of Sierpiński's Carpet and the Vicsek Cross are called **box fractals**: Start with a square, or some other basic geometric shape, subdivide it, remove some of the parts, then repeat on the remaining pieces. Try using this strategy to design your own box fractal. Tips:

- Change which subsquares are colored in (and with what colors) and which are recursively processed.
- Try doing more than nine subsquares.

- Don't limit yourself to equal-sized subunits. What if you use an asymmetric division?
- You can work with shapes other than squares. A rectangle is an easy extension, but you could use a triangle or hexagon if you want a challenge.
- Pay attention to the dimensions. To avoid visual artifacts, make the starting size a power of the divisor. For example, if you want to split a dimension in half at each step, start with a power of two.

9.4 The Mandelbrot Set

The Mandelbrot set, named after the French-American mathematician Benoit Mandelbrot, is the iconic fractal image. It's famous for its intricate shape and the aesthetically interesting details that it contains; Figure 9.7 shows a top-level visualization of the entire set. This section will lead you through the creation of a viewing program to produce color images of the Mandelbrot set. Unlike our other fractals, the set is not actually recursively defined, but the project still serves as a capstone for all of our generative Java graphics programs.

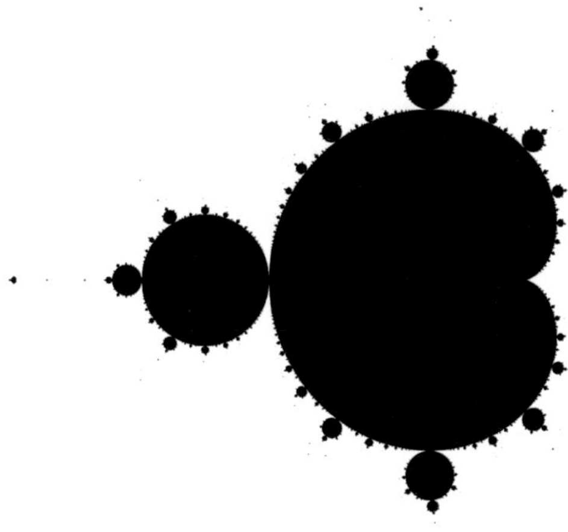

Figure 9.7 The Mandelbrot set.

9.4.1 Definition

The Mandelbrot set is defined over the set of complex numbers. Recall that a complex number has two parts, a **real part** and an **imaginary part**, and is written in the form

$$a + bi,$$

where a and b are both real numbers and i stands for the special **imaginary unit** satisfying

$$i^2 = -1.$$

That is, i represents $\sqrt{-1}$. Complex numbers can be visualized on the **complex plane**, where the horizontal axis represents the real part a of the number and the vertical axis represents the imaginary part b.

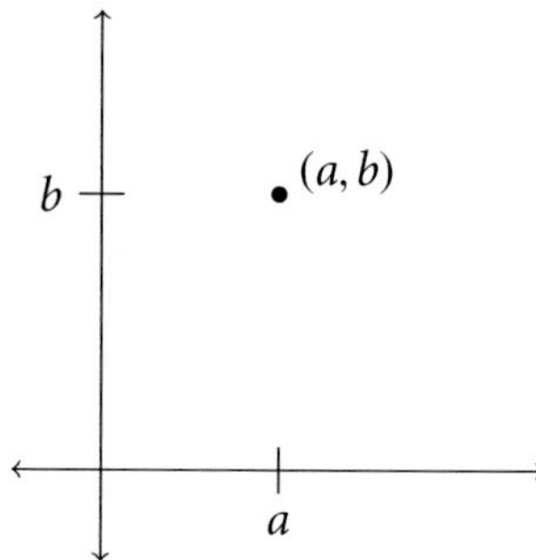

Now consider a complex number c and the following **iterative function**:

$$z_{n+1} = z_n^2 + c.$$

Beginning with a starting value of z_0, the iterative function uses z_0 and c to calculate z_1, then uses z_1 and c to calculate z_2, and so forth. For any given value of c and starting value of z_0, one of two things will happen to the sequence of z values produced by this process:

- The sequence will remain bounded; that is, the absolute magnitude of any z will remain less than some upper limit.
- The sequence *will not* remain bounded and will diverge to infinity. This may happen quickly or slowly.

The Mandelbrot set is defined to be the set of points c in the complex plane for which the iterative process *does not diverge to infinity* when starting from $z_0 = 0 + 0i$. For example, consider the point $c = 3 + 0i$. Starting from the origin, the sequence generated by the iterative function will be

$$z_1 = (0 + 0i)^2 + (3 + 0i) = 3 + 0i$$
$$z_2 = (3 + 0i)^2 + (3 + 0i) = 12 + 0i$$
$$z_3 = (12 + 0i)^2 + (3 + 0i) = 147 + 0i.$$

The sequence is clearly diverging to infinity so the complex point $(3, 0)$ is not included in the Mandelbrot set.

Try It Yourself

Evaluate the sequence for $c = -1 + 0i$. How does it behave? Is the point $(-1, 0)$ in the Mandelbrot set?

Starting from $z_0 = 0 + 0i$, the sequence alternates between -1 and 0:

$$z_1 = (0 + 0i)^2 + (-1 + 0i) = -1 + 0i$$
$$z_2 = (-1 + 0i)^2 + (-1 + 0i) = 0 + 0i.$$

Therefore, the sequence is bounded and the point $(-1, 0)$ is in the Mandelbrot set.

9.4.2 Visualizing the Set

Let's start by writing a class that can visualize the Mandelbrot set in the complex plane. The code below is similar to our previous examples. As before, `paint` calls a `draw` method that will actually perform the required graphics operations. The `inSet` method will test if a given complex point is in the Mandelbrot set.

```
/**
 * Visualize the Mandelbrot set
 */

import java.awt.Canvas;
import java.awt.Graphics;
import java.awt.Color;
import javax.swing.JFrame;

public class Mandelbrot extends Canvas {

  final int WIDTH = 800;
  final int HEIGHT = 800;
  final int THRESHOLD = 5000;

  /**
   * Constructor
   */
  public Mandelbrot() {
    setSize(WIDTH, HEIGHT);
  }

  /**
   * Iterate the complex Mandelbrot function on the point
   * (re, im)
   *
   * If the absolute value of the iterated point exceeds 2.0,
   * then it cannot be in the set
   *
   * @param re  the real part of the starting point
   * @param im  the complex part of the starting point
   *
   * @return  true if the absolute value of the iterated point
   * does not exceed 2.0 before THRESHOLD iterations,
```

```
   * false otherwise
   */
  public boolean inSet(double re, double im) {

  }

  /**
   * Visualize the Mandelbrot set
   *
   * @param  g  Graphics object for the drawable surface
   */
  public void draw(Graphics g) {

  }

  public void paint(Graphics g) {
    // Paint the background white
    g.setColor(Color.WHITE);
    g.fillRect(0,  0, WIDTH, HEIGHT);
    g.setColor(Color.BLACK);

    // Draw the image
    draw(g);
  }


  public static void main(String[] args) {
    Mandelbrot m = new Mandelbrot();

    JFrame frame = new JFrame();
    frame.add(m);
    frame.pack();
    frame.setVisible(true);
    frame.setDefaultCloseOperation(JFrame.EXIT_ON_CLOSE);
  }

}
```

The draw Method

The constructor, paint, and main methods should be familiar at this point. Let's start by implementing draw and then inSet. The basic drawing strategy relies on mapping each pixel in the image to a corresponding point in the complex plane. Given the complex coordinates associated with a pixel, we'll determine whether it belongs in the Mandelbrot set (using the inSet method), then color the pixel appropriately. Therefore, most of the complexity of the method is the mapping from pixel coordinates to their corresponding complex coordinates.

Start by setting limits on the real and imaginary axes. Initially, these limits will be set to view the entire set, but later we'll add the ability to zoom in on a point. The following lines, which are part of the draw method given below, set limits for the real line and calculate an appropriate range for the imaginary axis that keeps the image centered within the frame. The entire set fits within the real range $[-2.5, 0.75]$.

```
// Limits for the real axis
double minReal = -2.5;
double maxReal = 0.75;

// Center on the imaginary axis based on the real axis scale
double minImag = -(maxReal - minReal) / 2;
double maxImag = (maxReal - minReal) / 2;
```

If the size of the image is WIDTH by HEIGHT pixels, then the size of each pixel in the complex coordinate space is given by:

```
// Size of each pixel in the real and imaginary directions
double realStep = (maxReal - minReal) / WIDTH;
double imagStep = (maxImag - minImag) / HEIGHT;
```

Now consider a pixel with image coordinates (x, y). We need to map this pixel to its associated complex coordinates. This is slightly tricky because of the different geometries involved. Remember that in pixel space, increasing y corresponds to moving *down*, which is the opposite of the standard plane. Therefore, pixel coordinates (0, 0) correspond to the complex point (minReal, maxImag) in the upper-left corner of the visible region. Moving to the right on the image corresponds to increasing the complex real coordinate in units of realStep. Moving down the image corresponds to *decreasing* the complex imaginary coordinate in units of imagStep.

Try It Yourself

Based on the description above, write down the statements to convert from x and y to their corresponding real and imaginary coordinates.

Solution

Let `re` be the real coordinate corresponding to `x` and `im` be the imaginary coordinate corresponding to `y`. The conversions are given by:

```
double re = minReal + realStep * x;
double im = maxImag - imagStep * y;
```

The full `draw` method loops over all pixels in the image, converts each one to its real and imaginary coordinates, then calls `inSet` to determine if the point is in the Mandelbrot set or not.

```
/**
 * draw -- visualize the Mandelbrot set
 *
 * @param g Graphics object for the drawable surface
*/
public void draw(Graphics g) {
  // Limits for the real axis
  double minReal = -2.5;
  double maxReal = 0.75;

  // Center on the imaginary axis based on the real axis scale
  double minImag = -(maxReal - minReal) / 2;
  double maxImag = (maxReal - minReal) / 2;

  // Size of each pixel in the real and imaginary directions
  double realStep = (maxReal - minReal) / WIDTH;
  double imagStep = (maxImag - minImag) / HEIGHT;

  // Iterate through all pixels in the image
  for (int x = 0; x < WIDTH; x++) {
    for (int y = 0; y < HEIGHT; y++) {

      // Convert each pixel into its corresponding complex
      // plane coordinates -- REMEMBER: the vertical axis
      // is reversed!
      //
      // pixel (0, 0) corresponds to (minReal, maxImag)
      double re = minReal + realStep * x + realStep / 2;
      double im = maxImag - imagStep * y - imagStep / 2;
```

```
30
31         // If (re, im) is in the set, fill pixel (x, y)
32         if (inSet(re, im)) {
33           g.fillRect(x, y, 1, 1);
34         }
35       }
36     }
37 }
```

Lines 28 and 29 add one small optimization to the coordinate conversion: The extra half steps place the coordinate at the center of the pixel, rather than at its corner.

The `inSet` Method

The basic strategy for testing if a point is in the Mandelbrot set is to *iterate and quit*. It can be shown that a complex point in the Mandelbrot function will diverge to infinity once its magnitude exceeds 2.0. Our approach, therefore, is to simply evaluate the iterative sequence for the point and quit as soon as its magnitude exceeds 2.0. If we reach a preset iteration limit without quitting, we'll conclude that the point must be in the set. This approach is not perfect, because points can diverge at different rates – some exceed 2.0 almost immediately and others require thousands of iterations. We'll later exploit the rate of divergence to create interesting colored images showing the behavior of points that are on the boundary of the set.

```
/**
 * Iterate the complex Mandelbrot function on the point
 * (re, im)
 *
 * If the absolute value of the iterated point exceeds 2.0,
 * then it cannot be in the set
 *
 * @param re  the real part of the starting point
 * @param im  the complex part of the starting point
 *
 * @return  true if the absolute value of the iterated point
 * does not exceed 2.0 before THRESHOLD iterations,
 * false otherwise
 */
public boolean inSet(double re, double im) {

  double zReal = 0.0;
  double zImag = 0.0;
```

```
19
20   for(int i = 0; i < THRESHOLD; i++) {
21
22     // Calculate z ^ 2
23     double zSqReal = zReal * zReal - zImag * zImag;
24     double zSqImag = 2 * zReal * zImag;
25
26     // Next value of z
27     zReal= zSqReal + re;
28     zImag = zSqImag + im;
29
30     // Check the absolute value
31     double absSquared = zReal * zReal + zImag * zImag;
32     if (absSquared > 4.0) {
33       return false;
34     }
35
36   }
37
38   return true;
39 }
```

The square of a complex number is

$$(a + bi)^2 = (a^2 - b^2) + 2abi,$$

calculated on lines 23 and 24. Line 31 calculates the squared absolute value of the current z and then compares it to 4.0, avoiding the need to take a square root.

Try It Yourself

Implement `Mandelbrot` and then add the `draw` and `inSet` methods. Run the program and verify that you can visualize the Mandelbrot set.

9.4.3 Zooming in on a Point

The interesting details of the Mandelbrot set are located on the boundary. It's possible, for example, to find small fractal copies of the entire set by zooming in on its edge. Many Internet videos exploit these features by gradually zooming in on particular points of interest. Let's add the ability to focus the image on a particular point.

Add two variables to the beginning of `draw` called `targetReal` and `targetImag`. These will represent the complex plane coordinates of the central pixel of the image. For example, zooming in on the point

```
double targetReal = -1.4011;
double targetImag = 0.0;
```

will reveal the self-similar structure of the heart-shaped bulbs on the left side of the set. Create an additional variable called `zoom`, which will represent the magnification level of the image. Higher values of `zoom` correspond to greater levels of magnification.

```
double zoom = 100.0;
```

The following lines adjust `minReal` and `maxReal` to be centered on the target point. Increasing `zoom` reduces the range of the viewing window.

```
double minReal = targetReal - 2.0 / zoom;
double maxReal = targetReal + 2.0 / zoom;
```

You can then calculate `minImag` and `maxImag` to keep the window centered on the target point:

```
double minImag = targetImag - (maxReal - minReal) / 2.0;
double maxImag = targetImag + (maxReal - minReal) / 2.0;
```

The rest of the `draw` method remains unchanged.

Try It Yourself

Make the necessary changes to `draw`, then experiment with different `zoom` values. Figures 9.8(a) and 9.8(b) show example zooms with self-similar features.

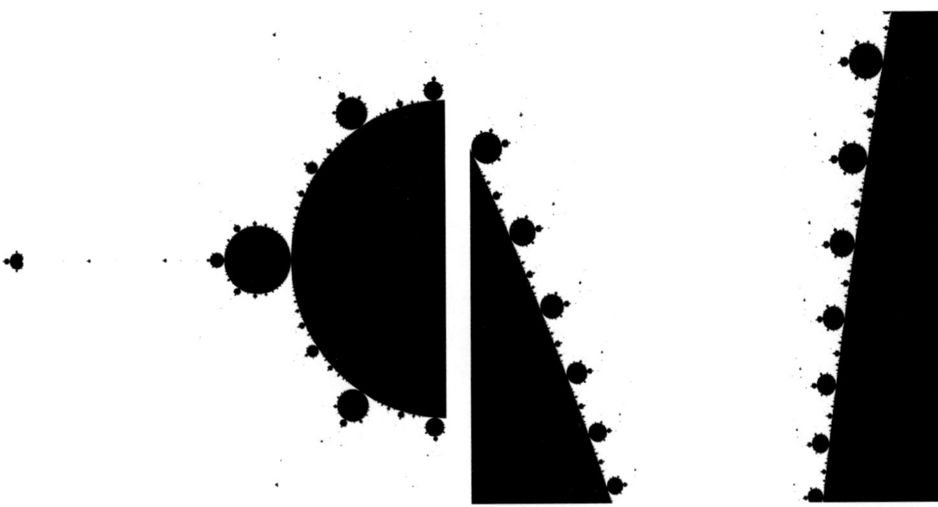

Figure 9.8 (a) View of $(-1.4011, 0.0)$, `zoom` = 100.0. (b) View of $(-0.755, 0.1)$, `zoom` = 100.0.

9.4.4 Adding Colors

The previous sections focused on visualizing only the points contained within the Mandelbrot set. This is great, but the most impressive visualizations use color to highlight not just the points within the set, but the behaviors of points on the boundary. The basic coloring strategy relies on testing not only whether a point is in or out of the set, but *how quickly the point diverges to infinity*, if it does so. Therefore, we can create a colorized version of the Mandelbrot set using the following strategy:

- Modify `inSet` to return the *number of iterations* required before the magnitude of the point exceeds the escape value of 2.0. For points in the set, which never escape, this will be the preset iteration limit.
- Map the number of iterations to a color, chosen according to some rule that highlights how quickly different points escape.

Try It Yourself

Modify `inSet` to return the number of iterations performed before the method returns. Change the method's return type to `int` instead of `boolean`. Points that are in the set will return a value of `THRESHOLD`.

At the beginning of `draw`, create a double array called `counts` that will keep track of the iteration count for each pixel.

```
int[][] counts = new int[WIDTH][HEIGHT];
```

You can then use `counts` to record the value returned by `inSet`.

```
counts[x][y] = inSet(re, im);
```

Determining colors offers more options. We need to decide on a pleasing color map and a means of mapping from iteration counts to colors. A popular approach to coloring the Mandelbrot set is the **histogram coloring algorithm** (Louvet and Martínez, 2003). It determines a pixel's color from its place in the *distribution of iteration counts.*

- Points that are at the bottom of the distribution, with proportionally low iteration counts (relative to other pixels in the same image), get "low" colors. These are the points that escaped quickly.
- Points that are at the top of the distribution, with proportionally high iteration counts, get "high" colors. These are the points that may have taken a long time to escape.

This strategy works well because it accounts for both cases where the range of iteration counts is wide – that is, there's a significant difference between the fastest diverging and slowest diverging pixels – and cases where the range is narrow.

The complete updated `draw` method is shown below. The first half is similar to the first version: it iterates through the pixels, converts each one to its corresponding complex coordinates, then records the number of iterations returned by `inSet`. The second half of the method implements the coloring algorithm, discussed below.

```
/**
 * draw -- visualize the Mandelbrot set
 *
 * @param g Graphics object for the drawable surface
*/
public void draw(Graphics g) {
  // Target point
  double targetReal = -1.4011;
  double targetImag = 0.0;
  double zoom = 100.0;

  // Limits for the real axis
  double minReal = targetReal - 2.0 / zoom;
  double maxReal = targetReal + 2.0 / zoom;

  // Center on the imaginary axis based on the real axis scale
  double minImag = targetImag - (maxReal - minReal) / 2.0;
  double maxImag = targetImag + (maxReal - minReal) / 2.0;

  // Size of each pixel in the real and imaginary directions
  double realStep = (maxReal - minReal) / WIDTH;
  double imagStep = (maxImag - minImag) / HEIGHT;

  // Matrix to keep track of iteration counts
  int[][] counts = new int[WIDTH][HEIGHT];

  // Iterate through all pixels in the image
  for (int x = 0; x < WIDTH; x++) {
    for (int y = 0; y < HEIGHT; y++) {

      // Convert each pixel into its corresponding complex
      // plane coordinates -- REMEMBER: the vertical axis
      // is reversed!
      //
      // pixel (0, 0) corresponds to (minReal, maxImag)
      double re = minReal + realStep * x + realStep / 2;
      double im = maxImag - imagStep * y - imagStep / 2;

```

```
    // Record the iteration count for pixel (x, y)
    counts[x][y] = inSet(re, im);
  }
}

// Construct histogram of counts
int[] hist = new int[THRESHOLD + 1];

for (int x = 0; x < WIDTH; x++) {
  for (int y = 0; y < HEIGHT; y++) {
    hist[counts[x][y]]++;
  }
}

// Convert each pixel to a color
for (int x = 0; x < WIDTH; x++) {
  for (int y = 0; y < HEIGHT; y++) {

    // Pixels in the set are colored black
    if (counts[x][y] == THRESHOLD) {
      g.setColor(Color.BLACK);
    }

    // Other pixels get mapped to a color
    else {
      // Number of pixels with count <= pixel (x, y)
      int cumSum = 0;
      for (int h = 0; h <= counts[x][y]; h++) {
        cumSum += hist[h];
      }

      // Convert cumSum to a percentile of the distribution
      float percentile = (float) cumSum / (WIDTH * HEIGHT);

      // Use getHSBColor to convert percentile to a hue
      Color c = Color.getHSBColor(percentile, 0.85f, 1.0f);
      g.setColor(c);
    }
```

```
77
78          // Fill pixel (x, y)
79          g.fillRect(x, y, 1, 1);
80      }
81    }
82 }
```

The coloring algorithm starts by constructing the histogram of pixel counts. Let `hist` be an `int` array, where each entry records the number of pixels with a given iteration count. For example, `hist[100]` records the number of pixels that achieved exactly 100 iterations before `inSet` terminated.

```
// Construct histogram of counts
int[] hist = new int[THRESHOLD + 1];

for (int x = 0; x < WIDTH; x++) {
  for (int y = 0; y < HEIGHT; y++) {
    hist[counts[x][y]]++;
  }
}
```

The size of `hist` is `THRESHOLD + 1` to allow `hist[THRESHOLD]` to record the number of pixels that achieved the maximum possible count and are therefore in the Mandelbrot set.

Now suppose that we want to color pixel (x, y). Lines 65–71 calculate the total number of pixels in the entire image with a result less than or equal to `counts[x][y]` and then convert that number to a percentile.

```
// Number of pixels with count <= pixel (x, y)
int cumSum = 0;
for (int h = 0; h <= counts[x][y]; h++) {
  cumSum += hist[h];
}

// Convert cumSum to a percentile of the distribution
float percentile = (float) cumSum / (WIDTH * HEIGHT);
```

The final step is to convert `percentile` into a color. This steps uses `Color.getHSBColor`, which generates colors using the hue–saturation–brightness color model.[3]

```
Color c = Color.getHSBColor((float) percentile, 0.85f, 1.0f);
```

3 See the old-school fire animation in Chapter 7.

Here, `percentile` is used to control the hue; the other two parameters are fixed.

Try It Yourself

Finish assembling the complete Mandelbrot program. You will need to modify `inSet` to return the number of iterations performed before the point diverges, then update the `draw` method to the color version. Once you've done that, you can experiment with zooming in on interesting boundary points. Figures 9.9(a) to 9.9(d) show examples generated by the final `Mandelbrot` program to give you some ideas. Try setting a relatively high threshold of iterations to bring out interesting structures in the image. Paul Bourke's overview of the Mandelbrot set provides other interesting points to investigate (Bourke, 2002).

(a) (b)

(c) (d)

Figure 9.9 (a) View of $(-1.4011, 0.0)$, `zoom` = 100.0, self-similar copy of the set on the left. (b) View of $(-0.755, 0.1)$, `zoom` = 100.0, the "Seahorse Valley". (c) View of $(-0.761574, -0.0847596)$, `zoom` = 800.0. (d) View of $(-0.761574, -0.0847596)$, `zoom` = 80,000.0.

Feel free to experiment with changing the color-mapping calculation. You can create a different palette by restricting the range of the hue. For example, try keeping the values between 0.0 and 0.15 to create a "hot" colormap of red, orange, and yellow; try 0.55 to 0.65 for a "cool" map of blue shades. Also try fixing the hue and letting the saturation and/or brightness vary to create a monochromatic look.

EXTENSIONS

Vicsek Saltire

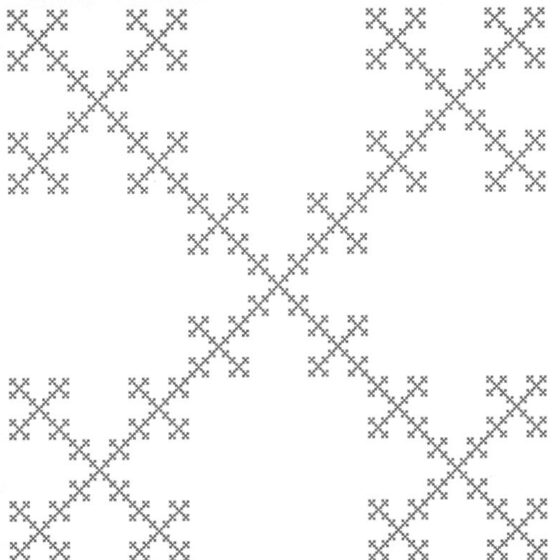

Figure 9.10 **Saltire form of the Vicsek fractal.**

A "saltire" is an X-shaped cross. Using the `vicsek` method as inspiration, write a program that draws the saltire form of the cross by recursively processing the four corner squares and the center square.

Haferman's Carpet

The Haferman carpet uses a similar approach to the Vicsek and Sierpiński box fractals, but uses *two different update rules*, depending on whether the subsquare being processed is white or black (Allouche and Shallit, 2003).

- Start with a black square.
- If a square is black, it's colored white in an X-shaped pattern, as in the saltire fractal. After the first iteration, the square looks like the following. Recursively process all nine subsquares.

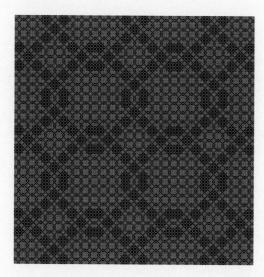

Figure 9.11 Haferman's carpet – this would literally make a nice carpet.

- If a square is white, color it completely black. After the second iteration, the figure looks like the following.

- Continue recursively dividing each square into its nine subsquares and processing each one, respecting the white–black update rules.

Using the `carpet` method as a starting point, implement a method named `haferman` that can draw the Haferman carpet.

The Burning Ship Fractal

The "Burning Ship" fractal is a variation of the Mandelbrot set. Like the Mandelbrot set, it's defined by iterating a complex function and identifying which inputs remain bounded and which escape to infinity. The Burning Ship function is

$$z_{n+1} = (|\operatorname{Re}(z_n)| + i|\operatorname{Im}(z_n)|)^2 + c,$$

where $|\operatorname{Re}(z_n)|$ and $|\operatorname{Im}(z_n)|$ denote the absolute values of the real and imaginary parts of z_n. That is, the Burning Ship fractal uses the same complex function as the Mandelbrot set, but uses the absolute values of both parts of z_n in the iterative calculation. Modify the `Mandelbrot` program to display the Burning Ship fractal. To do this, you'll need to make the following changes:

- Write a new method, `inBurningShipSet`, that has the same structure as the original `inSet` method, but calculates the absolute values of `zReal` and `zImag` at the beginning of each iteration. It should return the number of iterations performed before the point escapes, or the maximum number of iterations if the point never escapes.

(a)

(b)

Figure 9.12 **(a) The Burning Ship fractal, position ($-1.75, -0.03$), zoom = 50.0. (b) View of two ships on the real line, position ($-1.60, -0.03$), zoom = 40.0.**

- The default view of the fractal looks like an upside-down burning ship. To get the image of Figure 9.12(a), you'll need to reverse the y-axis coordinates. You can do this by either changing the mapping from pixel coordinates to complex plane coordinates, or by reversing the positions of pixels on the y-axis when you draw them.

The interesting details of the fractal are on the $y = 0$ line between $x = -1.8$ and $x = -1.4$. Figure 9.12(a) shows the main "burning ship" structure; 9.12(b) is a zoomed-out view of the real line with the main ship on the left.

NOTES AND FURTHER READING

For an introduction to mathematical fractals, examine Benoit Mandelbrot's early paper, "How long is the coast of Britain? Statistical self-similarity and fractional dimension" (Mandelbrot, 1967). The paper considers the "coastline problem" – the idea that the size of a geographic feature depends on the scale at which it's measured. On a high-level map, the coast appears to be a smooth line and is certainly bounded, but zooming in reveals more and more fine details, like bays and inlets, that make it hard to specify the length with certainty. **Chaos theory** is a general term for the branch of math and science that studies nonlinear systems that are highly sensitive to their initial conditions. In a chaotic dynamical system, very small changes in the starting state may lead to unpredictably radical changes as the system evolves. Weather systems can exhibit this property, which is the source of the famous "butterfly effect" – the meme that a butterfly flapping its wings can cause extreme weather in a distant location. For a historical overview of the development of chaos theory and its connection to fractals, see Gleick (2008).

10 Sorting

It becomes evident that sorting on the basis of Quicksort is somewhat like a gamble in which one should be aware of how much one may afford to lose if bad luck were to strike.
Niklaus Wirth, *Algorithms + Data Structures = Programs*

INTRODUCTION

No other computational problem has been studied in more depth, or yielded a greater number of useful solutions, than sorting. Historically, business computers spent 25% of their time doing nothing but sorting data (Knuth, 2014c), and many advanced algorithms start by sorting their inputs. Dozens of algorithms have been proposed over the last 80-odd years, but there is no "best" solution to the sorting problem. Although many popular sorting algorithms were known as early as the 1940s, researchers are still designing improved versions – Python's default algorithm was only implemented in the early 2000s and Java's current version in the 2010s.

LEARNING OBJECTIVES

This chapter presents:

- A collection of the most popular sorting algorithms: selection sort, insertion sort, Quicksort, merge sort, and radix sort. We'll discuss their design strategies and the trade-offs between them.
- Strategies for analyzing complex divide-and-conquer algorithms with randomization, focusing on Quicksort.
- Techniques used by real-world modern sorting routines in Java and Python.

Studying sorting will give you deeper appreciation for how *algorithms move from theory into practice*. Quicksort, in particular, is a great case study that illustrates how to transform the basic idea of an algorithm into a practical implementation.

10.1 Sorting Preliminaries

10.1.1 Comparing and Ordering Items

A standard sorting algorithm takes an array (or list) as input and rearranges its items in increasing order, such that no item is strictly smaller than its predecessor. We can also sort in decreasing order, such that no item is larger than its predecessor; the two problems are equivalent. Therefore, sorting depends upon some notion of *order* in the data. For some inputs, like integers, ordering is straightforward. Strings are ordered lexicographically based on the numeric codes of their characters.

Many applications need to sort *records* containing multiple pieces of related information about a person, item, or thing. Typically, one item is designated the **key** that's used to order the records. For example, we might sort student records using student names as the key. If equal keys are possible, we need to decide how to handle them:

- Some applications break ties using a secondary key. For example, we might sort records using student name as the primary key, then break ties using age as the secondary key.
- A **stable** sort is one that maintains the initial ordering of records with equal keys. That is, the record that came first in the initial unsorted data will still be listed first in the sorted output. Stability is important in some applications, but some of the most popular sorting algorithms, including Quicksort, are not stable by default.

We'll always assume that there is a way to compare two data items and discover their relative ordering. In Java, a class may define a `compareTo` method to compare its objects. The method returns a negative, zero, or positive integer if the first object is less than, equal to, or greater than the given object.

```
String s1 = "Rat";
String s2 = "Ratt";

// Test if s1 comes before s2
if (s1.compareTo(s2) < 0) {
  System.out.println(s1 + " comes before " + s2);
}
```

10.1.2 Standard Libraries Exist, So Why Are You Reading this Book?

Try It Yourself

Here's an interview question. You need to sort an array of 100 million elements. What algorithm should you choose?

Solution

There are a number of different ways of reasoning about this problem. You could ask what kind of data is in the array (integers, strings, objects, etc.), whether the values are bounded in a range, and whether they're randomized or perhaps partially sorted. Any of those factors might make you lean toward one algorithm versus another. The simplest answer, though, is to *just use the sorting method that's already in your language's standard library.*

Every modern programming framework includes built-in versions of common algorithms, as well as implementations of the standard data structures. These implementations are highly tuned and offer excellent performance. Unless you have an unusual case, it's usually a good idea to take advantage of the features provided by your language's designers. This fact poses an existential challenge for both the author and readers of a book on data structures and algorithms: How does studying code that you don't need to implement yourself make you a better programmer? Consider:

- The hardest and most interesting problems don't have standard answers. When you work in emerging domains, you'll have to use your individual skill and judgment to design good solutions. By studying core concepts, you're *building a foundation* that you can apply to new problems that don't already have fixed answers.
- Fundamental data structures and algorithms are required to work on advanced topics, including networking, security, and artificial intelligence. If you aspire to work or research at the cutting edge of the field, you have to be familiar with basic ideas like recursion and sorting.
- Studying well-known algorithms in depth illustrates important algorithm design concepts. These skills are *transferable*: Understanding a topic like sorting will build fundamental skills that will make you better at everything, even if you don't ever need to write a custom implementation of Quicksort.

10.2 Quadratic Sorting Algorithms

Having now convinced you that the study of established algorithms is not a complete waste of time, we can turn attention to our first pair of sorting algorithms: **selection sort and insertion sort**. Both algorithms have $O(n^2)$ complexity in the worst case, hence, they're **quadratic sorting algorithms**. The two methods share the approach of doing $O(n)$ work to position one item on each iteration.

10.2.1 Selection Sort

Selection sort scans the array from left to right to identify the smallest element, then swaps it into its correct position. Consider this array:

2	3	1	7	11	5

Selection sort loops through the array, identifies that 1 is the minimum value, and swaps it into the first position, where it doesn't need to be considered further.

1	3	2	7	11	5

A second scan of the remaining $n - 1$ elements identifies 2 as the second-smallest element and swaps it into the second position.

1	2	3	7	11	5

A third scan will identify that 3 is the next smallest element and already, as it turns out, in its correct position. Each pass through the remaining array elements identifies the smallest remaining element and swaps it into its correct position.

The method below implements selection sort on an `int[]` named `a`. Notice that the method has a return type of `void` – the input array is sorted *in place*, without creating a new array. The outer loop, using index `i`, iterates through each array position. The inner loop scans the positions greater than `i` to find the smallest remaining item and swap it into position `i`.

```
/**
 * Selection sort
 *
 * @param  a  the array to sort
 * @return  nothing, the array is sorted in place
 */
public static void selectionSort(int[] a) {
  // Outer loop: swap the smallest remaining element into position i
  for (int i = 0; i < a.length - 1; i++) {

    int minValue = a[i];
    int minIndex = i;

    // Inner loop: find the minimum remaining element
    for (int j = i + 1; j < a.length; j++) {
      if (a[j] < minValue) {
        minValue = a[j];
        minIndex = j;
      }
    }

    // Swap positions i and minIndex
    int temp = a[i];
    a[i] = a[minIndex];
    a[minIndex] = temp;
  }
}
```

How do we know that selection sort is $O(n^2)$? First, let's consider the work performed by a sorting algorithm. There are two different measurements of interest:

- The number of *comparisons* the algorithm makes between items. Selection sort, like most popular sorting algorithms, makes pairwise comparisons to put items in order.[1]
- The number of *data movements* the algorithm makes. Selection sort performs only one swap per iteration, but other algorithms may require multiple item exchanges to move one value into its correct position.

Comparisons usually dominate a sorting algorithm's workload, so standard analyses focus on bounding the number of comparisons as a function of n. It's also normal for every data movement to be preceded by one or more comparisons, so we'd expect the number of movements to add, at most, a constant factor to the number of comparisons.

Selection sort performs n iterations of the outer loop. The first pass examines all n items to find the smallest one, then performs a single swap to put that item at the front of the array. The second pass considers the remaining $n-1$ items to find the second-smallest item, and so forth. Therefore, the total amount of comparisons required for selection sort is

$$T(n) = n + (n-1) + (n-2) + \cdots + 3 + 2 + 1.$$

This is a popular summation,

$$T(n) = \frac{n(n+1)}{2}.$$

Therefore, the number of comparisons required for selection sort is $O(n^2)$. Each iteration performs one swap, so the total number of data movements is $O(n)$.

Try It Yourself

Make an argument that even the best case for selection sort still requires $O(n^2)$ comparisons.

Solution

Selection sort performs the same steps for every input. Even if the input array is already sorted, or becomes sorted before completing the full set of comparisons, there's no way to discover that, so selection sort never stops early.

10.2.2 Insertion Sort

The insertion sort algorithm iterates through the array from left to right. As it proceeds, it builds a partially sorted sequence, where the items in the front are in sorted order relative to each other and the items in the back are waiting to be processed. Consider the following example array:

3	9	1	2	5

Insertion sort first examines 3. A single item is automatically sorted, so there's no additional work to do on the first iteration. The algorithm next examines 9, and finds that the first two

1 Radix sort, discussed at the end of this chapter, is a non-comparison-based sorting algorithm.

elements are in sorted order relative to each other. The third item is out of place relative to the first two, so the algorithm swaps it backwards into its correct position; the first three elements are now in sorted order.

1	3	9	2	5

The fourth item, the 2, is also out of place relative to the first three, so the algorithm swaps it backwards into its correct position.

1	2	3	9	5

The final iteration identifies that 5 is out of position and swaps it backwards into its correct position between 3 and 9. The array is now sorted.

1	2	3	5	9

The implementation of insertion sort uses two loops: an outer loop that iterates over each element in the array and an inner loop that swaps the current item backwards into its correct position relative to the earlier items.

```
/**
 * Insertion sort
 *
 * @param  a  the array to sort
 * @return  nothing, the array is sorted in place
 */
public static void insertionSort(int[] a) {
  // Loop over the elements of the array
  for (int i = 1; i < a.length; i++) {
    // Swap item at position i into its correct position
    // relative to items 0 to i - 1
    int j = i;
    while (j > 0 && a[j - 1] > a[j]) {
      int temp = a[j - 1];
      a[j - 1] = a[j];
      a[j] = temp;
      j--;
    }
  }
}
```

The inner loop is tricky: The variable `j` is used to swap the current item backwards until it's in its correctly sorted position relative to the earlier elements in the list. Consider the following situation:

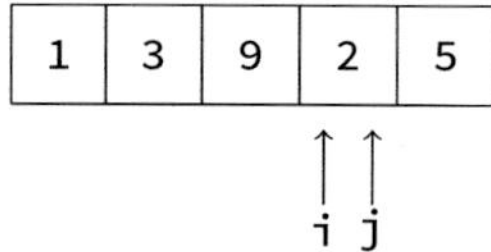

We need to swap 2 backwards into its correct position. The method compares `a[j]`, which is 2, to the previous element, 9, and finds that they're out of order. After swapping, the array is now:

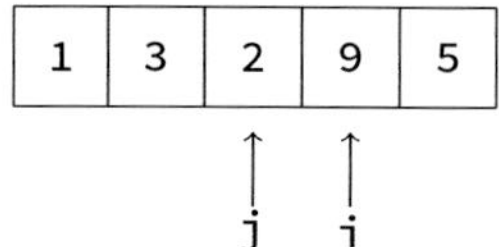

Another comparison between `a[j]` and `a[j - 1]` leads to a swap of 3 and 2, and the `while` loop terminates on the next iteration.

Insertion sort's analysis is similar to selection sort's analysis. In the worst case, the element at position k must swap $k - 1$ positions to find its correct location relative to its predecessors. For example, consider the reverse-sorted array

5	4	3	2	1

The first iteration considers 5 by itself and makes no changes. The second iteration compares 4 to 5 and does one swap. The third iteration moves 3 to the first position, requiring two comparisons and two movements, with the pattern continuing for the other elements. For an n-element array, the total amount of work is thus

$$T(n) = 0 + 1 + 2 + \cdots + (n - 2) + (n - 1).$$

This is the same standard summation form as selection sort, so the result is again $O(n^2)$. Unlike selection sort, which performed only one swap on each iteration, insertion sort may perform $O(n^2)$ swaps in the worst case.

Try It Yourself

Consider the *best* case for insertion sort, where the data are already sorted in the correct order. Give a result for the required number of comparisons.

Solution

If the array is already sorted, then the inner loop of insertion sort always terminates after making only one comparison. Therefore, the number of required comparisons is $O(n)$ in the best case, with no data movements. Insertion sort can be highly efficient on arrays that are close to sorted.

10.3 Quicksort

Quicksort, first described by C.A.R. (Tony) Hoare in 1961, is considered to be the fastest general-purpose sorting algorithm on typically occurring data sequences (Hoare, 1961a). Quicksort is a recursive algorithm that uses a **divide-and-conquer** approach. Its average complexity is $O(n \log n)$, but attaining that behavior requires careful engineering to deal with some tricky cases.

Before describing Quicksort,[2] let's consider the limitations of the quadratic sorting methods. Each iteration of selection sort makes an $O(n)$ pass through the input to move one element into its correct position. Insertion sort is a little more complicated, but has similar behavior – each linear pass through the data transports one item closer to its correct location. To sort more efficiently, we need to move *more than one item* on each $O(n)$ pass through the data. Items don't have to reach their final positions immediately, but ideally every item in the array should be closer to its final position after making a single pass through the input. Quicksort accomplishes this goal.

10.3.1 Sorting by Divide-and-Conquer

Quicksort uses the divide-and-conquer strategy: It solves a large problem by partitioning the input into smaller subproblems, which are themselves partitioned and solved recursively. The basic strategy is as follows:

- Choose one data item to be the **pivot**. There are several options for selecting the pivot, which we'll discuss in more detail shortly.
- Rearrange the input so that all items less than the pivot element are to its left and all items greater than or equal to the pivot are to its right. This is called the **partition** step, and it can be done in one pass through the array.
- The pivot element is now in its correct position relative to the other elements, with all smaller items to its left and all larger items to its right.
- Recursively Quicksort the left and right sides.

For example, consider the following array:

6	7	1	8	5	3	2	10	9	4

Suppose we choose the first element, 6, to be the pivot. Partitioning the array rearranges its elements so that the smaller values are to the left, the larger values are on the right, and the pivot is in the middle. Here's one possible partitioning result:

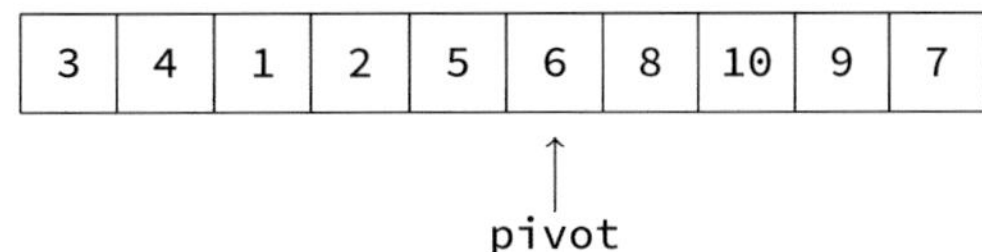

2 We'll follow the convention of the original paper by using "Quicksort" as the algorithm's proper name.

The array is not perfectly sorted, but both small and large items have moved closer to their eventual positions, with the pivot value in its correct final position. Also notice that it is fine for the left and right sides to have different lengths – it's unlikely that the pivot will be the true middle element. It's also possible for the array to contain duplicate elements, including duplicate copies of the pivot value. After completing this partition step, recursively sort the left side then the right side.

The standard Quicksort implementation takes three inputs: the input array, called `a` in the code below, and two index values, `left` and `right`, to keep track of the current region being recursively sorted. The code below uses a method called `partition` to select the pivot and rearrange the array, which we'll implement in the next section.

```
/**
 * Quicksort the region of input array a between left and right
 *
 * @param  a  the input array
 * @param  left  leftmost index of the partition region
 * @param  right  rightmost index of the partition region
 *
 * @return  nothing, the array a is sorted in place
 */
public static void quicksort(int[] a, int left, int right) {
    // Base case: no work is required for single element
    if (left >= right) {
        return;
    }

    // Partition the region between left and right
    //
    // Returns the final location of the pivot element
    int pivotIndex = partition(a, left, right);

    // Recursively sort the left and right sides
    quicksort(a, left, pivotIndex - 1);
    quicksort(a, pivotIndex + 1, right);
}
```

To call the method the first time, use:

```
quicksort(a, 0, a.length - 1);
```

10.3.2 Partitioning

Most of Quicksort's work is in the partition method. There are a number of partitioning strategies that differ in their details, but all require $O(n)$ time – that is, partitioning requires a linear scan through the region between `left` and `right`. The following popular partition method was developed by Nico Lomuto, described by Bentley (2016). Lomuto's partition chooses the *last element* in the region to serve as the pivot. It scans left to right, swapping any items smaller than the pivot toward the front of the region. After all elements have been examined, the pivot is swapped into its final position between the two groups.

```
/**
 * Quicksort partition
 *
 * @param  a  the input array
 * @param  left  index of the leftmost element in the partition
 * @param  right  index of the rightmost element in the partition
 *
 * @return the final position of the pivot value
 */
public static int partition(int[] a, int left, int right) {
  // Choose the last element for the pivot
  int pivot = a[right];

  // Swap index -- used to move smaller elements to
  // the front of the partition
  int swap = left;

  // Scan through the region from left to right
  for (int i = left; i < right; i++) {
      // Values smaller than the pivot swap to the front
      if (a[i] < pivot) {
          exchange(a, i, swap);
          swap++;
      }
  }

  // Swap the pivot into its final position
  exchange(a, swap, right);

  // Return the final pivot location
  return swap;
```

```
}

/**
 * exchange -- helper method that swaps two elements
 */
public static void exchange(int[]a, int s, int t) {
  int temp = a[s];
  a[s] = a[t];
  a[t] = temp;
}
```

The method is not that complicated, but can be difficult to visualize from the code alone. Consider the following example array, with `left = 0` and `right = 7`. The last element, 6, is the pivot.

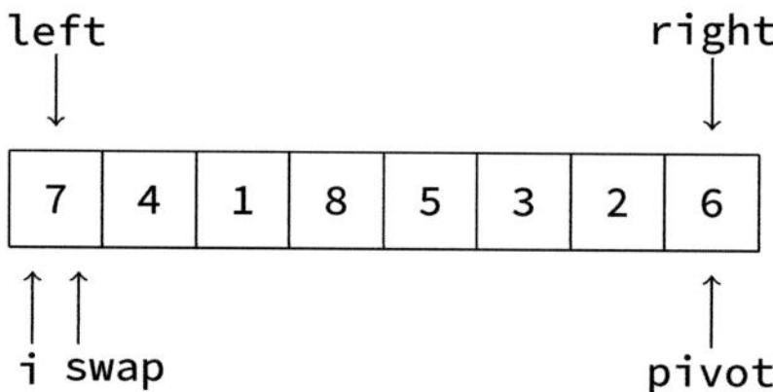

The first iteration checks if `a[i] < pivot`. This result is `false` (because `a[i] = 7`), so no swaps are made and `i` increments to 1. Notice that `swap` does not change.

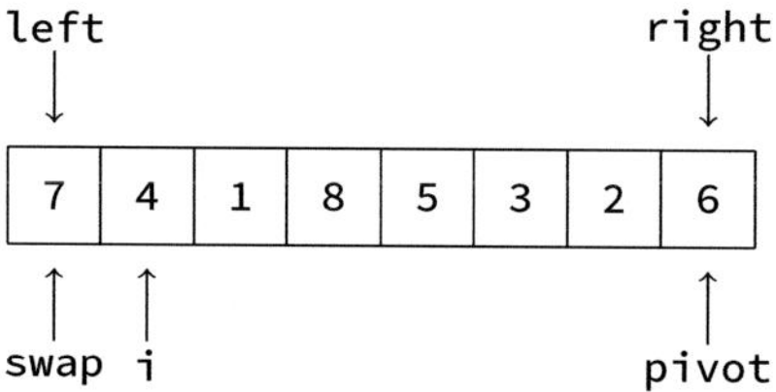

On the second iteration, `a[i]` is 4, which is less than the pivot value. The partition method exchanges the values at `swap` and `i`, which moves the 4 to the front of the array. After performing the exchange and incrementing both pointers, the array is now:

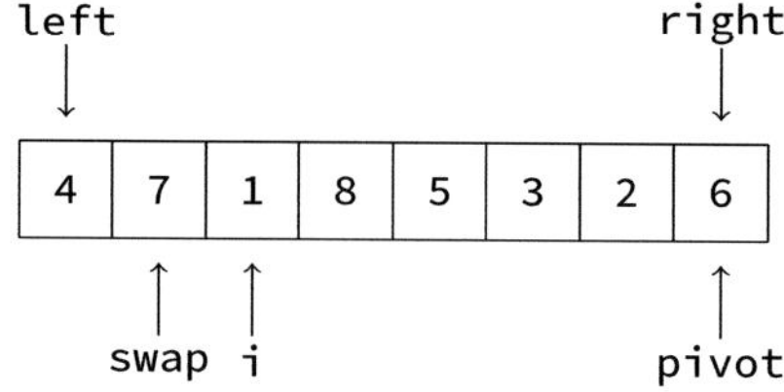

The next iteration again finds that `a[i]`, which is 1, is less than the pivot, so 1 swaps toward the front of the array, and both pointers are again incremented.

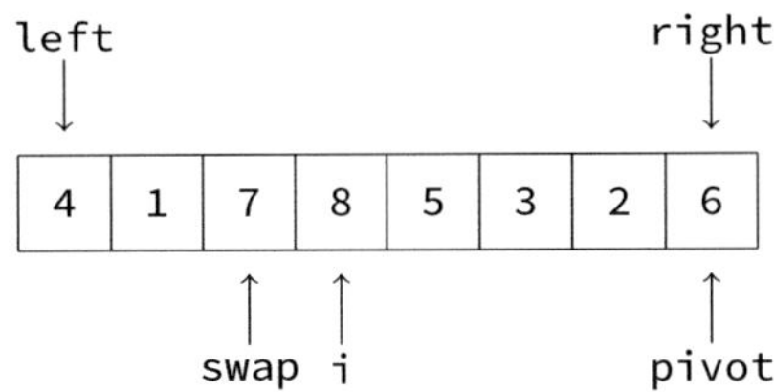

The value of `a[i]` on the fourth iteration, 8, is greater than the pivot, so no swap occurs.

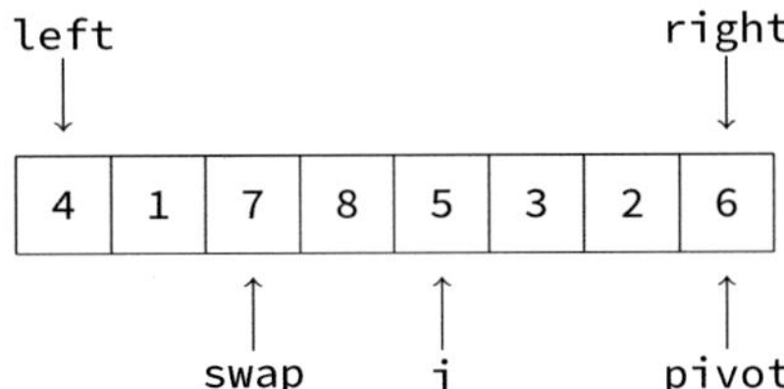

The following iteration finds that 5 is less than the pivot, which leads to another swap:

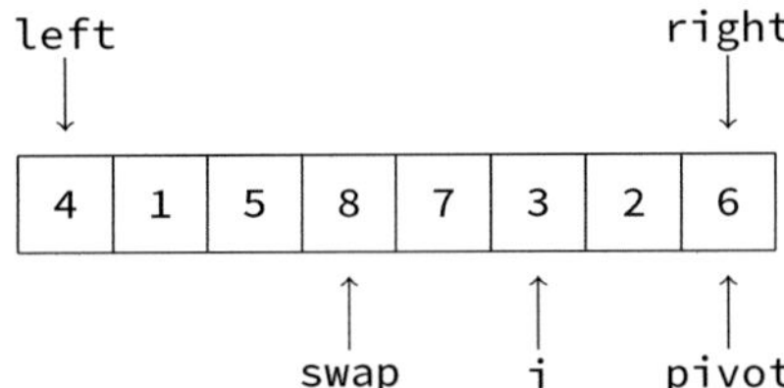

This process continues, with 3 and then 2 being swapped into the region toward the front of the array. When the loop ends, the array is in the following state:

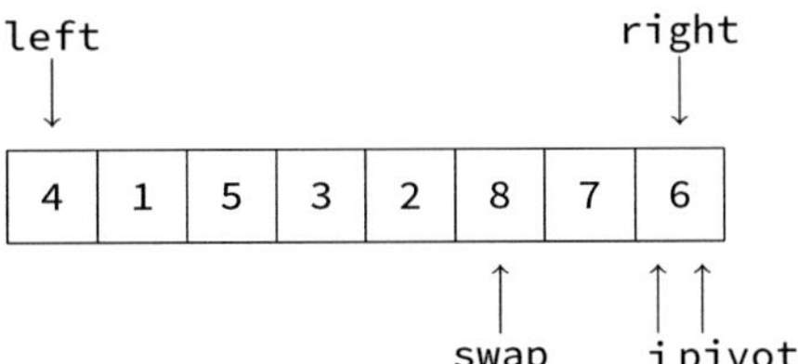

The final exchange moves the pivot value, 6, into the space between the two groups:

4	1	5	3	2	6	7	8

The array is now partitioned, with the pivot in its correct position relative to the other elements, all smaller elements to the left, and all larger elements to the right.

Try It Yourself

Make one pass of the partition algorithm over the left side of the array. Set `left = 0` and `right = 4`, so that 2 is the pivot element.

10.3.3 Correctness of `partition`

Before analyzing the complexity of Quicksort, let's consider an argument that it will, in fact, correctly sort its input. The key to showing the correctness of the algorithm is to reason about the `partition` procedure: If we can prove that the partition strategy is valid, then the recursive divide-and-conquer approach will result in a sorted array. Observe the state of the array at the end of a partition pass:

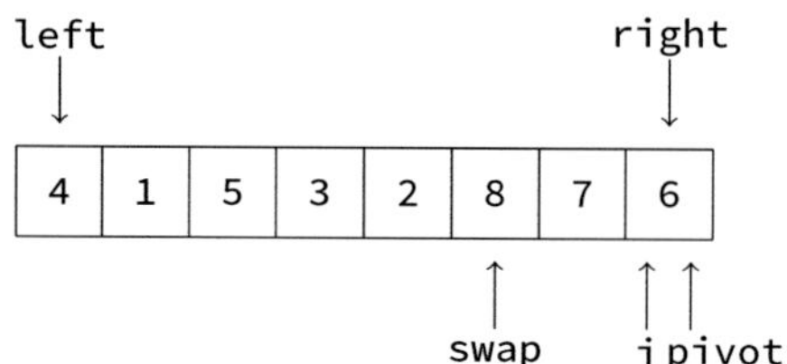

There are three properties of interest (Cormen et al., 2022):

1. The pivot is at position `right`. At the conclusion of the loop, `i == right`, so `i` is pointing to the pivot element.
2. Every index `k` with `left <= k < swap` has a value less than the pivot.
3. Every index `k` with `swap <= k < i` has a value greater than or equal to the pivot.

As long as the array is in this configuration at the end of the partition pass, we can exchange positions `swap` and `i`, which puts the pivot into its correct final position with the smaller and larger elements separated into the left and right sides.

We'll use the **loop invariant** strategy to prove the correctness of the partition method. Recall that a loop invariant describes a relationship that must hold at the beginning of the loop and then be maintained on every iteration. In this case, maintaining the three properties above will guarantee that the relationships among `i`, `swap`, the elements in the array, and the pivot value hold in such a way that the array must be in the desired state when the partition loop ends.[3]

The first step is to show that the invariant is satisfied on the first iteration. At the beginning of the loop, `i` and `swap` are both equal to `left`. There are no indices in the region less than either `i` or `swap`, or indices between the two, so the properties are satisfied. Now assume the invariant is true at the beginning of a loop iteration and consider what happens within the body of the loop. There are two cases to consider based on the relationship of `a[i]` and the `pivot`.

- The easier case occurs when `a[i] >= pivot`, as in the example below.

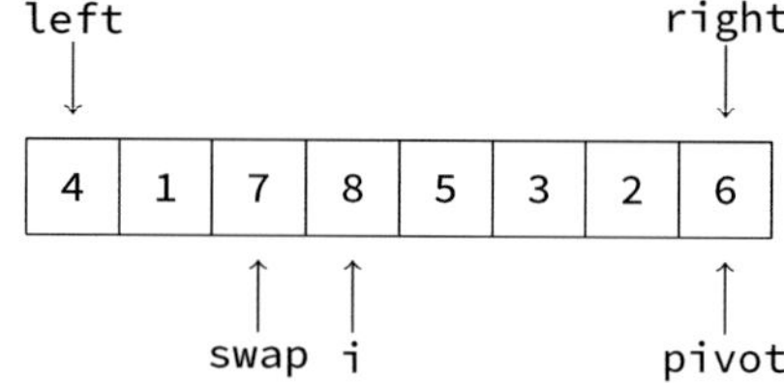

3 Review the proof of correctness for binary search in Chapter 5.

In this case, `i` advances to the next position and `swap` remains unchanged. Therefore, all items to the left of `swap` are the same as they were at the start of the iteration. The item pointed to by `i` (8 in this example) is greater than or equal to the pivot, so advancing `i` still guarantees that all items in the range `swap <= k < i` are greater than or equal to the pivot. Therefore, the invariant properties are maintained in this case.

- The other case occurs when `a[i] < pivot`, as in the example below:

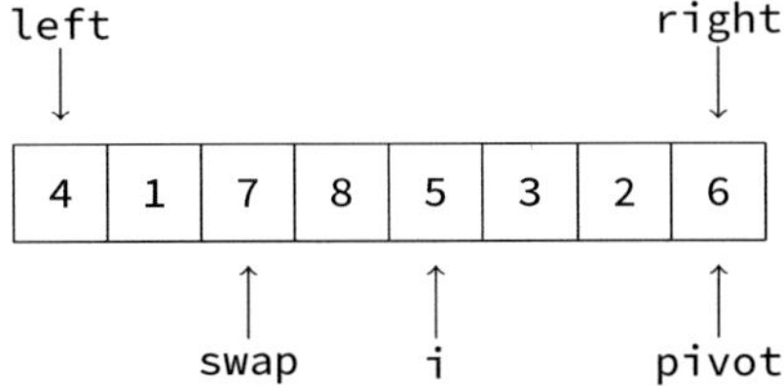

This case exchanges the elements at `i` and `swap` and increments both pointers. Note that, at the beginning of this iteration, we must have `a[swap] >= pivot`, by the third property. Therefore, immediately after the exchange, we know that `a[swap] < pivot` and `a[i] >= pivot`.

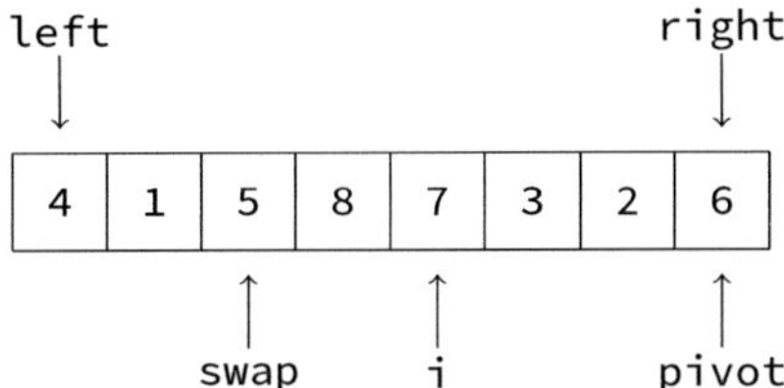

Incrementing `swap` restores the second property that all items left of swap are less than the pivot. It's also safe to increment `i` to maintain the third property that all items in the range `swap <= k < i` are at least as large as the pivot.

The final step is to argue that maintaining the invariants guarantees correct behavior for the procedure. If the invariant is maintained, then the loop will terminate with `i` equal to `right`, which is the position of the pivot. All values to the left of `swap` will be less than the pivot, and all other positions greater than or equal to the pivot. Therefore, we can exchange `a[swap]` and `a[i]` to place the pivot element into its correct position relative to the left and right sides.

10.3.4 Intuitive Analysis

Quicksort is, unsurprisingly, far more challenging to analyze than selection sort and insertion sort. In particular, the overall complexity depends on the choice of pivot value at each recursive step and its relationship to the rest of the data. First, observe that the best possible outcome is to always choose the *median element* at every partition step. Choosing the median results in the original array of size n being divided into two equal-sized subproblems.[4] Each of those problems will then be partitioned into two more equal-sized problems, and so forth. Graphically, the hierarchy of subproblems looks like the following:

4 The exact sizes of the recursive subproblems in the median pivot case depend on whether n is odd or even. If n is odd, both problems will have size $(n-1)/2$. If n is even, one subproblem will have $n/2$ elements and the other will have $(n-2)/2$. The average subproblem size is always $(n-1)/2$.

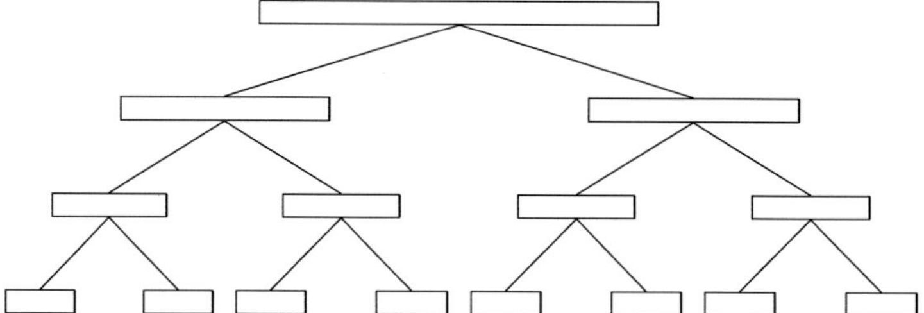

The first partition performs $O(n)$ work to place one item in its correct position and produce two subproblems with average size $(n-1)/2$. The second level of the recursion tree must partition those two subproblems, so the total amount of work at the second level is also $O(n)$, even if the two subproblems are being handled at different points in the recursive evaluation process. The same logic applies to the third level: Processing four problems, each of size approximately $n/4$, requires $O(n)$ total work. This pattern continues all the way down the tree.

Try It Yourself

If each level of the tree requires $O(n)$ total work, what is the total amount of work required for the entire process? How many levels are in the tree?

Solution

Dividing the problem in half at each step yields $\log n$ levels in the recursion tree, with the final level being a base case of single elements. Therefore, the total amount of work required for the entire process should be $O(n \log n)$.

Try It Yourself

Write down a recurrence relation for Quicksort in the case of equal partition divisions.

Solution

Recall that a recurrence relation expresses the amount of work required for a problem of size n in terms of the work required for the smaller subproblems. In Quicksort's best case, that means performing linear work for the partition step, then solving two recursive subproblems of equal size. Therefore, if $T(n)$ is the work required to Quicksort n elements, and we take the maximum subproblem size to be $n/2$, then

$$T(n) = n + 2\,T\left(\tfrac{n}{2}\right),$$

with a base case of $T(1) = 0$. Section 8.2.2 showed that this relation is satisfied by

$$T(n) = n \log n.$$

10.3.5 Worst-Case Analysis

So, intuitively, Quicksort is $O(n \log n)$ on average. It's possible, though, for a reasonable implementation to be *quadratic* in the worst case. Suppose that the pivot is the partition's minimum value. In that case, the partition step ends with the pivot in the leftmost position, with one subproblem of size $n-1$ and the other empty. A similar result occurs if the pivot is the maximum element. Now consider the worst case for Quicksort: choosing the maximum or minimum element in *every partition* at every level of the recursion tree.

- The first step partitions n elements to produce a subproblem of size $n - 1$.
- The second step processes those $n - 1$ elements to produce a subproblem of size $n - 2$.
- The third step produces a subproblem of size $n-3$, and so forth. Each step puts one item in its correct position, like selection sort.

Therefore, the total work required in Quicksort's worst case is $O(n^2)$:

$$T(n) = n + (n-1) + (n-2) + \cdots + 2 + 1.$$

Quicksort's performance depends on choosing "good" pivots at each step. The default strategy chooses the last element of the partition region as the pivot. If the array is random, this choice will, on average, yield pivots that are in the middle of the partition – some will be larger than the true median and some will be smaller, but the differences will even out. If the array is *already sorted*, though, the last element in a partition will be either the maximum or minimum, which guarantees worst-case $O(n^2)$ performance. It turns out that re-sorting data that is already almost sorted is a common case, so real-world Quicksort implementations need a better strategy than choosing the last element in the region to be the pivot.

Try It Yourself

Your friend argues that Quicksort is always $O(n^2)$ on sorted inputs. You argue that Quicksort may not be $O(n^2)$ even if the input is sorted, depending on the pivot selection algorithm. Give an example of a pivot selection strategy that could still yield $O(n \log n)$ performance even if the input array is sorted.

Solution

You could pick the center element at every step. If the array is sorted, that choice would result in pivots that consistently partition the array in half, so the overall work would still be $O(n \log n)$.

10.3.6 Average-Case Analysis with Random Pivots

The true median is the "best" pivot choice, but finding it requires checking every element in the partition region, which effectively doubles the time for the procedure. Rather than pay that overhead on every step, let's consider a version of Quicksort that chooses a *random element* as the pivot. The quality of the resulting partition then depends on *chance*: Some pivot choices will be close to the true median and yield a split that's close to equal, but others will lie close to the maximum or minimum value and yield an unbalanced division. The true average case analysis of Quicksort, therefore, requires reasoning about the performance of the algorithm when each level of the recursion tree may result in different splits, some good and others bad.

The following argument is based on one given by Steven Skiena (Skiena, 1998). Let's consider two classes of random pivot choices:

- "Good" pivots are those that lie closer to the median than to either end. Half of the possible pivots (the middle 50% of the data) belong to this category.
- "Bad" pivots are the other 50% of the data that lie closer to the minimum or maximum than to the median.

Each category consists of half the data, so *on average* we'd expect about 50% of randomly selected pivots to be good and the other 50% to be bad. The worst possible good pivot is one that partitions the data into groups of size $n/4$ and $3n/4$. The worst possible bad pivots are the maximum and minimum that split the input into subproblems of size $n - 1$ and 0.

Let's consider a sequence of random pivot choices that are consistently at the 25th or 75th percentile. These are "good" pivots, but only barely so, and each one produces subproblems of size $n/4$ and $3n/4$. The result is an unbalanced recursion tree:

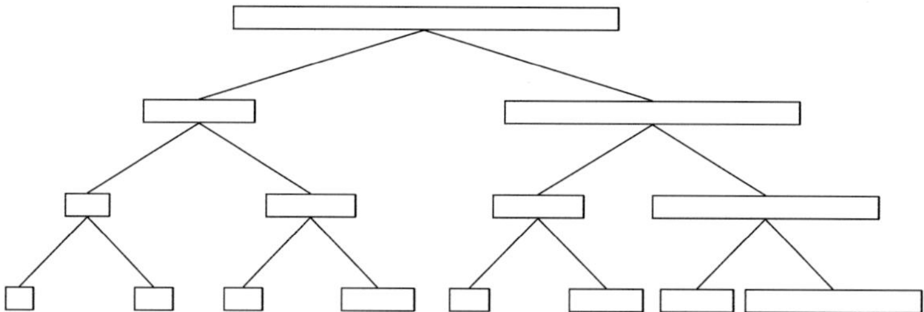

How deep is this tree? It turns out that the number of levels is still logarithmic in n! Specifically, the deepest branch has $\log_{\frac{4}{3}} n$ levels, which differs from $\log_2 n$ by only a constant factor. The total amount of work at each level of the recursion tree is still $O(n)$, so the overall Quicksort complexity under these assumptions is still $O(n \log n)$. In fact, any proportional split, no matter how unbalanced – 4 to 1, 10 to 1, 99 to 1, or worse – still results in an overall complexity of $O(n \log n)$ with only a constant factor difference from the optimal case.

What happens if we add in some "bad" splits? Suppose that 50% of our splits result in the absolute worst case of choosing the maximum or minimum value. These partitions do not meaningfully reduce the size of their subproblems, which effectively doubles the height of the tree – half of the partitions result in unbalanced, but still effective splits, and the other half do nothing. This result, while not great, only doubles the longest path through the tree. Therefore, even under an artificial construction where our randomized pivots are consistently of low (but not worst case) quality, the overall performance is still $O(n \log n)$.

Given these facts, how should pivot selection work in practice? A common rule is to choose the **median of three**. Examine the first, middle, and last elements of the partition and choose the median of those values to be the pivot. This strategy guarantees $O(n \log n)$ performance even if the array is sorted in increasing or decreasing order and requires only a constant amount of overhead on each partition step.

10.3.7 Improving Quicksort

There are a few other optimizations that real Quicksort implementations use. First, observe that the vanilla Quicksort algorithm makes a large number of recursive calls to sort very small partitions. To avoid that overhead, it's common to switch to a simpler sorting algorithm like insertion sort when the partition becomes small. Even if insertion sort is theoretically quadratic, it may still be faster than a fully recursive Quicksort.

Try It Yourself

Why is insertion sort a reasonable choice for a secondary sorting algorithm as opposed to, say, selection sort? Think about how the performance of each algorithm might depend on the distribution of the values in the partition.

Solution

Selection sort always requires $O(n^2)$ comparisons. Insertion sort can be faster if the data are already partially sorted. In the Quicksort case, we'd expect small partitions to be close to sorted, so insertion sort is a good choice.

A second optimization concerns arrays with repeated elements. Consider the following example:

0	1	1	0	0	0	1	1	0	1

Following the standard strategy of choosing 1 as the pivot and partitioning yields an array with a block of 0 followed by a block of 1. The pivot is the middle element between the two groups.

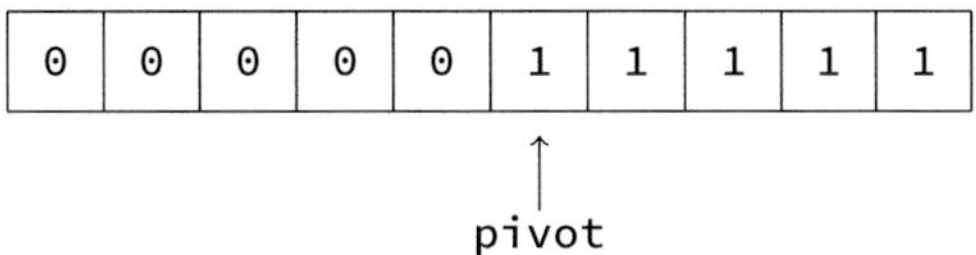

The recursive subarrays now have only same-valued elements. No matter how you choose the pivot element, Quicksorting a uniform array guarantees $O(n^2)$ performance. Arrays with many repeated elements are a problem for Quicksort because they can easily lead to uniform partitions.

The solution to this problem is a **three-way partition**, also called a "fat partition," which separates the input into three regions: values that are less than, equal to, or greater than the pivot.

< pivot	== pivot	> pivot

After the partition, values in the center region don't need to be considered any further. If the array has many duplicate values, the three-way partition can eliminate a significant number of elements at each step.

10.3.8 Java's `Arrays.sort`

`Arrays.sort` is a high-performance sorting routine with a hybrid approach. For object arrays, it uses Timsort, discussed in Section 10.4.3. For arrays of primitive types, it uses a **dual-pivot Quicksort** that chooses two pivots and partitions the array into three regions: those elements strictly less than the left pivot, those strictly greater than the right pivot, and those equal to or between the pivots.[5] It then recurses on each segment. On modern computers this approach can actually yield higher performance than the single-pivot version of the algorithm. The method includes other optimizations:

- The two pivots are chosen using a "tertiles of five" strategy. Pick five elements from the partition and sort them, then choose the second and fourth elements to approximately divide the partition into thirds.
- The method switches to insertion sort if the partition size is less than 48. The insertion sort implementation is also optimized to require fewer comparisons (OpenJDK, 2014).

Java's Quicksort is an interesting example of how even well-studied areas can still yield new innovations. Early versions of Java used a standard single-pivot Quicksort. In fact, multi-pivot Quicksorts were known in the 1960s and 1970s, but weren't widely used because they're theoretically no better than the conventional version. In 2009, Vladimir Yaroslavskiy published an updated dual-pivot algorithm, which was subsequently shown to yield empirically better performance than Java's existing Quicksort implementation (Yaroslavskiy, 2009). `Arrays.sort` switched to the dual-pivot algorithm in 2011. Subsequent research has shown that many of the benefits of Yaroslavskiy's method are due to better use of caching and the memory hierarchy on modern computers. Researchers have since proposed new versions of dual- and even triple-pivot Quicksorts (Kushagra et al., 2014; Nebel et al., 2016).

10.4 Merge Sort

Quicksort is a powerful and useful algorithm, but it isn't the only game in town for high-performance sorting. The merge sort algorithm, credited to mathematician and computing pioneer John von Neumann in 1945, is a pure divide-and-conquer sorting algorithm that is also $O(n \log n)$. Merge sort has advantages and disadvantages compared to Quicksort. It's generally more reliable and doesn't have the worst-case behavior and quirks of Quicksort, but it's usually two to three times slower on common workloads and requires allocating $O(n)$ extra space.

10.4.1 Implementation

Like Quicksort, merge sort uses a recursive divide-and-conquer strategy, based on the idea that it's easy to merge two sorted lists together in $O(n)$ time:

- Divide the input into its left and right halves.
- Sort the left half.

5 Note that this is different from the three-way fat partition. The fat partition also makes three regions, but uses only one pivot.

- Sort the right half.
- Merge the two sorted halves together.

How to sort the left and right halves? You guessed it: by recursively merge sorting them! The standard merge sort implementation creates new arrays to hold the two halves of the input data, then a new array to hold the sorted output. The implementation below uses the built-in `Arrays.copyOfRange` method, which takes a source array and two indices, then returns a new array containing a copy of those elements.

```
/**
 * Merge sort
 *
 * @param  a  the input array
 * @return  a new array containing the sorted input values
 */
public static int[] mergesort(int[] a) {
  // Base case: a single element is trivially sorted
  if (a.length == 1) {
    return a;
  }

  // Create new arrays for the left and right halves
     int[] left = Arrays.copyOfRange(a, 0, a.length / 2);
     int[] right = Arrays.copyOfRange(a, a.length / 2, a.length);

  // Recursively sort the left and right halves
  left = mergesort(left);
  right = mergesort(right);

  // Merge the two sorted halves
  int[] out = new int[a.length];
  int lPtr = 0;
  int rPtr = 0;
  int outPtr = 0;

  // Repeatedly copy the next smallest item from either the
  // left or right side to the output
  //
  // This loop runs until all of the elements on one side have
```

```
  // been processed
  while (lPtr < left.length && rPtr < right.length) {
    if (left[lPtr] < right[rPtr]) {
      out[outPtr] = left[lPtr];
      lPtr++;
    } else {
      out[outPtr] = right[rPtr];
      rPtr++;
    }

    outPtr++;
  }

  // At this point, one half (either the left or the right)
  // must have been completely merged into the output
  //
  // The loops below will copy the remaining data from the
  // unfinished side into the output

  // Copy any remaining values from the left side
  while (lPtr < left.length) {
    out[outPtr] = left[lPtr];
    lPtr++;
    outPtr++;
  }

  // Copy any remaining values from the right side
  while (rPtr < right.length) {
    out[outPtr] = right[rPtr];
    rPtr++;
    outPtr++;
  }

  return out;
}
```

Most of the work is in the merge operation, which is simpler than it appears. Consider the following array.

6	3	4	1	7	8	5	2

Dividing the array in half and sorting the two sides yields:

left: | 1 | 3 | 4 | 6 | right: | 2 | 5 | 7 | 8 |

The merge operation uses two pointers – called `lPtr` and `rPtr` in the implementation – to step through the sorted halves. At each step, it takes the smaller of the two values and copies it to the next open location in the output array.

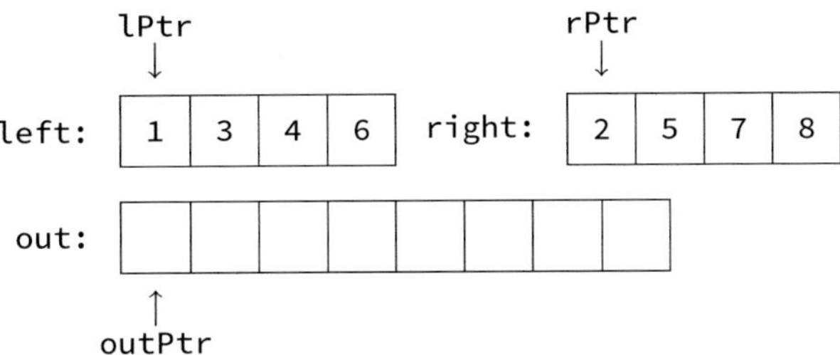

The first iteration compares 1 and 2 and discovers that 1 is smaller. The value is copied to `out` and both `lPtr` and `outPtr` advance.

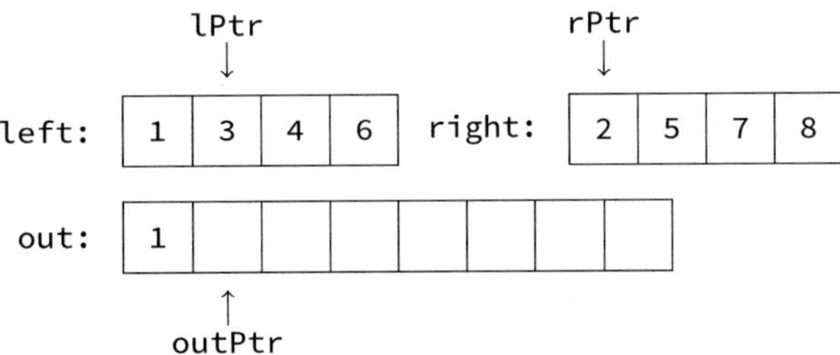

The second iteration finds that 2 on the right side is the next smallest value. After copying it to the output array, `rPtr` and `outPtr` advance.

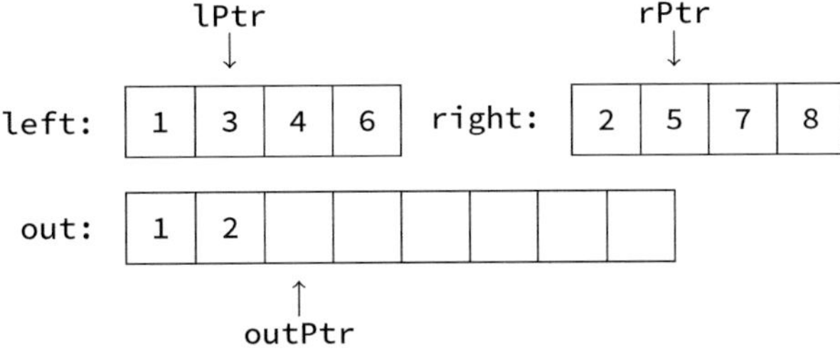

Try It Yourself

Continue the process until you reach the end of either the left or right array.

Solution

The first phase of the merge ends when all the elements from the left side have been copied over. There will be two elements from the right side remaining:

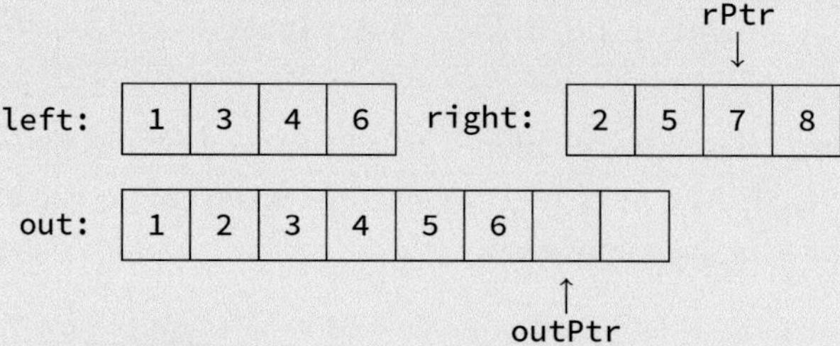

The final loop copies the last two elements from `right` to `out`.

Try It Yourself

Execute the complete recursive merge sort algorithm on the array

4	5	9	2	11	0	6	5	10	12	3

Tip: If the array length is odd, one side will be longer than the other; that's fine.

Solution

The first step splits the input array into two parts, one with six elements and the other with five. Each of those arrays is further subdivided until the method reaches the base case of single elements. Observe that, sometimes, a subarray may already be sorted, but merge sort doesn't identify that case and continues splitting.

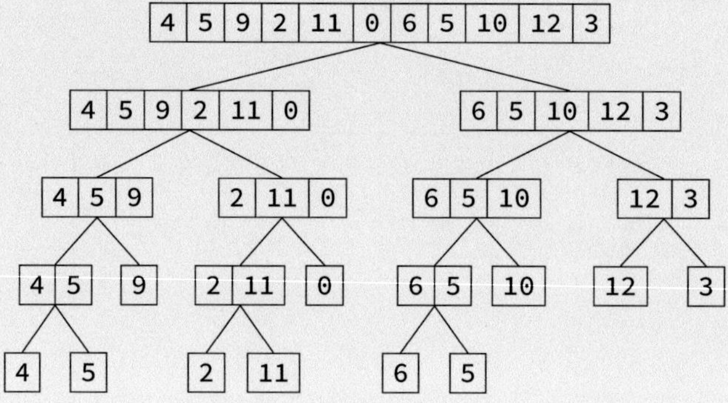

The merging starts at the bottom level and works its way back up, combining each pair of inputs to produce a sorted subarray.

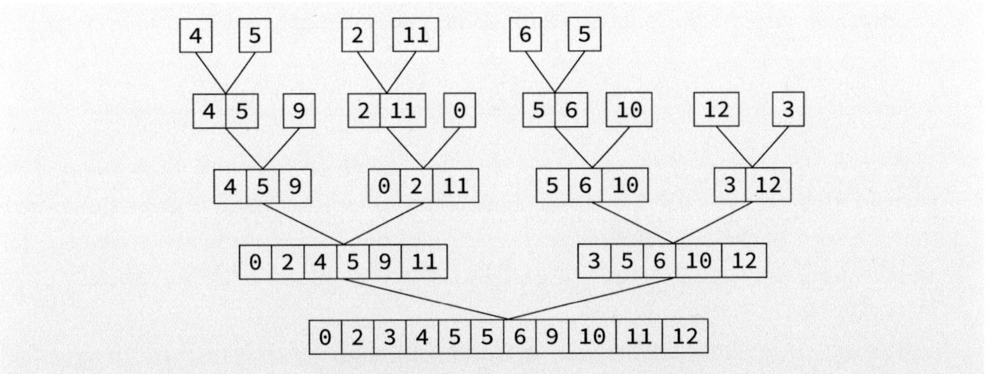

10.4.2 Analysis

Merge sort is a pure divide-and-conquer algorithm. It works by subdividing the input into smaller problems, recursively solving the subproblems, then doing $O(n)$ work to join the subproblem results together. Unlike Quicksort, which had an element of randomness due to the pivot selections, each recursive merge sort step produces equal-size subproblems (differing by only 1 if the total number of input values is odd). Therefore, the merge sort process is described by the recurrence relation

$$T(n) = 2T\left(\frac{n}{2}\right) + n,$$

which we know is $O(n \log n)$. You can arrive at the same result by reasoning about the recursion tree. Although merge sort is more consistent that Quicksort, it's generally slower because it spends more time copying data to the intermediate arrays. It also requires allocating $2n$ additional array elements to hold the left and right halves and the sorted output.

10.4.3 Merge Sort in Practice: Python's Timsort

Timsort, named after its creator, Tim Peters, is the default sorting algorithm in Python (Peters, 2002). It's also used by Java's `Arrays.sort` for arrays of non-primitive types. Timsort is a variation of merge sort: It generates sorted sequences in the data and merges them together. However, it takes advantage of the fact that many real-world data sets contain naturally occurring *runs* that are already sorted.

Like practical Quicksorts, Timsort uses a hybrid strategy. Small input arrays ($n < 64$) are sorted using insertion sort. Timsort breaks larger arrays down into a series of sorted runs of at least a set minimum length called `minsort`. The procedure is as follows:

- Start with the first element and look for a natural increasing or decreasing run.
- If the run is in decreasing order, reverse it to put it in increasing order.
- If the natural length of the run is less than `minsort`, add additional elements using insertion sort until you have a sorted run with at least `minsort` elements.
- Continue this process, looking for the next naturally occurring run.

For example, consider the following array and suppose that `minsort` is set to five:

4	2	1	3	7	5	6	8	9	10

The method would start by observing that the first three elements form a sorted strictly decreasing run and reorder them to be in increasing order. The length of that natural run is less than `minsort`, so the run would be extended by insertion sorting the next two elements to yield an increasing run of `[1, 2, 3, 4, 7]`. The second half of the array is a naturally occurring increasing run.

The algorithm continues this process, working through the array from left to right, building runs as it goes and merging consecutive pairs of runs with some clever bookkeeping.[6] Notice that for random data, the method is likely to result in a series of runs of length `minsort`, because random data should have few natural runs. If the data are already sorted, Timsort will simply recognize that the array consists of one continuous run and terminate.

Timsort is interesting in that it uses the basic concept of merge sort – merging sorted subarrays – but does so in a *non-recursive* way. Like Java's `Arrays.sort`, it's an interesting example of relatively recent progress in a well-established research area, as well as a further example of using detailed low-level optimizations to turn a theoretical algorithm into a real high-performance implementation.

10.5 Radix Sorting

And now for something completely different. All of the sorts we've considered so far, both the $O(n \log n)$ and $O(n^2)$ versions, are **comparison-based** sorting algorithms. That is, all of our methods have relied on the idea that it is possible to compare two data items and order them based on the result of the comparison. As we discussed at the beginning of the chapter, this is a good approach, because it makes no assumptions about the items being sorted – the algorithms we've discussed so far will work for anything, as long as there's a comparison method. An important result from the theory of sorting establishes that any comparison-based algorithm must be $\Omega(n \log n)$. However, in some cases it's possible to achieve *near-linear performance* with algorithms that don't rely on comparisons.

Radix sort (also called bucket sort or bin sort) orders items without ever comparing them to each other. It's one member of a family of distribution-based sorting algorithms that work by separating data into intermediate groups. The radix sort strategy separates data values based on their characters or digits. On each pass the method considers one position and bins items based on their values at that position. Suppose we want to alphabetize the following words:

```
alligator
zebra
aardvark
```

6 Specifically, it records references to the runs on a stack and monitors the relative sizes of the top elements to decide when it's appropriate to perform a merge (Peters, 2002).

```
echidna
elephant
squid
armadillo
snake
snail
squirrel
alpaca
```

The first pass of radix sort scans through the data items, separating them based on the value of the first letter. That is, all of the words starting with `a` are brought together, followed by the group of words that start with `e`, and so forth.

```
a: [alligator, aardvark, armadillo, alpaca]
e: [echidna, elephant]
s: [squid, snake, snail, squirrel]
z: [zebra]
```

Thus, with $O(n)$ work, we've roughly partitioned the list. Each item is now no more than four positions from its correct location. The binning process then repeats, subdividing the words in each bucket based on their second letter. Notice that `zebra` is in its own bin and doesn't need to be processed further.

```
aa: [aardvark]
al: [alligator, alpaca]
ar: [armadillo]
ec: [echidna]
el: [elephant]
sn: [snake, snail]
sq: [squid, squirrel]
z: [zebra]
```

The process continues, binning words based on the third letter (which separates `alligator` and `alpaca`), fourth letter (separating `snake` and `snail`), and fifth letter, which finally confirms the order of `squid` and `squirrel`. The final output list is the concatenation of the individual word lists.

Try It Yourself

Use the radix sorting approach, starting from the most-significant (leftmost) digit to sort the following integers. Remember that a number that has only three digits has an implicit leading zero.

```
8745, 3219, 358, 823, 8732, 8741, 342, 820, 3265, 3281
```

Repeat the problem, but now sort the digits starting from the *least-significant* (rightmost) digit. Radix sort can be implemented from either end. Starting at the significant digits will do a better job at quickly bringing the items into general order, but starting from the small end is useful for quickly processing short items.

Solution

Sorting from the most significant digit is conceptually easy. The first pass creates three groups for the numbers starting with 0, 3, and 8. The other passes further subdivide each bucket, as in the alphabetical example.

```
0: [358, 823, 342, 820]
3: [3219, 3265, 3281]
8: [8745, 8732, 8741]
```

Sorting from the least-significant digit is a bit trickier. Rather than dividing into buckets and then subdividing each bucket, it's easier to use a series of linear passes that partition on one digit at a time. The first pass organizes the values based on their ones digit. If you were to concatenate these lists, they would be sorted by the ones value.

```
0: [820]
1: [8741, 3281]
2: [8732, 342]
3: [823]
5: [8745, 3265]
8: [358]
9: [3219]
```

The second pass goes through the data in ones-digit order and moves each number to a new bucket based on its tens digit. For example, the first number processed in the second pass is 820, which is moved to the "20" bucket based on its second digit. The second number is 8741, which moves to the "40" bucket. Observe how everything is now sorted with respect to the lower two digits:

```
10: [3219]
20: [820, 823]
30: [8732]
40: [8741, 342, 8745]
50: [358]
60: [3265]
80: [3281]
```

The third pass continues with the hundreds digit; again the numbers are now sorted with respect to their lower three digits:

```
200: [3219, 3265, 3281]
300: [342, 358]
700: [8732, 8741, 8745]
800: [820, 823]
```

The final pass partitions on the thousands digits – 0, 3, and 8 – to bring everything into sorted order. The final output is the concatenation of the three buckets:

```
0000: [342, 358, 820, 823]
3000: [3219, 3265, 3281]
8000: [8732, 8741, 8745]
```

The complexity of radix sort depends on two parameters:

- n, the number of items; and
- d, the maximum length of an item, given in digits, characters, or other symbols that radix sort uses for the binning process.

Each $O(n)$ pass bins the items based on the value of one digit position. Therefore, in the worst case, radix sort must make d total passes to fully bin every item and the total number of operations is $O(nd)$. This is interesting: It's the first time we've seen an algorithm with a complexity that was not simply a function of one input size parameter. The performance of radix sort depends on the number of items that you need to sort, as expected, but also on the *size* of those items. In general, radix sort can be very fast in two cases:

- If the items have a known, small size. In this case, radix sort requires only a small number of passes over the input and the time required is effectively linear in n.
- If items are roughly uniformly distributed through the key space and n is small relative to the total number of possible keys. If so, it's unlikely to require very many passes through the data before the items are separated from each other. Ideally, you can avoid performing the full d binning passes and stop the sort once every item has been separated into its own bin.

Radix sort is not a good choice for data with long keys, highly variable lengths, or a nonuniform distribution, which leads to "clumps" of similar values that can't be distinguished without doing many comparisons.

10.6 Example Interview Questions Using Sorting

10.6.1 Problems Where You Sort and then Do Something

There is a large category of questions that can be summarized as "sort the input and then do something with the sorted values." For example:

- To find the median of an array, sort it and then get the middle element.
- To find the pair of elements that are closest to each other, sort the array and then examine pairs of consecutive elements, since the closest pair must be consecutive in the sorted array.
- To find the most frequently occurring item, sort the array and then perform a linear scan, keeping track of the length of runs of the same item and the length of the longest run overall.

In general, a question that asks about the relationships between items, or the relative position of an input compared to others, is a good candidate for a sort-first strategy.

Try It Yourself

Consider an array that has both positive and negative elements. Find the pair of elements with the maximum product. Remember that the maximum product could be formed by multiplying two negative values.

Solution

Sort the array, then compare the products of the last two elements (which must be the largest values) and the first two elements (which might have a larger product if both are negative). Notice that it's sufficient to perform two selection sort-style passes to identify the two largest and two smallest elements.

10.6.2 Finding the Median with Quickselect

Let's further consider the median-finding problem. Clearly you can solve this by sorting and then getting the middle element, but it's actually possible to find the median in $O(n)$ time using a clever recursive algorithm based on Quicksort partitioning. The algorithm is known as **Quickselect** and was created by Tony Hoare at the same time as the original Quicksort (Hoare, 1961b). Suppose that you perform a partition step on the input array. Let p be the final position of the pivot element.

- If you're lucky, $p = n/2$ and you can stop immediately: The pivot is the median element.
- If $p > n/2$, then the median is to the left of the pivot. Recursively partition the left side, checking for the item at position $n/2$.
- If $p < n/2$, then the median is to the right of the pivot. Recursively partition the right side, again looking for the item at position $n/2$.

This procedure can be generalized to find the item at position k in the sorted order:

```
/**
 * Find item at index k in the sorted ordering
 */
public static int quickselect(int[] a, int left, int right, int k) {
```

```
    // Base case for a single element
    if (left == right) {
      return a[left];
    }

    // Partition step
    int pivotIndex = partition(a, left, right);

    // Recursively search one side
    if (pivotIndex == k) {
      return a[pivotIndex];
    } else if (pivotIndex > k) {
      return quickselect(a, left, pivotIndex - 1, k);
    } else {
      return quickselect(a, pivotIndex + 1, right, k);
    }
}
```

Notice that Quickselect only recurses into one side of the partition. Therefore, if the pivot selection is good, it will be able to discard half of the remaining search space on each evaluation and the total required work will be at most

$$T(n) = n + \frac{n}{2} + \frac{n}{4} + \cdots + 4 + 2 + 1 = 2n,$$

which is $O(n)$.

10.6.3 National Flag Problems

Give an $O(n)$ algorithm for sorting an array that contains only 0, 1, and 2 values.

Edsger Dijkstra called this the *Dutch national flag problem*, after the flag of the Netherlands, which has horizontal stripes of red, white, and blue (Dijkstra, 1976). The goal is to make a linear pass over the array and separate the 0 values into the left-hand partition, 2 values into the right-hand partition, and 1 values in the middle. It's equivalent to performing the three-way fat Quicksort partition with 1 as the pivot element. The solution uses two pointers, `leftSwap` and `rightSwap`, to move 0 elements to the left and 2 elements to the right. Here's the core of the method:

```
// Dutch national flag partition

int leftSwap = 0;
int rightSwap = a.length - 1;
int i = 0;
```

```
int pivot = 1;

// Iterate through the array, swapping items left or right
while(i <= rightSwap) {
  // Values < pivot get swapped to the left
  if(a[i] < pivot) {
    exchange(a, i, leftSwap);
    leftSwap++;
    i++;
  }

  // Values > pivot get swapped to the right
  else if(a[i] > pivot) {
    exchange(a, i, rightSwap);
    rightSwap--;
  }

  // Values == pivot don't swap -- they collect in the middle
  else {
    i++;
  }
}
```

The tricky part is the handling of `rightSwap`. Notice that when `a[i] > pivot`, `i` is not incremented. This is required, because we don't know how the value being swapped into `i`'s position compares to the pivot. Keeping `i` unchanged means that the swapped value will be checked on the next iteration and moved to its appropriate spot.

Try It Yourself

Step through the solution on the array `[2, 2, 2, 0, 0, 0, 1, 1, 1]` and verify that it works as expected.

SUMMARY

This chapter has explored both the theoretical and practical aspects of sorting algorithms. Even if you never have to write your own high-performance sort routine, a solid understanding of sorting will prepare you for further work on advanced algorithms and data structures. As you're working through this chapter, keep the following in mind:

- Divide-and-conquer using recursion is an excellent building block for advanced algorithms, and we'll see more examples in future chapters. The quality of the solution depends, however, on generating good subproblems.
- An algorithmic technique can often be repurposed to solve many different problems. For example, the basic concept of a Quicksort partition can be reused for many problems where you need to split an array into groups. Learning common algorithmic strategies will help you build a mental library of techniques that you can draw on to solve new problems.
- There's no "best" sorting algorithm – there are many different algorithms that can be good in some contexts and poor in others.

Finally, there's one major sorting algorithm that we haven't discussed here: **Heapsort**, which we'll cover in Chapter 19 after introducing the heap data structure.

EXERCISES

Understand

1. Sort the following strings using insertion sort.

```
penguin
pangolin
eagle
chameleon
echidna
ermine
eider
```

2. Manually execute one Quicksort partition on the strings in the previous problem.
3. Modify insertion sort to work on an input `String[]`. Tip: Use the `String` class's built-in `compareTo` method.
4. Now modify insertion sort to work on an `ArrayList<Integer>`. Think about how to compare and swap elements.
5. Would radix sort be a good choice for names? Why or why not? Hint: Think about the length and distribution of real names. Are you likely to get an even distribution of names throughout the space of possible strings?
6. Modify insertion sort to sort in decreasing order.
7. Modify Quicksort to sort in decreasing order. Tip: Think about how to change the partition method so that larger elements are on the left and smaller elements are on the right.
8. Your friend says that Quicksort is bad on sorted arrays. How do you respond?
9. Next, your friend proposes starting every Quicksort with a linear pass over the input to determine if it's already sorted or not. Is this worth doing? Why or why not?

10. Consider a variation of selection sort that finds both the minimum and maximum element on each pass and swaps them into their appropriate locations. Analyze the complexity of this method and show that it's still $O(n)$.

11. Another fun algorithm is the **Shell sort**, named after its inventor, Donald Shell (Shell, 1959). Do some research and explain how Shell sort uses insertion sort but achieves $O(n \log n)$ average performance.

12. Give an example of a case where the standard Lomuto partition is not stable; that is, show how the order of two equal elements after a partition step may not match their order before the partition.

13. Suppose you have two sorted `ArrayList<Integer>`. Write a code fragment to merge both input lists into a sorted output list. You can allocate a new list to hold the output.

14. Explain how you could efficiently sort an array that contains repeated elements with only four distinct values, even if the values are not 0 to 3. Call this the Mauritian national flag problem.

15. **Bubble sort** is a well-known quadratic sorting algorithm whose "fame exceeds its usefulness" (Baecker, 1998). The method compares pairs of elements and "bubbles" the largest element to the end of the array on each pass. Here is a pseudocode version of the method:

```
void bubblesort(a) {
  swapped = true

  while (swapped) {
    swapped = false

    for (i = 1; i < a.length; i++) {
      if (a[i] < a[i - 1]) {
        swap a[i] and a[i - 1]
        swapped = true
      }
    }
  }
}
```

The algorithm runs until a pass completes with no swaps, which indicates the array is sorted. Execute the bubble sort algorithm on the following example array:

7	3	2	5	9	1

16. Make an argument that bubble sort is $O(n^2)$ in the worst case. What about its best-case behavior?

17. Implement bubble sort as a Java method.

Apply

18. Suppose that Quicksort repeatedly picks pivots that divide each partition into subproblems of size $n/4$ and $3n/4$. What is the expected number of levels in the most shallow branch of the tree?

19. What if the sizes of the subproblems are pn and $(1 - p)n$, for some $p \in (0, 0.5]$? What is the expected number of levels in the deepest branch of the tree?

20. Write a method called `compare` that takes an `int[] a` and `int[] b` as inputs. Your method should order the two arrays by returning `a[i] - b[i]`, where `i` is the first index where the two elements differ. You can assume that `a` and `b` have the same length.

21. Now use the `compare` method to sort the rows of an `int[][]`. You can pick any sorting algorithm you want to use. You can swap rows in a matrix like scalar values:

```
// Exchange rows i and j in int[][] a
int[] temp = a[i];
a[i] = a[j];
a[j] = temp;
```

22. Write a partition variation that takes an array with both positive and negative elements and separates them from each other, with the negative elements to the left and positive to the right.

23. Write a partition variation that places the even elements in an array on its left side and the odd elements on its right side. Tip: Think about doing a partition, but you're not partitioning on the actual value of `a[i]`.

24. Implement a method that sorts an array and then uses a linear scan to find the pair of elements that are closest to each other.

25. Implement a method that sorts an array and then performs a linear scan to find the most frequently occurring item.

Extend

26. Modify Quicksort to switch to insertion sort for small partitions.

27. Here's a variation on the strategy of switching to insertion sort for small partitions. Set a threshold k and modify the base case of Quicksort to immediately return when the partition size is less than or equal to k. After the recursive procedure completes, perform one pass of insertion sort over the entire array. No item should be more than k positions from its final location, so this should take $O(kn)$. Code this variation and experiment with timing it on random arrays to find a good value for k.

28. How does the strategy of making one insertion sort pass at the end compare to insertion sorting small partitions? Again, use timing experiments.

29. A variation on Quickselect is to return the k smallest items in the data set. Modify `quickselect` to find the pivot item at final position k, then return an array of the elements `a[0]` to `a[k - 1]`, which are the k smallest values in the array. Note that the items don't have to be in sorted order.

30. Explain how you could use the `quickselect` variant from the previous problem to find the top-k largest elements.

31. Suppose that you want to use radix sort on an array containing the integers from 1 to n. Make an argument that radix sort can't really do better than $O(n \log n)$ in this case. Tip: Think about the number of digits in a number n.

32. Suppose that you apply radix sort to the array in the previous problem but instead of binning on the base-10 digits 0–9 at each step, you bin on the value of each *byte* in a number. That is, on the first pass, bin values based on their most-significant byte, then subdivide those bins based on the second byte, and so forth. How many passes would you expect radix sort to take in this case?

33. Implement a variation of merge sort that switches to insertion sort on small partitions. How does it compare to the regular merge sort implementation?

34. Make an argument that the three-way partition method is guaranteed to execute correctly. Establish that the following three properties are initialized and maintained by the algorithm:

    - Any item at a position `k < leftSwap` is strictly less than the pivot value.
    - Any item at a position `k > rightSwap` is strictly greater than the pivot value.
    - Any item at a position `leftSwap <= k < i` is equal to the pivot value.

    The method terminates when `i > rightSwap`. Argue that this guarantees that positions `leftSwap <= k <= rightSwap` must all be equal to the pivot value.

35. Here's an idea: What if we made a three-way merge sort? Divide the input into three parts, recursively sort each part, and then merge the three sorted subarrays back together. How would you expect this algorithm to perform compared to conventional merge sort? Justify your answer.

36. Supposing that you did go through with the three-way merge sort idea, you'd need a way to merge three sorted lists. Write statements that can take three sorted arrays `a`, `b`, and `c` and merge them together into one sorted output array. You need to consider what happens when one of the input arrays is exhausted and there are two that still have elements waiting to be merged.

37. It turns out that multi-way merging is an important component of **external sorting** algorithms created to work with very large data sets that can't fit entirely within main memory. Do some research into external sorting and explain how an external merge sort can process huge data files.

NOTES AND FURTHER READING

As we said at the beginning of the chapter, sorting is the most well-studied computational problem. Every major algorithms text spends time on sorting algorithms. Robert Sedgewick carried out a detailed study of Quicksort implementation, including an investigation of pivot selection and partitioning methods (Sedgewick, 1978). See Bentley and McIlroy (1993) for an entertaining summary of the challenges encountered in redesigning `qsort`, the default sorting routine in C on UNIX systems. The authors discuss issues like the overhead of performing swaps, pivot selection (including different strategies for small, medium, and large arrays), switching to insertion sort, and more efficient three-way partitioning. Finally, there are a number of online tools and videos that will visualize sorting algorithms. The best visual overview of sorting algorithms is Ronald Baecker's *Sorting Out Sorting*, which should be regarded as a rite-of-passage for all computer science students (Baecker, 1998).

11 Stacks

It was when I found out I could make mistakes that I knew I was on to something.
Ornette Coleman

INTRODUCTION

The stack is the Incredible Hulk of data structures: superficially dumb, but so strong that it doesn't matter. Stacks have only a few basic operations and they're easy to implement, but they unlock a number of algorithms that are both theoretically powerful and practically important. You may recall that we previously discussed the role of the stack in recursion, and there's a connection between the stack as an explicit data structure and recursive methods that use a stack implicitly.

LEARNING OBJECTIVES

This chapter is an introduction to stacks, primarily focused on their implementation and key methods. At the end of it, you'll be able to:

- Describe the stack abstract data type, its operations, and how to implement a stack using linked and array lists.
- Use a stack to validate HTML tags.
- Evaluate prefix and postfix arithmetic.
- Use a stack to perform calculations and transform between notations.

This chapter's project is a tiny web browser with the ability to fetch and view web pages, click on links, and keep track of the history of visited pages using a stack. In addition to demonstrating a practical stack application, the tiny browser will give you an introduction to building graphical interfaces using Java Swing components.

11.1 The Stack Abstract Data Type

Recall that an abstract data type (ADT) is a description of the high-level behavior of a data structure – what it is and can do – separated from its internal implementation. The ADT describes the basic relationship among the data structure's elements and the methods that it provides to interact with those elements. A stack is a linear sequence of items that allows **last-in-first-out** (LIFO) access. Like a stack of pancakes, a stack data structure has a "top" item and stack operations interact only with that top element. This section discusses the basic stack methods, Java's `Stack` class, and then shows how to implement a stack using a list.

11.1.1 Stack Methods

The best thing about stacks is that they're mechanically simple. The stack abstract data type has two primary methods:

- `push`, which adds a new item to the top of the stack; and
- `pop`, which removes and returns the top item.

Unlike an array or list, you can't interact with any internal items. There are no `get`, `set`, or `remove` methods that interact with an element by its index. Many implementations, including Java's, have a small number of utility methods; the most common are:

- `size`, which returns the number of elements in the stack;
- `empty`, to test if the size is zero; and
- `peek`, which returns the top element without removing it.

11.1.2 Example: Validating HTML

Let's get started using stacks with a practical example: testing if tag pairs in an HTML page are properly matched. The World Wide Web, or just "the web," is a **hypermedia** system: Every web page is a document that can contain links to other documents. Web pages are written in HTML (the *Hypertext Markup Language*), which declares both the content and *tags* that specify the page's format and links. The idea of hypermedia existed in various forms going back to the postwar era,[1] but its introduction to the Internet is due to the British computer scientist Tim Berners-Lee. In 1989, while working at the CERN physics laboratory in Switzerland, Berners-Lee proposed creating an Internet-connected hypermedia document system for scientists to share their work (Berners-Lee, 1989), which would develop into the World Wide Web and become the dominant way of interacting with online content for billions of people.

Here's a small example web page:

```
<html>
  <head>
    <title>Page title</title>
  </head>

  <body>
    <h1>Top-level heading</h1>

    <p>Paragraph of text</p>
```

1 Vannevar Bush proposed the *memex* system, a pre-computer version of the concept, in 1945. See Chapter 16.

```
   </body>
</html>
```

Tags are enclosed in angle brackets. Most, but not all, tags come in pairs, where an opening tag, like <body>, is paired with a closing tag that begins with a forward slash, like </body>. Tags are hierarchical:

- The top-level <html> tag identifies everything it encloses as an HTML document.
- The <head> tag encloses meta-information about the page. The <title> tag is a meta-element that gives a heading that will be displayed in the browser's tab.
- The <body> tag encloses the page's content. Here, <h1> is used to identify a top-level heading, which will appear big and bold when it's displayed; <p> is the standard tag for denoting a paragraph of text. HTML ignores whitespace and uses tags to determine the page's layout.

HTML standards require that the tags in a page be properly nested and closed. It's one of a set of requirements that make a page "valid," which ensures that it can be properly displayed by browsers and indexed by search engines.

Try It Yourself

Verify that the example page has correctly matched tag pairs. Think about how you might approach the problem of testing if the tag pairs in a page are properly matched.

You might initially try testing if the outer symbols are matched, then recursively move inwards, but a quick check shows that method won't work. We need to *defer* making a decision about an opening tag until we've processed its interior tags. This turns out to be a perfect fit for a stack: Keep a record of data that you've seen, but don't want to process yet, so you can make a decision about it later. Suppose that we've scanned the page to extract all of its tags into an ArrayList<String> – we'll give a way to do that in a moment. The basic procedure for matching tag pairs is as follows:

- Process the list from left to right. Push each opening tag onto the stack.
- When you see a closing tag, it should be matched up with an opening one of the same type on top of the stack. Pop the opening tag and continue.
- If you reach the end of the input and the stack is empty, then everything has matched.

This process will fail if a closing tag doesn't have its correct partner on the top of the stack, or if you reach the end of the input with unmatched tags still on the stack. In either case, the sequence isn't valid.

Let's step through this algorithm on the example page to see how the stack works. After extracting the tag names, the input list is:

```
[html, head, title, /title, /head, body, h1, /h1, p, /p, /body, /html]
```

The method starts with the opening `html` tag and pushes it onto the stack, then pushes the opening `head`. Conceptually, think of the stack as a vertical sequence of items, where the oldest item is at the bottom and the most recent is at the top; the only reference is to the top element:

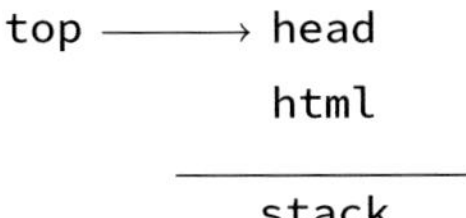

The next tag is `title`, which also goes on the stack:

```
top ——→ title
        head
        html
        ______
        stack
```

The fourth tag is `/title`, which closes the one on top of the stack. Pop it off, leaving the first two still waiting for their matches.

```
top ——→ head
        html
        ______
        stack
```

Try It Yourself

The fifth tag is `/head`, which closes that block and matches the one on top of the stack. Pop it off, then continue the algorithm to process the `body` block. Your result should show that the stack is empty when you finish the input.

Here's an example Java method that executes the matching algorithm on an input list of tag names.[2] It uses the built-in `Stack` class, which takes the type of the internal data in angle brackets – in this case, a `Stack<String>`. Import `Stack` using

```
import java.util.Stack;
```

at the top of the class.

```
/**
 * Match HTML tags
 *
 * @param  tags  ArrayList of tag names
 * @return  true if all tags match, false otherwise
 */
public static boolean validate(ArrayList<String> tags) {
  // Initialize the stack
```

2 This version assumes that all tags should be paired. The end-of-chapter questions ask about extensions to deal with single tags that don't have to be matched.

```
  Stack<String> stack = new Stack<String>();

  // Loop through the tag sequence
  for (String tag : tags) {
    // Closing tag should have a match on the stack
    if (tag.startsWith("/")) {
      // Get the name of the tag after the /
      String name = tag.substring(1);

      // Compare to the top of the stack
      if (!stack.pop().equals(name)) {
        return false;
      }
    } else {
      // Opening tags are pushed on the stack
      stack.push(tag);
    }
  }

  // If the stack is empty everything matched
  return stack.empty();
}
```

The method looks for tags starting with `/`. When it finds one, it extracts that name after the `/` using `substring`, then compares it to the top of the stack.

Try It Yourself

The program is not quite complete. Modify it to detect the case where the input is a closing tag and the stack is empty. Tip: Use the `empty` method.

Solution

Add an additional clause to the `if` statement, like so:

```
if (stack.empty() || !stack.pop().equals(name)) {
  return false;
}
```

How to extract the tag sequence? The method below uses a direct approach that can handle multiple tags on the same line:

- It reads each line of the input file using `Scanner`.
- On each line, it loops through the characters looking for an opening < character.
- When it finds one, it builds a string of all characters until the next closing >, then adds that string to the tag list.

```
/**
 * Extract HTML tags from a file
 *
 * @param  filename  name of the HTML file
 * @return  ArrayList of tag names
 */
public static ArrayList<String> getTags(String filename) {
  // Open the file
  Scanner scanner = null;
  try {
    scanner = new Scanner(new File(filename));
  } catch (FileNotFoundException e) {
    e.printStackTrace();
  }

  ArrayList<String> tags = new ArrayList<String>();

  // Read each line
  while (scanner.hasNextLine()) {
    String line = scanner.nextLine();
    String tag = "";
    boolean inTag = false;

    // Loop through the characters, looking for <
    for (int c = 0; c < line.length(); c++) {
      char ch = line.charAt(c);

      if (ch == '<') {  // Start of a tag
        inTag = true;
      } else if (ch == '>') {  // End of tag
        inTag = false;
        tags.add(tag);
```

```
33          tag = "";  // Clear the tag
34        } else if (inTag) {  // Part of tag
35          tag += ch;
36        }
37      }
38    }
39
40    return tags;
41 }
```

Lines 9–14 create a `Scanner` to read from the input file. This action can throw a `FileNotFoundException` so it has to be wrapped in a `try-catch` block.

11.1.3 Implementations

Like lists, stacks can be implemented using either a link-based or array-based approach. Both approaches are just subsets of the list implementations we've already described.

- An array-based stack maintains a single backing array, like an array list, and implements the `push` method by appending to the end of the array and the `pop` method by removing the last item. Both operations are $O(1)$ on average.
- Link-based stacks use the head of a singly-linked list as the top element. Pushing adds a new item to the front of the list and popping removes the current head. Again, both operations are $O(1)$.

Observe that the two implementations have reversed internal orderings: The array stack has its top value at the end, but the linked stack has it at the head.

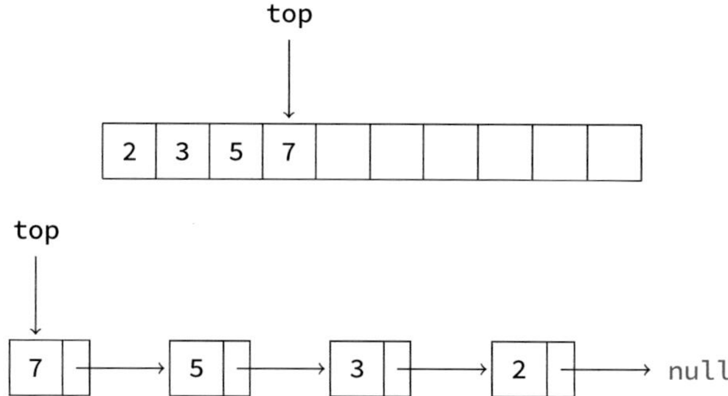

The simplest stack implementation is a wrapper around a list, with `push` and `pop` as aliases for the underlying list methods. Java's `Stack` class is an extension of `Vector`, which is an array-based list. The class below uses `ArrayList` as the internal data structure. `T` is the generic type for the stack's data.

```
/**
 * Example array-based stack
 */
```

```
import java.util.ArrayList;

public class Stack<T> {

  private ArrayList<T> items;

  public Stack() {
    this.items = new ArrayList<T>();
  }

  public void push(T newItem) {
    this.items.add(newItem);
  }

  public T pop() {
    return this.items.remove(this.items.size() - 1);
  }
}
```

Try It Yourself

Add implementations of `peek`, `size`, and `empty` to the example `Stack` class.

You can also implement a stack that interacts directly with the backing array without going through the intermediate list; see the end-of-chapter questions.

11.2 Stack-Based Arithmetic

Consider a complex arithmetic expression, like

$$(2 + 3 \times 4) + ((5 + 6) \times 7).$$

We know, by the rules of arithmetic, how to evaluate expressions like these using the standard order of operations. Our normal style of writing arithmetic expressions is called **infix notation**, which places each operator *between* its two operands. Although we know it well, infix notation can be ambiguous, which is why we need rules to determine the priority of operators and parentheses to group expressions. This section introduces two alternate notations, called *prefix* and *postfix* notation, which can be used to represent arithmetic unambiguously, with no need for parentheses. Both are used in computer science because they're easier to parse and decode than infix notation. We'll then see how a stack can be used to calculate postfix expressions and transform between a standard infix expression and its postfix equivalent.

11.2.1 Prefix and Postfix Notations

Prefix notation places each operator *before* its operands. The infix expression

$$(a+b)\times(c+d)$$

would be represented in prefix notation as

$$\times + a\,b + c\,d.$$

Here, each $+$ operator applies to the two values that follow it, so that $+a\,b$ is equivalent to $a+b$ and $+c\,d$ is $c+d$. The $\times$ operator multiplies the results of the two additions.

Try It Yourself

Evaluate the following prefix notation expressions:

- $+\;4\;+\;2\;3$
- $+\;\times\;5\;5\;+\;2\;2$
- $+\;\times\;\times\;2\;2\;3\;5.$

Solution

Let's look at the third expression. Move from right to left. When you encounter an operator, identify the two operands to its right, evaluate them, then put that result back at its position in the string and continue moving left. Following this process, the first calculation is $\times\;2\;2$, which gives

$$+\;\times\;4\;3\;5.$$

The next operator is $\times$, which applies to 4 and 3:

$$+\;12\;5.$$

The final result is 17.

Prefix notation is also called *Polish notation*, after the mathematician Jan Łukasiewicz (1878–1956), who first proposed it in the 1920s. Łukasiewicz was born in the city of Lviv, in present-day Ukraine. At the time of his birth, the city was part of Austria-Hungary and a center of Polish, Ukrainian, and Jewish cultures. The LISP family of languages and its descendants – including Scheme, Racket, and Clojure – is known for its use of prefix notation.

Postfix notation, also called *reverse Polish notation*, places each operator *after* its operands. The example statement

$$(a+b)\times(c+d)$$

would be written in postfix form as

$$a\,b + c\,d + \times.$$

The two additions are performed first, then used as the two multiplication operands.

Try It Yourself

Rewrite the example prefix expressions from the previous problem in postfix.

Solution

The third example, in postfix form, is

$$5\,3\,2\,2 \times \times +.$$

11.2.2 Evaluating Postfix Expressions with a Stack

Postfix expressions can be evaluated easily using only a single stack. The algorithm uses a similar strategy as the tag-matching solution, placing operands on the stack to store them until we encounter their associated operator. Here's the approach:

- Process the input string from left to right, separating it into tokens that represent operators and operands as you go.
- When you encounter an operand, push it on top of the stack.
- Upon reading an operator, pop the top two operands from the stack, apply the operator, and then push the result back onto the stack.

Let's use this approach to evaluate `50 20 40 + 10 - + 5 /`. The first three operands are 50, 20, and 40, which all get pushed on the stack:

top ⟶ 40 input: ~~50 20 40~~ + 10 - + 5 /
20
50
stack

The next token is +, which pops the top two items (40 and 20), adds them, and then pushes the result back on the stack. After pushing the next value, 10, the stack looks like this:

top ⟶ 10 input: ~~50 20 40 + 10~~ - + 5 /
60
50
stack

The subtraction operator pops the top two operands (10 and 60), takes their difference, and pushes the result. Order is important: The operation should be interpreted as 60−10, not 10−60; the top item is the second argument.

```
                        input: ~~50 20 40 + 10 -~~ + 5 /
top ───→ 50
         50
      ─────────
        stack
```

The next two actions add 50 + 50 and then push 5.

```
                        input: ~~50 20 40 + 10 - + 5~~ /
top ───→ 5
        100
      ─────────
        stack
```

The final operation calculates 100/5, which leaves the final result of 20 on the stack.

The Java method below implements this algorithm for a whitespace-delimited input string with `int` values, using `Scanner` to tokenize the inputs. The end-of-chapter questions will invite you to expand on the calculator and add some more features.

```
/**
 * Stack-based postfix calculator
 */
public static int postfix(String expr) {

  // Values are integers
  Stack<Integer> stack = new Stack<Integer>();

  // Tokenize with Scanner
  Scanner scan = new Scanner(expr);

  while (scan.hasNext()) {
    String token = scan.next();

    // Operators
    if (token.equals("+")) {
      int op1 = stack.pop();
      int op2 = stack.pop();
      stack.push(op1 + op2);
    }

    // Add cases for the other operators
```

```

    // If it's not an operator, it should be an integer
    else {
      int value = Integer.parseInt(token);
      stack.push(value);
    }
  }

  return stack.pop();
}
```

Try It Yourself

Finish the `postfix` method by adding support for the other basic operators.

11.2.3 Converting Infix Expressions to Postfix

It's possible to convert an infix expression to its postfix equivalent in linear time using a single stack. Consider an infix expression and its postfix equivalent,

$$a + b \times c - d$$

$$a\ b\ c\ \times\ + d\ -.$$

Observe that the operands are in the same left-to-right order in both expressions. The basic conversion algorithm scans the input expression from left to right, processing each token. Any operand is immediately appended to the output. Operators are processed using a stack, as follows:

- Examine the top of the stack. If the top operator has *equal or higher priority* to the current operator token, pop it and append to the output. Repeat this step until the stack is empty, or the operator on top of the stack has *lower priority* than the current operator token.
- Push the current operator token on top of the stack.

At the end of the input, pop and output any remaining operators from the stack. This method doesn't handle parentheses, but we'll address that in a moment.

Try It Yourself

Use the algorithm to convert the infix expression `a + b * c - d`.

Solution

The first token is a, which is passed immediately to the output. The second token is the + operator, which goes on the stack.

```
output = a
stack = [+]
```

The third token, b, goes to the output. The fourth token, *, has a higher priority than the + that's currently on top of the stack, so it's also pushed.

```
output = a b
stack = [+, *]
```

The next step adds c to the output.

```
output = a b c
stack = [+, *]
```

The - token finally triggers a series of changes to the operand stack:

- * has higher priority than - so it's popped and moved to the output;
- + has *equal* priority, so it's also popped.

Once the stack is empty, - is pushed on.

```
output = a b c * +
stack = [-]
```

The end of the method outputs d, then empties the stack to append - as the last operator.

```
output = a b c * + d -
stack = []
```

The conversion algorithm can be extended to include parentheses. Intuitively, every operator in parentheses should have higher priority than anything outside the parentheses, so closing a pair of parentheses triggers the output of any unprocessed operators in their enclosed expression. The rules are as follows:

- On encountering a left parenthesis, push it onto the stack.
- When you read a right parenthesis, pop and output all operators down to the matching left parenthesis, which can then be discarded.

Try It Yourself

Convert the expression `a * (b * c + d)`.

Solution

The first token is `a`, which goes immediately to the output. The second is `*`, which goes on the stack.

```
output = a
stack = [*]
```

The third token is `(`, which opens a parenthesized expression. Stack it.

```
output = a
stack = [*, (]
```

The next three tokens are `b`, `*`, and `c`, which are handled in the usual way.

```
output = a b c
stack = [*, (, *]
```

The next operator is `+`. The top of the stack is `*`, which is a higher priority operator, so we'll pop `*` and then push `+`. Note that being inside a parenthesized expression doesn't change this behavior.

```
output = a b c *
stack = [*, (, +]
```

The next token is `d` followed by the matching `)`. Pop and output `+` from the stack, then pop and discard the `(` token.

```
output = a b c * d +
stack = [*]
```

That's the end of the input, so the final step pops the last `*` from the stack. The result is `a b c * d + *`.

11.3 Project: Tiny Web Browser

This chapter's main project shows off another practical use for a stack: keeping track of the history of actions in a program. We're going to use Java's built-in Swing components to create a tiny browser that can automatically fetch and display HTML pages from the web. Our browser will have an address bar where the user can type in a URL and a back button that returns to the previous page. Beyond using a stack, this project demonstrates some core concepts of Swing graphical user interface (GUI) development: using built-in components, attaching them to an application window, and writing listeners that respond to input events. Figure 11.1 shows what our application will look like.

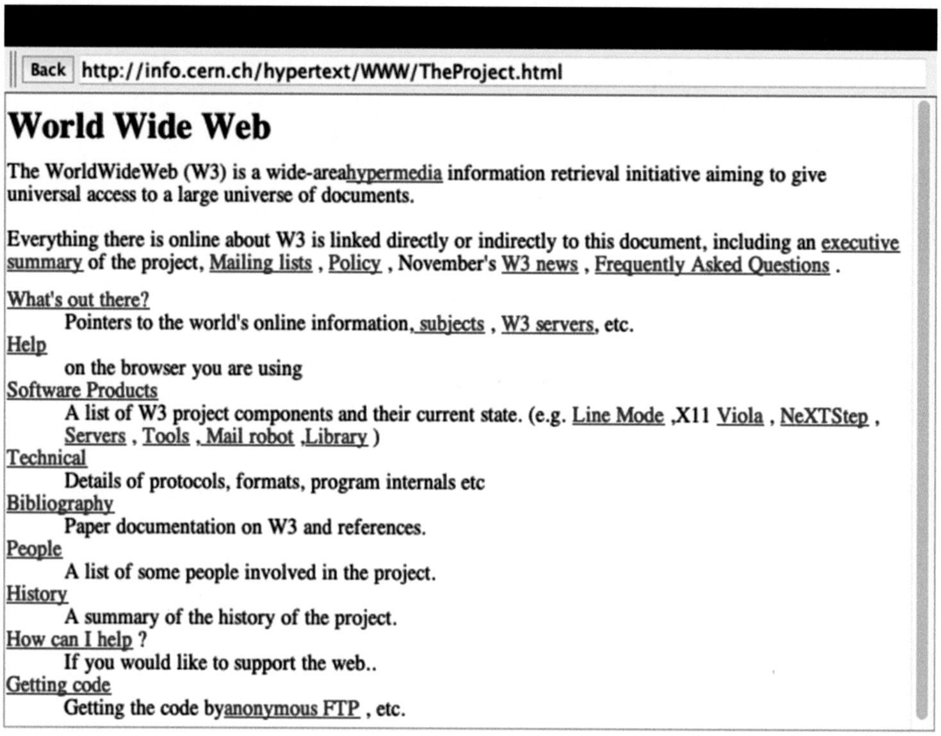

Back http://info.cern.ch/hypertext/WWW/TheProject.html

World Wide Web

The WorldWideWeb (W3) is a wide-areahypermedia information retrieval initiative aiming to give universal access to a large universe of documents.

Everything there is online about W3 is linked directly or indirectly to this document, including an executive summary of the project, Mailing lists , Policy , November's W3 news , Frequently Asked Questions .

What's out there?
Pointers to the world's online information, subjects , W3 servers, etc.
Help
on the browser you are using
Software Products
A list of W3 project components and their current state. (e.g. Line Mode ,X11 Viola , NeXTStep , Servers , Tools , Mail robot ,Library)
Technical
Details of protocols, formats, program internals etc
Bibliography
Paper documentation on W3 and references.
People
A list of some people involved in the project.
History
A summary of the history of the project.
How can I help ?
If you would like to support the web..
Getting code
Getting the code byanonymous FTP , etc.

Figure 11.1 The fully operational tiny web browser.

11.3.1 Viewing an HTML Page

Our web browsing program is built around two key classes. The first is `JFrame`, like our previous graphical applications. The other is `JEditorPane`, a Swing component for viewing and editing text that also has the ability to render HTML pages. `JEditorPane` is convenient, but has some limitations – it only displays basic HTML and styling, and it can't run embedded JavaScript, so it works best with first-generation web pages that don't rely on scripts for layout. The starting code is below. It imports and declares a number of components that we'll add during the following sections. It also includes three private `Listener` classes – leave them empty for now and we'll explain their role in the next section.

```
/**
 * HTML Viewer
 */

import javax.swing.*;
import javax.swing.event.*;
import javax.swing.event.*;
import java.awt.event.*;
import java.util.Stack;
import java.awt.BorderLayout;
```

```
import java.io.IOException;

public class TinyBrowser extends JFrame {

  final int WIDTH = 640;
  final int HEIGHT = 480;

  // Declare all of the components
  JScrollPane window;
  JEditorPane pane;
  JTextField urlField;
  JButton backButton;
  JToolBar bar;

  // Manage the history of visited pages with a stack
  Stack<String> history;
  String currentUrl;

  /**
   * Constructor: sets up the window and loads the start page
   *
   * @param  start  The URL of the starting page
   */
  public TinyBrowser(String start) {

  }

  /**
   * Load the given URL into the EditorPane
   */
  public void goToPage(String url) {

  }

  /**
   * Main -- create the window and make it visible
   */
  public static void main(String[] args) {
```

```
        TinyBrowser app = new TinyBrowser(
        "http://info.cern.ch/hypertext/WWW/TheProject.html");
        app.setSize(app.WIDTH, app.HEIGHT);
        app.setDefaultCloseOperation(JFrame.EXIT_ON_CLOSE);
        app.setVisible(true);
    }

    /**
     * Three helper event listener classes
     *
     * These will be filled in with their related components
     */
    private class LinkListener implements HyperlinkListener {
        public void hyperlinkUpdate(HyperlinkEvent event) {

        }
    }

    private class UrlFieldListener implements ActionListener {
        public void actionPerformed(ActionEvent e) {

        }
    }

    private class BackButtonListener implements ActionListener {
        public void actionPerformed(ActionEvent e) {

        }
    }
}
```

The `main` method is similar to our previous projects; it calls the constructor to initialize the application window, then makes it visible. Most of the work is in the constructor, which creates the `JEditorPane`, loads the starting URL, and then attaches it to the window to make it visible.

```
/**
 * Constructor: sets up the window and loads the start page
 *
 * @param  start  The URL of the starting page
```

```
  */
public TinyBrowser(String start) {
  // Set up the primary viewing window
  this.pane = new JEditorPane();
  this.pane.setEditable(false);  // required to view HTML

  // Load the starting page
  goToPage(start);

  // JScrollPane automatically adds scroll bars if
  // the content is too large for the window
  JScrollPane scroller = new JScrollPane(this.pane);

  // Attach the scrollable pane to the window
  JPanel container = (JPanel) this.getContentPane();
  container.add(scroller);
}
```

This method illustrates a core Swing concept: building a graphical interface by adding components. The `pane` object represents the main viewing window, but can't exist on its own. It has to be added to the top-level `JFrame` to become part of the visible window. `JScrollPane` is a quality-of-life upgrade that wraps around the `JEditorPane` and automatically adds scroll bars if the content is too big for the visible window. The last pair of lines get a reference to the `JFrame`'s content window, then call `add` to stick the scrollable viewing pane to it. This approach is typical for Swing: Create components that represent the different elements of the GUI, then `add` them to the content pane to make them visible.

The `goToPage` method is a simple wrapper that sets the URL of the editor pane. Doing so automatically fetches and loads the given page. This action can fail, so it's wrapped in a `try-catch` block.

```
/**
  * Load the given URL into the EditorPane
  */
public void goToPage(String url) {
  try {
    this.pane.setPage(url);
  } catch (IOException e) {
    e.printStackTrace();
  }
}
```

Fill in the constructor and `goToPage`, then run the program. You should see a copy of the oldest preserved web page from Tim Berners-Lee's original project at CERN.

11.3.2 Listening for Link Events

`JEditorPane` does not automatically load a new page when you click on a link. Recall how we handled keyboard and mouse events in previous projects:[3] Interacting with the window triggered calls to specific event-handling functions. In this case, clicking on a link in the `JEditorPane` triggers an event that can be processed by a `HyperlinkListener` object. Our project includes a private class called `LinkListener` that implements `HyperlinkListener`. First, add this line to the constructor, with the other code that initializes `pane`:

```
this.pane.addHyperlinkListener(new LinkListener());
```

Next, fill in the `hyperlinkUpdate` method to `LinkListener`. It takes a `HyperlinkEvent` object as input that includes the URL for the clicked link and is automatically called when the user interacts with a link. All we have to do is extract that, then call `goToPage` with the new URL.

```
public void hyperlinkUpdate(HyperlinkEvent event) {
  // The ACTIVATED event is triggered on a link click
  if (event.getEventType() == HyperlinkEvent.EventType.ACTIVATED) {
    String newUrl = event.getURL().toString();
    goToPage(newUrl);
  }
}
```

11.3.3 Implementing the Address Bar and Back Button

The address bar and back button combine ideas from the previous two sections: first, creating them in the constructor and attaching them to the content pane; second, writing listener methods that load new pages in response to interactions. Add the following lines to the constructor to create a `JTextField` and `JButton`, then add them to a `JToolBar`. Both objects have attached event listeners, which we'll complete in a moment.

```
// Text box to display and set the page URL
this.urlField = new JTextField();
urlField.setText(start);
this.urlField.addActionListener(new UrlFieldListener());

// Back button
this.backButton = new JButton();
```

3 See the *Snake* and Falling Sand examples in Chapters 6 and 7.

```
backButton.setText("Back");
backButton.addActionListener(new BackButtonListener());

// The back button uses a stack of URLs
this.history = new Stack<String>();

// Put the button and text field in a JToolBar container
this.bar = new JToolBar();
this.bar.add(backButton);
this.bar.add(urlField);
```

We also need to make the `JToolBar` visible. The updated code below uses `BorderLayout` to control the positioning of the tool bar and the scrollable content pane. Put it at the very end of the constructor, replacing the current lines that get the `container` and add the `scroller` to it.

```
// Add the tool bar and editor pane to the window
JPanel container = (JPanel) this.getContentPane();
container.add(this.bar, BorderLayout.NORTH);
container.add(scroller, BorderLayout.CENTER);
```

The address bar and back button are controlled by `UrlFieldListener` and `BackButtonListener`. Both classes have an `actionPerformed` method to respond to events on their respective objects. Let's start with `BackButtonListener`. The program uses a stack to keep track of the history of visited pages: When the user clicks the back button, pop the most recent visited page and go to it. Therefore, every time we transition to a new page, we should push the *old* URL onto the stack. The easiest way to do this is to modify `goToPage` to save the old URL and update the text in the address bar:

```
public void goToPage(String newUrl) {
  try {
    this.pane.setPage(newUrl);
  } catch (IOException e) {
    e.printStackTrace();
  }
  history.push(urlField.getText());  // Save previous URL
  urlField.setText(newUrl);  // Display new URL
}
```

`BackButtonListener` is now straightforward, with one small detail: Going backward should just pop the previous URL without saving anything new on the stack. Therefore, the method adds an extra `pop` to undo the `push` performed by `goToPage`.

```
private class BackButtonListener implements ActionListener {
  public void actionPerformed(ActionEvent e) {
    String newUrl = history.pop();
    goToPage(newUrl);
    history.pop();  // Undo the push performed by goToPage
  }
}
```

Try It Yourself

Finish implementing `UrlFieldListener`. The `actionPerformed` method triggers when the user presses ENTER while in the address bar. You should get the typed URL and then load it. Tip: Use `urlField.getText()` to retrieve the contents of the address bar.

Solution

Here is the `actionPeformed` method. Once it's implemented, you can travel to a new page by typing its URL in the address bar and pressing ENTER. Any pages you want to load through the address bar must include `http://` at the front of the URL.

```
public void actionPerformed(ActionEvent e) {
  String newUrl = urlField.getText();
  goToPage(newUrl);
}
```

11.4 Example Interview Questions Using Stacks

11.4.1 Removals to Make Matching Parentheses

Given a string of parentheses, determine which ones should be removed to make it balanced, without removing any balanced pairs.

The easy version of this question asks to scan a sequence of left and right parentheses and simply determine if they're properly matched or not. That can be done using the same strategy we used for HTML tags. This question asks for the *positions* of the unmatched parentheses:

- On seeing a left parenthesis, push its *index* onto the stack.
- A right parenthesis matches to the position on top of the stack; pop it off. If the stack is empty, then the right parenthesis is unmatched: output its index immediately.

- After reading the entire string, the stack will contain the indices of the unmatched left parentheses.

```
// Output the locations of unmatched parentheses

public static void unmatchedParens(String parens) {
  Stack<Integer> stack = new Stack<Integer>();

  for (int i = 0; i < parens.length(); i++) {
    char c = parens.charAt(i);

    // Push the index of a left
    if (c == '(') {
      stack.push(i);
    }

    // Right paren should match a left on top of the stack
    if (c == ')') {
        if (stack.empty()) {
          System.out.println(i);
        } else {
          stack.pop();
        }
    }
  }

  // Print remaining unmatched left indices
  while (!stack.empty()) {
    System.out.println(stack.pop());
  }
}
```

A variation is to keep track of the indices in a list, then return the cleaned-up string at the end of the method.

Try It Yourself

Run the removal algorithm on the input `((()())(()`.

11.4.2 Constant Time Minimum Operation

Design a data structure that implements push and pop operations like a stack, but supports an $O(1)$ `getMin` operation that returns, but doesn't remove, the minimum element. You can use $O(n)$ extra space.

The data structure in this question isn't really a practical one, but it does illustrate the idea of augmenting a basic data structure. The first idea is to use a normal stack and add a variable to track the minimum value. That approach fails, though, if you pop the minimum value – you would have to re-scan the entire stack to find the next smallest item and make it the new minimum. Instead, use *two stacks*: one as the regular stack of all items and a second one to maintain the history of the minimum value. The main stack operates as normal. A new item is pushed onto the `minHistory` stack if it's less than or equal to the current minimum:

```
// Pseudocode

push(value) {
  // Push onto the main stack
  mainStack.push(value)

  // Push onto the history stack if this is the new min
  if (value <= minHistory.peek()) {
    minHistory.push(value)
  }
}
```

On a pop, check if the top of the main stack is also the minimum element. If so, pop from both stacks, leaving the next smallest element as the new top of `minHistory`:

```
pop() {
  top = mainStack.pop();

  if (minHistory.peek() == top) {
    minHistory.pop();
  }
}
```

There is a gimmick variation of this question that asks for the same behavior without using the second stack – only a single variable is allowed. The solution is not obvious or practical, since it involves storing modified values on the stack so that you can always recalculate the current minimum value using only the top element.

SUMMARY

Stacks are our second major data structure and one that we'll return to multiple times in future chapters. So far, we've seen ways of using a stack to either defer decision-making on values or to maintain a history of items that were previously examined. We've also seen that stacks can show up in a variety of seemingly unrelated applications, including matching, arithmetic, and web browsing. In the next chapter, we'll build on these ideas and take a deep look at one of the most important stack-based algorithms: backtracking search and its applications to logical reasoning and game playing.

EXERCISES

Understand

1. Summarize the methods of the stack abstract data type.
2. Modify the `Stack` example to use a `LinkedList` as the internal data structure rather than an `ArrayList`.
3. Rewrite the example class to use an internal array that it manages directly, rather than wrapping around `ArrayList`. Tip: Review the implementation of `ArrayList`.
4. Add a method called `drop` that removes, but doesn't return, the top item.
5. Use a stack to reverse the elements in an `int[]`.
6. Repeat the previous problem, but reverse a `String`.
7. Evaluate `2 3 4 5 6 + - * +`.
8. Add a `swap` method to the `Stack` class that exchanges the top two elements.
9. Rewrite the expression `((10 + 2) + 3) * (5 - (3 - 1))` in both prefix and postfix forms.
10. Your friend wants to add a `get` method to the stack implementation that returns the element at a given position. Argue that this is not recommended. Tip: Think about the concept of the abstract data type. If we say something is a stack, what are we promising users?
11. The stack-based Forth language implemented a number of manipulation operations. Write a method called `rotate` that moves the third item in the stack to the top. If the stack has fewer than three items, do nothing.
12. Here's another Forth operation: Write a method called `over` that *duplicates* the second item to the top of the stack.
13. Write a function called `removeRepeats` that takes a string as input and removes any consecutive repeated characters. For example, the input `"ccaaatt"` would be reduced to `"cat"`.
14. Write a method that uses a stack to test if a string is a palindrome. Tip: You can assume that you get to keep access to the original string.

15. Write a program to check if a string containing regular parentheses, square brackets, and curly braces is balanced. For example, `({[]()})` is balanced.

Apply

16. Use `Scanner` and a stack to reverse a `String` without reversing the words it contains. For example, if the input is `"Pancake breakfast"` the output would be `"breakfast Pancake"`.

17. Modify the postfix calculator program to operate on `double` values.

18. Add a ~ operator to the postfix calculator that negates the previous operand. For example, `2 3 + ~` would yield −5.

19. Add a `^` operator to the calculator to perform exponentiation. For example, `2 10 ^` is 1,024.

20. Write a method to evaluate prefix expressions by scanning them right-to-left. Tip: Be careful with the order of the operands for subtraction and division. Use the `split` method to break the string into whitespace-delimited tokens.

21. Here's another popular interview question: Write a program that reverses a stack. You're allowed to use a second stack as intermediate storage. Tip: Think about taking the top element and moving it to the bottom. You must return the reversed values on the original stack.

22. Write a method called `toPostfix` that implements the infix-to-postfix conversion algorithm. You can assume that all tokens in the input string are separated by whitespace.

23. Design an algorithm to sort a stack in ascending order using a second stack. Tip: Use a strategy like selection sort. Move all n items to the second stack and identify the max as you go.

Extend

24. Modify the HTML validator to extract the tags and match them in one pass through the file, without constructing an intermediate list.

25. The <a> – short for "anchor" – specifies a link. The standard format is:

```
<a href="https://www.cam.ac.uk/">University of Cambridge</a>
```

The `href` parameter is the link's URL. Modify the validator to handle <a> tags.

26. Some tags are stand-alone and don't have to be paired with a closing tag. For example, the <img> tag inserts an image:

```
<img src="number_one.jpg" alt="Number One, 1950 (Lavender Mist)">
```

Modify the program to handle <img>. Note that the tag contains additional fields, not just `img`.

27. Suppose you wanted to implement an undo feature for a text editor. Think about what information you would want to store to keep track of the history of state changes. Is it necessary to save the contents of the entire document?

28. Write a complete calculator program that can take a whitespace-delimited infix expression as input and evaluate it.

29. Add a forward button to the tiny browser. You can use a second stack: Every time the user clicks the back button, save the old URL onto the forward stack. When the user wants to go forward, pop the top URL from the stack and load it. Empty the stack if the user clicks on a link or loads a new page.

NOTES AND FURTHER READING

The idea of stack-based computation turns out to be surprisingly flexible. A *stack-based programming language* is one that organizes all of its operations around a stack. Stack-based computation only requires a limited set of operations that take values off the stack and return results to the stack, so programs can be quite space-efficient. For this reason, stack-based languages have found a niche in environments where storage space is highly constrained. The best-known example is the Forth language, invented by Charles Moore in 1970, which has been used in embedded systems and aerospace programming; see Morgan (2015) for an accessible overview of its instructions. The JVM is, itself, a stack-based architecture: It uses an internal stack as its primary storage location and to perform all calculations. Most Java bytecode instructions interact with the stack in some way, either by pushing data or by performing actions on the top values, in a manner that's directly related to the postfix calculator.

During the first year of the World Wide Web project, Tim Berners-Lee implemented the first version of HTML, as well as

- the Hypertext Transfer Protocol (HTTP), which is used to fetch web pages from their servers;
- the first web browser, which could send HTTP requests and view the resulting HTML pages; and
- the concept of a Uniform Resource Locator (URL), the address that identifies a particular page somewhere on the Web.

Berners-Lee publicly released his World Wide Web project in 1991, after which it grew rapidly to become the dominant way of accessing Internet content. The Web was the right invention at the right time: It arrived just as the public commercial Internet was emerging and offered an improved way of navigating content compared to older systems. Berners-Lee was knighted for his work in 2004.

12 Project: Logic Puzzles

"Contrariwise," continued Tweedledee, "if it was so, it might be; and if it were so, it would be; but as it isn't, it ain't. That's logic."
Lewis Carroll, *Through the Looking Glass*

INTRODUCTION

Logic Theorist was the first artificially intelligent program, created in 1955 by Allen Newell and Herbert Simon, and actually predating the term "artificial intelligence," which was introduced the next year. Logic Theorist could apply the rules of symbolic logic to prove mathematical theorems – the first time a computer accomplished a task considered solely within the domain of human intelligence. Given a starting statement, it applied logical laws to generate a set of new statements, then recursively continued the process. Eventually, this procedure would discover a chain of logical transformations that connected the starting statement to the desired final statement. Applied naively, this process would generate an intractable number of possible paths, but Logic Theorist had the ability to detect and discard infeasible paths that couldn't lead to a solution.

LEARNING OBJECTIVES

Writing a program on the scale of Logic Theorist, even with modern techniques, would be ambitious, but we can still explore the tools of early AI and practice using them to solve logic puzzles. This chapter introduces **backtracking search**, a fundamental algorithm for solving constraint satisfaction problems. Backtracking search incrementally builds up a solution, abandoning any partial solution path that it discovers can't lead to a full solution. As we'll see, the method has a close connection to both stacks and recursion. At the end of this chapter, you will:

- Understand the backtracking search strategy.
- Be able to apply backtracking to solve grid-based logic puzzles.
- Adapt your methods to solve new logic puzzles with written constraints.

12.1 Solving Puzzles by Backtracking

Puzzle Communication Nikoli is a Japanese magazine that specializes in symbolic and numeric logic puzzles. You may be familiar with their most popular export: Sudoku, which was introduced in the 1970s and became massively popular worldwide starting in the 2000s. A Sudoku puzzle is a 9 × 9 grid filled with the numbers 1 through 9. Each number must appear exactly once in each row, each column, and in each of nine 3 × 3 subsquares. For example, the puzzle on the left below has the solution on the right (Nikoli, 2021):

8					5	1		
		1				8		
	4		2				9	
				3				2
1	2	3	4		6	7	8	9
6				1				
	8				9		5	
		2				4		
		7	6					1

8	3	9	7	6	5	1	2	4
2	6	1	3	9	4	8	7	5
7	4	5	2	8	1	3	9	6
5	9	4	8	3	7	6	1	2
1	2	3	4	5	6	7	8	9
6	7	8	9	1	2	5	4	3
3	8	6	1	4	9	2	5	7
9	1	2	5	7	3	4	6	8
4	5	7	6	2	8	9	3	1

Most people solve Sudoku using a combination of logical elimination and trial-and-error. It's possible, though, to solve logic puzzles like Sudoku *algorithmically* using recursive backtracking search. This section introduces the backtracking search technique and shows how to use it to solve Nikoli-style number puzzles.

12.1.1 Latin Squares

Before jumping into Sudoku and its siblings, let's look at a much older problem: **Latin squares.** A Latin square is an $n \times n$ matrix containing copies of n distinct symbols. Each symbol appears exactly one time in each row and one time in each column. Sudoku puzzles are 9 × 9 Latin squares with the 3 × 3 subsquares added as an additional constraint. Here's an example 4 × 4 square with letters as the symbols:

b	a	d	c
d	c	b	a
c	b	a	d
a	d	c	b

Although, they've been studied and derived by numerologists since antiquity, the "Latin" title comes from the work of Leonhard Euler, who produced some of the first formal results on their properties in the 1780s. Euler's first examples used combinations of Greek and Latin letters as the symbols in the squares (Euler, 1782).

Try It Yourself

Let's consider the problem of completing a partial Latin square. Given the matrix below, fill it in with the numbers 1–5 to make a valid Latin square:

2		1		4
	4		2	3
		4		
4		3	5	
	1			5

Solution

Here's one possible solution:

2	5	1	3	4
1	4	5	2	3
5	3	4	1	2
4	2	3	5	1
3	1	2	4	5

What if you wanted to write a program to automatically complete the square? One option is to try every possible arrangement of digits and check for any that have the required properties, but that's obviously infeasible since the number of potential arrangements grows exponentially with n. A better strategy is to *systematically explore the space of possible solutions*. Let's start by defining a generic search problem:

- There is a set of *decision variables*. In the Latin square example, each entry in the square is one variable.
- There are one or more sets of *values* that can be assigned to each variable. In our example, these are the digits 1 to n. Right now, we have only one value set, but it's possible to create problems with multiple value sets, each applying to a different subset of the variables.
- Finally, there are *constraints* that determine what combinations of variables and values are valid.

The overall goal, then, is to find an assignment of values to variables that respects the constraints: This is a **constraint satisfaction problem**. Note that we're not seeking the "best" solution – there's no objective function to minimize or maximize. The only requirement is to find a satisfying solution.

12.1.2 The Backtracking Search Strategy

Backtracking search is guaranteed to test each possible configuration of variables and values at most one time. Unlike brute force search, it immediately abandons infeasible paths as soon as they're identified, so you never waste time checking solutions that can't possibly satisfy the constraints. Each step of method performs the following actions:

- Choose a variable v that has not yet been assigned a value. If all variables have been assigned, then we've reached a satisfying solution and the search can terminate.
- Determine the set of values that can be assigned to v without violating the constraints. Choose one, assign it, and then recursively continue the search.

- If there are no valid values for *v*, then the search has reached a dead end. Backtrack to the previous decision and try a different assignment.

The pseudocode version of the method is below. The input to the method is `state`, a structure that represents an in-progress solution to the problem.

```
// Pseudocode for backtracking search

search(state) {
  v = choose the next unassigned variable

  // All variables are assigned: this is a solution
  if (v == null) {
    output current state as a solution and exit
  }

  // Recursively explore all valid assignments to v
  for (each value s) {
    if (s is a valid assignment to v in the current state) {
      state[v] = s
      search(state)
    }
  }

  // There was no solution on this path
  //
  // Reset v, then backtrack to the previous decision
  // and try a different value
  state[v] = null
}
```

Try It Yourself

How does the backtracking procedure maintain the history of visited states?

Solution

The method is recursive, so the history of all `search` calls is stored on the program stack. Backtracking, in this case, means returning from `search` back to the previous frame saved on the stack.

Let's work through an example to fill in a small Latin square manually, then we'll look at the Java implementation. Suppose we want to complete the following 4×4 square:

	2	3	
	4		
	3	4	2
	1		4

The first step chooses an empty square to fill; the upper-left corner is a reasonable choice. The method checks each possible value for that location and finds that 1 and 4 are valid options. Try placing 1, then move to the next open position.

1	2	3	
	4		
	3	4	2
	1		4

The only option for the last item on the first row is 4, which is already in the column. Therefore, the initial choice of 1 must have been incorrect: Backtrack to the first square and put 4 there, which allows the last square of the first row to be assigned 1:

4	2	3	1
	4		
	3	4	2
	1		4

Try It Yourself

Continue to the first position on the second row, which could be either 1, 2, or 3. What happens if you place a 1 there?

Solution

If you place a 1, then you're forced to place 2 and 3 to complete the second row:

4	2	3	1
1	4	2	3
	3	4	2
	1		4

This appears to be fine, but you'll run into a problem on the next row, where the first square has no valid assignment. Backtrack to the last decision point and place 2 at the beginning of the second row. You can then complete the rest of the puzzle with no conflicts:

4	2	3	1
2	4	1	3
1	3	4	2
3	1	2	4

12.1.3 Implementation

The main challenge of implementing backtracking search is not usually the method itself. Instead, the hard part is deciding how to represent the variable set and implement the constraints. For the Latin square puzzle, this is straightforward – we'll use an `int[][]` to represent the grid. The `solve` method below translates the recursive backtracking search pseudocode into Java. It uses two methods, `findOpenPosition` and `valid`, that we'll discuss in a moment.

```
/**
 * Filling a Latin square with backtracking search
 */
public static void solve(int[][] square) {
  // Find the next open position
  int[] nextPosition = findOpenPosition(square);

  // If there is no open position, output solution
  if (nextPosition == null) {
    print(square);
    System.exit(0);
  }

  int r = nextPosition[0];
  int c = nextPosition[1];

  // Loop through all N options
  for (int i = 1; i <= square.length; i++) {
    // If i is allowed for position (r, c), recursively explore
    if (valid(square, i, r, c)) {
      square[r][c] = i;
      solve(square);
    }
  }

  // If we made it here, then there was no solution on this path --
```

```
27   // reset any choices made by this call to search and then backtrack
28   square[r][c] = 0;
29 }
```

The input to the method is an `int[][]` representing the current partially filled square with `final int N` representing its dimensions. Line 6 calls `findOpenPosition`, which checks for an open square by looping through the matrix until it finds a 0:

```
/**
 * Find the next open position
 *
 * @param  square  the partially filled square
 * @return  an int[] of the next square's (row, col) position
 */
public static int[] findOpenPosition(int[][] square) {
  for (int r = 0; r < square.length; r++) {
    for (int c = 0; c < square.length; c++) {
      if (square[r][c] == 0) {
        int[] result = {r, c};
        return result;
      }
    }
  }

  return null;
}
```

The `valid` method takes the current square, the proposed value, and the row and column indices, and checks if the value already exists in either the row or the column:

```
/**
 * Test if value i is valid for square[r][c]
 */
public static boolean valid(int[][] square, int i, int r, int c) {
  for (int j = 0; j < square.length; j++) {
    if (square[r][j] == i || square[j][c] == i) {
      return false;
    }
  }

  return true;
}
```

Try It Yourself

Implement a class containing the three methods and use it to complete the following 6×6 square:

			2	1	3
	4		5		
6			4		
2					6
	2	6			
5					2

```
public static void main(String[] args) {
  int[][] square = new int[6][6];

  // Fill in the starting conditions
  square[0][3] = 2;
  square[0][4] = 1;
  square[0][5] = 3;
  square[1][1] = 4;
  square[1][3] = 5;
  // Etc.

  // Solve
  solve(square);
}
```

You'll also need to add a small method to print the solution.

12.1.4 Sudoku

Now you're ready for Sudoku! Modify the Latin square solver to create a backtracking Sudoku solver. You have almost all of the pieces; you only need to modify the `valid` method to check that a digit can't occur more than once in a subsquare.

Try It Yourself

Suppose that you have the position at indices (r, c) in the square. Calculate the row and column indices of the upper-left corner of its associated subsquare.

Solution

Use integer division by 3:

```
int ulRow = (r / 3) * 3;
int ulCol = (c / 3) * 3;
```

For example, the square at row 4, column 7 is mapped to the subsquare with (3, 6) as its upper-left corner.

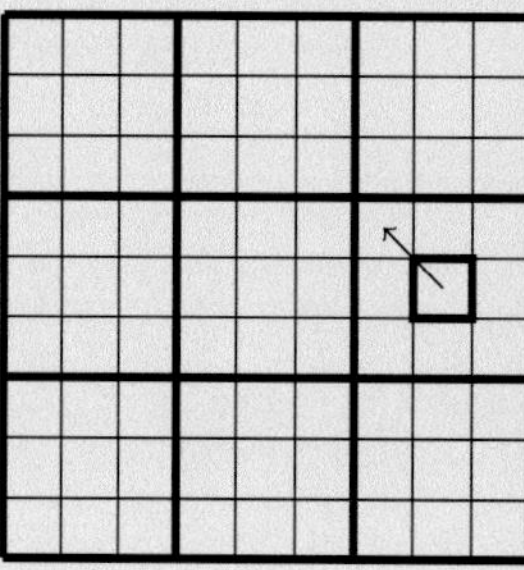

Once you know the upper-left corner of the relevant subsquare, you can add a test that loops through the 3×3 box and tests all nine elements to determine if a particular assignment is valid.

12.2 Who Owns the Fish?

This is my all-time favorite assignment. It's often attributed to Einstein – there's no actual evidence he created it, of course – but various versions of the puzzle have been published since at least the mid-1960s (Yeomans, 2003).

> There are five houses in a row, each painted a different color. In each house lives a person with a different nationality. The five owners each drink a different drink, smoke a different brand of tobacco, and keep a different pet. One of the pets is a walleye pike.
>
> - The Brit lives in the red house.
> - The Swede keeps dogs as pets.
> - The Dane drinks tea.
> - The green house is on the left of and next to the white house.
> - The green house owner drinks coffee.
> - The person who smokes Pall Malls keeps birds.
> - The owner of the yellow house smokes Dunhills.
> - The man living in the house right in the center drinks milk.
> - The man who smokes Blends lives next to the one who keeps cats.

- The Norwegian lives in the first house.
- The man who keeps horses lives next to the one who smokes Dunhills.
- The owner who smokes Bluemasters drinks beer.
- The German smokes Princes.
- The Norwegian lives next to the blue house.
- The man who smokes Blends has a neighbor who drinks water.

Who owns the fish?

This section illustrates how to solve a more complex logic problem with backtracking search. We can use the same metastrategy as the Latin square and Sudoku puzzles: Choose an unassigned variable, try to fill it with a value that satisfies the constraints, then recursively continue the solution path; if you get stuck, backtrack to the last decision and try a different value. The challenge is how to represent the in-progress solution and how to check the constraints.

12.2.1 Representing the Solution

Begin with an image of the five houses in a line. Each house is like a basket of five attributes: *Nationality*, *Color*, *Drinks*, *Smokes*, and *Pet*. You can represent the solution in a table where each row is house and each attribute is a column – this will map to the matrix solution we'll use in the program. Some starting facts are given in the clues.

	Nationality	*Color*	*Drinks*	*Smokes*	*Pet*
1	Norwegian				
2		Blue			
3			Milk		
4					
5					

Try It Yourself

Work on the puzzle by hand. Try teaming up with a friend.

Stop reading here if you don't want any hints.

Here are some tips to help you get started.

- The first house can't be blue, red (the Brit lives in the red house), green (the green house must be next to the white house), or white (the white house can't be in the first position). Therefore, it must be yellow.
- The center house can't be green (the green house owner drinks coffee) or white. Therefore, it must be red.
- The owner of the yellow house smokes Dunhills and the Brit lives in the red house.

	Nationality	*Color*	*Drinks*	*Smokes*	*Pet*
1	Norwegian	Yellow		Dunhills	
2		Blue			
3	Brit	Red	Milk		
4					
5					

Let's consider how to convert this tabular model of the solution to code. One option is to use OOP, with a `House` class that has five fields and a `House[]` representing all five houses in a row. That could get cumbersome, though, particularly if we decide to use enumerated types to represent the assignments for each field. Instead, let's use the direct approach:

- Represent the houses as a 5×5 `int[][]`, as in the Latin square puzzle.
- Define a set of constants that map each assignment to an integer.

```
/**
 * Who Owns the Fish?
 */

import java.util.Arrays;

public class WhoOwnsTheFish {

  // Constants for each possible value
  final int NONE = -1;

  final int NATIONALITY = 0;
  final int COLOR = 1;
  final int DRINKS = 2;
  final int SMOKES = 3;
  final int PET = 4;

  final int NORWEGIAN = 0;
  final int DANE = 1;
  final int BRIT = 2;
  final int GERMAN = 3;
  final int SWEDE = 4;

  // And so forth for the other types

```

```
  //*** We'll complete these methods ***//

  /**
   * Check if assigning value to houses[h][a] is valid
   */
  public boolean valid(int[][] houses, int h, int a, int value) {

  }

  /**
   * Find the next open position in the houses matrix
   */
  public int[] findNext(int[][] houses) {

  }

  /**
   * Backtracking search
   */
  public void search(int[][] houses) {

  }

  /**
   * Start the solution process
   */
  public void solve() {

  }

  public static void main(String[] args) {
    WhoOwnsTheFish who = new WhoOwnsTheFish();
    who.solve();
  }
}
```

The `main` method calls `solve`, which sets up the initial conditions and then starts the search.

```
/**
 * Start the solution process
```

```
  */
public void solve() {
  // Empty 5x5 solution grid
  int[][] houses = new int[5][5];
  for (int[] house : houses) {
    Arrays.fill(house, NONE);  // Initialize to NONE
  }

  // Norwegian lives in the first house
  houses[0][NATIONALITY] = NORWEGIAN;

  // Norwegian lives next to the blue house
  houses[1][COLOR] = BLUE;

  // Center house drinks milk
  houses[2][DRINKS] = MILK;

  // Search for a solution
  search(houses);
}
```

Try It Yourself

Finish defining the constants for the other four attributes.

12.2.2 Search Procedure

Before jumping into coding the constraints, let's verify that we can produce a solution that simply avoids duplicating any assignments – for example, once `NORWEGIAN` has been used, no other house can have that nationality. The `search` method checks for an open position, then tries to assign each possible value 0 to 4 into that location. Observe that this is almost identical to the Latin square version.

```
/**
 * Backtracking search
 */
public void search(int[][] houses) {
  int[] result = findNext(houses);
  if (result == null) {
    // TODO: solution found, print houses
```

```

    // Exit
    System.exit(0);
  }

  int h = result[0];  // house
  int a = result[1];  // attribute

  // Test all possible assignments to houses[h][a]
  for (int i = 0; i < 5; i++) {
    if (valid(houses, h, a, i)) {
      houses[h][a] = i;
      search(houses);
    }
  }

  // No solution on this path, backtrack
  houses[h][a] = NONE;
}
```

Try It Yourself

Using the Latin square solution as a model, add `findNext`, which should return the row and column indices of the next open position. The `valid` method should ensure that each value 0 to 4 is used only one time in each matrix column. Finally, add the code to print the solution once the entire grid has been filled. You should be able to run the program and produce a Latin square matrix with the initial constraints in their correct positions. Tip: Remember to test for `NONE` when you're looking for an open position.

12.2.3 Coding the Constraints

Now let's consider writing a function to check if a single constraint is satisfied. For example, the first clue of the puzzle says that the Brit lives in the red house. Given a `houses` array, we can check if the condition is satisfied.

```
/**
 * Check if the Brit lives in the red house
 */
public boolean britLivesInRedHouse(int[][] houses) {
  for (int i = 0; i < houses.length; i++) {
```

```
    int[] house = houses[i];

    if (house[NATIONALITY] == NONE || house[COLOR] == NONE) {
      continue;
    }

    if ((house[NATIONALITY] == BRIT && house[COLOR] != RED)
        || (house[NATIONALITY] != BRIT && house[COLOR] == RED)) {
      return false;
    }
  }

  return true;
}
```

The method loops through the five houses, checking each one. If either variable is unassigned, the constraint doesn't apply, and the loop moves on to the next house. If `NATIONALITY` is `BRIT`, then `COLOR` must be `RED` and vice versa. If those conditions don't hold, then the method returns `false`. If no violation is found, then the method returns `true`.

Suppose that we have one method per constraint, which returns `false` if the constraint is violated and `true` if it's either satisfied or not applicable yet. The `valid` method needs to check all of the constraints and ensure that none are violated.

```
/**
 * Check if assigning value to houses[h][a] is valid
 */
public boolean valid(int[][] houses, int h, int a, int value) {
  // Use each value one time per column
  for (int i = 0; i < houses.length; i++) {
    if (houses[i][a] == value) {
      return false;
    }
  }

  // Provisional assignment
  houses[h][a] = value;

  // Check the constraints
```

```
    boolean constraints =  britLivesInRedHouse(houses)
                           && swedeKeepsDogs(houses)
                           && daneDrinksTea(houses);
                           // etc.

    // Undo test assignment
    houses[h][a] = NONE;
    return constraints;
}
```

Try It Yourself

This is a hard problem! But you now have all the pieces that you need to solve it. The most important tip is to proceed incrementally.

- Start with *only* the `britLivesInRedHouse` constraint. Run your search and verify that you can produce a solution with the Brit in the red house. The other assignments will probably be incorrect, but that's okay.
- Then add *one more constraint*, like `swedeKeepsDogs`. Run the solution again and verify that you're now satisfying both constraints.
- Continue, adding just one constraint at a time until you have all 15 in place.

Who owns the fish?

SUMMARY

Backtracking search isn't a single algorithm that solves a specific problem, but rather a general framework that can be adapted to produce solutions to a variety of problems. As you're working on these projects, keep the following ideas in mind:

- Backtracking search is a great opportunity to further develop your recursive thinking skills. If you need to practice recursion, review Chapters 8, 9, and 10.
- The real difficulty of backtracking search is in the implementation details – choosing how to represent the solution and enforce the constraints. Deciding to use backtracking is only the beginning of solving the problem.
- Develop incrementally! Add one constraint at a time, verify that it works, and then continue building up your solution.

EXTENSIONS

Sudoku Variants

There are a variety of Sudoku puzzles with additional or different constraints. *X-Sudoku* adds the requirement that the numbers 1–9 must appear exactly once on each of the two matrix diagonals. *Even/Odd Sudoku* marks squares that must contain even numbers. Another common variant is to use irregular regions:

1					6	7		
		1				3		
	5		2				9	
				2				7
3		5	9		7	4		8
2				4				
	7				4		5	
		8				2		
		6	5					2

Think about how to write a backtracking search solver for irregular Sudoku:

- Does the core algorithm change? No! The basic search method follows the exact same outline as the conventional version.
- What *does* change is the `valid` method and the way the constraints are encoded. Now, you need to specify which squares belong to which region, so you can verify that each number appears only once per region.

Suppose that you start by defining an `int[][]` that records the region of each position. For example, in the problem above, cells in the upper-left region are assigned the value 1, and likewise for the other regions:

1	1	1	2	2	2	3	3	3
1	1	2	2	2	3	3	3	3
1	1	1	5	2	2	3	6	3
4	1	4	5	2	5	6	6	6
4	4	4	5	5	5	6	6	6
4	4	4	5	8	5	6	9	6
7	4	7	8	8	5	9	9	9
7	7	7	7	8	8	8	9	9
7	7	7	8	8	8	9	9	9

After defining this matrix, iterate over it and construct an array of lists, where each list contains the row and column positions for each region.[1]

1 You could also use a `HashMap`, which we'll discuss in Chapter 15.

```
// Pseudocode

regionLists = array of 9 empty lists

for r = 0 to 9 {
  for c = 0 to 9 {
    region = regionMatrix[r][c];
    regionLists[region].add((r, c));
  }
}
```

Given a (row, column) position that you want to test, you can look up its region in `regionMatrix`, then retrieve that region's list of neighbor cells from `regionLists`.

The Officers Problem

There are six military regiments, each of which has six officers, one for each of six different ranks. The officers must present themselves in formation for an official event. Is there a way to arrange the officers into a 6×6 grid such that no two officers of the same regiment appear in any row or column, *and* no two officers of the same rank appear in any row or column?

This is the problem that Leonhard Euler used to commence his study of Latin squares in his 1782 paper. The problem asks for a double Latin square where each cell holds two values and all combinations appear exactly once. These matrices are called *Euler squares* or *Graeco-Latin squares*, after the notation that Euler used in his paper, which combined Greek and Latin letters. Here's an example square with $n = 4$.

A1	B3	C4	D2
B4	A2	D1	C3
C2	D4	A3	B1
D3	C1	B2	A4

Try It Yourself

It's clear that an Euler square can be decomposed into two Latin squares, one for the letters and one for the numbers. Therefore, it might seem like you could just generate two Latin squares and overlay one on the other to obtain an Euler square. Try some experiments and explain why that won't work.

Solution

Experimentation will show that overlaying two independent squares won't guarantee unique combinations in every cell. For example, the matrix below is made from two Latin squares, but isn't an Euler square because some combinations are repeated.

B1	C4	A2	D3
A3	D2	B1	C4
D4	A1	C3	B2
C2	B3	D4	A1

Modify the Latin square solver to generate Euler squares. Use the digits 1 to n and the first n letters of the alphabet as your values. You'll need to decide how to represent the entries in each square and decide how to perform assignments. A good strategy is to choose a square and then assign it a valid letter–number combination. For example, if you make the upper-left square A1, then no other square in the same row or column can use any combination with A or 1.

What about Euler's original problem? He was unable to find a solution to the $n = 6$ version and conjectured that no such square existed for any $n = 4k + 2$. The French mathematician Gaston Tarry finally showed there was no solution for $n = 6$ in 1901 by checking all possible solutions by hand. Euler's conjecture was not disproven until 1960, when it was shown that squares exist for all n except 2 and 6! See Young (2007) for a nice overview of results related to Euler squares.

Futoshiki

Futoshiki ("inequality") is another number puzzle game that has appeared in *Puzzle Communication Nikoli.* Like Sudoku, the goal of Futoshiki is to complete an $n \times n$ Latin square with the digits 1 to n. Rather than using the 3×3 subsquares of Sudoku, the puzzle contains inequality constraints specifying that some cells must be greater than or less than their neighbors.

Try It Yourself

Try to solve the following puzzle. Tip: Start with the four squares in the lower-left.

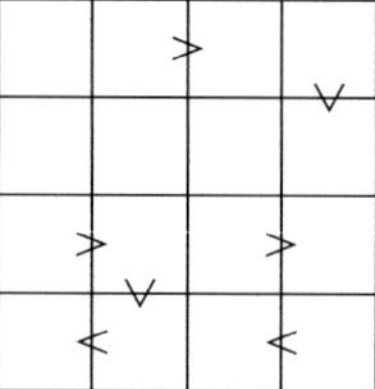

Solution

The four squares in the lower-left must contain 4-3-2-1 in a cycle. Checking will show that the top-middle squares must then contain 4 and 1.

2	4 >	1	3 ∨
3	1	4	2
4 >	3 ∨	2 >	1
1 <	2	3 <	4

Modify your Sudoku solving program to solve Futoshiki puzzles. Again, the key is encoding the constraints. The simplest approach is to make a `valid` method with one check per inequality. Remember that you'll need to distinguish between constraints where both variables have been assigned and constraints where one or both variables are still undetermined.

NOTES AND FURTHER READING

Latin squares have important practical applications in experimental design. They're one of a family of techniques called *orthogonal arrays* that can be used to plan experimental treatments. For example, suppose an industrial baker wants to test the quality of cakes produced by the interaction of three experimental factors: five different cake recipes, baked at five different temperatures, and for five different baking times. There are 125 possible combinations of the recipe–temperature–time factors, which might be too many to test. The baker could use a 5×5 Latin square, where the row corresponds to temperature, the column to time, and the symbol to recipe:

	12 min	15 min	18 min	21 min	24 min
275°	A	B	C	D	E
300°	B	C	D	E	A
325°	C	D	E	A	B
350°	D	E	A	B	C
375°	E	A	B	C	D

Every recipe is tested once at each time and temperature. This setup requires only 25 trials and balances the effect of each factor across trials. Statistical analysis can then be used to isolate the effect of each variable on the quality of the resulting cakes.

13 Queues and Buffers

I could give you no advice but this: to go into yourself and to explore the depths where your life wells forth.
Rainer Maria Rilke, *Letters to a Young Poet* (1903)

INTRODUCTION

The previous two chapters showed how the concept of last-in-first-out data processing is surprisingly powerful. We'll now consider the stack's counterpart, the **queue**. Like a waiting line, a queue stores a set of items and returns them in **first-in-first-out** (FIFO) order. Pushing to the queue adds a new item to the back of the line and pulling retrieves the oldest item from the front. Queues have a lower profile than stacks, and are rarely the centerpiece of an algorithm. Instead, queues tend to serve as utility data structures in a larger system.

LEARNING OBJECTIVES

After completing this chapter you will be able to:

- Discuss Java's `Queue` and `Deque` interfaces and their important methods.
- Implement a queue or deque as a linked list.
- Describe and implement the **circular buffer**, an array-based queue used for I/O processing; it demonstrates how to build an array-based data structure that is different from `ArrayList`.

The second half of the chapter demonstrates how to use a queue to implement a flood-filling algorithm, a common feature of painting programs. It demonstrates a common pattern for queue-based algorithms and also shows how processing a set of items with a queue differs from using a stack.

13.1 The Queue Abstract Data Type

Fundamentally, any data structure that has two "ends" can implement queue operations: The only requirement is being able to add items to the "back" end and remove them from the "front" in first-come-first-serve order. The primary consideration with queues is whether the structure is single-ended, like a traditional waiting line, or *double-ended*.

13.1.1 Queue and Deque Methods

The queue abstract data type represents an ordered sequence of items that returns values in FIFO order. Its basic operations are:

- `offer`: add a new item to the end of the queue. May be called `push`, `add`, or `enqueue`.
- `poll`: remove and return the next item from the front of the queue. May also be called `pop`, `remove`, or `dequeue`.

Like stacks, queues generally implement utility methods, including `size`, `empty`, and `peek` to return the front element without removing it. Also like stacks, you do not generally have access to the internal values of a queue – it isn't possible to get or remove an item by its index. Java uses `offer` and `poll` for its queue methods, so we'll follow that convention here.

A queue that allows adding or removing from *either end* in $O(1)$ time is called a **double-ended queue** or "deque," pronounced as "deck." It may be helpful to think of a deque like a deck of cards: It's easy to add or remove cards at the bottom or top of the pile, but you don't have direct access to the internal cards. The standard deque has methods to insert and remove at either end; typical names are `offerFirst`, `offerLast`, `pollFirst`, and `pollLast`.

13.1.2 Java's `Queue` and `Deque` Interfaces

In Java, `Queue` and `Deque` are *interfaces*. Recall that a Java interface functions like a contract: A class that implements a particular interface guarantees to other classes that it will provide certain behaviors. A class that implements `Queue` must provide a set of methods that includes `offer`, `poll`, and `peek`. A `Deque` must provide the `First` and `Last` versions of each method. `LinkedList` implements both interfaces and provides the full suite of `offer` and `poll` methods. Note that `LinkedList` also has `add` and `remove` methods for list interactions and `push` and `pop` for stack behaviors[1] – make sure you don't confuse the three sets of methods. Another built-in class is `ArrayDeque`, which, as its name implies, is a deque built on top of an array. There are also a number of specialized queue-related classes intended for multi-threaded applications, where you need to handle multiple parallel updates; `ConcurrentLinkedDeque` is one example.

Try It Yourself

Take a look at the documentation for Java's `Queue` interface and you'll see that it includes the `offer` and `poll` methods, but also `add` and `remove`. What is the difference between the two sets of methods?

Solution

The `offer` and `poll` methods return a result that the caller can check to see if the operation was successful; `add` and `remove` both *throw exceptions* if their operations couldn't complete. In general, `offer` and `poll` are better choices when failure is an accepted outcome. For example, calling `poll` is appropriate when the queue might be empty and checking an empty queue is not an error; `remove` is a better choice if the application logic dictates that you should never even attempt to remove from an empty queue.

1 `LinkedList` is like the Swiss Army chainsaw of data structures.

13.2 Queue and Deque Implementations

There are two basic strategies for implementing a queue or deque: a link-based approach, which is really the same as a linked list, and the array-based circular buffer.

13.2.1 Using `LinkedList`

Recall that a basic singly linked list had a head reference and forward links to other nodes in the chain. That list could add or remove from the head end in $O(1)$ time, but required $O(n)$ to access the tail. The improved doubly linked list has both head and tail pointers and contains both forward and backward links between nodes.[2] With these additions, it's now possible to interact directly with the tail element.

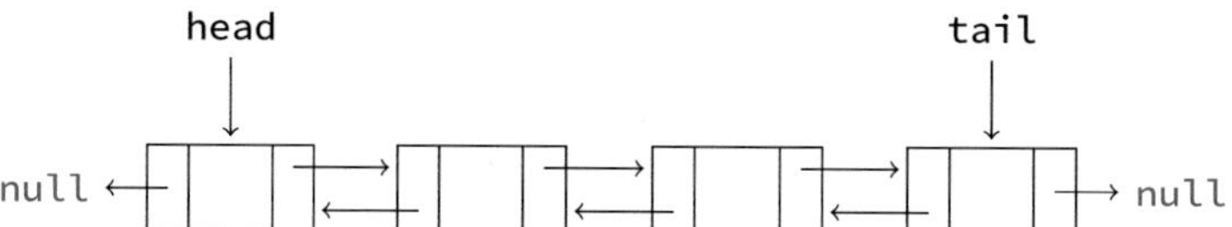

This setup can insert or remove at either end in $O(1)$ time.

Try It Yourself

Review the section on doubly linked lists in Chapter 6. Write your own versions of the `offer` and `poll` methods based on the examples there.

Try It Yourself

Explain why an `ArrayList` is a bad choice for a queue or deque implementation.

Solution

Recall that `ArrayList` can append to its end in average $O(1)$ time by increasing the size of the backing array when it becomes full. However, interacting with the head of the list requires shifting every element, which is $O(n)$.

13.2.2 Array-Based Circular Buffers

Despite the fact that a basic `ArrayList` can't serve as a queue or deque, it is possible to build an array-based queue or deque using a different strategy. Consider the following diagram: It shows an array with two references, one for the "end" of the queue and one for the "front."

2 It may also be circular, but that isn't required to implement deque operations.

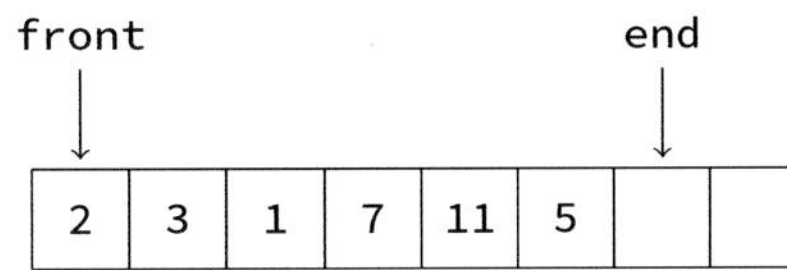

Here, the `front` and `end` references keep track of the active ends of the queue.

- The `end` reference always points to the next open array position. The basic `offer` operation fills the open location, then advances `end` to the next position.[3]
- The `front` reference points to the next unconsumed item; `poll` retrieves that item, then advances `front` to the next position. Note that this setup allows us to poll the queue in $O(1)$ without shifting any elements.

When a reference reaches the end of the array, it loops back to the beginning and begins reusing positions there. Java's `ArrayDeque` implements the `Queue` and `Deque` interfaces using this type of circular buffer. In the example below, `front` has advanced to the third array element and `end` is pointing to the final array position, which is currently empty. The first two array values, 4 and 9, have already been consumed and are no longer part of the active queue.

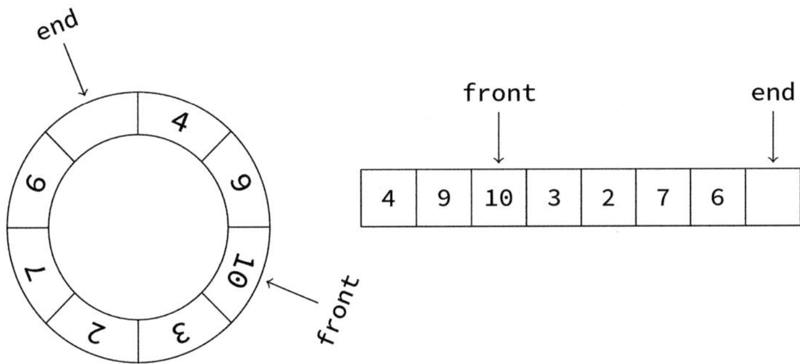

Now consider what happens when we offer a new value of 1 to the end of the queue. The operation fills the open position, then advances `end` to the next circular location by resetting it back to the front of the array.

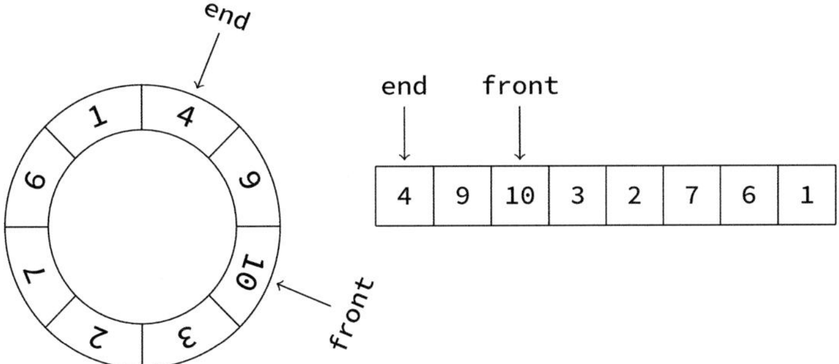

The next `offer` operation will fill the position currently occupied by 4. Old values don't have to be removed or cleared; they just move out of the active region of the queue once they're read and can be safely overwritten when the `end` pointer loops back through the array.

3 It's also possible to make `end` point to the last item instead of the next open position.

"But wait!" you interject, "what if the buffer completely fills with unpolled items?" There are three basic options:

- Don't add new data and indicate that the queue is full, by either throwing an exception or returning a `boolean` to indicate that `offer` couldn't complete.
- Use the `ArrayList` approach of allocating a larger array and copying the old data over to it, creating new space for additional elements.
- Simply overwrite the oldest value, which will now be lost.

`ArrayDeque` uses a combination of the first and second approaches: It will resize itself when the buffer fills, but also returns a `boolean` value to indicate if `offer` succeeded.

13.2.3 A `CircularBuffer` Class

Let's write a circular buffer class with the basic `offer` and `poll` methods. Like our earlier example classes, this one will use a generic type `T` to represent the kind of objects stored in the buffer.

```
/**
 * Circular Buffer with offer and poll methods
 */

public class CircularBuffer<T>{

  // Internal array
  private T[] buffer;

  // References
  private int front;
  private int end;

  // Number of active elements in the queue
  int size;

  /**
   * Constructor -- allocate default buffer
   */
  @SuppressWarnings("unchecked")
  public CircularBuffer() {
    this.buffer = (T[]) new Object[10];
    this.front = 0;
    this.end = 0;
```

```
    this.size = 0;
  }

  /**
   * offer -- add a new object to the queue
   *
   * @param  value  item to add (has generic type T)
   * @return  true if offer completes, false otherwise
   */
  public boolean offer(T value) {
    // If array is full, return false
    if (this.size == buffer.length) {
      return false;
    }

    this.buffer[this.end] = value;
    this.size++;
    this.end = (this.end + 1) % buffer.length;
    return true;
  }

  /**
   * poll -- remove the next item
   *
   * @return  the next item or null if the queue is empty
   */
  public T poll() {
    // Return null for an empty queue
    if (this.size == 0) {
      return null;
    }

    T next = this.buffer[this.front];
    this.size--;
    this.front = (this.front + 1) % buffer.length;
    return next;
  }
}
```

The details of this class should be familiar from our previous implementations:

- The class has a single `T[]` that serves as the backing storage for the queue. Notice that the constructor uses the same technique we previously used for `ArrayList`, declaring an `Object[]` and then casting it to type `T`.[4]
- The `offer` method returns `false` if the buffer is full; `poll` is similar.
- Both methods use modular arithmetic to update `end` and `front`.

Try It Yourself

Your friend says the `size` variable is unnecessary because we could calculate the number of active elements from the difference between `end` and `front` (allowing for wrapping back to the beginning). Is there a situation where using this approach could lead to an ambiguity about the size of the queue?

Solution

If `front == end`, the queue could be empty or it could be full, but we can't tell the difference from the pointers alone. It isn't possible to implement `offer` and `poll` correctly without distinguishing between those two cases. A variation handles this problem by making the array size $n + 1$ but never allowing the buffer to hold more than n elements; see the end-of-chapter questions.

13.3 Application: Flood-Filling

Flood-filling is a general term for algorithms that automatically identify and modify all points in an image or graph that are connected to a starting point – the change "floods" out from the starting location to every point it can reach. A well-known application is coloring pixels in a paint program: Given a starting pixel, the flooding tool sets all similar-valued pixels that are connected to the start to a new value. In the example below, the flood starts at the center of the image and expands outwards until it's filled the white pixels inside the ring.

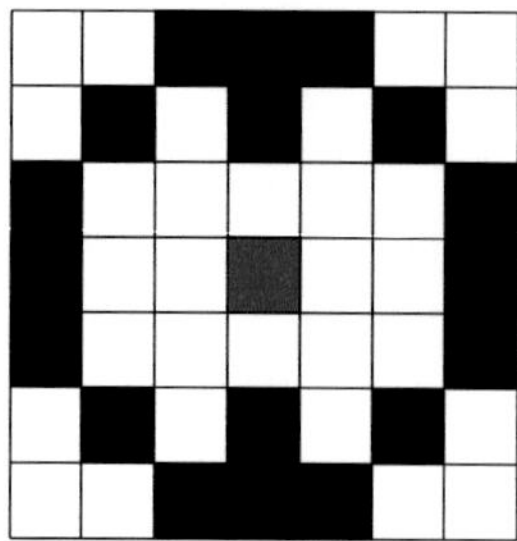

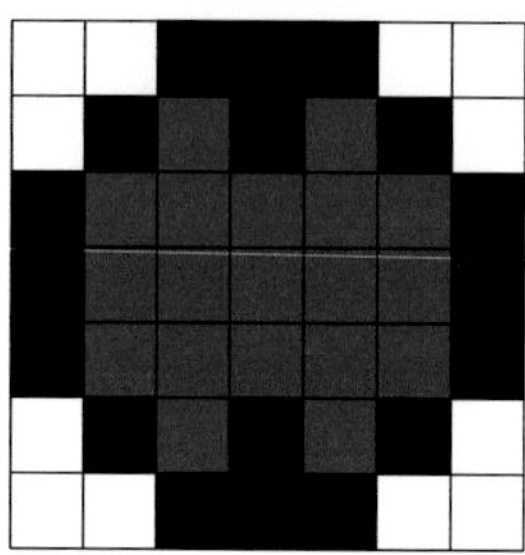

4 Review `ArrayList` in Chapter 6 for why this generates a compiler warning that we suppress.

13.3.1 The Breadth-First Flooding Algorithm

The basic flooding strategy is simple, but characteristic of queue-based algorithms. It has the following steps:

- Initialize a queue that contains the starting square.
- While the queue is not empty, remove the next square, fill it, then add its unfilled neighbors to the queue.
- Keep track of squares that have already been added to the queue so you don't attempt to visit the same square more than once.

Working through the previous example, the algorithm begins with the unfilled matrix. The starting square is the center at position (3, 3), which goes into the initial queue.

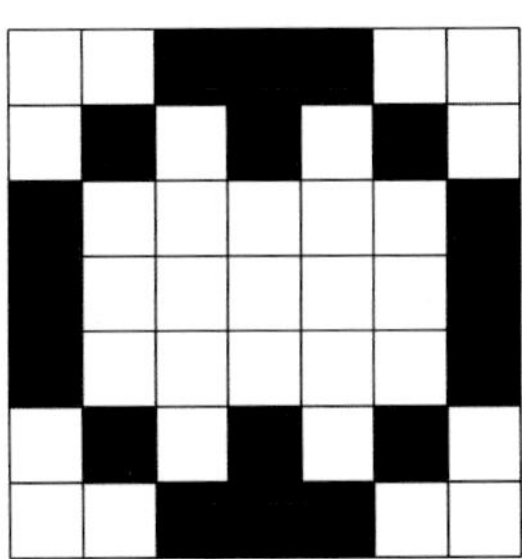

```
queue
(3, 3)
```

The first iteration removes the starting square from the queue, fills it, then adds its eight neighbors (shown in gray) to the queue, which are now waiting to be processed.

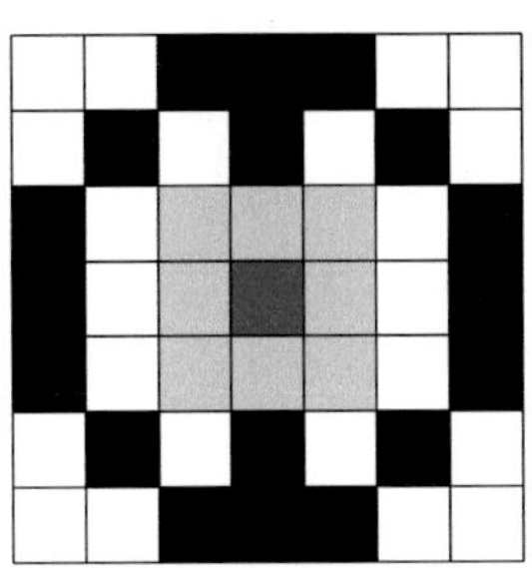

```
queue
(2, 2)
(2, 3)
(2, 4)
(3, 2)
(3, 4)
(4, 2)
(4, 3)
(4, 4)
```

The next iteration removes the first item in the queue – position (2, 2) – fills that square, then generates its neighbors. Notice that of (2, 2)'s neighbors, two are black squares that can't be filled, two are already in the queue, and one is the starting central square that's already been filled. Therefore, only three of (2, 2)'s neighbors actually need to join the queue. The result after processing (2, 2) is the following:

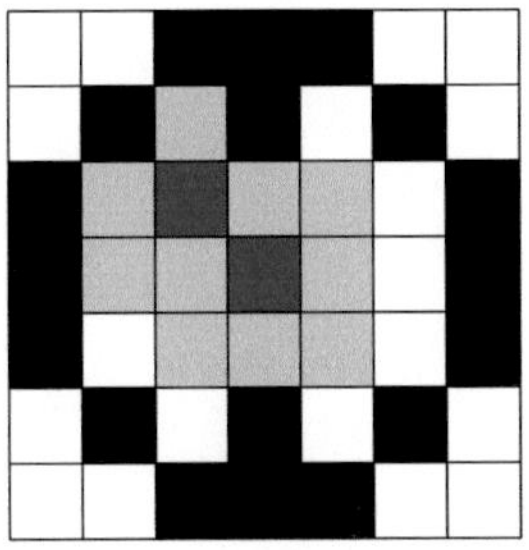

```
queue
(2, 3)
(2, 4)
(3, 2)
(3, 4)
(4, 2)
(4, 3)
(4, 4)
(1, 2)
(2, 1)
(3, 1)
```

This process continues: (2, 3) will be the next square filled, followed by (2, 4) and so forth. Notice how the method works outwards, first processing the starting square, then all neighbors one step away from the starting square, then all squares two steps away, and so forth. At each step, the next layer of unprocessed neighbors is added to the back of the queue, where they can wait for their turn to be processed. This behavior is characteristic of queue-based algorithms.

1. There is some starting location or point. Processing the initial location generates further locations for the algorithm to process.
2. Each new location is placed into the queue.
3. The queue is first-come-first-served, so entries are processed in order of their creation. Locations closer to the start are always processed before locations that are further away.
4. The method marks or tracks locations that have already been processed so it doesn't revisit them.

Step 3 distinguishes queue-based algorithms from similar stack-based algorithms. In a stack-based backtracking search, the *most recent* unvisited location is always processed next, in last-in-first-out order. In this case, both the stack- and queue-based versions of flooding would eventually visit the same locations, but in different orders.

Try It Yourself

Repeat the flood-fill algorithm on the example starting from position (1, 2).

13.3.2 Flood-Filling in a Matrix Using `ArrayDeque`

The Java implementation below takes an `int[][] a`, an `int[] start` for the starting location, and a `fill` as the new value. It uses an `ArrayDeque` to manage the set of remaining locations and fills all matrix locations that are connected to `start` and share its initial value.

```
/**
 * Example flood-fill on a matrix of integers
 *
 * @param  a  the matrix
 * @param  start  starting row and column for the fill
 * @param  fill  set pixels to this value
 *
 * @return  nothing, changes are made to a
 */
public static void flood(int[][] a, int[] start, int fill) {
  // Record the initial value of the start location
  int initialValue = a[start[0]][start[1]];

```

```
  // Initialize queue and add the starting location
  ArrayDeque<int[]> q = new ArrayDeque<int[]>();
  q.offer(start);

  // Keep track of visited locations
  boolean[][] visited = new boolean[a.length][a[0].length];
  visited[start[0]][start[1]] = true;

  while (!q.isEmpty()) {
    // Pop the next location from the queue
    int[] next = q.poll();

    // Fill the location
    int row = next[0];
    int col = next[1];
    a[row][col] = fill;

    // Check eight neighbors
    for (int r = row - 1; r <= row + 1; r++) {
      for (int c = col - 1; c <= col + 1; c++) {
        // Skip locations outside the matrix
        if (r < 0 || c < 0 || r >= a.length || c >= a[r].length) {
          continue;
        }

        // Add unvisited locations to the queue
        if (a[r][c] == initialValue && !visited[r][c]) {
          visited[r][c] = true;
          int[] neighbor = {r, c};
          q.offer(neighbor);
        }
      }
    }
  }
}
```

The `visited` array keeps track of the locations that have already been inserted into the queue. Array locations with `visited[r][c]` set to `true` have either been filled or are currently in the queue and waiting to be filled on a future iteration. In either case, skip the location to avoid creating a duplicate queue entry.

13.4 Example Interview Questions Using Queues

The majority of queue-based questions are related to tree and graph traversals. We'll see examples of those applications in future chapters. This section presents a few common questions that focus on queues themselves.

13.4.1 Count the Number of Islands

Given a matrix containing only 0s and 1s, let the 0s represent "water" and the 1s represent "land." Count the number of islands in the matrix, where an island is a group of entries with one or more adjacent 1s (Chea, 2018). For example, the matrix below has five islands.

1	1	0	0	1	0
1	1	0	1	1	1
0	0	0	0	0	1
0	1	0	0	0	0
0	0	0	1	0	0
1	0	1	1	0	0

This problem uses a variation on the flood-filling concept. It's easy to iterate through the matrix and identify land squares – the challenge is identifying that a group of land squares are part of the same connected component. Here's a strategy:

- Iterate through the matrix, checking for a land square. When you find one, initiate a flood-fill from that point. The flood will mark all connected 1 squares as being part of the same component.
- If, on a future iteration, you find a square that's already been marked by a flood-fill, skip it, because it must be part of a component you've already considered.
- Return a counter of the number of flooded components you found.

The code fragment below operates on an `int[][]` named `map` and uses the `flood` method from the previous section.

```
// Counter of the connected islands
int islands = 0;

// Scan the horizon for land
for (int r = 0; r < map.length; r++) {
  for (int c = 0; c < map[r].length; c++) {

    // Land ho!
    if (map[r][c] == 1) {
      // Initiate a flood-fill from position (r, c)
      // Mark all connected squares with another value
```

```
            int[] start = {r, c};
            flood(map, start, 99);

            // Count the new island
            islands++;
        }
    }
}

return islands;
```

13.4.2 Fairy Chess Pieces

In chess, a **fairy piece** is a novel piece with nonstandard movement rules. They're created for chess variants and problems, or derived from older historical pieces that existed before modern chess was standardized. Consider the following fairy piece, which has three possible moves.

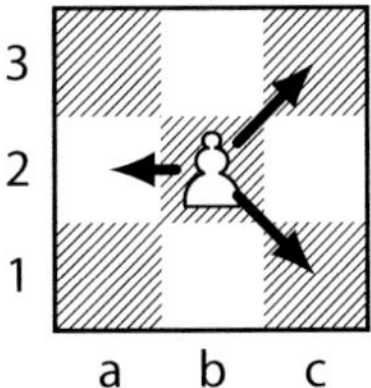

Given a starting square on a chess board s and a finishing square f, determine the minimum number of moves that this piece would need to move from s to f, or return -1 if it's not possible to reach f from s.

This problem seems wonky, but is in fact another variation of the flood-filling algorithm. From the starting location, the piece can reach at most three neighbor squares – the up-right, down-right, and left neighbors.

Try It Yourself

Imagine the piece is at the center of a 5×5 grid. Work out the sets of squares accessible within one, two, and three moves from the central starting square.

Moving the chess piece, then, is like a flooding algorithm that's limited to *only visiting certain neighbors*. The method, therefore, uses the same structure as flood-filling. Omitting the setup steps, the main loop of the solution is:

```
// Visit every position reachable from the starting square
while (!queue.isEmpty()) {
```

```
  // Get the next visited position from the queue
  int[] pos = queue.poll();

  // Success
  if (pos[0] == finish[0] && pos[1] == finish[1]) {
    // Return the number of moves from the starting square
  }

  // Generate three possible moves
  int[] rowMoves = {-1, 0, 1};
  int[] colMoves = {1, -1, 1};
  for (int i = 0; i < rowMoves.length; i++) {
    int r = pos[0] + rowMoves[i];
    int c = pos[1] + colMoves[i];

    // Verify (r, c) is on the board and unvisited
    if (r < 0 || c < 0 || r > 7 || c > 7 || visited[r][c]) {
      continue;
    }

    // If (r, c) is valid, put it in the queue
    int[] neighbor = {r, c};
    queue.offer(neighbor);
    visited[r][c] = true;
  }
}

// Failure: the loop ended without reaching the goal
return -1;
```

This method will begin at the start square then expand outward, first visiting the squares that are one move away, then those that are two moves away, and so forth. It will reach the destination square, if possible, in the minimum number of moves. However, we still need a way to keep track of the moves used to reach each position. Add an additional counter to each queue entry:

```
// Get the next visited position from the queue
int[] pos = queue.poll();

// Number of moves required to reach this position
int moves = pos[2];
```

```

// Success
if (pos[0] == finish[0] && pos[1] == finish[1]) {
  return moves;
}
```

The start location has a move count of 0, and each subsequent move is one more than its parent's count:

```
int[] neighbor = {r, c, moves + 1};
queue.offer(neighbor);
```

SUMMARY

We've now considered all three of the important sequential data structures: lists, stacks, and queues. All three maintain a *linear relationship* among their data items, with different ideas about how items can be added and removed. As you're working through this chapter, keep in mind the two key roles of the queue:

- First, serving as *intermediate storage*: A queue holds a set of items that are waiting to be processed. A stack can fulfill the same purpose (whether explicit or as part of a recursive implementation) but the order of evaluation will be different.
- Second, algorithms that expand outwards from a starting location, exemplified by flood-filling. We'll apply this strategy to both trees and graphs in future chapters.

EXERCISES

Understand

1. Write a code fragment that initializes an `ArrayDeque` of `String` and populates it with five values.
2. Your friend says that a queue and a stack have the same abstract data type because they both implement `push` and `pop` operations. How do you respond?
3. What is the difference between `offer` and `add` in the Java `Queue` interface?
4. Both the linked deque and circular buffer provide $O(1)$ operations at both ends. Can you think of any reason why you might prefer one over the other in some cases?
5. Add `peek`, `size`, and `isEmpty` methods to the `CircularBuffer` class.
6. Here's another popular interview question, albeit a non-useful one: Describe how to implement a queue using two stacks. Tip: One end of the stack is readily accessible; treat that as the front of the queue so that polling is always $O(1)$. Think about how to use the second stack to insert a new element.

7. The mirror of the previous question: Implement a stack using only queue operations. Assume you have only a single-ended queue that adds to the end and removes from the front, not a deque.
8. Use a queue and a stack to reverse the order of the items in the queue.
9. Write a method called `swap` that takes an `ArrayDeque` and reverses the order of the two elements at the front, or does nothing if there are fewer than two elements.
10. Write a pseudocode method that takes a `String s` as input and uses a queue and a stack to test if `s` is a palindrome.
11. Repeat the previous problem, but use a single `ArrayDeque`.

Apply

12. Write a `pollLast` method for the `CircularBuffer` that removes from the end in $O(1)$ time. Tip: You'll need to determine the index of the last element and update the `end` reference, which may require moving it from the front to the end of the array.
13. Now write a `offerFront` method that adds to the front in $O(1)$ time. Again, you'll have to think about how to modify the `front` reference. Remember to check the size before adding a new element.
14. Write a `contains` method that takes a `T value` as input, iterates through the `CircularBuffer`, then returns `true` if it finds an item equal to `value` and `false` otherwise. Use the `equals` method to test if two objects are equal. Remember to only check the active region, not the entire array.
15. Repeat the island counting problem, but consider only neighbors to the north, south, east, and west.
16. Modify the island counting solution to mark each island with a unique number, so printing the map will show which squares are part of which islands.
17. Repeat the flood-fill example (by hand) using a stack. How does the order of visited locations compare to the queue-based version?
18. Write a method called `lookup` that takes an `int index` as input and returns the item in the `CircularBuffer` queue at that position, or `null` if there is no such item. This is not a standard queue operation, but will help you think about how to iterate through the buffer. Tip: This is the *queue* position, not the *array* position.

Extend

19. Update the `CircularBuffer` implementation to expand the backing array when it becomes full. Tip: You'll need to think about how to copy the elements between `front` and `end` and then where to set `front` and `end` in the new array. A reasonable choice is to reset `front` to the first item.
20. Make an argument that `offer` on an `ArrayDeque` is $O(1)$ on average, including the time required to expand the backing array when it fills.
21. Section 13.2.3 argued that the `size` field was required to distinguish between a full queue and an empty one. Another option is to allow the backing array to have $n + 1$ elements, but never store more than n items (Shaffer, 1997). Write a new version of `offer` that

uses this approach. You should determine the distance between `front` and `end` (allowing for wrapping around the buffer) then perform the insertion only if there are n or fewer elements queued. Don't use the `size` field.

22. Consider the following fairy chess piece, which can move one square down or one square diagonally. What is the minimum number of moves required to move it from the upper-left to the lower-right of the chessboard?

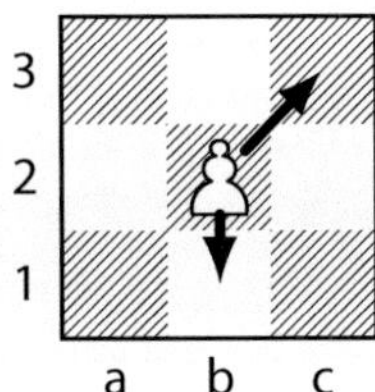

23. Are there any squares on the board that the piece can't reach?

24. One more deque method, and then you can rest. `ArrayDeque` has a method called `toArray`, which returns the elements of the deque as a `T[]`, where `T` is the deque's data type. Write your own version of this method. Remember that you can't just return the backing array.

25. Here's another variation on the islands problem. Suppose that you have a matrix of 0s and 1s, where the 1s represent land. Determine if it's possible to move from the upper-left to the lower-right of the matrix while stepping only on land squares. Tip: This is again like a flooding problem, but a neighbor square must contain a 1 to be a valid move.

26. The last series of questions will lead you through the design of a modified `ArrayDeque` that allows insertion and removal at both ends *and in the middle.* First, consider the problem of making $O(1)$ modifications to the middle of a circular buffer: Why is it not sufficient to keep track of the middle position between `front` and `end` and insert or remove items from there?

27. Here's the approach: Maintain two `ArrayDeque`, one for the front half of the queue and the other for the back (Poitevin, 2020). With this setup, it's possible to interact with either end or the middle in $O(1)$. To begin, write a class that contains an `ArrayDeque<T> frontHalf` and an `ArrayDeque<T> backHalf`. Implement a basic `offer` that adds a new item to the end of `backHalf` and a `poll` that takes the first item from the `frontHalf`.

28. Let's adopt the rule of keeping the two deques balanced so that the middle position, at index `size / 2`, is always the first element of the back deque. If we maintain this condition, the sizes of the two deques must be equal or differ by at most one, with the back deque being larger. For example, if the total queue has seven elements, three should be in the front half and four in the back half.

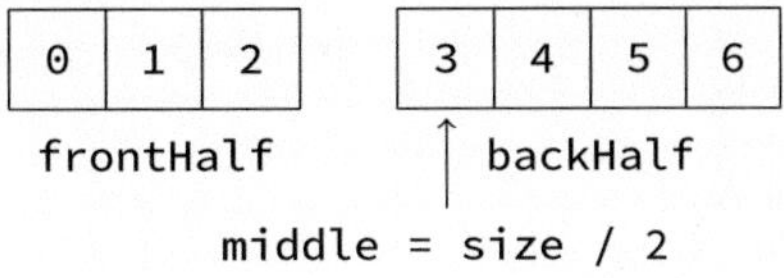

Modify the `offer` and `poll` methods from the previous problem to rebalance the two deques if necessary. If `offer` makes the back deque longer than `size / 2`, move an element to the front deque, and vice versa if `poll` makes the front deque too short.

29. Implement the `offerMiddle` method: Insert a new item at the front of `backHalf` and then rebalance the two deques if necessary.

30. `pollMiddle` is similar: Remove the first item from the back deque and then rebalance if the back deque is too short.

31. Finally, implement the `offerFront` and `pollBack` methods.

NOTES AND FURTHER READING

Queueing theory is the branch of mathematics that analyzes systems with waiting lines. The invention of queueing models is credited to the Danish telephone engineer Agner Erlang, who first used stochastic techniques to model the Copenhagen telephone system in the early 1900s. At the time, telephone calls were connected manually by operators patching wires on a switchboard. If a call arrived, but all available operators were busy servicing other calls, then that call would be *blocked* and rejected by the system. Erlang derived formulas for calculating the expected blocking probability based on the number of operators and the statistical properties of the call arrival and service time distributions. Communication engineers measure call load in units of Erlangs, and a statistical distribution and programming language are also named for him.

Queueing theory was important in the development of the Internet: In the 1960s, Leonard Kleinrock used queueing methods to analyze waiting times in computer networks. His work established that *packet switching* – transmitting data through a network one step at a time in self-contained units, as opposed to reserving an entire end-to-end circuit for a communication – was viable for the ARPANET, which would become the predecessor of the modern Internet. Harchol-Balter (2013) is an introduction to queueing theory and its application to computer performance modeling.

14 Hashing

HASH, x. There is no definition for this word—nobody knows what hash is.
Ambrose Bierce, *The Unabridged Devil's Dictionary*

INTRODUCTION

A hash, in culinary terms, is a dish made of mixed foods – often including corned beef and onions – chopped into tiny pieces. In the early twentieth century, it became a shorthand for something of dubious origin, probably unwise to consume. In computer science, a **hash function** is an operation that rearranges, mixes, and combines data to produce a single fixed-size output. Unlike their culinary namesake, hash functions are wonderfully useful. A hash value is like a "fingerprint" of the input used to calculate it. Hash functions have applications to security, distributed systems, and – as we'll explore – data structures.

LEARNING OBJECTIVES

This chapter introduces hash functions, including:

- The important properties of hash functions and some key examples, including Java's `hashCode` and the SHA family of cryptographic functions.
- Using hash functions to implement message authentication.
- The role of hashing in password systems, which we'll explore by writing a *password cracking* program.
- The proof-of-work problem and its application to the Bitcoin blockchain.

After building our knowledge of hash functions in general, the next chapter will introduce **hash tables**, a data structure built around using hash values to index information and perform fast lookups.

14.1 Hash Functions

A hash function maps an input of arbitrary length to a fixed-size output. The input is often called the *key* and the output is the hash of that key. The primary use of hash functions is *summarizing data*. A hash function can condense a string, file, or other input into a single output value. If two hash values differ, by even a single bit, then they must have been generated from different inputs. There is no single "best" hash function – there are many options and the right choice depends on the application. Therefore, a good place to start is by learning how hash functions work with Java classes that we've already seen. After that, we'll consider some more advanced hashes and good all-around properties that hash functions should have.

14.1.1 Java's `hashCode`

Every Java class implements a method called `hashCode`, which returns an `int` hash value for objects of its type. Any class that doesn't provide its own `hashCode` implementation inherits the default one from the top-level `Object` class, which converts the object's internal memory address to an integer.[1] Any custom `hashCode` method should obey the following two requirements:

- Two objects that are equal according to their `equals` method must also have the same `hashCode` value.
- An object's hash value should not change between consecutive calls to `hashCode` if none of the object's data used in an `equals` comparison have changed.

Therefore, the basic contract of `hashCode` is that *equal objects must have equal hashes.* Note that *unequal* objects aren't required to return different hash codes, but doing so is recommended.

Many of the built-in Java classes we've already worked with provide their own `hashCode` methods:

- `Integer` simply returns its underlying `int` value as the hash. This is an example of an *identity hash function*, where the hash of a key is simply the key itself.
- `String` uses a more complex calculation that takes into account the values of each character and their positions. For a string s with n characters, the hash value is given by:

  $$h(s, n) = \sum_{i=0}^{n-1} s_i\, 31^{n-1-i} = s_0\, 31^{n-1} + s_1\, 31^{n-2} + \cdots + s_{n-1},$$

  where s_i is the value of the character located at position i.
- The `List` interface defines that the hash code of any `List` must be calculated from the hash codes of its elements according to the following code fragment:

  ```
  int hashCode = 1;
  for (E e : list)
    hashCode = 31 * hashCode + (e==null ? 0 : e.hashCode());
  ```

  The ternary condition checks if `e` is `null`. If so, it uses 0 for the hash value.

Observe that the `String` and `List` codes both calculate the overall hash value by combining lower-level pieces of data into one result – the individual characters for a string and the element hashes for a list.

1 If you print an object that doesn't have a `toString`, you'll see this default hash output, which will have a form like `[I@31befd9f`.

Try It Yourself

Consider the following two lists. Would they generate the same hash value? Assume that they use the iterative calculation given above and that each `Integer` returns its underlying `int` value for its hash code.

```
a = [1, 2, 3, 4]
b = [null, 33, 4, -27]
```

Solution

a's hash evaluates to 955,331. Starting with 1, the iterations are as follows:

$$31 \cdot 1 + 1 = 32$$
$$31 \cdot 32 + 2 = 994$$
$$31 \cdot 994 + 3 = 30,817$$
$$31 \cdot 30,817 + 4 = 955,331$$

`b` calculates the same final result.

Try It Yourself

I wrote the following code fragment. When I ran it, it printed `false`. What's going on?

```
int[] a = {1, 2, 3, 4};
int[] b = {1, 2, 3, 4};

System.out.println(a.hashCode() == b.hashCode());
```

Solution

Recall the difference between *reference equality* and *value equality*. The two arrays have the same values, but are different objects in memory. Arrays use the default `hashCode` based on memory address, so the two arrays generate different hash values.

14.1.2 A Real-World Hash Function: MurmurHash3

Let's look at another general-purpose hash function that illustrates how a hash can be computed from arbitrary-length input data. **MurmurHash3** is a widely used hash algorithm invented by Austin Appleby (Appleby, 2008). It's been adopted into a number of programming languages and open-source projects, so it provides a good illustration of a general-purpose modern hash function designed to be fast and uniform. *Murmur* is short for *multiply–rotate–multiply–rotate*, which is a high-level (but not quite complete) description of the operations it performs. The core MurmurHash3 algorithm produces a 32-bit output, which is calculated from:

- The input data, which can be any number of bytes. The algorithm processes data in *four-byte chunks*, where each chunk is put through a series of calculations, then incorporated into the hash value, which we'll discuss below. If the data length is not divisible by four, there's a finishing step at the end to incorporate any extra bytes into the hash.
- A 32-bit *seed*, which is used as the starting hash value. An application can change the seed to get different hashes for the same input data.
- A set of fixed-value constants used in the multiply and rotation steps. Their values are set as part of the algorithm's specification and don't change.

Notice how the algorithm processes data in blocks of bytes that are the same size as the output. This is typical for complex hash functions: The input can be of any length because the function only operates on a small chunk of bytes at a time. Also observe that MurmurHash3 doesn't care about the *type* of its input data – it just crunches up bytes, whatever they represent, to produce its output.

The method maintains a running hash value, which is initially set to the seed. Each iteration of the loop updates the hash using one four-byte chunk of the input. At the conclusion an iteration, its output is fed back to be used with the next four-byte chunk. In block form, the core calculation looks like the following:

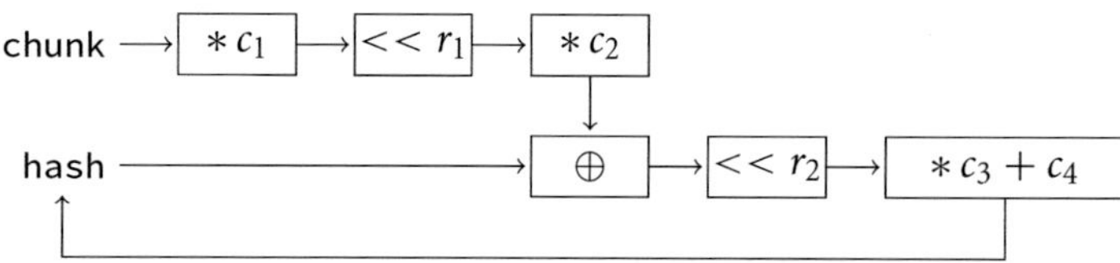

The chunk is multiplied, rotated, and multiplied again by the algorithm's constants, then XORed with the current hash value. The result is rotated one more time (completing the multiply–rotate–multiply–rotate process), then scaled and shifted by two more constants. That output hash value is then used as the input to the next round, to be combined with the next four-byte chunk. After every chunk has been processed, the algorithm performs a last step that incorporates any remaining bytes and the length of the input to produce the final output hash.

Although the details are different, MurmurHash3 is conceptually similar to the `String` class's `hashCode` method. Both start with an initial hash value, then process the input data in fixed-size chunks. Each chunk gets manipulated through a combination of relatively simple operations – one multiplication for `String`, multiplies and rotates for MurmurHash3 – then incorporated into the running hash value. If the sequence of operations and constants are well-designed, the result is an output that takes into account every bit of the input, such that even small changes in the input percolate through to affect every bit of the output.

Try It Yourself

Your friend proposes a hash function that simply divides the input into `int`-sized 32-bit chunks and adds them together.

```
int hash = 1;
for x = each int-sized chunk of the input {
```

```
    hash += x
}
```

Identify some problems with this approach.

Solution

First, the method needs a way to deal with inputs that aren't evenly divisible into `int`-sized chunks. Here's another more subtle issue: The method doesn't use the *position* of the chunk, so inputs that have the same chunk values but in a different order would generate the same hash value. This would be like a string hash function that returned the same values for all anagrams.

14.1.3 Properties of Good Hash Functions

Choosing an appropriate hash function depends on the application and the particular type of data that you're hashing. Any good hash function, though, should satisfy a few basic properties.

- It should be *deterministic*: For a given input, the function always computes the same output. Hash functions are never randomized.
- It should be as efficient as possible. Most practical hash functions are linear in the length of the input data.

In many applications, it's also important for the function to be *uniform*. Given an input x, the output $h(x)$ should behave as if it's chosen uniformly at random from the set of output values. Uniformity helps avoid clustering hash values into only part of the output range and avoids mapping similar keys to similar outputs.

Try It Yourself

Consider a function that takes a string as input and returns its first character. Is this a hash function? If so, is it a good one?

Solution

The function takes a variable-length input and returns a fixed size output – one `char` – so it satisfies the definition of a hash function. It's also deterministic and $O(1)$. However, it will cluster all strings with the same starting character, regardless of length, into the same hash value, so it isn't uniform. In general, the hash calculation should use every byte of the input data.

A **collision** occurs if two nonidentical inputs x and y generate the same hash value; that is, if $h(x) = h(y)$. Note that, in a hash function with an output size of b bits, there are 2^b possible hashes. Therefore, if the input size is allowed to be longer than b bits, then it must be possible for two different inputs to collide and produce the same output. Uniform hashing minimizes the probability of collisions.

Try It Yourself

Suppose you have a uniform hash with an output size of b bits. What's the probability that two randomly chosen inputs x and y hash to the same output value?

Solution

The first hash could land on any of the 2^b outputs. The probability that the second hash lands on any other randomly chosen output is

$$\frac{2^b - 1}{2^b}.$$

Therefore, the probability the second hash hits the same output as the first is

$$1 - \frac{2^b - 1}{2^b} = \frac{1}{2^b}.$$

14.1.4 Cryptographic Hash Functions

Cryptographic hash functions have even stronger properties that make them suitable for secure applications, like password protection and message authentication. Informally, the key property of cryptographic hash functions is that given an output $h(x)$, an attacker has no way of determining x (or any other input that also generates $h(x)$) other than the brute-force approach of trying every possible input. More specifically, a cryptographic hash should have the following features:

- *One-way*: Given a hash value v, it should be computationally infeasible to invert the function and find an input x that gives $h(x) = v$. That is, knowing the output reveals no information about the input used to generate it. A stronger version of this property prevents an attacker from deriving *any information* about the input x from observing v.
- *Collision avoidant*: It should be computationally infeasible for an attacker to find two nonidentical inputs x and y that have $h(x) = h(y)$. This is stronger than basic uniformity, because it protects against deliberately engineered collisions.

There are only a limited number of popular cryptographic hash functions, which have to undergo extensive testing and validation before they can be deployed. The most widely used are the *Secure Hash Algorithm* (SHA) family of functions, which are based on published standards issued by the US National Institute of Standards and Technology. The first version, SHA-1, was introduced in the early 1990s and calculated a 160-bit output. It was succeeded in the 2000s by the SHA-2 algorithm, which has several variants that produce different-sized outputs. SHA-256, which calculates a 256-bit output, is currently the most widely deployed cryptographic hash function and is used in many major applications, including the Bitcoin blockchain. A third function, SHA-3, was introduced in 2015 as an alternative to SHA-2 and based on a different algorithm.

14.1.5 Application: Message Authentication

Sending data over computer networks is inherently unreliable. Packets can, of course, be dropped due to problems like network congestion, but it's also possible for the data in a message to be corrupted in transit by, for example, electrical noise. Therefore, it's important to include extra information with a message so that the recipient can verify that it was actually transmitted correctly. Lower-level networks often use *error-correcting codes* that can detect if a message was corrupted and, in some cases, detect and fix the error without requiring a retransmission. Another type of message authentication, typically used at the application level, relies on the data-summarizing properties of hash functions.

Suppose that Alicia wants to send a message to her partner, Bobbie, and that Bobbie wants to be able to verify that the message has been transmitted without errors. Alicia can do the following:

- Take her message – call it m – and calculate its hash value $h(m)$. The hash is a fingerprint of m and summarizes the information it contains.
- Alicia sends the pair $(m, h(m))$ to Bobbie.
- Bobbie receives the message and now needs to validate it – call the version she received m'. She calculates $h(m')$ and compares it to the received $h(m)$ value that Alicia sent. If the two hashes match, Bobbie concludes that the message she received is likely valid; it's unlikely that the message could have been corrupted and still produce the same hash.

The hashed message, $h(m)$, is sometimes called the *authenticator* or *message digest*.

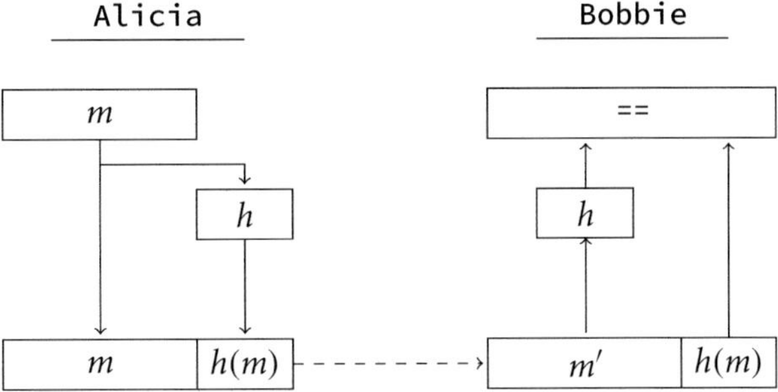

Try It Yourself

Suppose that the message m arrives correctly, but the authenticator $h(m)$ is somehow corrupted in transmission. What happens in this case?

Solution

In this case, Bobbie would detect that the $h(m)$ she received and the $h(m')$ she calculated don't match, so she'll know that something went wrong. She can't determine if the problem is with the message or the received hash value, though, so she would still have to ask Alicia to retransmit the message.

Note that this version, by itself, doesn't allow for *secure* message exchange, because it doesn't allow Bobbie to verify that the message really comes from Alicia, as opposed to an adversary impersonating her. It also can't stop an adversary from intercepting Alicia's communication and replacing the contents with a new message and its hash. A stronger version of this system uses cryptography to construct a *digital signature*. By signing her message and its hash with a cryptographic key, Alicia can protect it from being manipulated by an adversary and Bobbie can confirm that it really was sent by Alicia and not a malicious third party.

14.2 Project: Password Cracking

You've probably read guidelines for creating secure passwords: at least eight characters, use a combination of upper- and lowercase letters and digits, include at least one special character, and so forth. Password security is important for both users and designers, since weak passwords are one of the easiest ways for attackers to gain access to systems. Hashing is an important part of password protection. In this project, we'll write an example **password cracker** using Java's built-in hashing features. After completing this project, you'll be familiar with:

- shadow password files and the role of hashing in password security;
- Java's `MessageDigest` class;
- brute-force and dictionary-based password cracking approaches; and
- more refined guidelines for creating strong passwords.

14.2.1 Shadow Password Files

The earliest Unix systems stored users' passwords in a special file called `passwd`. When a user needed to perform an action that required authentication, like logging in or running a command with elevated privileges, the system would prompt the user to enter a password, then compare it to the `passwd` file. However, these early systems stored users' passwords in *cleartext*, with no encryption or obfuscation, with entries matching each user ID with its password (Morris and Thompson, 1979). As you might expect, this was a problem, since any user that gained the ability to read `passwd` could see every other user's password.

Modern Unix/Linux systems don't store passwords in cleartext, of course. Instead, they store the *hash* of each user's password in a file called `shadow`, the **shadow password file**. When a user needs to authenticate, the system calculates the hash of the input password and compares it to the real hash in `shadow`. If the hashes match, the system assumes the user has entered a valid password and allows the action.

What if the `shadow` file is compromised? This isn't great, but it's not as bad as leaking users' real passwords. An attacker who manages to obtain the `shadow` file would know the hash of each user's password, but not the real passwords themselves. Therefore, the attacker faces a reverse-engineering problem: Given a password hash, try to generate an input to match it. Secure hash functions are one-way, so the attacker's only option is to try many candidate passwords, looking for one that produces a collision with the target hash.

Try It Yourself

Your friend thinks an attacker can defeat the login system by simply entering the stolen password hash in place of the real password. Explain why this won't work.

Solution

Assuming you can enter the stolen password hash as a character string, the system will treat it as an input password and then hash it, which transforms it to a different hash value that won't match the expected one in the `shadow` file.

14.2.2 Cryptographic Hashing with `MessageDigest`

`MessageDigest` is a built-in Java class that can calculate secure hash functions. Here's an example that takes a password string and prints its SHA-256 hash:

```
/**
 * Password hashing with MessageDigest
 */

import java.security.MessageDigest;
import java.security.NoSuchAlgorithmException;

public class PasswordExample {
  public static void main(String[] args) {
    String password = "password1";
    MessageDigest md = null;

    // Initialize the message digest calculator
    try {
      md = MessageDigest.getInstance("SHA-256");
    } catch (NoSuchAlgorithmException e) {
      e.printStackTrace();
    }

    // Compute the hash of the password string
    // md.digest takes a byte[] as input and returns a byte[]
    byte[] hashBytes = md.digest(password.getBytes());

    // Convert byte array to hexadecimal string
```

```
25     StringBuilder hexString = new StringBuilder();
26     for(byte b: hashBytes) {
27       hexString.append(String.format("%02x", b));
28     }
29     String hashedPassword = hexString.toString();
30     System.out.println(hashedPassword);
31   }
32 }
```

The first set of statements creates the `MessageDigest` object, specifying that it should use the SHA-256 algorithm. Java is guaranteed to support SHA-256, but the initialization will fail if you ask for an unsupported algorithm, so it must be wrapped in a `try-catch` block. The `digest` method performs the hash calculation; notice that it takes a `byte[]` as input and returns the result as a `byte[]`. Lines 25–30 convert each byte in the result array into hexadecimal digits using `String.format` as a helper method to convert each byte into a two-digit representation.

Although SHA-256 is an important secure hash function, it's not a good choice for password security, because it's actually *too easy* to calculate. As we'll discuss next, real password systems want to prevent attackers from testing hashes too quickly, so they use special resource-intensive hash functions that are deliberately inefficient.[2] One hash function in this category is `bcrypt` (Provos and Mazieres, 1999).

14.2.3 Brute-Force Cracking

The simplest password cracking approach is a **brute-force** attack: Simply generate all candidate passwords and test each one. This is guaranteed to eventually succeed, but may take a long time. Let's assume that you have a target hash available in `byte[]` form and want to brute-force search passwords of *k* characters. Take a look at the following two functions, which recursively generate all combinations of *k* characters from a given constant string called `ALPHABET`:

```
/**
 * Recursively generate candidate passwords
 *
 * @param  target  the target password hash in byte[] format
 * @param  k  password length
 * @param  candidate  the in-progress candidate password
 */
public void generate(byte[] target, int k, String candidate) {

  // Base case: the candidate string has length k
  //
  // Test if it's a match for the target
```

2 This is the only time I'll tell you inefficiency is a good thing.

```
13   if (candidate.length() == k) {
14     byte[] candidateHash = hash(candidate);
15
16     if (Arrays.equals(candidateHash, target)) {
17       System.out.println("Cracked: " + candidate);
18       System.exit(0);
19     }
20     return;
21   }
22
23   // Recursive case: extend candidate by each alphabet character
24   for (int i = 0; i < ALPHABET.length(); i++) {
25     char next = ALPHABET.charAt(i);
26     generate(target, k, candidate + next);
27   }
28 }
29
30 /**
31  * Entry function to generate candidate passwords
32  */
33 public void crack(byte[] target, int k) {
34   generate(target, k, "");
35 }
```

If the length of `candidate` equals the goal length `k`, then the method calculates the candidate string's hash value and compares it to the `target`. Finding a match ends the program, although we could allow it to continue running to search for additional matches. Lines 24–27 are the recursive case: Call `generate` with one more character appended to the candidate string. The `crack` function is simply a wrapper to start the process with an empty input.

Here's a class framework that includes an example `main` that generates a practice target hash. It uses a `MessageDigest` class member to implement the `hash` function.

```
/**
 * Brute-force Password Cracking
 */

import java.security.MessageDigest;
import java.security.NoSuchAlgorithmException;
import java.util.Arrays;

```

```
public class BruteForceCracker {

  private MessageDigest md;
  private final String ALPHABET = "abcdefghijklmnopqrstuvwxyz";

  public BruteForceCracker() {
    // Initialize this.md
    try {
      md = MessageDigest.getInstance("SHA-256");
    } catch (NoSuchAlgorithmException e) {
      e.printStackTrace();
    }
  }

  public byte[] hash(String data) {
    return this.md.digest(data.getBytes());
  }

  public static void main(String[] args) {
    try {
      // Generate a test byte[] from an example password
      MessageDigest md = MessageDigest.getInstance("SHA-256");
      byte[] test = md.digest("hello".getBytes());

      // Brutally crack it
      BruteForceCracker cracker = new BruteForceCracker();
      cracker.crack(test, 5);
    } catch (NoSuchAlgorithmException e) {
      e.printStackTrace();
    }
  }
}
```

Try It Yourself

Add `crack` and `generate` to the class and verify that you can crack five-character target passwords. Experiment with longer passwords and with adding more characters to the alphabet. How do those changes affect the cracking time?

The effectiveness of a brute-force attack is tied to the complexity of the user's password. A simple password of five lowercase characters only has $26^5 \approx 11.8$ million possible options. Eight lowercase characters has $26^8 \approx 208.8$ billion potential combinations, which is a lot, but a cracking system using a small number of graphics processing cards to implement the hash algorithm could practically test tens to hundreds of millions of hashes per second. Increasing the length, character variety, and randomness of a password reduces its vulnerability to brute-force attacks. For example, a 12 character password consisting of any combination of uppercase letters, lowercase letters, and digits has $62^{12} \approx 3.2$ sextillion possible combinations. Even if you could test one billion hashes per second, it would take, on average, more than 5,000 years to brute-force crack such a password.

14.2.4 Dictionary Attacks

For the most part, though, attackers don't need to resort to brute-force attacks. Users rarely pick complex passwords, and the same kinds of passwords tend to show up repeatedly on different systems. The classic, of course, is setting your password to `password`, but even savvy users still tend to choose passwords that are based on common words, short phrases, or cultural tropes.

For example, suppose a user picks a password based on a Bible verse, like `2Timothy3:16`. This seems strong by ordinary password rules: It's long and contains a mixture of characters, digits, and symbols. A smart attacker, though, knows that passwords based on Bible verses are common. Even with capitalization and spelling variations, there are only a few million options, so generating and testing passwords based on the Bible is a low-cost attack that will probably crack a few passwords in a large database. The same logic applies to passwords based on other religious texts, band names, movies, and common phrases.

A **dictionary attack** starts with a list of candidate passwords, which might consist of real passwords leaked from other systems, and then tests each one. In a large shadow file, it's likely that some users will have picked passwords that are already in the dictionary. An attacker can get more passwords for low cost by applying *mangling rules* to the dictionary entries. For example, taking a short phrase and appending a number (e.g., `pumpkinspice1`) is a common password heuristic, but it's easy for an attacker to generate 10 variations on each dictionary entry. Toggling the case of the first letter is an easy mangle (only one character needs to change), as are common substitutions, like replacing the lowercase letter `o` with `0` (Munroe, 2011).

Try It Yourself

Do some research and find the number of unique words in a common English dictionary. How long might it feasibly take an attacker to test the hash of each one? What about two-word combinations? How about two-word combinations with a digit appended?

Writing a dictionary-based cracker is easy: Get a file of pre-existing passwords (or a dictionary of common words), read each line and then hash it, checking for matches with the target hash. The more interesting challenge is adding mangling rules to test variations on each candidate. Here's an example function that reads a dictionary file with `Scanner` and hashes each word. The end-of-chapter questions will let you practice implementing some mangling rules.

```
/**
 * Dictionary attack
 *
 * @param  dict  dictionary file name
 * @param  target  the target has in byte[] format
 */
public void crack(String dict, byte[] target) {

  // Open the dictionary file
  Scanner s = null;
  try {
    s = new Scanner(new File(dict));
  } catch (FileNotFoundException e) {
    e.printStackTrace();
  }

  // Loop through the dictionary passwords
  while (s.hasNext()) {
    String candidate = s.next();

    //*** Apply mangling rules here ***//

    // Test the candidate word: exit if it's a match
    byte[] candidateHash = hash(candidate);
    if (Arrays.equals(candidateHash, target)) {
      System.out.println("Cracked: " + candidate);
      System.exit(0);
    }
  }
}
```

Observe that this method loops through the entire file to test one target hash. If you wanted to test multiple targets – which a real attacker would – it's inefficient to hash each candidate password more than once. A better strategy would be to process the file one time and store each candidate password's hash in a lookup data structure. Then, given a target hash, you could check if there's a match in the lookup structure and retrieve the associated password. If lookups are fast, then this approach would allow you to pay the one-time up-front cost of hashing every dictionary entry then quickly test lots of passwords. A **rainbow table** is a special data structure optimized to quickly look-up password matches in a large dictionary. It's a variant of the hash table, the most important lookup structure, which we'll discuss in the next chapter.

The basic defense against pre-computed lookup tables is to make passwords even longer, so that it becomes infeasible to compute and save every possible password hash. To do this, password systems generate an extra value called the **salt**, which is unique for each user and stored in the `shadow` file with the user's password. When the user needs to authenticate, the system takes the input password, appends the salt value, then hashes the password–salt combination, rather than only the password by itself. Adding the salt string effectively increases the length of the user's password before it's hashed, so that an attacker can't precompute all possible combinations of dictionary passwords and salts.

14.3 Application: Proof-of-Work and Bitcoin

The Bitcoin system was proposed in a 2008 white paper written by a person or persons using the pseudonym "Satoshi Nakamoto," whose real identity is still unknown (Nakamoto, 2008). Nakamoto proposed creating a "peer-to-peer electronic cash system" that would allow participants to conduct irreversible cash-like transactions without relying on a bank or payment processor. The key innovation of Bitcoin is the **blockchain**, a distributed peer-to-peer system that validates and orders transactions without relying on a centralized third party. A key element of the Bitcoin system is a computational problem built around hashing, called the **proof-of-work** problem.

14.3.1 Fighting Email Spam with Hashing

Before discussing Bitcoin, let's talk about spam. Email suffers from a problem of asymmetry: It's easy for anyone to send you an email, whether you want to receive it or not. Several authors have proposed that we fight spam by *making users pay* to send email. Adam Back proposed the Hashcash anti-spam system in 2002 (Back, 2002). Rather than paying with money, it asks senders to pay with *computational time*. Before sending any email, the sender has to solve a little problem, which we'll describe in a moment, and include the answer in the header of their email message. The problem is designed so that the receiver can check the provided answer and confirm that the sender really did invest the time to calculate it.

As its name implies, Hashcash's problem is built around hashing.

- The sender prepares an email header containing the recipient's address, a timestamp, and a randomized counter value, then calculates:

$$h = hash(\text{address} + \text{timestamp} + \text{counter}).$$

- If the first 20 bits of h are 0, the result is accepted and the message transmits.
- If the first 20 bits aren't all 0, the sender increments the counter and tries again.
- This process repeats until the sender finds a counter value that produces a hash output with 20 leading zeros.

Observe that the recipient can check the result by simply computing the hash of the message header, which includes the sender's final counter value. If the result has 20 leading zeros, then the messsage is accepted; if not, it's rejected. This is a proof-of-work problem: Supplying the answer allows the receiver to easily verify that the sender really did expend effort to solve the problem.

Try It Yourself

Back proposed using a SHA-1 hash function, which is one-way, so the sender has no option except to try many different counters until one works. If the SHA-1 hash is 160 bits, on average how many tries would you need to find a hash with 20 leading zeros?

Solution

There are 2^{140} hashes with 20 leading zeros, so the probability of success is

$$\frac{2^{140}}{2^{160}} = \frac{1}{2^{20}}.$$

Therefore we'd expect to need $2^{20} \approx 1$ million attempts on average.

14.3.2 Proof-of-Work in the Bitcoin Blockchain

Hashcash itself didn't really catch on, but it provided a key inspiration for Bitcoin and, by extension, other blockchain-based cryptocurrency systems. The main challenge faced by blockchains is the ordering of transactions: There needs to be a mechanism to force the peers making up the network to agree on what the next accepted set of transactions should be, so that peers don't disagree on the state of the distributed database. For Bitcoin, the proof-of-work problem provides that mechanism.

In the Bitcoin system, transactions are grouped into *blocks*. The blockchain is the ordered history of all transaction blocks that have been validated and accepted by the peers making up the Bitcoin network. Peers in the Bitcoin network – called "miners" – compete to add new blocks to the chain by trying to solve a proof-of-work problem similar to Hashcash:

- Each miner gathers a block of pending transactions and prepares a header containing data for their block.
- The miner then solves a proof-of-work hash problem:

  $$hash(\text{block header} + \text{reference to previous block} + \text{counter}) < threshold.$$

  The goal is to find a counter value (also called a *nonce*) that produces a hash less than a preset threshold, which requires evaluating millions of hashes. The system adjusts the threshold over time to keep the solution time to 10 minutes per block on average.
- A miner that finds a qualifying hash broadcasts their block to the network. Other miners quickly verify it meets the proof-of-work requirement, then move on to compete over the next block. The miner of an accepted block is awarded a prize of newly created Bitcoins.

The proof-of-work problem paces the introduction of new blocks into the network. By using a reference to the old block in the hash calculation, it cryptographically ties each new block onto the history of previous blocks. This connection is what creates the "chain" and also what makes it infeasible for attackers to modify the blockchain – attempting to change a historical transaction would require resolving the entire history of proof-of-work problems after that point. One of the key results of Satoshi's paper is that such an attack is infeasible if at least 50% of the computing power in the network is controlled by legitimate participants.

Try It Yourself

The proof-of-work problem forces peers to expend resources to process transaction blocks, and hence it provides a way of achieving trustless distributed consensus, which was the entire goal of the blockchain. What are the disadvantages of relying on proof-of-work?

Solution

The main problem of proof-of-work is that it is literally, by design, *an enormous waste of time.* The hashing calculations serve no purpose other than to waste computational cycles and expend energy. As a result, the Bitcoin network is massively, stupendously wasteful – estimates are that it consumes as much electricity as the entire country of Belgium (Neumueller, 2023). Further, it's unclear that the core feature of the blockchain – trustless consensus – is really that useful for real-world problems. Despite its interesting technology, it's still unclear if the crypto ecosystem can transition away from speculation to legitimate value creation.

SUMMARY

Hashing is an important building block of complex algorithms. As you're reviewing this material, keep the following ideas in mind:

- There are many hash functions, and choosing the right one depends on the data and applications. Uniformity is an important property, which we'll discuss more in the next chapter.
- Every Java class implements a `hashCode` method, which returns a hash based on an object's data. Remember, though, that pushing the hash calculation into the object means that other parts of the application shouldn't make assumptions about its properties, beyond the basic `hashCode` contract.
- Secure applications depend on well-defined standards that have been rigorously validated. You should be *very careful* when working with passwords and encryption. As we've seen, techniques that seem safe may not be – don't rely on your intuition.

EXERCISES

Understand

1. List the desirable properties of a hash function.
2. How is the `hashCode` of a `String[]` determined?
3. Summarize some guidelines for choosing good passwords.

4. What are the requirements for the `hashCode` method in Java?
5. Implement your own version of the String `hashCode` method. Verify that the values produced by your method are the same as the one in the `String` class.
6. Implement a method that takes a `List` as input and calculates a `hashCode` for it by combining the `hashCode` results of its elements.
7. I set my password to `asdf;lkj`. Is that a good choice? Why or why not?
8. Consider again the example of a string hash function that just returns the first character. Would this function satisfy the contract for Java's `hashCode`?
9. The Java documentation specifies that "any class that overrides `Object.equals` must also override `Object.hashCode` in order to satisfy the general contract for the `Object`." What does that mean? Why do you have to write your own `hashCode` method if you create your own `equals` method?

Apply

10. Add a mangling rule to the dictionary-based cracker that toggles the case of the first character in the candidate password if it's a letter. Add a `boolean toggleCase` input to the method that controls whether this option is active.
11. Add a mangling rule that appends each of the digits 0 to 9 to the candidate password and tests each variation. Control it with a `boolean appendDigit` flag.
12. Add a mangling rule that replaces `e` with `3`. Again, add a flag.
13. Create one more mangling rule of your own choice and add it to the program.
14. Finally, if you haven't done so, modify the program so that you can test any combination of the mangling rules together by setting the input flags to the *crack* method.
15. The Diceware approach to password generation, proposed by Arnold Reinhold, creates passphrases by randomly choosing n words from a list and appending them together (Reinhold, 1995). Reinhold's original system uses physical dice to choose the word, but the system can be implemented electronically if you have a high-quality random number generator. Write your own version of the Diceware system. Your program should read in a large list of words, select k of them at random (where k is a parameter), and output the passphrase.

Extend

16. An alternative to proof-of-work is **proof-of-stake**, which serves similar goals in a less wasteful way. Do some research on proof-of-stake. What is it and how is it used by blockchain systems?
17. The next set of questions will lead you through some reasoning related to the *Birthday Paradox*, a problem in probability that has connections to secure hashing. First, consider two people. What is the probability that they have different birthdays? Assume that there are 365 possible birthdays (ignore leap years) and that each person could be born independently on any day with equal probability. Tip: The first person could be born on any of the 365 out of 365 days, but the second person has to be born on one of the other 364 days.

18. What if you have three people? Write a formula for the probability that they're all born on different days. The first person can be born on any day, the second has to be born on a different day, and the third has to be born on a different day from the first two.
19. What about n people?
20. Implement a method that can calculate your formula for a given value of n.
21. Use your method to test increasing values of n. What is the value of n for which the probability drops below 50%? That is, how many people do you need before the probability of at least two of them having the same birthday drops below 50%? Tip: The answer should be 23.
22. Suppose you have a uniform hash function that produces a 16-bit output. How many inputs might you need to test to make the probability of finding two with the same hash more than 50%? Tip: This is like the birthday paradox with 2^{16} possible choices.
23. Do some research on the Birthday Attack, which uses a large pool of candidates to find any two that have the same hash value. Explain how an attacker could use this to compromise a system.

NOTES AND FURTHER READING

Entropy is a concept from the field of information theory that can be used to quantify the strength of a password. Information theory is concerned with analyzing the "information" – that is, the useful, meaningful content – present in data. Consider a 1 GB file that contains only zero-valued bytes: It's large, but doesn't contain much information. You could compress it to only a few bytes by storing the equivalent of "0 repeated 1G times."

Entropy quantifies how many bits would be required to encode every possible outcome of a random process, which can be used to compare password-generation strategies. A choice between two random values corresponds to one bit of entropy; four random values can be encoded in two bits, and so forth. If you have a password of length n generated at random from a collection of c symbols, the entropy is

$$\log c^n = n \log c.$$

For example, a password composed of eight random lowercase letters has

$$\log 26^8 = 37.6$$

bits of entropy. Picking three random entries from a list of the 5,000 most commonly used words would have

$$\log 5,000^3 = 36.9$$

bits of entropy, so the two strategies are comparable in terms of strength, but a three-word phrase is probably easier to remember than a random sequence of eight letters.

The concept of entropy is due to Claude Shannon, who published the definition and formula in a Bell Labs technical report in 1948, almost single-handedly creating the entire field of information theory (Shannon, 1948). Shannon had already done pioneering work in the 1930s on designing Boolean logic circuits that could perform addition and other operations, which would become the foundation of post-war digital computer designs. The 1948 report focused on the problem of encoding messages in a communication system: How much data needs to be transmitted to ensure the receiver can interpret the message? Intuitively, more complex messages require more bits of data to be sent to encode their information content. Since Shannon's publication, information theory and entropy calculations have been applied to data compression, linguistics, and machine learning.

15 Hash Tables

It is not down on any map; true places never are.
Herman Melville, *Moby Dick; or, The Whale*

INTRODUCTION

So far, we've considered four data structures: arrays, lists, stacks, and queues. All four could be described as *linear*, in that they maintain their items as ordered sequences: arrays and lists are indexed by position, stacks are LIFO, and queues are FIFO. In this chapter, we'll consider the new problem of building a lookup structure, like a table, that can take an input called the *key* and return its associated *value*. For example, we might fetch a record of information about a museum artifact given its ID number as the key. None of our previous data structures are a good fit for this problem.

LEARNING OBJECTIVES

This chapter introduces the **map** – a new abstract data type that can represent a lookup table – and one of its primary implementations, the hash table. In addition to tables, maps can also be used to represent sets and other collections. At the end of this chapter, you will be able to:

- Discuss the map abstract data type, its methods, and Java's `HashMap` class.
- Describe strategies for implementing hash tables, including direct addressing, chaining, and linear probing.
- Perform an aggregate analysis of chained hashing.
- Use a hash table to represent sets and solve matching problems.

15.1 The Map Abstract Data Type

In linguistics, a *hapax legomenon* is a word that occurs only one time in a body of text. The term can apply to words in a single work or in the corpus of an entire author. One well-known example occurs in Shakespeare's *Love's Labour's Lost*, where the comic character Costard deploys the word *honorificabilitudinitatibus*. Meaning "capable of receiving honors," it's the longest word in any of Shakespeare's works.[1] It turns out that *hapaxes* are surprisingly common: In large bodies of text, around 50% of unique words are expected to occur only one time, with another 10–15% occurring only two times. This result applies across languages and historical periods, which causes problems for textual scholars, since *hapaxes* can't be easily translated.[2]

Suppose that you want to write a program to scan through a text and identify the words that are *hapax legomena*. You'll need to record the words you encounter and count the number of occurrences for each word. The best data structure for this problem would be a *lookup table* that allows us to associate a *key* – in this case, a word from the document – with a *value*, the count of occurrences for that word, and quickly look-up the value for a given key. The **map** abstract data type provides this behavior.

15.1.1 Map Methods

The map ADT corresponds to a data structure that stores a set of <key, value> pairs. Examples of maps are ubiquitous:

- A dictionary maps a word to a list of its definitions.
- Rainbow tables, which we discussed in the previous chapter, are a map specialized to look up a password given its precomputed hash.
- A course-scheduling system might map a course's ID number to a record of information about the course, like its instructor, enrollment, and meeting time.
- A search engine can be thought of as a map that takes a search query string as the key and associates it with a list of relevant results.

Maps are also called *dictionaries* (used by Python for its built-in map data structure), and *symbol tables*. JavaScript has *objects*, but they're actually implemented internally as maps. The fundamental map operations are:

- `put`, which inserts a new <key, value> pair into the map – duplicates are generally not allowed, so trying to `put` a new value for a key replaces the old value;
- `get`, which takes a key as input and returns its value, or `null` if the map has no entry for that key; and
- `remove`, which takes a key as input and removes its associated entry, if present.

Most implementations also support utility methods, like `isEmpty`, `size`, and `clear`. Another important method is `keySet`, which returns the set of all keys, and is the primary way to iterate over the contents of a map.

Java has two primary map classes: `HashMap` and `TreeMap`. This chapter focuses on `HashMap`, which is implemented using a hash table. `TreeMap` uses a binary search tree, which we'll talk about in Chapters 17 and 18. Both classes implement the `Map` interface and provide the same behaviors, but with different complexities and trade-offs, which we'll discuss once we've introduced both implementations.

1 And also the longest word in English literature that alternates consonants and vowels.

2 This can even be a problem in modern English. In *Dracula*, the vampire's servant Renfield is described as "mixed up with the Count in an indexy sort of way." No one knows what Bram Stoker meant by "indexy" (Smyth, 2018).

15.1.2 Java's HashMap

The program below demonstrates how to use `HashMap` in a word-counting program. It declares a variable called `counts` that maps from a `String` key to an `Integer` value. The declaration uses angle brackets to specify types; the first type is for the key and the second for the value. The following line declares `counts`:

```
HashMap<String, Integer> counts = new HashMap<String, Integer>();
```

```
/**
 * Word counting with HashMap
 */

import java.util.HashMap;
import java.util.Scanner;
import java.io.*;

public class WordCount {
  public static void main(String[] args) {
    // Declare the count data structure
    HashMap<String, Integer> counts = new HashMap<String,  Integer>();

    // Open a text file
    Scanner s = null;
    try {
      s = new Scanner(new File("moby_dick.txt"));
    } catch (FileNotFoundException e) {
      e.printStackTrace();
    }

    // Loop through all whitespace-delimited words in the file
    while (s.hasNext()) {
      String word = s.next();

      // TODO: clean up the word before putting it in the map

      // Make an entry for the word if it's not in the map
      if (!counts.containsKey(word)) {
        counts.put(word, 0);
      }

```

```
33         // Increment the count
34         int newCount = counts.get(word) + 1;
35         counts.put(word, newCount);
36       }
37
38       // Print the final counts
39       //
40       // keySet returns an iterable set of all keys in the map
41       for (String word : counts.keySet()) {
42         System.out.println(word + "\t" + counts.get(word));
43       }
44     }
45 }
```

This program illustrates some common patterns for `HashMap`. Lines 29–31 add an entry for new words.[3] The next statements get the current count, increment it, and put the updated count back into the map. Lines 41–43 use `keySet` to iterate through the keys and print the stored count for each word.

Try It Yourself

Make a small text file and try running the program on it. Is there any ordering on the output?

Solution

If you run the program, you'll probably see that the output keys have no apparent order. This is a basic property of `HashMap`: It makes *no guarantee* on the ordering of the keys it contains. Some maps have different behaviors – Python dictionaries generally return keys in the order they were inserted – but it's wise to avoid assumptions when retrieving keys from a map.

Line 26 is a placeholder for two improvements. First, string keys are case-sensitive; you can push a string to lowercase using the `toLowerCase` method:

```
word = word.toLowerCase();
```

Second, if you're processing raw text, the `word` string might contain punctuation that should be removed. The `replaceAll` method can be used to remove or replace characters. Here's an example that removes punctuation marks from the word:

```
word.replaceAll("[,;!?.]", "");
```

3 This check can be removed. See the end-of-chapter exercises.

The first input is a **regular expression** that lists a set of characters in square brackets. The second input is the replacement string, which in this case is the empty string. Any character in `word` that matches any element of that set – that is, any character that's one of the five punctuation symbols – triggers the replacement action. A full discussion of regular expressions is beyond the scope of this chapter, but becoming familiar with them can help you solve text processing and matching problems.[4]

15.2 Implementing Hash Tables

A hash table is built on top of a 1D backing array, similar to an `ArrayList`. It gets its name because it uses a hash function to transform the input key into an array index, then stores the <key, value> pair at that position in the backing array. This section works through the details of this process, starting with the simplest implementation, then building up to a table that can handle nonnumeric keys and deal with collisions. The last part of the section shows off a few fun and theoretically interesting variants.

15.2.1 Direct Addressing

Let's start by assuming the key value is either a number or another type, like a `char`, that can be interpreted as a number – we'll relax this requirement in a moment. Allocate a backing array of m elements to store the items in the table. By tradition, each array position in a hash table is called a **bucket**. The simplest hash table takes a <key, value> pair and uses the numeric key as the bucket index:

```
this.buckets[key] = value;
```

Lookups use the same process: Given a key, return the value stored at its associated bucket, or `null` if the bucket is empty. Both insertions and lookups are $O(1)$ accesses to the bucket array. This technique is called **direct addressing** because the key itself determines the bucket index.

Try It Yourself

What if the maximum key is larger than the number of buckets?

Solution

Use the modulus operator to transform the key to a bucket index in the range 0 to $m - 1$:

```
int index = key % m;
this.buckets[index] = value;
```

4 A famous programming joke: You have a problem. You decide to solve it using regular expressions. Now you have two problems.

For example, suppose $m = 7$ and we wish to insert the pairs <1, v_1>, <3, v_3>, and <9, v_9>, where v_i denotes some arbitrary value mapped to key i. The state of the table after performing those insertions would be as follows:

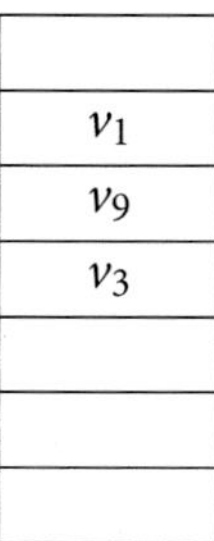

Try It Yourself

Add the pairs <13, v_{13}> and <70, v_{70}> to the table.

Solution

Key 13 is mapped to bucket 6 and key 70 is mapped to bucket 0.

v_{70}
v_1
v_9
v_3
v_{13}

You probably have a question at this point: What happens if two keys land in the same bucket? We'll deal with that problem in the next section. Before doing so, though, let's put the "hash" into our hash table and consider the problem of nonnumeric keys. Given a pair <k, v> to insert into a hash table and a hash function h, first calculate $h(k)$, which can then be interpreted as a number.[5] Map the key to one of the m hash buckets using

```
int index = h(k) % m;
```

and store the value at that location.

```
this.buckets[index] = v;
```

5 In Java, this will be a 32-bit `int`, but the same principle applies if the hash value is a different size.

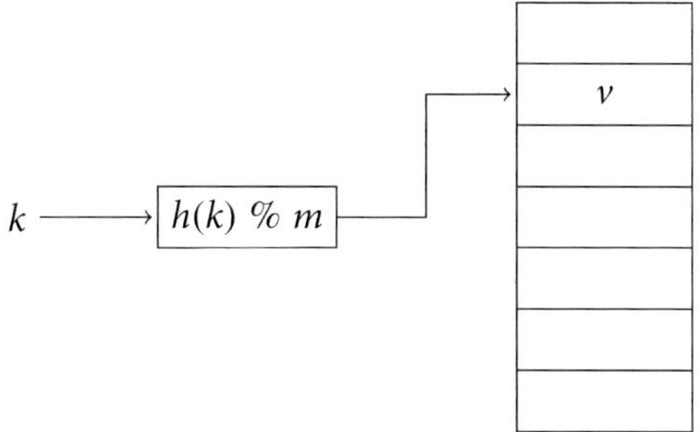

Try It Yourself

Describe the process for performing a lookup in a direct-addressed table with a hash function. Given a lookup key k, how do you find the bucket containing k's value, or verify that it doesn't exist in the table?

Solution

Use the same process as insertion. Calculate the bucket as

```
int index = h(k) % m;
```

and return the value at that location, or `null` if the bucket is empty.

A table that uses hashing and direct addressing can perform $O(1)$ insertions and lookups. We have to pay the overhead for the `hashCode` method, but that doesn't depend on the number of items in the table.

15.2.2 Chained Hashing

Basic direct addressing only works if the entries in each bucket are unique. A practical hash table must have a way of resolving **collisions**, where two keys map to the same bucket. We'll start by considering one of the most popular techniques, **chaining**, then describe some alternatives. In a chained hash table, each bucket holds a *linked list* of <key, value> pairs, rather than only a single pair. Here's an example showing a table with integer keys and their associated values. Keys that hash to the same bucket, like 2 and 9, are now stored as nodes in that bucket's list.

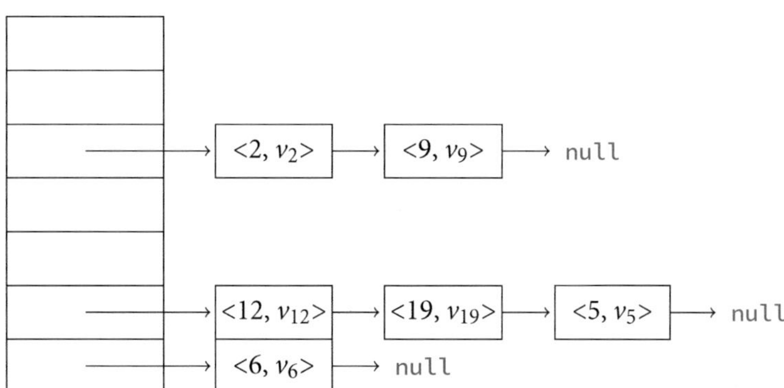

Inserting a new pair <*k*, *v*> requires identifying the appropriate bucket, then adding a new node containing <*k*, *v*> into the bucket's list.

- Calculate the target bucket using the same rule as direct addressing: $b = h(k) \% m$.
- Create a new node and set its fields to *k* and *v*.
- Insert a new entry for the pair into bucket *b*'s list.

The direct address table didn't need to store the keys, but the chained table does, because the lookup operation must iterate through the list to search for the matching key. The lookup fails if it reaches the end of the list without finding the key.

The program below shows a `ChainedHashTable` class with `put` and `get` methods. It uses several of the techniques in our previous data structure implementations, including an inner class to represent each entry in the chained linked lists. Notice the use of two generic types, `K` and `V`, to represent the types of the keys and values.

```
/**
 * Example chained hash table implementation
 */

import java.util.LinkedList;

public class ChainedHashTable<K, V> {

  // The table is an array of linked lists
  LinkedList<HashNode>[] table;

  /**
   *  Constructor - creates a LinkedList[] for the buckets
   */
  @SuppressWarnings("unchecked")
  public ChainedHashTable() {
    this.table = new LinkedList[7];
    for (int i = 0; i < this.table.length; i++) {
      this.table[i] = new LinkedList<HashNode>();
    }
  }

  /**
   * Insert a new <key, value> pair
   *
   * @param  newKey  the new key of generic type K
```

```
   * @param  newValue  the new value of generic type V
   */
  public void put(K newKey, V newValue) {
    // Calculate the bucket
    int bucket = newKey.hashCode() % this.table.length;

    // Inserting at the head of the list is easy, but is it correct?
    HashNode newNode = new HashNode(newKey, newValue);
    this.table[bucket].addFirst(newNode);
  }

  /**
   * Get the value associated with a particular key
   *
   * @param  lookupKey  the search key
   * @return  The associated value if it exists, or null
   */
  public V get(K lookupKey) {
    int bucket = lookupKey.hashCode() % this.table.length;

    // Look for a matching key in the bucket's chain
    for (HashNode node : this.table[bucket]) {
      if (node.key.equals(lookupKey)) {
        return node.value;
      }
    }

    return null;  // Failure
  }

  /**
   * Private class representing a single <key, value> pair
   */
  private class HashNode {
    K key;
    V value;

    public HashNode(K newKey, V newValue) {
```

```
            this.key = newKey;
            this.value = newValue;
        }
    }
}
```

Try It Yourself

The example `put` given above inserts the new pair at the front of its list, so it's possible to insert the same key more than once with different values – although only the first match would be returned on a lookup. Rewrite the `put` method to iterate through the list and check for a matching key that's already present. If you find one, update its associated value. If you reach the end of the list without finding a matching key, insert a new entry there.

15.2.3 Analyzing Chaining

The complexity of the lookup operation depends on the distribution of items across the hash table's buckets. In the best case, each bucket has no more than one item, and a lookup requires checking at most one node to determine if it matches the search key or not. This case is functionally equivalent to an $O(1)$ lookup in a direct addressed table. The worst case occurs when all entries are hashed to the same bucket, which makes lookups equal to searching a linked list in $O(n)$ time. Therefore, it's important to have a uniform hash function that evenly distributes keys throughout the table and avoids clustering similar inputs together in the same bucket.

Consider a hash table with m buckets and n items. The **load factor** α is the expected number of items per bucket:

$$\alpha = \frac{n}{m}.$$

Now consider the time required to search a list of average length α for a particular key. If you get lucky, the key of interest may be the first item, in which case the search terminates immediately. If you are less lucky, you may need to check all α items before determining that the key isn't present in the bucket. Therefore, an unsuccessful lookup is $O(\alpha)$.

Try It Yourself

Make an intuitive argument that the average time required for a successful lookup is approximately $\alpha/2$.

Solution

On average, if all orderings of keys are equally likely, you'd expect to find the key halfway through its bucket's list, after checking $\alpha/2$ entries.

Let's make that argument more rigorous, using a technique called **aggregate analysis**. Rather than reasoning about one lookup in isolation, let's consider the total work required to perform a series of lookups and then take their average. Suppose that we insert n items into a hash table, with a uniform hash function that distributes them equally, and that new items are added to the end of their bucket's linked list. What is the total time required to then lookup all n items?

Try It Yourself

The first item was inserted into the initially empty table, so it must be at the head of its bucket's list. Now consider item i. What position would you expect it to have in its bucket's list?

Solution

At the time item i is inserted, there must be $i-1$ items already in the table, so the expected number of items *before* item i is

$$\frac{i-1}{m}.$$

The time required to look-up item i is therefore the time required to iterate through, on average, $\frac{i-1}{m}$ items in the linked list, plus one more operation to access item i itself. The expected total lookup work across all items is:

$$T = n + \sum_{i=1}^{n} \frac{i-1}{m}.$$

The leading n represents the time spent accessing the n items once you find them, and the summation is the total number of operations spent searching the linked lists. The summation is equivalent to summing from 1 to $n-1$, which yields

$$T = n + \frac{n(n-1)}{2m}.$$

That's the total work for all n items. Divide by n to find the average:

$$T_{avg} = 1 + \frac{n-1}{2m}.$$

This equation states that a random item is in a bucket that contains, on average, $(n-1)/m$ other items. An expected lookup requires iterating through half the bucket, then doing one operation to process the item itself, which supports our earlier intuition that the expected work for a successful lookup is approximately $\alpha/2$.

A standard strategy is to track the load factor as the table fills; when it becomes too high, **rebalance** the table by allocating a new, larger backing array and then rehashing all items into new buckets. By default, `HashMap` increases the number of buckets when $\alpha > 0.75$, which is more conservative than the theoretical limit, but reduces the probability of any bucket having more than one item. As with `ArrayList`, it's possible to show that the overhead of rebalancing doesn't affect the amortized $O(1)$ expected lookup time.

15.2.4 Open Addressing with Probing

Open addressed tables are an alternative to chained hash tables that can often be faster. This type of table stores all of its entries directly in the 1D backing array, without using linked lists or other supplementary data structures. As long as no collisions occur, these tables behave exactly like the original direct addressed table. When a collision does happen, the table uses a **probing strategy** to search the array for an alternative empty location where the colliding entry can be stored. The simplest probing strategy is **linear probing**: On a collision, simply scan forward in the array one position at a time, looking for the next open spot. For example, suppose we have this table:

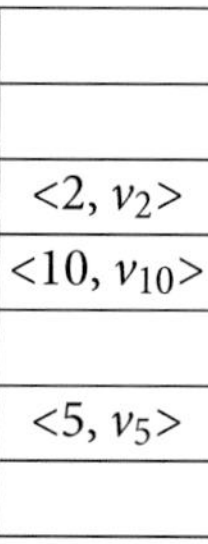

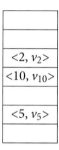

Inserting <9, v_9> would cause a collision with <2, v_2>, so the algorithm instead inserts it at the next empty position:

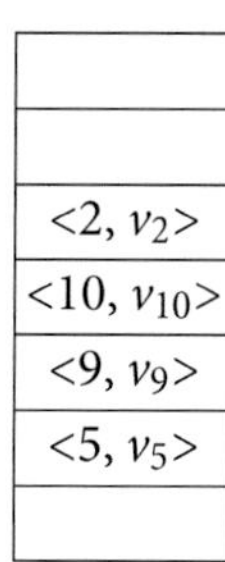

Inserting <3, v_3> would cause another collision, and the linear probing method would scan forward to find the next open position at bucket 6. On a lookup, the key is first hashed to give the starting bucket for the search and the method performs a linear scan until it either finds a matching key or fails by finding an empty location or circling the entire table.

Like chaining, the performance of linear probing depends on the load factor. On average, probes in a lightly loaded table should require checking only one bucket. As the load factor increases, entries tend to cluster into groups, which can then overlap with each other to create large blocks of consecutive elements. Like with chaining, the standard strategy is to resize and rehash the table when the load factor exceeds a set threshold.

Try It Yourself

In practice, linear probing is usually faster than chaining, even if they require the same number of comparisons on average. Can you suggest why?

Solution

Linear probing stores all elements in a single 1D array. We'd therefore expect it to have better memory performance than chaining. The first access of a lookup may cause a cache miss, but the subsequent array accesses will likely be cache hits, which is faster than performing the same number of random memory accesses to nodes in a linked list.

Variations on linear probing focus on spreading the probing sequence out over the table to avoid clustering items together. In *quadratic probing*, the step size increases quadratically. The probe for the ith step is given by

$$p(x, i) = (h(x) + i^2) \mod m,$$

where $i = 0$ is the starting location. The probe sequence starts close to the home bucket, then takes progressively larger steps to find an open location. For example, suppose we want to insert $<16, v_{16}>$ into this table using quadratic probing:

$<2, v_2>$
$<10, v_{10}>$
$<9, v_9>$
$<5, v_5>$

The first iteration sets $i = 0$ to check the home bucket for key 16, which is position 2. That spot is occupied, so the next iteration sets $i = 1$ and checks bucket 3, which is also occupied. The third iteration sets $i = 2$ and checks bucket 6 to find an open space:

$<2, v_2>$
$<10, v_{10}>$
$<9, v_9>$
$<5, v_5>$
$<16, v_{16}>$

The *double hashing* approach functions like linear probing, but with a step size chosen by a second hash function. Suppose that h_1 is the primary hash function and let h_2 be a second hash function. The position of the ith probe for input key x is given by

$$p(x, i) = (h_1(x) + i\,h_2(x)) \mod m.$$

Intuitively, two keys can hash to the same starting bucket, but have different probe sequences. If $h_2(x)$ is uniform, then every probe sequence will be a permutation of the table's buckets, and keys will be uniformly distributed throughout the table. Double hashing allows the load factor to be higher than would be desirable for linear probing, but at the cost of calculating the second hash function.

15.2.5 Cuckoo Hashing

Cuckoo hashing is a clever approach to hash table construction that combines multiple tables and multiple hash functions. The technique gets its name from the common cuckoo bird, *Cuculus canorus*, which practices *brood parasitism*. Cuckoos do not raise their own young. Instead, the female lays each of her eggs in the nest of another bird. Cuckoo eggs hatch quickly, and the newborn cuckoo chick instinctively pushes its rival chicks out of their nest, leaving it to exploit the undivided attention and food provided by its host parents.

Cuckoo hashing uses two equal-sized tables, which we'll denote T_A and T_B, and two hash functions h_A and h_B to index buckets in T_A and T_B respectively. Keys may be stored in either table. To perform a lookup for a key x, calculate $h_A(x)$ and $h_B(x)$, modulo the table size, then check to see if x is stored at either position.

To insert x, first check $h_A(x)$. If that position is open, store x there and stop. If $h_A(x)$ is already filled, the table invokes the cuckoo metaphor and *kicks out the current occupant* to make room for x. The old occupant – let's call it y – is moved to its alternative location in T_B, and the process repeats: If position $h_B(y)$ is occupied, *that* key is kicked out and moved to its alternative location in T_A, and so forth. In the illustration below, inserting x kicks out y, which then kicks out z, which finds an open spot in T_A.

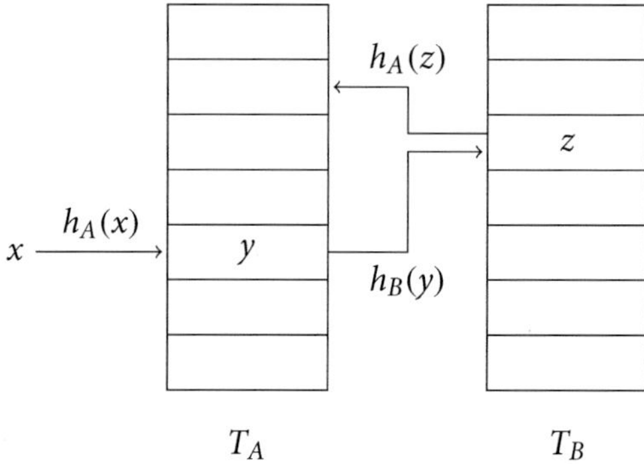

An insertion may cause a chain of kick-outs, moving keys between the tables, until one of the following occurs:

- A kicked-out key lands in an empty location, which means that every item now has an appropriate place and the process terminates. In the figure above, z will move to an empty spot, which allows y and x to move to their locations.
- The process reaches a preset maximum number of iterations, indicating that there might be an unresolvable cycle. In this case, the tables are enlarged and the keys are rehashed before trying the insertion again. It might be necessary to rehash more than once for the insertion to succeed.

Theoretically, cuckoo hashing's main benefit is a *worst case* $O(1)$ lookup time: Key x must be at either $h_A(x)$ or $h_B(x)$, so the lookup operation never needs to check more than two positions. This is better than chained hashing or probing, which were both $O(1)$ *on average*, but might need to check more than two positions in the worst case. The main challenge, of course, is analyzing the cuckoo insertion algorithm. It turns out that if the load factor is less than 0.50, cuckoo insertions are still amortized $O(1)$ (Pagh and Rodler, 2004).

15.3 Example Interview Questions Using Hash Tables

15.3.1 Representing a Set

Design a data structure that can represent an unordered set of items. Your structure should allow an application to insert items into the set and check if an item is in the set, both in expected $O(1)$ time.

Representing sets is an important component of many algorithms. This could be done by putting items into a list, but then checking if an item is in the set would be $O(n)$. In general, the request to do something in $O(1)$ time is a strong indication that a hash table should be involved. In this case, let the keys in the table be the items in the set, and either remove the need to store a value, or insert a dummy value with each key. Here's a small class that wraps around a `HashMap`:

```
/**
 * Hash-based set
 */

import java.util.HashMap;

public class HashBasedSet<K> {
  private HashMap<K, Object> set;

  public HashBasedSet() {
    this.set = new HashMap<K, Object>();
  }

  // Insert a new key with a dummy value
  public void add(K item) {
    this.set.put(item, null);
  }

  // Check if the set contains an item
  public boolean contains(K item) {
    return this.set.containsKey(item);
  }
}
```

Note that `HashMap` disallows duplicate keys, which is correct for sets. Java has a built-in `HashSet` class that provides exactly this functionality, which you should use any time you need to represent an unordered collection.

15.3.2 Find the Pairs with a Given Sum

Given an integer array and a target value, find the pairs of items in the array that add to the target. Your solution must be $O(n)$.

The easy solution is to check all pairs of items, but that would be $O(n^2)$. The requirement for a linear time solution is an indication that a hash table is involved. If you make a single pass over the input data, you can use a hash table (or set) with $O(1)$ lookups for bookkeeping and still have a solution that's $O(n)$ overall. In this case, iterate through the array and use a `HashSet` to keep track of the items you've seen. When you examine item `i`, check if the set contains `target - a[i]`. If so, you've found a pair that adds to the target.

```
HashSet<Integer> set = new HashSet<Integer>();

for (int i = 0; i < a.length; i++) {
  // Check if a[i] pairs with an element we've already seen
  if (set.contains(target - a[i])) {
    System.out.printf("%d   %d\n", a[i], target - a[i]);
  }

  // Insert into the set -- HashSet uses add instead of put
  set.add(a[i]);
}
```

15.3.3 Finding Anagrams

Write a method that takes a `String[]` as input and returns all of the anagrams in contains. For example, if the input is `["art", "rat", "taco", "cato", "tar"]` the output should be

```
["art", "rat", "tar"]
["taco", "cato"]
```

Once again, the straightforward solution is to compare all pairs of strings and check if they're anagrams, which can be done by sorting their letters and seeing if the results are equal. Like the last question, one pass through the array is sufficient if you use a hash table for bookkeeping. In this case, we're going to create a `HashMap<String, ArrayList<String>>`, where the key will be the sorted letters of a word and the value will be the list of all strings having those letters. This is a common configuration, since you often need to map one key to a list of related values. The code excerpt below gives the core of the solution.

```
HashMap<String, ArrayList<String>> anagrams =
                            new HashMap<String, ArrayList<String>>();

for (String s : words) {
```

```
  // Sort the letters of s
  char[] letters = s.toCharArray();
  Arrays.sort(letters);
  String key = new String(letters);

  // Case for new entries
  if (!anagrams.containsKey(key)) {
    anagrams.put(key, new ArrayList<String>());
  }

  // Add the word to its anagram list
  ArrayList<String> values = anagrams.get(key);
  values.add(s);
  anagrams.put(key, values);
}
```

You can then step through the keys of `anagrams` and print each list.

SUMMARY

Each new data structure gives us a new tool for representing information in programs. Now that we have hash tables, we finally have the ability to create lookup tables and efficiently manage sets of items. As you're reviewing this material, keep the following ideas in mind:

- The superpower of the hash table is its ability to perform expected $O(1)$ lookups. This property allows us to convert algorithms that would have been $O(n^2)$ with a list representation into $O(n)$, simply by avoiding the need to search the list on every iteration. We'll see further examples where changing the internal data structure of an algorithm makes a difference to its performance.
- The value in a `HashMap` can be another data structure, like a list or even another map. Sometimes you need to map a single key to an entire collection of values.
- Hash tables are not the only map implementation – we'll see binary search trees in a couple of chapters. Hash tables themselves allow for a variety of different implementations. Knowing the internal implementation of a data structure can help you understand its behaviors; for example, the fact that keys in a hash table are not normally ordered.

The next chapter will allow you to practice these ideas by building a textual search engine for the plays of William Shakespeare.

EXERCISES

Understand

1. List the methods of the map abstract data type.
2. Give three additional examples of data that could be well-represented by a map.
3. Suppose you need to create a data structure that represents a word in a dictionary with its list of definitions. How could you declare that in Java?
4. Consider a direct addressed table with $m = 11$. Show the state of the table after inserting keys 22, 37, 108, 111, and 8.
5. List the methods for `HashSet`.
6. Explain why hash tables don't maintain an ordering on their keys.
7. I wrote the following fragment in the word-counting program, but it outputs a value of 0 for every count. What's the problem and how can I fix it? Tip: Think about the semantics of the ++ operator.

```
int oldCount = counts.get(word);
counts.put(word, oldCount++);
```

8. Rewrite the word-counting program to use the `getOrDefault` method, which removes the need to initialize an empty entry for every new key.
9. Write a program that takes an `int[] a` and an `int value` as input and returns all pairs of elements that multiply to `value`. Start by writing the $O(n^2)$ solution that compares every element to every other element.
10. Now solve the previous problem in $O(n)$ using a `HashSet`.
11. Modify the example hash table to keep track of the number of pairs it contains and add a `size` method.
12. Add a `containsKey` method to the example hash table.
13. Add a `remove` method to the example hash table that takes a key as input and removes its associated pair, if it exists.

Apply

14. Add a `keySet` method to the example hash table that returns a `HashSet` containing all of the keys in the table.
15. Write a method called `removeDuplicates` that takes a `String` as input and uses a `HashSet` to remove any duplicate letters it contains.
16. Recall the concept of frequency analysis in classical code breaking from Chapter 1. Modify the word-counting program to count letters instead.
17. Run your letter-counting program on a large text file and report the distribution of letters you obtain.
18. Give an algorithm that uses a hash table to check if a linked list contains a cycle.
19. Write a method called `union` that takes two `int[]` as input and returns an `int[]` containing one entry for each unique value found in either array.

20. Write a method called `intersection` that also takes two `int[]` as input but returns only the unique items found in *both* arrays. Tip: First find the set of unique items in each array.

21. Repeat the `union` question, but let the inputs be `List<T>`, where `T` is the generic type of data in the list.

22. Write a method that takes two `String` as input and return `true` if they contain the same distribution of letters. Don't do any sorting.

23. Write a code fragment that takes an `int[]` and constructs a map from each value in the array to all of the positions where that value occurs.

24. Repeat the previous problem, but for an `int[][]`.

25. Write a method to find the first element in an `int[]` that occurs only one time. Tip: Make two passes over the array.

Extend

26. Do some research on hash table sizing. Why is it often considered a bad idea to make the table size a power of 2? What should you do instead?

27. What's the difference between Java's `HashMap` and `LinkedHashMap`? How is `LinkedHashMap` implemented internally?

28. What about `ConcurrentHashMap`? When would you prefer a `ConcurrentHashMap` to the non-concurrent version?

29. It's certainly possible to make a `HashMap` that contains `HashMap` values, but can such a `HashMap` contain *itself* as a value? Tip: Check the official documentation for the `Map` interface.

30. Suppose you insert n items into a hash table with m buckets using a uniform hash function. What's the probability all of the items land in the same bucket? Assume the table doesn't rebalance itself. Tip: The items are inserted independently.

31. Modify the example hash table to track the load factor, then automatically resize the table and rehash every item when it exceeds 0.75.

32. Modify the example hash table to use the linear probing strategy instead of chaining.

33. Implement a variation of the open addressing table that uses the Fibonacci sequence to choose the distance between steps. After first checking the home bucket $h(x)$, the sequence should advance in step sizes of 1, 1, 2, 3, 5, etc., wrapping around the table if necessary.

34. The remaining questions will lead you through building a `Spellchecker` class. First, write a class called `Spellchecker` that contains a `HashSet<String> words`. Write a constructor for the class that takes a dictionary file containing a list of words as input, opens it, and inserts all the words it contains into the set.

35. Add a method called `check` that takes a `String` and returns `true` if it's in the set of words and `false` if it isn't.

36. Now write a method called `spellcheck` that takes a filename as input, opens it, then uses `Scanner` to break it into whitespace-delimited words. Call `check` on each word and print the ones that return `false`.

37. If a word is misspelled, add a method that will make suggestions. Here's a code fragment that generates all possible words that could be created by substituting one letter with another:

```
// Find all valid words that can be created by substitution
String letters = "abcdefghijklmnopqrstuvwxyz";

for (int i = 0; i < word.length(); i++) {
  for (int j = 0; j < letters.length(); j++) {
    // Construct a candidate word
    //
    // The first substring gets the letters 0 to i - 1
    // The letter at position i is replaced
    // The second substring gets the remaining letters
    String candidate = word.substring(0, i) + letters.charAt(j)
                     + word.substring(i+1, word.length());

    // Output valid candidate words
    if (check(candidate)) {
      System.out.println(candidate);
    }
  }
}
```

38. Modify the example above to identify all candidate words that could be created by removing a letter from a misspelled word, or by inserting a letter.

NOTES AND FURTHER READING

As noted at the beginning of the chapter, *hapax legomena* are surprisingly common. A basic fact of word distributions is that natural languages contain a few high-frequency words that are used all the time – *the*, *you*, *and*, and so forth – and many more low-frequency words that are used only occasionally, like *floccinaucinihilipilification*.[6] The distribution of natural language words is described by a result known as **Zipf's Law**, after the linguist George Zipf who stated it in the 1930s. Zipf's result, which he based on empirical observation, says that the second most common word in a corpus occurs with about half the frequency of the most common, the third most common with about one-third the frequency of the most common, and so forth. In general, the kth most frequent word should occur with probability $1/k$ that of the most frequent. The exact reason why the Zipf distribution exists is still unclear; linguists and others have repeatedly proposed explanations for why it might emerge spontaneously as a property of language (Piantadosi, 2014).

6 The act of regarding something as having no value.

16 Project: Ye Olde Shakespearean Search Engine

Once more, search with me.
The Merry Wives of Windsor

INTRODUCTION

The previous two chapters introduced hash functions and hash tables. In this chapter, we'll combine hash tables with lists to construct a *search engine index*. Our index will map a search word to the list of locations where that word occurs in a set of text documents. The data for our example search engine will come from the plays of William Shakespeare, the most influential English-language dramatist in history. We'll work primarily with the text of *Macbeth*.[1] The play provides a good development example because the text is rich enough to be interesting, but the structured script format makes it easy to extract everything we need with a reasonable amount of code.

LEARNING OBJECTIVES

After completing this project chapter, you will be able to:

- Describe the architecture of a text-based search engine.
- Implement an inverted index using Java's built-in `HashMap` and `ArrayList`.
- Design a custom object that stores information about each search engine record, and automatically extract information for each record by reading the input text file.
- Use the index structure to insert new entries and look-up the results of search queries.

16.1 Building a Search Index

Building search systems for historical texts has been an active area of investigation since the early days of information retrieval. For Shakespeare's works, the Open Source Shakespeare (OSS) project is a full-featured search engine that allows filtering queries by work, character, and genre (Johnson, 2005). OSS uses a database of information parsed from the plays and takes advantage of the fact that Shakespeare's corpus is small enough to manually tag search information, like

1 Or "The Scottish Play" if you're reading this book out loud in a theater.

the character speaking each line, to aid the parsing process. The ultimate goal of our project is to build an index containing search terms for a collection of documents – in this case, *Macbeth* or other plays. Just like a regular book index, which maps the book's important words to their locations in the text, our search engine's index is a data structure that maps words and phrases to locations in the documents where they appear.

Consider three example documents containing the names of sharks. These documents form the *corpus*, the body of documents that will be the raw material for our search index.

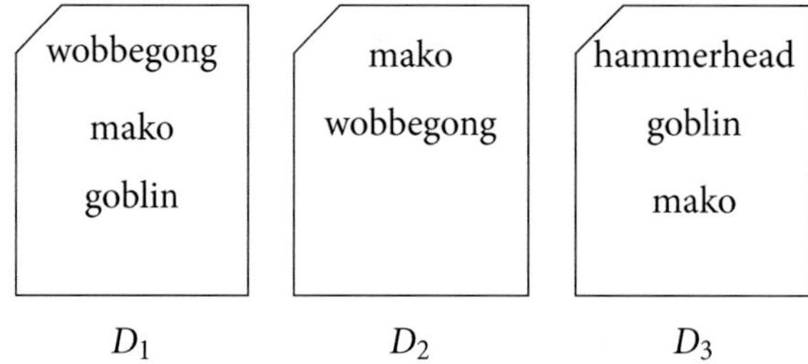

Typically, each document is assigned a unique identifier and the system maintains a database of meta-information (name, last retrieval time, size, etc.) associated with each document.

Once the documents have been collected, the basic indexing procedure has three steps (Brin and Page, 1998):

1. For each document, extract a list of individual words and multi-word phrases that are likely to be search terms. The simplest approach is to extract all individual words, then all pairs of consecutive words (*2-grams*), then all triples of consecutive words (*3-grams*), and so forth. In practice, we should filter common words and phrases that are unlikely to be good search terms.
2. Given the list of search terms for each page, construct the *forward index*, a data structure that stores mappings from each document ID to its search terms.
3. Finally, construct the *inverted index*, which maps every search term to its list of associated documents. This index is the one used for search lookups: Given an input word or phrase, the inverted index returns the list of pages that contain it.

The output of this process is a table where each entry maps from a keyword to a list of documents where that word occurs. In this example, the keywords are shark names and the data structure is a hash table where each value is a list.

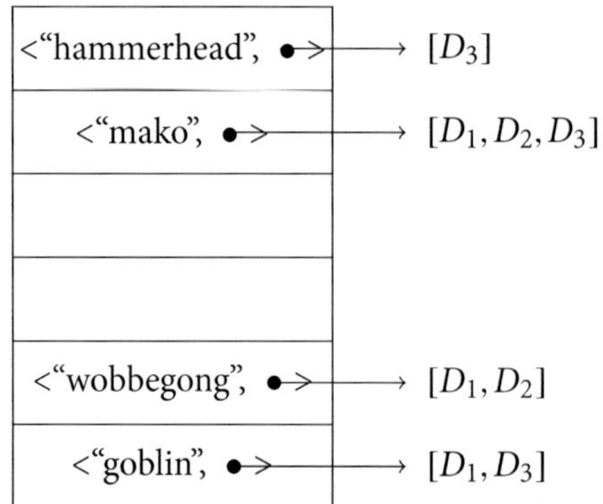

Recall that the mapping of keys to hash buckets depends on the choice of hash function, the size of the table, and the collision-handling strategy. Here, the example lists record the document identifiers, but each list entry could be expanded to store more information about the location where each word occurs. The relevant Java object for this search index is a

```
HashMap<String, ArrayList<DocumentIdentifier>>
```

where `DocumentIdentifier` is a class that stores information about each document.

Try It Yourself

Suppose we add a new document D_4 to the set, containing entries for *goblin*, *hammerhead*, and a new keyword, *megalodon*. Modify the example index to show how it could incorporate the new entries.

Solution

Here's an updated index with D_4 added to the relevant lists and new table entry created for *megalodon*.

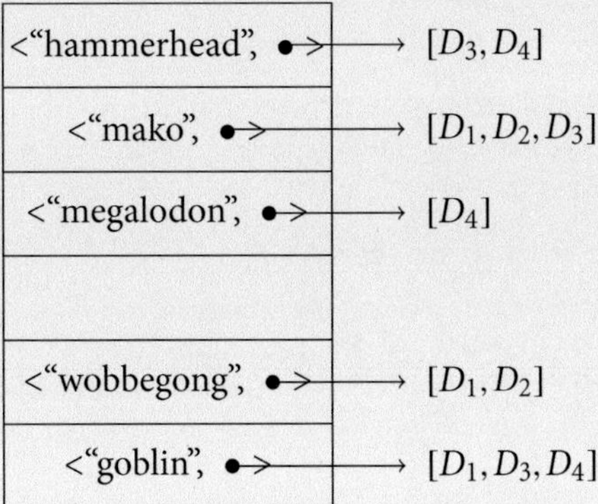

16.2 Implementation

Let's implement a program that can extract and index words and phrases from *Macbeth*. Given a search word, our engine will report each location where the word occurs, including the play, act, and scene. As we discussed in the previous section, the main data structure for our system will be a `HashMap` of lists. The map's keys will be the search words, represented as `String` objects. Each key will map to an `ArrayList` of custom `Location` objects. The complete program will have three classes:

- `Location`, representing a single occurrence of a word or phrase and storing information about the location in the script where it occurs.
- `Index`, representing the search index data structure. This class will have methods to read an input script file (discussed in more detail below), then extract its contents and add

them to the index, as well as a lookup method that returns the list of `Location` objects associated with a given search term.

- Finally, `Driver`, which will function as the `main` method for the entire program. It will initialize the `Index`, call its methods to process the set of required input files, and then run an input loop to prompt the user to enter search terms and view the results.

16.2.1 Getting the Text

Texts of all of Shakespeare's works are available in royalty-free plain text form from Project Gutenberg. Here is an excerpt from the start of *Macbeth* (Project Gutenberg, 1998). If you want to work with a short example while you're developing, copy it into a file named `macbeth.txt`. If you choose to work with the complete document, edit the text file to remove any starting or ending material that isn't part of the play's script.

```
ACT I

SCENE I. An open Place.

Thunder and Lightning. Enter three Witches.

FIRST WITCH.
When shall we three meet again?
In thunder, lightning, or in rain?

SECOND WITCH.
When the hurlyburly's done,
When the battle's lost and won.

THIRD WITCH.
That will be ere the set of sun.

FIRST WITCH.
Where the place?

SECOND WITCH.
Upon the heath.

THIRD WITCH.
There to meet with Macbeth.
```

Observe that the file has a clear structure, with easily identifiable act, scene, and speaking character transitions.

Try It Yourself

Copy the excerpt into a text file and add it to your programming environment. Write a short program that uses `Scanner` to open the file and print it.

Solution

When you're working with files, it's often a good idea to simply open and interact with the file's contents before writing any additional code. We've already seen examples of using `Scanner` to read typed user input, but it can also read from files. The code example below constructs a new `Scanner` to read from `macbeth.txt`, then uses a `while` loop to iterate through its lines.

```
/**
 * Open and iterate through a file
 */

import java.util.Scanner;
import java.io.File;
import java.io.FileNotFoundException;

public class FileReaderExample {
  public static void main(String[] args) {
    Scanner fileReader = null;

    try {
      fileReader = new Scanner(new File("macbeth.txt"));
    } catch(FileNotFoundException e) {
      e.printStackTrace();
    }

    while (fileReader.hasNext()) {
      String line = fileReader.nextLine();
      System.out.println(line);
    }
  }
}
```

Constructing the new `Scanner` might throw a `FileNotFoundException`, so it's wrapped in a `try-catch` block. The `hasNext` method returns `true` as long as the `Scanner` has unread input.

16.2.2 The `Location` Class

`Location` is a straightforward class that wraps up a set of variables relating to one occurrence of one single word from the play.

```
/**
 * Class representing the occurrence of a single phrase
 * in a single text location
 */
```

```
public class Location {

  private String phrase, act, scene, play, line;

  /**
   * Constructor -- initialize instance variables
   */
  public Location(String phrase, String act, String scene,
                  String line, String play) {
    this.phrase = phrase;
    this.act = act;
    this.scene = scene;
    this.line = line;
    this.play = play;
  }

  /**
   * toString -- return fields as a String
   */
  public String toString() {
    String output = String.format("%s  %s  %s\n%s\n", this.play,
                                  this.act, this.scene, this.line);
    return output;
  }
}
```

The `toString` method uses `String.format` to produce formatted output. Recall that formatted printing replaces each `%s` specifier with one of the given variables. Printing a `Location` produces output like the following:

```
Macbeth  I  I
In thunder, lightning, or in rain?
```

16.2.3 The `Driver` Class

Before tackling the `Index` class, which is the heart of the program, let's look at the `Driver` class and the `main` method.

```
/**
 * Driver for the Shakespearean search engine
 */

```

```
import java.util.Scanner;

public class Driver {

  public static void main(String[] args) {

    // Create a new SearchEngine object
    Index searchIndex = new Index();

    // Add plays to the index structure - call addPlay for each script
    searchIndex.addPlay("macbeth.txt", "Macbeth");

    // Run an input loop to prompt for search terms
    Scanner input = new Scanner(System.in);

    while (true) {
      System.out.println("Enter a search term: ");
      String searchPhrase = input.nextLine();

      // Look up and print search results
      searchIndex.printResults(searchPhrase);
    }
  }
}
```

The method constructs a new `Index`, then calls the `addPlay` method to process an input script. The final part of `main` runs a loop that repeatedly prompts for an input search term and then queries the engine to print the locations where the term occurs.

16.2.4 The `Index` Class

The `Index` class is responsible for managing the search index data structure. It has three primary methods:

- `addPlay`, which takes a script file as input and extracts its words and locations;
- `addToIndex`, which takes an entry identified by `addPlay` and puts it in the index data structure; and
- `printResults`, which takes a search word as input, looks it up in the index, and prints the search results.

Here's a shell of the class, which the rest of this section will fill in step-by-step.

```java
/**
 * Class that encapsulates the search index structure
 */

import java.util.HashMap;
import java.util.ArrayList;
import java.util.Scanner;
import java.io.File;
import java.io.FileNotFoundException;

public class Index {

  /**
   * The search index is a HashMap with List values
   */
  private HashMap<String, ArrayList<Location>> index;

  /**
   * Constructor -- create the index structure
   */
  public Index() {
    this.index = new HashMap<String, ArrayList<Location>>();
  }

  /**
   * Add a new entry to the index
   */
  public void addToIndex(String phrase, String act, String scene,
                         String line, String play) {

  }

  /**
   * Process an input file and add its words to the index
   */
  public void addPlay(String fileName, String playName) {

  }
```

```

  /**
   * Helper method to query the index
   */
  public ArrayList<Location> lookup(String searchPhrase) {

  }

  /**
   * Print the results of a search
   */
  public void printResults(String searchPhrase) {

  }
}
```

Let's start by filling in `lookup`, which is a wrapper around the index's `get` method.[3] We'll adopt the convention that all search words should be in lowercase.

```
/**
 * Helper method to query the index
 */
public ArrayList<Location> lookup(String searchPhrase) {
  return this.index.get(searchPhrase.toLowerCase());
}
```

The `printResults` method simply calls `lookup`, then prints the list that it returns:

```
/**
 * Print the results of a search
 */
public void printResults(String searchPhrase) {
  ArrayList<Location> results = lookup(searchPhrase);

  for (Location loc : results) {
    System.out.println(loc);
  }
}
```

3 Sharp-eyed readers will notice that this operation could return `null` if the search phrase does not have an entry. One of the end-of-chapter questions asks you to resolve this issue.

16.2.5 Adding a Script to the Index

Most of the work is in `addPlay`. We're going to use the strategy of opening the file with `Scanner`, then using a second `Scanner` to parse each line. The version below prints each whitespace-delimited word on each line.

```
/**
 * Process an input file and add its search phrases to
 *   the index
 */
public void addPlay(String fileName, String playName) {

  Scanner fileReader = null;

  try {
    fileReader = new Scanner(new File(fileName));
  } catch(FileNotFoundException e) {
    e.printStackTrace();
  }

  // Variables to track the act and scene
  String act = null;
  String scene = null;

  while (fileReader.hasNext()) {
    String line = fileReader.nextLine();
    Scanner lineReader = new Scanner(line);

    while (lineReader.hasNext()) {
      String token = lineReader.next();
      System.out.println(token);
    }
  }
}
```

Try It Yourself

At this point, you should have code for `Location`, `Driver`, and the basic version of `Index`. Verify that you can compile all three classes together and run the program by running the `main` method of `Driver`. The program should open `macbeth.txt` and print all of its words. End the program when it prompts you for a search word.

Try It Yourself

Add statements to the `while` loop to identify changes in the act and scene.

Solution

Changes are identified by the words `ACT` and `SCENE`. Check the value of `token` at the beginning of the line-reading `while` loop.

```
while (lineReader.hasNext()) {
  String token = lineReader.next();

  // Identify lines that mark act and scene transitions
  if (token.equals("ACT")) {
    act = lineReader.next();
  } else if (token.equals("SCENE")) {
    scene = lineReader.next();
  } else {
    System.out.println(token);
  }
}
```

The final step is to call `addToIndex` to put an entry for the new word into the index structure – we'll finish that method in a moment. Replace the current line-reading loop with the following:

```
while (lineReader.hasNext()) {
  String token = lineReader.next();

  // Identify lines that mark act and scene transitions
  if (token.equals("ACT")) {
    act = lineReader.next();
  } else if (token.equals("SCENE")) {
    scene = lineReader.next();
  } else {
    // Add the new token to the index
    token = token.toLowerCase();
    addToIndex(token, act, scene, line, playName);
  }
}
```

16.2.6 Constructing the Index

The `addToIndex` method takes information about a single search result, constructs a new `Location` object, and then inserts it into the `HashMap`.

```
/**
 * Add a new entry to the index
 */
public void addToIndex(String phrase, String act, String scene,
                       String line, String play) {

  // Construct a new Location object
  Location loc = new Location(phrase, act, scene, line, play);

  // Look up the list of entries for this phrase
  //
  // getOrDefault returns a new list if this phrase does not
  // have a current entry
  ArrayList<Location> list = this.index.getOrDefault(phrase,
                                        new ArrayList<Location>());

  // Add the new Location to the list of entries
  list.add(loc);

  // Insert the updated list back into the HashMap
  this.index.put(phrase, list);
}
```

Notice the use of `getOrDefault`: It's used to return a default value if the given key isn't in the map. In this case, if a search term isn't present we'll make a new list for it.

Try It Yourself

After updating the program, run it again and verify that you can construct and then query the index to look-up entries for words from the script.

Try It Yourself

Look at the following lines. What problems do you foresee if you add them to the index?

```
FIRST WITCH.
When shall we three meet again?
In thunder, lightning, or in rain?
```

Solution

Our current program doesn't remove punctuation, so a token like `again?` is treated as different from the plain word `again`.

We dealt with this problem in the word-counting program of the previous chapter. Use `replaceAll` with a regular expression that identifies punctuation marks:

```
// Token-processing loop
while (lineReader.hasNext()) {
  String token = lineReader.next();

  // Remove punctuation
  token = token.replaceAll("[,;!?.]", "");

  //*** Remainder of token-processing loop ***//
```

16.2.7 Putting It All Together

You should now have all three classes assembled: `Location`, which stores information about where each word occurs in the play text, `Index`, which builds and manages the index data structure, and `Driver`, which provides the `main` method and the interactive input loop. Run the complete program and verify that you can look-up words. For example, a search for "thunder" against the sample excerpt will produce the following output:

```
Macbeth  I  I.
 Thunder and Lightning. Enter three Witches.

Macbeth  I  I.
In thunder, lightning, or in rain?
```

Experiment with several different queries. What happens if you search for a word that doesn't have an entry?

16.3 Extending to Web Search

Finding useful and relevant information online has been a challenge since the beginning of the Internet. In the mid-1990s – the early days of the public Internet – there were a number of search engines, as well as website directories that grouped listings of pages into hierarchical categories. However, all of these early approaches struggled to make online information easily accessible. According to a famous anecdote, only one of the top four early commercial search engines was capable of returning its own homepage in response to a search for its own name (Brin and Page, 1998).

Building a real web search engine requires grappling with the problem of *scale*. Google's search index, for example, contains hundreds of billions of documents and over 100 petabytes of data and can continue to grow as the service indexes more and more information (Google, 2022b). There is no fixed listing of pages to use as the corpus for a web search engine. The raw documents must come from "crawling" the web to find and retrieve pages that can then be analyzed and incorporated into the index. A **web crawler** is a program that knows how to fetch pages from the Internet (using HTTP or other protocols), extract their contents, and then follow their hypertext links to find more pages. The basic crawling procedure is recursive:

- The crawler starts with a known page, retrieves it, and reads its content.
- It extracts any links that lead to other pages.
- It then recursively follows those links to reach more pages, extracts *their* links, which lead to more pages, and so forth, until the crawler has explored the segment of the web reachable from its starting location.
- This process repeats (or runs in parallel) from many different starting locations with the goal of capturing a high fraction of the total reachable pages on the web.

Modern crawlers try to do this in an intelligent way by prioritizing pages that are likely to be high-value. Site owners are also allowed to supply instructions to crawler programs. Major search engine crawlers look for a file called `robots.txt` at the root of every site, which can supply instructions for how to crawl the site effectively.

Once the corpus has been assembled, the process of building the index is not that different from the one we just implemented: parse each document, extract search terms, and then construct the inverted index mapping each term to its locations. However, because the corpus is huge, these steps have to be done in parallel across a complex distributed system. Google's architecture includes a number of customized file and data formats to facilitate storing and processing hundreds of billions of web documents. Search engines also need to rank their results by relevance, so that users see the best results first. We'll return to this question in Chapter 21, which discusses building recommendation engines.

SUMMARY

Information retrieval is a fundamental problem in computer science and, indeed, fundamental to how people interact with computer systems every single day. This project has illustrated some important concepts and design principles that are used, on a much bigger scale, to create major Internet search engines. After working through the two previous chapters and this project, you should have a good idea of how Java's `HashMap` works and how to reason about hash table applications. The next set of chapters will introduce a new information organization technique – the binary tree – which can also be used to implement another kind of map data structure.

EXTENSIONS

Additional Features

Here are some ideas for additional features to add to the engine:

- Add a new method called `delete` to the `Index` class. Your method should take a `String` named `searchPhrase` as the input and remove it from the index if it exists.
- Add another method called `isCommonWord` to `Index` to filter out high-frequency words. You can decide what counts as a common word. Modify the rest of the program so that common words are filtered and don't get inserted into the index.
- As we noted earlier, it's possible for a search lookup to fail and return `null`. Modify your code to handle this case and output a reasonable message when a search phrase has no results. Note that this is not an error, so don't terminate the program or throw an exception.
- Modify your input-processing code to identify the speaking character, then modify the `Location` class to keep track of and report the character speaking each phrase. In the example Project Gutenberg *Macbeth* text, speaker names occur on their own lines, are capitalized, and end with a period (e.g., `FIRST WITCH.`).

Stemming

The current search engine treats all word variations as unique search terms. For example, *attack*, *attacked*, and *attacking* are regarded as distinct even though they are variations on the same underlying word. *Stemming* is the process of stripping suffixes to combine related words into one group for information retrieval applications. It's a standard problem in linguistics that has been studied since the early days of computer science (Sanderson and Croft, 2012). The most popular method for English-language stemming is the *Porter Stemming Algorithm*, named after its author, Martin Porter (Porter, 1980), which is used in the Open Source Shakespeare search engine. Do a little research into the Porter algorithm. How does it work, at a high level?

Suppose you had access to a prewritten method that could take a `String` as input and return its stemmed counterpart. How would you modify your program to use that method and incorporate stemmed searches? If you're feeling ambitious, Java implementations of the Porter algorithm are available (Porter, 2006).

Multi-word Searches

Finally, let's consider the challenge of multi-word searches. The example program tokenizes and indexes only single words. One option is to extend the program to capture and store all pairs of words, triples of words, and so forth, but this approach can't scale beyond small word clusters. A more robust approach is to perform a separate lookup for each individual word in the search phrase, then *merge* the results together, returning only the results that contain every word in the search phrase. With this approach, the index still only stores the results of individual words. You need to address two major questions to implement merged multi-word searches.

- First, what criteria should you use to merge results? One reasonable option is to treat multiple words as being part of the same result if they belong to the same line.
- Second, how do you actually implement the merging operation?

Modify the `lookup` method to allow for a multi-word `String` as input, then return an `ArrayList` containing only `Location` results that match every word in that `String`.

NOTES AND FURTHER READING

Shakespeare authored at least 38 plays and over 150 poems. He is the world's most influential dramatist and his works have been translated into every major living language and some fictitious ones (Nicholas and Strader, 2000). He is credited with inventing or popularizing a mind-boggling number of phrases that have made their way into everyday speech, including: *in my mind's eye, break the ice, bated breath, good riddance, one fell swoop, all that glitters is not gold, foregone conclusion, brave new world, wild-goose chase, swagger*, and *Knock, knock. Who's there?*[4] (Vernon, 2010). He died in 1616 in Stratford-upon-Avon, where he had returned after retiring from theater a few years earlier, and is buried there.

An important historical predecessor for the modern search engine was Vannevar Bush's **memex**, proposed near the end of World War II (Bush, 1945). During the war, Bush directed the Office of Scientific Research and Development, which oversaw American military research projects. In that position, he played a major role in convincing President Roosevelt to fund the ultra-secret, high-priority program in atomic weapons development that would become the Manhattan Project. In July 1945 – after the end of the European war but before the bombings of Hiroshima and Nagasaki – Bush published an influential essay titled "As We May Think," which advocated for scientists turning their attentions away from "strange destructive gadgets" and toward new challenges (Bush, 1945). In particular, he argued that the future of scientific advancement depended on making information more accessible and searchable.

Short for "memory expansion," the memex was imagined as a desk-sized device that could store a library of books, records, and correspondence.[5] Further, it would make all of this information linked and searchable, so that the user could easily find information on a topic and then move quickly between related documents. Historians credit "As We May Think" with predicting the arrival of many modern information processing technologies, including hypertext, the World Wide Web, search engines, and online encyclopedias (Nyce and Kahn, 1991). Douglas Engelbart, a pioneer of human–computer interaction, credited Bush's vision with helping begin the stream of research that would eventually lead to the creation of the personal computer, graphical user interface, and mouse (Engelbart, 1986).

---

4 He did not, however, invent the knock-knock joke, which didn't come into vogue until the 1930s.

5 Electronic data storage didn't exist in the mid-1940s, so Bush envisioned that the memex would keep its documents on some type of super-efficient microfilm.

17 Binary Trees

I like to think
(right now please!)
of a cybernetic forest
filled with pines and electronics
where deer stroll peacefully
past computers
as if they were flowers
with spinning blossoms.
Richard Brautigan, "All Watched Over by Machines of Loving Grace"

INTRODUCTION

After the linear data structures and hash tables, we're now ready to introduce the third major kind of structure: trees, which represent *hierarchical* data. Computer science, like nature, delights in trees: There are a huge number of tree-based structures customized for different problems. In particular, trees are used to construct map data structures that provide useful alternatives to hash tables.

LEARNING OBJECTIVES

After reading this chapter, you'll be able to:

- Understand the important terms used to describe trees.
- Perform traversals that iterate through the nodes of a tree.
- Implement and analyze the binary search tree, our second major map data structure, and the starting point for more specialized trees.

After completing this chapter, you'll be ready to dig into advanced trees in Chapters 18 and 19.

17.1 Representing Hierarchical Data

17.1.1 Dendrology

Trees represent hierarchical data. Figure 17.1 shows an example tree depicting the descent of the Romance languages from Latin. You've likely seen similar charts that show family genealogies, animal pedigrees, and biological classifications. A tree is a set of *nodes*. If the set is not empty, then

- there is one node designated the **root** of the tree; and
- the non-root nodes may be partitioned into zero or more disjoint sets that are themselves trees. These trees are the **subtrees** of the root node.

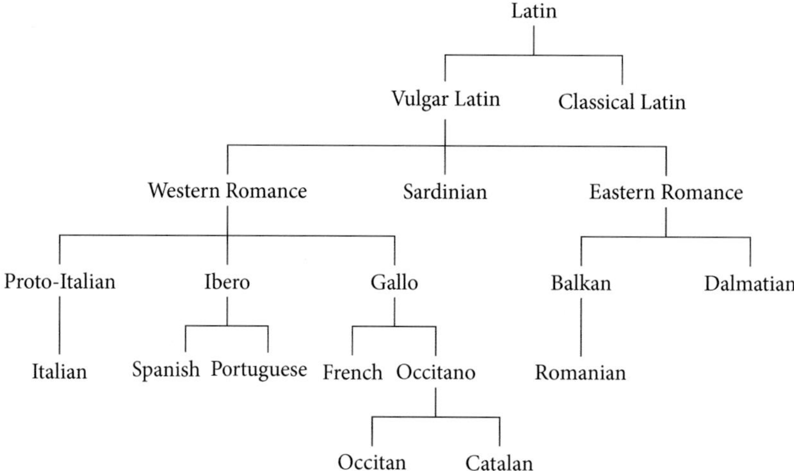

Figure 17.1 Tree showing the descent of some of the Romance languages from Latin.

This is a recursive definition: Each subtree is itself a tree, so it has a root, which is its topmost node, and may have one or more subtrees.[1] In the Romance language tree, *Latin* is the top-level root node with two subtrees: Their roots are *Vulgar Latin* and *Classical Latin*. The *Classical Latin* subtree consists of only that node with no further subtrees. *Vulgar Latin* has three subtrees.

There are a number of terms used to describe tree structure. Most are straightforward generalizations of terms from family trees.

- The *descendants* of a node n are the nodes that lie below n in its subtrees.
- The *ancestors* of n are the nodes that lie on the path from n to the top-level root.
- The immediate descendants of a node are its *children*. Likewise, the immediate ancestor of a node is its *parent*. Note that, by our definition, a node may have only one parent, and the top-level root has no parent.
- Children of the same parent are *siblings*. We'll sometimes refer to other family relationships, like grandparents, cousins, etc.

A few terms describe properties of individual nodes:

- The *degree* of a node is its number of children.
- *Leaves* are terminal nodes that have no children; that is, a leaf has degree zero.
- The *level* of a node is the number of edges on its path to the root. By convention, the top-level root is considered level 0, the children of the root make up level 1, their children are level 2, and so forth.
- The *height* of a node is the maximum number of edges connecting it to a leaf. The height of the tree as a whole is the height of its top-level root node.
- A subtree is *balanced* if its child subtrees have approximately equal height. That is, no child subtree is significantly deeper than another. A common definition is that the heights of the subtrees differ by no more than 1.

1 It would make more sense, of course, to put the root at the *bottom* of the tree, but computer scientists have decided to just do the opposite of biologists.

Try It Yourself

Identify the leaves of the Romance language tree. What is the height of the tree? Which level contains the most nodes? What are the ancestors of French? Which nodes have only one child?

17.1.2 Binary Trees

The most important type of tree, and the starting point for all of our hierarchical data structures, is the **binary tree**. Every binary tree node has either zero, one, or two children.

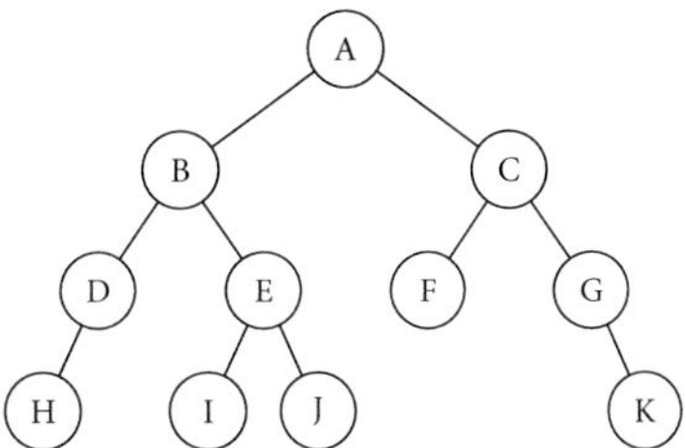

Try It Yourself

Is a linked list a binary tree?

Solution

Yes, a linked list meets the definition: The head of the list is the root and every node has only one child.

A *perfect binary tree* is one where every node has either zero or two children and all leaves are on the same level; that is, it's a binary tree containing the maximum number of nodes for its height.

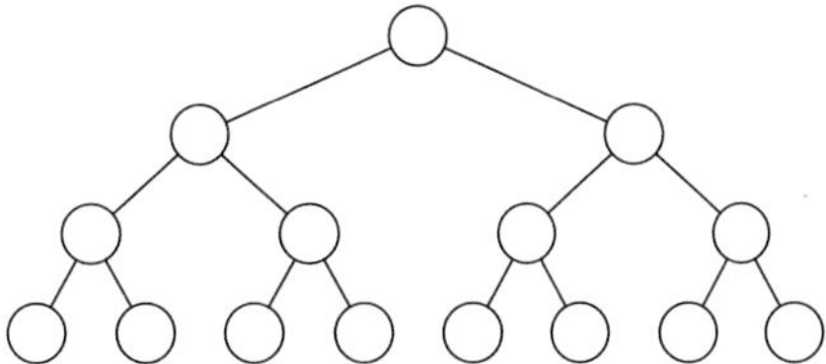

Try It Yourself

How many nodes are in a perfect binary tree with a height of h?

Solution

Consider some cases and look for a pattern:

- A tree with only a root node has height zero, by the definition of tree height.
- The perfect tree with a height of one has three nodes.
- The tree with a height of two has seven nodes.
- The tree with a height of three has 15 nodes.

If h is the height, the perfect tree has $2^{h+1} - 1$ nodes.

Try It Yourself

What is the height of a perfect binary tree with n nodes?

Solution

Inverting the previous expression gives

$$h = \log(n + 1) - 1.$$

In Big-O terms, $h = O(\log n)$. The logarithmic relationship between the number of nodes and tree height in a balanced tree is important for analysis. Keep it in mind and we'll return to this fact later in the chapter.

Some authors consider a *full* binary tree to be one where every node has either zero or two children, without requiring the leaves to be on the same level.

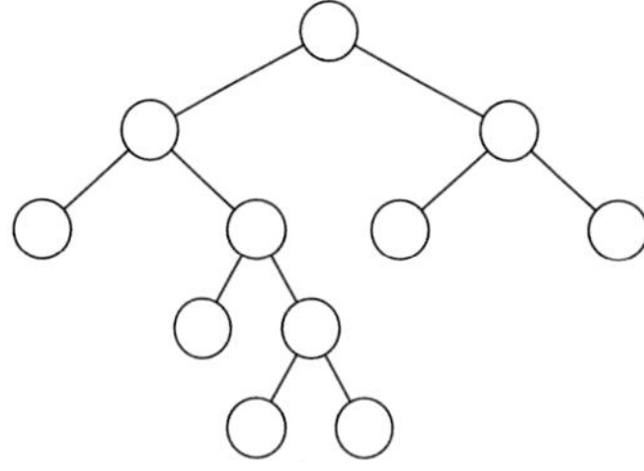

This is confusing, though, because it's too easy to use "full" when you mean "perfect." If you need to describe a tree, make sure to clearly define your terms.

17.1.3 Implementation

The standard binary tree implementation uses the link-based representation. Every node maintains two references, one for its left child and one for its right child. Nodes may also store data depending on the application. We'll call the node's internal data its *key*, similar to the hash table. The class below shows a generic linked binary tree parameterized by a type `T`. Similar to our other linked data structures, it uses an internal private `TreeNode` class. We'll extend this class and add methods in Section 17.5.

```
/**
 * Example linked binary tree
 */
public class BinaryTree<T> {
  // The tree maintains a reference to its root
  private TreeNode root;

  private class TreeNode {
    TreeNode left;
    TreeNode right;
    T key;

    // Construct a new unconnected TreeNode
    TreeNode(T newKey) {
      this.key = newKey;
      this.left = null;
      this.right = null;
    }
  }
}
```

Try It Yourself

Given a `TreeNode`, how could you determine if it's a leaf?

Solution

A leaf node has no children, so its `left` and `right` references are both `null`.

```
if (node.left == null && node.right == null) {
  // node is a leaf
}
```

Try It Yourself

Write a code fragment to start at the root and find the leftmost node in the tree.

Solution

This is a standard pattern: Use a `node` variable that starts at the root and repeatedly move to the left child.

```
TreeNode node = root;
while (node.left != null) {
  node = node.left;
}
```

Try It Yourself

What modification would we need to make if we wanted to *ascend* the tree toward the root starting from a given node?

Solution

Some applications require moving upwards in the tree. A variant implementation adds a `parent` field to `TreeNode`. The constructor takes the parent as input and sets it when the node is created. The parent of the root is `null`. For example, to ascend to the root:

```
// Rise from a starting node to the root
while (node.parent != null) {
  node = node.parent;
}
```

17.2 Tree Traversals

A **traversal** is a procedure that iterates through every node in a tree. There are two basic traversal strategies:

- the recursive *depth-first* traversal, which has three variants; and
- the *level-order* traversal, also called the breadth-first traversal.

Depth-First Traversals

Suppose that we want to print all of the keys in a binary tree. Consider the following recursive procedure:

```
/**
 * Depth-first traversal
```

```
   */
public void traverse(TreeNode node) {
  if (node == null) {
    return;
  }

  System.out.println(node.key);
  traverse(node.left);
  traverse(node.right);
}
```

Given a node, the method first prints its key, then recursively processes the left subtree, then the right subtree. Each time the method encounters a new node it performs some action on it – printing in this example – which is called *visiting* the node. The traversal typically has a wrapper method that calls `traverse` on the root:

```
public void depthFirstTraversal() {
  traverse(this.root);
}
```

Try It Yourself

Run the example traversal on the following tree starting from the root.

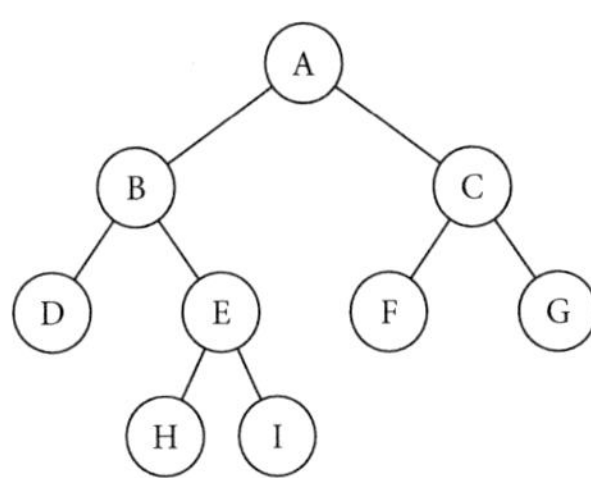

Solution

- The traversal procedure begins at the root A and visits it, then recursively descends to the left subtree.
- The second node visited is B, followed by another descent to the left to D.
- D is a leaf. After visiting it, the method checks its left child, which is `null`, and its right child, also `null`. The subtree rooted at D is now complete, so the recursion unwinds back to B and moves into the right subtree at E.
- The method visits E, then H, then I. After the visit to I, the entire left subtree rooted at B has been processed.

- The recursive procedure unwinds back to A, and then moves to the right subtree rooted at C. After visiting C, the traversal visits F and then G.

The order in which the nodes are visited is `A B D E H I C F G`.

The traversal is "depth-first" because it always explores one path to completion, then backs up and explores the next-deepest unvisited path. There are three variations of depth-first traversal that alter when the node is visited during the method.

- A *pre-order traversal* visits the node first, then recursively processes each of its child subtrees. The example above is the pre-order traversal.
- An *in-order* traversal first processes the left subtree, then visits the node, then processes the right subtree. To perform an in-order traversal, simply move the visiting action in between the recursive calls.

```
// In-order traversal
traverse(node.left);
System.out.println(node.key);  // Visit the node
traverse(node.right);
```

- A *post-order* traversal processes both subtrees, then visits the node on the way out.

```
// Post-order traversal
traverse(node.left);
traverse(node.right);
System.out.println(node.key);  // Visit the node
```

Let's work through the in-order traversal on the example tree:

- Begin at the root A, but don't visit it yet. Descend into the left subtree rooted at B.
- Don't visit B yet, either. Keep going left to D.
- Check D's left child, which is `null`, ending that recursive path. Return to D, visit it, then check D's right child, which is also `null`. D is now complete.
- Return back to B and visit it, then descend to the right subtree at E.
- The nodes of E's subtree are visited in the order H, then E, then I.
- The left subtree has been traversed. Unwind the recursion back to the root A, visit it, then move to the right subtree rooted at C.
- The nodes of the right subtree are visited in the order F, then C, then G.

The final output is `D B H E I A F C G`.

Try It Yourself

What about the post-order traversal?

Solution

The post-order traversal visits each node only after exploring both its subtrees. The root is always the last node visited. The output will be `D H I E B F G C A`.

Level-Order Traversal

A level-order traversal starts at the root and works down the tree one level at a time, processing all nodes on the second level, then all nodes on the third level, and so forth. For the example tree, level-order traversal visits the nodes in alphabetical order: `A B C D E F G H I`. The method uses a queue to keep track of the nodes that are waiting to be visited and processes them in first-come-first-served order. Here's an example implementation that uses `ArrayDeque`:

```
/**
 * Level-order traversal
 */
public void levelOrderTraversal() {
  ArrayDeque<TreeNode> q = new ArrayDeque<TreeNode>();
  q.add(this.root);

  while (!q.isEmpty()) {
    // Get the next unvisited node
    TreeNode next = q.remove();

    // Perform the visiting action
    System.out.println(next.key);

    // Add the children to the queue
    if (next.left != null) {
      q.add(next.left);
    }
    if (next.right != null) {
      q.add(next.right);
    }
  }
}
```

Notice how the level-order traversal is similar to our previous queue-based algorithms. From the starting point, the traversal expands outward one step at a time, processing all nodes that are one step away from the root, then the nodes two steps away, and so forth.

Try It Yourself

What's the complexity of level-order traversal? How about depth-first traversal?

Solution

Queue operations are $O(1)$ and each node is visited one time. Therefore, the traversal is $O(n)$. All three depth-first traversals are likewise $O(n)$.

17.3 Application: Syntax Trees

The linguist Noam Chomsky proposed the sentence *Colorless green ideas sleep furiously* as an example of an English sentence that's grammatical, but makes no sense (Chomsky, 1956). His example illustrates the distinction between *syntax* – the organization and form of statements – and *semantics* – their actual meaning. As you may have seen in a language class, tree diagrams can be used to illustrate sentence structure:

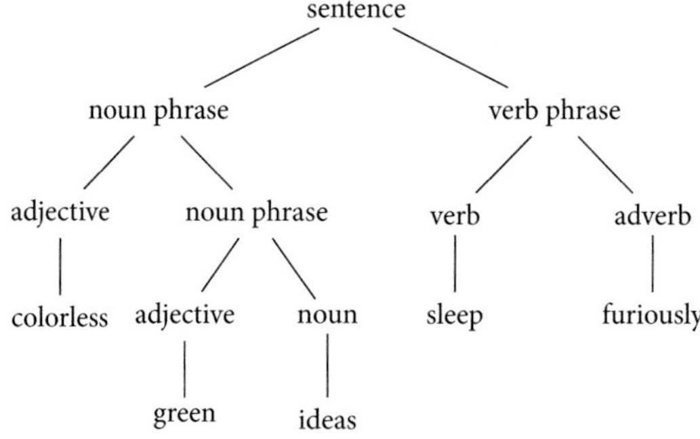

In computer science, a **syntax tree** – sometimes called an *abstract* syntax tree – is a tree showing the structure of an expression or program. For example, consider an arithmetic expression like

$$2 \times 3 + 4 \times 5.$$

Basic arithmetic expressions can be represented in tree form by making the operators internal nodes and the operands leaves. The structure of the tree respects order of operations: Higher-priority operators occur lower in the tree:

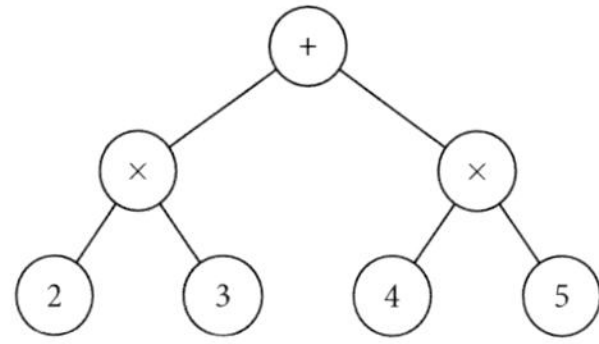

The evaluation of a syntax tree works from the bottom-up: Each node operates on the values represented by its subtrees. First evaluate the two multiplications:

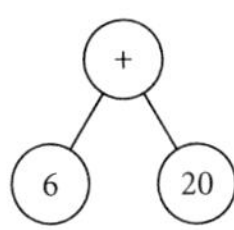

Then perform the top-level addition to obtain 26.

Try It Yourself

Construct the syntax tree for

$$(2 \times 3 + 4 \times 5) + (8 - 4),$$

then evaluate it from the bottom-up.

Solution

The tree is shown below. The order of operations given by the parentheses is represented implicitly by the structure.

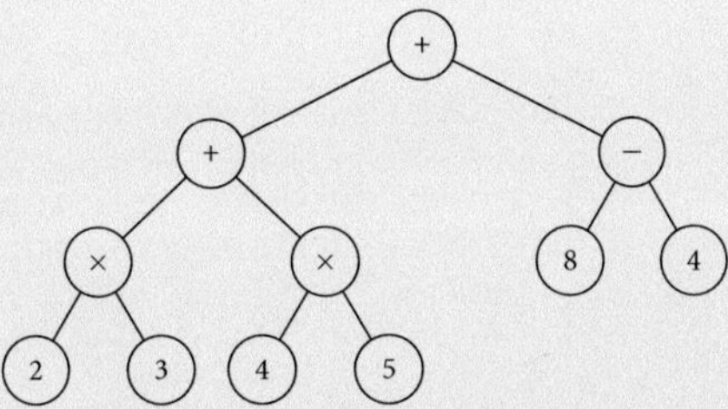

Try It Yourself

What happens if you traverse the arithmetic syntax tree? Perform pre-order and post-order traversals on the tree from the previous question. What expressions do you obtain?

Solution

The pre-order result is

$$+ \; + \; \times \; 2 \; 3 \; \times \; 4 \; 5 \; - \; 8 \; 4,$$

and the post-order result is

$$2 \; 3 \; \times \; 4 \; 5 \; \times \; + \; 8 \; 4 \; - \; +.$$

Well, if it isn't our old friends *prefix and postfix notation*!

The in-order traversal is trickier. Simply iterating through the nodes in order will reconstruct the infix arrangement, but the result may not have the correct order of operations. To obtain a valid infix expression, you have to *fully parenthesize* the output by surrounding every operation with a pair of parentheses:

- When you descend into a subtree, output a left parenthesis.
- Then, when exiting a subtree, output the matching right parenthesis.

If you apply this strategy to the example tree, you'll obtain a messy, but valid, infix expression:

$$(((2) \times (3)) + ((4) \times (5))) + ((8) - (4)).$$

Try It Yourself

Think about how to implement the evaluation algorithm. You'll need to evaluate each subtree, then pass its result up to its parent.

Solution

The post-order strategy is appropriate. If a node is an operand, simply return its value. If it's an operator, evaluate its two subtrees, then apply the operator and return the result. In pseudocode, the general method could look like this:

```
// Arithmetic syntax tree evaluation

evaluate(node) {
  // Base case: operands are in leaves
  if node is an operand {
    return node.value
  }

  // Otherwise, this is an operator node

  // Recursively evaluate subtrees
  leftResult = evaluate(node.left);
  rightResult = evaluate(node.right);

  // Apply this node's operator and return the result
  return node.operator(leftResult, rightResult)
}
```

Syntax trees are used in programming language translation to represent the structure of programs in a way that's higher-level than the literal source code. For example, consider the following simple program fragment:

```
sum = 0
i = 100
```

```
while (i > 0) {
  sum = sum + i
  i--
}
```

This code could be represented conceptually in a syntax tree like the following:

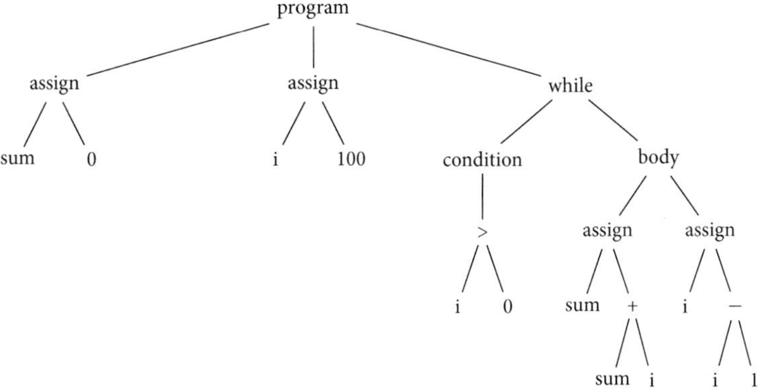

The structure of the tree captures the structure of the code:

- The root represents the program as a whole. Its children are the three statements.
- The first two statements are assignments, with left and right children representing the left and right sides of the statement.
- The third statement is the while loop, which has a condition and a body of statements.
- The body has two children, which represent the two assignments inside the loop.

A major job of a compiler is to analyze input source code and transform it into a syntax tree based on the grammar of the programming language:

- The compiler first scans the source file's text and turns it into a sequence of *tokens* that are meaningful in the language – keywords, operators, variable names, and so forth.
- The second stage analyzes the tokens according to the rules of the language and constructs the syntax tree; this is called **parsing**. If the program is not well-formed – that is, it has a syntax error – the parser will fail, print the error, and terminate.

The syntax tree is an *intermediate representation*: It captures the meaning of the program, but in a way that's more abstract than the raw source code.

The intermediate representation serves as a bridge between the "front-end" of the compiler that does program analysis and the "back-end" that generates lower-level code. A typical strategy is to traverse the tree and translate each node into instructions in the output language. For example, a compiler targeting the JVM could translate the syntax tree into JBC instructions. A **tree-walk interpreter** would dispense with generating output code and execute each statement directly. Nystrom (2021) is an excellent, accessible overview that uses Java to build a tree-walk interpreter for a simple programming language and then adapts it to generate byte code for a virtual machine.

17.4 Binary Search Trees

The **binary search tree** is the most important tree data structure. Search trees implement the map abstract data type: They store a set of <key, value> pairs and allow for both quick insertion of new pairs and fast lookups of a value given its key. Unlike hash tables, trees *maintain an internal ordering* on their keys. This ordering adds some overhead, so binary search trees are not as fast as hash tables in the typical case, but they can perform operations that aren't possible on a hash table, like returning all keys in sorted order, or finding the predecessor of a key. Java has two built-in tree classes, `TreeMap` and `TreeSet`, which are the search tree counterparts to `HashMap` and `HashSet`.

17.4.1 Properties

A binary search tree is a binary tree where the arrangement of nodes is determined by their keys:

- The keys in every left subtree are *less than* the parent's key.
- The keys in every right subtree are *greater than or equal to* the parent's key.

For example, the integer keys in the following tree obey the binary search tree property:

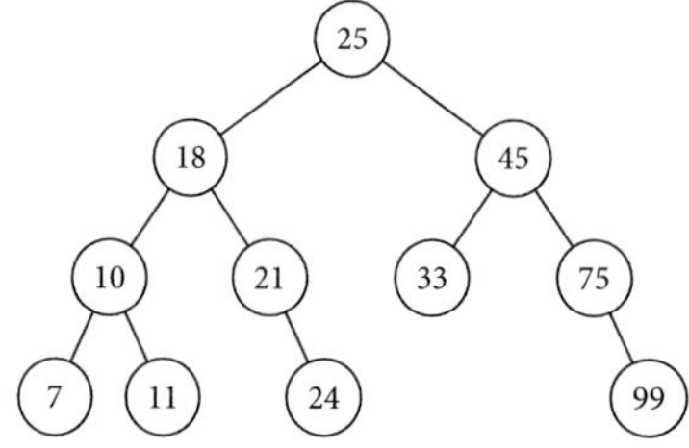

The contents of the node depend on the application. In a `TreeMap`, each node stores both a key and a value. A `TreeSet` stores only keys. When we visualize search trees, we'll always show the keys for each node, without worrying about the values. Like a hash table, duplicate keys are generally not allowed.

Try It Yourself

Arrange the following keys into a binary search tree: 7, 11, 25, 31, 17, 19, 5.

Solution

Here's one possible balanced configuration:

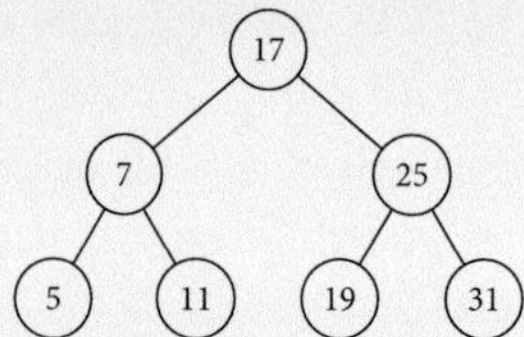

Try It Yourself

What if the keys aren't integers? For example, how would the arrangement be determined in a map with `String` keys?

Solution

There's no requirement that the keys be numeric, as long as it's possible to compare keys and determine their relative ordering. Recall that Java uses the `Comparable` interface with a `compareTo` method to define custom ordering rules for a class. For `String`, `compareTo` uses lexicographic ordering.

Try It Yourself

Perform an in-order traversal on one of the example search trees.

Solution

This is a useful result. You'll find that an in-order traversal of a binary search tree visits the keys *in sorted order*. We couldn't do that with a hash table! Likewise, the ordering makes it possible to perform actions like finding the predecessor or successor of a given key, which we'll examine shortly.

17.4.2 Searching

The search procedure takes a key as input and looks for its associated node. Searching a `TreeMap` returns the value stored at that node, or `null` if the key isn't present. In a `TreeSet`, searching returns a `boolean` indicating whether the key is or is not in the set. The basic procedure is as follows:

- Begin at the root. If the search key is stored there, stop and return the result.
- Compare the search key to the root key. If the search key is less than the root key, descend into the left subtree; otherwise, descend into the right subtree.
- Continue this process until you either find the node containing the search key, or reach a `null` endpoint, in which case the key isn't present in the tree.

For example, suppose we want to search for 24 in this example set:

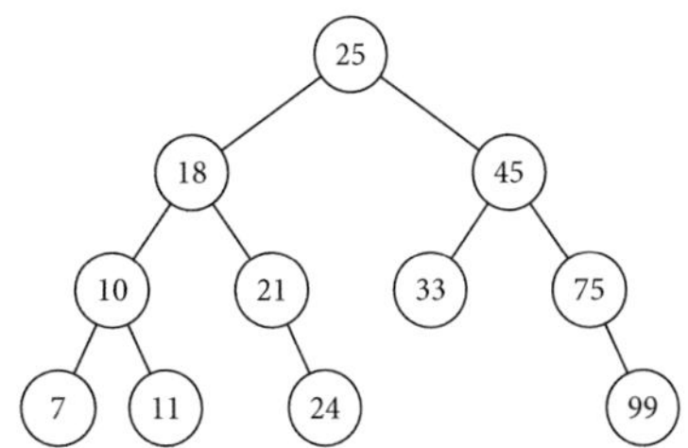

Begin at the root: 24 is less than 25, so the key, if present, must be in the left subtree. The next step compares 24 to 18 and moves right. The third step compares 24 to 21 and moves right again. The fourth step finds 24 in the leaf and returns `true` to indicate that the search succeeded.

Try It Yourself

Suppose that you want to search the tree for 39. What happens?

Solution

The first step compares 39 to 25 and moves right. The second step finds that $39 < 45$, and moves left. The third step checks that $39 > 33$, so the search key should be located in 33's right subtree. However, 33 is a leaf and its right subtree is `null`, so the search fails and the method returns `false`.

Let's implement the search algorithm in Java. The class below is our starting point: a binary tree that stores a set of keys. It's almost the same as the one in Section 17.1.3:

```
/**
 * BST-based set class
 */
public class BinarySearchTree<K extends Comparable<K>> {

  TreeNode root;

  private class TreeNode {
    K key;
    TreeNode left;
    TreeNode right;

    TreeNode(K newKey) {
      this.key = newKey;
      this.left = null;
      this.right = null;
    }
  }
}
```

You're probably wondering about that class declaration:

```
public class BinarySearchTree<K extends Comparable<K>>
```

K is the generic type for the key. It could be, in theory, *any* class, but the binary search tree must be able to *compare* keys. Declaring `K extends Comparable<K>` allows the compiler to enforce a requirement that `K` have a `compareTo` method.

With that out of the way, the search code is straightforward. Begin at the root and descend the tree, checking for the key at each step and moving left or right.

```
/**
 * Search the tree for a key
 *
 * @param  key  the search key
 * @return  true if the key is present, false otherwise
 */
public boolean search(K searchKey) {
  TreeNode current = this.root;

  while (current != null) {
    int comparison = searchKey.compareTo(current.key);

    if (comparison == 0) {
      return true;  // Success
    } else if (comparison < 0) {
      current = current.left;  // Go left
    } else {
      current = current.right;  // Go right
    }
  }

  // Failure: reached null without finding the key
  return false;
}
```

17.4.3 Insertion

Inserting a new key into a binary search tree is similar to searching:

- Make a new `TreeNode` containing the new key.
- Begin at the root. If the root is `null`, make the new node the root and stop.
- Otherwise, descend the tree, moving left or right at each level, until you reach a `null` endpoint. This location is the new key's correct position in the tree's ordering.
- Insert the new node at that position.

For example, suppose we begin with this tree of letter keys and want to insert L.

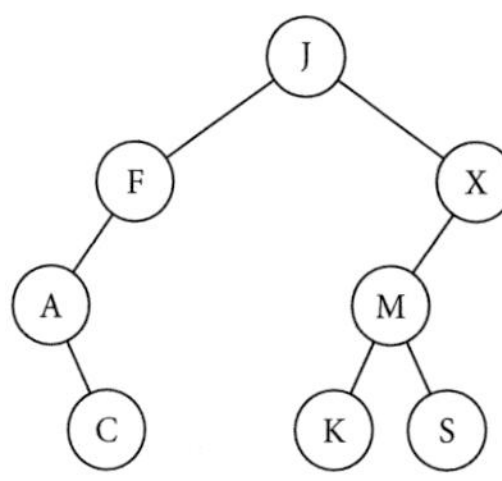

Start at the root and find that L should be right of J. The next step checks X and moves left, followed by checking M and moving left again. The last comparison checks K and discovers that L should become its new right child.

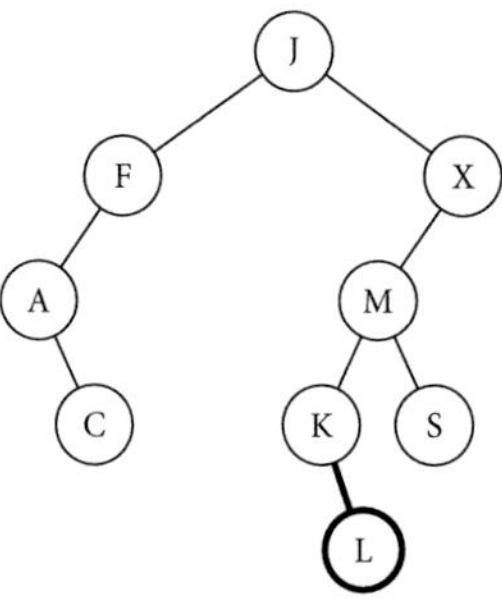

Try It Yourself

Insert Z, H, and B into the tree.

Solution

Z becomes the right child of X, H becomes the right child of F, and B becomes the left child of C.

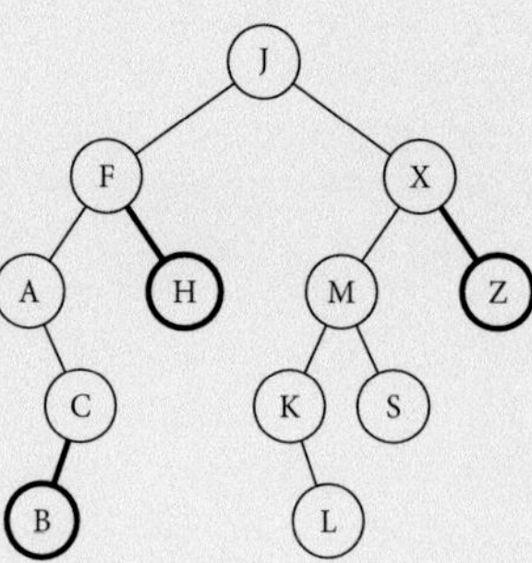

The iterative `insert` implementation uses two references to descend the tree: `current` to keep track of the node being considered, and `parent` to keep track of `current`'s parent. The descent ends when `current` becomes `null`, at which point the new node is connected to `parent`.

```
/**
 * Insert a new key
```

```
 *
 * @param  key  the new key
 */
public void insert(K key) {
  TreeNode newNode = new TreeNode(key);
  TreeNode current = this.root;
  TreeNode parent = null;

  // Descend the tree looking for an open position
  while (current != null) {
    parent = current;
    int comparison = key.compareTo(current.key);

    if (comparison == 0) {
      return;  // Key is already present
    } else if (comparison < 0) {
      current = current.left;  // Go left
    } else {
      current = current.right;  // Go right
    }
  }

  // Insert the new node
  if (this.root == null) {
    this.root = newNode;  // Insert into an empty tree
  } else if (key.compareTo(parent.key) < 0) {
    parent.left = newNode;  // New left child
  } else {
    parent.right = newNode;  // New right child
  }
}
```

Notice, again, the use of `compareTo` to check whether the key should go in the left or right subtree. Also observe that the method doesn't allow duplicate keys, so it returns immediately without making any changes if it finds the key during the descent.

17.4.4 Deletion

Deleting a key is more complex, because it requires removing the key in a way that maintains the tree's ordering. The removal process depends on whether the deleted key's node has zero, one, or two children. The first case is the easiest: If the deleted node is a leaf, simply remove it. For example, suppose we want to delete Z from the previous tree. Locate Z's parent X, then set its right pointer to `null`.

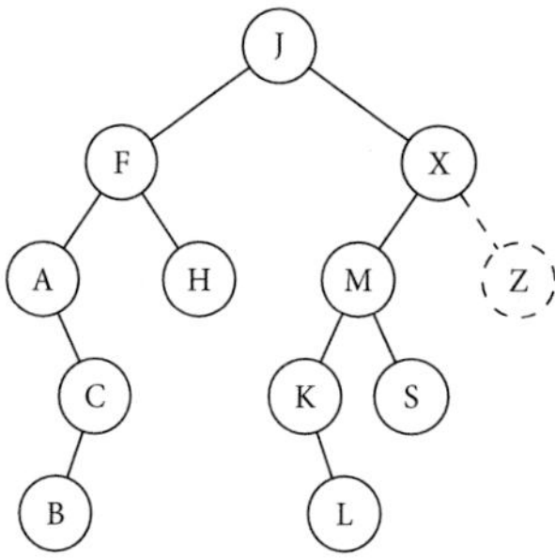

If the deleted node has only one child, then promote the child to take the place of its parent. For example, suppose that, after deleting Z, we now want to delete X.

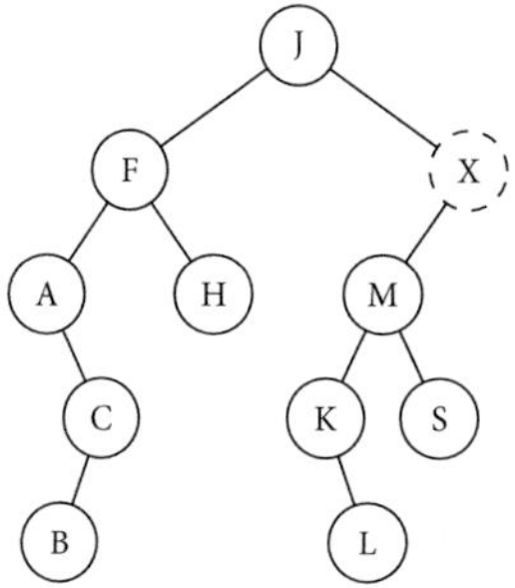

Promoting M to X's position as the right child of J maintains the structure of the tree.

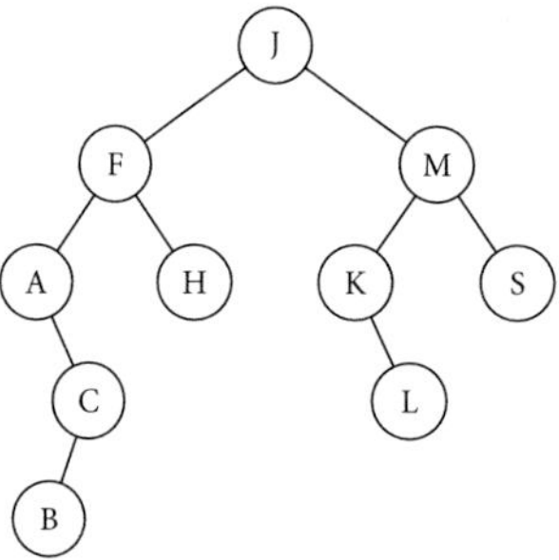

The hard case occurs when the deleted node has two children. In this case, we need to replace the deleted key with either its *predecessor* or *successor*:

- The predecessor is the largest key in the left subtree. It's smaller than the deleted key, but bigger than everything else in the left subtree.
- Likewise, the successor is the smallest key in the right subtree. It's larger than the deleted key, but smaller than everything else in the right subtree.

For example, J could be replaced with either H (its predecessor) or K (its successor). Either replacement maintains the structure of the tree.

Try It Yourself

Describe a procedure for finding the predecessor of a given key.

Solution

The predecessor is the largest value in the left subtree, which can be found by going left one time, then repeatedly going right until you reach a `null` endpoint. Likewise, the successor is found by going to the right subtree, then repeatedly going left as far as possible.

Suppose we choose to use the predecessor key for the deletion. The basic procedure is to swap the predecessor key with the deleted key, then delete the old predecessor node. Consider, for example, deleting 15 from the tree below:

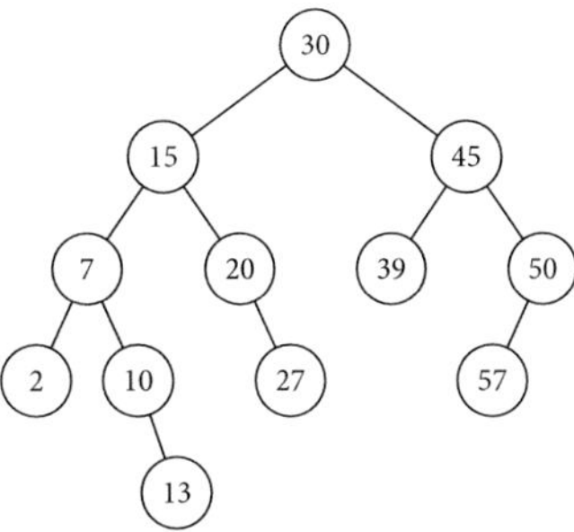

- First identify 15's predecessor, which is 13. Swap the two keys. Here, 15 moves down and 13 moves up.

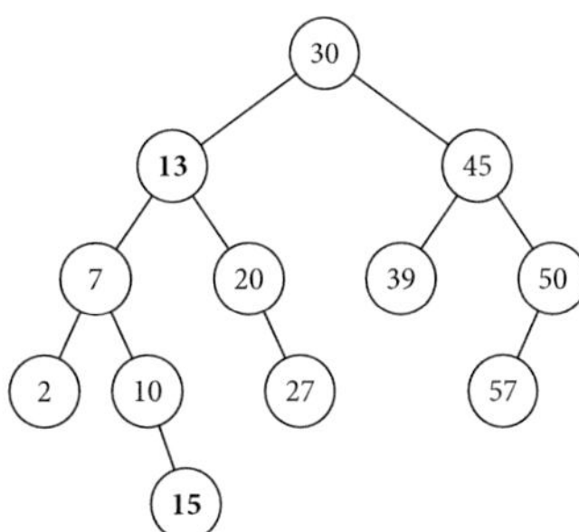

- 15 is now a leaf, and can be removed without affecting the rest of the tree. The result is valid binary search tree.

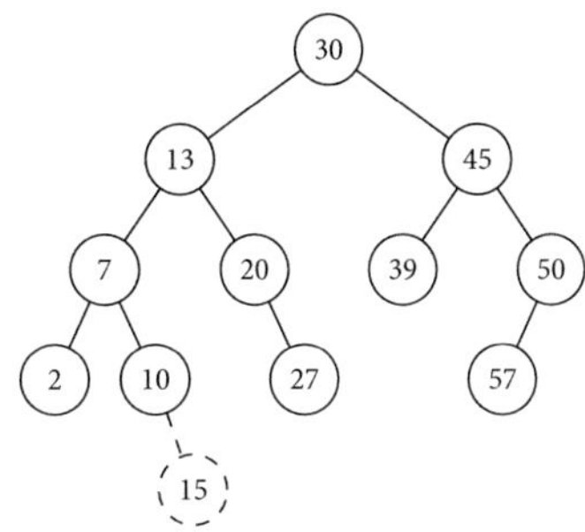

The general deletion procedure starts by selecting the replacement key, which will be either the predecessor or successor. It then swaps the deleted key with its replacement, then removes the replacement key's old node.[2] The next question considers what happens if the swap node has a child.

Try It Yourself

Repeat the deletion of 15 from the original tree, but use the successor key instead.

Solution

15's successor key is 20 – it's the leftmost node in the right subtree, but it isn't a leaf. Move 20 up to 15's position, then delete 20's old node, which moves 27 up to take its place.

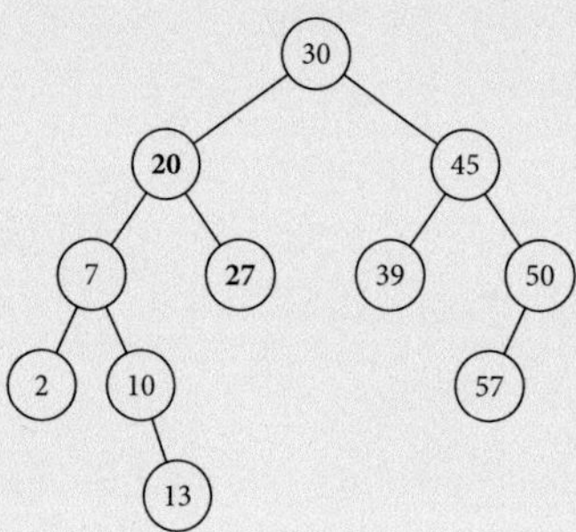

Here's an implementation of the full deletion method. The code is long, but uses the same techniques as `search` and `insert` – look at each small section and think about how it relates to the examples. The beginning of the loop descends the tree until it finds the node containing the deleted key. Once the key has been found, the `else` block makes the appropriate changes based on whether the key has zero, one, or two children. The first three cases replace `current` with either `null` or its only child. The last case implements the swap with the successor node. After swapping, the method continues descending the tree until it finds the swapped key in the old successor's node, where it has either zero or one child and can be safely deleted.

```
/**
 * Delete a key
 *
 * @param  key  the key to delete
 */
public void delete(K key) {
  TreeNode parent = null;
```

2 There's a bit of subtlety to key deletion: The procedure we've described deletes *the key* from the tree, but may not delete *the node containing that key*. Some applications need to maintain references to specific nodes within the tree, and a deletion step that swap keys can make those references invalid. There are more complex deletion strategies that will delete *the key and its node* and rearrange the tree to maintain a valid ordering without swapping any keys to different nodes (Cormen et al., 2022).

```
TreeNode current = this.root;

// Descend, looking for the key
while (current != null) {
  int comparison = key.compareTo(current.key);
  if (comparison < 0) {  // Go left
    parent = current;
    current = current.left;
  } else if (comparison > 0) {  // Go right
    parent = current;
    current = current.right;
  } else {
    // Found the key: consider three deletion options

    // 1. No children -- replace current with null
    if (current.left == null && current.right == null) {
      if (parent == null) {
        this.root = null;
      } else {
        replace(parent, current, null);
      }
      return;
    }

    // 2a. No left child -- replace current with right child
    else if (current.left == null) {
      if (parent == null) {
        this.root = this.root.right;
      } else {
        replace(parent, current, current.right);
      }
      return;
    }

    // 2b. No right child -- replace current with left child
    else if (current.right == null) {
      if (parent == null) {
        this.root = this.root.left;
```

```
        } else {
          replace(parent, current, current.left);
        }
        return;
      }

      // 3. Two children -- swap with successor key
      else {
        // Find the successor -- minimum in the right subtree
        TreeNode successor = current.right;
        while (successor.left != null) {
          successor = successor.left;
        }

        // Swap keys
        K temp = current.key;
        current.key = successor.key;
        successor.key = temp;

        // Continue descending towards the right -- the method
        // will keep going until it finds the swapped key in the
        // old successor node, then delete that node
        parent = current;
        current = current.right;
      }
    }
  }

  return;  // Never found the key
}

/**
 * Helper method -- replace current node with newNode
 */
public void replace(TreeNode parent, TreeNode current,
                    TreeNode newNode) {
  // Test if current is the left or right child of parent
  // This is one case where comparing with == is useful!
```

```
    if (current == parent.left) {
      parent.left = newNode;
    } else {
      parent.right = newNode;
    }
}
```

17.4.5 Analysis

The complexity of binary search tree operations depends on the number of levels in the tree. Search, insert, and delete all require traversing the tree from the root to, in the worst case, a `null` endpoint, checking one node at each level.

Try It Yourself

Suppose the tree is perfect. What is the complexity of a method that performs $O(1)$ work at each of its levels?

Solution

As we saw earlier, a perfect tree with n nodes has $\lceil \log n \rceil$ levels and operations on it are $O(\log n)$ in the worst case.

Try It Yourself

But what if the tree isn't perfect? In that case it depends on how the nodes are arranged. What happens if you build a search tree by inserting keys in sorted order?

Solution

Inserting values in sorted order builds a "tree" with only a single branch. For example, inserting 2, 3, 5, 7, in that order, yields:

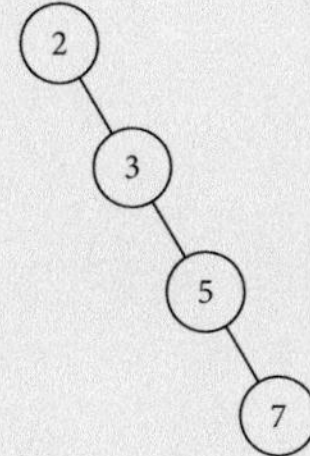

This search tree is equivalent to a linked list, and operations on it will be $O(n)$.

To get $O(\log n)$ behavior, the tree needs to be roughly *balanced*, so that the left and right subtrees of every node have approximately equal height. In most cases, it's considered reasonable if no sibling subtrees have a height difference greater than 1.

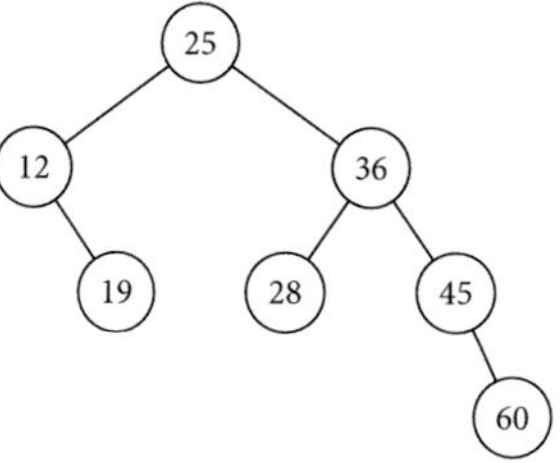

Key ordering in a basic binary search tree depends only on insertion order, so there's no way to guarantee that it remains balanced. All real search tree implementations, therefore, use special balanced variants that do extra work to keep the height of the tree within a constant factor of $\log n$. Java's `TreeMap` uses the **red–black tree**, which we'll examine in detail in the next chapter.

17.5 Example Interview Questions Using Trees

17.5.1 Mirror a Binary Tree

Given a binary tree, which does not have to be a search tree, convert it to its mirror image by flipping it along its vertical axis. For example, the tree on the left has the mirror on the right.

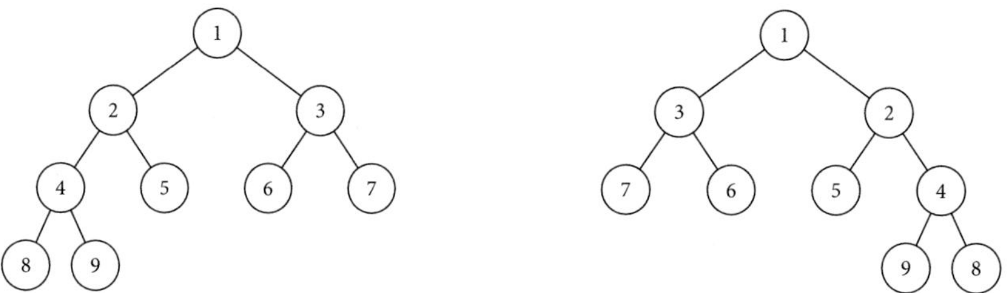

Trees are defined recursively: Every subtree has a root and its own set of subtrees. Therefore, lots of tree problems have recursive solutions. The general strategy is to perform an action at the root, then recursively repeat on the child subtrees, until the entire tree has been processed. In this case, observe that you could mirror a one-level tree by just exchanging its left and right child. The general strategy is to exchange the root's two children, then recursively repeat on each subtree.

```
/**
 * Mirror a binary tree
 */
public void mirror(TreeNode root) {
  // Base case
  if (root == null) {
    return;
  }
```

```

  // Swap children
  TreeNode temp = root.left;
  root.left = root.right;
  root.right = temp;

  // Recursively repeat on the two subtrees
  mirror(root.left);
  mirror(root.right);
}
```

Try It Yourself

Here's a variation: Given two trees, T_1 and T_2, check if they are mirrors of each other. Think about how to approach this problem recursively. If the two trees are mirrors, they must have identical values stored at their roots. What relationships need to exist among the subtrees?

Solution

If the trees are mirrors, then the *left* subtree of T_1 must be a mirror of the *right* subtree of T_2 and vice versa.

```
public boolean areMirrors(TreeNode t1, TreeNode t2) {
  // Base case: both are null
  if (t1 == null && t2 == null) {
    return true;
  }

  // Recursive case: nodes must be non-null, have equal
  // data, and have mirrored subtrees -- if any of
  // those conditions fails, return false.
  return (t1 != null) && (t2 != null)
          && (t1.key == t2.key)
          && areMirrors(t1.left, t2.right)
          && areMirrors(t1.right, t2.left);
}
```

17.5.2 Checking If a Tree Is Height Balanced

Suppose you'd like to verify if a given tree is roughly height balanced, which we'll define as having the left and right subtrees of every node differ by no more than one.

Try It Yourself

Write a recursive method to calculate the height of a node.

Solution

If you know the heights of its left and right subtrees, the height of the node is:

```
int height = Math.max(leftHeight, rightHeight) + 1;
```

This leads to a short recursive method:

```
public int height(TreeNode t) {
  // Base case: null nodes and leaves have height 0
  if (t == null || (t.left == null && t.right == null)) {
    return 0;
  }

  int leftHeight = height(t.left);
  int rightHeight = height(t.right);
  return Math.max(leftHeight, rightHeight) + 1;
}
```

To answer the question, we need a way to report whether any node in the tree is unbalanced. The solution below recursively calculates the height of each node. If a node is balanced, return its height, but if it's unbalanced return –1 instead. If any node is unbalanced, the –1 value will propagate up the tree to the root.

```
// Find the height of a node
public int height(TreeNode<K> t) {
  if (t == null || (t.left == null && t.right == null)) {
    return 0;
  }

  int leftHeight = height(t.left);
  int rightHeight = height(t.right);

```

```
  if (leftHeight < 0 || rightHeight < 0) {
    return -1;  // At least one subtree contains an imbalance
  } else if (Math.abs(leftHeight - rightHeight) > 1) {
    return -1;  // This node is unbalanced
  } else {
    return Math.max(leftHeight, rightHeight) + 1;  // Default
  }
}

// Check if the tree is balanced by finding the height
// If height < 0 then at least one node is unbalanced
public boolean isBalanced() {
  return height(this.root) >= 0;
}
```

SUMMARY

This entire chapter has engaged in a little sleight of hand. Binary search trees *are* a major data structure, but mostly because they introduce concepts that are fully realized by advanced trees. As you're reading, keep the following ideas in mind:

- There's a strong connection between trees and recursion. If you still aren't solid on recursive thinking, review the earlier chapters.
- Recursive tree traversal is a key algorithm. We'll see further variations of it in Chapters 20–22, when we consider graphs.
- Search trees are a kind of map and can serve as an alternative to hash tables.

The next chapter introduces three advanced self-balancing search trees that are widely used in practice.

EXERCISES

Understand

1. Return to the language tree and list all the descendants of *Vulgar Latin*. What is the height of *Vulgar Latin*?
2. List all the sets of siblings in the language tree.
3. How many nodes are on level k of a perfect binary search tree?
4. Construct a binary search tree from the following keys by successive insertion: 20, 15, 35, 18, 12, 19, 28, 32, 24, 45.

5. Show the tree that results after deleting 35.
6. Review the Java documentation for `TreeMap` and `HashMap`. What behaviors does a `TreeMap` provide that a `HashMap` does not?
7. Describe the advantages a `HashMap` has over a `TreeMap`.
8. Your friend says that a binary search tree has worst-case $O(\log n)$ performance for searches, insertions, and deletion. How do you respond?
9. Write methods called `max` and `min` that return the maximum and minimum keys in a search tree.
10. Modify the in-order traversal algorithm to return a search tree's keys in reverse sorted order, from the largest down to the smallest.
11. Write a method called `depth` that takes a `TreeNode` as input and returns its distance from the top-level root. Assume that each node has a `parent` field.
12. Write a method to find the lowest common ancestor of two nodes. Again, assume that you have a `parent` field to move up the tree.
13. Two nodes are *first cousins* if their closest ancestor is a grandparent. Write a method that takes two `TreeNode` objects as input and returns `true` if they're first cousins and `false` otherwise.
14. Modify the `BinarySearchTree` example class to store <key, value> pairs at each node, then update the `search` method to return the value for the search key.
15. Modify the `insert` method to insert a new <key, value> pair into the tree.
16. Add a `size` field to the class. Think about where to update the size in the insert and remove methods.
17. Represent $(1 + (2 \times (3 - (4 \times 5))))$ as a syntax tree.
18. Convert the following code fragment to a syntax tree. You can decide how you want to label the internal nodes.

```
for (int i = 1; i <= 100; i++) {
  if (i % 2 == 0) {
    System.out.println(i);
  }
}
```

Apply

19. Write a method called `predecessor` that takes a key as input and returns its predecessor key, or `null` if there is no predecessor.
20. Repeat the previous question to find the successor key.
21. Write a method called `numLeaves` to count the number of leaves in a binary tree.
22. Find an expression for the number of leaf nodes in a perfect binary tree.
23. Recall that a full tree has either zero or two children at every node. Write a method to test if a tree is full.

24. Let's say that a tree is *degenerate* if every node except the last has only one child. In that case, the tree behaves like a list. Write a method to test if a tree is degenerate. Tip: The tree could have a mixture of left and right children.

25. Suppose you have a tree with integer keys. Write a method to calculate the sum of the keys in a tree.

26. Now let's say that the tree is "sum balanced" – a term we just made up for this question – if the left and right subtrees of every node have equal sums. Write a recursive method that checks if a tree is sum balanced.

27. Let's say that a tree is "left skewed" if there is any node where the height of the left subtree exceeds the height of the right subtree by two or more. Write a method to test if a tree is left skewed.

28. Suppose that you want to create a *nonbinary* tree. Let each `TreeNode` have an `ArrayList<TreeNode>` that stores its children. Write a method to perform pre-order traversal on such a tree.

29. `TreeMap` has a method called `lowerKey` that takes a key as input and returns the largest key that is still strictly less than the given key, or `null` if there is no such key. Implement this method.

30. Find an expression for the minimum number of nodes in a *full* binary search tree with a height of h.

31. What is the worst-case complexity for a search operation on a full binary search tree with n nodes? Is it linear or logarithmic?

32. Write a method called `paths` that recursively prints all the root-to-leaf paths in a binary tree. Tip: Use two inputs, `TreeNode current` and `String path`, where `path` records the sequence of keys from the root to `current`.

33. Suppose that you want to test if a tree is a valid binary search tree. "Easy," you say, "I'll simply write a recursive method to test if the left and right children of every node obey the search tree property." Come up with a counterexample to show that this approach doesn't work.

34. Now write a *correct* method to test if a binary tree is a valid binary search tree.

Extend

35. Modify the depth-first traversal algorithm to use an explicitly declared `Stack<TreeNode>` rather than a recursive implementation.

36. Modify the in-order traversal algorithm to output the k largest keys in a search tree.

37. Write a method called `printRange` that takes `low` and `high` keys as input and prints all keys in the tree that are in the range [`low`, `high`].

38. Develop a method to construct a roughly balanced search tree from a sorted input array. Assume you're going to use the basic insertion algorithm.

39. Suppose that you have a `List` that contains all the keys of a perfect binary search tree in *level order*. Design a method to reconstruct the tree.

40. An *order statistic* tree is a variant binary search tree that allows quickly finding the rank of any node in the tree – that is, its position in the sorted ordering of the tree's keys. The tree

adds an extra field to each node to track the size of the node's subtree, which is defined to be the total number of nodes in its left and right subtrees, plus one for the node itself:

```
node.size = node.left.size + node.right.size + 1;
```

A leaf node has a size of 1 and a `null` node has a size of 0. Suppose that you update `TreeNode` to include this `size` field. Use it to implement the `rank` method that takes a key as input and returns its rank among the tree's keys.

41. Next, modify the `insert` method to update the `size` field.

42. Modify the `delete` method to update the `size` field. This is much easier if you also use a `parent` field to move back up the tree.

43. Implement another method called `select` that takes an `int index` as input and returns the key at that position in the sorted ordering of the tree's keys.

NOTES AND FURTHER READING

An unexpected application of binary trees occurs in the classic PC game *Doom*. One of the first games to combine 3D graphics with intense action, it established the first-person shooter as a commercially dominant genre. *Doom*'s 3D rendering engine, written by lead programmer John Carmack, used an algorithm called **binary space partitioning** to speed up its calculations. To perform real-time rendering, the engine needed to be able to quickly determine which objects were visible from the player's position (and hence which ones needed to be rendered), and the relative positions of objects, so that background and foreground objects were drawn in the correct order.

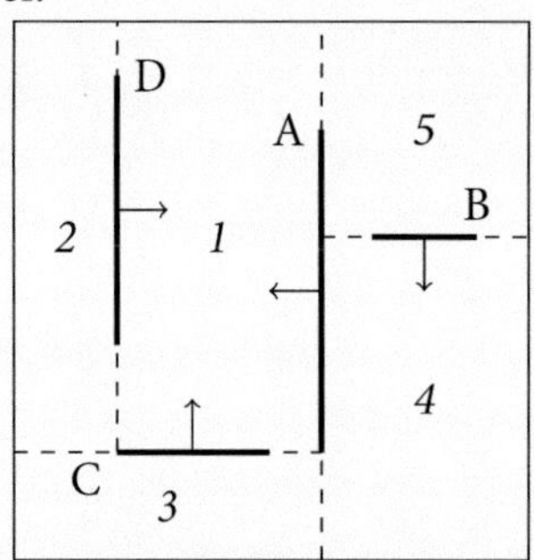

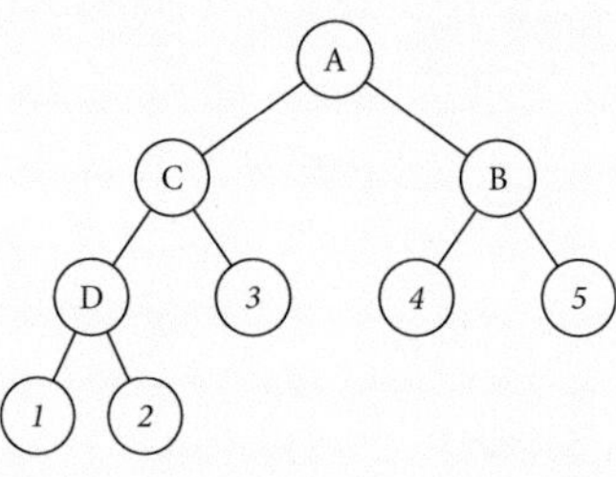

The BSP algorithm splits space into regions by recursively dividing it in two.[3] The method begins by picking one object and using it to split the space into two parts: those in front of the object and those behind it. The room above has four walls, each labeled with an arrow indicating its front direction. If wall A is chosen as the first split, then C and D will be in the front set and B will be in the back set. This process then continues recursively, until the entire space has been divided into nonoverlapping regions.

In the tree on the right, every internal node corresponds to a split, with the left child representing objects in front and the right child representing those behind. The numbered leaves

3 Similar to the Mondrian art generator in Chapter 9.

represent regions of the 2D room. For example, anything in region 4 is behind A, but in front of B. Given a point in the room, you can discover its containing region by descending the tree from root to a leaf, checking whether it's in front of or behind each wall to determine whether to move to the left or right child at each step.

Doom extends this idea to 3D scenes, where the space is divided by planes instead of lines, and the objects are polygons instead of walls. The BSP algorithm works similarly, but it also handles cases where a polygon is cut by a partition plane, creating two new polygons. *Doom* traverses the BSP tree according to the position and orientation of the player's viewpoint, drawing only the polygons that are visible and in the correct order. Target (2019) provides an accessible overview of the implementation and historical context of the BSP algorithm. An interesting detail is that Carmack adopted the method after reading about it in a research paper that was itself inspired by earlier US Air Force research on flight simulation.

18 Self-Balancing Search Trees

So, friends, every day do something that won't compute.
Wendell Berry

INTRODUCTION

The last chapter ended on a down note, when we realized that the standard binary search tree can't guarantee $O(\log n)$ performance if it isn't balanced. This chapter introduces **self-balancing search trees**. All three of the trees we'll examine – 2-3-4 trees, B-trees, and red–black trees – implement search tree operations, but perform *extra work* to ensure that the tree stays balanced.

LEARNING OBJECTIVES

At the end of this chapter, you will be able to:

- Describe the properties of the nonbinary 2-3-4 tree and apply its insertion and deletion rules to example trees.
- Discuss the B-tree, how it relates to the 2-3-4 tree, and its role in building disk-based indices. Insert and delete from example B-trees.
- Explain the characteristics of the red–black tree and how it relates to the 2-3-4 tree. Analyze red–black insertion and deletion operations, and understand the argument that the tree's height is $O(\log n)$.

This material is hard! Red–black trees are the most complex data structure that we'll encounter in this book. On the positive side, by comparison, everything else is easy. Our discussion will focus mostly on the principles of the different trees and working through examples; once you're familiar with the principles you can dig into the implementation details, like the source code for Java's `TreeMap` (OpenJDK, 2013).

18.1 2-3-4 Trees

Our first self-balancing tree is the **2-3-4 tree**. It's a *nonbinary* search tree, where each node is allowed to have more than two children. As we'll see, the tree's update rules ensure that no path ever becomes deeper than any other. Working with 2-3-4 trees will prepare you for B-trees and red–black trees, which are both based on the 2-3-4 concept.

18.1.1 Nonbinary search trees

The **2-3-4 tree** is a nonbinary search tree where each node can have up to four children:

- A *2-node* holds one value and has two children, equivalent to a standard binary search tree node.
- A *3-node* holds two values and has three children.
- A *4-node* holds three values and has four children.

To stay balanced, the tree also enforces a rule that *all leaf nodes appear on the same level.* Therefore, no subtree can ever become deeper than its siblings.

Consider the example 2-3-4 tree below. Each node implements a *multi-way split* based on its keys. For example, all keys less than 5 lie in the root's left subtree, keys greater than 25 are in the right, and keys between 5 and 25 are in the middle.

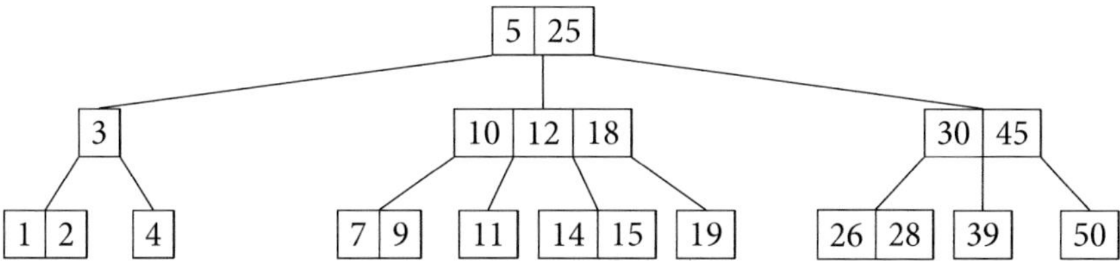

Looking up a key in a 2-3-4 tree is similar to the standard binary search tree procedure. Compare the search key against the current node's keys and choose the appropriate branch to move to the next level. To search for 19, for example, begin at the root: 19 is between 5 and 25, so it must be in the middle subtree. Descend to the middle node, compare 19 to the keys 10, 12, and 18, and take the rightmost branch. The search then finds 19 in its leaf node and terminates.

Try It Yourself

Suppose you have a balanced search tree where each node has degree c – that is, each node has c children. Make an argument that this reduces the height of the tree, but doesn't change the worst-case complexity of the search method.

Solution

If each node has c children, then the expected height of the balanced tree with n nodes is $\log_c n$. This is better than the $\log_2 n$ levels in a binary search tree, but by only a constant factor:

$$\log_c n = \frac{\log_2 n}{\log_2 c}.$$

Therefore, the time to search for a key is still $O(\log n)$. Also, observe that each node now requires $c-1$ comparisons. Therefore, using our standard analysis techniques, search trees with high-degree nodes don't outperform binary trees.

That answer, though, assumes there's no overhead involved in accessing each node. What if we change the problem and make the *cost of accessing nodes* much higher than the cost of checking their keys? In that case, reducing the height of the tree is now valuable – we want a *short, wide tree*[1] that has to visit as few nodes as possible.

This is an important problem for disk-based systems like databases. Disks are slow, so you can't practically search a large database by performing a linear scan of its records. A **database index** is a lookup structure that maps search keys to their associated on-disk records. All databases use indexing to speed up their queries. However, if the database is large, then the index itself may be too large to fit in memory. If the index is stored on disk, then every node visited during a lookup might still require a separate disk access, which makes the height of the tree the dominant driver of lookup times. Therefore, multi-way tree structures that store lots of keys in each node and keep the tree as short as possible are a good choice for database indexing. The B-tree, which we'll discuss in Section 18.1.4, is the most popular database indexing structure.

18.1.2 Insertion

The 2-3-4 tree builds itself from the bottom upwards. The first insertion to an empty tree creates a new root node:

10

Subsequent insertions, whatever their values, go into that node until it fills. Keys in the node are kept in sorted order:

3	10	20

Attempting to insert another key triggers a split. Suppose that we attempt to insert 30. The split procedure chooses one of the middle keys and promotes it to become a new root. The remaining three keys become a child 3-node and 2-node.[2] If 20 is promoted to become the new root, the result is the following:

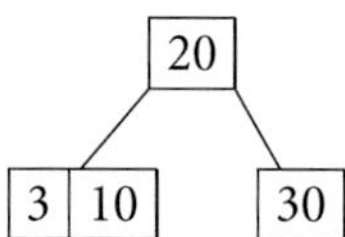

Further insertions travel down the tree and add the new key to the appropriate leaf. For example, inserting 15 and 27:

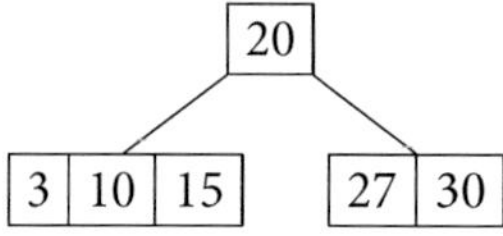

Now consider what happens if we try to insert 7. It should go into the left child, but that would create a node with four keys: 3, 7, 10, and 15. The response is to split the node again and promote

1 A bush?

2 Remember that the node name refers to the number of children. A 3-node has three children and *two keys*; a 2-node has two children and one key.

one of its middle values up to become a new key at the root. In the tree below we've promoted 10 up to join 20 and make the root a 3-node. The other three keys (3, 7, and 15) split to make a new 3-node and a 2-node. The tree now has three leaves, all on the same level.

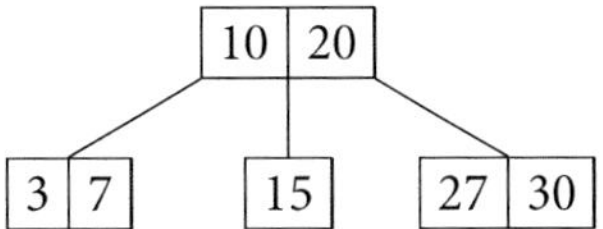

Try It Yourself

Insert 5, 45, and 99.

Solution

Here, 5 joins the leftmost leaf and 45 joins the rightmost leaf. Inserting 99 triggers a split on the right leaf, which causes one of the middle keys to promote up and make the root a 4-node. Here's the result if 45 is promoted:

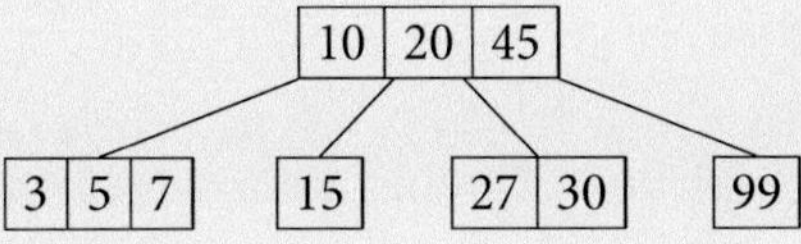

The top-level root is now full. Trying to promote another key to the root triggers a second-level split to create a new higher-level root and increase the height of the tree. For example, suppose we insert 2:

- It should go in the left leaf, which would then contain four keys: 2, 3, 5, and 7. Split it and promote one of the middle keys – we choose 5 – up.
- But the root is also full, so *it* needs to split. Again, one of the middle keys, say 20, moves up to become the new top-level root and the other three keys (5, 10, and 45) become a 3-node and 2-node at the middle level.

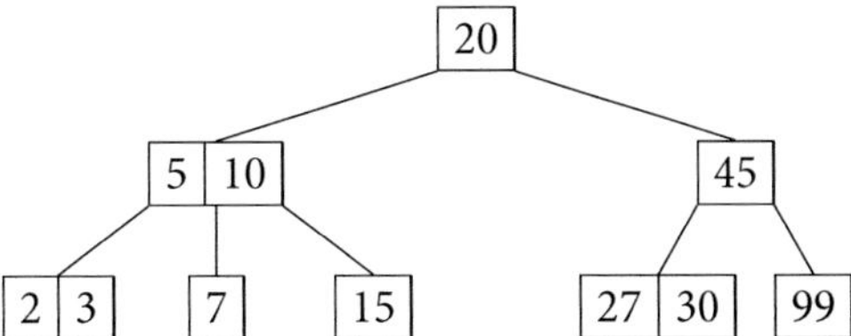

Again, notice how the insertion procedure never creates new leaves *below* the level of the current leaves, only new roots *above* the current nodes. The 2-3-4 tree insertion method is self-balancing because it keeps all leaves on the same level.

18.1.3 Deletion

Deleting from a 2-3-4 tree starts off like deleting from a standard binary search tree. First, search the tree to find the key that you want to delete, then:

- If the key is in a leaf, delete it from that leaf.
- If the key is in an internal node, identify its predecessor key (or, alternatively, successor key). Swap the deleted key with its predecessor, then delete the predecessor's old node. Review Chapter 17 for examples on the standard binary tree.

However, in a 2-3-4 tree, deleting a node may require additional work to *rebalance* the tree. We'll first consider a few easy examples showing how to resolve changes at the leaf level, then look at the general strategy that can make changes further up the tree.

The easiest case occurs when deleting from a leaf that has more than one key. For an example, suppose we want to delete 45 from the previous example tree: 45 is at an internal node, so it's swapped with 30 (its predecessor key in its left subtree), which moves it to a leaf position that can then be deleted. The resulting tree is still a valid 2-3-4 tree, so no further work is necessary.

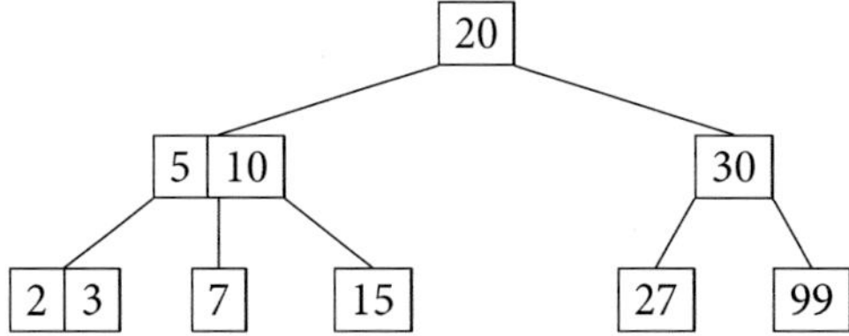

Challenges arise when deleting a key that is the only member of its leaf. Suppose we delete 7 from the example tree. Leaving an empty space at the leaf level isn't allowed, so we need to move a key into 7's position. The first strategy for resolving deficient nodes is to steal a key from a sibling that has more than one. In this case, 7's left sibling has an extra key, so we can do a rotation: move 5 down from the parent to take 7's place, then move the largest sibling key, 3, up to become the parent's new separating value. It's then safe to delete 7.

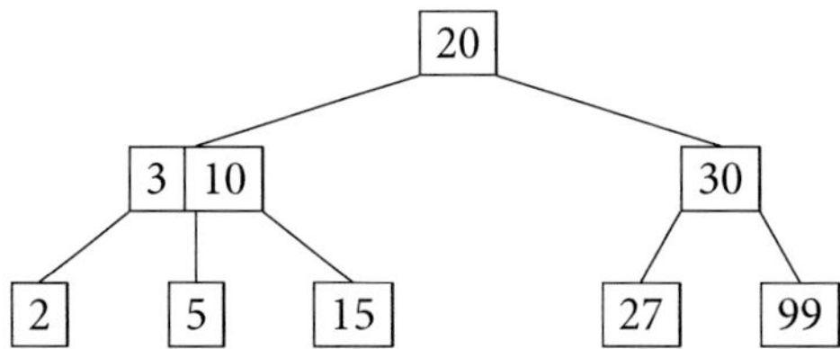

Now consider deleting 15. Its immediate sibling is 5, which doesn't have any extra keys. The parent, however, has two keys, so we can take one and *merge* it with the children to create a new node. Here, we'll take 5, 15, and their common parent, 10, and merge them together to create a new leaf with three keys, after which 15 can be deleted. This change reduces the number of keys in the parent by one.

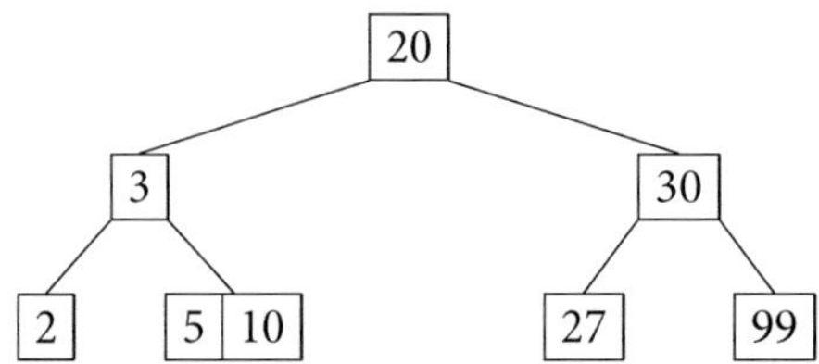

The hard case occurs when neither the sibling nor the parent have extra keys. Look at the tree below and consider deleting 2 from it. The simple borrowing approach doesn't work for this example: both 2's sibling and parent are themselves 2-nodes.

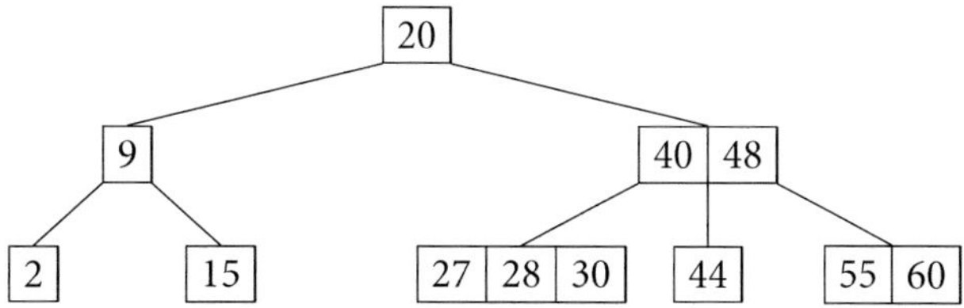

There are two ways to deal with general deletion in a 2-3-4 tree:

- The *bottom-up approach*, which starts at the leaf, performs the deletion there, then ascends back up the tree to perform rebalancing operations at higher levels if necessary.
- The *top-down* approach, which starts at the root and works down the tree, fixing any nodes that might lead to problems before you reach the leaf level.

The top-down strategy is preferred for 2-3-4 trees, so we'll discuss it in more detail.

- As you descend the tree, check for any 2-nodes on the path to the relevant leaf. These are the nodes that have only one key and might lead to deletion problems.
- Whenever you encounter a nonroot 2-node, *fix it* so that, when it's time to delete at the leaf level, there won't be any problems higher in the tree.

There are three different fix-it cases that can apply, depending on the relationship between the 2-node, its parent, and its sibling. Let x be the 2-node that we're going to fix. The first two strategies are generalizations of the key-borrowing approach:

- If x has an immediate left or right sibling with more than one key, rotate one of that sibling's keys over to make x into a 3-node.
- If x's immediate left and right siblings are also 2-nodes, but their parent is a 3- or 4-node, take one key from the parent and merge x, one of its siblings, and the parent key to create a new 4-node.

Let's apply these rules to delete 2 from the example tree. The deletion procedure starts at the root, which is allowed to be a 2-node. Go left to check 9, which is a 2-node and needs to be fixed up before proceeding deeper. This is the first case: 9 is a 2-node, but its sibling has an extra key. Rotate 20 down to join 9, and move 40 up to become the new root.

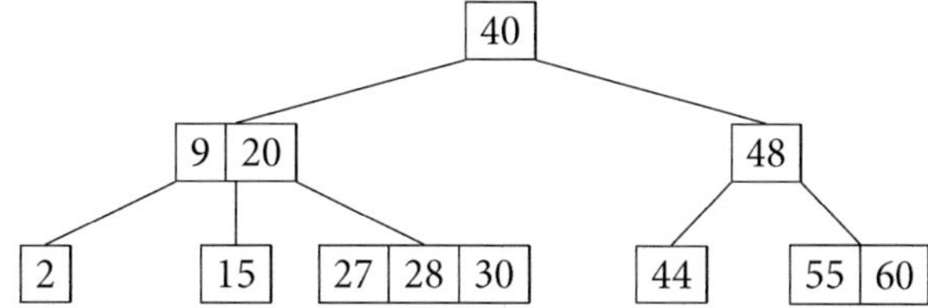

Observe the subtree that moved from the right to the left to stay between 20 and 40.

After fixing 9, the method descends to 2. This is the key we want to delete, but it's a 2-node, so we'll fix it before performing the deletion. The second case applies: Take 9 from the parent and merge 2, 9, and 15 to create a new leaf:

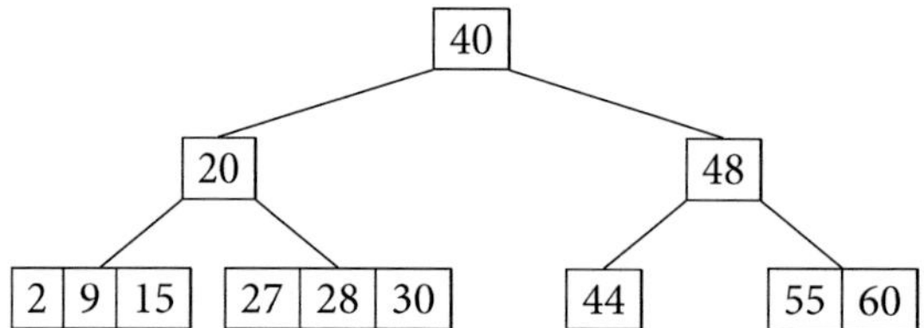

It's now safe to delete 2.

There is a third fix-up case, which occurs when x, its sibling, and their parent are all 2-nodes. This case only occurs when the parent is the root of the tree. The solution is to merge all three values together to create a new 4-node, which becomes the new root, reducing the height of the tree by one. For example, suppose we want to delete 44 from the example tree. Starting from the root, go right to 48, which is a 2-node and needs to be fixed. In this case, 20, 40, and 48 are all 2-nodes, so they're merged to create a new 4-node:

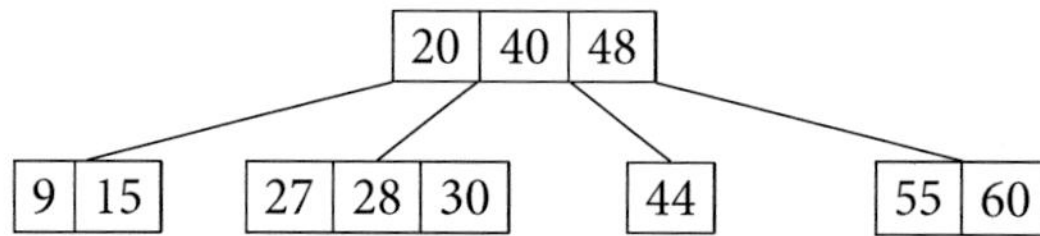

Deleting 44 is an application of the first case: rotate 40 down and 30 up, then remove 44.

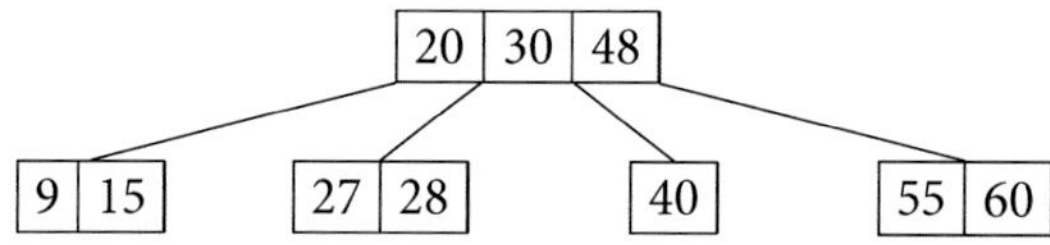

Try It Yourself

Delete 50 from the following 2-3-4 tree, made from only 2-nodes:

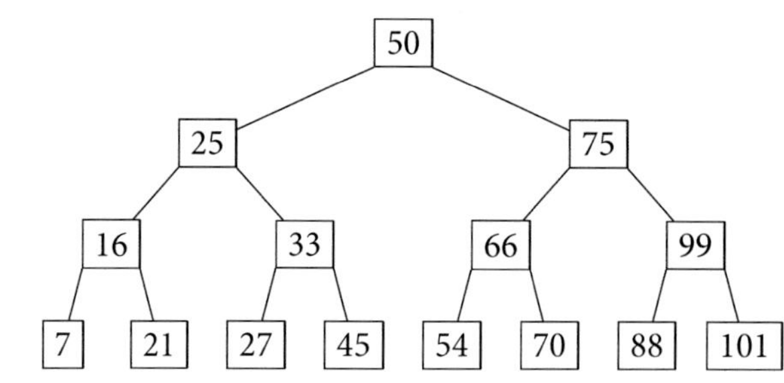

Solution

The overall goal is to swap 50 with its predecessor leaf, 45, and then delete that leaf. The method descends the tree toward the required leaf, fixing up any nonroot 2-nodes it encounters on the way. First, 25, which is in case 3: Merge 25, 50, and 75 to create a new root and reduce the height of the tree:

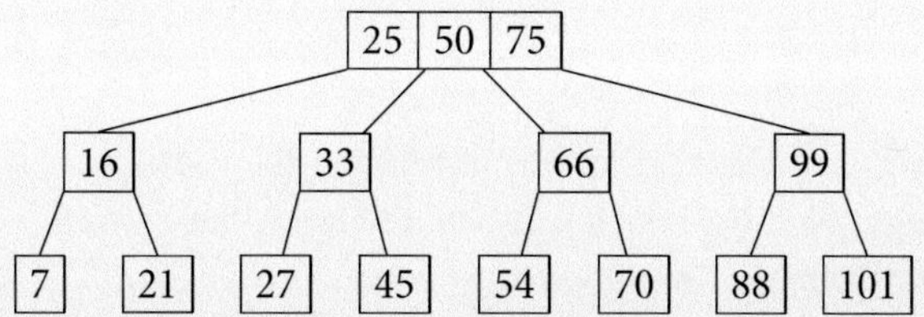

Continuing down, the next 2-node is 33, which is in case 2: Merge 33, one of its siblings, and their parent to create a new middle-level 4-node. In the tree below, we've chosen to merge 16, 25, and 33. This step reduces the number of keys in the root, but that's okay because we fixed the root on the previous step:

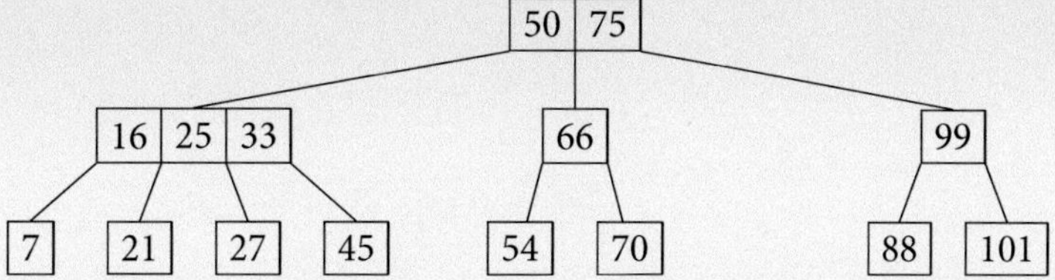

Continuing the descent, we come to 45, the desired leaf. Before performing the deletion, we'll first fix it up by merging 27, 33, and 45 into a new 4-node:

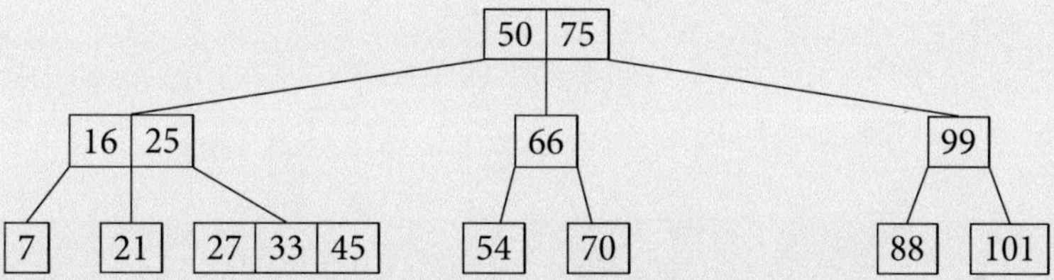

Every 2-node on the path from the root to the leaf has been fixed, so we can now safely perform the deletion. The last step swaps 45 and 50, then deletes 50 from the leaf. The final tree is:

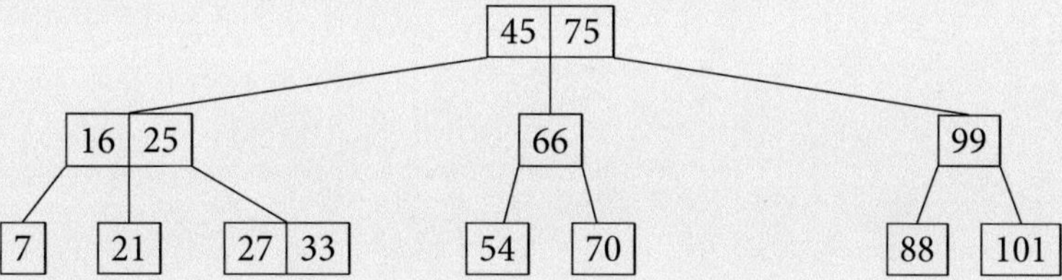

18.1.4 Going Wider: B-trees

B-trees, which generalize the 2-3-4 tree to allow arbitrarily wide nodes, are the most popular data structure for disk-based indices. They were invented in 1970 by Rudolf Bayer and Edward McCreight of Boeing Research (Bayer and McCreight, 1970). Amusingly, Bayer and McCreight never specified what "B" stands for.[3] A B-tree is characterized by its *order*, defined as the maximum number of children that a node may have. A 2-3-4 tree is equivalent to a B-tree of order 4. A B-tree maintains the following invariants on its structure:

3 Suggestions include *Boeing*, *Bayer*, and my personal favorite, *bushy*.

- All leaves appear on the same level.
- If the tree is not empty, the root has at least one key.
- In a B-tree of order m, all nodes other than the root must have at least $m/2$ children, which might be `null` leaves if the node lies on the bottom level. This is equivalent to saying that every nonroot node must contain at least $m/2 - 1$ keys.[4] For example, a tree with $m = 5$ must have at least two keys and three children at every nonroot node.

Compared to a 2-3-4 tree, the main difference is the last property, which is like a density requirement that prevents nodes from becoming too empty.

B-tree insertion uses the same rule as the 2-3-4 tree: Insert new keys into the appropriate leaf until the node fills, then split it. For example, suppose we insert 7 into the following tree of order 5:

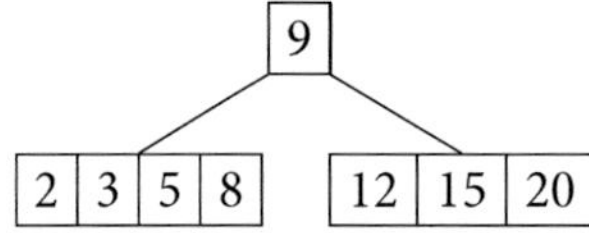

Inserting 7 makes the left leaf full, so it splits in half. The median is promoted up to the parent and the remaining nodes divide into two new leaves:

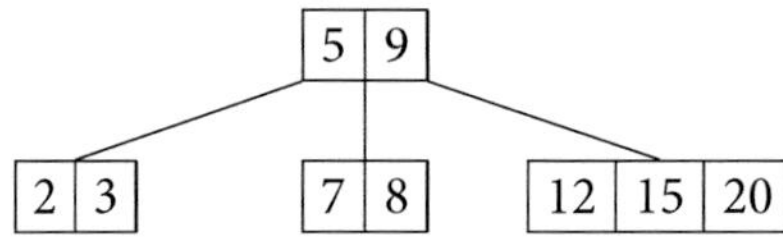

Try It Yourself

Continue inserting 30 and then 18 into the example tree.

Solution

Here, 30 becomes the fourth key in the right leaf. Inserting 18 triggers a split. The two smaller keys, 12 and 15, become one leaf, and 20 and 30 become the other.

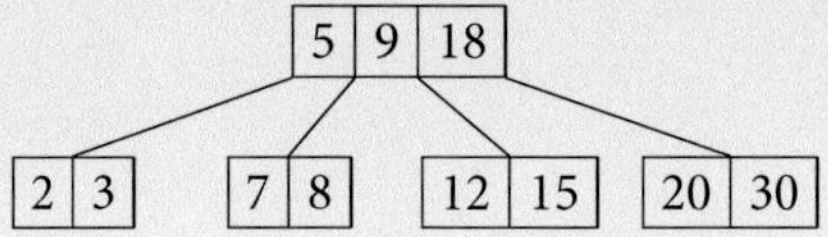

Deletion is again similar to 2-3-4 tree deletion, but with the requirement to maintain at least $m/2 - 1$ keys in every node. For example, suppose we remove 12 from the tree above:

- Deleting 12 would leave 15 alone in a leaf. A B-tree of order 5 needs at least two keys in every node.
- Both of 15's siblings have only two keys, so stealing isn't possible.

4 If this number is fractional, then round up to get the minimum number of keys.

- The next choice is to take a key from the parent and merge it into a new leaf node. If we merge 15 with its left sibling and their shared parent, then delete 12, the result is the tree below, which is valid.

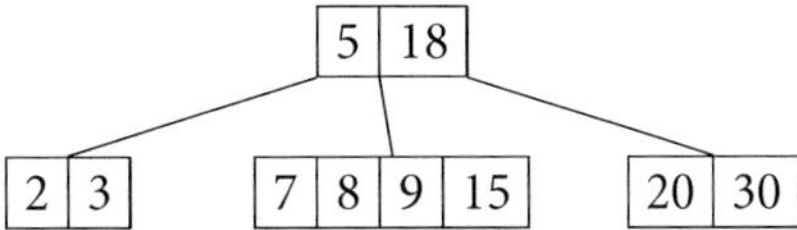

B-trees can use either bottom-up or top-down deletion. The bottom-up case first deletes the key, then ascends the tree to fix any deficiencies. The top-down strategy is similar to the 2-3-4 approach: As you descend the tree, look for any nodes that have the minimum number of keys and fix them up so that you can safely remove at the leaf level.

18.2 Red–Black Trees

The **red–black tree** is a binary search tree that uses coloring rules to ensure the tree stays balanced. Every node is colored either "red" or "black," and the tree enforces rules on the ordering of red and black nodes. As we'll discuss, following these rules guarantees that the tree must be roughly balanced: Specifically, the longest path in the tree can never be more than twice as long as the shortest path. Red–black trees are widely used in practice; Java's `TreeMap` class uses one for its internal implementation. Red–black trees are complicated, but at this point you have all the tools you need to master them. There are five things you need to understand to handle red–black trees:

- How the tree handles `null` references, which differs from our previous trees.
- The rules for maintaining red–black relationships in the tree, and how these rules relate red–black trees to 2-3-4 trees.
- The argument that maintaining the red–black relationships keeps the tree balanced.
- The detailed rules for insertion and deletion, which include steps for rotating a subtree to restore the correct red–black relationships when they break. The connection to 2-3-4 trees is very helpful for understanding the different cases.

18.2.1 Red–Black Ordering Rules

Leaf nodes are handled a bit differently in a red–black tree than our previous search trees. Recall that we defined a leaf to be a node that has no children – that is, a node whose `left` and `right` references are both `null`. For the most part, we've ignored these `null` references, and treated them as implicitly present, even if we didn't draw them in our example trees. In a red–black tree, these `null` values are part of the structure of the tree. They're treated as extra nodes that are always colored **black**. We'll call these nodes the *`null` leaves*. The figure below shows an example red–black tree with its black `null` leaves at the end of every path.[5]

5 In practice, it's common to allocate one bottom-level `null` leaf node and make all paths end with a reference to it, rather than separate `null` leaves for every path.

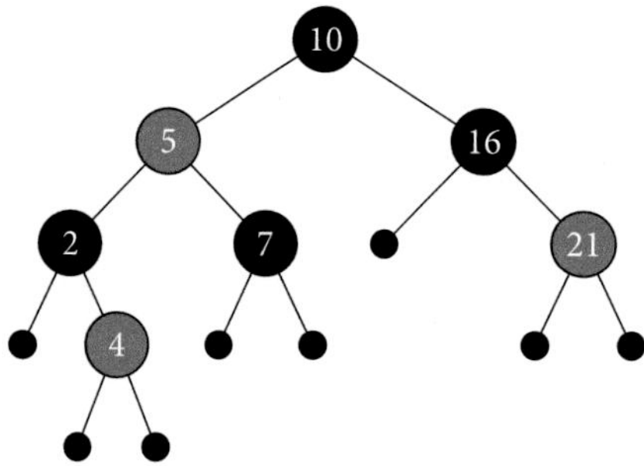

The arrangement of red and black nodes obeys the following rules:

- Every node is colored either red or black.
- The root is black.
- Every `null` leaf is black.
- Every red node has only black children.
- All paths from any node to its descendant `null` leaves contain the same number of black nodes.

It's not clear why any of this is helpful. Consider the following intuitive argument for why the red–black tree is balanced:

- For any node, all paths descending from it have the same number of black nodes. Therefore, the tree can't become unbalanced by one subtree having a longer path of black nodes than its sibling – we'll have to describe how to maintain this property, of course, but for now let's assert that it's possible.
- Therefore, if the tree is unbalanced, it must be from adding additional *red* nodes.
- But the rules of the tree don't allow consecutive red nodes, so the longest possible path through the tree is one that alternates black and red nodes. That path is at most twice the height of the shortest possible path containing only black nodes.

Taken together, the red–black coloring rules guarantee that paths through the tree must be approximately balanced. In the tree above, observe how the difference in height at every level is bounded.

Try It Yourself

Color the tree below according to the red–black rules.

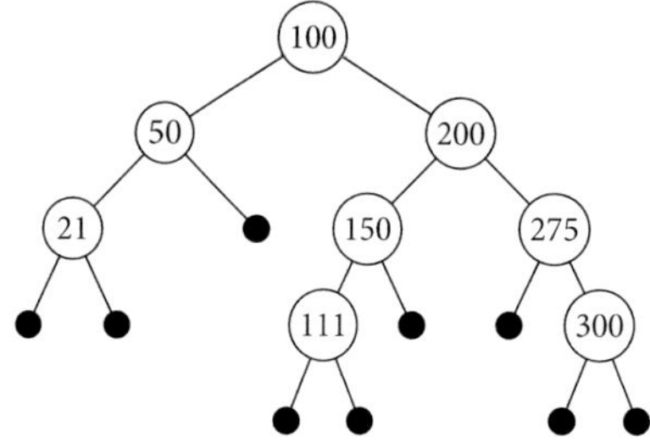

18.2.2 Connection to 2-3-4 Trees

The red–black tree was originally invented by converting the 2-3-4 tree into a binary tree (Guibas and Sedgewick, 1978). Although the 2-3-4 tree is balanced, implementing it requires managing all of the cases for the different kinds of nodes, orderings of keys, and so forth. As we'll see, the red–black tree has its own set of cases that have to be considered, but it's easier to implement the required operations in the binary tree format. In a red–black tree, a 4-node corresponds to a black node with two red children. Observe how the ordering of nodes in the binary tree matches that in the 2-3-4 tree: *a* is less than *x*, which is less than *y*; *b* is greater than *x*, but less than *y*, and so forth.

A 3-node becomes a black node with one red child, which can be on either the right or left, depending on the arrangement of the keys.

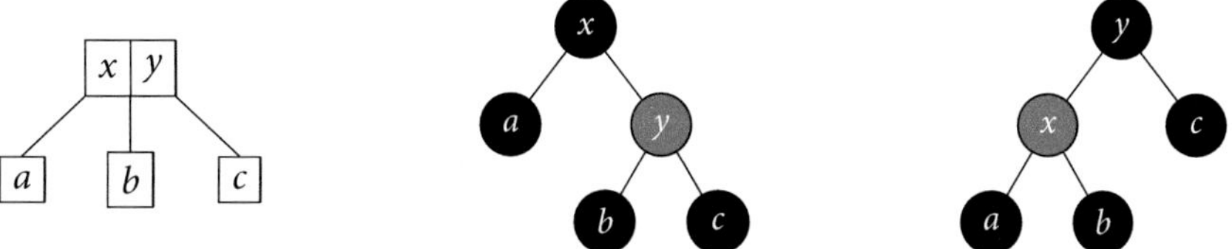

A 2-node is a black node with no red children, as in a regular binary tree.

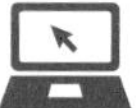

Try It Yourself

Convert the following 2-3-4 tree to its red–black equivalent.

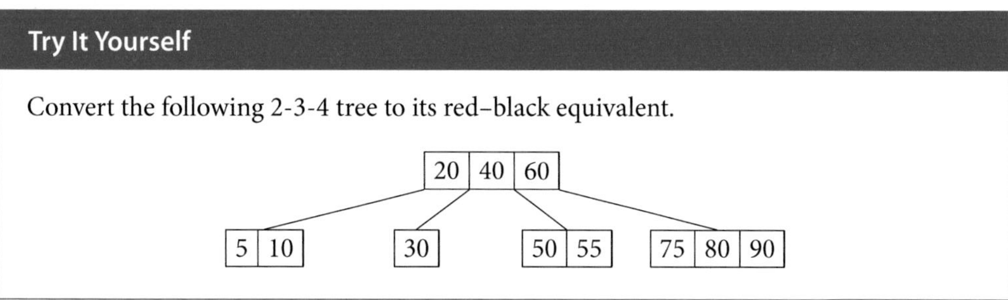

Solution

Multiple solutions are possible, depending on how you convert the 3-nodes. Here's a version that puts the red child of each 3-node on the left side. Tip: Always draw the `null` leaves! Remember that `null` leaves are always black and count toward the number of black nodes on a path.

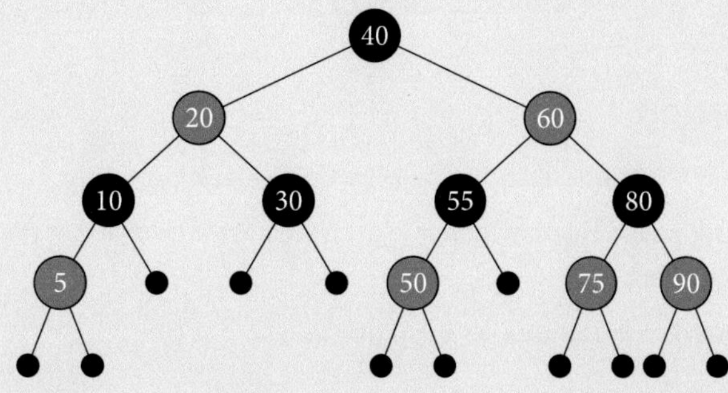

18.2.3 Bounds on the Height of the Tree

We established informally that the tree can't become *too* unbalanced. However, that isn't enough to show that operations on the tree are efficient. This section makes a stronger argument: If the tree has n nodes, then its maximum height is $O(\log n)$ and therefore searches run in logarithmic time. The proof has two parts:

- First, we'll reason about the relationship between the height of the longest path in the tree and the number of black nodes that path could contain. This will yield an inequality that bounds the height of the tree.
- Second, we'll consider the relationship between the number of nodes in the tree, n, and the number of black nodes. This will allow us to restate the first inequality and bound the height h in terms of n.

Define the *black height* of a node x to be the number of black nodes on any path from x to one of its descendant `null` leaves, not including x itself (so it doesn't matter whether x is colored red or black). Let $bh(x)$ be the black height of node x and h be the height of x's subtree. We've already established that the minimum length path from x to a `null` leaf contains only black nodes, and the longest possible path alternates red and black nodes. Therefore,

$$bh(x) \leq h \leq 2\,bh(x).$$

Now let $n(x)$ be the number of internal non-`null` nodes in x's subtree, including x itself. What is the relationship between $n(x)$ and the black height? Intuitively, $n(x)$ is minimized if the subtree contains only black nodes, because adding any red nodes would allow us to increase $n(x)$ without increasing the black height. Recall that all paths from x to any of its leaves must have the same number of black nodes, so this case occurs if the subtree is a perfect binary search tree with only black nodes. Experiment with a few trees of different black heights, and you can verify that

$$n(x) \geq 2^{bh(x)} - 1.$$

For example, a subtree with a black height of 3 must have at least 7 internal non-`null` nodes. Rearranging gives a bound on the black height in terms of $n(x)$:

$$bh(x) \leq \log(n(x) + 1).$$

Applying this relationship to the root and n nodes in the entire tree gives a logarithmic bound on the height:

$$h \leq 2 \log(n + 1).$$

Therefore, a red–black tree with n nodes has a height that is $O(\log n)$.

18.2.4 Insertion

There are two ways to think of inserting into a red–black tree:

- as inserting into a regular binary search tree, with additional steps to maintain the red–black properties; and
- in terms of the operations on the equivalent 2-3-4 tree.

Try It Yourself

Suppose that we begin with the following red–black tree and want to insert 99. Where should it go and what color should it be?

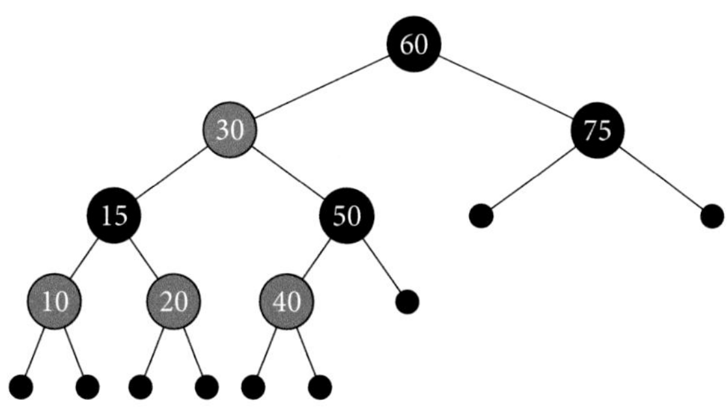

Solution

Clearly, 99 should become the right child of 75, just like in a regular binary search tree. Coloring it red maintains the black height of every path. This is the first rule of red–black insertion: Place the new node using the standard binary search tree procedure and always color it **red**.

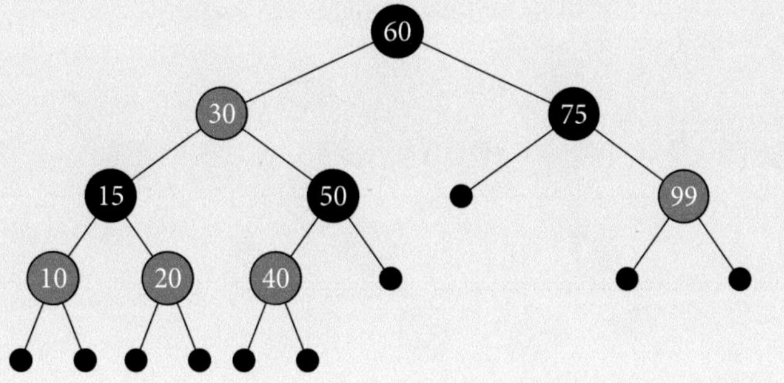

From a 2-3-4 tree perspective, adding a new red node corresponds to adding a new key into a leaf. The tree above is equivalent to the following 2-3-4 tree:

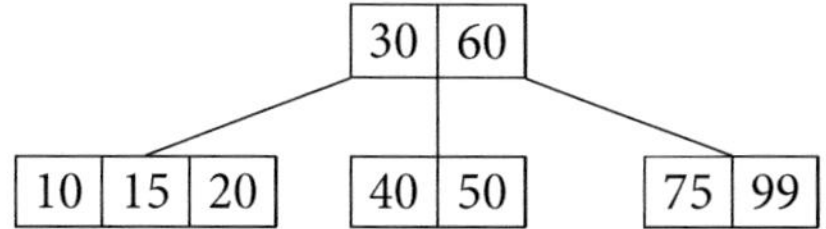

Try It Yourself

Adding a new red node can't change the black height, but how could it cause a problem?

Solution

Consecutive red nodes aren't allowed, so adding a red node will cause a problem if the parent is also red. Therefore, if the insertion *doesn't* create two consecutive red nodes, no further work is required and the procedure ends immediately.

In general, though, we may need to fix up the tree to deal with consecutive red nodes. Suppose that we insert 35:

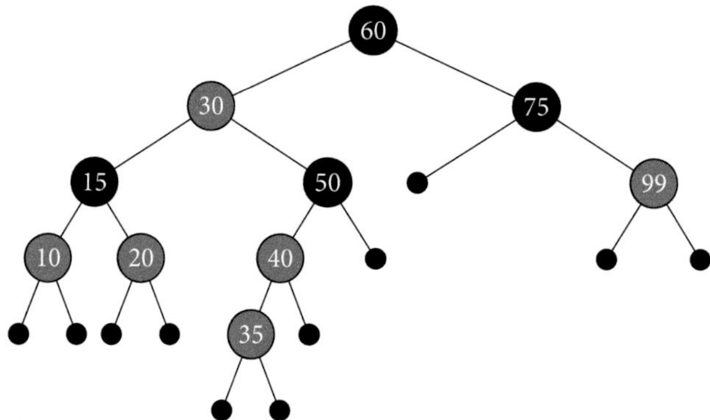

From a 2-3-4 perspective, adding 35 corresponds to making the 3-node containing 40 and 50 into a 4-node.

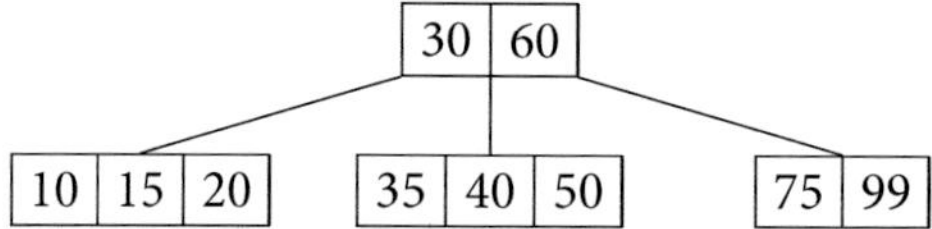

The double-red problem can be resolved by rotating the subtree to bring 40, the median key, up to the top, then recoloring 50 to maintain the black height:

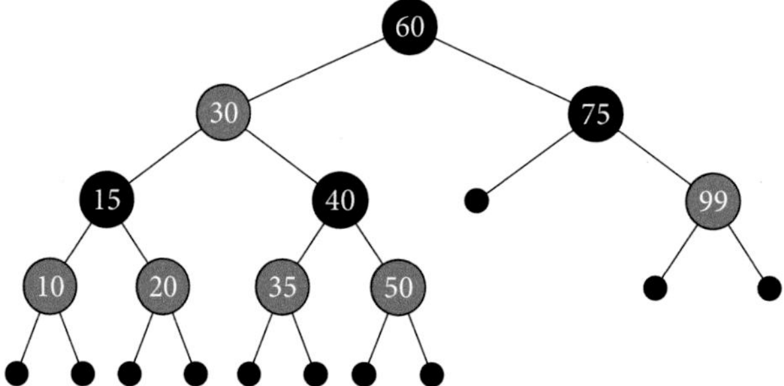

This is the first complex insertion case: consecutive red nodes that can be fixed by performing a subtree rotation. There are four possible cases, shown in Figure 18.1, which depend on the orientation of the new node to the other nodes in the subtree. The relevant players are:

- x, the new node, which is always colored red;
- p, the parent of x, which must also be red – if p was black, there would be nothing to fix;
- g, which must be black, because p is red and the tree couldn't have had consecutive red nodes before inserting x;
- u, the uncle of x, which in these cases must also be black, because we're assuming p and g correspond to a 3-node in the equivalent 2-3-4 tree. Note that u could be a `null` leaf, as it was in the last example; and
- any other attached subtrees, a, b, c, d, and e. The exact nature of these attachments depends on the configuration and where we are in the fix-up process. If x is at the bottom level, like it was in the last example, these will be `null` leaves or not present, but they may be non-`null` subtrees if we're performing operations higher in the tree.

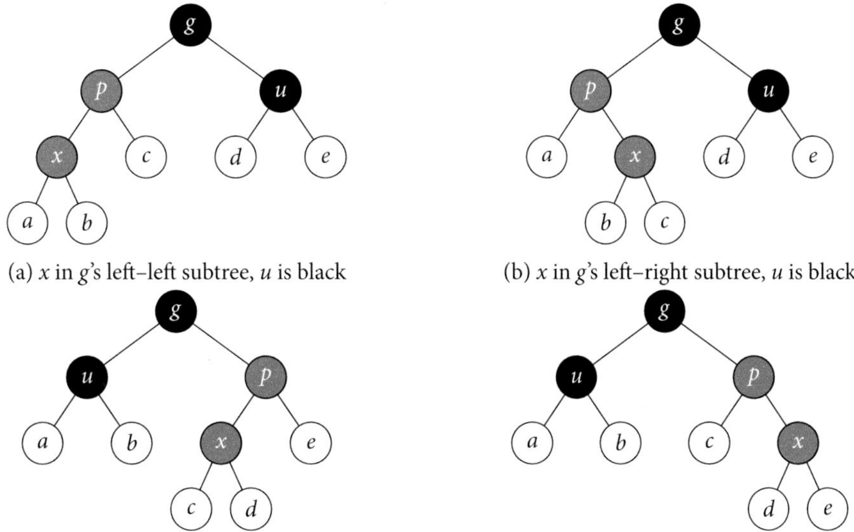

(a) x in g's left–left subtree, u is black (b) x in g's left–right subtree, u is black

(c) x in g's right–left subtree, u is black (d) x in g's right–right subtree, u is black

Figure 18.1 The four cases where x has a red parent p and a black uncle u

In every case, the goal is to rotate the subtree so that the median of x, p, and g moves up to become the new root. Start by considering case (a), the "left–left" case, where x is in g's leftmost subtree. Here, p is the median, so it should move up to the top. Recoloring g maintains the black height.

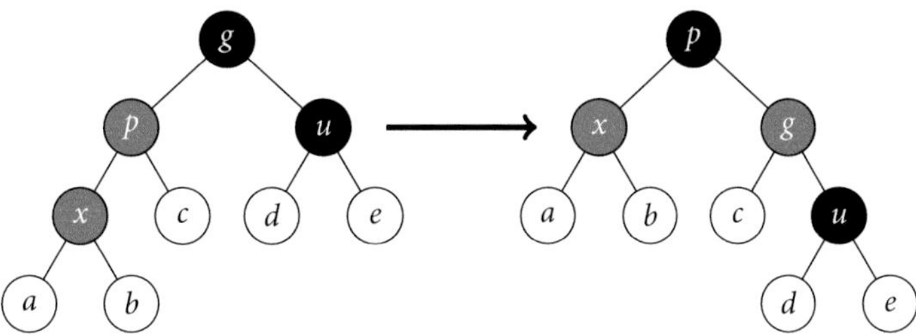

Case (b) is the "left–right" case, where x is the left inner grandchild. Observe that, in this case, x is the median, so it should move up to the top. The left–right rotation first turns p's subtree to the left to bring x up. Observe how subtree b moves to maintain the correct ordering.

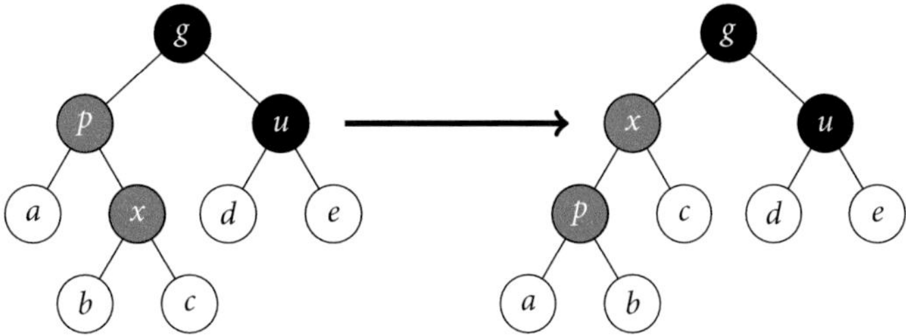

The tree is now in the left–left case, where p is in the position of the new node. Perform the right rotation to bring x to the top and g to the right, then color g red. Notice that c moves to remain in the position of being greater than x but smaller than g.

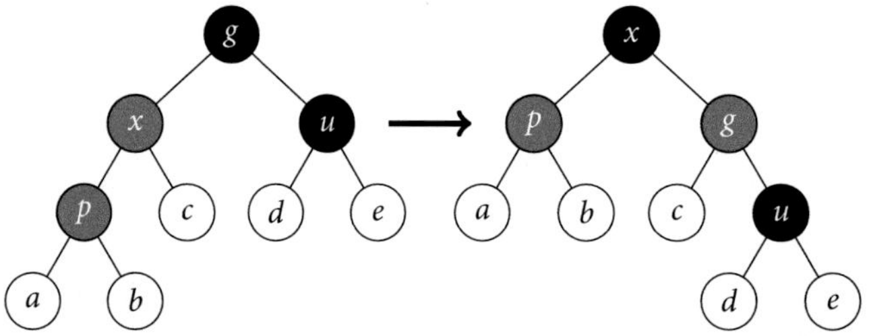

Try It Yourself

Cases (c) and (d) are the right-side mirrors of (a) and (b) and use the same rotations, just from the other side. Modify the left–right case to fix up the following tree, which is in case (c).

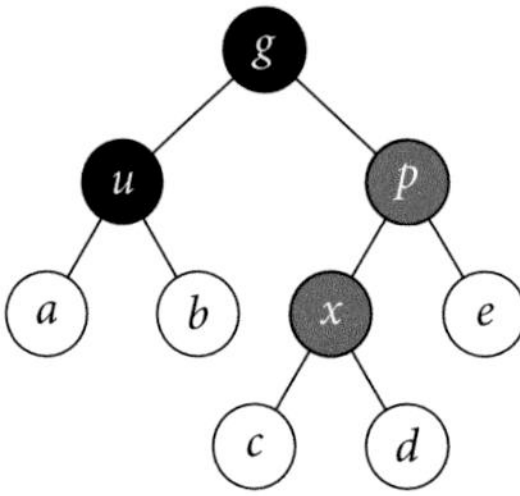

Solution

First, rotate p's subtree to the right to bring x up and p down. Then rotate the entire tree to the left to make x the new root and recolor to obtain the solution:

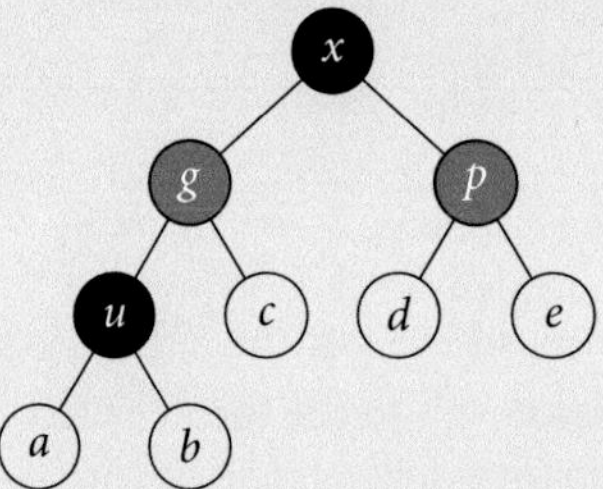

All four cases in Figure 18.1 had a black uncle u. The other insertion case occurs when u is red. Suppose that we insert 12 into the example tree. It becomes a new red leaf with 10 as its red parent and 20 as its red uncle.

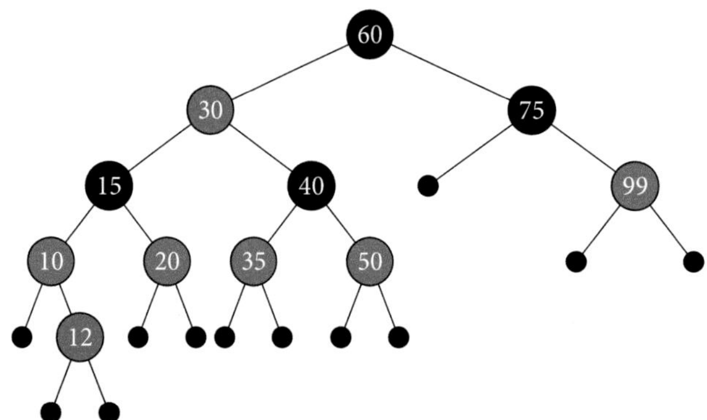

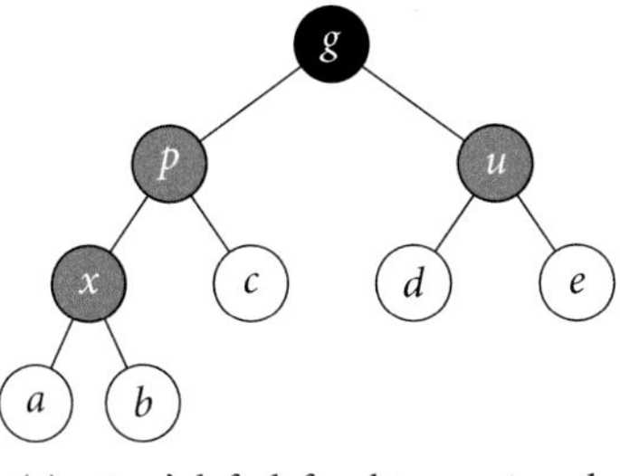

(a) x in g's left–left subtree, u is red

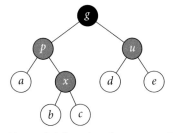

(b) x in g's left–right subtree, u is red

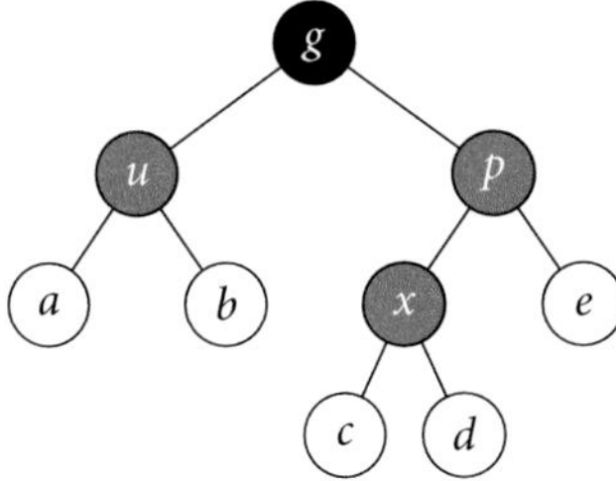

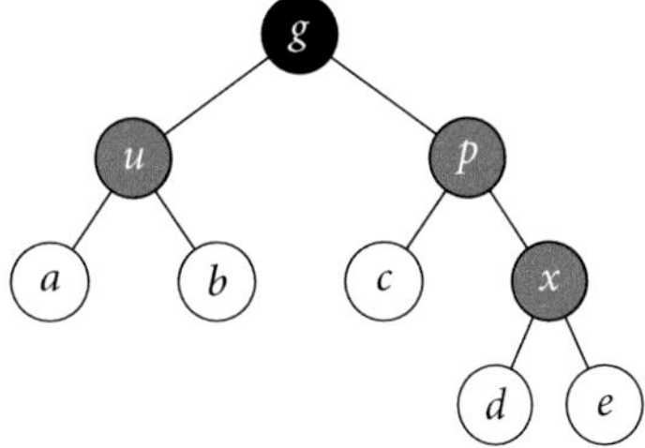

(c) x in g's right–left subtree, u is red

(d) x in g's right–right subtree, u is red

Figure 18.2 The four cases where x has a red uncle u

In the 2-3-4 tree, this corresponds to inserting a key that overfills a 4-node, which was resolved by splitting the node and moving one of its keys up to the parent level.

Figure 18.2 shows the four possible red-uncle cases, which again depend on the four possible relationships between p and x. All four cases use the same resolution strategy: Recolor p and u to black and g to red. In the 2-3-4 tree, this corresponds to promoting g up one level and splitting its children into separate leaves.

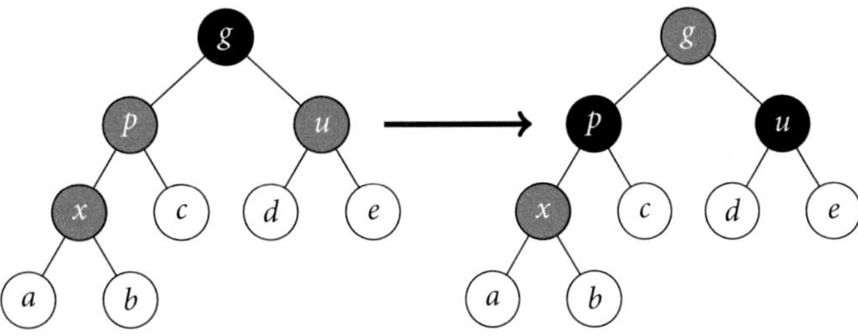

Try It Yourself

Explain why recoloring g might cause a problem.

Solution

If g's parent is black, then making g red causes no issue, but if g's parent is red then we've just created consecutive red nodes. Therefore, after recoloring, move up the tree by making g the active node and checking its parent to determine if further changes are required. If so, treat g as if it was a newly inserted node and apply the appropriate case.

Try It Yourself

Use the fix-up rules to restore the tree after inserting 12.

Solution

The fix-up procedure starts by considering 12. It has a red uncle, so the immediate fix is to recolor 10, 15, and 20.

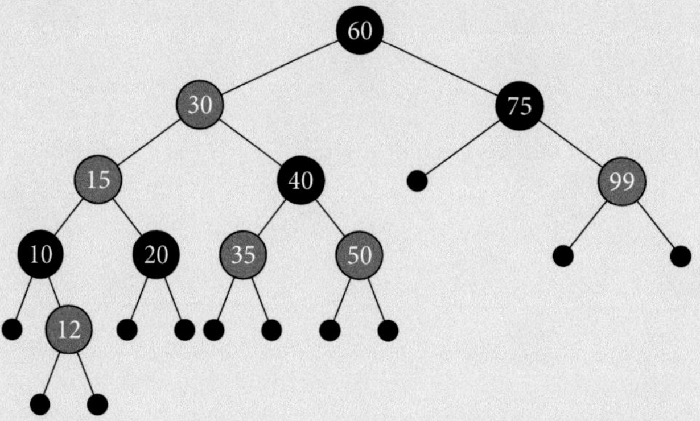

This is not a stable solution, though, because recoloring 15 creates consecutive red nodes. Make 15 the active node and consider the tree as if it was just inserted; 15's uncle, 75, is black, and it's the left–left grandchild of 60, so the solution is to rotate to the right. The challenge with the higher-level rotation is keeping track of the subtrees. A good strategy is to reduce the tree to only the essentials, with placeholders for the subtrees:

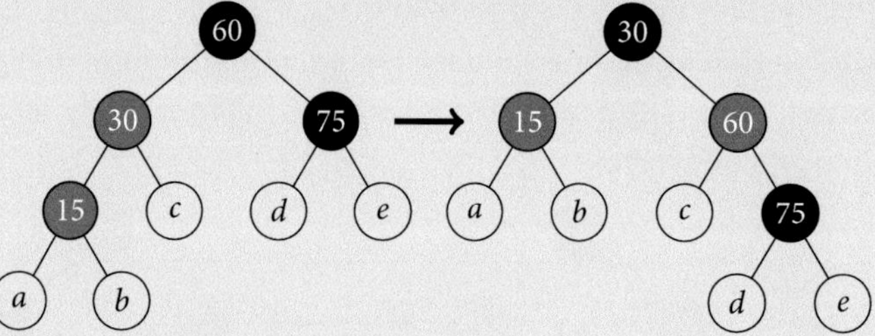

You can then substitute the subtrees back in to recover the complete tree.

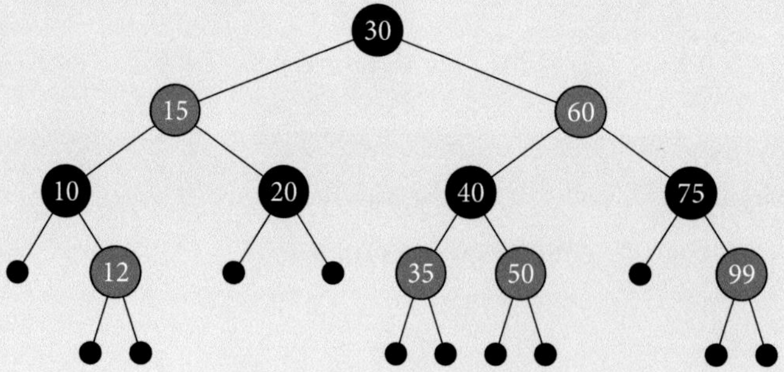

18.2.5 Deletion

Red–black deletion starts with the same approach as a regular binary search tree. First, locate the key; if it's in an internal node, swap it with its successor key in its right subtree.[6] After those steps, we'll have identified a node x that's ready to delete. Note that x can't be an internal node, by how the process works, so it has at most one non-`null` child. There are three cases to consider:

6 Or predecessor in the left; we'll use the successor in this section.

- x is red with two `null` children, like 99 in the tree above.
- x is black with one red child, like 10.
- x is black with two `null` children, like 20.

Note that a red node can't have only one non-`null` black child, because then one subtree would have more black nodes than the other, which isn't allowed.

Try It Yourself

Explain how to resolve the first two cases.

Solution

If x is red it can be removed with no other changes. If x is black with a red child, move the child up to take x's place, then color it black. In both cases, x is removed without reducing the black height of any path.

However, if x is black without a red child, then deleting it *will* reduce the black height. In 2-3-4 tree terms, this action corresponds to deleting a 2-node, which creates a hole in the tree that has to be filled. The exact steps to take depend on:

- x, which must be black;
- s, the sibling of x, which could be red or black;
- s's children – the major distinction here is if s has at least one red child vs. no red children; and
- p, the parent, which could be red or black.

Try It Yourself

Suppose you delete 5 from the following tree. Perform a rotation to move 10 into 5's old position and make 12 the new parent, then delete 5. Do you need to do anything different if 10 is red?

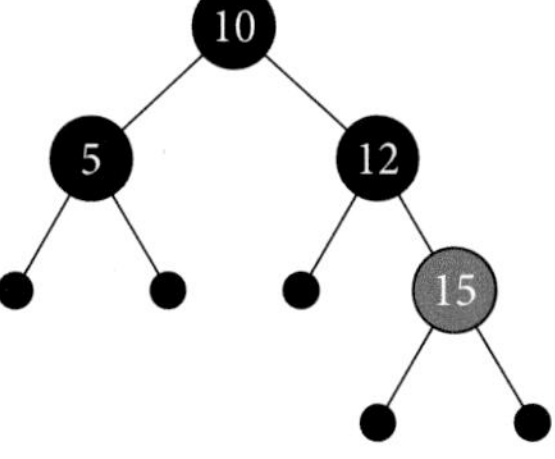

Solution

The rotation turns the tree to the left, and recolors the nephew, 15, from red to black. In 2-3-4 terms, this action corresponds to taking a key from the right subtree and rotating it over to the left to fill 5's position.

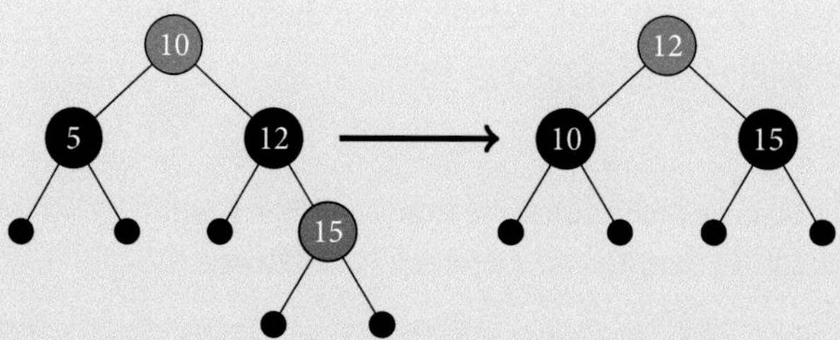

The color of the parent doesn't matter. If it was originally black, we'll keep it black and likewise if it's red. Observe that the black heights through the tree remain the same in either case.

Figure 18.3 shows the general cases where x has at least one red nephew.[7] As before, the letters a through d correspond to any attachments that may be present, depending on where we are in the fix-up process. The parent can be red or black: The value that moves up keeps the parent's old color.

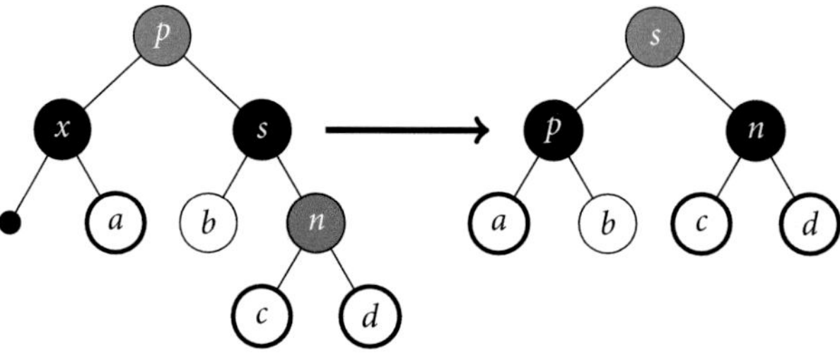

(a) Deleting x when its far nephew n is red. Observe that the roots of any subtrees attached at a, c, and d must be black.

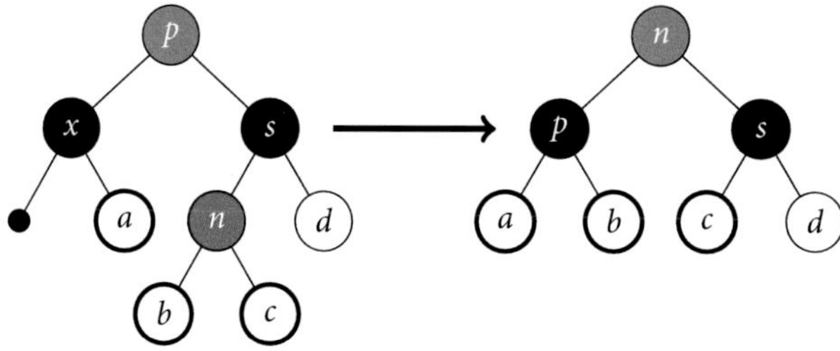

(b) Deleting x when its near nephew n is red. The two-step rotation first turns s's tree to the right to bring n up, then turns the entire tree to the left to make n the new root. If both nephews are red, apply this case.

Figure 18.3 Deleting x by rotating a key from the sibling subtree. The parent p can be either red or black and the color of its node remains the same

Try It Yourself

Consider the trees of Figure 18.3. What 2-3-4 configurations do these correspond to? Explain what the red–black deletion is doing in terms of the equivalent 2-3-4 tree.

7 A tricky detail: The figures show x's left child as `null`, which will be the case if x was selected as the successor node of the deleted key. If you work out the equivalent cases when x was selected as the predecessor node, your professor is required by secret computer science law to give you an automatic A.

Solution

The case where s is black with at least one red child corresponds to the situation where x is a 2-node and its sibling node has an extra key. Ignoring any extra subtrees, here's the case where n is the inner child:

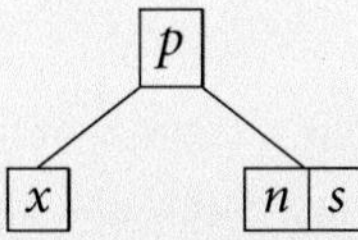

The solution corresponds to deleting x, which makes a hole that's filled by rotating p down and moving n, which is the smallest key in the sibling node, up:

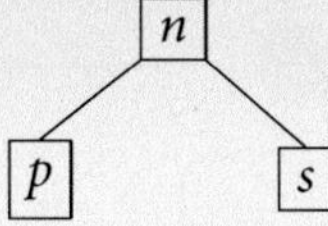

This example has p as a 2-node in the 2-3-4 tree, which would correspond to black. If we made p one key in a 3- or 4-node, then it would be colored red, but that wouldn't change anything. Taking a key from the 2-3-4 sibling doesn't change the number of keys in the parent, so the red–black color is unaffected.

The third easy case occurs when s is black with black children, but p is red. Deleting x removes one black node from the left side, which is balanced by recoloring s to red and making p black. All black heights through the subtree remain unchanged. This is the 2-3-4 merging case: p and s have created a new 3-node.

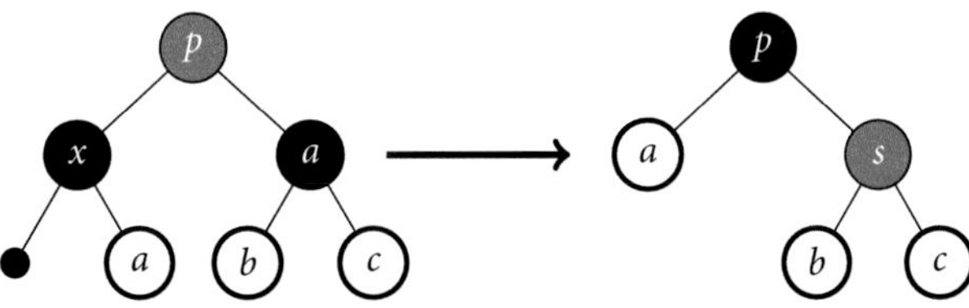

Try It Yourself

Again, explain how that case relates to the equivalent 2-3-4 tree.

Solution

If s is black with black children, then it's a 2-node. If p is red, then it must be part of a 3- or 4-node with at least one other key. Here, let q be some other parent key and t be some other leaf:

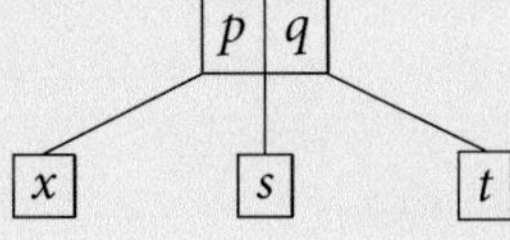

The solution corresponds to merging p and s into a new 3-node.

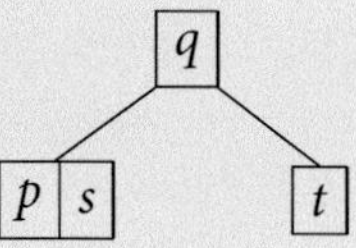

In some cases, though, making one change is not enough to fully rebalance the tree. The first such case occurs if s is black with black children, but p is also black. Recoloring s to red balances the black node lost by deleting x:

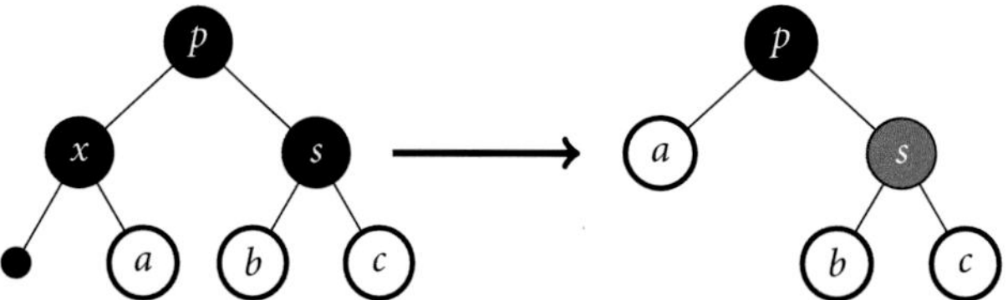

However, the black height of the entire subtree has been reduced by one, so it won't be in balance with the rest of the tree. The only choice is to continue the rebalancing process one level higher. To make this easier to track, we'll add a "phantom" node as a new parent of p. This isn't a real node and it doesn't have a key – it's a placeholder that represents the black node that was lost by deleting x. Choosing the operations that delete the phantom node will balance the tree.

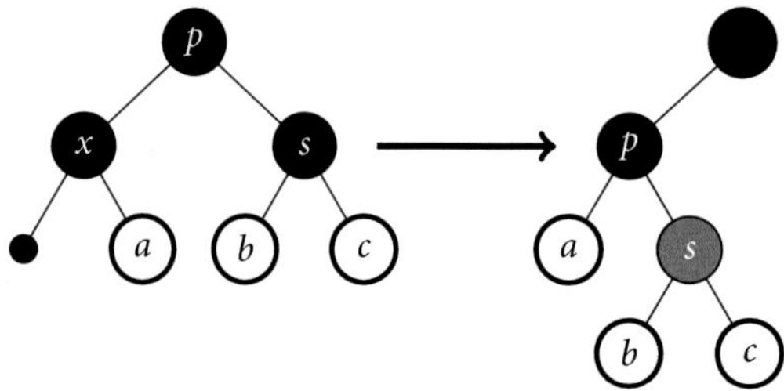

Try It Yourself

Delete 5 from the following tree.

Solution

Here, 5 has a black sibling, black nephews, and black parent. Recoloring 12 to red will balance the deletion, but we have to move one level higher to fix the black heights. Using the "phantom" node technique, we'll add an extra black node above 7 and then choose the operation required to delete it.

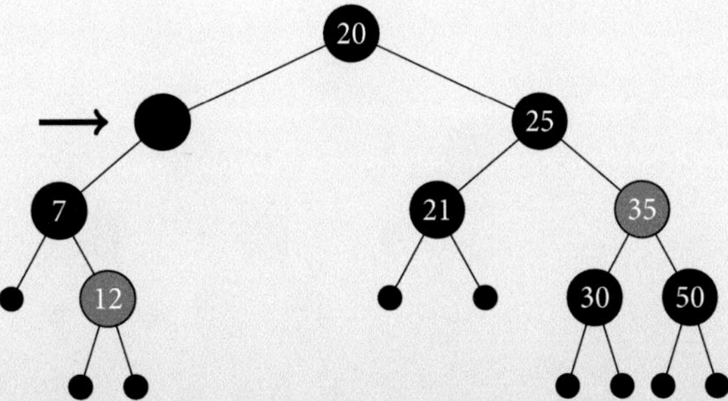

The phantom node has a black sibling (25) and a red far nephew (35), so we can apply a left rotation to delete the phantom node and bring 20 down, which balances the tree.

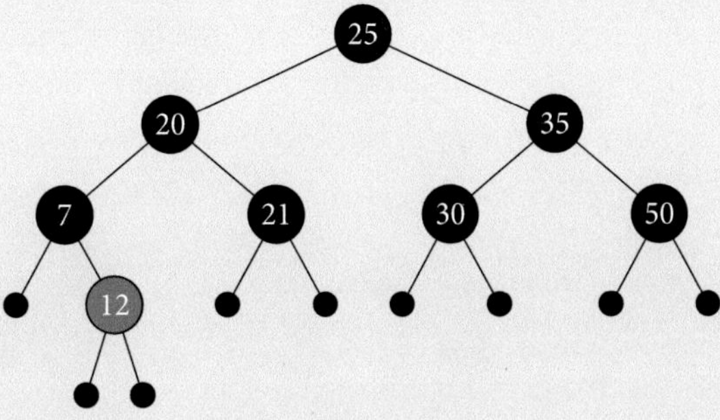

The final case occurs when s is red with black children. Deleting x removes a black node from the left side, which we'll balance by rotating p down and coloring it red.

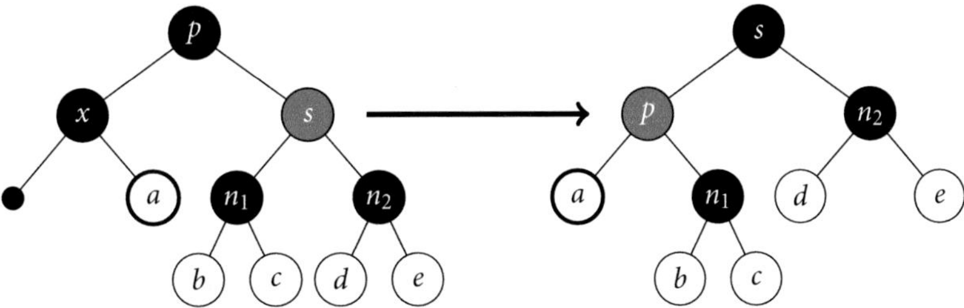

Look carefully: The subtree rooted at a has one less black node than n_1. Previously, n_1's subtree was balanced by both x and a together, but we just deleted x. Therefore, we now need to consider the position occupied by a and apply one of the other changes to bring it into balance. Again, the phantom node concept is helpful: We'll make an extra black node to represent the black node that was lost by removing x, then choose the operation that deletes it to balance the tree.

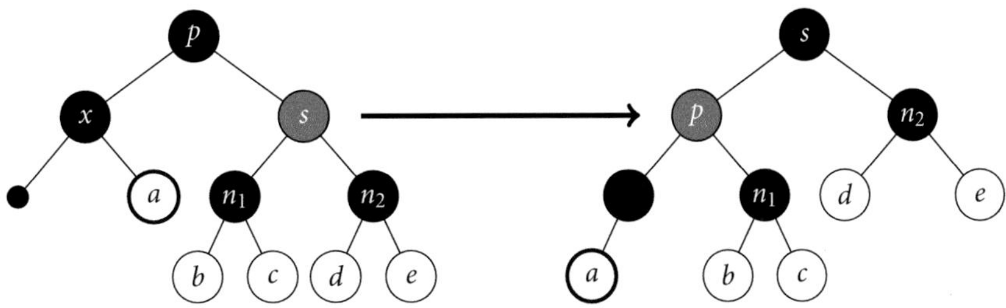

Try It Yourself

Delete 25 from the following tree.

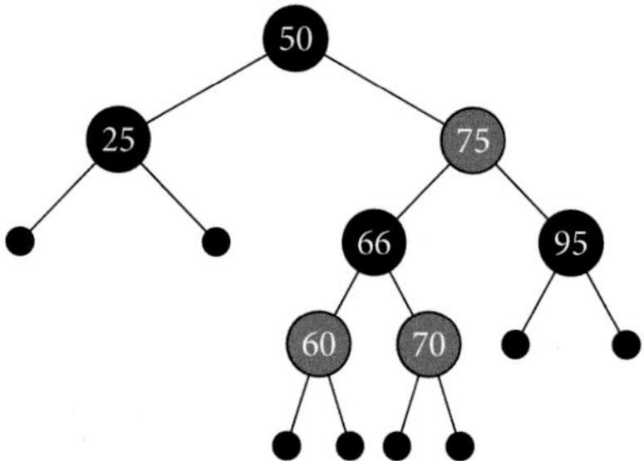

Solution

Here, 25 has a red sibling with black children, so the first move is to rotate the red color over to the left side. This will leave 50's left side deficient by one black node, so we'll add a phantom black node and then choose the operation required to delete it.

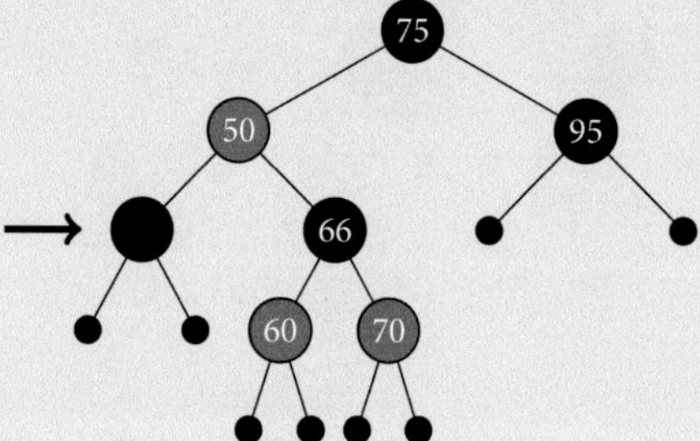

The sibling, 66, is black with red children, so we can do another left rotation to bring 50 down. There are two red nephews, so we'll choose the inner one, 60, to promote to the new root because it's the smallest key in its group.

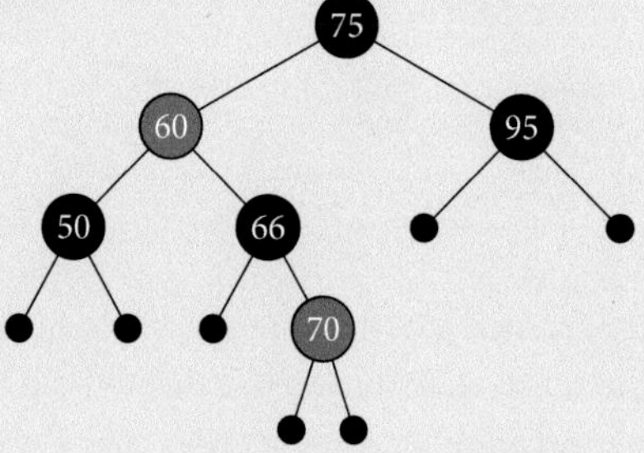

Try It Yourself

Make an argument that insertions and deletions in red–black trees are $O(\log n)$.

Solution

We previously argued that the height of the tree from the root to any leaf is $O(\log n)$. Therefore, the standard binary search tree insertion and deletion procedures are $O(\log n)$. The cost of any extra time required to rebalance the tree is bounded:

- Each rotate and recolor operation manipulates a fixed number of references and fields and therefore takes constant time.
- If we need to ascend the tree to perform rebalancing operations at higher levels, then the maximum number of steps required is still bounded by log n, because the rebalancing procedure performs at most one operation at each level up the tree.

Therefore, adding up all the work required to insert or delete is still $O(\log n)$.

SUMMARY

Self-balancing trees are challenging, but the time you invest in studying them will be well spent. As you work on the exercises, keep these ideas in mind:

- Start by understanding the motivating problem, then the general solution each data structure takes toward addressing that problem.
- Many advanced data structures use an "update then fix" approach, where you perform an operation, then do some extra work to keep the structure in the desired configuration. Updates cost extra time, but are worth it to keep the structure balanced and the overall average operation time low.
- Understanding the intellectual heritage of the tools you use can help you understand them better. In this case, learning about 2-3-4 trees makes it easier to understand both B-trees and red–black trees.

The next chapter introduces the final tree-based data structure: the heap.

EXERCISES

Understand

1. Why do we need self-balancing search trees?
2. List the invariants for a 2-3-4 tree. How does that compare to the invariants for a B-tree?
3. Summarize, in your words, the rules for inserting into a 2-3-4 tree.
4. Repeat the previous question, but for deletion.
5. Color the tree below according to the red–black rules.

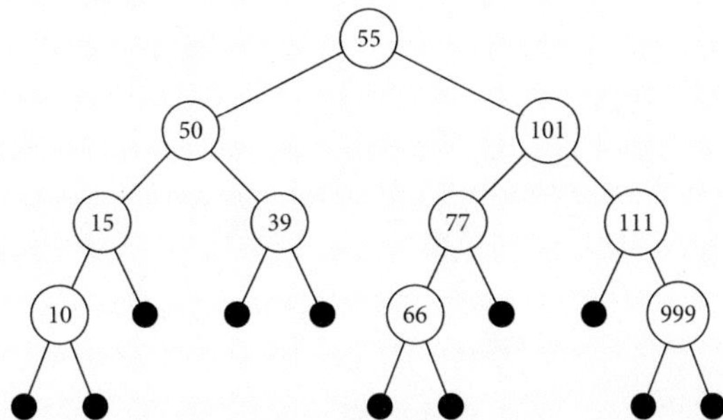

6. What are the minimum and maximum number of keys in a B-tree node of order 333?

7. Write pseudocode for the 2-3-4 lookup procedure. Assume that you have a `TreeNode` that contains a `K[]` containing the node's keys of type `K` and a `TreeNode[] children` containing the references to the next level.
8. Does traversing a red–black tree with an in-order traversal still return the keys in sorted order?
9. Write a method to traverse a red–black tree and verify that it doesn't contain consecutive red nodes. Assume that each node is a `TreeNode` with a `boolean black` field that's `true` if the node is black. Tip: Think recursively.
10. Your friend says that a red node can have a `null` leaf and non-`null` black child. Explain why that's wrong.
11. Your friend has updated their priors and now says that a red node must always have two black children. Is that correct?

Apply

12. Convert the following red–black tree to its 2-3-4 equivalent.

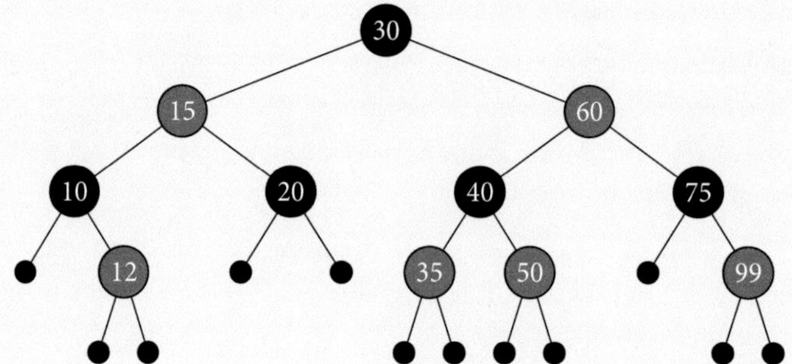

13. Convert the following 2-3-4 tree into its red–black equivalent.

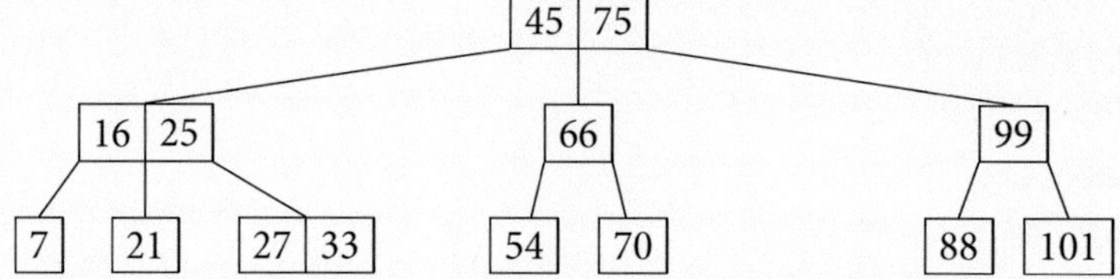

14. How many different valid red–black trees could you make for the 2-3-4 tree in the previous question?
15. Insert 5 into the following red–black tree Tip: Start by fixing the tree rooted at 12, then you'll need to move up the tree.

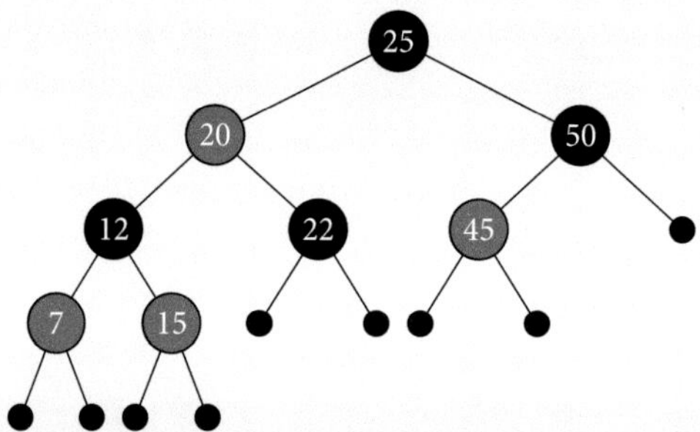

16. Insert the following values, in order, into a 2-3-4 tree: 2, 3, 5, 7, 11, 13, 17, 19.
17. Repeat with a B-tree of order 6.
18. Repeat again with a B-tree of order 3. That is, each node may have at most two keys and have three children.
19. Repeat again with a red–black tree.
20. Delete 8 from the following tree:

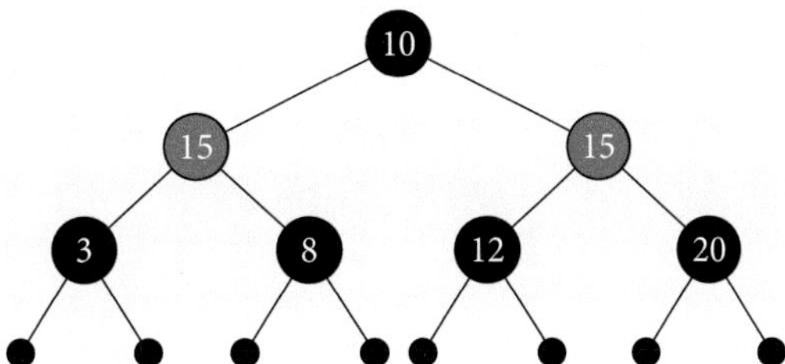

21. Show the 2-3-4 tree corresponding to your solution to the previous problem.
22. Delete 1 from the following tree. Tip: Keep track of which node is active; consider its parent, sibling, and nephews when deciding what case applies.

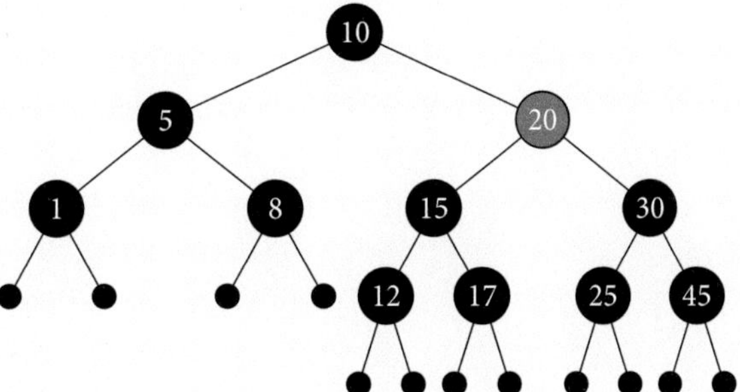

23. Draw out the 2-3-4 tree for the previous problem, before and after performing the deletion. Explain your red–black tree changes in terms of the changes to the corresponding 2-3-4 tree.
24. Write a method called `blackHeight` that takes a red–black `TreeNode` as input and returns the black height of its subtree.
25. Modify your method to check if the black heights of every pair of subtrees are equal. Tip: Look at the example for checking if a tree is balanced in Chapter 17.

Extend

26. Write pseudocode for the insertion rotations from Figure 18.1. Assume that you have references to x, p, g, and u and that each node has a `key` and `color` field.
27. Repeat with Figure 18.2.
28. Write pseudocode to traverse a 2-3-4 tree in sorted order using an in-order traversal. Assume that you have a `TreeNode` that contains a `K[]` containing the node's keys of type `K` and a `TreeNode[] children` containing the references to the next level. Tip: Start with a concrete example.

29. Your friend proposes using a hash table for a disk-based index instead of a B-tree. Do some research into hash-based indexing structures. What are the advantages of a hash table vs. a B-tree and vice versa?

30. Do some more research. What is the preferred way to store the keys and pointers in a B-tree node?

31. Many indexing systems use a variant called the B+-tree. How does it differ from the regular B-tree and what are its advantages?

NOTES AND FURTHER READING

The first self-balancing search tree was the AVL tree, named for its inventors, Georgy Adelson-Velsky and Evgenii Landis (Adelson-Velsky and Landis, 1962). The AVL tree takes a direct approach to keeping the tree balanced: It tracks a *balance factor* for every node, which is the difference in the heights of the node's right and left subtrees.

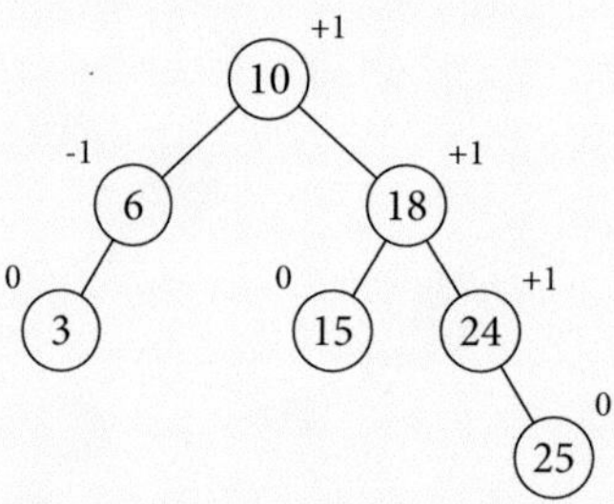

A node with a factor of -1, 0, or $+1$ is considered balanced. If an insertion or deletion ever makes a node unbalanced, perform a rotation to return its subtrees back to balance. AVL rotations are similar to the ones used in the red–black tree.

There is a vast world of self-balancing data structures that you can now explore. A fun variant on the balanced tree concept is the *splay tree* (Sleator and Tarjan, 1985). After every update, the tree does a special "splay" operation that rotates recently accessed nodes toward the top-level root. The tree isn't guaranteed to remain balanced, but promoting recently accessed nodes upward makes them faster to access on future queries, so splay trees are efficient on workloads that exhibit reference locality.

19 Heaps and Priority Queues

Science is built up of facts, as a house is with stones. But a collection of facts is no more a science than a heap of stones is a house.
Henri Poincaré

INTRODUCTION

A **heap** is a tree-based data structure that's designed to quickly return the maximum or minimum of its items. Like a search tree, it maintains a special ordering among its nodes, and takes advantage of the hierarchical nature of binary trees to perform its operations in $O(\log n)$ time. Heaps are the primary implementation of the **priority queue** abstract data type. Like the first-in-first-out queues we studied in Chapter 13, a priority queue supports operations to insert and remove elements, but also maintains an ordering among its items. Polling the queue returns the next item according to the underlying ordering, rather than strictly returning items in FIFO order. Priority queues are used in applications that need to continually fetch the "next" item of a dynamic set that may change over time. A common application is ordering events by time in a simulation program.

LEARNING OBJECTIVES

After studying this chapter, you'll be familiar with:

- The definition and major operations of a heap, including insertion, removing the maximum or minimum item, and initialization.
- Implementing a heap as an *implicit tree packed into an array*. This is a clever technique that is practically important, because it makes heaps a viable solution to problems that require finding the maximum or minimum of an array.
- **Heapsort**, the third major $O(n \log n)$ sorting algorithm.

19.1 Tree-Based Heaps

A heap is a special type of binary tree. A **max heap** is structured so that the root is always the element with the maximum key; likewise, the root of a **min heap** is the element with the minimum key. There are advanced heaps that can track both the maximum and minimum element at the same time, but the standard heap, which we're discussing here, must be either a max heap or a min heap. The basic operation on a heap is to remove and return the current root, then adjust the heap so that the next largest (in a max heap) or smallest (in a min heap) value is promoted to the top.

19.1.1 Definition

A heap is a binary tree that obeys two properties:

- It is *almost-complete*: Every level except possibly the last one is filled, and the nodes on the last level are packed as far to the left as possible. The name indicates that every level has the maximum number of nodes except possibly the last.[1]
- It obeys the *heap property*: In a max heap, every node has a value greater than or equal to its children; likewise, in a min heap every node has a value less than or equal to its children.

Here is one possible min heap constructed from the values `[2, 3, 5, 7, 1, 9]`:

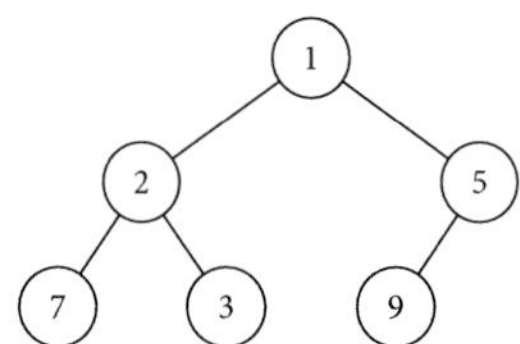

Notice that the heap property doesn't require any particular relationships among nodes in different subtrees. For example, 3 is on a lower level than 5, but this doesn't violate the heap property. A heap isn't a search tree and nodes aren't required to obey any particular left–right ordering. Therefore, checking if the heap contains a particular internal value requires iterating over all the nodes in $O(n)$ time.

Try It Yourself

Construct (by hand) a max heap from the same values.

19.1.2 Inserting into a Heap

Suppose that we have the example heap above and would like to insert the new value 0, which would be the new minimum value and should therefore become the new root of the tree. The insertion process uses two steps:

- Insert the new item at the next open position on the last level. If the last level is full, insert at the first position on the next level.
- Perform an *upward pass* (also called a "heap-up" or "swim" operation) to move the new item into its correct position relative to the other values. The upward pass compares the

1 Many authors use the term "complete" with no qualifications for this property. Others use "complete" to mean a perfect tree that has the maximum number of nodes, which seems more in line with the common definition of the word. Given this inconsistency, we'll use "almost-complete" to make it clear that a heap may have missing nodes, but only on the last level.

new element to its parent, swaps them if they are out of order, then repeats until the element is in a position that satisfies the heap property.

The first step inserts the new item, 0, at the next free position on the bottom level:

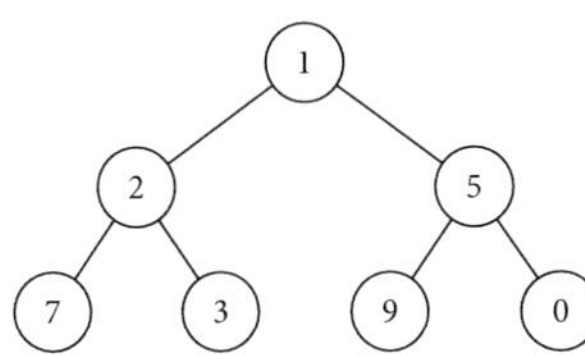

This tree is not a heap, but only because 0 is not in its correct position. The upward pass compares 0 to its parent, 5, finds that 0 is smaller, and swaps the two values:

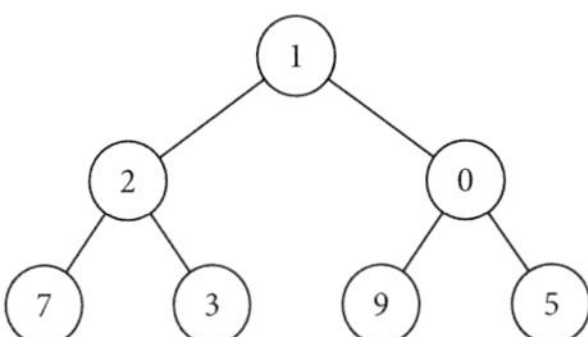

The upward pass continues, comparing 0 to 1 and making 0 the new root.

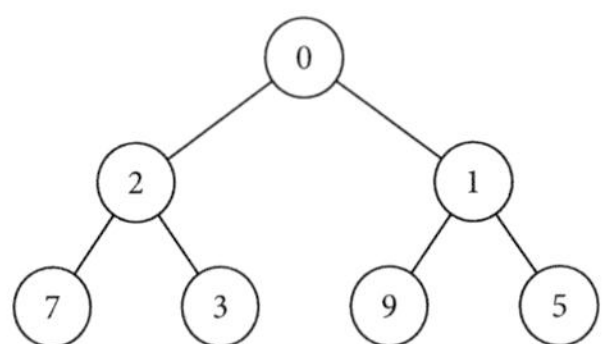

Try It Yourself

Using your example max heap from the previous question, insert the value 10 and perform an upward pass to move it up to the root of the tree.

Try It Yourself

What is the worst-case complexity of the insertion operation? Tip: Think about how many comparisons might be required.

Solution

The insertion operation starts at the bottom level of the tree and, in the worst case, has to rise all the way to the root. The heap is a balanced binary tree, so this requires performing at most $O(\log n)$ operations.

19.1.3 Removing the Root Element

The key operation on a heap is to remove the root element, which represents the min or max of the items and requires two steps:

- Swap the root to the last position in the heap, where it can be delinked from the rest of the tree. The value that was previously at the last position swaps up to the root, where it may violate the heap property.
- Perform a *downward pass* ("heap-down" or "sink") to put the swapped value into its correct position and restore the heap property. The downward pass compares the value to its children and performs a swap if they're out of order, then continues until the value reaches its correct position in the tree.

Suppose that we want to remove the minimum element from the following heap:

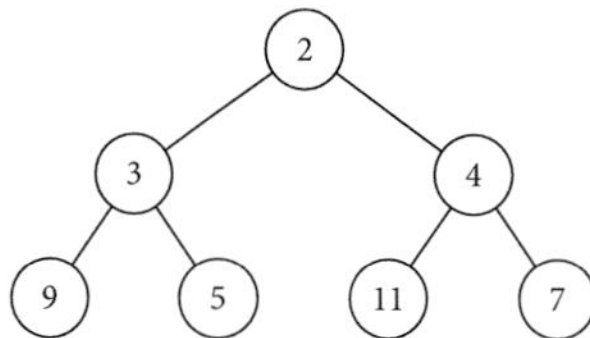

First, swap the root, 2, with the last element, 7, so that 2 can be delinked without affecting the rest of the tree.

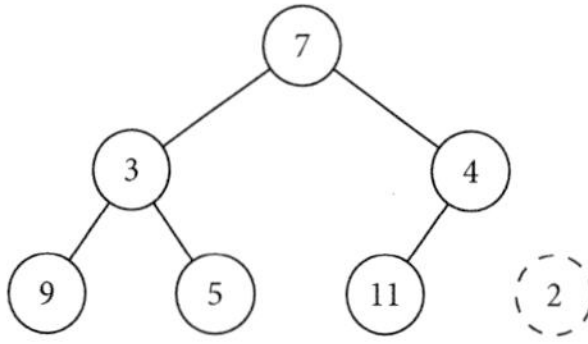

Before returning 2 as the result, we have to restore the heap by putting 7 into its correct position. The downward pass compares 7 to its children, discovers 3 is the smallest, and promotes it to the new root.

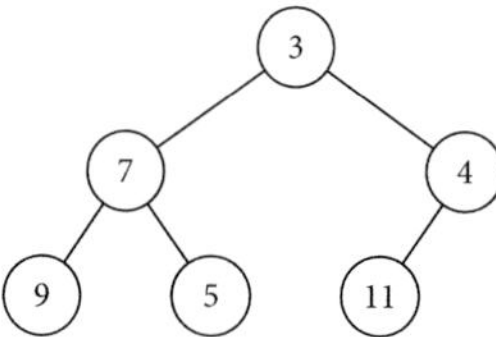

The pass continues, comparing 7, 9, and 5 to discover that 5 should be promoted.

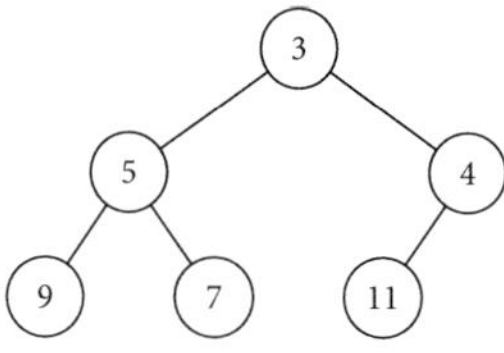

Like the upward pass, the worst case for a downward pass might require traversing the entire height of the heap, so it's also $O(\log n)$.

Try It Yourself

Remove the root of the following max heap and then perform a downward pass to restore the heap property.

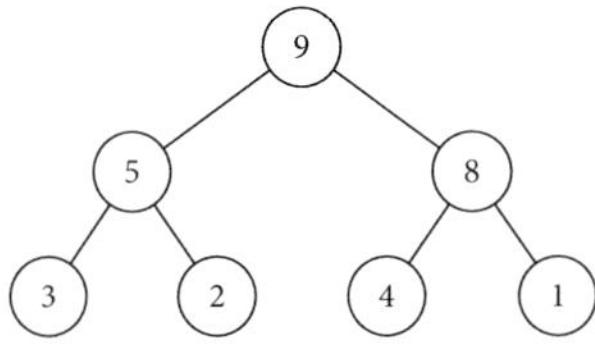

19.1.4 Initializing a Heap

In some cases you have a collection of items given as a list or array and want to turn them into a heap. You could do this by *successive insertions*: Start with an empty heap and insert the items one at a time. Each insertion is $O(\log n)$, so the total cost of constructing a heap by repeated insertion is $O(n \log n)$.

Try It Yourself

Build a min heap from the following values using successive insertion: `[3, 7, 5, 2, 1, 9]`.

It isn't obvious that this method can be improved, but it turns out that we can do better using a different strategy:

- Arrange the items into an almost-complete binary tree in level order, with the first item as the root, the second and third items as the first two children, and so forth. This tree will probably not be a heap.
- Starting from the leaves and working up, perform a downward pass *on each subtree*. This method starts with small subtrees that are close to the bottom, then works its way up, heapifying[2] larger subtrees at each level. The final downward pass starts at the root and confirms that the entire tree is a heap.

Let's heapify the array `[2, 10, 3, 5, 9, 7, 1, 6, 4, 8, 0]`. Arrange the values into a binary tree, starting from the root and working in level order:

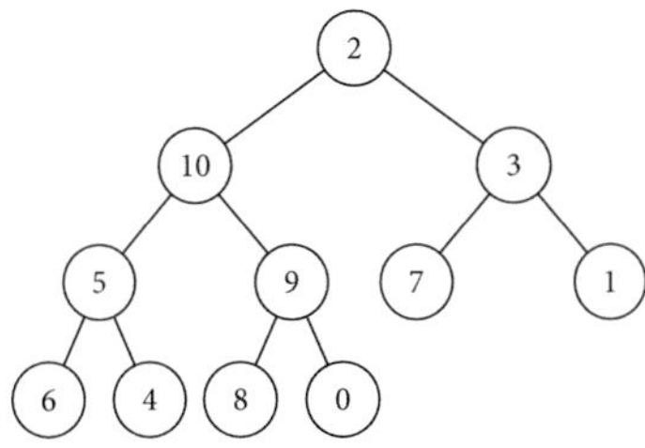

2 This is a valid term for the action of turning data into a heap. You can also use "heapification" if you want more syllables.

The six leaf nodes (7, 1, 6, 4, 8, and 0) have no children and are therefore trivially heaps. The method considers the subtrees rooted at 5 and 9 and heapifies them:

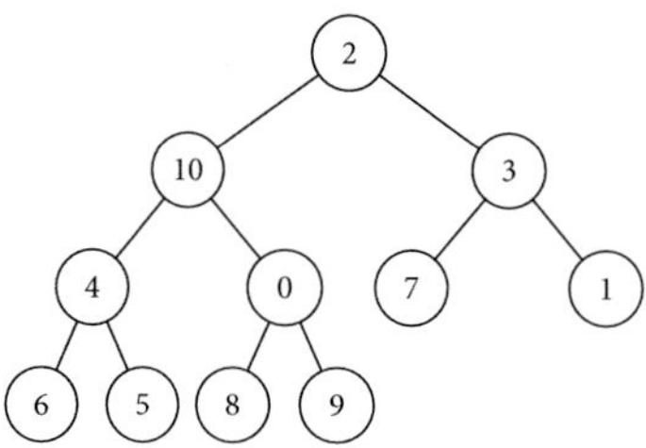

The method then moves up to the next level to perform downward passes on the trees rooted at 10 and 3.

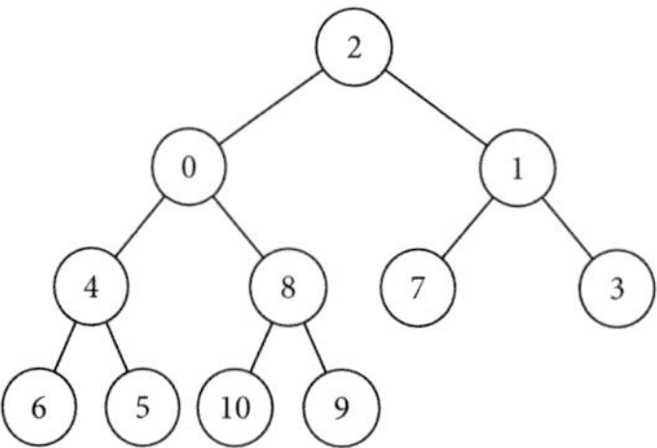

The final downward pass starts at the root and moves the 2 to its correct position, making the entire tree into a heap:

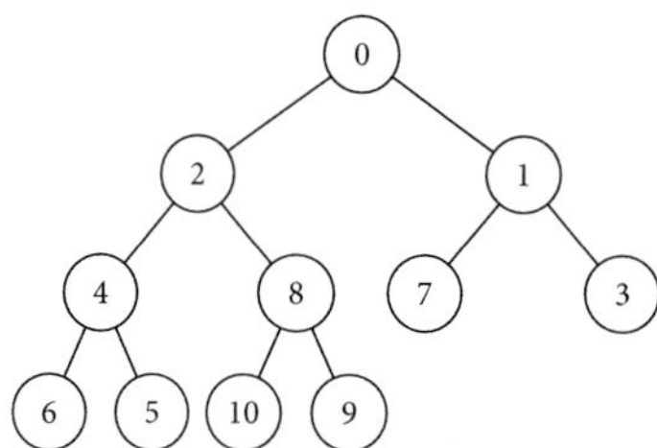

19.1.5 Analysis of Bottom-Up Initialization

It's not obvious, but this method initializes the heap in $O(n)$ operations, rather than the $O(n \log n)$ that would be required for successive insertions. An outline of the argument is as follows (Floyd, 1964):

- About half the nodes in the almost-complete tree are leaves, which require no work on a downward pass (experiment with trees of various numbers of nodes and convince yourself that this is correct). Specifically, there are at most $\lceil n/2 \rceil$ leaves.
- Approximately one-quarter of the nodes are the roots of subtrees that contain at most one other level. Therefore, a downward pass starting at one of these nodes requires at most one compare-and-swap step to turn its subtree into a heap.
- The next level of nodes comprises about one-eighth of the tree and their subtrees contain at most two levels, which requires at most two operations.

This pattern continues up the tree. If we let the work required at level k be proportional to k, the total number of compare-and-swap operations is approximately:

$$T(n) \approx \frac{n}{2}(0) + \frac{n}{4}(1) + \frac{n}{8}(2) + \frac{n}{16}(3) \cdots$$
$$= n\left(\frac{1}{4} + \frac{2}{8} + \frac{3}{16} + \cdots\right).$$

The sum is bounded by 1 and the expression is $O(n)$. Therefore, we expect the work required by bottom-up initialization to be linear in n. This is better than successive insertion, because the work on each subtree is bounded. Most nodes are close to the bottom of the tree and don't have to move far to find their correct position. With successive insertion, the earliest nodes are inserted close to the root, but half of the insertions happen at the bottom of the tree and, in the worst case, might need to rise the full $\log n$ height of the tree.

19.2 Implementing a Heap in an Array

Although a heap is conceptually a tree, it's rare to implement a heap as a binary tree using nodes and links. Instead, it's more common to implement a heap as a *specially ordered array*. In this framework, the tree structure is implicitly represented by packing its keys into the array in level order: The root is the first element, its children are the second and third elements, and so forth.

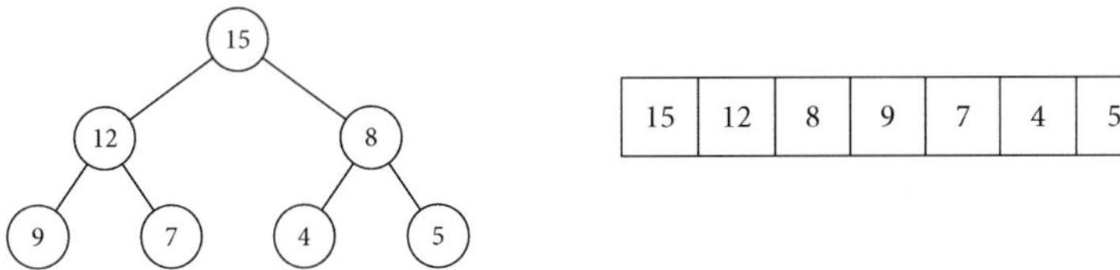

Because the heap is an almost-complete binary tree, there are no holes in its array representation.

19.2.1 Parent–Child Relationships

Every operation that could be performed on a tree-based heap can be done on an array-based one. First, let's consider how parent–child relationships work in the array representation. If a node is at position k in the array, its left child is at $2k+1$ and its right child is at position $2k+2$. Take a moment to work through some examples and verify that these relationships are correct.

Try It Yourself

If a tree node is mapped to index k, what is the index of its parent?

Solution

Consider some example values for k and its associated parent.

- $k = 1$ and $k = 2$ are the children of the root, so their parent is at index 0.

- $k = 3$ and $k = 4$ are the root's left grandchildren, so their parent is the root's left child at index 1.
- $k = 5$ and $k = 6$ are the root's right grandchildren, so their parent is the root's right child at index 2.

A little experimentation shows that k's parent must be at index

$$p = \left\lfloor \frac{k-1}{2} \right\rfloor.$$

19.2.2 A Heap Class

The following class outlines an array-based min heap. It uses an internal array called `heap` to store the implicit tree. We'll complete the upward and downward pass methods, `offer` and `poll`.

```
/**
 * Array-based heap
 */
public class Heap<K extends Comparable<K>> {

  private K[] heap;
  private int size;

  /**
   *  Basic constructor -- default internal array
   */
  @SuppressWarnings("unchecked")
  public Heap() {
    this.heap = (K[]) new Comparable[10];
  }

  /**
   * Index calculation methods
   */
  public int leftChild(int k) {
    return 2 * k + 1;
  }

  public int rightChild(int k) {
      return 2 * k + 2;
  }
```

```

public int parent(int k) {
  return (k - 1) / 2;  // integer division
}

/**
 * Exchange values at two positions
 */
public void swap(int a, int b) {
  K temp = this.heap[a];
  this.heap[a] = this.heap[b];
  this.heap[b] = temp;
}

/**
 * Upward heap pass for a min heap
 *
 * @param  k  the starting index of the pass
 * @return  nothing, changes are made to the heap array
 */
public void upwardPass(int k) {

}

/**
 *  Downward pass for a min heap
 *
 * @param k  the starting index of the pass
 * @return  nothing, changes are made to the heap array
 */
public void downwardPass(int k) {

}

/**
 * Add a new value to the heap
 *
 * @param value
```

```
   * @return  nothing
   */
  public void offer(K key) {

  }

  /**
   * Remove the minimum value and restore the heap
   *
   * @return  the current minimum of the items in the heap
   */
  public K poll() {

  }
}
```

Like the earlier `BinarySearchTree`, the class declaration uses a generic parameter `K` and enforces the requirement that it be `Comparable`, so that there's a `compareTo` method for ordering the heap's elements. The constructor allocates a default backing array and casts it to the required `K[]` type, similar to our previous generic data structures.

Most of the work is in the upward and downward pass methods. Each takes in index `k` as input and performs a pass starting from that position. The upward pass compares element `k` to its parent and swaps them if necessary. It continues moving up the tree until it either reaches the root or finds that item `k` is in its correct position relative to its parent.

```
/**
 * Upward heap pass for a min heap
 *
 * @param  k  the starting index of the pass
 * @return  nothing, changes are made to the heap array
 */
public void upwardPass(int k) {
  while (k > 0) {
    int parent = parent(k);

    // Compare to parent and swap upwards if necessary
    if (this.heap[k].compareTo(this.heap[parent]) < 0) {
      swap(k, parent);
      k = parent;  // Move up
    } else {
      break;  // k is in the correct position, end
```

```
    }
  }
}
```

The downward pass is a bit more complicated. It first checks the left child of `k` and ends immediately if `k` has no children. The interior of the loop determines if `k` also has a right child, and if so, which of the two children is smaller. If that child is smaller than node `k`, swap and continue downward. Otherwise, node `k` is in its correct position and the loop ends.

```
/**
 *  Downward pass for a min heap
 *
 * @param k  the starting index of the pass
 * @return  nothing, changes are made to the heap array
 */
public void downwardPass(int k) {
  int left = leftChild(k);

  while (left < this.size && k >= 0) {
    int smaller = left;

    // If there is a right child, determine which is smaller
    int right = rightChild(k);
    if (right < this.size
        && this.heap[right].compareTo(this.heap[left]) < 0) {
      smaller = right;
    }

    // Compare the smaller item to item k and swap if necessary
    if (this.heap[smaller].compareTo(this.heap[k]) < 0) {
      swap(k, smaller);

      // Move down to the next level and continue
      k = smaller;
      left = leftChild(k);
    } else {
      break;  // k is in the correct position, end
    }
  }
}
```

With those two methods complete, `offer` and `poll` are straightforward. Notice that `offer` doesn't extend the array when it fills up. One of the end-of-chapter questions will invite you to fix this problem.

```
/**
 * Add a new key to the heap
 *
 * @param  key  the new key
 */
public void offer(K key) {
  // TODO: allocate a larger array if the current one fills

  // Add the new value at the next open position
  this.size++;
  this.heap[this.size - 1] = key;

  // Upward pass to put the new value into its correct position
  upwardPass(this.size - 1);
}

/**
  * Remove the minimum value and restore the heap
  *
  * @return  the current minimum of the items in the heap
  */
public K poll() {
  // Swap the last item into the root position
  swap(0, this.size - 1);

  // Remove the old root and reduce the heap size
  K result = this.heap[this.size - 1];
  this.size--;

  // Downward pass starting from the root
  downwardPass(0);

  return result;
}
```

Try It Yourself

Write a method called `heapify` that takes a `K[]` as input and builds a heap by successively inserting its elements.

19.3 Application: Heapsort

Chapter 10 introduced two major divide-and-conquer sorting algorithms: Quicksort and merge sort. Heapsort[3] is the third important $O(n \log n)$ sorting algorithm (Williams, 1964). Heapsort's basic strategy is similar to selection sort: Use a heap to repeatedly find the maximum item and move it into its correct position.

- Given an input array, arrange its items as a max heap, which can be done in $O(n)$ using the bottom-up initialization technique.
- The root of the heap is now the largest item. Swap it to the end of the array, where it's now in its correct position and doesn't need to be considered any further. Perform an $O(\log n)$ downward pass to restore the heap.
- Repeat, successively swapping the root into its correct position as the largest of the remaining elements, then restoring the heap.

This strategy requires $O(n)$ start-up work to prepare the heap, followed by n steps that each require an $O(\log n)$ downward pass. Therefore, Heapsort runs in $O(n \log n)$. This is better than selection sort, because the heap maintains a partial ordering that reduces the time required to find the next largest element on each step.

The method below shows an implementation of Heapsort, assuming the existence of static `heapify` and `downwardPass` methods.

```
/**
 * Heapsort an array
 *
 * @param  a  an int array
 * @return  nothing, the sort is performed in place
 */
public static void heapsort(int[] a) {
  // Turn a into a heap
  heapify(a);

  // Keep track of the number of remaining elements
```

3 Like Quicksort, we'll follow the convention of using the capitalized name from the original paper that described the algorithm.

```
  int size = a.length;

  // Repeatedly remove the max value
  for (int i = a.length - 1; i > 0; i--) {
    // Swap root to position i
    swap(a, 0, i);

    // Downward pass on the remaining elements to restore the heap
    size--;
    downwardPass(a, 0, size);
  }
}
```

The `downwardPass` method is similar to the previous version, but takes the array and the size of the remaining heap as parameters. This version constructs a max heap, so it identifies the largest element at each step. We'll leave the implementation of `heapify` for an end-of-chapter exercise.

```
/**
 * Downward pass for a max heap
 *
 * @param  a  the array
 * @param  k  the starting index for the pass
 * @param  size  the maximum index of the heap
 * @return  nothing, changes are made in place
 */
public static void downwardPass(int[] a, int k, int size) {
  int left = leftChild(k);

  while (left < size && k >= 0) {
    int larger = left;

    // Identify the larger child
    int right = rightChild(k);
    if (right < size && a[right] > a[left]) {
      larger = right;
    }

    // Swap the larger child with k if necessary
```

```
    if (a[larger] > a[k]) {
      swap(a, k, larger);

      // Move down to the next level and continue the pass
      k = larger;
      left = leftChild(k);
    } else {
      break;  // k is in its correct position, end
    }
  }
}
```

How does Heapsort compare to our other $O(n \log n)$ sorting algorithms? In practice, Heapsort is usually slower than a well-tuned Quicksort. Its primary advantage is consistency: Heapsort performs similarly on all input sequences. It requires no special engineering to avoid worst-case behavior, but it also can't perform significantly better on good input sequences. Merge sort shares the property of consistent performance that doesn't depend on its inputs, but requires allocating $O(n)$ additional space. Heapsort does all of its operations in place on the original array. There are a few other points of comparison that are worth noting:

- Quicksort is a divide-and-conquer algorithm that puts most of its work into *generating subproblems*. Throughout our discussion of Quicksort, we focused on how to perform efficient partitions and avoid choosing bad pivots.
- Mergesort is also a divide-and-conquer method, but puts most of its work into *assembling the results of subproblems*.
- Heapsort, by contrast, puts most of its work into *the data structure*. Once you have the concept of a heap, adapting it to sorting is straightforward.

Try It Yourself

From a performance perspective, Heapsort's main disadvantage is poor reference locality. What does that mean and why does Heapsort exhibit it? Tip: Think about how the heap structure distributes values throughout the array.

Solution

Reference locality refers to the tendency for programs to access memory locations that are close to each other. Optimizations like hardware caching take advantage of locality to speed up memory accesses. The heap structure distributes values throughout the array, so every downward pass operation tends to access elements that are far apart from each other, rather than iterating through a sequence of consecutive array locations. The Quicksort partition operation, on the other hand, is a linear scan through a segment of the array, which is a highly localized operation that benefits from caching.

19.4 Example Interview Questions Using Heaps

19.4.1 Verify If a Binary Tree Is a Heap

This question has two parts: verify that every node in the tree satisfies the heap property and that the tree is almost-complete. Checking that every node obeys the heap property is easy and similar to the other recursive tree algorithms from Chapter 17. The pseudocode method below takes a `TreeNode` object as input and verifies that its subtree obeys the heap property for a min heap.

```
// Check if a tree is a heap

checkHeap(TreeNode node) {
  // Base case
  if (node is null or node has no children) {
    return true;
  }

  // Failure
  if (either child key is less than the node key) {
    return false;
  }

  // Recursively check the children
  return checkHeap(node.left) && checkHeap(node.right);
}
```

Checking for completeness is more challenging. You might initially attempt to verify that each node has either zero, two, or only a left child, but this is not sufficient.

Try It Yourself

Construct a tree with no single right children that is not almost-complete.

If the tree is almost-complete, then it can be packed into an array. To do so, there must be one array element per node, and every node must obey the parent–child index relationships given in Section 19.2. The code below descends through the tree, calculating the array index associated with each node. If the tree is complete, then the maximum index is `size - 1`. If any node's index exceeds that, then there must be a hole somewhere in the tree.

```
public boolean checkCompleteness(TreeNode node, int index) {
  // Base case: a null node is complete
  if (node == null) {
    return true;
  }

  // Failure: the calculated index of this node is too large
  // There must be a hole somewhere in the tree
  if (index >= this.size) {
    return false;
  }

  // Recursive case: verify that the left and right children
  // are at valid indices
  return checkCompleteness(node.left, 2 * index + 1)
         && checkCompleteness(node.right, 2 * index + 2);
}
```

To start the procedure, begin at the root node:

```
checkCompleteness(this.root, 0);
```

19.4.2 Merging Sorted Lists

Given an input of k linked lists, each sorted in ascending order, merge them together into one sorted list.

This problem illustrates a strategy similar to Heapsort, where a straightforward method can be made more efficient by choosing a better data structure. Let n be the total number of values in the final list. It would be easy to merge the lists in $O(nk)$ time using a strategy similar to merge sort.

- Maintain k pointers that are initially set to the heads of the lists.
- Identify the smallest value among the k references and copy it to the output.
- Advance the minimum element's pointer to the next entry in its list.
- Repeat, with each step choosing the next smallest value from the k references.

This approach uses n iterations, each with k comparisons. The solution can be improved to $O(n \log k)$ by using a priority queue that stores the active set of k values. On each step, remove the minimum value from the queue, copy it to the output, then insert the next element from its list. The entire process requires n remove and replace operations that can each be done in $O(\log k)$.

19.4.3 Find the Top-k Largest Elements in an Array

This question is representative of a number of problems that involve using a heap to manage a set of some size k. The basic strategy is as follows:

- Initialize a min priority queue containing the first k elements of the array.
- Iterate through the remaining elements. For each element, check if it's greater than the current minimum (this can be done in $O(1)$ by peeking at the root). If so, remove the current minimum and insert the new element.
- After processing all elements, the heap contains the k largest elements in the array, with the kth largest at the root.

Another approach is to turn the array into a heap and then run k iterations of Heapsort, which will move the k largest items to the end of the array.

Try It Yourself

Here's a variation: Find the top-k *most frequently occurring* elements in an array. Tip: Use one pass over the input to count the occurrences of each item.

Solution

This problem combines two data structures: a hash table and a heap. The first step iterates through the input and builds a table mapping each unique value to its count of occurrences, a standard problem that we saw in Chapter 15. You can then use the entries in the set to build a max heap, ordered by item counts. Polling k times returns the k most frequently occurring items. If there are v distinct values, this method requires $O(n)$ to count the items, $O(v)$ to build the max heap from the counts for each value, and $O(k \log v)$ to poll the top-k items.

SUMMARY

The heap is the last of our tree-based data structures. As you're studying the material in this chapter, keep the following points in mind:

- Sometimes an alternative representation offers advantages: A heap is conceptually a tree, but implemented as an array.
- Heapsort is a simple concept made efficient by an intelligent choice of data structure.
- Any problem that requires repeatedly finding the minimum or maximum of a group of items is a good candidate for a heap. We've seen multiple examples of improving an algorithm from linear to logarithmic time by switching from an array to a heap.

This chapter also illustrated how an idea evolves from theory to application, starting with the general idea of a heap, the theoretical tree model, the actual implementation in an array, and finally the practically useful Heapsort algorithm.

EXERCISES

Understand

1. Construct a max heap from the following array: `[0 2 4 1 5 6 3]`.
2. Show the result after removing the maximum and restoring the heap.
3. Show the result after adding 10 to the heap.
4. Run the bottom-up initialization procedure on the following array: `[2, 6, 8, 3, 5, 4, 0, 9, 1, 10, 11, 7]`.
5. Is it possible for a tree to be both a heap and a binary search tree?
6. Is a heap guaranteed to be a balanced binary tree? Tip: Think about the maximum possible difference between any pair of left and right subtrees.
7. Your acquaintance wants to build a priority queue class that uses a linked list as its data structure instead of a heap. How do you respond?
8. Write a function called `grandparent` that takes an `int k` as input and returns the index of `k`'s grandparent node in an array-based heap.
9. Give expressions that calculate the indices of the four grandchildren of a node in an array-based heap.

Apply

10. Add a method to the `Heap` class that implements the bottom-up initialization method.
11. Modify the `offer` method of `Heap` to expand the backing array when it fills.
12. Make an argument that heap insertion on an array is still $O(\log n)$ on average, even if you include the overhead of increasing the size of the backing array.
13. Consider the problem of building a heap by insertion when the input array is correctly sorted – for example, building a min heap from an array sorted in increasing order. What is the complexity of this case?
14. Make an argument that the bottom-up heap initialization method is $\Omega(n)$. Tip: Think about a *lower bound* for the amount of work.
15. Find a nontrivial input array where successive insertion and bottom-up initialization create the same heap.
16. Do the successive insertion and bottom-up initialization methods always create the same heap when run on the same inputs?
17. Suppose you have an n-element array and you'd like to test if its entries are arranged according to the heap property. Write an $O(n)$ *nonrecursive* method that does this.
18. Suppose you have a large number of files that need to be merged into one output file. You can only merge files two at a time and the cost of merging any two files is the sum of their sizes. Using a priority queue, design an algorithm that computes the sequence of

merges that have minimal total cost. For example, if the file sizes are `[5, 2, 4, 1, 3]`, the minimum cost sequence is:

- Merge the second and fourth files for a cost of 3, creating a new file of size 3. You now have four files with sizes `[5, 4, 3, 3]`.
- Merge the two files of size 3 at a cost of 6. You now have three files with sizes `[5, 4, 6]`.
- Merge the files of size 4 and 5 at a cost of 9. The final step merges the files of size 9 and 6 for a cost of 15.

The complete cost of the merging sequence is $3 + 6 + 9 + 15 = 33$.

Extend

19. Write a method for the `Heap` class called `merge` that takes a second `Heap` as input and merges it into the current `Heap` by successively inserting each node.

20. If the primary heap has n_1 elements and the second heap has n_2 elements, what is the complexity of the `merge` method?

21. Consider another merging strategy: Allocate a backing array of size $n_1 + n_2$, fill it with the elements of both heaps, and then run bottom-up initialization. Analyze the complexity of this method. Tip: Assume that you have a method that can return a heap's underlying array.

22. Describe a method for implementing a first-in-first-out queue using a heap. Tip: Think about the priority of items in the queue.

23. Suppose that you want to create a heap that is an almost-complete *ternary tree*, where each node has at most three children. This tree can still be represented in an array: The root is at position 0, its children are at positions 1 to 3, and so forth. Given a node at position k in the tree, what are the indices of its children?

24. Given a node at position k in the ternary heap, what is the index of its parent?

25. Repeat the two previous questions for a general c-ary heap.

26. What are the complexities of insertion and removal on a c-ary heap? Make an argument that this isn't a significant improvement over a binary heap.

27. An advanced heap called a **min-max heap** can keep track of both the minimum and maximum of its elements and return both in constant time. It can be used to build a **double-ended priority queue** that allows interacting with both the min and max priority elements. Do some research on min-max heaps. How are they organized? How does the heap identify the min and max values?

NOTES AND FURTHER READING

Heaps and Heapsort were both invented by J.W.J. Williams in 1964 (Williams, 1964). His original description of both, including implementations of the upward and downward pass methods, is less than one page long.

The standard binary heap has one major weakness: There is no easy way to merge two heaps together in sublinear time. As a result, there are a number of advanced heap variations that are designed to allow on-average constant time merges. One fun example is the **Fibonacci heap**, which gets its name due to the fact that its complexity analysis depends on the Fibonacci sequence (Fredman and Tarjan, 1987). The **treap** is another interesting heap-like structure that combines a binary search tree with the heap property (Seidel and Aragon, 1996). A treap is organized like a binary search tree, but every node is also assigned a random priority when it's inserted. The treap performs rotations to both maintain BST ordering among its real keys and maintain the heap property among the random priorities. The result is that every insertion or removal effectively randomizes the tree, as if its keys had been inserted in random order, and therefore maintains a height of log n on average.

20 Graph Algorithms

I want to inspire you to raise your quality standards. I mean, if 10 years from now, when you are doing something quick and dirty, you suddenly visualize that I am looking over your shoulders and say to yourself: "Dijkstra would not have liked this", well that would be enough immortality for me.

Edsger Dijkstra

INTRODUCTION

We live in a networked world. Professional networks, social networks, neural networks – we're all familiar with the idea that connections matter. This chapter introduces graphs, our last major topic. Graphs are the primary tool for modeling connections or relationships among a set of items; binary trees, for example, are a special type of graph. Graph models illustrate the power of *abstraction*: They capture the underlying structure of a network, independent of what the elements actually represent. Therefore, graph algorithms are flexible – they're not tied to one particular application or problem domain.

LEARNING OBJECTIVES

This chapter introduces graphs and presents two important algorithms, which we'll use for projects in the next two chapters. After this chapter, you'll be able to:

- Describe the structure and properties of graphs.
- Represent a graph in matrix and list forms, and implement a graph in Java.
- Use breadth-first and depth-first traversals to process a graph.
- Understand Dijkstra's shortest-path algorithm, including its complexity analysis and proof of correctness.

20.1 Graph Basics

Figure 20.1 shows an example graph: a map of the sites connected to the ARPANET – the historical predecessor of the modern Internet – in 1981 (Cerf and Kahn, 1990). Each vertex represents a university or research center and the edges represent existing network connections. This section introduces the key concepts of graph theory: What graphs are, how to describe them, and how to represent them in programs. Over time, theorists have created many variations on the basic graph model and a vocabulary of properties used to describe the structure of graphs. Remember to refer back to this section if you need help remembering the definition of a specific property.

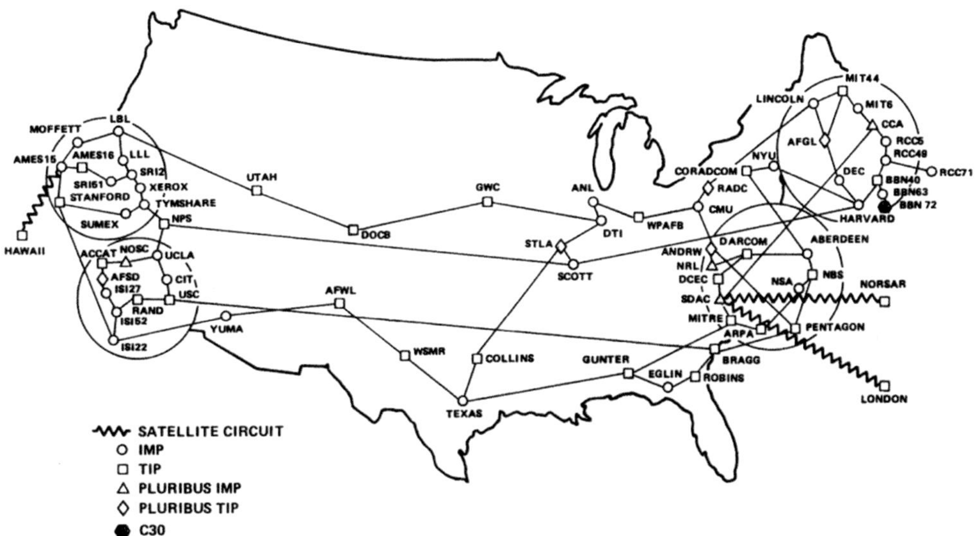

Figure 20.1 Map of the ARPANET in 1981, originally produced by the network engineering firm BBN, which developed the earliest Internet routers. The ARPANET grew rapidly in the 1970s and would later merge with the National Science Foundation's NSFNET to transition into the modern Internet.

20.1.1 Some Important Graph Terms

Formally, a graph $G = (V, E)$ consists of two sets. V is the set of **vertices** and E is the set of **edges**, with each edge representing a connection between two vertices. Edges may be **directed** or **undirected**, depending on the application. Directed edges are used in models where the path or flow from the start to the finish is one-way; undirected edges represent two-way connections. A graph having only directed edges can be called a **digraph**.

Try It Yourself

Decide whether each of the following models might be better represented using directed or undirected edges:

- a social network that allows users to befriend each other vs. a network that allows user to follow high-profile accounts;
- a map showing all international airline flights from the United States to other nations;
- the stations and lines on the Tokyo metro; and
- a food web for a marine ecosystem.

Here are some important graph properties that we'll refer to in future sections:

- The **degree of a vertex** in a graph refers to the number of edges incident to that vertex. In a directed graph, it is often helpful to distinguish between the *in-degree* (number of incoming edges) and the *out-degree* (number of outgoing edges).
- A **self-loop** is an edge that joins a vertex to itself. Both vertices in the digraph below have a self-loop.

- A graph is **connected** if it contains a path from every vertex to every other vertex. A directed graph is **strongly connected** if there is a directed path from every vertex to every other vertex, and weakly connected if there is only an undirected path between vertices.
- A **cycle** is a path that starts and ends at the same vertex without visiting any intermediate vertex or edge more than once. A graph with no cycles is **acyclic**.
- A **tree**, in graph theory, is an acyclic connected graph – that is, there is exactly one path from any node to any other node. The binary trees we've already seen are a modification of this definition – they're directed acyclic graphs with a special root node, and unique paths exist from the root to every other node.[1] In graph theory, trees are usually considered to be undirected and aren't required to have a root; the graph below is a tree, but isn't a rooted binary tree.

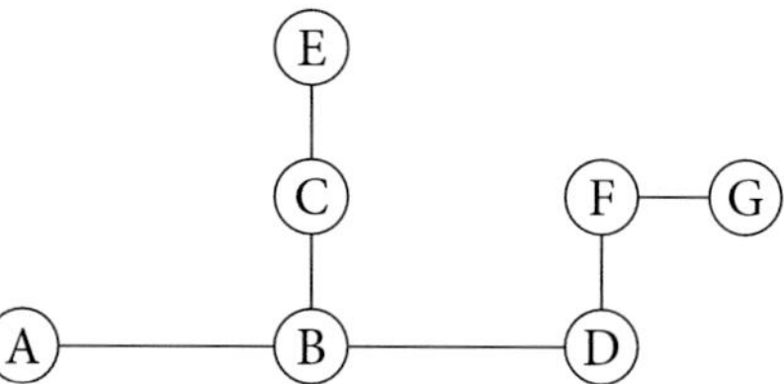

- A **weighted graph** assigns a number to each edge, which may represent the distance between the vertices or the strength of their relationship. Weights can be negative or zero if it's appropriate for the model. Finding shortest paths in a weighted graph is an important problem that we'll investigate in Section 20.3.

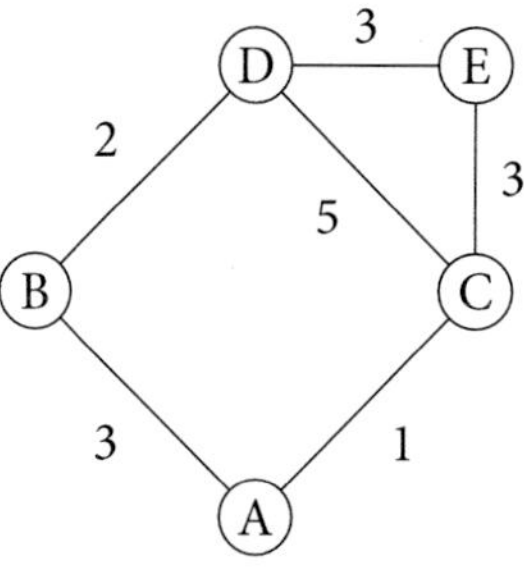

Try It Yourself

Consider three different graph properties: directed vs. undirected, weighted vs. unweighted, and cyclic vs. acyclic. Draw eight example graphs having each combination of the three properties.

A **simple graph** has at most one edge between each pair of vertices and no self-loops. In some cases, it makes sense to allow multiple edges between the same pair of vertices; for example,

1 If you want to be fancy, which you do, a directed acyclic graph with a root node can also be called an **arborescence** (Gross and Yellen, 2003).

multiple airline routes flying between the same pair of cities. A graph that allows these kinds of multiple edges is called a **multigraph**.

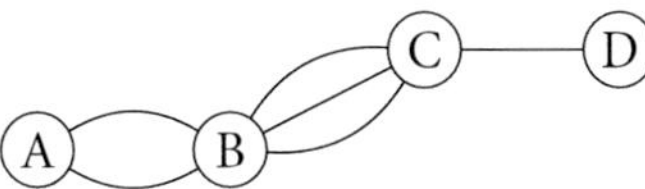

A multigraph with self-edges is sometimes called a *pseudograph* (Gross and Yellen, 2003). We'll assume throughout the following sections that the graphs we're representing are simple.

20.1.2 Representing Graphs

The two standard options for representing graph data structures are **adjacency matrices** and **adjacency lists**. An adjacency matrix encodes the graph as a square matrix, where each entry indicates the presence or absence of an edge between two vertices. In the figure below, vertex A is connected to all four other vertices, B is connected to A, C, and E, and so forth.

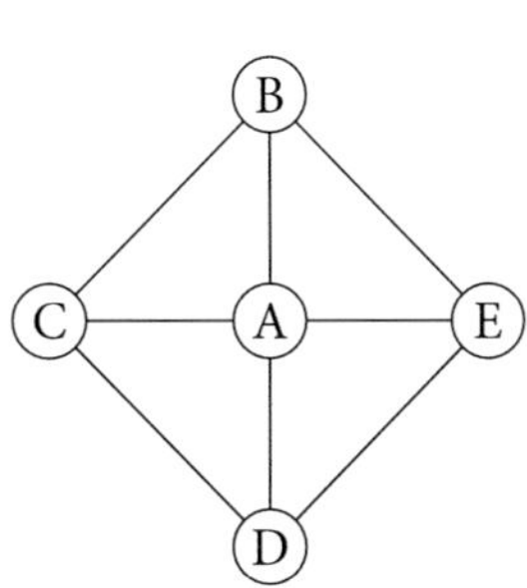

	A	B	C	D	E
A	0	1	1	1	1
B	1	0	1	0	1
C	1	1	0	1	0
D	1	0	1	0	1
E	1	1	0	1	0

The adjacency list representation uses an array of lists, one per vertex. Each vertex's list contains references to all of its neighboring vertices. For example, the previous graph could have the following structure if it was encoded as an array of linked lists:

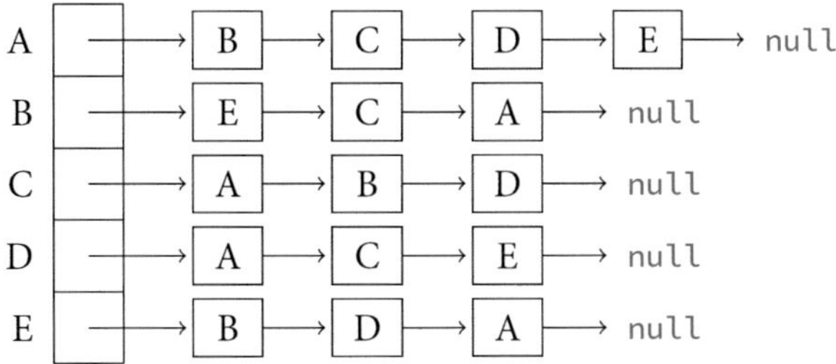

Adjacency lists are conceptually simple, but the actual implementation details can be tricky. The choice of outer data structure depends on how you intend to identify the vertices. Referring to vertices by name (rather than numeric index) requires either a map or some other way of converting between a node's name and its underlying position in the array of lists. Note that the entries in each list don't have to be sorted.

Both methods can represent weighted graphs.

- In an adjacency matrix, each entry stores the weight of the edge between its two associated vertices. Missing edges can be encoded as zero, or as a null value if zero is a valid weight.

- In an adjacency list, the weights are stored as an additional data field in each list entry, along with any other edge properties that might need to be recorded.

Try It Yourself

Convert the following weighted digraph to its list and matrix representations.

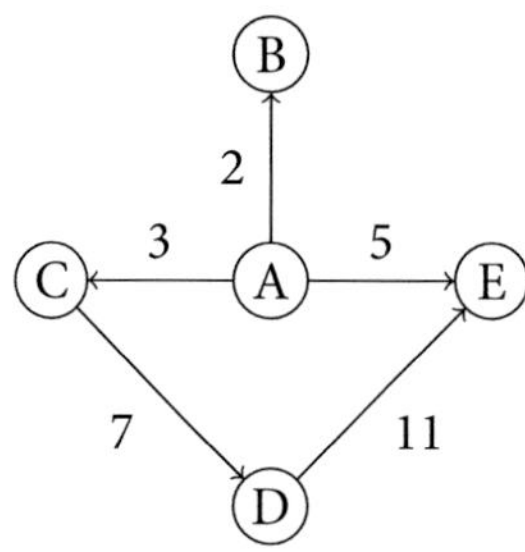

Solution

Here's the adjacency matrix. The row identifies the starting vertex and the column identifies the destination; zero entries indicate unconnected vertices.

	A	B	C	D	E
A	0	2	3	0	5
B	0	0	0	0	0
C	0	0	0	7	0
D	0	0	0	0	11
E	0	0	0	0	0

How do the two representations compare? In general, adjacency matrices are easier to work with than lists and preferable for storing small graphs. Their main disadvantage is the need to store V^2 entries, where V is the size of the vertex set.[2] If the graph is *sparse*, with many fewer edges than vertices, this can waste a lot of space. For undirected graphs, it's sufficient to store only half the entries (because the graph is symmetric), and a fancy implementation could pack the entire matrix into a `byte[]` and use only one bit to store each entry. Weighted graphs need to store the edge weights (or a null value) for every entry.

Lists are harder to manipulate and search, but their space requirements are proportional to the number of edges, at most E in a directed graph. Even with the overhead of storing references for each entry, adjacency lists are preferred for large sparse graphs that have many vertices but relatively few edges.

2 This is a casual notation that's often used when working with graph algorithms. If V is a set, the number of items it contains is more formally written $|V|$.

20.1.3 Graphs (or the Lack Thereof) in Java

Bad news: Java doesn't have a built-in `Graph` class. Good news: There are third party libraries that provide graph implementations.[3] Bad news: Graph libraries are complex, because different kinds of graph models and applications need different features. Good news: You can write your own `Graph` class!

Let's consider a class that represents an unweighted, undirected graph; we'll think about options for extending it to other models later. Before jumping into designing the implementation, we should consider how applications will interact with our class. In particular, we need to specify how users will identify vertices and edges, and what methods the graph will support. Here are some starting assumptions:

- Vertices are identified by index numbers rather than by names.
- Users can add and remove edges between vertices and check if an edge exists.
- We'll implement one constructor, which constructs an empty graph with a given number of vertices and no edges.

The class below uses an adjacency matrix as its internal representation. The constructor takes the number of vertices as input and initializes a square `boolean[][]` to store the edges. The `addEdge` method takes vertex identifiers `u` and `v` as input, then sets the appropriate matrix locations – remember that the matrix is symmetric!

```
/**
 * Unweighted, undirected graph using adjacency matrix
 */

public class Graph {

  private boolean[][] edges;

  /**
   * Initialize empty n x n adjacency matrix
   */
  public Graph(int n) {
    this.edges = new boolean[n][n];
  }

  /**
   * Add an edge
   *
   * @param  u, v  id numbers of the vertices
   */
```

---

3 JGraphT is one example (Michail et al., 2020).

```
  public void addEdge(int u, int v) {
    this.edges[u][v] = true;
    this.edges[v][u] = true;  // Edges are symmetric!
  }
  /**
   * Check if two vertices are neighbors
   */
  public boolean neighbors(int u, int v) {
    return this.edges[u][v];
  }
}
```

Try It Yourself

Add `removeEdge` that takes `u` and `v` as input and set their associated matrix locations to `false`.

Simply managing connections is straightforward. Let's make the class more complex by allowing each vertex to store a value of some generic type `T`. If the number of vertices is fixed, a `T[]` can hold the value for each vertex, with `set` and `get` methods that wrap around the array accesses.

```
/**
 * Updated Graph with array of vertex values
 */
public class Graph<T> {
  private boolean[][] edges;
  private T[] vertices;
  @SuppressWarnings("unchecked")
  public Graph(int n) {
    this.edges = new boolean[n][n];
    this.vertices = (T[]) new Object[n];
  }
  public T getVertexValue(int i) {
```

```
        return this.vertices[i];
    }

    //*** Add other methods ***//
}
```

Try It Yourself

Finish the updated `Graph` class. Copy `addEdge` and `removeEdge`. Add a `setVertexValue` method that sets the value of a given vertex.

Often, the real complexity of a program isn't in the actual code, but in the decisions you need to make *before* writing anything. Consider some ways this program could be modified:

- To implement weighted graphs, change the `boolean[][]` to an `int[][]` or `double[][]`. Add methods to get and set the weight of an edge.
- To implement directed graphs, modify `addEdge` and `removeEdge` to ignore symmetry.
- To disallows self-loops, make `addEdge` ignore the case where `u` and `v` are equal.
- Allowing dynamic addition of vertices is more challenging, but can be done by adding a new row and column to the adjacency matrix and a new entry to the vertex list. Removing is similar: Delete the associated row and column from the matrix and remove the vertex's entry.

20.2 Traversals

A **traversal** is an algorithm that sequentially visits every node in a graph. Traversals can be used to enumerate all of the vertices in the graph, to search for a specific value stored at a vertex, or to update vertices. Recall that there were two basic kinds of tree traversals:

- *level-order traversal*, which used a queue to order the nodes, and processed all nodes on a level before moving down to the next level; and
- *depth-first traversals*, which recursively explored each path to completion before moving to the next-deepest path.

Both strategies can be adapted from trees to general graphs.

20.2.1 Breadth-First Traversal

Breadth-first traversal is the general graph counterpart of level-order tree traversal, using a queue to manage the vertices waiting to be processed. In pseudocode, the basic procedure is as follows:

```
// Breadth-first graph traversal

choose a starting vertex s
mark s as discovered
queue.offer(s)

while the queue is not empty {
  v = queue.poll()

  for each undiscovered neighbor u of v {
    mark u as discovered
    queue.offer(u)
  }
}
```

Breadth-first traversal gets its name because it works outward from the starting vertex, visiting all vertices that are one edge from the starting vertex, then all vertices two edges away, and so forth. It's possible for multiple paths to a vertex to exist, so the method keeps track of which vertices have been discovered to avoid adding a vertex to the queue more than once. Consider the following example. Suppose that A is the starting vertex. The initialization marks it as discovered, then adds it to the queue.

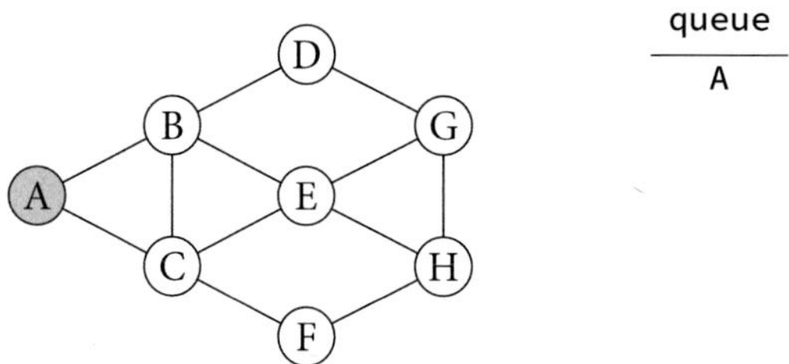

The first iteration of the main loop pops A, then identifies its two neighbors, B and C. They're marked as discovered, then added to the queue.

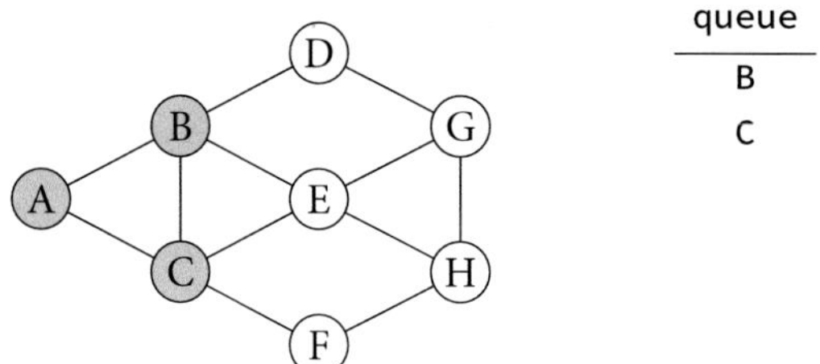

The vertex at the head of the queue is now B. Its neighbors are A, C, D, and E, but A and C have already been marked as discovered, so they're ignored. D and E are added to the queue.

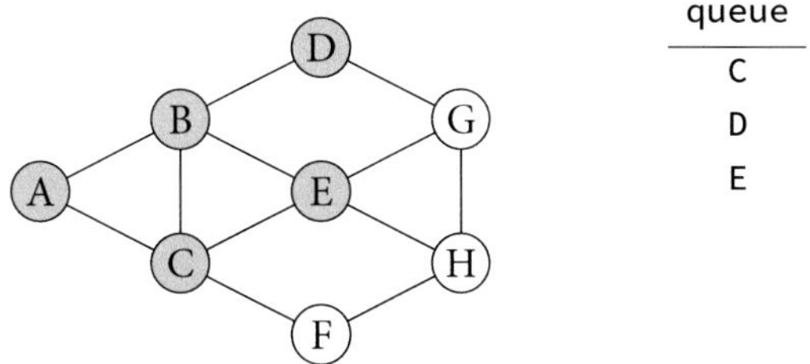

The remaining steps will discover F (via C), G (via D), and finally H (via E).

Try It Yourself

Marking nodes as discovered when they're first added to the queue prevents the method from processing the same node more than once or getting stuck in a cycle. What is an efficient way to keep track of the set of discovered nodes? Explain why you need something other than the queue to keep track of the discovered vertices.

Solution

A `HashSet` is a reasonable choice, which would allow checking if a node has been visited in $O(1)$ time. The queue itself only supports FIFO access; it isn't a map, so it can't provide efficient lookups.

20.2.2 Depth-First Traversal

A depth-first traversal uses a stack (explicitly declared or recursive) to store the nodes that are waiting to be processed. The method proceeds down one path at a time, exploring it to completion before backing up and moving to the next closest path. The stack-based version of the algorithm is almost identical to the breadth-first method:

```
// Stack-based depth-first graph traversal

choose a starting vertex s
mark s as discovered
stack.push(s)

while the stack is not empty {
  v = stack.pop()

  for each undiscovered neighbor u of v {
    mark u as discovered
    stack.push(u)
  }
}
```

Like its tree-based counterpart, depth-first traversal can also be implemented in a compact recursive form. The method takes a vertex as input and recursively processes its neighbors. The method begins by calling `dft` on the starting vertex.

```
// Recursive depth-first graph traversal

dft(v) {
  mark v as discovered

  for each undiscovered neighbor u of v {
    dft(u)
  }
}
```

Let's apply the explicit-stack version to the graph below. If A is the starting node, the process begins by marking A as discovered, then pushing it onto the stack.

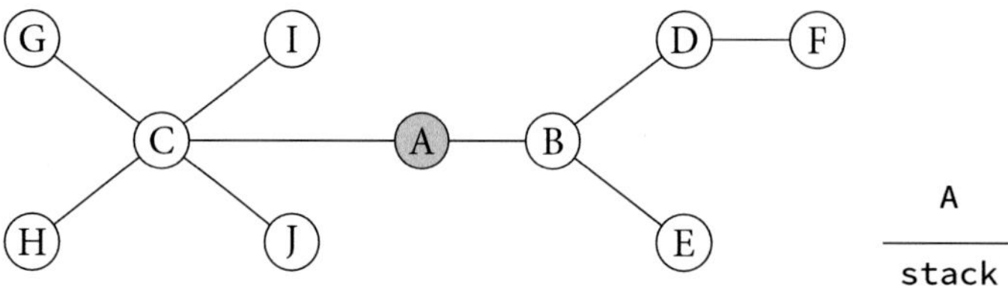

The method pops A, then pushes its undiscovered neighbors onto the stack. Let's suppose B is pushed first, then C. Vertices are processed in LIFO order, so C will be processed next.

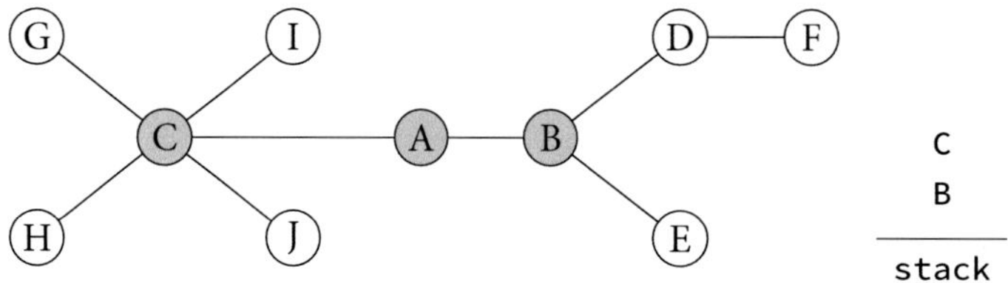

The next iteration pops C, then adds its four neighbors to the stack.

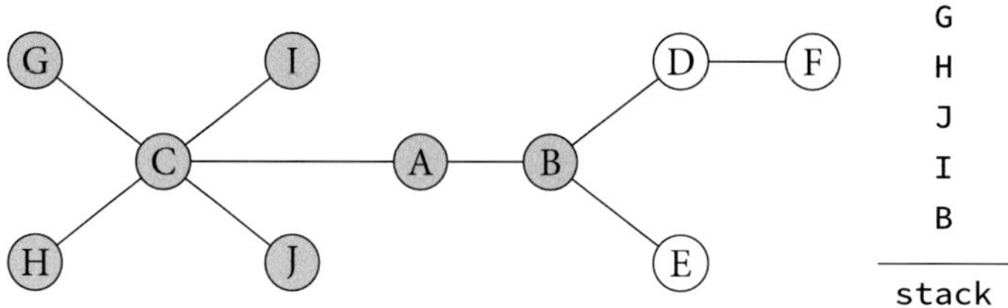

The four nodes generate no new undiscovered vertices, so the method will quickly check them and then move to expand B on the right side.

Try It Yourself

Apply a depth-first traversal to the following graph, starting from A.

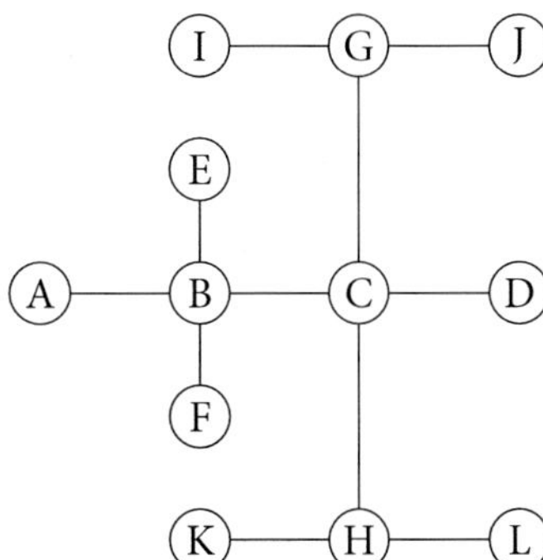

20.2.3 Application: Garbage Collection

Memory management refers to how a programming language handles the allocation and deallocation of space for dynamic data, including objects and arrays. Allocated memory comes from a region of main memory called the **heap**, which is usually managed by the language's runtime execution environment, subject to oversight from the operating system (Arpaci-Dusseau and Arpaci-Dusseau, 2018).

In older languages like C, programmers were responsible for *manually* freeing memory they allocated. This can easily lead to a *memory leak* bug, where programmers forget to free memory that then goes out of scope and can never be reclaimed. Left unchecked, the system eventually runs out of free memory, can't allocate new objects, and crashes. Java's designers chose to implement *automated memory management*, which is used by all modern programming languages. When you use the `new` keyword to call a constructor, the Java runtime automatically determines the amount of memory needed for the new object, then allocates it from the pool of available heap memory. Periodically, the system runs a routine called the **garbage collector** that scans the heap and reclaims memory from objects that are no longer in use. The core problem of garbage collection is deciding what objects are safe to reclaim, because you should never reclaim an object if it might be used in the future.

Think of the objects in memory making a directed graph, where each edge represents a reference from one object to another. For example, the following code fragment makes an `ArrayList<Object>`. The list is referred to by the variable `a`, and in turn has references to the objects it contains.

```
// Variable a refers to the ArrayList
ArrayList<Object> a = new ArrayList<Object>();

// It maintains references to its internal items
a.add(new Object());
```

```
a.add(new Object());
a.add(new Object());

// o1 is now an additional reference to the first item
Object o1 = a.get(0);

// Remove the third object without assigning it to a variable
a.remove(2);
```

The first part of the fragment creates the list and assigns `o1`:

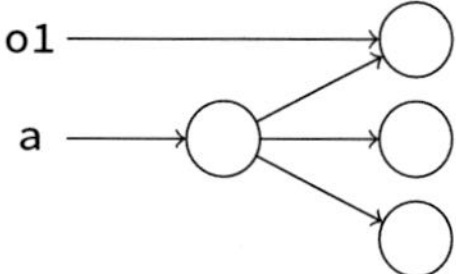

The final line takes the third object out of the list, but it's not immediately deleted from memory. Instead, it's now hanging out, disconnected from the rest of the reference graph.

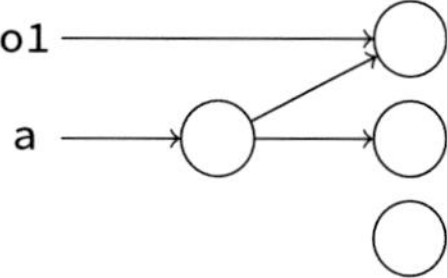

Mark-and-sweep is the classic garbage collection algorithm. It distinguishes between *reachable* objects, which have at least one external reference pointing to them, and *unreachable* objects, which have no external references. Intuitively, if an object has no references, no part of the program can find it or interact with it, so it's safe to reclaim. An object is reachable if either:

- It's part of the *root set* of data that can be accessed without needing to follow a reference. In Java, the root set includes all static class members and all variables on the program stack (Aho et al., 2007).
- It's referenced by another reachable object.

The mark-and-sweep algorithm runs in two phases. Phase 1 traverses the graph of object references, marking every object that it reaches. After marking, phase 2 "sweeps" the heap and frees all the unmarked objects.

The marking phase is a depth-first traversal. Beginning with each item in the root set, the collector traverses the reference graph and marks every encountered object, usually by setting a special reserved bit inside the object. After marking is complete, the sweep phase checks every allocated object on the heap. If an object is marked, the sweeper simply clears its bit and moves on. If it's unmarked, then it must have never been discovered by the traversal, so it's unreachable and can be reclaimed.

```
// Pseudocode for the marking graph traversal

// Depth-first search from the object referred to by r
mark(r) {
  mark object referenced by r
  for each unmarked neighbor v of r {
    mark(v)
  }
}

// Recursively traverse the graph of object references
mark-phase {
  for each reference r in the root set {
    mark(r);
  }
}
```

Reclaiming objects may leave gaps in memory, so it's common to combine sweeping with *compaction*, which repositions objects in memory to reduce fragmentation.

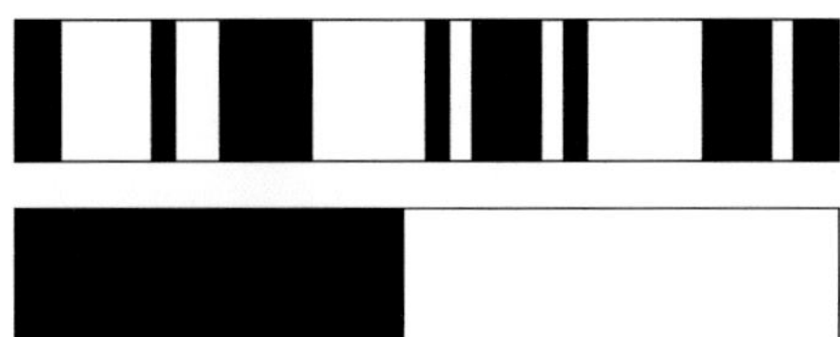

The major limitation of basic mark-and-sweep is the high overhead of scanning everything in memory. Running the collector requires "stopping the world" – the rest of the program has to pause while the collector computes the reachability of every object. This can lead to huge, unpredictable performance penalties, so designers would like to reduce the overhead of garbage collection, particularly the time required for the final sweeping scan.

One technique for reducing the variability of sweep times is *generational garbage collection*, which is used by the HotSpot JVM (Oracle, 2023). The generational approach partitions objects into different sets based on their age. Program analysis shows that most objects are like mayflies: They live brief, glorious lives and then die young. Therefore, it makes sense to prioritize collecting recent objects. The generational strategy partitions the heap into numbered regions, then manages it according to rules like the following:

- All new objects go into region 0.
- When region 0 fills, it's garbage collected and any surviving objects are promoted to region 1. This takes only a fraction of the time required for a full sweep.
- This process – allocating new objects to region 0, then running the collector and promoting survivors – continues until region 1 fills, at which point both regions 0 and 1 are collected.

- Region 1 survivors are then promoted to region 2. When that region eventually fills, it will trigger a collection of regions 0, 1, and 2, and promotion to region 3, and so forth for all higher-numbered regions.

The highest-numbered region holds the longest-tenured objects, which are likely to continue surviving.[4] It is still possible for the top-level partition to fill, which would trigger a complete collection pass over the entire heap.

20.3 Shortest Paths

As we've discussed, weighted graphs can be used to model networks where each edge has a distance or cost. This section discusses the problem of finding shortest paths in weighted graphs, where the sum of the edge weights along the path is minimized. There are different versions of the shortest path problem that require different algorithms, including:

- Single-source shortest path: Find the shortest path from one starting vertex to every other vertex in the graph. A variation asks for the shortest path to only one particular ending vertex.
- All-pairs shortest path: Find the shortest paths between every pair of vertices.
- Nonnegative edge weights vs. general edge weights: Nonnegative weights are normal if the edges represent physical links, but some problems allow for negative edge weights.

This section looks at Dijkstra's algorithm, the most well-known shortest-path method. Take the time to really understand its implementation and analysis: Both are good preparation for working with more complex graph algorithms.

20.3.1 Dijkstra's Algorithm

If you remember only one graph algorithm, it might as well be this one. **Dijkstra's algorithm** is the canonical solution to the single-source shortest-paths problem. The algorithm is named for Edsger Dijkstra, who we have encountered a few times before.[5] Dijkstra was born in Rotterdam, the Netherlands in 1930 and studied math and physics before entering the very new field of computer science in the early 1950s. During his life, he made contributions to almost every area of computing, including operating systems, compilers, and algorithms. He also played a major part in introducing the concept of *structured programming* using variables, functions, loops, and other features that are standard elements of modern languages.

Dijkstra's algorithm takes the weighted graph and the starting vertex as inputs. The standard version runs until it finds the shortest paths from the start to every other vertex, but it's possible to stop early if you only need the path to one particular vertex. The graph may be directed or

---

4 In reliability analysis this is called a *decreasing failure rate* – the longer something has functioned the more likely it is to keep functioning. Program run times also have this property: most are short, but long-running programs are likely to be system daemons that never terminate. (Immortal Daemon Program is a great name for a band.)

5 The quote at the beginning of Chapter 2 – about object-oriented programming being "an exceptionally bad idea" – is attributed to him.

undirected, but it must have *nonnegative* edge weights. Let's first consider a concrete example, then we'll look at the implementation details. Let A be the source vertex in the following graph.

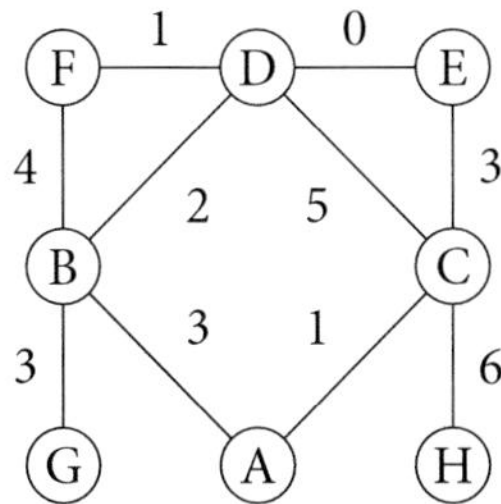

The method keeps track of which vertices have been visited and the shortest known distance to each unvisited vertex. At the beginning of the method, the distance to the starting vertex A is set to 0 and no other vertices have been reached yet.

Vertex	Visited	Best known distance	Predecessor
A		0	Source

Each iteration confirms the shortest path to one vertex, as follows:

- Identify the unvisited vertex *v* with minimum known distance. This is *v*'s shortest path. Mark *v* as visited so it isn't considered further.
- If there are undiscovered vertices adjacent to *v*, add them to the table. Their best known path is the path through *v*.
- Update the distances to each neighbor of *v* if the path through *v* is better than what was previously known.

The first step processes the source, A, and adds its neighbors, B and C, to the table.

Vertex	Visited	Best known distance	Predecessor
A	✓	0	Source
B		3	A
C		1	A

The next step identifies the vertex with minimum distance, C, and marks it as visited. The neighbors of C are D, E, and H.

Vertex	Visited	Best known distance	Predecessor
A	✓	0	Source
B		3	A
C	✓	1	A
D		6	C
E		4	C
H		7	C

B is processed next, which adds F and G to the table – at this point, every vertex has been discovered, but we have not yet confirmed the shortest paths. Notice: The path to D via B improves on the old path through C.

Vertex	Visited	Best known distance	Predecessor
A	✓	0	Source
B	✓	3	A
C	✓	1	A
D		**5**	**B**
E		4	C
F		7	B
G		6	B
H		7	C

The process continues, marking one vertex on each iteration and then updating its neighbors if necessary.

Try It Yourself

Finish executing Dijkstra's algorithm on the example graph.

Dijkstra's algorithm is easy to understand and execute by hand, but can be tricky to formulate as a program. The pseudocode implementation below uses three arrays, `visited`, `dist`, and `pred`, corresponding to the columns of the table. It also uses a structure called `frontier` to keep track of the nodes that have been discovered but not yet finalized. The `frontier` structure has the ability to find the vertex of minimum distance – the implementation of this method turns out to be important for the complexity of the algorithm.

```
// Dijkstra's algorithm

dijkstra(matrix of edge weights, starting vertex s) {

  // Initialization -- no distances are known at the start
  for each vertex i {
    dist[i] = infinity
    pred[i] = null
    visited[i] = false
    frontier.insert(i, infinity)
  }

  // Starting vertex is initialized to distance 0
  dist[s] = 0
  frontier.update(s, 0)

  // Main loop
  while the frontier is not empty {
```

```
    // Get the nearest unvisited vertex
    u = frontier.removeMin()
    visited[u] = true

    // Check all unvisited neighbors of u
    for each unvisited neighbor v of u {

      // d is the cost of reaching v through u
      d = dist[u] + weight[u][v]

      // The path through u is an improvement on the previous
      // best known distance to v
      if d < dist[v] {
        dist[v] = d
        pred[v] = u
        frontier.update(v, d)
      }
    }
  }
}
```

Look at the code carefully. This version inserts all entries into the `frontier` structure at the start of the program, but it's also possible to insert entries for vertices as they're discovered. Entries in `frontier` are updated as the algorithm finds new paths.

Try It Yourself

What's a good choice for the `frontier` data structure?

Solution

A priority queue is a logical choice, since it returns the minimum of its items in $O(\log n)$. The simple heap-based priority queue still requires $O(n)$ for the update operation, though, because finding the entry for a given vertex requires traversing its internal tree. The next section discusses options for representing the frontier set that are better than a binary heap.

20.3.2 Analyzing Dijkstra's Algorithm

Complexity

The complexity of Dijkstra's algorithm depends on the implementation of the frontier set. Let's use an *aggregate analysis* and reason about the total work performed by the method. The key operations are the removes and updates performed on the frontier set. Let V be the number of vertices and E be the number of edges.

- Observe that each iteration of the algorithm finalizes the distance to one vertex, so the main loop executes V times. Each iteration requires one call to the frontier's `removeMin` method.
- The inner loop examines the edges from each vertex u to its neighbors. Dijkstra's algorithm considers each edge one time, on the first iteration that one of its endpoints is visited. Therefore, the `update` method is called at most E times.

If T_r is the average time required for `removeMin` and T_u is the average time required for `update`, the total work is

$$T(V,E) = V\,T_r + E\,T_u.$$

Try It Yourself

If the frontier is an array, updates are $O(1)$, but finding the minimum requires a linear search. If $T_r = O(V)$, what is the complexity of the algorithm?

Solution

The running time is dominated by performing the linear `removeMin` on each vertex, so the result is $O(V^2)$.

Try It Yourself

If the frontier is a standard binary heap, T_r becomes $O(\log V)$, but T_u is now $O(V)$. What is the complexity in this case?

Solution

$O(V \log V + EV)$.

Doing better requires reducing the time for updates. One option is to maintain an extra reference from each vertex to its position in the binary heap. With this change, each update can find the correct entry in the heap in $O(1)$ and then perform an $O(\log V)$ pass to move it to its new position, so that $T_u = O(\log V)$ and

$$T(V,E) = (V+E)\log V.$$

If every vertex is reachable, then there must be at least one edge on each path from the source, so $V + E = O(E)$ and the expression can be simplified to $O(E \log V)$. Even better performance is possible with an advanced heap that allows $O(1)$ updates. The best known example is the Fibonacci heap, which gets its name from the fact that its complexity analysis uses the Fibonacci series (Fredman and Tarjan, 1987). With an advanced heap, the total complexity is $O(V \log V + E)$.

Proof of Correctness

Proving that Dijkstra's algorithm is correct means showing that it terminates having confirmed the true shortest path to every vertex. The proof has two parts:

- First, we'll state a hypothesis that every iteration of the method chooses the correct shortest path to a previously unvisited node. If this is true, then the method must eventually find the shortest path to *every* node.
- Second, to show that this is correct, we'll consider the possibility that the algorithm makes a wrong decision – that there could be some iteration where the method selects a vertex, but hasn't found its true shortest path. We'll then argue that this is impossible and Dijkstra's algorithm never makes a mistake.

The proof is a bit complex, but it's worth going through in detail. It illustrates a common strategy for proving the correctness of algorithms that make decisions on each step. Let's call it the "Three Act" proof structure:

- Act 1: Establish the scene. Assert that the algorithm makes a correct decision on each iteration. Show that this is true for the first decision.
- Act 2: Rising tension. Consider the possibility that the algorithm makes a series of correct decisions, but then makes a bad one. Show that this is impossible.
- Act 3: Denouement. As a consequence of Acts 1 and 2, the algorithm starts off with a good decision and must keep making good decisions on every iteration until it eventually finishes successfully.

You may recognize this structure as a variation of the induction/invariant method we've used in previous proofs. We're going to need some notation to describe the different elements of the algorithm:

- Let V be the set of all vertices.
- Let Q_i be the set of vertices that have been visited at the *start* of iteration i.
- At any point in the method, let d_v be the best known distance to vertex v from the source vertex, which we'll call s.
- Let w_{uv} be the edge weight connecting vertices u and v.

Consider the following statement:

For every vertex $v \in Q_i$, d_v is the shortest path from s to v.

That is, at the beginning of some iteration i, the algorithm must have found the true shortest path to all vertices marked as visited. The initial iteration of the algorithm visits the source node s with $d_s = 0$, so this is clearly true at the start.

Now consider some iteration i. The set Q_i contains all of the vertices the algorithm has visited up to that point and – by the inductive hypothesis – we know that it's found the correct shortest path to each one. Suppose that the algorithm picks a vertex u to visit, asserting that d_u is the length of the true shortest path from s to u. We need to argue that this is the correct choice – that d_u *really is* the shortest distance to u, and that therefore the hypothesis is still true on the next iteration of the algorithm.

A common strategy for proofs like these is to use *contradiction*. Let's suppose that u is a bad choice and that d_u really *isn't* the shortest path to u – there's some better path out there that the algorithm didn't identify. There are two ways this could happen, and we're going to argue that both are impossible.

First, there could be a better path to u that uses only visited vertices in the set Q_i. If this is the case, there must be some visited vertex t, such that

$$d_t + w_{tu} < d_u.$$

That is, taking the shortest path to t, then an edge from t to u, is better than the path chosen by Dijkstra's algorithm. The figure below illustrates this setup, where the squiggly lines indicate a path that might go through multiple other vertices between its source and destination.

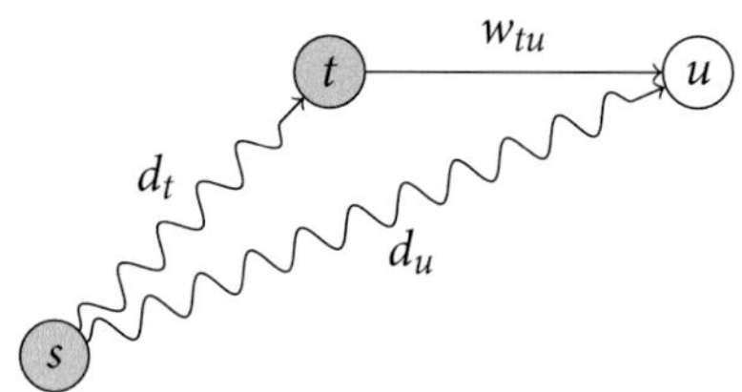

Think about how Dijkstra's algorithm works. If t has already been visited, then the algorithm must have considered its edges and evaluated $d_t + w_{tu}$. If that distance was really better, *Dijkstra's algorithm would use it as the distance to u*. Therefore, this case can't occur: There can't be a better path from s to u that goes through only visited vertices. If such a path existed, the algorithm would have found it.

The other option is that there is a better path through some *unvisited* vertex, let's call that vertex y and think step-by-step about this path:

- It must start at the source s, which is in the visited set.
- It might then pass through additional visited vertices. Let x be the last visited vertex on the path immediately before y. By the induction hypothesis, we know that d_x is the shortest distance from s to x.
- It then goes from y to u, possibly passing through some more vertices. Let's assume the length of this part is ℓ. Weights are nonnegative, so $\ell \geq 0$.

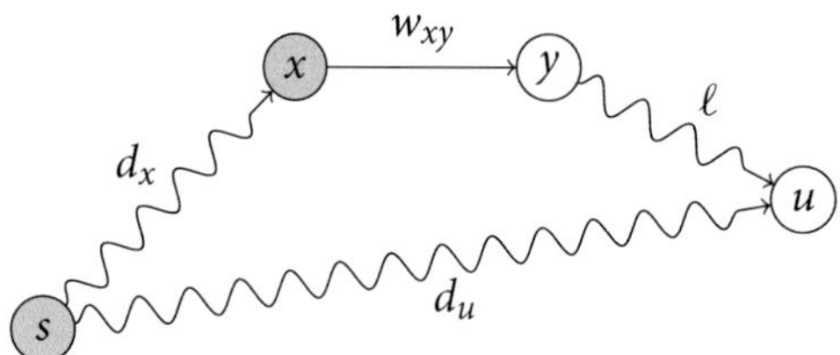

If the hypothetical path through y is better, then

$$d_x + w_{xy} + \ell < d_u.$$

Recall that d_y is the algorithm's estimate of the best known path to y. Vertex x has been visited, so the algorithm has already considered its edges and evaluated $d_x + w_{xy}$, so we can reason that

$$d_y \leq d_x + w_{xy}.$$

We also know that the algorithm is trying to visit u and not y, so

$$d_u \leq d_y.$$

Putting all these facts together:

$$\begin{aligned} d_x + w_{xy} + \ell &< d_u \\ d_y + \ell &< d_u. \\ d_u + \ell &< d_u \end{aligned}$$

This is a contradiction! Weights are nonnegative, so $d_u + \ell$ can't be less than d_u itself. Therefore, our original assumption – that there was a better path to vertex u than the one picked by Dijkstra's algorithm – is false. When the algorithm selects u to visit next, d_u must be its true shortest distance. Thus, on every iteration, the algorithm correctly identifies the shortest path to one previously unvisited vertex, which guarantees that it will eventually find the shortest path to all vertices.

20.4 Example Interview Questions Using Graphs

20.4.1 Snakes and Ladders

Snakes and ladders is a traditional board game played on a grid with 100 squares. Players start at square 1 and the first player to reach square 100 is the winner. On each turn, a player rolls a six-sided die and moves ahead that many squares. Some squares are marked with "ladders" that move the player to a higher-numbered square. If a player's turn ends on a ladder square, he immediately advances up to the higher-numbered square. Other squares are "snakes" that move the player to a lower-numbered square. Determine the minimum number of die rolls needed to complete a given snakes and ladders board. For example, in the small board below, the minimum number of required moves is 3.

21	22	23	24	25
20	19	18	17	16
11	12	13	14	15
10	9	8	7	6
1	2	3	4	5

This problem uses a variation of the breadth-first search technique; it's also similar to the queue-based grid exploration problems we considered in Chapter 13. Problems having to do with routes or paths are often a good fit for a graph traversal algorithm, even if the question doesn't actually mention a graph.

Try It Yourself

How can you convert the snakes and ladders board into a graph model? Tip: Think about each square as a vertex.

Solution

Each die roll moves the player from a starting square to one member of a set of destination squares. For example, in the board above, a player starting at 1 can reach 2, 14 (via the ladder from 3), 4, 5, or 6 on a roll. Construct a graph that has one vertex per square, then add edges from each vertex to the other vertices that are reachable on a single die roll. For example, vertex 1 would have edges to vertices 2, 14, 4, 5, and 6.

Breadth-first search will find the path to the destination square that follows the minimum number of edges, which corresponds to finishing the game in the minimum number of die rolls. The pseudocode solution below maintains each path as a list; the first list that reaches the goal square is the minimum length sequence of moves.

```
// Snakes and Ladders

start = [1]
queue.offer(start)

while queue is not empty {
  path = queue.poll()
  s = last entry in path

  for each square r reachable from s {
    if r == goal {
      output path + r
      return
    }

    queue.offer(path + r)
  }
}
```

You could also view this solution as using Dijkstra's algorithm on the movement graph when all edges have a weight of 1.

20.4.2 Finding Cycles

Design a method to detect if a graph is acyclic.

Checking a graph's properties is another common problem type. As in the previous problem, the key is to adapt a technique that you already know. Cycles and traversal are clearly related: If you traverse the graph and encounter the same vertex more than once, you must have reached it via a cycle. So consider a solution like this, using depth-first search:

```
// Return true if a graph is acyclic

stack.push(start)
while stack is not empty {

  u = stack.pop()
  mark u as visited

  for each neighbor v of u {
    if v is already marked visited {
      return false
    }

    stack.push(v)
  }

  return true
}
```

Try It Yourself

This is almost correct, but has a bug. What's the problem? Tip: Think carefully about the line that checks if v has been previously visited.

Solution

As written, the program will always identify the immediate predecessor of u as a visited neighbor and return `false` immediately. The method should only detect a cycle if v has been previously visited and is not the immediate predecessor of u:

```
for each neighbor v of u {
  if v is already marked visited and v != pred[u] {
    return false
  }
```

```
        pred[v] = u
        stack.push(v)
    }
```

SUMMARY

As you're learning about graphs, it's easy to become overwhelmed by the variety of definitions and variations. For now, stay focused on the primary algorithms – traversals and shortest paths in this chapter – and think about how they can be applied to different kinds of problems. As you're reading, keep the following ideas in mind:

- Many graphs are *implicit*: The problem doesn't obviously feature a network of nodes and edges, but there is an underlying graph structure.[6]
- Breadth-first and depth-first traversals are the main building blocks of graph-related algorithms. Often, the solution to a graph question is resolved by taking a traversal and adding a little extra bit on top of it.[7]
- Dijkstra's algorithm is practically important, and also illustrates how the complexity of an algorithm can depend on its internal data structures. Take some time to understand both the complexity analysis and the proof of correctness.

EXERCISES

Understand

1. List methods that could be part of a graph abstract data type.
2. Define the following graph terms: acyclic, connected, weighted, multigraph.
3. Perform breadth-first and depth-first traversals on the graph below starting from A:

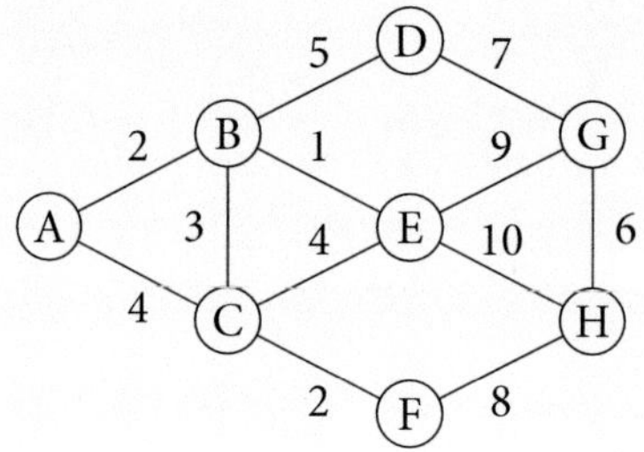

6 Here's a fun example: determining if a Rubik's Cube is solvable (Skiena, 1998). Let each state of the Cube be a vertex and let edges represent the transitions between states that are possible by rotating the Cube. The set of vertices connected to the ending state represents the set of solvable configurations.

7 In fact, many of the algorithms we've already encountered – including backtracking search, flood filling, and tree traversals – are just variations of the basic traversal strategies.

4. Determine the graph's adjacency matrix and adjacency list representations.
5. Run Dijkstra's algorithm on the graph starting from E.
6. Draw out the portion of the movement graph showing all moves starting from any of the first six squares on the example snakes and ladders board.
7. Draw a directed graph representing the object references for the following code fragment:

```
ArrayList<Integer[]> a = new ArrayList<Integer[]>();

Integer[] i1 = {1, 2, 3};
Integer[] i2 = {4, 5};
Integer[] i3 = {6};

a.add(i1);
a.add(i2);
a.add(i3);
```

8. Add a method to the example `Graph` class to calculate the in-degree of a vertex in a directed graph using an adjacency matrix representation.
9. Repeat the previous question for the out-degree of a vertex.
10. Why can't `System.out` be garbage-collected?
11. Write a method called `neighbors` for the `Graph` class that takes a vertex index as input and returns a `List` of that vertex's neighbors. Use the adjacency matrix representation.
12. Modify the example `Graph` class to use an adjacency list representation. Rewrite the constructor to take the number of vertices `n` as input and initialize an array containing that many empty lists.
13. Rewrite the `addEdge` method for the adjacency list representation.
14. Rewrite the `removeEdge` method for the list representation.
15. Your friend wants to apply depth-first traversal to the snakes and ladders problem. Explain why this is probably not a good idea.

Apply

16. Implement Dijkstra's algorithm using arrays to keep track of the distances to each vertex. Test your implementation on a small input graph.
17. Design a method to check if a graph is connected. Assume you know the number of vertices.
18. Write a method called `addVertex` that adds a new unconnected vertex to the `Graph` class by expanding the adjacency matrix.
19. Write a `removeVertex` method that takes a vertex index as input and deletes its entries from the adjacency matrix.
20. Make an argument that the complexities of both breadth-first and depth-first traversals are $O(V + E)$.

21. Write a method called `path` that takes an `int vertex`, `int source`, and the `int[] pred` of predecessors produced by Dijkstra's algorithm, then outputs the sequence of vertices defining the shortest path from `source` to `vertex`.

22. Suppose your friend gives you the `dist` and `pred` arrays produced by running Dijkstra's algorithm. Design a method that can check the results and verify that every shortest path determined by the `pred` array has the distance given by `dist`.

23. Write a method for the `Graph` class called `search` that takes a `T value` as input and uses a breadth-first search to return the index of the first vertex having that value, or `-1` if no such vertex exists.

24. Create another version of `search` that uses a depth-first traversal.

Extend

25. Do some research on multigraphs. Describe the preferred ways to represent the edges in a multigraph.

26. Design a method to check if a graph is a spanning tree.

27. Rewrite the depth-first cycle checking method to be recursive. Tip: Think about when it's okay to return `true`. If you've explored all of u's neighbor vertices and none of them returned `false`, that means you never found a cycle on any path from u.

28. Write a method that can construct the adjacency matrix for a snakes and ladders game given a list of its ladder and snake squares. Assume that the list is an `ArrayList<Integer[]>`, where each array entry describes one snake or ladder in the form `[start square, end square]`. For example, the ladder going from square 3 to square 14 would be entered as `[3, 14]`. Take the maximum number of squares as a second input to the method. Return the adjacency matrix as a `boolean[][]`, where the entry at position `(r, c)` is true if square `c` is reachable in one move from `r`.

29. Modify your method to read the snakes and ladders from a file with one entry per line, like the following:

```
3, 14
10, 2
12, 20
23, 15
```

30. Suppose you wanted to determine the *average* number of moves required to win a given snakes and ladders game. Write a Monte Carlo simulation that takes a snakes and ladders adjacency matrix as input and uses simulation to estimate the expected number of turns a player needs to complete the board. Test your method on the example board.

31. Implement a version of `search` that uses Dijkstra's algorithm to find the occurrence of the value of interest that has minimal distance from the source. You could consider this a variation of breadth-first search that uses a priority queue to explore nodes in terms of distance. In the AI literature, this technique is known as *best-first search*; it's often implemented with a heuristic function that estimates how close each node is to the goal value (Russell and Norvig, 2020).

32. Design and implement a version of Dijkstra's algorithm that uses a custom heap implementation that allows for $O(\log V)$ updates. Tips: Assume that you know the number of vertices and maintain a mapping from each vertex's index number to its current position in the heap. Implement the heap using the array-packing approach (Chapter 19). To update a vertex's minimum distance, change its associated value in the heap array, then perform an upward pass.

33. A **connected component** in an undirected graph is a set of vertices that are all reachable from each other. If a graph is connected, in the sense that we defined at the beginning of the chapter, then it is one connected component, but a graph may also consist of multiple independent connected components. Design a method that will find and return all of the connected components in a given input graph. Return the indices of the vertices of each component as a list, and the complete set as a list of those lists.

NOTES AND FURTHER READING

The introduction of graph theory is credited to Leonhard Euler, who introduced some of its earliest results when he solved the *Königsberg bridge problem* in 1736. In Euler's day, Königsberg was a city in the German state of Prussia; in the present, it's Kaliningrad, Russia. The city includes two islands in the Pregel River that were joined to each other and the mainland by seven bridges. The problem asked if it was possible to walk a route that crossed all seven bridges, but only one time each. Euler simplified the problem to what we would now call a multigraph. In the figure below, A and B represent the islands and C and D represent the north and south banks of the river, respectively:

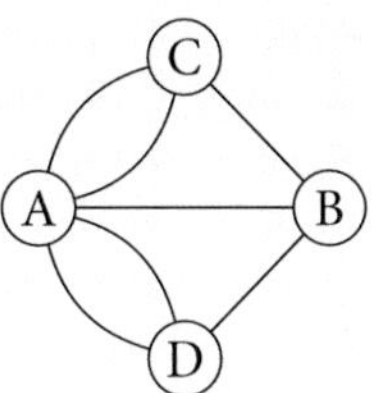

If a bridge can only be walked one time, it must be used to either *enter* one of the vertices on the graph or *exit* one of the vertices. Therefore, any vertex that isn't the start or end point of the walk must have an even degree – the number of edges you use to enter it must equal the number you use to leave. In the Königsberg graph, all of the vertices have odd degree, so there's no way to construct a path that uses every edge only once; you'll eventually get stuck at a vertex with no way to leave. An *Eulerian path* is a path on a graph that uses every edge exactly once.

21 Project: Graph-Based Recommendation Engine

Once you become predictable no one's interested anymore.
Chet Atkins

INTRODUCTION

Pinterest is a social media platform that allows users to assemble images or other media into customized lists, then share those lists with others. Pinterest calls these lists "pinboards" and the items added to each board "pins," analogous to real-world physical bulletin boards. Like other social media systems, Pinterest wants to recommend new content to its users to keep them engaged with the service. In 2018, Pinterest introduced a system called **Pixie** as a component of their overall recommendation infrastructure (Eksombatchai et al., 2018). It uses a graph model to represent the connections among items, then explores that graph in a randomized way to generate recommendations. In this chapter, we'll build our own system based on the graph algorithms used by Pixie.

LEARNING OBJECTIVES

By the end of this project, you'll be able to:

- Give the definition of a bipartite graph.
- Understand the concept of graph coloring, and use breadth-first coloring to test if a graph is bipartite.
- Construct a bipartite graph model to represent the connections between items and user-generated lists.
- Implement a recommendation program that uses a random walk over a bipartite graph to find clusters of related nodes.

21.1 Bipartite Graphs

There are two basic approaches to recommender systems:

- *Content filtering*, which extracts key descriptive features from each item, then uses those features to find new items similar to those that a user already likes. For example, a music system might categorize songs based on high-level features such as artist, genre, and language, but also on more specific audio details, such as tempo and brightness. Given a user's preferences, the system can recommend songs that are "close" in feature space, often by using a machine learning model.

- *Collaborative filtering*, which uses the social graph to find related items. Users that consistently engage with similar content are likely to have similar preferences. The system finds connections between content a user has already liked and new content liked by similar users in similar ways.

In practice, commercial systems are often hybrids. Pixie uses its graph-based collaborative model to generate a set of initial recommendations that are then given more detailed scoring by machine learning. We're going to explore the collaborative component, which is based on connections between pinned items. Intuitively, if two pins appear on the same board, then that provides evidence for a relationship between them. Pixie models the connections between pins and boards using a special type of graph called a **bipartite graph**. This section presents background on bipartite graphs, and their connection to a new concept, **graph coloring**.

21.1.1 Definition

In a bipartite graph, the vertices can be partitioned into two sets, V_1 and V_2, such that every edge connects a vertex in V_1 to a vertex in V_2, and no edge connects two vertices in the same set. For example, in the graph below every edge connects one vertex on the left side to a vertex on the right side, but there are no intra-side connections.

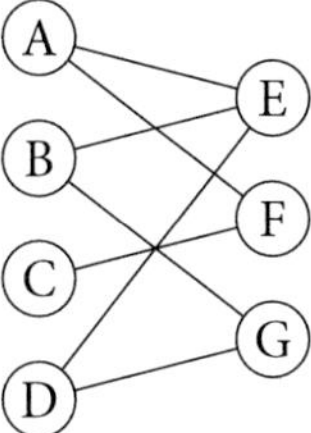

Try It Yourself

In some cases, the vertices are not clearly divided into "sides" but it's still possible to partition the vertices into sets. Partition the grid below into two bipartite sets.

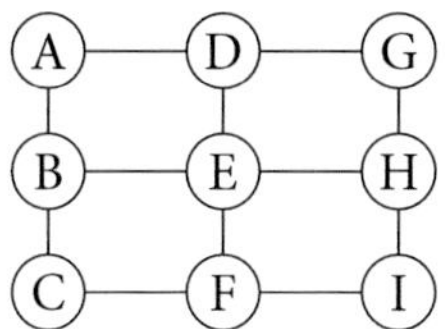

Solution

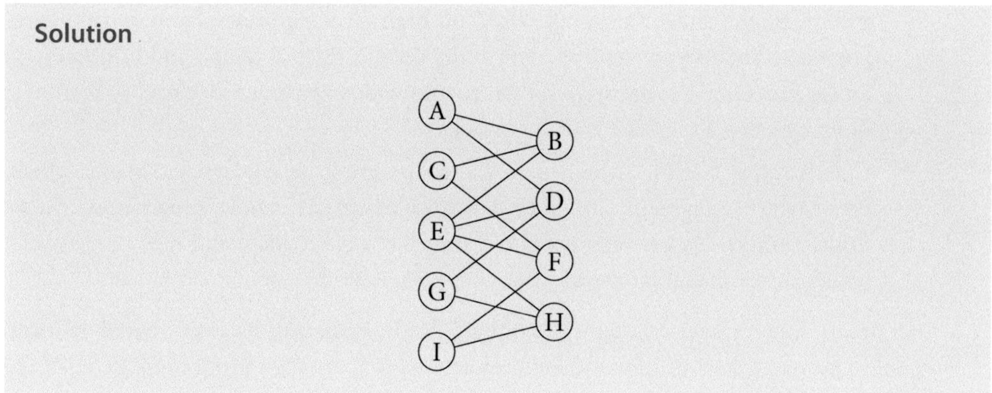

21.1.2 Testing If a Graph Is Bipartite

Now consider the problem of testing if a graph is bipartite, which requires discovering if it can be partitioned into the two sets V_1 and V_2. In addition to being a possible interview question, this turns out to be another nice application of breadth-first graph traversal. Observe that it's possible to visualize the two groups by coloring the vertices:

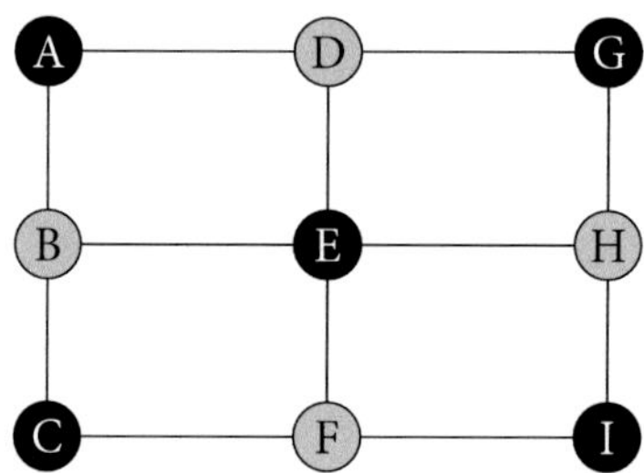

Graph coloring assigns an additional property – the color – to each vertex so that no two adjacent vertices have the same color. Coloring can be used to find groupings of vertices, with the requirement that vertices connected by an edge be in different color groups. The number of distinct colors required to color a graph is called its *chromatic number*; bipartite graphs have a chromatic number of 2. This fact can be combined with graph traversal to determine if G is bipartite:

- Choose the starting vertex and assign it the first color. This could be a literal color, like black, but it could also just be a number or other value that serves as a label.
- Perform a breadth-first traversal of the graph, assigning each new uncolored vertex the opposite color to its parent. If we begin at A in the example above, it will be colored black and its neighbors B and D will be colored gray. B's neighbors C and E will be colored black, and so forth.
- If you ever discover an edge that connects two vertices with the same color, then the graph is not bipartite.
- If the method completes without finding any such edge, then the graph has been successfully 2-colored and is therefore bipartite.

Try It Yourself

Use the breadth-first coloring algorithm to test if the following graph is bipartite:

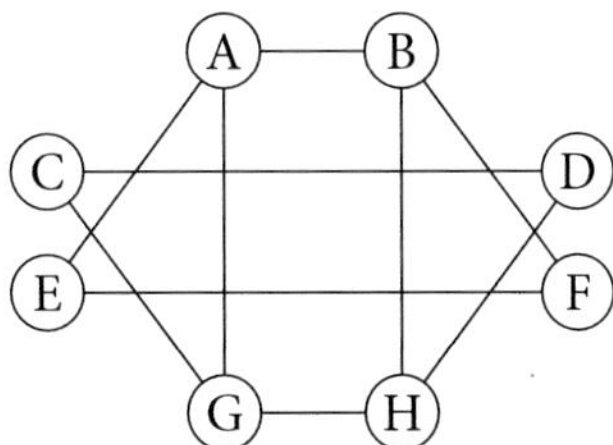

Solution

Choose a starting vertex, say A, and assign it the first color. The breadth-first procedure assigns the opposite color to all of A's neighbors.

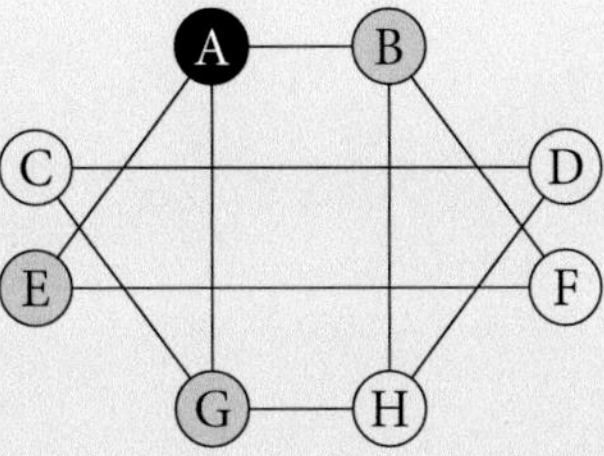

The next iteration chooses one of those neighbors, say B, and colors *its* neighbors black. Note that A has already been colored so it isn't processed again.

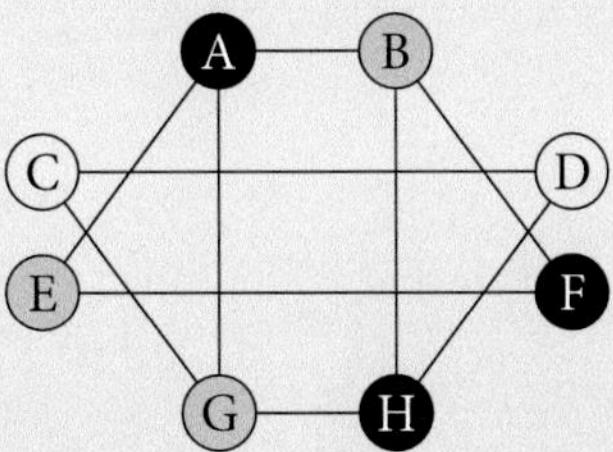

Continuing the algorithm will show that C is colored black and D is gray. The two sets are {A, C, F, H} and {B, D, E, G}.

Try It Yourself

Write a pseudocode method to implement bipartite testing. Use the breadth-first graph traversal as a starting point.

21.2 Building the Recommendation System

We're now ready to apply the theory from the previous section to implement a graph-based recommendation system. This section works with an example set of music playlists, with songs organized by theme. Pixie extends this idea to general pinboards, where the entries can be arbitrary images or links.

21.2.1 The Object Graph and Random Walks

Suppose that the entire universe of music consists of four small playlists:

Boy Bands
"Bye Bye Bye" – *NSYNC
"Dynamite" – BTS
"Everybody" – Backstreet Boys

Summer Jams
"Everybody" – Backstreet Boys
"Despacito" – Luis Fonsi feat. Daddy Yankee
"Mambo #5" – Lou Bega
"Dynamite" – BTS

Latin Party
"Despacito" – Luis Fonsi feat. Daddy Yankee
"Mambo #5" – Lou Bega
"Gasolina" – Daddy Yankee

90s
"Mambo #5" – Lou Bega
"Everybody" – Backstreet Boys
"Bye Bye Bye" – *NSYNC

The collection can be represented as a bipartite graph, where one set of vertices is the individual songs and the other is the playlists; an edge exists if a song appears on a list. The Pixie system refers to this structure as the *object graph*.

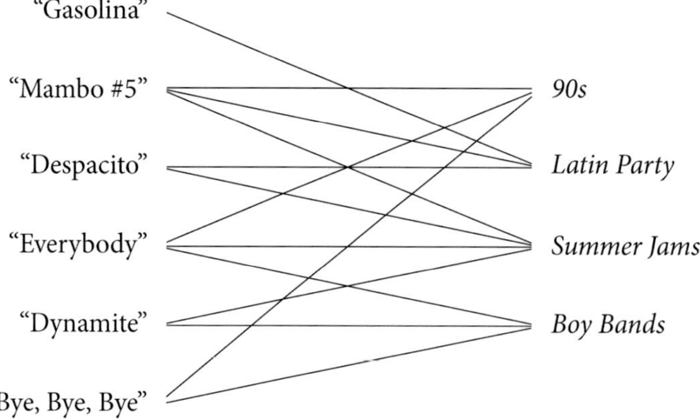

The basic recommendation algorithm is a **random walk** over the object graph. Given a starting vertex, jump to one of its associated playlists at random, then jump to one of that list's items. The result is a randomly chosen item that's one shared list away from the starting vertex. The process then repeats, jumping from the second item to one of *its* lists, then to an item, to

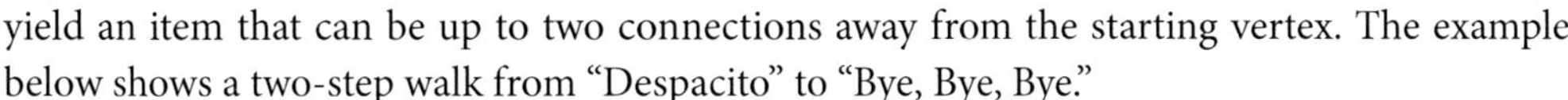

yield an item that can be up to two connections away from the starting vertex. The example below shows a two-step walk from "Despacito" to "Bye, Bye, Bye."

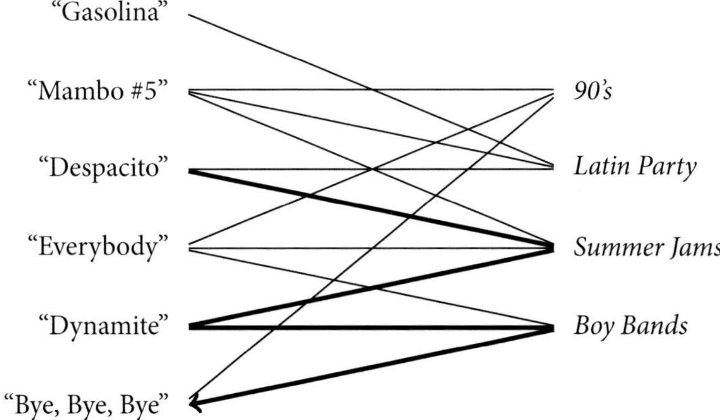

To generate recommendations for items similar to a starting vertex, Pixie runs the random walk process and keeps count of the number of times each item is visited. Once the walk finishes, it returns the top-k most visited items as the set of recommendations.

Many walks will remain within subgraphs of closely related items, but if the object graph is connected, it's possible to eventually walk to items that are only dimly related to the starting vertex. To avoid wandering too far, Pixie periodically resets the walk back to the starting vertex after each step with a fixed probability p. The parameter can be tuned to control how far the search is allowed to wander; the published Pixie system uses $p = 0.50$, which makes the average walk two steps from the source. The pseudocode below summarizes the random walk method:

```
// Random walk recommendation using the bipartite model
item = starting node;

counts = empty table storing <item, visit count> pairs

for (i = 1 to MAX_STEPS) {
  list = item.getRandomNeighbor();
  item = list.getRandomNeighbor();
  counts[item]++;
  if (Math.random() < p) {
    reset item to starting node;
  }
}

return top-k items of counts
```

Try It Yourself

By hand, simulate the algorithm on the example playlist graph. Perform 20 total iterations, but reset to the starting vertex with a 50% probability after each step. Try working with another person and compare your results to see if you obtain similar outcomes.

21.2.2 Implementation

Once the background model is in place, the implementation is not too difficult. The main design challenge is choosing an appropriate representation for the graph. Let's assume that each node in the graph – representing either an item or a list – has an associated identifier. In our example, these identifiers will be the names of the song or playlist, but in a more general system you might choose to use unique URLs, identifier numbers, or hash codes.

We'll represent the graph using the *adjacency list* approach. Let the main data structure be a `HashMap<String, ArrayList<String>>`, where each entry maps an ID name to a list of its connected IDs. Each song name is mapped to its associated playlists and each playlist is mapped to the songs it contains, like in the following pseudocode declarations:

```
graph["Despacito"] = {"Latin Party", "Summer Jams"}
graph["Latin Party"]= {"Despacito", "Mambo #5", "Gasolina"}
graph["Dynamite"]= {"Summer Jams", "Boy Bands"}
```

The code below shows the starting class. We'll fill in the `addEdge` and `recommend` methods. The constructor initializes the empty graph and calls `addEdge` to create connections.

```
/**
 * Graph-based recommendation system
 */

import java.util.ArrayList;
import java.util.HashMap;

public class Recommender {

  // The graph model
  HashMap<String, ArrayList<String>> graph;

  final int MAX_STEPS = 10;
  final double RESET_PROB = 0.50;


  /**
```

```
   * Constructor
   */
  public Recommender() {
    this.graph = new HashMap<String, ArrayList<String>>();

    // Add some example nodes and edges
    addEdge("Despacito", "Latin Party");
    addEdge("Despacito", "Summer Jams");
    addEdge("Dynamite", "Summer Jams");
 addEdge("Dynamite", "Boy Bands");
  }

  /**
   * Add a new edge to the graph
   *
   * @param  item  name of the item
   * @param  list  name of the list containing the item
   */
  public void addEdge(String item, String list) {

  }

  /**
   * Perform a random walk on the object graph
   *
   * @param  start  id of the starting vertex
   * @return  id of the most frequently visited item
   */
  public String recommend(String start) {

  }

  public String toString() {
    return this.graph.toString();
  }

  public static void main(String[] args) {
    Recommender r = new Recommender();
```

```
    String rec = r.recommend("Despacito");
  }
}
```

The `addEdge` method takes two ID strings as input and adds each to the list of connections for the other; this corresponds to adding an undirected edge between their associated vertices in the graph.

```
/**
 * Add a new edge to the graph
 *
 * @param  item  name of the item
 * @param  list  name of the list containing the item
 */
public void addEdge(String item, String list) {
  // Connect the list to the item
  ArrayList<String> itemEdges = this.graph.getOrDefault(item,
                                    new ArrayList<String>());
  itemEdges.add(list);
  this.graph.put(item, itemEdges);

  // Connect the item to the list
  ArrayList<String> listEdges = this.graph.getOrDefault(list,
                                    new ArrayList<String>());
  listEdges.add(item);
  this.graph.put(list, listEdges);
}
```

Notice the use of `getOrDefault`, which either returns the `ArrayList` associated with the given ID, or otherwise creates a new `ArrayList` for a new entry.

Try It Yourself

Implement the `recommend` method. Use the pseudocode from the previous section as a starting point. Here are some tips:

- Create a `HashMap<String, Integer>` to count the visits to each item.
- On each step, look up the `ArrayList` associated with the current ID, then select one of its elements at random.
- Use a loop that runs for a preset maximum number of iterations.

Solution

Here's an example implementation. The `counts` map records the number of times each item is visited. The version below returns the top-visited item as the result; getting the top-*k* items is covered in the end-of-chapter extensions.

```
/**
 * Perform a random walk on the object graph
 *
 * @param  start  id of the starting vertex
 * @return  name of the top result
 */
public String recommend(String start) {
 HashMap<String, Integer> counts = new HashMap<String, Integer>();

  String item = start;
  String list = null;

  for (int iter = 0; iter < 10; iter++) {
    // Choose a random list
    list = randomChoice(this.graph.get(item));

    // Choose a random item from the list
    item = randomChoice(this.graph.get(list));

    // Increment visit count
    int count = counts.getOrDefault(item, 0);
    counts.put(item, ++count);

    // Randomly reset
    if (Math.random() < RESET_PROB) {
      item = start;
    }
  }

  // Return the top-visited item
  String maxItem = null;
  int maxCount = 0;
  for (String id : counts.keySet()) {
```

```
    int count = counts.get(id);
    if (count > maxCount) {
      maxItem = id;
      maxCount = count;
    }
  }

  return maxItem;
}
```

`randomChoice` is a helper method that takes an `ArrayList` as input and returns one of its elements at random.

```
public String randomChoice(ArrayList<String> a) {
  if (a.size() == 0) {
    return null;
  }

  int r = (int) (Math.random() * a.size());
  return a.get(r);
}
```

Try It Yourself

There's one more subtle issue that can occur when choosing the random edge to take for the next transition. Can you spot it? Tip: Think about the relationship between the incoming and outgoing edges.

Solution

The example method doesn't prevent the walk from immediately returning to the previous item that it just left. We could update the random choice method to ensure the randomly chosen outgoing edge is different from the edge that was used to enter the current vertex.

Try It Yourself

Finish implementing the system and add all of the edges for the example graph. Verify that you can run the program and make recommendations. After that, gather some custom playlist data and experiment with building a larger recommendation graph.

SUMMARY

The recommendation system is a nice example of how data structures and algorithms work together to enable a useful application. As we move into the final chapter, keep the following ideas in mind:

- We started by reasoning about the underlying data relationships, which led naturally to the random walk algorithm. When working with connected or networked data, spend time thinking about the structure of their connections. If your solution seems very difficult to implement, you might not have found the right abstraction yet.
- `ArrayList` and `HashMap` – or their counterparts – never go out of style. As we've now seen multiple times, the map-of-lists construction is quite flexible.

EXTENSIONS

Top-*k* Results

The example solution returns the name of the most-visited item. Modify the `recommend` method to return an `ArrayList<String>` containing the top-*k* items, where `K` is a constant defined at the top of the class. Two reasonable strategies are:

- extract the entries of the `counts` map into a list, sort it, then return a sublist with the top entries; and
- insert all of the items into a max `PriorityQueue`, then remove *k* times.

Observe that you ultimately want to return a list of name IDs as the recommendations, but entries are ordered based on the *counts for each name*. Therefore, your solution has to keep track of the <name, count> pairing as it finds the top-*k* items.

Map Coloring

The most famous graph coloring result is the *Four Color Theorem*, which says that any planar map can be colored using at most four colors. The theorem was first stated in 1852 by Francis Guthrie and investigated by Augustus De Morgan, but wasn't proven until 1976. The theorem is notable for being the first major result relying on a computer-assisted proof. Kenneth Appel and Wolfgang Haken, the researchers, used a program to test all potential counterexamples and show that they could all be four-colored, and hence, no counterexample was possible (Appel and Haken, 1989).

Consider a two-dimensional map divided into contiguous nonoverlapping regions. Let each region be a vertex in a graph, and if two regions share a boundary, connect them with an edge. For example, the map on the left has the graph on the right.

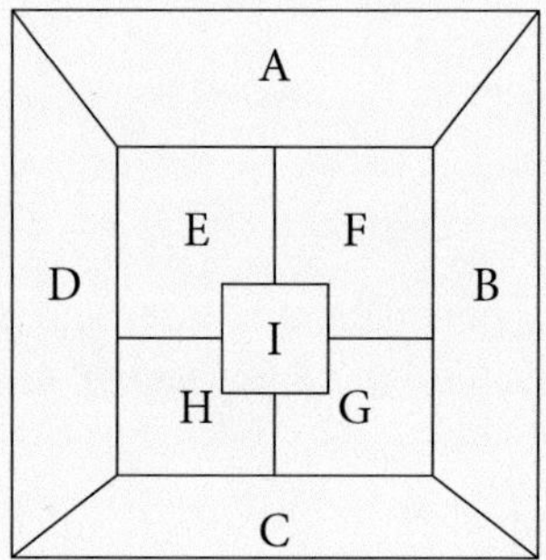

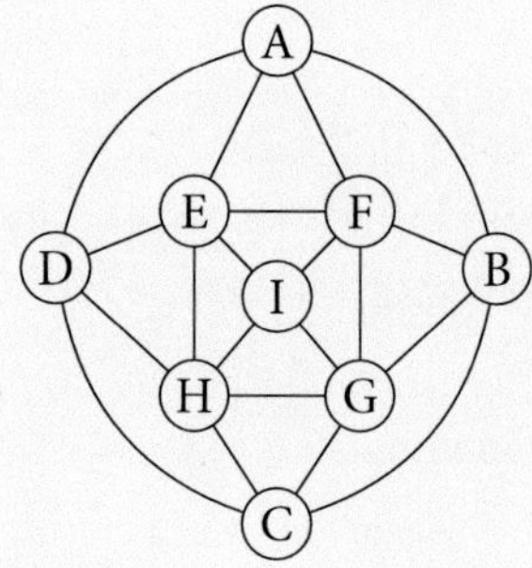

A *planar graph* is one that can be embedded in the 2D plane, such that no edges cross each other. The theorem states that the chromatic number of a planar graph is at most four.[1]

Try It Yourself

Find a coloring for the example graph.

Solution

Here's one possible solution:

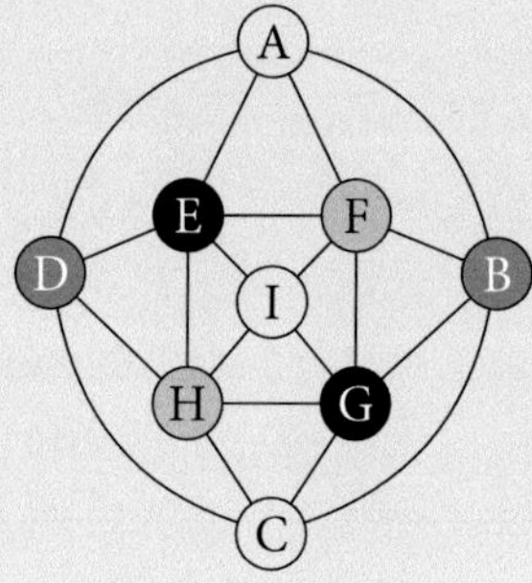

Suppose that you have a planar graph constructed from a map and represented as an adjacency list. Write a program that can find a valid coloring for the graph. The basic strategy is backtracking search.[2]

- Choose an uncolored vertex *v*. If all vertices are colored, then you've reached a solution; stop.
- Choose one valid color that doesn't conflict with any of *v*'s neighbors and assign that color to *v*.
- Recursively explore from that point.
- If *v* has no valid colors, then this path can't lead to a solution; backtrack to the previous vertex and try a different color.

1 This can get tricky with real-world maps. Real countries can have noncontiguous regions, like the continental United States and Alaska, or Kaliningrad Oblast, a noncontiguous part of Russia located on the Baltic Sea. If you want noncontiguous parts of the same country to be the same color, then the map may not correspond to a planar graph, and it's possible to construct examples that need more than four colors.

2 Review the examples in Chapter 12.

The main challenge with backtracking search is in representing the state of the problem and enforcing the constraints. Let each vertex in the problem have an integer identifier, so the first vertex is numbered 0, the second is 1, and so forth. You can then use a `HashMap<Integer, Integer[]>` to store the adjacency list representing the set of edges connecting the vertices. You can use the class below as a starting point:

```
/**
 * Starting code for four coloring
 */

import java.util.HashMap;

public class FourColor {

  // Fixed number of vertices
  final int N = 9;

  // The graph adjacency list
  HashMap<Integer, Integer[]> edges;

  // Constructor
  public FourColor() {
    // Initialize the edges structure

    // Fill edges with the data for the problem
  }

  // Search for a coloring
  public void color(int[] coloring) {
    int v = findUncoloredVertex(coloring);
    if (v == -1) {
      // Output current coloring and stop
    }

    for (int c = 1; c <= 4; c++) {
      // Test if c is valid for vertex v in the in-progress coloring
      if (valid(c, v, coloring)) {
        // Recursively explore this path
        coloring[v] = c;
        color(coloring);
```

```
      }
    }

    // If you make it here there was no solution on this path,
    // backtrack to the previous solution
    coloring[v] = 0;
  }
}
```

The example code uses integers 1–4 to represent the coloring and 0 to indicate an uncolored vertex. You'll need to add `findUncoloredVertex`, `valid`, and a `main` that creates the `FourColor` object and calls `color` with an empty array.

NOTES AND FURTHER READING

There's a connection between Pixie and search engine ranking results. The final step in a web search is to order the results so that the most relevant pages are at the top of the output. Early search engines were notoriously bad at this! Early search ranking was based mostly on context and heuristics – for example, a search term appearing in a page's title meant the page was a relevant result. Larry Page and Sergey Brin, the founders of Google, gave search a significant boost when they introduced the PageRank algorithm in the late 1990s (Page et al., 1999). Another important early link-based search engine was RankDex, developed in 1996 by Robin Li, who went on to found the major Chinese search engine Baidu.

PageRank was inspired by research on academic research paper citations and uses *links between pages* to determine relevance. Intuitively, "good" pages with high-quality content are more likely to link to other "good" pages. The network of page links forms a directed graph: If page A links to page B, then the graph has an edge pointing from A to B. At Internet scale, this graph is *very* large, but also very sparse, since most pages link to only a few other pages.

Like Pixie, PageRank models web surfing as a *random walk* over the page graph. Conceptually, the process follows random edges from page to page, representing a user randomly clicking through the link graph. If the user reaches a page with no outgoing links, the walk resets to a random vertex and then continues. Consider: Frequently visited pages are those that have high numbers of incoming links from other frequently visited pages. That is, the most visited pages are likely to be "good" pages and should appear at the top of the search results. In practice, Google doesn't perform a random walk to order the results of every search. Instead, you can use techniques from stochastic analysis and linear algebra to estimate the long-run fraction of visits the random walk would make to each page (Harchol-Balter, 2013).

You are in a maze of twisty little passages, all alike.
Will Crowther, *Colossal Cave Adventure*

22 Project: Twisty Little Passages

INTRODUCTION

Minecraft is the most popular video game in history. Created by Markus "Notch" Persson using Java, it has sold more than 250 million copies since its first release in 2011. *Minecraft* is a sandbox-style game with no plot or required goals: Players explore an open three-dimensional world made of cubic blocks, and can mine for resources, craft items, and build. Every *Minecraft* world is effectively infinite and **procedurally generated**. Rather than having a fixed map, the game automatically generates new terrain as the player explores the world. The idea of procedurally generated game worlds goes back to some of the earliest computer games, including the highly influential *Rogue* (1980), which sent the player on a crawl through a brutally difficult random dungeon and inspired an entire genre of successors.

LEARNING OBJECTIVES

In this chapter, we'll look at one example of procedural generation: creating mazes using graph algorithms. We'll introduce our final major algorithm, minimum-weight spanning trees, then show how they can be used to automatically construct and visualize mazes. After finishing this – *the final project* – you'll be able to:

- Define the concept of a minimum spanning tree in a weighted graph.
- Use Kruskal's and Prim's algorithms to build spanning trees.
- Discuss how the complexities of the two algorithms depend on their data structures.
- Implement a Java program that uses minimum spanning tree to generate and visualize randomized perfect mazes.

The end-of-chapter extensions will allow you to try out some additional maze-generation techniques.

22.1 Minimum Spanning Trees

A **spanning tree** of an undirected graph is an acyclic subgraph that has paths from every node to every other node. The tree is like a "skeleton" that preserves the essential structure of the graph, but removes unnecessary edges. Spanning trees are important in networking and path-finding applications, where the first step is often to reduce a complex graph by removing its cycles, then using the tree skeleton to find efficient routes between the nodes. Here is an example unweighted graph, with the bolded edges forming one possible spanning tree:

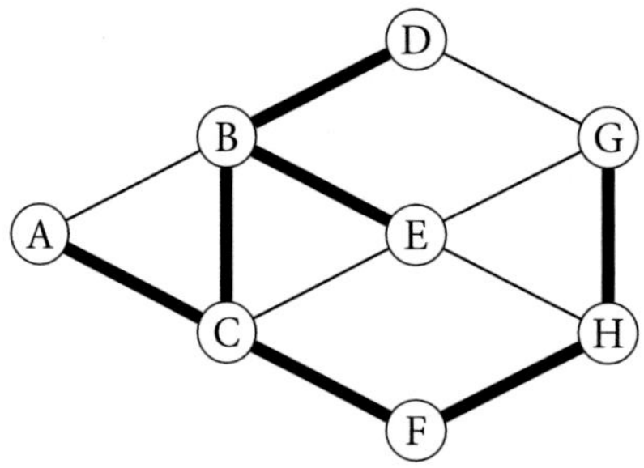

Try It Yourself

Create at least two other spanning trees for the example graph.

In a weighted graph, we're often interested in finding the **minimum-weight spanning tree**, for which the sum of edges in the tree is minimal. The two classic minimum spanning tree methods are Kruskal's and Prim's algorithms. Both algorithms grow the tree by starting from a disconnected set of vertices, then adding one edge on each iteration, but they differ in how they decide which edge to add.

22.1.1 Kruskal's Algorithm

Kruskal's algorithm is named for Joseph Kruskal, who first described it in 1956 (Kruskal, 1956). It builds a *forest* of disconnected subtrees, then gradually connects the subtrees to create the complete minimum-spanning tree. The algorithm starts with all of the vertices disconnected, then repeatedly adds the remaining minimum-weight edge that joins two disconnected parts of the graph. As we'll see, this process can never create a cycle and it's guaranteed to generate the tree with minimum total weight. Here is a pseudocode description of the method :

```
// Kruskal's algorithm
kruskal(list of edges E) {
  E = sort(E)
  initialize each vertex as its own set
  for each edge (u, v) in E {
    if u and v are in different sets {
      add edge (u, v) to the spanning tree
```

```
        union the sets containing u and v
      }
    }
}
```

Kruskal's algorithm is one of the canonical examples of a **greedy algorithm**: It makes a series of *locally optimal* decisions that result in an overall optimal solution. Let's look at a concrete example for the graph below.

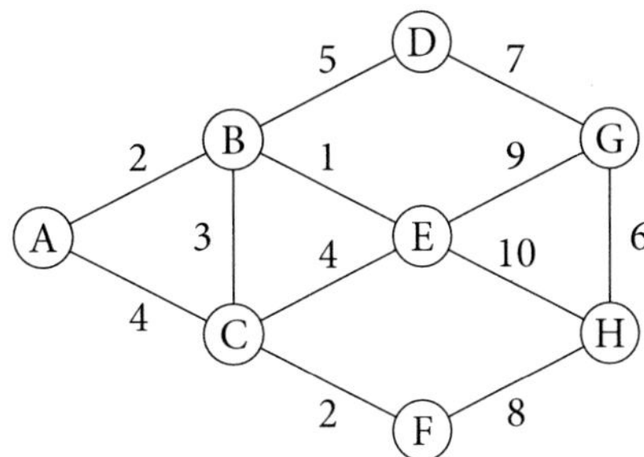

Kruskal's algorithm first initializes a collection of sets, one set per vertex. We'll discuss in a moment the options for representing these sets – this turns out to be an important detail for the performance of the algorithm. The minimum-weight edge is (B, E) with a weight of 1; the algorithm adds it to the spanning tree and unions B and E into a single set.

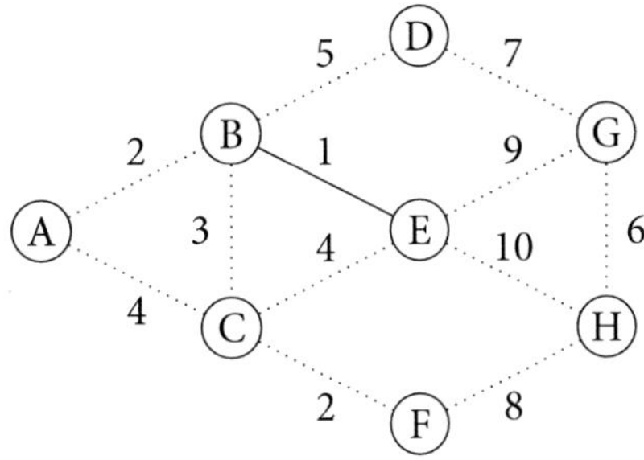

There are two edges with weight 2, (A, B) and (C, F). Both edges connect vertices in different sets, so it's safe to add them both to the tree as the next two iterations.

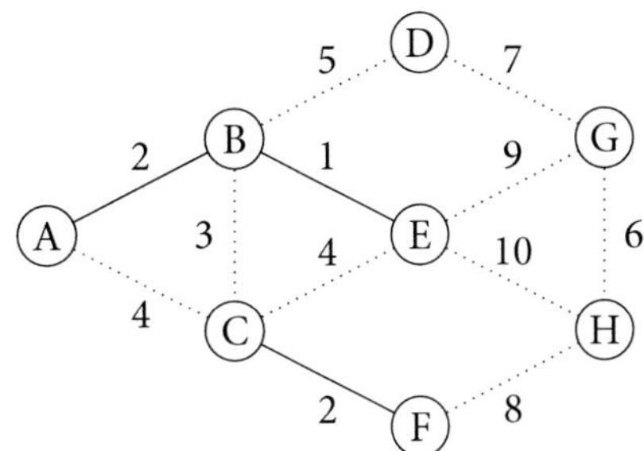

The next edge is (B, C), with a weight of 3, which joins the two connected components together.

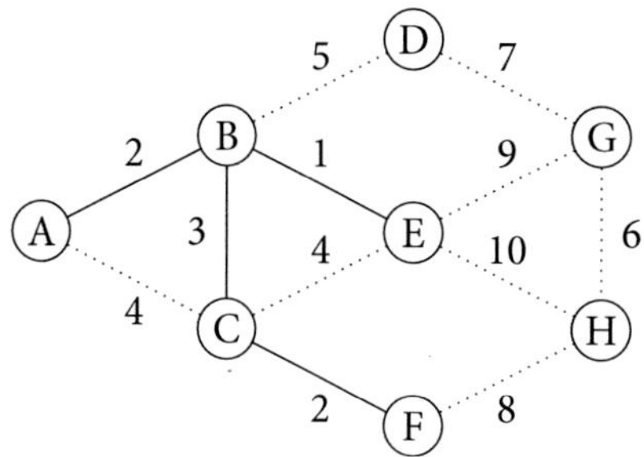

Now consider edges (A, C) and (C, E), which both have a weight of 4. A, C, and E are already in the same component, so adding either edge would create a cycle. Kruskal's algorithm skips both edges.

Try It Yourself

Continue the process and finish constructing the spanning tree.

Solution

The next edge is (B, D), with a weight of 5, followed by (G, H) and then (D, G) to complete the tree. The final result has a weight of 26.

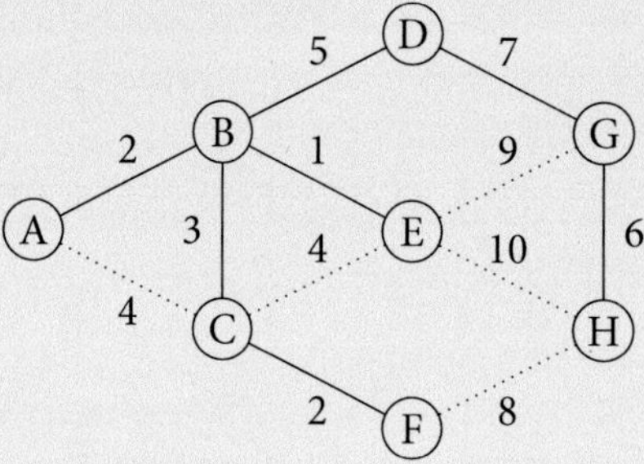

The first step of Kruskal's algorithm requires sorting the edges, so the complexity is at least $O(E \log E)$, where E is the size of the edge set, but we also have to account for the time required to manage the sets of vertices. First, every vertex is initialized into its own set; if creating a set is $O(1)$ (which it is for all practical solutions) then this step is $O(V)$. Every iteration of the method checks an edge to determine if its endpoints are already in the same set. If so, the edge is skipped; if not, the sets of the two endpoints are merged together.

Let T_c be the average time required to check if two edges are in the same set and T_u the average time required to union two sets together. In the worst case, every edge requires both a check and a merge, so the total required time is

$$T = E \log E + V + E(T_c + T_u).$$

Try It Yourself

What are the complexities of T_c and T_u if the sets are represented as lists? What about hash tables? Assume that the worst case for both operations is a function of V, the number of vertices.

Solution

If the sets are represented as lists of vertices, then unioning sets can be done in $O(1)$ by appending one list to the other. However, checking if two vertices are in the same list requires an $O(V)$ scan. Using a hash table to keep track of the set for each vertex allows $O(1)$ lookups (by checking if the two vertices are mapped to the same set or not), but merging now requires linear time to update the mappings for every vertex in the merged sets. Therefore, if we relied on either lists or hash tables, the time would be

$$T = E \log E + V + E(1 + V).$$

Every edge connects at most two unique vertices, so $V \leq 2E$ and the overall complexity can be simplified to $O(E^2)$.

Better performance requires performing both operations in sublinear time. The solution to this problem is a special data structure called the **disjoint set forest**, which represents a collection of sets as a forest of trees. Each set has one element designated as its "representative" which is the root of its tree. Unlike our normal binary trees, where each node maintains references to its children, a disjoint set tree has each child point to its *parent*. The root of the tree is its own parent and each node is allowed to have any number of children.

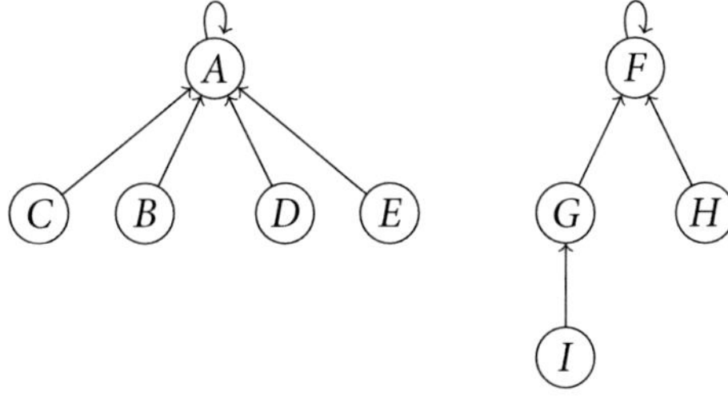

This setup allows efficiently testing if two elements are in the same set: Given a reference to an element, follow its parent pointer and return the root of its tree. If two nodes have the same root, they belong to the same set. For example, to test if C and I are in the same set:

- Start at C and follow its pointer up to the root of its tree, which is A. Return A as the representative of C's set.
- Start at I and follow the pointers up to the root of its tree, which is F. Return F.
- C and I have different set representatives, so they must be in different sets.

This operation is $O(1)$ if the trees are flat. Merging sets is done by making one tree a child of the other, which requires changing only one pointer. For example, merging F's tree into A's could be done like this:

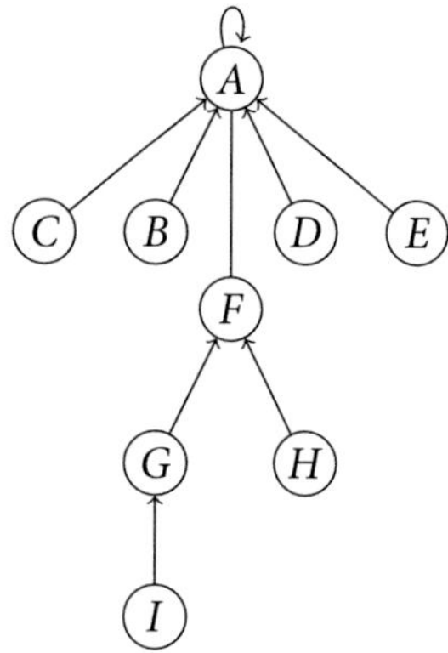

Merging initially increases the height of the tree, which makes checking set membership slower, but the disjoint set has the ability to rebalance itself to keep the tree flat.[1]

The amortized analysis of disjoint set operations is complex, but it's been shown that any sequence of n operations – create, merge, or check – is no more than $O(n\alpha(n))$, where $\alpha(n)$ is the special *inverse Ackermann function*, which grows extremely slowly.[2] In fact, $\alpha(n)$ grows so slowly that $\alpha(10^{80}) < 4$, and that input is roughly the number of elementary particles in the entire universe. Therefore, if we use the disjoint set forest, all of the set operations for Kruskal's algorithm are effectively $O(1)$, the complexity is dominated by the time to sort the edges, and the algorithm is $O(E \log E)$. This can be rewritten as $O(E \log V)$ by using the fact that there are no more than V^2 edges if the graph is fully connected.

22.1.2 Prim's Algorithm

Prim's algorithm is named for Robert C. Prim, who published it in 1957 (Prim, 1957), but was independently discovered by the Czech mathematician Vojtěch Jarník in the 1930s and by Edsger Dijkstra[3] at about the same time as Prim. Kruskal's algorithm grew the spanning tree by adding edges to a forest of disconnected subtrees, gradually connecting them into a single spanning tree. Prim's algorithm grows the tree outward from a single starting node, so that each step connects one new vertex to the in-progress spanning tree.

The algorithm begins with the starting vertex as the only element of the spanning tree. At each step, it chooses the minimum-weight edge that connects any vertex in the tree to a vertex that is currently outside the tree. This process repeats until every vertex is connected. Let's work through an example, starting from A in the graph below.

1 An example: Checking the set of I requires rising up the tree through G and F to identify that A is its root element. Once that's done, we'll just make I and G point directly to A, so future checks will be immediate. This is called *path compression*.

2 See the Chapter 8 exercises for its noninverse version that grows extremely fast.

3 Truly the main character of mid-twentieth-century computer science.

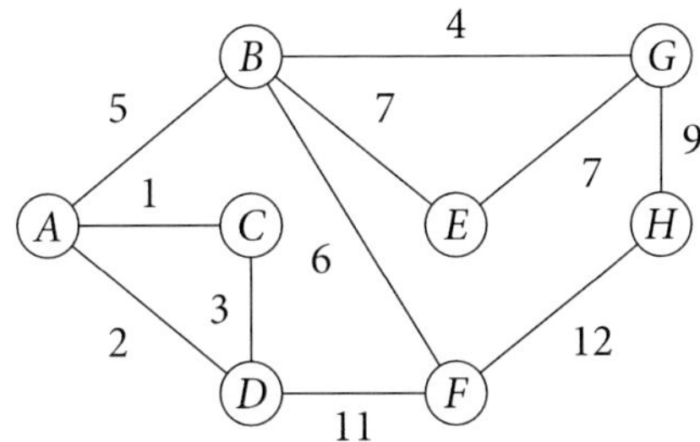

After initializing A as the only vertex in the tree, the first iteration checks A's neighbors, discovers that C is the closest, and adds it to the tree.

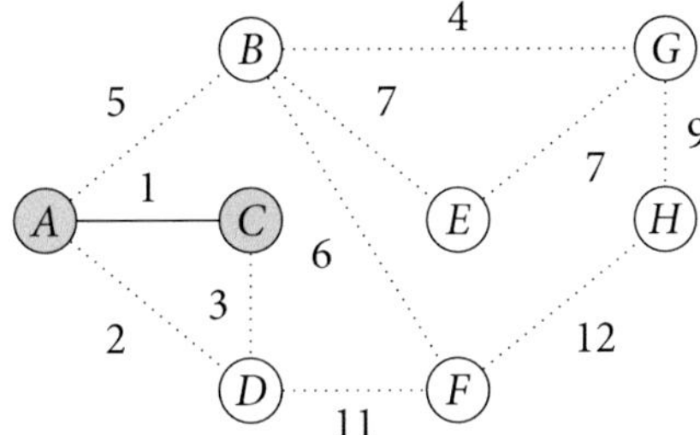

The next iteration finds the node closest to A or C, which is D via the edge (A, D).

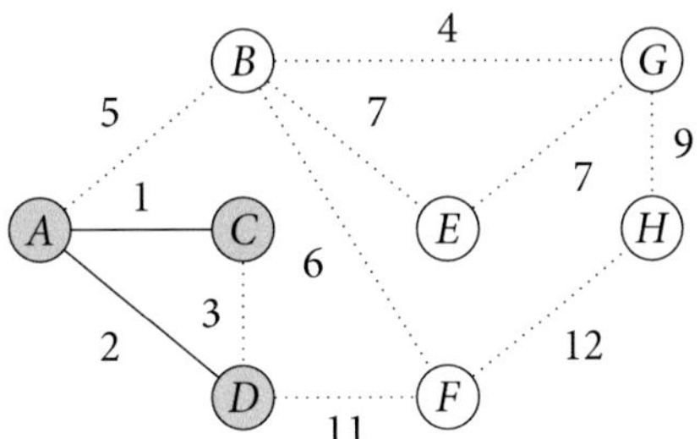

The process continues: For the nodes in the tree (A, C, and D), what is the closest node not already in the tree? The answer is B, with a distance of 5 from A. Notice that (C, D) has a weight of 3, but it would connect two nodes already in the tree and create a cycle, so Prim's algorithm ignores it. The next iteration will add G, with a distance of 4 from B.

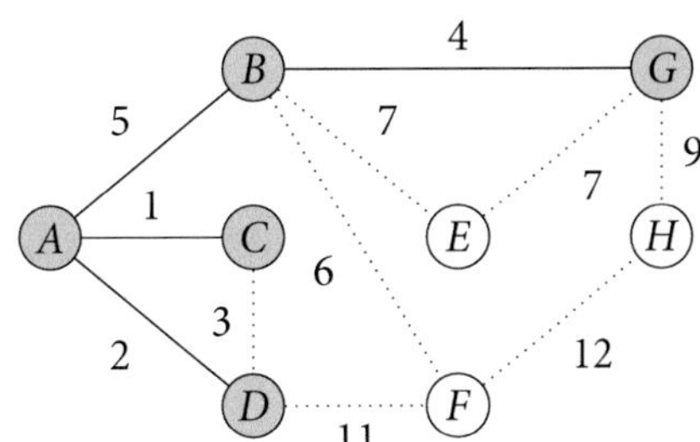

The remaining iterations will add (B, F) with a weight of 6, (B, E), and then (G, H) to complete the tree.

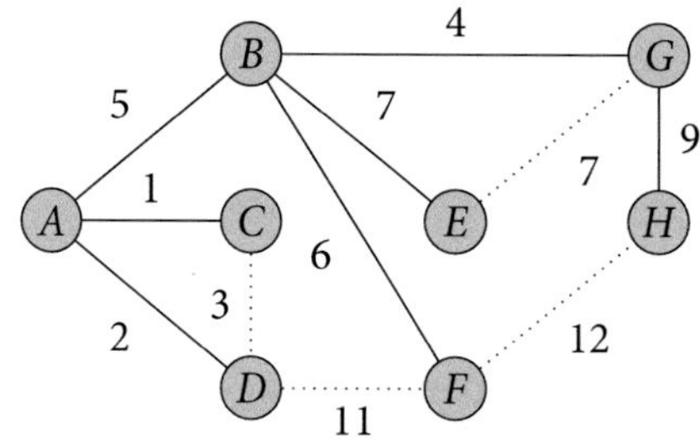

Try It Yourself

Run Prim's algorithm on the graph used to illustrate Kruskal's algorithm. You'll obtain the same minimum spanning tree.

Prim's algorithm is similar to Dijkstra's algorithm, in that it grows outward from a starting node and always connects one new vertex to the visited set. We can use a similar strategy by maintaining a frontier structure that records the minimum-cost edge to all vertices that have been discovered but not yet visited. For example, in the graph above, the state of the frontier after processing A would be the following:

Vertex	Visited	Minimum edge	Predecessor
A	✓	0	Source
B		5	A
C		1	A
D		2	A

Each iteration identifies the frontier node with the minimum-cost edge (C in this case), marks it visited, then examines its edges to update the minimum cost weights and add any newly discovered vertices to the frontier. The pseudocode implementation below is similar to Dijkstra's algorithm; the primary difference is that we're not maintaining the length of the total path to a vertex, only the minimum cost edge that joins it to the in-progress tree.

```
// Prim's algorithm

prim(matrix of edge weights, starting vertex s) {

  // Initialization -- no distances are known at the start
  for each vertex i {
    edge[i] = infinity
    pred[i] = null
    visited[i] = false
    frontier.insert(i, infinity)
```

```
  }

  tree = empty spanning tree

  // Starting vertex is initialized to distance 0
  dist[s] = 0
  frontier.update(s, 0)

  // Main loop
  while the frontier is not empty {
    // Get the unvisited vertex that's closest to the tree
    u = frontier.removeMin()
    visited[u] = true

    // Connect u to the in-progress tree
    add edge (u, pred[u]) to tree

    // Update its neighbors
    for each unvisited neighbor v of u {
      // The edge (u, v) is better than the best known edge
      // connecting v to any vertex in the tree
      if weight[u][v] < edge[v] {
        edge[v] = weight[u][v]
        pred[v] = u
        frontier.update(v, weight[u][v])
      }
    }
  }
}
```

The complexity of Prim's algorithm depends on the implementation of the frontier set. Observe that the main loop executes V times and each iteration requires finding the minimum. The inner loop performs at most E total updates, because it considers each edge only once over the life of the program. Recall from our discussion of Dijkstra's algorithm that a binary heap can be adapted to perform both removals and updates in logarithmic time, giving a total time that is $O(V \log V + E \log V)$, which is asymptotically $O(E \log V)$, the same as Kruskal's algorithm.[4]

4 An advanced heap, like the Fibonacci heap, can achieve $O(1)$ updates, which makes the complexity $O(V \log V + E)$.

22.1.3 Correctness

Let T be the tree constructed by either Kruskal's or Prim's algorithm for a graph G. It's easy to verify that T must be a spanning tree:

- If G is connected, then T must be connected, because the algorithms only terminate after reaching every vertex.
- Prim's algorithm only adds edges that connect new vertices to the in-progress tree and Kruskal's algorithm only adds edges that connect vertices in different sets, so T can never contain a cycle.

But how are we going to prove that T is the *minimal* spanning tree? *The same way we prove everything*. The proofs of Kruskal's and Prim's algorithms are similar to the one developed for Dijkstra's algorithm in Chapter 20. Recall how that proof used a three-act structure to argue that every iteration of the algorithm made a good choice.

- Act 1: State an invariant and show that it's true at the beginning of the method.
- Act 2: Assume that the algorithm has made a series of correct decisions, but then makes a bad decision on some iteration. Show that making a bad decision is not actually possible, and therefore the invariant must remain true on every iteration.
- Act 3: If the invariant is maintained, then the algorithm will eventually terminate with a correct solution.

In this case, we want to argue that every iteration always selects a valid edge that builds toward a correct minimum spanning tree. Here's an outline of the proof for Prim's algorithm; Kruskal's algorithm uses similar reasoning.

Let T_k be the in-progress spanning tree at the beginning of iteration k. Our invariant property is the following:

T_k is always a subset of some minimum spanning tree for the graph G.

If this is true when the algorithm begins and remains true on every iteration, then the final tree (after adding $V - 1$ edges to connect all the vertices) must be a minimum spanning tree and we've achieved our goal. The starting tree T_0 is just the disconnected set of vertices, which is trivially a part of any minimum spanning tree, so the property holds at the beginning of the algorithm.

Now suppose that the algorithm has reached iteration i and now wants to add edge e to the spanning tree. We're assuming that all of the edges in T_i – by the induction hypothesis – are good, but that e is a bad edge. We now need to argue that this assumption is wrong and that, in fact, e is a splendid edge. Specifically, we'll argue that e is at least as good as any other edge the algorithm could have picked on step i.

Let's reason step-by-step about edge e and its relationship to the in-progress tree T_i:

- Prim's algorithm always connects a new vertex on every iteration, so there must be some node on the other end of edge e that isn't part of the in-progress tree. Call that node y.
- Any spanning tree must have a path that connects the nodes in T_i to y. If edge e, which directly connects some vertex in T_i to y, isn't that path, then there must be some *other* edge on a path from some vertex in T_i to y. Call that edge f.

The figure below shows an example of this situation. The shaded nodes are part of the in-progress spanning tree. Prim's algorithm has chosen e as the next edge and we're considering the possibility that some different edge f should have been selected instead. Both edges offer a way to connect the nodes in the tree to y – either directly via e, or using some other path that contains f.

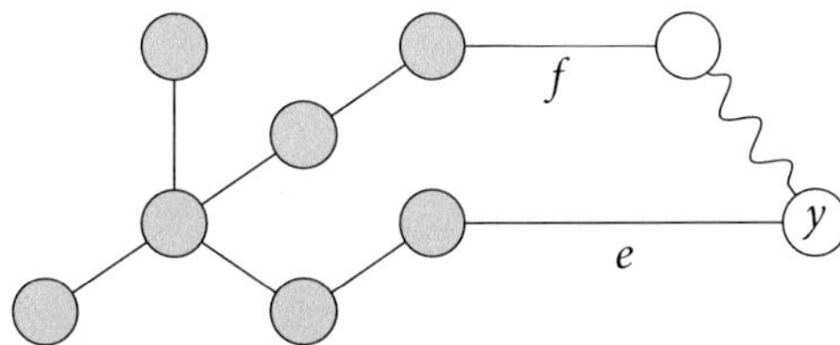

What do we know about the edge weights w_e and w_f? Well, both edges connect a vertex in T_i to a vertex outside it, so Prim's algorithm could have chosen either one to add on iteration i. However – and this is the key – *the algorithm chose to add e instead of f*. Prim's algorithm always chooses the minimum weight edge, so if it wants to add e, we can conclude that $w_e \leq w_f$.

Now we can bring things home. Suppose that we have the correct final minimum spanning tree T. If e is a bad edge, then it should not be part of T because f was the correct choice. Take T and swap f for e:

- e connects one vertex in the set T_i to one vertex outside it, the same as f, so swapping the edges keeps the overall tree connected and doesn't create a cycle.
- The weight of e is no worse than f, so we haven't increased the total weight of the tree by making the swap.

Therefore, swapping edge e in place of f must create a new tree *that is still a minimum spanning tree*. It turns out edge e couldn't have been a bad choice at all! If the in-progress tree T_i is the subset of some minimum spanning tree, then e is at least as good as any other edge we could have selected, and must result in a new tree that is still a subset of a minimum spanning tree. This is the invariant that we set out to prove: The in-progress tree constructed by Prim's algorithm is always a subset of some minimum spanning tree, so the method must terminate with a complete minimum spanning tree.

22.2 Maze Generation

There are a number of algorithms for generating mazes, including ones based on random walks, genetic algorithms, and cellular automata (Pullen, 2022). We're interested in algorithms that can generate **perfect mazes** using minimum spanning trees. Imagine that the maze is built from a grid of cells, with walls dividing the cells. A perfect maze is one in which there is exactly one path from each cell to any other cell – exactly like a spanning tree. This section describes how to construct perfect spanning tree-based mazes, then shows how to visualize them using Java.

22.2.1 Perfect Mazes and Spanning Trees

The starting point for our mazes is a square graph like the following. Each vertex corresponds to a cell in the maze and every nonboundary cell has connections to its north, south, east, and west neighbors.

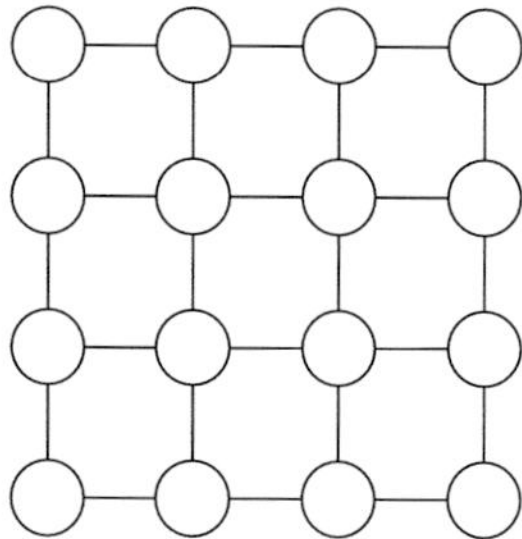

We'll adopt the convention that the *presence* of an edge indicates a path between cells; the *absence* of an edge indicates a wall. For example, the small maze on the left below corresponds to the graph on the right. Each edge in the graph corresponds to an open path between its two endpoint cells – the cells are outlined to make it easier to see how the maze matches the structure of the graph.

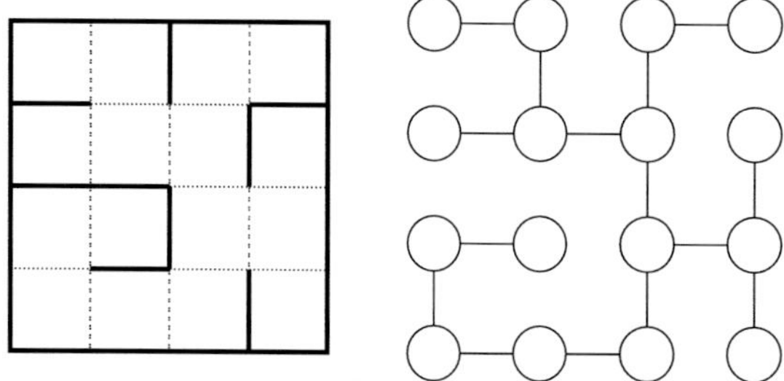

A spanning tree algorithm starts with a disconnected set of vertices and adds edges until the set of vertices is connected. This corresponds to starting with a grid of walled-off maze cells and *removing* walls until there is a path from every cell to every other cell. We'll assume that the maze is square, with every cell connected to its four neighbors, but this detail is easy to change if you want to. We'll also give the edges randomized weights, so that the program makes different choices every time it's run.

22.2.2 Implementation

The code below shows an outline of the program. There are three important methods:

- The constructor creates the matrix of random edge weights. We're assuming that the weights have `double` values in the range $[0, 1)$.
- `build` will use Prim's algorithm to construct the spanning tree. The output will be a `boolean[][]` called `maze` that marks the open passages between cells.
- `draw` will create an image that visualizes the maze.[5]

The parameter `N` controls the size of the maze. The complete graph has `N * N` vertices.

5 We're not using a `JFrame` for this project, but an awesome variation is to create an application that draws the in-progress maze to the screen on every iteration, so you can see how the spanning tree is built. Use the code from `draw` as a base for the `paint` method and have `build` call `repaint` on every iteration, with a suitable delay.

```
/**
 * Spanning tree maze generator
 */

import java.awt.Color;
import java.awt.image.BufferedImage;
import java.awt.Graphics;
import java.io.File;
import javax.imageio.ImageIO;

public class MazeGenerator {

  // Create a square maze with N * N total nodes
  final int N = 40;
  final int NUM_NODES = N * N;

  // The maze is represented as a boolean matrix
  boolean[][] maze;

  // Matrix of edge weights
  double[][] weights;

  // Side length of output image in pixels
  final int SIZE = 400;


  // Initialize adjacency matrix and generate random weights
  public MazeGenerator() {

  }

  // Map a given node number to its corresponding row or column
  // in the matrix configuration
  public int row(int k) {
    return k / N;
  }

  public int col(int k) {
```

```
      return k % N;
    }

    // Build the maze with Prim's algorithm
    public void build() {

    }

    // Draw the completed maze
    public void draw() {

    }

    // Build a maze and then draw it to an image
    public static void main(String[] args) {
      MazeGenerator mg = new MazeGenerator();
      mg.build();
      mg.draw();
    }
}
```

Constructor

The `weights` matrix is an `N * N` array of `double` values. We're assuming the graph is undirected, so we want to create a symmetric matrix of randomized values, representing the randomized edge weights. Your first inclination might be to try the following, which fills all N^2 entries in the matrix with random entries:

```
weight = new double[N][N];

// Fill in the matrix with random values
for (int r = 0; r < N; r++) {
  for (int c = r + 1; c < N; c++) {
    double w = Math.random();
    weight[r][c] = w;
    weight[c][r] = w;  // Symmetric entry
  }
}
```

Try It Yourself

Explain why randomizing every entry in the matrix is not correct. Tip: Think about what entry `weights[r][c]` represents if `weights` is an adjacency matrix.

Solution

Simply filling in the matrix is equivalent to making a *fully connected* graph, where every node has an edge to every other node. For the maze problem, each node must only have connections to its four neighbors.

Let each cell be numbered like the following:

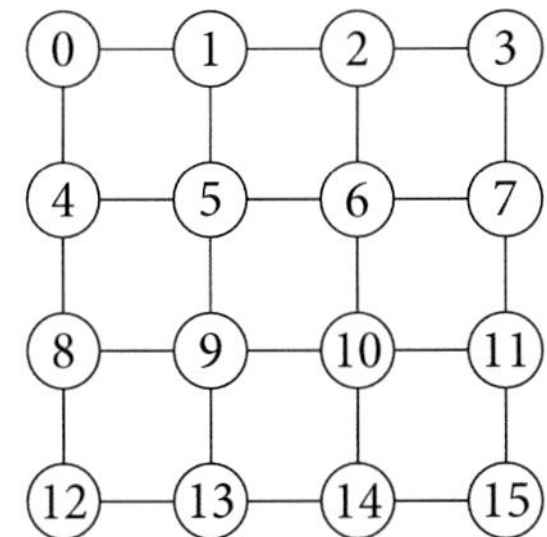

Observe that the eastern neighbor of node n has index number $n+1$ and the southern neighbor has index $n + N$, where $N = 4$ in the figure. The method below iterates through the upper triangle of the adjacency matrix and connects each node to its eastern and southern neighbors in the maze graph. North–south and east–west pairs are symmetric, so mirroring the upper triangle to the lower triangle constructs the full undirected graph.

```
// Initialize adjacency matrix and generate random weights
public MazeGenerator() {
  maze = new boolean[NUM_NODES][NUM_NODES];
  weights = new double[NUM_NODES][NUM_NODES];

  // Loop through the upper triangle
  for (int n = 0; n < NUM_NODES; n++) {
    for (int i = n + 1; i < NUM_NODES; i++)  {

      // Connect each vertex to its east and south neighbors, then
      // mirror to the lower triangle
      if ((i == n + 1 && row(i) == row(n)) || i == n + N) {
        double w = Math.random();
        this.weights[n][i] = w;
        this.weights[i][n] = w;
```

```
      }
    }
  }
}
```

build

The `build` method is an implementation of Prim's algorithm. It follows the outline of the pseudocode given in Section 22.2. Despite the time we spent talking about using efficient heaps to keep track of the minimum cost distances, the method just uses an array – the cost of linearly searching a small array is trivial. Each iteration adds an edge to the `boolean[][]` maze.

```
// Build the maze with Prim's algorithm
public void build() {
  double[] distance = new double[NUM_NODES];
  boolean[] visited = new boolean[NUM_NODES];
  int[] parent = new int[NUM_NODES];
  int numVisited = 0;

  for (int i = 0; i < NUM_NODES; i++) {
    distance[i] = Double.MAX_VALUE;
  }

  // Start from vertex 0
  distance[0] = 0.0;
  parent[0] = 0;

  while (numVisited < NUM_NODES) {
    // Find the unvisited node with minimum distance
    double minDist = Double.MAX_VALUE;
    int nextNode = -1;
    for (int i = 0; i < NUM_NODES; i++) {
      if (!visited[i] && distance[i] < minDist) {
        minDist = distance[i];
        nextNode = i;
      }
    }
    visited[nextNode] = true;
    numVisited++;

```

```
    // Add the edge connecting the closest node to its parent
    // to the spanning tree matrix
    int parentNode = parent[nextNode];
    maze[nextNode][parentNode] = true;
    maze[parentNode][nextNode] = true;

    // Check the edges from nextNode to its unvisited neighbors
    for (int i = 0; i < NUM_NODES; i++) {
      // Skip if i has been visited or is not a neighbor
      if (visited[i] || this.weights[nextNode][i] == 0.0) {
        continue;
      }

      // Update distances if necessary
      if (this.weights[nextNode][i] < distance[i]) {
        distance[i] = this.weights[nextNode][i];
        parent[i] = nextNode;
      }
    }
  }
}
```

draw

The `draw` method iterates through all of the maze cells and draws each one to a `BufferedImage`. The first part of the loop determines each cell's position on the image, which requires converting its index into an (x, y) position on the image coordinate system. The second section checks the adjacency matrix and draws a wall on any edge of the cell that *isn't* connected to its neighbors. Once the drawing is complete, the method uses the built-in `ImageIO` class to save the `BufferedImage`.

```
// Draw the completed maze
public void draw() {
  BufferedImage im = new BufferedImage(SIZE, SIZE, BufferedImage.
     TYPE_INT_RGB);
  Graphics g = im.getGraphics();

  // Paint the background white
  g.setColor(Color.WHITE);
  g.fillRect(0,  0, SIZE, SIZE);
```

```

  // Wall color and outer boundary
  g.setColor(Color.BLACK);
  g.drawRect(0, 0, SIZE - 1, SIZE - 1);

  // Side length of each maze cell in pixels
  int side = SIZE / N;

  // Loop through the maze cells
  for (int i = 0; i < NUM_NODES; i++) {
    // Calculate the upper-left (x y) position of the cell
    //
    // Remember: (0, 0) is in the upper-left corner
    int x = col(i) * side;
    int y = row(i) * side;

    // Check the four edges adjacent to the cell
    //
    // Draw walls for any edges that AREN'T connected
    int north = i - N;
    if (row(i) > 0 && this.maze[i][north] == false) {
      g.drawLine(x, y, x + side, y);
    }

    //*** Add cases for the east, west, and south walls ***//
  }

  // Save as an image
  File f = new File("maze.png");
  try {
    ImageIO.write(im, "png", f);
  } catch(Exception e) {
    e.printStackTrace();
  }
}
```

Try It Yourself

Add three more cases to draw walls to the east, west, and south of a cell. For each case, calculate the index of the neighbor cell, verify that it's in bounds, and then check if there is or is not an edge. The `drawLine` method should draw one side of a box that has (`x`, `y`) in its upper-left corner and (`x + side`, `y + side`) in its lower-right corner.

Solution

Here's a case for the east neighbor:

```
int east = i + 1;
if (col(i) < N - 1 && this.maze[i][east] == false) {
  g.drawLine(x + side, y, x + side, y + side);
}
```

Figure 22.1 shows an example maze for a 40 × 40 node grid. Notice how the maze has lots of short corridors and a high degree of branching. This is characteristic of mazes built with Prim's algorithm.

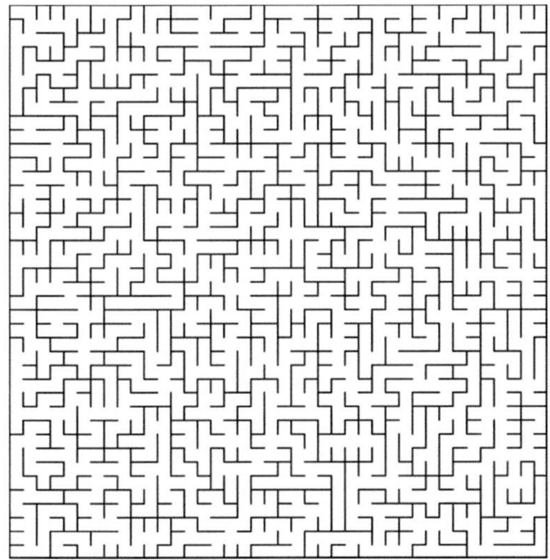

Figure 22.1 An example maze generated by Prim's algorithm.

Try It Yourself

Implement the maze generation program and experiment with creating mazes of different sizes. Once you have the program working, you can consider a few variations:

- Change, or randomize, the starting cell.

- Add a bias to the weights to make the maze favor one direction – if you make the east–west weights consistently bigger, paths will be more horizontal.
- Change the shape of the maze to a rectangle.
- Incorporate different colors.

SUMMARY

As you're reviewing the material for this chapter – and the entire book – keep the following ideas in mind:

- Algorithms + Data Structures = Programs. That is, the information that your program processes must be organized in some way. You can't separate the work that a program does from how its data is represented.
- There is often no "best" solution to a particular programming problem, but rather multiple solutions with their own trade-offs. Understanding data structures and algorithm analysis will help you evaluate these trade-offs in an intelligent way.
- Learning the history and development of the field allows you to understand how each technique fits into the broader evolution of computer science.
- Programming and computer science are like an iceberg. Some aspects of the field are highly visible, but are supported by a deeper layer of fundamental knowledge.

EXTENSIONS

Depth-First Traversal

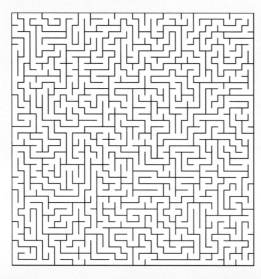

Figure 22.2 An example maze generated by depth-first carving.

Prim's algorithm created a maze with a short, branch-heavy structure. If you want longer passages, you can create a maze that carves its paths using depth-first traversal. The recursive version is as follows, where u is a reference to a maze cell.

```
// Maze generation with depth-first traversal

depthFirstCarving(u) {
  mark u as visited

  while u has unvisited neighbors {
    randomly choose an unvisited neighbor v
    add an edge from u to v
    depthFirstCarve(v)
  }
}
```

Given a cell, the method randomly chooses one of its unvisited neighbors, carves a path to it, then recursively continues exploring from the neighbor. If the path reaches a dead end, it backs up to the last cell that still has unvisited neighbors and then continues carving from there. Figure 22.2 shows an example maze made by this method. The structure is clearly different from the one produced by Prim's algorithm. In fact, the depth-first method tends to generate one very long path that winds through the entire maze with short branches. The recursive method is not difficult to implement, but you'll need to add a `visited` array to the class and add steps to select a random neighbor.

Escape with Backtracking Search

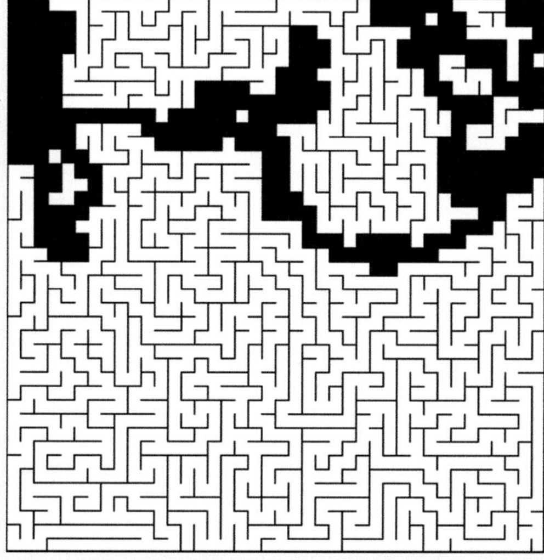

Figure 22.3 Finding a path through a maze.

Finally, tie everything together by using a recursive backtracking search to escape from the maze you've generated. Pick a starting square and an ending square and perform a depth-first traversal from the start looking for the end.

```
// Escape!

escape(u) {
  mark u as visited

  if u is the ending cell {
    freedom!
    exit
  }

  for each neighbor v of u {
    if v is still unvisited and (u, v) is an edge {
      escape(v)
    }
  }
}
```

Figure 22.3 shows an example path in the depth-first maze starting at the upper-left and searching for the upper-right, with all of the squares visited during the search filled in. For a fun variation, make an animation that draws the maze and the set of visited cells on each iteration. You'll be able to see when the algorithm reaches a dead end and backtracks.

NOTES AND FURTHER READING

Colossal Cave Adventure was one of the first computer games to become a bona fide viral hit. First written by Will Crowther, an engineer and caver, then improved by Don Woods, a Stanford student, it spread rapidly through the universities and research centers connected to the early ARPANET after it was published in 1977. Allegedly so popular that it "set the entire computer industry back by two weeks" (Reed, 2021), *Adventure* inspired an entire genre of text-based adventure and interactive fiction games. Two of the game's famous puzzles involve mazes made of "twisty little passages." In the first, the player enters a series of rooms that are "all alike" and has to navigate by leaving a trail of items to tell them apart. In the second, the passages are "all different," and the description changes as the player moves around the maze: "a little twisty maze of passages," "a twisty maze of little passages," and so forth. Nick Montfort's *Twisty Little Passages* takes its title from the game and surveys the history of the interactive fiction genre (Montfort, 2005).

One important practical application of spanning trees is the **Spanning Tree Protocol** for network bridges, invented by Radia Perlman. A bridge is a networking device that connects multiple local area networks (LANs) and allows them to exchange messages with each other. In the early days of networking, bridges had to be manually configured by network administrators. Connecting a group of bridges in a loop would lead to a "packet storm," where the bridges repeatedly circulated multiple copies of every message. Perlman's protocol allows bridges to *automatically* configure themselves into a spanning tree, where there's a path from every LAN to every other one, but no loops. Unlike Kruskal's and Prim's algorithm, there is no top-level supervisor with global knowledge of the network. Instead, the bridges exchange messages among themselves to designate one bridge as the root of the tree, then learn the minimum weight links connecting each bridge to the root. The bridges will automatically reconfigure the spanning tree if the network topology changes, so engineers are free to add or remove devices without manually updating every device. Perlman memorialized her work with the following poem (Perlman, 1985):

I think that I shall never see
A graph more lovely than a tree.
A tree whose crucial property
Is loop-free connectivity.
A tree that must be sure to span
So packets can reach every LAN.
First the root must be selected.
By ID it is elected.
Least cost paths from root are traced.
In the tree, these paths are placed.
A mesh is made by folks like me,
Then bridges find a spanning tree.

References

Adelson-Velsky, Georgy Maksimovich, and Landis, Evgenii Mikhailovich. 1962. An algorithm for organization of information. *Doklady Akademii Nauk*, **146**: 263–266.

Aho, Alfred V., Sethi, Ravi, Ullman, Jeffrey D., et al. 2007. *Compilers: Principles, Techniques, and Tools*, vol. 2. Addison-Wesley.

Allouche, Jean-Paul, and Shallit, Jeffrey. 2003. *Automatic Sequences: Theory, Applications, Generalizations*. Cambridge University Press.

Anderson, Julie, and Franceschi, Hervé J. 2014. *Java Illuminated: An Active Learning Approach*. Jones & Bartlett Publishers.

Appel, Kenneth I., and Haken, Wolfgang. 1989. *Every Planar Map is Four Colorable*. American Mathematical Society.

Appleby, Austin. 2008. *SMHasher*. Online: Accessed July 4, 2023 from https://github.com/aappleby/smhasher.

Arpaci-Dusseau, Remzi H., and Arpaci-Dusseau, Andrea C. 2018. *Operating Systems: Three Easy Pieces*. Arpaci-Dusseau Books LLC.

Atwood, Jeff. 2007. *The Danger of Naïveté*. Online: Accessed August 1, 2022 from https://blog.codinghorror.com/the-danger-of-naivete/.

Bachmann, Paul. 1894. *Die Analytische Zahlentheorie*, vol. 2. Teubner.

Back, Adam. 2002. *Hashcash: A Denial of Service Counter-Measure*. Online: Accessed November 28, 2023 from www.hashcash.org/papers/hashcash.pdf.

Baecker, Ronald. 1998. Sorting out sorting: A case study of software visualization for teaching computer science. *Software Visualization: Programming as a Multimedia Experience*, **1**, 369–381.

Bayer, Rudolf, and McCreight, Edward. 1970. Organization and maintenance of large ordered indices. Pages 107–141 of: *Proceedings of the 1970 ACM SIGFIDET (Now SIGMOD) Workshop on Data Description, Access and Control*.

Bentley, Jon. 2016. *Programming Pearls*. Addison-Wesley Professional.

Bentley, Jon L., and McIlroy, M. Douglas. 1993. Engineering a sort function. *Software: Practice and Experience*, **23**(11), 1249–1265.

Berners-Lee, Timothy J. 1989. *Information Management: A Proposal*. Technical Report.

Berto, Francesco, and Tagliabue, Jacopo. 2006. *Cellular Automata*. The Stanford Encyclopedia of Philosophy (Spring 2022 edition), Edward N. Zalta (ed.) Online: Accessed October 30, 2022 from https://plato.stanford.edu/archives/spr2022/entries/cellular-automata/.

Bloch, Joshua. 2006. *Extra, extra – read all about it: Nearly all binary searches and mergesorts are broken*. Online: Accessed October 30, 2021 from http://googleresearch.blogspot.com/2006/06/extra-extra-read-allabout-it-nearly.html.

Bourke, Paul. 2002. *The Mandelbrot set at a glance.* Online: Accessed 30 August 2022 from http://paulbourke.net/fractals/mandelbrot/.

Brin, Sergey, and Page, Lawrence. 1998. The anatomy of a large-scale hypertextual Web search engine. *Computer Networks and ISDN Systems*, **30**(1–7), 107–117.

Bush, Vannevar. 1945. As we may think. *The Atlantic Monthly*, **176**(1), 101–108.

Cerf, Vinton, and Kahn, Bob. 1990. Selected ARPANET Maps. *Computer Communications Review (CCR)*, **20**, 81–110.

Chea, Rattanak. 2018. *Amazon's Interview Question: Count Island.* Online: Accessed December 21, 2022 from https://dev.to/rattanakchea/amazons-interview-question-count-island-21h6.

Chomsky, Noam. 1956. Three models for the description of language. *IRE Transactions on Information Theory*, **2**(3), 113–124.

Collavo, Alberto, Glew, Robert H., Huang, Yung-Sheng, et al. 2005. House cricket small-scale farming. *Ecological Implications of Minilivestock: Potential of Insects, Rodents, Frogs and Snails*, **27**, 515–540.

Conway, John Horton. 1973. Tomorrow is the day after doomsday. *Eureka*, **36**, 28–31.

Cormen, Thomas H., Leiserson, Charles E., Rivest, Ronald L., and Stein, Clifford. 2022. *Introduction to Algorithms.* MIT Press.

Dahl, Ole-Johan. 2004. The birth of object orientation: The Simula languages. Pages 15–25 of: *From Object-Orientation to Formal Methods.* Springer.

Deitel, H.M., and Deitel, P.J.C. 2005. *How to Program.* Pearson Education.

Dijkstra, Edsger Wybe. 1976. *A Discipline of Programming.* Prentice-Hall.

Doctorow, Cory. 2007. *Famous poems as limericks.* Online: Accessed May 26, 2022 from https://boingboing.net/2007/07/23/famous-poems-as-lime.html.

Droste, Magdalena. 2002. *Bauhaus, 1919–1933.* Taschen.

Eckhardt, Roger. 1987. Stan Ulam, John von Neumann, and the Monte Carlo method. *Los Alamos Science*, **15**(131–136), 30.

Eksombatchai, Chantat, Jindal, Pranav, Liu, Jerry Zitao, et al. 2018. Pixie: A system for recommending 3+ billion items to 200+ million users in real-time. Pages 1775–1784 of: *Proceedings of the 2018 World Wide Web Conference.*

Engelbart, Christina. 1986. *A lifetime pursuit: A brief history of Doug Engelbart's work by Christina Engelbart.* Online: Accessed June 12, 2022 from https://dougengelbart.org/content/view/183/ .

Euler, Leonhard. 1782. Recherches sur un nouvelle espéce de quarrés magiques. *Verhandelingen uitgegeven door het zeeuwsch Genootschap der Wetenschappen te Vlissingen*, 85–239.

Everson, Michael, McGowan, Rick, Whistler, Ken, and Umamaheswaran, V.S. 2021. *Roadmap to the basic multilingual plane.* Online: Accessed August 28, 2022 from https://unicode.org/roadmaps/bmp/.

Floyd, Robert W. 1964. Algorithm 245: Treesort. *Communications of the ACM*, **7**(12), 701.

Fredman, Michael L., and Tarjan, Robert Endre. 1987. Fibonacci heaps and their uses in improved network optimization algorithms. *Journal of the ACM (JACM)*, **34**(3), 596–615.

Freeman, Eric, Robson, Elisabeth, Bates, Bert, and Sierra, Kathy. 2004. *Head First Design Patterns: A Brain-Friendly Guide.* O'Reilly Media.

Friedman, Daniel P., and Felleisen, Matthias. 1995. *The Little Schemer.* MIT Press.

Gandz, Solomon. 1926. The origin of the term "Algebra." *The American Mathematical Monthly*, **33**(9), 437–440.

Gardner, Martin. 1970. The fantastic combinations of John Conway's New Solitaire Game of Life. *Scientific American*, **223**, 20–123.

Gardner, Martin. 2001. *The Colossal Book of Mathematics*. W.W. Norton.

Geiling, Natasha. 2014. *The World's Longest Beard Is One of the Smithsonian's Strangest Artifacts*. Online: Accessed August 28, 2022 from www.smithsonianmag.com/smithsonian-institution/smithsonian-home-worlds-longest-beard-180953370/.

Gleick, James. 2008. *Chaos: Making a New Science*. Penguin.

Goldberg, Adele, and Robson, David. 1983. *Smalltalk-80: The Language and Its Implementation*. Addison-Wesley Longman.

Google. 2022a. *Google Java style guide*. Online: Accessed August 28, 2022 from https://google.github.io/styleguide/javaguide.html.

Google. 2022b. *How Google Search organizes information*. Online: Accessed May 14, 2022 from www.google.com/search/howsearchworks/how-search-works/organizing-information/.

Gross, Jonathan L., and Yellen, Jay. 2003. *Handbook of Graph Theory*. CRC Press.

Guibas, Leo J., and Sedgewick, Robert. 1978. A dichromatic framework for balanced trees. Pages 8–21 of: *19th Annual Symposium on Foundations of Computer Science (SFCS 1978)*. IEEE.

Harchol-Balter, Mor. 2013. *Performance Modeling and Design of Computer Systems: Queueing Theory in Action*. Cambridge University Press.

Hoare, Charles Antony Richard. 1961a. Algorithm 64: quicksort. *Communications of the ACM*, **4**(7), 321.

Hoare, Charles Antony Richard. 1961b. Algorithm 65: find. *Communications of the ACM*, **4**(7), 321–322.

Hofstadter, Douglas R. 1979. *Gödel, Escher, Bach: An Eternal Golden Braid*. Basic Books.

Johnson, Eric M. 2005. *Open Source Shakespeare: An Experiment in Literary Technology*. Ph.D. thesis, George Mason University.

Kennedy, James, and Eberhart, Russell. 1995. Particle swarm optimization. Pages 1942–1948 of: *Proceedings of ICNN'95 – International Conference on Neural Networks*, vol. 4. IEEE.

Knuth, Donald E. 1972. Ancient Babylonian algorithms. *Communications of the ACM*, **15**(7), 671–677.

Knuth, Donald E. 1976. Big omicron and big omega and big theta. *ACM Sigact News*, **8**(2), 18–24.

Knuth, Donald E. 2014a. *Art of Computer Programming, Volume 1: Fundamental Algorithms*. Addison-Wesley Professional.

Knuth, Donald E. 2014b. *Art of Computer Programming, Volume 2: Seminumerical Algorithms*. Addison-Wesley Professional.

Knuth, Donald E. 2014c. *Art of Computer Programming, Volume 3: Searching and Sorting*. Addison-Wesley Professional.

Kraitchik, Maurice. 1942. *Mathematical Recreations*. W.W. Norton.

Kruskal, Joseph B. 1956. On the shortest spanning subtree of a graph and the traveling salesman problem. *Proceedings of the American Mathematical Society*, **7**(1), 48–50.

Kushagra, Shrinu, López-Ortiz, Alejandro, Qiao, Aurick, and Munro, J. Ian. 2014. Multi-pivot quicksort: Theory and experiments. Pages 47–60 of: *2014 Proceedings of the Sixteenth Workshop on Algorithm Engineering and Experiments (ALENEX)*. SIAM.

LifeWiki. 2022. Online: Accessed October 30, 2022 from https://conwaylife.com/wiki/Main_Page.

Louvet, Jean-Pierre, and Martínez, Juan Luis. 2003. *Fractal art FAQ*. Online: Accessed August 30, 2022 from www.fractalus.com/fractal-art-faq/index.html.

Lyons, James. 2012. *Practical cryptography*. Online: Accessed May 26, 2022 from https://practicalcryptography.com/.

Mandelbrot, Benoit. 1967. How long is the coast of Britain? Statistical self-similarity and fractional dimension. *Science*, **156**(3775), 636–638.

Martin, Keith M. 2012. *Everyday Cryptography*. Oxford University Press.

Michail, Dimitrios, Kinable, Joris, Naveh, Barak, and Sichi, John V. 2020. JGraphT: a Java library for graph data structures and algorithms. *ACM Transactions on Mathematical Software*, **46**(2).

Montfort, Nick. 2005. *Twisty Little Passages: An Approach to Interactive Fiction*. MIT Press.

Morgan, Nick. 2015. *Easy forth*. Online: Accessed July 4, 2023 from https://skilldrick.github.io/easyforth/.

Morris, Robert, and Thompson, Ken. 1979. Password security: A case history. *Communications of the ACM*, **22**(11), 594–597.

Munroe, Randall. 2011. *Password strength*. Online: Accessed July 4, 2023 from https://xkcd.com/936/.

Nakamoto, Satoshi. 2008. *Bitcoin: A peer-to-peer electronic cash system*. Online: Accessed November 28, 2023 from https://bitcoin.org/bitcoin.pdf.

Nebel, Markus E., Wild, Sebastian, and Martínez, Conrado. 2016. Analysis of pivot sampling in dual-pivot quicksort: A holistic analysis of Yaroslavskiy's partitioning scheme. *Algorithmica*, **75**(4), 632–683.

Neumueller, Alexander. 2023. *Bitcoin electricity consumption: An improved assessment*. Online: Accessed November 28, 2023 from www.jbs.cam.ac.uk/2023/bitcoin-electricity-consumption/.

Nicholas, Nick, and Strader, Andrew. 2000. *The Klingon Hamlet*. Pocket Books.

Nikoli. 2021. *Nikoli puzzles*. Online: Accessed September 4, 2023 from www.nikoli.co.jp/en/puzzles/.

Nyce, James M., and Kahn, Paul. 1991. *From Memex to Hypertext: Vannevar Bush and the Mind's Machine*. Academic Press Professional.

Nystrom, Robert. 2021. *Crafting Interpreters*. Genever Benning.

OpenJDK. 2013. *TreeMap.java*. Online: Accessed September 10, 2023 from https://hg.openjdk.org/jdk8/jdk8/jdk/file/tip/src/share/classes/java/util/TreeMap.java.

OpenJDK. 2014. *DualPivotQuicksort.java*. Online: Accessed October 29, 2022 from http://hg.openjdk.java.net/jdk8/jdk8/jdk/file/tip/src/share/classes/java/util/\DualPivotQuicksort.java.

Oracle. 2023. *HotSpot garbage collection basics*. Online: Accessed August 27, 2022 from www.oracle.com/webfolder/technetwork/tutorials/obe/java/gc01/index.html.

Page, Lawrence, Brin, Sergey, Motwani, Rajeev, and Winograd, Terry. 1999. *The PageRank citation ranking: Bringing order to the web*. Technical Report. Stanford InfoLab.

Pagh, Rasmus, and Rodler, Flemming Friche. 2004. Cuckoo hashing. *Journal of Algorithms*, **51**(2), 122–144.

Papert, Seymour A. 1980. *Mindstorms: Children, Computers, and Powerful Ideas*. Basic Books.

Perlman, Radia. 1985. An algorithm for distributed computation of a spanning tree in an extended LAN. *ACM SIGCOMM Computer Communication Review*, **15**(4), 44–53.

Peters, Tim. 2002. *Timsort*. Online: Accessed October 30, 2022 from https://svn.python.org/projects/python/trunk/Objects/listsort.txt.

Peyrott, Sebastian. 2017. *A brief history of JavaScript*. Online: Accessed August 28, 2022 from https://auth0.com/blog/a-brief-history-of-javascript/.

Piantadosi, Steven T. 2014. Zipf's word frequency law in natural language: a critical review and future directions. *Psychonomic Bulletin Review*, **21**, 1112–1130.

Poitevin, Pierre-Marie. 2020. *Leetcode 1670: Design front middle back queue*. Online: Accessed December 21, 2022 from https://poitevinpm.medium.com/leetcode-1670-design-front-middle-back-queue-7ee2ce386d0d.

Porter, Martin F. 1980. An algorithm for suffix stripping. *Program*, **14**(3), 130–137.

Porter, Martin F. 2006. *The Porter stemming algorithm*. Online: Accessed May 27, 2022 from https://tartarus.org/martin/PorterStemmer/.

Prim, Robert Clay. 1957. Shortest connection networks and some generalizations. *The Bell System Technical Journal*, **36**(6), 1389–1401.

Project Gutenberg. 1998. *Macbeth*. Online: Accessed May 26, 2022 from www.gutenberg.org/ebooks/1533.

Provos, Niels, and Mazieres, David. 1999. A future-adaptable password scheme. Pages 81–91 of: *USENIX Annual Technical Conference, FREENIX Track*.

Pullen, Walter. 2022. *Think labyrinth*. Online: Accessed July 3, 2023 from www.astrolog.org/labyrnth/algrithm.htm.

Python. 2022. *dis — Disassembler for Python bytecode*. Online: Accessed August 28, 2022 from https://docs.python.org/3/library/dis.html.

Reed, Aaron. 2021. *50 years of text games*. Online: Accessed July 3, 2023 from https://if50.substack.com/.

Reeves, William T. 1983. Particle systems: A technique for modeling a class of fuzzy objects. *ACM Transactions on Graphics (TOG)*, **2**(2), 91–108.

Reinhold, Arnold. 1995. *The Diceware passphrase home page*. Online: Accessed July 3, 2023 from https://theworld.com/reinhold/diceware.html.

Reynolds, Craig W. 1987. Flocks, herds and schools: A distributed behavioral model. Pages 25–34 of: *Proceedings of the 14th Annual Conference on Computer Graphics and Interactive Techniques*.

Reynolds, Craig W. 2001. *Boids: background and update*. Online: Accessed March 15, 2023 from www.red3d.com/cwr/boids/.

Russell, Stuart, and Norvig, Peter. 2020. *Artificial Intelligence: A Modern Approach*, 4th edn. Prentice Hall.

Sanderson, Mark, and Croft, W. Bruce. 2012. The history of information retrieval research. *Proceedings of the IEEE*, **100**(Special Centennial Issue), 1444–1451.

Sedgewick, Robert. 1978. Implementing quicksort programs. *Communications of the ACM*, **21**(10), 847–857.

Seidel, Raimund, and Aragon, Cecilia R. 1996. Randomized search trees. *Algorithmica*, **16**(4), 464–497.

Shaffer, Clifford A. 1997. *A Practical Introduction to Data Structures and Algorithm Analysis*. Prentice Hall.

Shannon, Claude Elwood. 1948. A mathematical theory of communication. *The Bell System Technical Journal*, **27**(3), 379–423.

Shell, Donald L. 1959. A high-speed sorting procedure. *Communications of the ACM*, **2**(7), 30–32.

Skiena, Steven S. 1998. *The Algorithm Design Manual*, vol. 2. Springer.

Sleator, Daniel Dominic, and Tarjan, Robert Endre. 1985. Self-adjusting binary search trees. *Journal of the ACM (JACM)*, **32**(3), 652–686.

Smyth, A.S.H. 2018. *The weird world of the hapax legomenon*. Online: Accessed July 3, 2023 from www.spectator.co.uk/article/the-weird-world-of-the-hapaxlegomenon/.

St. John, James. 2016. *Conus textile (textile cone snail) 3*. Online: Accessed October 30, 2022 from www.flickr.com/photos/jsjgeology/31207880866.

Stephenson, Brian. 2018. *Random Mondrian art*. Online: Accessed August 30, 2022 from http://nifty.stanford.edu/2018/stephenson-mondrian-art/.

Stroethoff, Karel. 2014. Bhaskara's approximation for the sine. *The Mathematics Enthusiast*, **11**(3), 485–492.

Sullivan, Andrew. 2009. *The beard-second*. Online: Accessed August 26, 2022 from www.theatlantic.com/daily-dish/archive/2009/11/-a-beard-second/194602/.

Target, Sinclair. 2019. *How much of a genius-level move was using binary space partitioning in Doom?* Online: Accessed September 4, 2023 from https://twobithistory.org/2019/11/06/doom-bsp.html.

V8 Dev. 2010. *Digging into the TurboFan JIT*. Online: Accessed August 28, 2022 from https://v8.dev/blog/turbofan-jit.

Vandevenne, Lode. 2007. *Lode's computer graphics tutorial*. Online: Accessed March 15, 2023 from https://lodev.org/cgtutor/fire.html.

Vernon, Jennifer. 2010. *Shakespeare's coined words now common currency*. Online: Accessed June 12, 2022 from www.nationalgeographic.com/culture/article/shakespeares-coined-words-now-common-currency.

Williams, John William Joseph. 1964. Algorithm 232: Heapsort. *Communications of the ACM*, 7, 347–348.

Wirth, Niklaus. 1976. *Algorithms + Data Structures = Programs*. Prentice-Hall.

Wolfram, Stephen. 1983. Statistical mechanics of cellular automata. *Reviews of Modern Physics*, **55**(3), 601.

Yan, Xiang, Diaconis, Persi, Rusmevichientong, Paat, and Roy, Benjamin. 2004. Solitaire: Man versus machine. *Advances in Neural Information Processing Systems*, **17**.

Yaroslavskiy, Vladimir. 2009. Dual-pivot quicksort. *Research Disclosure*.

Yeomans, Julian Scott. 2003. Solving "Einstein's riddle" using spreadsheet optimization. *INFORMS Transactions on Education*, **3**(2), 55–63.

Young, Elaine. 2007. *Euler squares*. Online: Accessed June 12, 2022 from https://maa.org/press/periodicals/convergence/euler-squares-introduction.

Index

Printed in the United States
by Baker & Taylor Publisher Services